On and Off the Beaten Path

The Central and Southern Bahamas Guide

From South Florida to the

Turks and Caicos

by

Stephen J. Pavlidis

Part I-*On The Beaten Path*
includes

The Biminis, Andros, The Berry Islands, New Providence, Eleuthera, Little San Salvador, Cat Island, Long Island, Conception Island, Rum Cay, and San Salvador

Part II-*Off The Beaten Path*
includes

The Jumentos, The Crooked/Acklins District, Samana, The Plana Cays, Mayaguana, Inagua, and Hogsty Reef

Published in the USA by Seaworthy Publications, Inc. 507 Sunrise Dr., Port Washington, WI 53074
Phone: 414-268-9250, Fax: 414-268-9208, e-mail: publisher@seaworthy.com

On the World Wide Web at:
www.seaworthy.com

CAUTION: The author has taken extreme care to provide the most accurate and reliable charts possible for use in this guide. Nevertheless, the charts in this guide are designed to be used in conjunction with DMA, NOAA, and other government charts and publications. The Author and Publisher take no responsibility for their misuse.

A publication like this is actually the result of a blending of many people's knowledge and experiences. Kelly Becker, how can I thank you enough, you have been with me through the thick and thin of this, tossing the lead, shooting photos, investigating all the best places to shop, your suggestions always seem to keep me on the right path when I stray, the people reading this book will never understand how large a part you played in its production, but you and I know; Andy and Star on the S/V *Moria*, for their help with the dive sites, Capt. Lee Bakewell on the S/V *Winterlude* for his help with programming; A1 Broadshad of Spanish Wells; Gene Ballou on the S/V *Harrison*; BASRA Nassau, Chris Lloyd, Ken Waton, and Courtney Curtis; Steven Clareridge; Craig and Paige on the S/V *Caribbean Soul*; Pete Davidson and Adam Musial of the *Forfar Field Station*; Roger and Beth Day on the S/V *42*; Doug and LouAnn on the Schooner *Whisper*; Dan Doyle, skipper of the R/V *Sea Dragon* for once again making his vast knowledge of these waters available to all; Ann Francone, S/V *Calypso Poet*, for her editorial assistance; Tom Gill on the S/V *Windrider* for his help with the hardware; Rev. David Goodrum on the S/V *Ephesians*; Manny and Ora Mae Lacour at *Hawks Nest Resort and Marina*, thanks for making us feel right at home; Louis and the staff at the *Nassau Land and Surveys Department* for their help and for putting up with me in those long hours of research at their office; John McKie, *Sunseeker*, for sharing his vast knowledge, what little John has forgotten about these islands is more than many of us will ever know about them; Bob Rader (NU4P) and Anita Martinec (WZ4U) for enriching this publication by sharing the wisdom of their years of experience and experiences in The Bahamas; Carolyn Wardle for her help with the section on ham radio and weather broadcasts, and let us not forget her tireless efforts on the Bahamas Weather Net which benefits all mariners plying these waters; Jan and Carol on the S/V *Asapwal*; Gene Zace on the S/V *Joshua*; John DeCarion of the S/V *Packadreams*; and Gordon and Jane Groves of the S/V *Goombay*. Last but not least, I would like to thank my publisher for making this work possible. If there is anybody that I have neglected to mention here, rest assured that it is an oversight and I sincerely apologize.

Cover designed and painted by Jack Blackman.
Sketches that appear on section pages are courtesy of Don Reynolds.

Library of Congress Cataloging-in-Publication Data
Pavlidis, Stephen J.
    On and off the beaten path : the central and southern Bahamas
guide : from south Florida to the Turks and Caicos / by Stephen J.
Pavlidis.
        p.   cm.
    Includes bibliographical references and index.
    ISBN 0-9639566-9-8
    1. Boats and boating—Bahamas—Guidebooks.   2. Nautical charts-
-Bahamas.   3. Bahamas—Guidebooks.   4. Bahamas—Description and
travel.   I. Title.
GV776.24.P38 1997
917.29604—dc21   97-36533
                                                  CIP

Other books by:
Stephen J. Pavlidis
A Cruising Guide to the Exuma Cays Land and Sea Park; with Ray Darville, ISBN 0-9638306
The Exuma Guide, A Cruising Guide to the Exuma Cays 2nd Edition; ISBN 0-9639566-7-1
The Turks and Caicos Guide; ISBN 1-892399-01-6

On and Off the Beaten Path

The Central and Southern Bahamas Guide

From South Florida to the

Turks and Caicos

by

Stephen J. Pavlidis

Seaworthy Publications, Inc.
Port Washington, Wisconsin

Table of Contents

PART I

ON THE BEATEN PATH

THE CENTRAL BAHAMAS

PART II

OFF THE BEATEN PATH

THE SOUTHERN BAHAMAS

DEDICATION

In memory of

Ron Turner

Cruiser, Artist, Teacher, Friend

I first met Ron Turner (KA4FNP) and his wife Linda (WD4OCI) in the Abacos a decade ago where they were cruising on their ketch *Moonshadow*. We were in Marsh Harbour watching some escaped dolphins from Guana Cay cavort in the shallows while waiting for their trainers to arrive as the Turners dinghied over. Over the years my relationship with Ron grew from acquaintance to friend. Patient Ron was always handy with sound advice for highly impatient me. Quite a few projects on *IV Play* may not have gotten accomplished without Ron's help and direction. Sometimes we forget to tell those we care about how we feel about them until it is too late. I am guilty of that. I miss you Ron. May you always sail circles around me.

Steve

INTRODUCTION

It's funny how things will snowball if you give them half a chance. This cruising guide to the Central and Southern Bahamas is the latest turn in the process.

It started in 1993 when I met Ray Darville, then the new Warden of Exuma Park in the Exumas, and volunteered my services as an Assistant Warden. Trying to create something of use to the Park, Ray and I decided to share our knowledge of the waters with incoming boaters. We were dog tired of pulling them off sandbanks and giving them waypoints or directing them in by VHF. We figured that the *Cruising Guide to the Exuma Cays Land and Sea Park* would change all that. That project completed we returned to concentrating on Park problems.

Ray had innocently planted a thought in my mind that the guide should be expanded to cover the entire Exumas. Being basically a lazy person, the idea of such a project seemed like an immense amount of work that I did not care to get involved with at the moment, especially since I was having too much fun simply letting the wind blow me where it will. To quote Dashiell Hammett I was, and still am, *". . . a two-fisted loafer. I can loaf longer and better than anyone I know. I did not acquire this genius. I was born with it."* Well, *The Exuma Guide* **was** an immense amount of work but it was well worth it. With the publication of *The Exuma Guide* anchorages opened up that were hitherto unknown to many cruisers, much to the dismay of those who wanted their favorite spots to remain secret.

In keeping with that tradition I have now turned my attention, and yours too perhaps, to the rest of the Central and Southern Bahamas. These areas I have divided up into two sections that I call *On and Off the Beaten Path*.

The Central Bahamas are what I regard as *on the beaten path*. Most cruisers simply heading to George Town in the Exumas for the winter will visit places like Bimini and the Berrys on the way south and then Conception, Rum Cay, Long Island, Cat Island, Little San Salvador, and Eleuthera on the way back north in the Spring. These islands get a considerable amount of boat traffic.

Those hardier souls who may be headed for the Caribbean, or those that are just looking for someplace different, are indeed the ones who take the road less traveled, *off the beaten path*. For those skippers I offer my knowledge of the Southern Bahamas, the Jumentos, The Crooked/Acklins District, Mayaguana, and Inagua. There are few boats visiting these cays and their people are not as dependent on the tourist dollar for survival. Here you will find a different breed of Bahamians, independent, yet just as warm and friendly, even more so at times, than their neighbors who cater so well to the tourists.

Readers will notice that the charts are no longer referred to as "sketch charts." The acquisition of a computer based hydrographic system and a fast 16' boat has given me the ability to record a vast amount of data in a very short time. This high tech approach allows me to construct highly accurate charts with properly placed latitude and longitude lines. While taking my soundings throughout The Bahamas over the last three years I have found many discrepancies between the existing charts and data, and what is really out there. You will find these errors corrected by this guide. A few charts in this guide are noted as "not for navigational purposes." These are the *Index Charts* for each region and island group. Also the chart labeled *Routes Across the Great Bahama Bank* from Bimini to the Berry Islands as size alone restricts accuracy when reduced to 7.5" x 10".

For the most part, the routes to be found within this publication are nothing new. They have been around in different forms for years, generously given to us by Linton Rigg, Harry Etheridge, and Harry Kline. A few of these routes and anchorages have not been presented before in any publication. For instance, the routes through the reef west of Man Of War Cay in the Jumentos are the same routes the Bahamians have been using for years and years, nothing new, except that now you have access to this database of local knowledge. What is new is that you can now enter an area and have a detailed, and geographically correct chart that was unavailable even a few years ago. I hope you enjoy this book and its charts. There is no greater compliment than cruisers telling me they used my work and that it enabled them to have a safer journey and to enjoy the area they visited. Enjoy your cruise, few things in life are as rewarding.

Stephen J. Pavlidis
S/V IV Play

THE BASICS

ANCHORING

Just as important as getting your vessel moving and keeping her heading along your chosen courseline quickly and efficiently is the fine art of keeping your vessel from moving. Many of the anchorages in this book are swept by swift tidal currents, sometimes up to 3 knots, and to avoid bumping into your neighbor in the middle of the night or putting your vessel on the rocks or beach, two anchors, such as in a Bahamian Moor, are required.

Anchor choice is basically a personal preference. Some skippers prefer CQRs, while others swear by a Bruce or a Danforth. Of the "Big Three," you will find that a Danforth holds as well or better than a CQR or Bruce in sandy bottoms while the CQR or Bruce is preferred when anchoring in rocky bottoms. Whatever your choice of anchor, you must deploy your anchor correctly and with sufficient scope to hold you when the tide changes, if a front approaches, or if a squall should blow through at 2:00 A.M. (which seems to be the time they choose to blow through). Your anchor should have a length of chain (at least 15') shackled to your anchor to keep your rode from chafing against coral or rocks and to create a catenary curve that helps absorb shock loads while lowering the angle of pull on your anchor. Too high an angle may cause your anchor to pull up and out of the bottom. Some cruisers prefer all chain rodes with a nylon snubber to absorb the shock loads. This is an excellent arrangement but a windlass may be needed unless you prefer the workout involved with hauling in the chain and anchor every time you move.

In many of the lee side anchorages in The Bahamas you will find that you can lie quite comfortably to only one anchor. When setting your anchor do not just drop it and let your rode run out, piling itself on top of your anchor. Lower your anchor to the bottom and deploy the rode as you fall back with the current or wind until you have at least a 5:1 scope out, 7:1 is preferable but not always possible. When calculating the amount of scope required, be sure to allow for high tide as well as the height of your anchor roller or fairlead above the water. Without being precise, you can figure on a 2½'-4' tidal rise in The Bahamas although occasionally you may find a 4½' rise such as during Spring tides, a little more during a full moon, and a little less at new moon. When you have secured your rode, back down with the engine at about ½ throttle to set the anchor. If you have not succeeded in securing your anchor, try again. To check the set it is best to dive on your anchors or at the very least, look at their set through a glass bottom bucket from your dinghy. You may find that you will have to set them by hand, especially in rocky areas.

If there are other boats in the anchorage when you arrive and they are riding to two anchors, or if you are in an area beset by tidal currents, it is best to set two anchors in a Bahamian Moor. Although one anchor may be fine if you have the swinging room, when the tide changes it may pull out and fail to reset. These anchorages are often very crowded and while you may swing wide on your one anchor and not find yourself endangered by the rocks or beach, you and your neighbor may go bump in the night because his two anchors have kept him in one spot. If unsure the best thing to do is follow the lead of those boats that are there before you. Conversely, if you arrive at an anchorage and everyone is on one anchor and you choose to set two, do so outside the swing radius of the other boats. If you are riding on one anchor and find that you are lying to the wind but that the swell is rolling you, position another anchor at an angle off the stern so as to align your bow into the swell making for a more comfortable night.

To set a Bahamian Moor you must first decide where you wish for your vessel to settle. You will lay out two anchors, one up-current and one down-current of that spot which will keep you swinging in a small circle. Head into the current to where you will drop your first anchor and set it properly. Let out as much scope as you can, setting your anchor on the way by snubbing it, until you are at the spot where you are to drop your down-current anchor. If the wind has pushed you to one side or the other of the tidal stream, you will have to power up to the position where you will set your second anchor. Lower your second anchor and pull your vessel back up current on your first rode, paying out the rode for the second anchor and snubbing it as you maneuver back up current to your chosen spot. You may want to dive on your anchors to check their set. Keeping your rodes tight will keep you swinging in a tighter circle. Check your anchor rodes daily as they will twist together and make it extremely difficult to undo them in an emergency.

In some tight anchorages you will be unable to set your anchors 180° apart. An alternative is to set them 90° apart in a "Y" configuration perpendicular to the wind. A skipper with a large swing radius in very tight quarters is apt to find out what his neighbors think of his anchoring technique as soon as the wind shifts. Responsible anchoring cannot be over-stressed.

Always set an anchor light. Some cruisers feel this is unimportant in some of the more isolated anchorages. What they probably do not understand is that many locals run these islands at all hours of the night, even on moonless nights, and an anchor light protects your vessel as well as theirs.

It is important to note that the lee-side anchorages, especially those in the outer islands (Inagua, Plana, etc.), can get rolly at times (yes, you will learn a new dance, "The Out Island Roll"). The Atlantic Ocean surge seeks out any way it can to round the tips of these islands to cause you seemingly no end of discomfort and there is not much you can do about it except possibly use a second anchor or bridle arrangement to keep your bow or stern into the swell. If using a bridle, set up your line on the opposite side that you wish to turn your vessel. For instance, if you need to turn your bow to port to face the incoming swells and make for a calmer ride, run your bridle line from a winch to a block on your starboard quarter and then forward outside your shrouds to your anchor line. Either tie it to your rode or, if you use all chain, attach it to the shackle where your nylon snubber (be sure to use a long one, at least 10'-20' if you are setting up for a bridle arrangement) hooks to your chain. After your anchor is set, simply crank in your bridle line bringing your bow to port and off the wind.

Anchorages on the eastern shores of the Bahamian Out Islands are all daytime anchorages only due to the prevailing winds and should be used only in settled or westerly weather.

Never anchor in coral, even with your dinghy anchor. An anchor can do a great deal of damage to a very fragile ecosystem that will take years to recover if it is to recover at all. Besides, sand holds so much better anyway.

In summer months and on into the early fall, or when there is no wind, you may wish to anchor a good distance from shore to keep away from the relentless biting insects. Cays with a lot of vegetation or mangroves will have a higher concentration of biting insects.

Proper anchoring etiquette should by practiced at all times. For instance, if the anchorage is wide and roomy and only one boat is at anchor, do not anchor right on top of them, give your neighbor a little breathing room and some solitude. You would probably appreciate the same consideration should the situation be reversed. All too often cruisers exhibit a herding instinct where they seek the comfort of other nearby cruisers, anchoring much too close at times. Many boaters, after a long, hard day in rough seas or bad weather, anxiously await the peace and tranquility of a calm anchorage. The last thing they want is noise and wake. If you have a dog aboard that loves to bark, be considerate of your neighbors who do not wish to hear him. They do have that right. Jet skis can be a lot of fun, but only when you are astride one. Many cruisers have little tolerance for the incessant buzzing back and forth of high speed jet skis. It is a good show of manners to slowly leave the anchorage where you can have your high speed fun and games and not disturb anyone. The same can be said of water skiing which is prohibited within 200' of the shoreline in The Bahamas unless the skier is approaching or leaving the shore at a speed of 3 knots or less. If at all possible, try not to run your generators at sunset or after dark. At sunset, many cruisers are sitting in their cockpits enjoying cocktails and watching the sun go down and do not want a generator disturbing their soft conversations. Many powerboats use a lot of electricity by running all sorts of lights at night. Some will leave on huge floodlights for one reason or another with no idea of the amount of glare and light it produces in nearby cockpits to other boaters. This is not an incrimination of all powerboaters, only the careless few. The vast majority of powerboaters are very considerate and professional and do not approve of their noisy, blinding, cousins. Courtesy shown is usually courtesy returned.

CHARTERING

The only true charter company operating in the Outer Islands is Marine Services of Eleuthera and Charter Cats of Eleuthera in Hatchet Bay, Eleuthera. They have a fleet of Cabo Rico's and some newly acquired catamarans. You can contact them in the United States at 800-446-9441.

Flyfishing Charters operates a 47' Catamaran in the Bight of Acklins where up to three couples can stay for a week or two and enjoy bonefishing or tarpon fishing on a daily basis. Anglers stay aboard the sailing Catamaran *Blue Lagoon* sailing in the protected waters of the Bight of Acklins. For more information call 410-280-0859 in the United States.

Students wishing to do research in The Bahamas, particularly from New Providence to the Turks and Caicos, should contact Nicolas and Dragan Popov of Island Expeditions at P.O. Box CB11934, Love Beach #4C, Nassau, N.P., The Bahamas, 242-327-8659. Island Expeditions has several sailing trips each year through the Exumas and the Southern Bahamas on the way to the Dominican Republic and the Silver Banks as part of a humpback whale study program.

CHARTS

The BBA, the Better Boating Association, Box 407, Needham, Ma. 01292, makes an excellent 17" x 22" chart kit covering The Bahamas with reproductions of U.S. government charts and color photographs. Be sure to get as late a version as possible as some of the earlier versions are not corrected for WGS84 datum and many of the lat/lon lines are up to as much as .3' off.

CLOTHING

If you are heading to The Bahamas, especially the more southerly Out Islands you will enter a tropical climate where the theme for clothing is light. You will most likely live in shorts and T-shirts (if that much). Long pants and sturdy, comfortable shoes are preferred when hiking for protection from the bush and the rugged terrain. Long sleeved shirts (or old cotton pajamas) and wide brimmed hats are important in keeping the sun off you. Polarized sunglasses (helpful for piloting) and suntan lotion (suntan oil tends to leave a long lasting greasy smear all over everything) should be included in your gear. In winter months it is advisable to bring something warm to wear, especially in the evenings. Long pants and sweaters are usually adequate and a light jacket would be a good idea as some frontal passages will occasionally drop the temperature to 60° F.

It is important that men and women dress appropriately when entering settlements. Skimpy bathing suits for men as well as women are excellent for the beach or boat but in town they are not apropos. Men should wear shirts in town as some local inhabitants are quick to remind you to cover up. Remember, you are a visitor here and that entails a certain responsibility.

CURRENCY

The legally acceptable currency of The Bahamas is the Bahamian dollar whose value is on par with the American dollar. American money is readily acceptable throughout the islands at all stores, marinas, and hotels. Bahamian coins come in 1¢, 5¢, 10¢, and 25¢ denomination while Bahamian paper money comes in $.50, $1, $3, (yes, a three dollar bill), $5, $10, $20, $50, and $100 denominations.

CUSTOMS AND IMMIGRATION

Bahamian Ports of Entry

ABACO: Green Turtle Cay, Marsh Harbour, Spanish Cay, Walker's Cay
ANDROS: Congo Town, Fresh Creek (*Lighthouse Marina*), Mangrove Cay, Morgan's Bluff
BERRY ISLANDS: Chubb Cay (*Chubb Cay Marina*), Great Harbour Cay (*Great Harbour Cay Marina*)
BIMINI: Alice Town (*any marina*)
CAT CAY: *Cat Cay Marina*
CAT ISLAND: Smith's Bay, New Bight
ELEUTHERA: Governor's Harbour, Harbour Island, Hatchett *Bay (Marine Services of Eleuthera),* Rock Sound, Spanish Wells, Powell Point (*Cape Eleuthera Marina*)
EXUMA: George Town
GRAND BAHAMA: Freeport Harbour, *Lucaya Marina*, Port Lucaya, West End, *Xanadu Marina*
INAGUA: Matthew Town
LONG ISLAND: Stella Maris
NEW PROVIDENCE: Nassau (*any marina*)
MAYAGUANA: Abraham's Bay
RAGGED ISLAND: Duncan Town
SAN SALVADOR: Cockburn Town (*Riding Rock Marina*)

All vessels entering Bahamian waters must clear in with Customs and Immigration officials at the nearest port of entry listed above. Failure to report within 24 hours may subject you to a penalty and make you liable for confiscation and forfeiture of your vessel. When approaching your selected port of entry be sure to fly your yellow "Q" flag. Tie up to a dock or marina and await the officials if directed. In places like Bimini (where the dockmasters will usually have the necessary forms for you) or Green Turtle Cay, only the captain of the vessel may go ashore to arrange clearance and no other shore contact is permitted until pratique is granted. Some of the marinas that you use may levy a charge for using their dock, Cat Cay in particular. If they do not charge you, good manners suggest that you at least make a fuel purchase. Most southbound vessels usually clear in long before reaching the outer islands while those northbound skippers have a choice of ports of entry.

During normal working hours, 9:00 A.M. to 5:30 P.M., Monday through Friday, no charge other than necessary transportation costs is charged for the clearance of pleasure vessels. If arriving outside these hours or on holidays you may expect to pay overtime charges of 1½-2 times the normal pay of the officer. These charges are per boat so don't expect to split them up amongst the members of your flotilla. U.S. citizens need proof of citizenship, a passport (not required) or Voter Registration Card. Canadian and British visitors also do not need passports. Visas are not required for visitors from the U.S., Canada, and persons from any British Commonwealth country. If you are flying in and returning by way of a boat in transit you need some proof that you are able to leave the country. It is suggested that you purchase a round trip ticket and leave the return reservation open. When you return aboard your boat you may then cash in your unused ticket or use it for a future flight. Check with the airline when buying your ticket as to their policy in this matter.

If yours is a pleasure vessel with no dutiable cargo, the captain will fill out a Maritime Declaration of Health, Inwards Report for pleasure vessels, and a crew list. Do not mistakenly call your crew "passengers" or it may be interpreted that you are running a charter. An International Marine Declaration of Health in duplicate will be accepted in lieu of a Bill of Health from vessels arriving in The Bahamas. Smallpox vaccination certificates and cholera inoculation certificates are required only if the vessel is arriving directly from an infected area.

Each crew member will fill out and sign an Immigration Card. You will be asked to keep the small tab off the card and return it by mail after you leave The Bahamas. You can ask for and receive a stay of up to eight months however some Immigration Officials will only give three or four months for reasons that are clear only to them. This is an inconsistency that one sees every now and then as you talk to different cruisers and find out about their clearing-in adventure. An Immigration official in Nassau explained that it is up to the individual officer to determine how long a stay to permit. If you have guests flying in they also must have a return trip ticket and proof of citizenship.

The captain will be issued a Cruising Permit (Transire) for the vessel that is valid for up to 12 months. This permit must be presented to any Customs official or other proper officer (if requested) while in The Bahamas. If you wish to keep your vessel in Bahamian waters for longer than one year without paying import duties, special arrangements must be made with Customs. The owner may extend the one year stay for up to three years by paying a fee of $500 per year after the first year. Import duties are now 7.5% for vessels of 30'-100' while vessels less than 30' are charged 22.5%. Spare parts for installation aboard your vessel are duty free. If the parts are imported as cargo they are subject to a 6% duty.

If you plan to do any fishing during your stay you must purchase a Fishing Permit that is good for up to six reels. The permit now costs $20 and is valid for three months. As you approach its expiration date you should visit a Customs Office to purchase another if you intend to stay longer. Acquiring a permit for more than six reels is costly and only for the serious fisherman. Please familiarize yourself with the rules and regulations on the reverse side of the permit. There are strict penalties if you are caught fishing without a permit so pay the man the $20.

If you have pets on board they must have an import permit. An application for the permit may be requested by writing to the Director of the Department of Agriculture, P.O. Box N-3704, Nassau, Bahamas (242-325-7413, fax # 242-325-3960). Return the completed application with a $10.00 fee in the form of a Postal Money Order or International Money Order payable to the Public Treasury. This will hasten the process of obtaining your permit although you should allow three to four weeks processing time. Rabies certificates are required of all animals over three months old and must be more than 10 days but less than 9 months old and should be presented when you clear Customs and Immigration.

Non-residents of The Bahamas entering aboard a foreign vessel are not required to obtain permits nor pay duties on firearms during their visit to the islands. This exemption is for three months following the arrival of the vessel at a designated port of entry. After three months a certificate must be obtained from the Commissioner of Police. All firearms must be kept safe from theft under lock and key and be declared on your cruising permit with an accurate count of all ammunition. Firearms may not be used in Bahamian waters nor taken ashore. Hunters should contact the Department of Agriculture and Fisheries in Nassau for information on hunting in The Bahamas. Completely forbidden are tear gas pens, military arms such as artillery, flame-throwers, machine guns, and automatic weapons. Exempt are toy guns, dummy firearms, flare guns, and spear guns designed for underwater use.

Certain items may be brought in duty free including personal effects such as wearing apparel, ship's stores, 1 quart of alcoholic beverage, 1 quart of wine, 1 pound in weight of tobacco or 200 cigarettes or 50 cigars.

As soon as the captain has cleared Customs, you may take down your yellow "Q" flag and replace it with the Bahamian courtesy flag.

American flag vessels are not required to obtain clearance when departing U.S. ports. If you are clearing back into the United States you must, upon entry, call the U.S. Customs Service to clear in. You are required to go to a nearby telephone immediately upon arrival and dock nearby. You can dial 1-800-432-1216, 1-800-458-4239, or 1-800-451-0393 to get a Customs Agent on the line to arrange clearance. When you have Customs on the phone you will need to give them your vessel's name and registration number, the owner's name, the Captain's name and date of birth, all passenger names and date of births, a list of all foreign ports visited and the duration of your stay there, a list of guns aboard, the total value of all purchases, and your Customs User Fee decal number if one has been issued, and whether you have anything to declare (total of all purchases, fresh fruit, vegetables, or meat). If you do not have a decal you may be directed to the nearest U.S. Customs station to purchase one within 48 hours. Decals may be purchased prior to departing on your voyage by ordering an application (Customs Form #339) and submitting the completed application with a $25.00 fee (Money Order or check drawn on U.S. bank) to U.S. Customs Service, National Finance Center, P.O. Box 198151, Atlanta, Georgia 30384.

Each resident of the United States, including minors, may take home duty-free purchases up to $600 U.S. if they have been outside the U.S. for more than 48 hours and have not taken this exemption in 30 days. This includes up to 2 liters of liquor per person over 21 provided that one liter is manufactured in The Bahamas or a member of the Caribbean Basin Initiative (CBI). A family may pool their exemptions. Articles of up to $1000 in excess of the duty-free $600 allowance are assessed at a flat rate of 10%. For example, a family of four may bring back up to $2400 worth of duty-free goods. If they were to bring back $6400 worth of goods, they would have to pay a duty of $400 on the $4000 above the duty-free allowance. This flat rate may only be used once every 30 days. If the returning U.S. resident is not entitled to the duty-free allowance because of the 30 day or 48 hour restrictions, they may still bring back $25 worth of personal or household items. This exemption may not be pooled. Antiques are admitted to the U.S. duty-free if they are over 100 years old. The Bahamian store selling the antique should provide you with a form indicating the value and certifying the age of the object. Importation of fruits, plants, meats, poultry, and diary products is generally prohibited. More than $10,000 in U.S. or foreign coin, currency, traveler's checks, money orders, and negotiable instruments or investment securities in bearer form must be reported to Customs. Importation of Bahamian tortoise or turtle shell goods is prohibited. Many medicines purchased over the counter in The Bahamas such as 222, a codeine-aspirin-caffeine compound, are not allowed entry. Although you can buy Cuban cigars in Nassau, enjoy them on your cruise and do not attempt to bring them back into the U.S. The U.S. Customs Service frowns on Americans spending money on Cuban products. Hopefully that will change in time.

Any number of gifts may be sent to the U.S. from The Bahamas and the recipient will pay no duty provided that the gift is worth U.S. $50 or less. If the value is over U.S. $50, duty and tax is charged on the full value. The following regulations must be complied with. Only $50 worth of gifts may be received by the U.S. addressee in one day. The value of the gifts must be clearly written on the package as well as the words "Unsolicited Gift." No alcoholic beverages or tobacco may be sent. Perfume with value of more than $5 may not be sent. Persons in the U.S. are not allowed to send money to The Bahamas for gifts to be shipped to them duty-free, the gifts must be unsolicited. Persons may not mail a gift addressed to themselves. For more information, contact the U.S. Customs Service before you leave or call them in Nassau at 242-327-7126.

Canadian residents may take advantage of three categories of duty-free exemption. If you have been out of Canada for 24 hours, you may make a verbal declaration to claim a CDN$20 duty-free allowance any number of times per year. This exemption does not include alcohol or tobacco. If you have been out of the country for 48 hours, any number of times per year, a written declaration must be made and you may claim a CDN$100 allowance. This allowance can include up to 200 cigarettes, 50 cigars, or 2 lbs. of tobacco, and 1.1 liters of alcohol per person. If you have been out of Canada for over 7 days, you may make a written declaration and claim a CDN$300 exemption including the above mentioned amounts of tobacco and alcohol. After a trip abroad for 48 hours or more you are entitled to a special 20% tax rate on goods valued up to CDN$300 over and above the CDN$100 and CDN$300 personal exemption. For importation of tobacco the claimant must be 16 years of age. For alcohol, the claimant must have attained the legal age prescribed by the laws of the provincial or territorial authority at the point of entry.

Unsolicited gifts may be sent to Canada duty-free as long as they are valued under CDN$400 and do not contain alcoholic beverages, tobacco products, or advertising matter. If the value is above CDN$400 the recipient must pay regular duty and tax on the excess amount.

THE DEFENCE FORCE

The Royal Bahamas Defence Force came into existence officially on March 31, 1980. Their duties include defending The Bahamas, stopping drug smuggling, illegal immigration, poaching, and providing assistance to mariners whenever and wherever they can. They have a fleet of 26 coastal and inshore patrol craft along with 2 aircraft. The Defence Force has over 850 personnel including 65 officers and 74 women.

I have been associated with a number of Defence Force personnel through my efforts at Exuma Park and I have developed a healthy respect for these men and women. Every officer and seaman that I have met has been highly intelligent, articulate, dedicated, and very professional in regards to their duties. These are not the thugs and hoodlums that so many cruisers have come to fear over the last few years. As late as 1991, horror stories were coming out of Nassau concerning improprieties during routine boardings. The Defence Force has taken corrective steps and reports of trouble caused by boarding parties are almost non-existent now. What complaints I have heard I have found to have two sides, and quite often cruisers take the boaters side instinctively while giving no thought to the other side of the coin. There is no reason to dread the gray boats as they approach. The Defence Force has a very difficult job to do and it often becomes necessary for them to board private pleasure vessels in routine searches. The boarding party will do everything they can to be polite and professional, however, due to the violent nature of the criminals they seek, standard procedure is to be armed. Unfortunately, in the process of protecting themselves, they inadvertently intimidate cruisers. Please do not be alarmed if a crewman bearing an automatic weapon stays in your cockpit while the officer conducts a search below decks in your presence. If you are boarded you will be asked to sign a statement saying that the search was carried out politely and in the presence of the owner or skipper. I have been boarded and found the boarding officer and crew to be courteous and professional. It is not unusual for the Defence Force to enter an anchorage and board all the vessels anchored there. Normally they will not board a vessel that is unoccupied, preferring to keep an eye out for your return.

Cruisers often ask why single me out, why search my boat? What are they looking for? Besides the obvious problem with drugs, The Bahamas has problems with people smuggling illegal weapons and ammunition into the country. With bullets selling for $5 and more apiece on the street in Nassau a boater could fatten his or her cruising kitty very easily. You must keep accurate records on all your weapons and ammunition and make sure you record them on your cruising permit when you check in.

The Defence Force also must defend the richness of the marine fisheries in The Bahamas. It is not unknown for a boat to cross over from the states without a permit and fill up its freezers with Bahamian caught fish, conch, and lobster. In 1997, a boat from south Florida was boarded upon its return to Florida and the owners and crew arrested and charged under the Lacy Act. The Defence Force, if they board your vessel, will probably want to see your fishing permit and ask you whether you have any fish aboard. For most cruisers this does not pose a problem. If, however, you have 100 dolphin aboard, you will find yourself in a world of well deserved trouble. You might have a better understanding of what the Defence Force goes through if you learn about the four Defence Force Marines who died a decade ago when Cuban MIGs sank their boat after the rest of the crew boarded Cuban fishing boats illegally operating in Bahamian waters along the southern edge of the Great Bahama Bank. This is serious business.

DINGHY SAFETY

Most cruisers spent a considerable amount of time in their dinghies exploring the waters and islands in the vicinity of their anchorage. It is not unknown for a dinghy engine to fail or a skipper to run out of gas miles away from the mother vessel. For this reason I urge boaters to carry some simple survival gear in their dinghies. First, I would recommend a handheld VHF radio for obvious reasons. If there are any other boats around this may be your best chance for getting some assistance. A good anchor and plenty of line are also high on the list. I do not mean one of those small three pound anchors with thirty feet of line that is only used on the beach to keep your dinghy from drifting to Cuba. It may pay to sacrifice the onboard room and use a substantial anchor with a couple of feet of chain and at least 100' of line. Just as you would go oversize on your mother vessel do the same with your dinghy. If you are being blown away from land a good anchor and plenty of line gives you a good chance of staying put where someone may find you. Next, a dinghy should have a supply of flares. Local boaters often carry a large coffee can with a rag soaked in oil lying in the bottom. If they get in trouble lighting the rag will produce an abundant amount of smoke that can be seen from a quite a distance. A dinghy should be equipped with survival water, a bottle or some small packages manufactured by a company called DATREX. It would be a good idea to throw in a few MRE's. These are the modern, tastier version of K-Rations that our armed forces survived on for years. Each MRE also contains vital survival components such as matches and toilet paper. Another handy item that does not take up much room is a foil survival blanket. They really work and take up as much space as a couple of packs of cigarettes.

Please don't laugh at these suggestions. I have seen people forced to spend a night or two in a dinghy and these few items would have made their experience much more pleasant if not entirely unnecessary. I have run out of gas and used flares to attract some local attention even though one of my boat mates was ready to dive in and swim for the nearest island to fetch some help. Now, I never leave in my dinghy without my little survival bag stashed away in the dink. It doesn't take much effort to prepare a small bag for your dinghy and it will be worth it's weight in gold should you need it.

One final word, if you find the need to skirt a large sandbank lying to leeward of a cay remember that even though the sandbanks stretch out quite a way to the west, there is usually a channel of slightly deeper water nearer the shoreline of the cays.

DIVING

From shallow water reef dives to deep water wall drop-offs, the diving in The Bahamas is as good as it gets anywhere and much better than most places. You don't need scuba equipment to enjoy the undersea delights that are available, many reefs lie in less than 30' and are easily accessible to those with snorkels, dinghies, and curiosity.

Although the waters in The Bahamas are crystal clear and the obstructions plainly visible in the ambient light, divers must take proper precautions when diving in areas of current. Experienced divers are well aware of this but it must be stated for novices and snorkelers. Tidal fluctuations can produce strong currents which must be taken into account when diving. Waves breaking over and around inshore reefs can create strong surges which can push or pull you into some very sharp coral. For safety's sake, only experienced divers should penetrate wrecks and caves.

FISHING

Fishing in The Bahamas is hard to beat. Trolling in the Gulf Stream, the Atlantic Ocean, Exuma Sound, or Crooked Island Passage you are likely to hook a dolphin, wahoo, or tuna, all excellent eating. Trolling on the banks you will usually catch a barracuda although it is possible to bring up a snapper, jack, or grouper. Bonefish can be found in the tidal flats scattered throughout the islands. Chris Lloyd of BASRA in Nassau offers this little ditty to those who are unsure what color lure to use for trolling offshore. Chris says:

> *Red and black-*
> *Wahoo attack.*
> *Yellow and green-*
> *Dolphin fishing machine.*

Chris works Monday through Friday and BASRA HQ in Nassau Harbour and is quite an authority on fishing Bahamian waters. If you have any questions stop in and ask Chris. He loves visitors and is a wealth of fishing and diving information. Chris reminds us that the cooler months are ripe for wahoo while dolphin are more abundant from March through May.

The back of your fishing permit will have a brief but incomplete description of the fishing regulations in The Bahamas. Only six lines are permitted in the water at one time unless you have paid for a commercial permit (very expensive). SCUBA is illegal for the taking of marine life and an air compressor such as a

Third Lung or similar type of apparatus, must have a permit issued by the Minister of Agriculture. Spearguns are illegal for fishing in The Bahamas and are illegal to have aboard. You may only use a Hawaiian Sling or pole spear for spearfishing. It is illegal to use bleach, firearms, or explosives for fishing. Spearfishing is illegal within one mile of New Providence and within 200 yards of any family island (defined as any cay with a residence). The capture of bonefish by net is illegal as is their purchase or sale. Conch, with a daily limit of 10 per person, may not be taken if they do not have a well formed, flared lip. Possession of a hawksbill turtle is prohibited. The minimum size for a green turtle is 24" and for a loggerhead, 30". The bag limit for kingfish, dolphin, and wahoo is a maximum combination of 6 fish per person aboard.

Crawfish, the spiny lobster that is such a treat as well as being a large part of the economy for local fishermen, has a closed season from April 1-August 1. The minimum limits are a carapace length of 3 3/8" and a 6" tail length. It is illegal to possess a berried (egg laying) female or to remove the eggs from a female. You may not take any corals while in the Bahamas.

In the Out Islands there are far fewer jobs than there are people looking for jobs. The people here must eke out a living the best way they can. Remember that when you are fishing. Please catch just enough to eat and maybe put some away for tomorrow. So often cruisers come through this area with huge freezers just waiting to be filled to the brim to help their owners offset vacation costs. If you over-fish an area you may be taking food out of the mouths of children. To protect the livelihood of the people of The Bahamas, some of richer fishing spots will not be mentioned in this guide.

Conch can usually be found on the bottom in beds of sea grass or soft corals where they prefer to feed. They are usually in areas with a swift current such as in the cuts between cays. The conch that you don't plan to eat right away can be left in a dive bag hanging in the water or may be put on a stringer. Punch or drill a small hole in the lip of the conch shell and string four or five together and set them on the bottom, they won't go far. After you clean the conch, save the tough orange colored skin and put it in your freezer for later, it is an excellent fish bait and a small piece of it should be placed on all lures to give them an attractive aroma to fish.

The reefs in The Bahamas can provide you with a plentiful supply of fish such as grouper, snapper, hogfish, turbots (trigger fish), and grunts. How many you can get is dependent on your skill with the spear. Groupers are especially wary and prefer holes to hide in.

When near cays, the drop-offs are excellent for game and food fish. You may find yourself hooking a dolphin, wahoo, shark, kingfish, or tuna.

Crawfish, the clawless spiny lobster, is the principal delicacy that most cruisers search so hard for and which are getting increasingly difficult to find. They prefer to hide during the day under ledges, and rocks, and in holes where the only visible sign of them will be a pair of antennae resembling some sort of sea fan jutting out from their hiding spot. If you are fortunate enough to spear a few, and they are large enough, do not overlook the succulent meat in the base of the antennae and in the legs. So many cruisers ignore these pieces and just take the tail. Watch a Bahamian as they prepare a lobster, very little goes to waste.

FLIGHTS

Flying in and out of the Central or Southern Bahamas poses little problems. Nassau's international airport is the hub of flying activity in The Bahamas with numerous flights per day to the US and points beyond. Paradise Island airport also is quite busy on a daily basis. Almost all the outer islands have some sort of daily service, whether regular or charter, it is possible to get to any island group. See the relevant chapter for the particulars on flights for that island group.

GARBAGE

When I first began cruising I had this naive idea that all cruisers lived in a certain symbiosis with nature. My bubble finally burst with the bitter realization that many cruisers were infinitely worse than common litterbugs. So often they have the attitude of "out of sight, out of mind." I sometimes wonder if they believe in supernatural beings, hoping that if they dump their trash somewhere imaginary garbage fairies will come along and take care of the disposal problems for them. One cruiser leaves a few bags of garbage in some secluded (or not so secluded) spot and the next cruiser says "My, what a good spot for a garbage dump. Ethel, bring the garbage, I've found the dump!" This is why you often go ashore on otherwise deserted islands and find bags and piles of bags of garbage. Nothing is worse than entering paradise only to discover some lazy, ignorant, slob of a cruiser (no, I have not been too harsh on this type of person, I can still think of plenty of other adjectives without having to consult a thesaurus) has dumped his bags of garbage in the bushes. Please do not add to this problem. Remember, your garbage attracts all kinds of foul creatures such as rats (and other careless cruisers).

Nobody likes storing bags of smelly garbage aboard but if you cannot find a settlement nearby to take your garbage for free, you will have to make an allowance in your budget to pay for the local garbage disposal service. If you are nowhere near a garbage facility you should stow your trash aboard separated into three groups for easier disposal. First cans and bottles (wash them first to remove any smells while being stored), then into another container stow the organic stuff such as food scraps, rinds, and eggshells, and finally paper and plastic trash. Your food scraps, you can store them in a large coffee can with a lid, should be thrown overboard daily on an outgoing tide. The paper and plastic should be burned completely when necessary and the ashes buried deep and not on the beach. Cans and bottles should be punctured or broken and dumped overboard in very deep water at least a few miles offshore. Cut off both ends of the cans and break the bottles overboard as you sink them. If you cannot implement a garbage disposal policy aboard your vessel, stay home, don't come to these beautiful islands. Do not abuse what we all use.

GPS

Even with today's crop of sophisticated Loran receivers, accuracy of this system south of Nassau should be viewed as suspect at best. In the search for reliable positioning, skippers have turned to that electronic marvel called GPS as their main source of navigational data. Nowadays anyone with a couple of hundred dollars can become an instant navigator and there are very, very few boats cruising without a GPS unit. Let's face it, it is the standard for navigation today and in the foreseeable future.

The GPS waypoints listed in this guide are for general usage only. I do not intend for you to follow a string of waypoints to an anchorage. Instead, I will bring you to the general area where you can pilot your way in the rest of the way. Do not attempt to maneuver your vessel from waypoint to waypoint without a constant lookout. The GPS is truly a marvel but I have yet to find one that will locate and steer around a coral head or sandbar. Any skipper who attempts to navigate a tricky channel such as The Devil's Backbone in Eleuthera the inside passage at Andros, or the entrance to George Town, Exuma, at Conch Cay Cut by using only GPS waypoints deserves whatever ill fortune befalls them. The inherent error in such waypoints due to the Selective Availability (SA) of the system is too great to make such dangerous routes viable. The positions plotted on the charts in this guide are taken with the help of a GPS based hydrographic system (see *Using The Charts*) with its inherent SA error of 100 meters, approximately 328'. In the worst case scenario, if you couple the inherent error of my GPS during soundings, and your GPS when you are cruising the same locale, it is theoretically possible to have a maximum error of 200 meters, 656', or a little over .1 nautical mile! That much of a possible error could be disastrous. Until the SA is turned off and I can resound these areas I repeat: <u>use these waypoints only as a guideline, trust your eyes and your depthsounder!</u>

GPS datum used in all areas of The Bahamas is WGS 84.

HAM RADIO

All amateur radio operators will need a Bahamian Reciprocal licensee (C6A) to operate legally in the waters of The Bahamas. To obtain an application write to Mr. T. M. Deveaux, Batelco, P.O. Box N-3048, Nassau, N.P., Bahamas, or if you have questions call 242-323-4911, ext. 7553. Return the application with a photocopy of your license and a money order for $6 (payable to Batelco, money order or certified check, no personal checks) and allow two months for processing of a new application. Do not arrive in Nassau thinking that you can apply for and get a new C6A. Although you may apply at the office, it will still take almost two months to process the application. Renewals, good for one year, are also $6 and can be walked through the Batelco Office on John F. Kennedy Drive in Nassau or handled by mail usually within approximately 2-3 weeks. It is best to handle this prior to your cruise. If you change your call sign with an upgrade you only need to send Mr. Deveaux a letter explaining the situation, it would probably be a good idea to enclose a photocopy of your new license.

The Bahamas does not have a third-party agreement with the United States, this means that you cannot make a phone patch from The Bahamas to the U.S. If you head offshore three miles you will be in international waters and can make a phone patch from there without using your C6A, you will be MM2

(Maritime Mobile) once you are three miles out. Currently, Bahamian regulations state that international waters begin three miles out from the nearest Bahamian land mass. The Bahamas is currently considering a plan to classify all waters within the Bahamian archipelago as being Bahamian waters. This would mean that if you were three miles out on the Banks you would not be in international waters, you would still be in Bahamian waters. Hams will want to stay abreast of this situation and check with Batelco as to the status of the ruling. An excellent source of information on the topic would be Carolyn Wardle, C6AGG, who runs the Bahamas Weather Net every morning. If you have any questions give her a shout after the net, she will be happy to share any information she has on the subject.

A Bahamian reciprocal license offers expanded frequency allocations compared to domestic U.S. regulations. Some amateurs may not be allowed to use these frequencies unless they have a C6A or the proper class of U.S. license. For example, if you possess a General Class license in the U.S., you will be unable to participate in the Bahamas Weather Net (7.096 MHz) unless you have a C6A and are within Bahamian territorial waters. You could listen but not transmit. Remember to always use your C6A call suffix when you transmit in Bahamian waters.

Domestic U.S. FCC regulations have recently been slackened concerning business communications on a personal basis but in The Bahamas this is still a gray area. Batelco has made no rulings concerning this situation so use caution when broaching the subject if you are using a Bahamian reciprocal call sign.

There is a 2 meter repeater in Nassau that operates on 146.940 MHz (down 600). Until recently there was a second 2-meter repeater in Nassau on 146.640 MHz (down 600), it is currently off-line and its future is uncertain.

The following is a listing of frequency allocations permitted by a Bahamian reciprocal license. Please note that the a maximum output power of 250 watts (Peak Envelope Power) is allowed for A3A and A3J emissions only.

BAND	CW-MHz A1	VOICE -MHz A3, A3H	VOICE -MHz A3A	VOICE -MHz A3J
160M	1.800-2.000	1.800-2.000	1.800-2.000	1.800-2.000
80 M	3.500-4.000	3.600-4.000	3.600-4.000	3.600-4.000
40M	7.000-7.3000	7.040-7.300	7.040-7.300	7.040-7.300
30M	10.100-10.150			
20M	14.000-14.350	14.050-14.350	14.050-14.350	14.050-14.350
17M	18.068-18.168	18.110-18.168	18.110-18.168	18.110-18.168
15M	21.000-21.450	21.050-21.450	21.050-21.450	21.050-21.450
12M	24.890-24.920	24.930-24.990		24.930-24.990
	24.930-24.990			
10M	28.000-29.700	28.050-29.700		28.050-29.700
6M	50.000-54.000	50.000-54.000	50.000-54.000	50.000-54.000
2M	144.000-148.000	144.000-148.000	144.000-148.000	144.000-148.000
70CM	430.000-440.000	430.000-440.000	430.000-440.000	

Emission Types:
A1-CW-telegraphy by on-off keying of a carrier without the use of a modulated tone.
A3-Telephony, double sideband.
A3A-Telephony, single sideband, reduced carrier.
A3H-Telephony, single sideband, full carrier.
A3J-Telephony, single sideband, suppressed carrier.

The following is a listing of ham nets you may wish to participate in during your Bahamas cruise.

NET NAME	FREQUENCY KHz	TIME
Waterway Net	7268	0745-0845 ET
Computer Net	7268	0900 ET-Fridays
CW Net-slow	7128	0630 ET-Mon., Wed., and Fri.
CW Net-fast	7128	0630 ET-Tues., Thurs., Sat., and Sun.
Bahamas Weather Net	3696	0720 ET
Bah. Amat. Radio Soc.	3696	0830-Sundays
Intercontinental Net	14300-14316 (changes often)	1100 UTC
Maritime Mobile Net	14300-14316 (changes often)	After Intercon. until around 0200 UTC
Caribbean Net	7240 (changes often)	1100-1200 UTC
Hurricane Watch Net	14325, 14275, 14175	When needed

HOLIDAYS

The following public holidays are observed in The Bahamas:
New Year's Day-January 1
Good Friday
Easter Sunday
Easter Monday
Whit Monday-six weeks after Easter
Labour Day-first Friday in June
Independence Day-July 10
Emancipation Day-first Monday in August
Discovery Day-October 12
Christmas Day-December 25
Boxing Day-December 26

Holidays that fall on Sunday are always observed on Monday. Holidays which fall on Saturday are also usually observed on Monday. Bahamians are very religious people so expect stores and services to be closed on Sundays as well as on Holidays. Some businesses may be open all day on Saturday but may close for a half day on Wednesdays. A must see is the Junkanoo Parade that begins about 4:00 A.M. on Boxing Day and New Years Day in Nassau and Freeport.

HURRICANE HOLES

If you are going to be cruising in The Bahamas from June through November, hurricane season, you should always keep a lookout for a safe hurricane hole. You'll want to know where they are, what you can expect when you get there, and how far you are away from your first choice. Personally, this skipper prefers a narrow, deep, mangrove lined creek but if one isn't available I'll search for something equally suitable. In the northern and central Bahamas you're never too far away from some sort of refuge. Some holes are better than others but like the old adage advises: *Any port in a storm.* With that in mind let me offer a few of the places I consider hurricane holes. Bear in mind that if you ask ten different skippers what they look for in a hurricane hole you're likely to get ten different answers. Some of these holes may not meet your requirements. I offer them only for your consideration when seeking safety for your vessel. The final decision is yours and yours alone. For the best information concerning hurricane holes always check with the locals. They'll know the best spots.

To begin with, there is no such thing as a truly safe hurricane hole, in fact, the term hurricane hole itself is quite misleading. I believe that given a strong enough hurricane, any harbour, hole, or creek can be devastated. Keep this in mind as the places that I am going to recommend offer the best protection and, under most circumstances, give you a better than average chance of surviving a hurricane, but are by no means "safe" in the true meaning of the word. Although you may feel quite safe in your chosen hole please remember that no hurricane hole comes with a guarantee. Many factors will contribute to your survival. The physical location and protection the hole offers is your primary line of defense. But hand in hand with that is the way you secure your vessel, the tidal surge, other vessels around you, and the path and strength of the hurricane. Allow yourself plenty of time to get to your chosen location and to get settled. Only a fool would attempt to race a hurricane. One more thing, in The Bahamas, owners of cays who chain off or otherwise restrict entry to a harbour, are required by law to make their harbour open and available to mariners seeking shelter in an approaching hurricane, not just in bad weather or a front, but only in a hurricane.

Abaco

Abaco offers quite a few decent hurricane holes. The best protection lies in places like Treasure Cay where you can anchor in the narrow creeks surrounding the marina complex. There is a man-made canal complex called Leisure Lee lying just south of Treasure Cay on Great Abaco. Here you will find excellent protection from seas in 8' but you will have to tie off to the trees along the shore as the entire complex is dredged and the holding is not good. Green Turtle Cay offers White Sound and Black Sound. I much prefer White Sound though there is a bit more fetch for seas to build up. Black Sound, though smaller, has a grassy bottom and a few concrete mooring blocks scattered about. At Man Of War you can choose either anchorage. Just to the south on Elbow Cay, Hope Town Harbour boasts very good protection. If you arrive early enough and your draft is shallow enough you may be able to work you way up the creek for better protection. There is an old hurricane chain stretched across the harbour that you may be able to secure your vessel to. Ask any local where to find the chain. Just a few miles away lies Marsh Harbour with that wonderful sand/mud bottom that anchors so love. The holding here is great but the harbour is open to the west for a fetch of over a mile. For small shallow draft (3') monohull vessels there is a small creek on the eastern side of the harbour just to the east of the Conch Inn Marina. Get there early. Farther south you might consider Little Harbour though it is open to the north with a 3' bar across the mouth. Between Marsh Harbour and Little Harbour lies Snake Cay which has excellent protection in its mangrove lined creeks. In the more northern Abacos you can try Hurricane Hole on the southeast end of Allan's Pensacola Cay. Here excellent protection can be found in 6'-8' of water but the bar at the entrance will only allow about 4' at high water. Small shallow draft vessels can work themselves well up into the creeks at Double Breasted Cay if unable to get to better protection to the south.

Andros

The numerous creeks that divide Andros into hundreds of tiny isles are only suitable for small, shallow draft vessels. An excellent spot for vessels drawing less than 4' is in the small pocket at Stafford Creek that lies north of the bridge. Enter only at high tide. If you draw over 6' and are in Andros when a hurricane threatens you would be better off to get to New Providence or someplace in the Exumas.

The Berry Islands

There are only three places to consider in the Berry Islands and two of them were hit hard by powerful Hurricane Andrew. Chub Cay Marina is a possibility if you didn't mind a slip or perhaps tying off between pilings. The marina was devastated by Andrew and quite a few boats destroyed. Something to remember when it's decision making time. Another possibility would be to work your way into Little Harbour. There is a winding channel into the inner anchorage where you can tuck into a narrow channel just north of the Darville's dock in 8'-11' of water with mangroves to the east and a shallow bar and a small cay to the west. Little Harbour is open to the north but there is a large shallow bank with 1'-3' over it just north of the mangroves. Ask the Darville's where they found their refrigerator after Andrew. By far the best place to be in a hurricane is in Bullock's Harbour at Great Harbour Cay Marina. Check with the dockmaster prior to arrival to make sure there is room at the marina as the holding in the harbour is poor.

Bimini

The best protection in the Biminis is up the creeks of South Bimini by way of Nixon's Harbour. Seven feet can get in over the bar at high tide where you'll find plenty of secure water inside. On the west side of South Bimini lies the entrance to the Port Royal canals. Five feet can make it over the bar with spots of 7'-10' inside. Be sure to tie up in vacant areas between houses. On the north side of South Bimini is another entrance to some small canals with a 4' bar at the entrance from the harbour at North Bimini. Take into consideration that these canals have plenty of wrecks lining the shores along with old rotten pilings jutting up here and there. The surrounding land is very low and the canals may become untenable in a high storm surge. From Bimini Harbour you can follow the deep water channel, 5' at MLW, northward to Bimini Bay Resort where you can find protection in a deep mangrove lined creek. There is only room for two or three boats here at best. As with any hurricane hole, get there early.

Cat Island

Unless you have a small, shallow draft vessel and can get up Orange Creek or Bennett's Creek along the western shore of Cat Island, your only choice may be Hawksnest Creek on the southwestern tip of Cat Island. Six feet can enter here at MLW and work its way up the creek. Bennett's Harbour offers good protection but it is small and open to the north.

Crooked/Acklins

The only protection here will be found in the maze of creeks between French Wells and Turtle Sound for boats with drafts of 3' or less, or by going through The Going Through towards the Bight of Acklins. Here you will find a maze of shallow creeks leading to numerous small mangrove lined holes, perfect little hidey-holes for the shallow draft cruiser (up to 4' or less draft) seeking shelter.

Eleuthera

There are a few holes in Eleuthera but they all suffered considerable damage from Andrew. Royal Island offers excellent protection and good holding with a number of large concrete moorings. During Andrew the fleet washed up on one shore only to be washed up on the other shore after the eye passed. Hatchet Bay is often considered a prime hurricane hole but it too has a history of damage as the hulls along the shore will testify. At Spanish Wells you will find Muddy Hole lying off the creek between Russell Island and St. George's Cay. Muddy Hole is the local hurricane hole and 4'-5' can enter here at MLW if you get there early. Every boat (and there are a lot of them) at Spanish Wells will be heading there also.

Some skippers like Cape Eleuthera Marina at Powell Point, but I wouldn't use it as shelter unless I had no other choice. The dogleg marina channel is open to the west and large seas easily work their way into the basin rocking and rolling everybody. The huge concrete breakwater at the bend in the dogleg has suffered considerable damage and offers testimony to the power of the seas that enter the marina. Just south of Powell Point lies No Name Harbour, Un-Named Harbour on some charts. Eight feet can enter here at MLW, and 6' can work their way farther up the small coves that branch off and offer fair protection. You might consider tying your lines to the trees and setting your anchors ashore here, the holding is not that great being as this is a dredged harbour.

Exumas

The Exuma Cays are home to some of the best hurricane holes in The Bahamas. From the north you should consider the inner pond at Norman's Cay. The pond offers excellent protection and good holding although there is a mile long north-south fetch that could make things rough at best. Shroud Cay has some excellent creeks with a reputation as good hurricane holes. Dr. Evans Cottman rode out a fierce hurricane here as documented in his book *Out Island Doctor*. Compass Cay has a snug little cove for protection with moorings, a marina, and creeks for shallow draft vessels. Farther south at Sampson Cay you may be able to tie up in the marina on the eastern side of the complex in the shallow and well-protected basin. I have known people to anchor between the Majors just north of Staniel Cay for hurricane shelter though I personally would try to find someplace a little more protected. At the north end of Great Guana Cay lies a small, shallow creek that gives fair to good protection for one or two small vessels drawing less that 5'. Cave Cay is an excellent hurricane hole with room for four boats in 6' at MLW. Many experienced captains like the pond at Rudder Cut Cay as a refuge, but I see the eastern shore as being very low. I believe a strong hurricane with a large storm surge and high tide might make this anchorage a death trap. If I had time to choose I would go north for five miles to Cave Cay and hope it wasn't too crowded. The George Town area is home to what may be the finest holes in The Bahamas. Holes #0, #2, and #3 at Stocking Island are excellent hurricane holes in every sense offering protection from wind and wave. The only problem here is that these holes will be crowded and Hole #3 is usually full of stored boats with absentee owners. The inner cove at Red Shanks offers good protection if you can get in close to the mangroves. Another possibility is inside the western arm of Crab Cay.

Grand Bahama

If you're in the area of Grand Bahama Island you might consider tying up at Old Bahama Bay Marina at West End. Although the Old Bahama Bay Marina offers excellent protection, a direct hit by a major hurricane would likely do some considerable damage to this complex. From the north of Grand Bahama you can consider entering Hawksbill Creek though it only has 2' over the bar at its entrance with 5'-6' inside at MLW. The Grand Lucayan Waterway offers very good protection. You can tie up anywhere deep within its concrete lined canals but you cannot pass under the Casuarina Bridge unless your height is less than 27' at high water. The canal has a fairly uniform depth of 5' throughout although the northern entrance has shoaled to around 4'-4.5' at MLW. Another option for some very good protection would be to tie up at Lucayan Marina or in the small coves surrounding the complex.

New Providence

Here, in the capitol of The Bahamas, Nassau Harbour has good holding along with a long east-west fetch. There are two hurricane chains crossing the harbour whose approximate locations are shown on the chart for Nassau. If you are fortunate enough to know someone in Coral Harbour you may be able to use their dock to escape the seas. On the southwestern shore of Rose Island is the entrance to a very good hurricane hole shown as Salt Pond on charts. It is a circular harbour with a small island in the center. The water is easily 50'-60' wide and 7'-9' deep. Anchor and tie off between the shore and the island. Get there early as everyone in Nassau and the northern Exumas will have the same idea.

Long Island

If I had to find a place to hide from a hurricane while visiting Long Island my first choice would be in the canals that wind behind the marina at Stella Maris. Some skippers have suggested Joe's Sound but I find the land to the west too low and a tidal surge like the one in Hurricane Lili (9'-14') would make this anchorage untenable. Another consideration is in the mangrove tidal creeks in the Dollar Harbour area but the best protection is hard to get into unless you have a draft of less than 4'.

The Jumentos and Ragged Island

There are only two possibilities here and both are in the vicinity of Ragged Island. A boat with a draft of less than 5' can work its way up the mangrove lined channel to anchor off the dock at Duncan Town. Here you will 4'-6' at high water with mangroves and cliffs surrounding you. This would be a fantastic hurricane hole if it were just a couple of feet deeper. The people of Duncan Town are in the process of having their channel re-dredged, perhaps they will do something with the harbour area also. Just south of Ragged Island is a small hole called Boat Harbour that some Ragged Islanders use as a hurricane hole. There is 9' inside but there is a winding channel with a 3' bar at the entrance. Ask any Ragged Islander to help you find your way in if necessary; they'll be more than happy to help.

Southern Bahamas

If you are cruising the southern Bahamas from Crooked-Acklins to Mayaguana or Inagua you will not find a truly safe hole. Although I have heard about a large sailboat riding out Hurricane Klaus lying between Samana and Propeller Cay I would not attempt to test my luck. I would either head north to better protection at George Town or continue on to The Turks and Caicos for protection at Sellar's Pond or up the canals at Discovery Bay lying northeast of Five Cays, at Leeward Going Through, or up North Creek at Grand Turk. If I had enough time I would try to make Luperon, D.R., which is as good a hole as any in the Caribbean.

JUNKANOO

The culture of The Bahamas, its heart and soul, the eyes through which it sees and is seen, is Junkanoo, with its spirit, music, dancing, singing, costumes and color. Standing along Bay Street in Nassau in the early hours of Boxing Day or New Years Day, one cannot help getting caught up in the frenzy that is Junkanoo. Junkanoo must be experienced on the street, where the clamor of the bells, whistles, and goombay drums approaching in the distance creates an electric feeling in the crowd who sway and jostle with the building excitement. Its source of all this energy is the participants, organized groups and "scrap gangs," throbbing forward to the rhythm of the music. Groups vie in a heated competition for awards for best music, costumes, and dance.

Junkanoo was introduced to the American colonies by slaves from Africa's western coast. From there it quickly spread to Jamaica and The Bahamas. Its exact origins are unknown and the numerous derivations of the name *John Canoe* further complicate the matter. The West African name *Jananin Canno* was derived from a combination of the Quojas tribe's *Canno*, a supreme being, and *Janani*, who were the dead who became spirits and were seen as patrons or defenders of the tribe. The Jamaican *John Canoe* was known in eastern North Carolina as *John Kuner, John Kooner, John Canoe, Who-Who's, and Joncooner*. A West African trait often attributed to the origin of Junkanoo was an Ashanti figure know as *Jankomo*. *Jankomo* was famed for his dance where he took two steps forward and one step back, a form of Junkanoo dancing prevalent in today's festival. Some researchers theorized that the name is a corruption of the French *gens innconnus* which, roughly translated, means u*nknown people* or *masked people*.

Junkanoo developed as a celebration during the pre-emancipation days when slaves were allowed a special Christmas holiday. Not wanting to waste any of their holiday, they took to beginning their celebration well before dawn. It is said that the wild costumes, masks, and makeup were used by the slaves as a way to disguise themselves while exacting revenge upon masters and settling grudges with fellow slaves. During the late 1800's, Junkanoo began taking on added dimensions and significance for Bahamian people. It became a vehicle for political expression and a catalyst for social change. The Street Nuisance Act of 1899 was aimed directly at Junkanoo attempting to reduce the amount of noise and length of celebration of the event in the hopes that Junkanoo would extinguish itself. Junkanoo continued, albeit a little quieter. During the economic depression of the early 1900's, Junkanoo was characterized by rival masked and costumed gangs from the various districts of New Providence. Money was scarce and the costumes changed from cloth to papier-mâché and became more frightening and grotesque.

World War I saw the suspension of Junkanoo when the white inhabitants of Nassau felt the celebrations were unsuitable considering the wartime conditions and Junkanoo was banned from Bay Street until well after the war. It moved to the "over the hill" section of Nassau where it grew and prospered. The prosperous bootlegging period of the 1920's in The Bahamas was reflected in more flamboyant costumes and headdresses. Junkanoo moved back to Bay Street in 1923 when its potential for increasing tourism revenue became apparent. It was at this time that Junkanoo became a competition with prizes being awarded.

Junkanoo was again banned from Bay Street in 1942 when riots broke out due to labor unrest and all public gatherings were banned. Junkanoo still thrived on various parts of New Providence however and was back on Bay Street by 1947.

Junkanoo today is basically the same with some minor changes. It is no longer considered a social taboo to participate in Junkanoo and more and more women are parading in this once male dominated event. Junkanoo is a national event on the edge of becoming an international festival.

The heart of Junkanoo is the music which has changed little over the last 50 years. A typical Junkanoo band consists of lead drums, second or bass drums (goombay), cowbells, clappers, bugles, trumpets, horns, conch shells, and whistles. A few obscure instruments, such as the fife, are no longer used. The drum is the core of the music. Drums are made every year from goat or sheep skin and represent a sacrifice, the spilling of blood to make a drum. Drummers often place a flame inside the drum, "called bringing it up," to help produce various drum tones. The combined effect of the music, the bells and drums and horns, all fueled by the emotion of the participants, is overwhelming.

The costumes create a tremendous visual effect and are painstakingly manufactured by hand. The costumes are brightly colored and usually represent some theme. There are no weight restrictions on costumes and one single piece may weigh over 200 pounds. Competition among the various groups is fierce and members are very secretive about their upcoming productions.

If you plan to be in Nassau or Freeport around Christmas or New Year's, do not miss Junkanoo.

MAILBOATS

You do not have to own a yacht to see The Bahamas, by sea. You will find you can go almost anywhere within by mailboat. One need only approach the dockmaster on Potter's Cay (pronounced Porter's Cay in the Bahamian dialect) for schedules and costs. Shipping times are announced three times daily on ZNS radio in Nassau. The mailboats are subsidized by the Bahamian government for carrying the mail but they also take on freight and passengers. It is an inexpensive and rewarding way to see the Out Islands. If you book passage you will gain a different view of the Bahamian people as travel by mailboat is a cultural experience as well as being a mode of transportation. People on the outer islands would find life hard indeed if not for the mailboats, they are the lifeline of the Bahamian Out Islands and the arrival of the mailboat is somewhat of a celebration. Costs range from a little over $30.00 to George Town, Exuma and slightly more to Inagua. Some mailboats include food in the fare.

MEDICAL EMERGENCIES

There are two hospitals in Nassau, Princess Margaret Hospital on Shirley Street and Doctor's Hospital on the corner of Shirley Street and Collins Ave. On Lyford Cay, also on the island of New Providence, is the Lyford Cay Hospital and Bahamas Heart Institute.

If more medical assistance is needed the patient will be flown into Nassau, usually to Princess Margaret Hospital. National Air Ambulance out of Ft. Lauderdale, Florida (305-359-9900 or 800-327-3710), can transport patients from The Bahamas to the United States. If you join DAN, the Divers Alert Network, for a small yearly fee, you are covered under their *Assist America Plan.* This program offers emergency evacuation for any accident or injury, diving related or not, to the nearest facility that can provide you with adequate care. After you have been stabilized to the satisfaction of the attending physician and the *Assist America* doctor, *Assist America* will arrange your transportation back to the United States, under medical supervision if necessary.

The Bahamas Air-Sea Rescue Association, BASRA, has stations in Nassau, Black Point, and George Town in the Exumas, Salt Pond in Long Island, and at Landrail Point on Crooked Island. All BASRA stations monitor VHF ch.16. BASRA Nassau, monitors VHF ch.16 and 2182 KHz and 4125 KHz on marine single sideband from 9:00 A.M.-5:00 P.M. Monday through Saturday. BASRA, Nassau, can be reached by phone at 242-322-3877.

PHONING HOME

If you are expecting speedy phone connections you will find that the telephone service in The Bahamas to be quite frustrating. Although there is a Marine Operator in Nassau monitoring VHF ch. 27, there are no marine operators in the Out Islands and public phones are few and far between. If you are in an emergency situation you may find a helpful Bahamian with a cellular phone in their home but these are very expensive and usually out of the reach of the average person. If you have a cellular phone contact your nearest Batelco office to arrange for service while in The Bahamas.

Amateur radio operators may not patch through phone calls by ham radio from The Bahamas. Most cays with settlements will have a Batelco office where you may place a phone call. If you call the States, try to get an *AT&T USA Direct* line (1-800-872-2881), the quality and rates are much better.

If you are calling The Bahamas the area code for all islands is 242.

PROVISIONING

If you are on a tight budget, it would be best for you to stock up on provisions in the United States prior to your Bahamas cruise. Take enough for the length of your cruise and then some. The cheapest place after the U.S. for provisioning is Puerto Plata in the Dominican Republic. With few exceptions, prices in The Bahamas are considerably higher than American prices. Beer and cigarette prices will seem outrageous with cigarette prices some 2-3 times higher than in the States. The local Bahamian beer, *Kalik* (named after the sound that cow bells make when clanged together), is very good and more reasonably priced than foreign beers. Try the Kalik Gold Label, it is more full bodied and a little stronger. Rum, as one would think, can be very inexpensive while American whiskies and certain Scotches are very high. Staples such as rice, beans, flour, and sugar are just slightly higher than U.S. prices. Vegetables can be quite reasonable in season. The vegetable market on Potter's Cay in Nassau is a good spot to pick up a large box of mixed vegetables for around $15.00 in season. Meats, soft drinks, and milk all are considerably higher than in America. As you shop the various markets throughout The Bahamas you will find some delightful items that are not sold in the U.S., foreign butter and meats for example. The shopping experience will give you the opportunity to purchase and enjoy some new treats. Of course, the prices on fresh fish, conch, and lobster are all open to bargaining with the local fishermen.

Good drinking water is available throughout the islands from some of the cisterns and wells on various cays. Well water will have a higher salt content than cistern water which is rainwater. Always check with the owners before you remove any water. Most stores sell bottled water and you can buy reverse osmosis (watermaker) in quite a few places.

I have found prices on Long Island, particularly at Salt Pond and southward to Mangrove Bush, to be equivalent to and sometimes better than prices in George Town, Exuma. Prices in Provo, Turks and Caicos, are equivalent to Nassau prices and sometimes better with some prices near stateside levels.

If you plan to dine out while in the islands, you will find the prices to be comparable to or higher than at home. It is common for dining establishments in The Bahamas to include a 15% gratuity in the check.

TIDES AND CURRENTS

The islands of The Bahamas are affected by the west setting North Equatorial Current on both their eastern and western extremities. After entering the Caribbean the North Equatorial Current splits into two branches, the northern branch flowing northeast of The Bahamas off Abaco, Eleuthera, Cat Island, and Long Island as the Antilles Current with an average velocity of approximately ½ knot. To a lesser extent the Antilles Current also flows through the Old Bahama Channel along the northern coast of Cuba and through the islands of The Bahamas themselves. The more southern branch of the North Equatorial Current makes its way around the Caribbean and the Gulf of Mexico and enters the Straits of Florida as the Gulf Stream with an average velocity of approximately 2.5 knots in a northward direction. Once north of The Bahamas the stronger Gulf Stream merges with the weaker Antilles Current and bears off north and northeastward across the North Atlantic. For more information on the Gulf Stream see the chapter *Crossing The Gulf Stream*. The *Sailing Directions for the Caribbean Sea* (DMA# SDPUB147) advises that the eastern entrance to the Northwest Providence Channel has a northwest setting current of approximately 2-3 knots which may reverse to a southeast set after strong northwest to north winds. Within the Northeast and Northwest Providence Channels themselves the current is nominal although after strong northerly winds the set may be easterly with a velocity of approximately one knot.

Where the shallow banks drop off to deeper ocean waters in such areas as The Abacos, The Berry Islands, The Biminis, The Exumas, and The Jumentos, tidal currents flow in and out of the passes and cuts sometimes reaching 2-4 knots in strength and even more in a few of the more narrow passes. Some cuts may be impassable in adverse wind conditions or in heavy swells that may exist with or without any wind. Even in moderate conditions, onshore winds against an outgoing tide can create very rough conditions.

As a rule of thumb you can estimate the tidal rise and fall to be about 2½'-4' at most times. Where the banks drop off to the deeper waters of the Atlantic Ocean, the Straits of Florida, the Tongue Of The Ocean, or Exuma Sound for instance, the tides flow in and out of the passes and cuts with ferocity in places, sometimes reaching 2-4 knots in strength and even more in a few of the more narrow passes. All tides in The Bahamas are based on the tides in Nassau which have a mean rise of 2.6'. Neap tides, those after the first and last quarter of the moon, rise approximately ½' less, while tides after new and full moons rise approximately ½' more. During Spring tides, when the moon is nearest the Earth, the range is increased by another ½'. Cruising through The Bahamas during Spring full moon tides will give you some of the lowest lows and highest highs. It is quite easy to run aground at this time on some of the Banks routes. Boats with drafts of 5' have reportedly run aground in what is normally a 6' depth at low water during this time. To receive tidal information while in The Bahamas see the section *Weather*.

When attempting to predict the state of tide at any time other than at slack tide, you can use the *Rule of Twelfths* for a generally reliable accuracy. To do this take the amount of tidal fluctuation and divide it into twelfths. For example, if high tide in Nassau is expected to be 3.0' and the low water datum is 0.0', the tidal fluctuation is 3', and each twelfth is 0.25' or 3". To predict the state of tide at different times you can use the *Rule of Twelfths* in the following table. The table is merely to demonstrate a point and uses an imaginary charted high tide of 3'. Always consult your chart tables or listen for tide information broadcasts and calculate accordingly.

TIME OF LOW WATER	TIDE DATUM-0 FEET
1 hour after low, add 1/12	¼ foot above datum-3"
2 hours after low, add 3/12	¾ feet above datum-9"
3 hours after low, add 6/12	1½ feet above datum-18"
4 hours after low, add 9/12	2¼ feet above datum-27"
5 hours after low, add 11/12	2¾ feet above datum-33"
6 hours after low, add 12/12	High Water-3'*

Caution: *assumes a 3' tidal fluctuation as an example.*

Chart tables give the times and heights of high and low water but not the time of the turning of the tide or slack water. Usually there is little difference between the times of high and low water and the beginning of ebb or flood currents, but in narrow channels, landlocked harbours, or on tidal creeks and rivers, the time of slack water may vary by several hours. In some places you will find that it is not unusual for the currents to continue their direction of flow long after charted predictions say they should change. Strong winds can play havoc on the navigator attempting to predict slack water. The current may often appear in places as a swift flowing river and care must be taken whenever crossing a stretch of strong current to avoid being swept out to sea or onto a bank or rocks. Some of the currents may flow from 2.5 to over 4 knots in places and in anchorages with a tidal flow two anchors is a must. Some cuts may be impassable in adverse wind conditions or in heavy swells that may exist with or without any wind. Even in moderate conditions, onshore winds against an outgoing tide can create very rough conditions. Some of the passes, cuts, and anchorages shown may be a real test of your ability. If in doubt, stay out. As with cruising anywhere, if you exercise caution you will have a safe and enjoyable cruise in The Bahamas.

VHF

The regulations pertaining to the proper use of VHF in The Bahamas are basically identical to those in the United States. Batelco, The Bahamas Telecommunications Co. oversees all licensing for VHF, SSB, and Ham radio. Channel 16 is the designated channel for hailing and distress. Please shift all traffic to a working channel when you have made contact with your party.

People throughout The Bahamas use the VHF as a telephone. Almost every household has a VHF while few can afford the luxury of a cellular phone. You will often hear businesses announcing their latest deals, or the local restaurant describing the delights of their upcoming seafood night and inviting you for a meal in exchange for a small amount of cash. Technically this is illegal and improper by American as well as Bahamian laws. Bear in mind that this is a way of life in the Bahamian Out-Islands and that you are a visitor here and only temporary. There are a few cruisers who bring with them into this paradise the very things that many of us are here to escape. Some of these people insist on playing radio vigilante, sitting by the VHF anxiously awaiting an opportunity to spring into action and place the restrictions of the dreaded "proper radio etiquette" that have been placed on them, upon someone else. If you are one of the *Radio*

Police, please relax. You are doing nothing but making an unpleasant situation intolerable and increasing your blood pressure in the process. This is just the way it is on ch.16 in The Bahamas and you had best learn to live with it. There is absolutely nothing that you, the Bahamian Government, or Batelco can do to change things. Besides, you will find few other cruisers that will agree with you. If you don't wish to hear the ads or traffic, simply turn your radio off.

When you are using your VHF assume that at least a half-dozen of your neighbors will follow your conversation to another channel. Even if you have a "secret" channel it will not take too long to find you. It is a fact of life that everybody listens in to everybody else.

WEATHER

The weather throughout The Bahamas is tropical with a rainy season from June through October, coinciding with hurricane season. In the winter, temperatures in the Out Islands rarely fall below 60°F and generally are above 75°F in the daytime. During the summer months the lows are around 75°-78°F while the highs seldom rise above 90°F. Sea water temperatures normally vary between 74°F in February and 84°F in August.

Humidity is fairly high all year long, especially during the summer months, but there is usually a breeze to lessen the effect. In the summer, winds tend to be light, 10 knots or less from the southeast with more calms, especially at night. In the winter, the prevailing winds are east-southeast and stronger. It is not unusual to get a week of strong winds, 20 knots or better, during the winter months as fronts move through. These fronts tend to move through with regularity during the winter months and become more infrequent as spring approaches. The wind will usually be in the southeast or south before a front and will often be very light to calm. As the front approaches with its telltale bank of dark clouds on the western and northwestern horizon, the winds will steadily pick up and move into the southwest, west, and northwest as the front approaches. Strongest winds are usually from the west and northwest. After the front passes the winds will move into the north and northeast for a day or two before finally settling back into an east/southeast pattern until the next front. Winds just after the front tend to be strong and the temperature a little cooler. A front passing off the southeast Florida coast will usually be in Nassau in about 12-24 hours and from there it may arrive in the Exumas within 12-36 hours and points south a little later.

In the summer the weather pattern is typically scattered showers with the occasional line squall. Although the main concern during June through November is hurricanes, The Bahamas are more often visited by a tropical wave with its strong winds and drenching rains. Tropical waves, sometimes called easterly waves, are low pressure systems that can strengthen and turn into a tropical depression or hurricane. Cruisers visiting The Bahamas during hurricane season are advised to monitor weather broadcasts closely and take timely, appropriate action (also see previous section on *Hurricane Holes*).

Staying in touch with weather broadcasts presents little problem in The Bahamas, even if you don't have SSB or ham radio capabilities. From Nassau you can receive the local Bahamian radio station ZNS I at 1540 KHz which also broadcasts simultaneously on FM at 107.1 MHz. ZNS II on 1240 KHz and ZNS III at 810 KHz can usually be picked up in the northern Exumas. WINZ, 940 KHz from Miami, is on the air 24 hours with weather for southern Florida approximately every 10 minutes. Unfortunately this station is difficult to pick up at night. WGBS also from Miami at 710 KHz has weather four times an hour 24 hours a day. In New Providence you will be able to pick up *Ranger* giving the weather and tides at 0715 every morning. *Ranger* will place a call on VHF ch.16 and then move to ch. 72 for weather information. Skippers can contact the Nassau Marine Operator on VHF ch. 27 and ask for the latest weather report from the Nassau Meteorological Office.

If you have ham radio capabilities you can pick up the Bahamas Weather Net every morning at 0720 on 3.696 MHz, lower sideband. Carolyn Wardle, C6AGG, whose husband Nick is *Ranger* in Nassau, begins with the local weather forecast and tides from the Nassau Met. Office. Next, hams from all over the Bahamas check in with their local conditions which Carolyn later forwards to the Nassau Met. Office to assist in their forecasting. If you are interested in the approach of a front you can listen in and hear what conditions hams in the path of the front have experienced. All licensed amateur radio operators with current Bahamian reciprocals are invited to participate. The local conditions in the weather reports follow a specific order so listen in and give your conditions in the order indicated. If requested, Carolyn will send you some information on the types of clouds and their descriptions along with a log sheet. Be sure to thank Carolyn for her tireless efforts that benefit all mariners, not only those with ham licenses. Thanks Carolyn.

At 0745 on 7.268 MHz you can pick up the Waterway Net. Organized and maintained by the Waterway Radio and Cruising Club, this dedicated band of amateur radio operators begin the net with a synopsis of the weather for South Florida and then proceed to weather for The Bahamas (with tides), the southwest north Atlantic, the Caribbean Sea, and the Gulf Of Mexico. For a listing of marine weather frequencies, see *Appendix F: Weather Broadcast Frequencies.*

If you have marine SSB capabilities you can pick up BASRA's weather broadcasts every morning at 0700 on 4003 KHz, upper sideband. Later in the day you can pick up the guru of weather forecasters, Herb Hilgenberg, *Southbound II*, from Canada. After a short interruptions of Herb's service, he is once again operating, this time from his home in Canada. You can tune in to Herb on 12.359 MHz, upper sideband, at 2000 Zulu. On 6.501 MHz you can pick up the voice weather broadcasts from NMN four times a day at 0530, 1130, 1730, and 2300 EST.

Starting in the Southern Bahamas and continuing on throughout the entire Caribbean, an SSB equipped vessel can pick up David Jones, *Misstine*, call sign ZHB, who operates out of Venezuela waters. David is on the air each day at 0815-0830 AST (1215-1230 UTC) on 4.003 MHz and then moves up to 8.104 MHz from 0830-0915. He begins with a 24-48 hour wind and sea summary followed by a synoptic analysis and tropical conditions during hurricane season. After this he repeats the weather for those needing fills and finally he takes check-ins reporting local conditions. During hurricane season David relays the latest tropical storm advisories at 1815 AST on 6.224 MHz.

USING THE CHARTS

For soundings I use a computer-based hydrographic system in my 16', 90hp, Data Acquisition Vessel, DAV for short. The system consists of an off-the-shelf GPS and sonar combination that gives a GPS waypoint and depth every two seconds including the time of each observation. The software records and stores this information in an onboard computer. When I begin to chart an area, I first put the DAV's bow on a well-marked, prominent point of land and take GPS lat/lons for a period of at least twenty minutes. I use the average of all these positions to check against the lat/lon shown on the topos, which are very accurate by the way. I also use cross bearings to help set up control points for my own reference. At this point I then begin to take soundings.

My next objective is to chart the inshore reefs. Then I'll plot all visible hazards to navigation. These positions are recorded by hand on my field notes as well as being recorded electronically. I rely primarily on my on-site notes for the actual construction of the charts. The soundings taken by the system are later entered by hand, but it is the field notes that help me create the basis for the chart graphics. The computer will not tell me where a certain reef ends or begins as accurately as I can record it and show it on my field notes. Next, I will run the one-fathom line as well as the ten-fathom line (if applicable) and chart these. Here is where the system does most of the work, though I still stop to take field notes. Finally, I will crisscross the entire area in a grid pattern and hopefully catch hazards that are at first glance unseen. It is not unusual to spend days sounding an area of only a couple of square miles. This takes a lot of fuel as well as a lot of time when transferring the data to the chart!

Due to the speed of the DAV, each identical lat/long may have as many as ten or twenty separate soundings. Then, with the help of NOAA tide tables, the computer gives me accurate depths to one decimal place for each separate lat/long pair acquired on the data run. A macro purges all but the lowest depths for each lat/long position (to two decimal places). At this point the actual plotting is begun including one fathom and ten fathom lines. The charts themselves are still constructed from outline tracings of topographic maps purchased at the Nassau Land and Surveys Dept. and the Turks and Caicos Land Office. The lat/long lines are placed in accordance with these maps which are known for their accuracy. These topos are drawn from aerial photos and are geographically located using ground plane markers at known positions on each of the islands.

These charts are as accurate as I can make them and I believe them to be superior to any others. They are indeed more detailed than all others showing many areas that are not covered, or are incorrectly represented by other publications. However, it is not possible to plot every individual rock or coral head so pilotage by eye is still essential. On many of the routes in my guides you must be able to pick out the blue, deeper water as it snakes between sandbanks, rocky bars, and coral heads. Learn to trust your eyes. Remember that on the banks, sandbars and channels can shift over time so that what once was a channel may now be a sandbar. Never approach a cut or sandbar with the sun in your eyes, it should be above and behind you. Sunglasses with polarized lenses can be a big help in combating the glare of the sun on the water. With good visibility the sandbars and heads stand out and are clearly defined. As you gain experience you may even learn to read the subtle differences in the water surface as it flows over underwater obstructions.

All courses shown are magnetic. All GPS latitude and longitude positions for entrances to cuts and for detouring around shoal areas are only to be used in a general sense. They are meant to get you into the general area, you must pilot your way through the cut or around the shoal yourself. You will have to keep a good lookout, GPS will not do that for you. The best aids to navigation when near these shoals and cuts are sharp eyesight and good light. The charts will show both deep draft vessel routes as well as some shallow draft vessel routes. Deep draft vessel routes will accommodate a draft of 6' minimum and often more with the assistance of the tide. Shallow draft vessel routes are for dinghies and small outboard powered boats with drafts of less than 3'. Shallow draft monohulls and multihulls very often use these same routes.

Not being a perfect world, I expect errors to occur. I would deeply appreciate any input and corrections that you may notice as you travel these waters. Please send your suggestions to Stephen J. Pavlidis, C/O Seaworthy Publications, Inc., 507 Sunrise Drive, Port Washington, WI 53074, Phone 414-268-9250, Fax 414-268-9208, e-mail publisher@seaworthy.com. If you see me anchored nearby, don't hesitate to stop and say hello and offer your input. Your suggestion may help improve the next edition of this guide.

LIST OF CHARTS

CAUTION:

*The prudent navigator will not rely solely on any
single aid to navigation, particularly on floating aids.
The Approach and Index charts are designed strictly for orientation,
they are not to be used for navigational purposes.
All charts are to be used in conjunction with the text.
All soundings are in feet at Mean Low Water.
All courses are magnetic.
Projection is transverse Mercator.
Orientation of all Charts-North is up.
Datum used is WGS84.
Differences in latitude and longitude may exist between these charts and other charts of the area;
therefore the transfer of positions from one chart to another should be done by
bearings and distances from common features.
If attempting to measure distances, remember: one minute of latitude =1 nautical mile (approx.).*

The author and publisher take no responsibility for errors, omissions, or the misuse of these charts. No warranties are either expressed or implied as to the usability of the information contained herein.

Note: Some official NOAA and DMA charts do not show some of the reefs and heads charted in this guide. Always keep a good lookout when piloting in these waters.

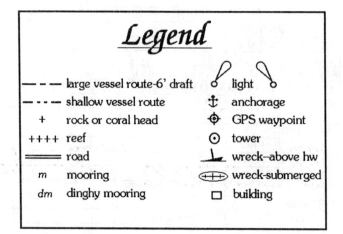

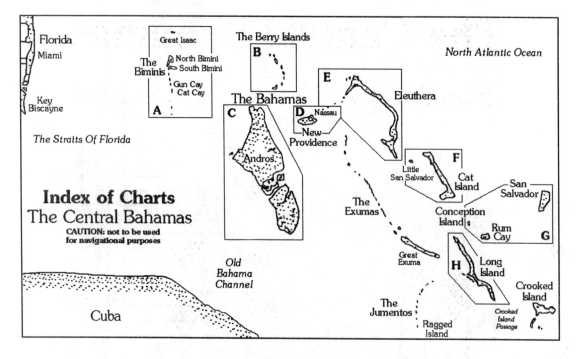

Index of Charts
The Central Bahamas
CAUTION: not to be used for navigational purposes

Index Chart	Region	Page
A	The Biminis	41
B	The Berrys	62
C	Andros	84
D	New Providence	115
E	Eleuthera	140
F	Cat Island	174
G	Conception Is. Rum Cay San Salvador	193
H	Long Island	210

PART I

On the
Beaten Path

The Central Bahamas
South Florida to Long Island

Part I

On The Beaten Path

THE CENTRAL BAHAMAS

South Florida to Long Island

The islands in the central Bahamas, from Bimini to Long Island, are some of the most visited islands in the entire Bahamian archipelago. Many cruisers stop and enjoy the Biminis, the Berrys, Andros, and New Providence on their way to spend their winters in George Town, Exuma. Working out of George Town they'll make short jaunts to places like Long Island, Conception, Rum Cay, San Salvador, or the Jumentos prior to heading back northward via Cat Island, Little San Salvador, and Eleuthera. From Eleuthera, Abaco is just a short hop across open water. Add to this the lists of long distance cruisers on their way to or from the Caribbean and you can work up quite a boat count visiting these islands.

These island's various charms appeal to all manner of boaters. The cays offer solitude, secluded beaches, great diving and fishing, and all usually within a day's sail of places like Miami, Nassau, Spanish Wells, Governor's Harbour, Fresh Creek, or George Town where the convenience of provisions, fuel, repairs, telephones, marinas, and air flights can ease the burden on an already overstressed captain or crew.

Solitude and convenience...quite a pair. The proverbial best of both worlds. But solitude and convenience are not all. Let's not forget the culture. Not all of these islands are as tourist-oriented as New Providence. If you just look around you will still find a lot of Bahamians living in traditional ways, holding on somewhat to older, almost forgotten values; the men till working the fish traps or farming, the ladies still plaiting top. On Cat Island for instance, *Obeah*, a form of magic, is still said to be practiced and a few Cat Islanders still use an outside, stone oven.

The Bahamas are steeped in history and Bimini and Nassau are history lessons in themselves. You'll walk in the footsteps of Henry Morgan, Blackbeard, Woodes Rogers, and scores of pirates that roamed The Bahamas almost three centuries ago. You'll stroll the docks that Ernest Hemmingway prowled in Alice Town, boxing and fishing his life away. And you'll sail the same waters as various gun runners, rum runners, and the more modern drug runners did in their quest for fortune. Even as you find rare old bottles spilled from a rum runner's wreck, one day divers will stare in awe at the wrecks of Cigarette-type boats with four outboards across the stern or sunken planes with the crews and cargoes still aboard.

Yes, these cays are on the beaten path, but they have not been trampled, their high points have not been beaten down. There is a tremendous amount to enjoy here without venturing far from what many of us see as civilization.

CROSSING THE GULF STREAM

DEALING WITH THE GULF STREAM-WHEN DO I CROSS?

The Gulf Stream is a powerful ocean current that flows northward off the eastern shore of the United States between south Florida and The Bahamas. The Stream is comparable to a mighty river in the ocean moving a thousand times more water than the widest, longest, deepest rivers on Earth through the narrow bottleneck known as the Straits of Florida. At its narrowest point between Miami and Bimini, the Stream may be 44 miles wide and up to 2500' deep. Its waters are a beautiful deep indigo blue with a warm temperature that averages 76° even during the winter months.

Crossing the Gulf Stream provokes the most uneasiness and presents the greatest challenge, and danger, for anyone headed to The Bahamas. Not only do you have to worry about the seas created by opposing wind and current, bear in mind that if you break down the Stream will move you northward away from your present position at 2-4 knots. However, for a well equipped and crewed vessel, the inherent dangers in the crossing can be lessened immensely by doing only one simple thing-waiting for weather. I'm not going to tell you what type of vessel to take on your adventure and how to equip her. There are far too many naval architects and maritime experts who can do a far better job than I. Only you can testify to the seaworthiness of your vessel. Make sure you know her well and that she is sound and equipped with current charts (#'s 26320 and 26324) and up to date safety devices. I have seen boats as small as 15' plywood sloops with no engines make the crossing. Whatever type of vessel you take, the most important thing to remember is to wait for the right weather window.

Since the Stream is a northward flowing current, an opposing wind (from any northerly direction-NW through NE) can cause some truly dangerous seas to build up. The Gulf Stream is no place to be in a frontal passage so unless you absolutely have to go (I can't imagine a single reason to make a skipper want to cross the Stream in a norther although some would probably thrive on the challenge), stay put and wait on the weather. Most veteran skippers will wait until the seas are down and the wind is somewhere between east and south at less than 15 knots. An east or southeast wind of 15 knots or more can build up quite a chop that will have to be bucked for the entire trip. Winds from south to west would be quite favorable for sailing vessels but they are rare and can be the forerunners of a frontal passage during the months from October through May. When the wind seems right for you, and you have given the Stream enough time to settle down if it has been boisterous, it may be time to go. Personally I prefer to look out upon the water from a high vantage point before I leave. If I see what appears to be camel humps on the horizon I will postpone my departure for a while no matter what the wind is forecast to be. When you do get a weather window don't delay, take advantage of it and enjoy your cruise.

NAVIGATING THE GULF STREAM-HOW DO I CROSS?

From Fort Lauderdale to Miami there are several jumping off spots for sailors heading to the central and southern Bahamas. Some skippers prefer to leave from Angelfish Creek at Key Largo or even Marathon to make the most of the advantage that the Gulf Stream has to offer. That's definitely a good idea but most boats choose to depart the States via Hillsboro Inlet, Port Everglades, Government Cut, or Cape Florida at the south end of Key Biscayne. Passages from points north of Hillsboro Inlet will be bucking the Gulf Stream too much, it would be better to head south to Fort Lauderdale or Miami to get a better angle to cross to Bimini.

The south Florida National Weather Service radio broadcasts on VHF weather ch. 1 give the latest Gulf Stream information 6 days a week. Mondays, Wednesdays, and Fridays from 4:00 P.M. until 8:00 P.M. and on Tuesdays, Thursdays, and Saturdays from 4:00 A.M. until 8:00 A.M. The broadcasts give the approximate position of the western edge of the Stream, its width, and the average northward flow in knots across the Stream. The Gulf Stream is usually slower in October and November and generally stronger in July and August with a mean difference of approximately .5 knots. The speed at the edges of the Stream may be as little as ½ knot or less while the speed at the axis, the "hump," may be as high as 4 knots or more. For the most part, strong northerly winds will slow the Stream while strong southerly winds will increase its speed. Normally though you can figure on an average speed of 2.5 knots across the Stream in a direction of 010°.

Crossing the Gulf Stream poses a nifty navigational problem in vectors that we all probably learned to solve in high school geometry. You remember high school geometry, don't you? Due to the northward flow of the Stream a certain amount of compensatory southerly heading must be employed. For example, steering the rhumb line course from Fort Lauderdale to Bimini in a sailboat making 5-6 knots will cause you to make landfall somewhere in the vicinity of Great Isaac Light in normal conditions. By applying a certain amount of southerly heading to offset the strength of the Stream your vessel will travel the shortest, straightest path to Bimini.

The navigational problem is a classic one of finding the course to steer to make good an intended track given the set and drift of the current and your vessel's speed. For solving you will need a plotting sheet or a current chart of the area, a pencil, a compass, and parallel rules. As in the diagram, plot point A as your position on the western edge of the Gulf Stream on your plotting sheet or chart. Next, pencil in line AB of an indefinite length on the bearing that is your direct course to Bimini. Next plot vector AC, representing the Gulf Stream current, in the direction of the set of the Stream, approximately 010°, for a distance equivalent to the estimated drift, (be sure to listen to the NOAA weather broadcasts for the latest information, see above paragraph). Next take your compass with the center on C and swing an arc of radius equal to your vessel's speed, if you will be making 6 knots set it for 6 nautical miles. This will intersect line AB at point B. The line CB will be your course to steer allowing for the set and drift of the Gulf Stream. Use your parallel rules to measure the angle. The length

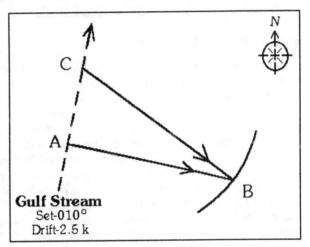

Gulf Stream
Set-010°
Drift-2.5 k

of line AB in *nautical* miles, will be your speed of advance towards Bimini. In other words, you might be making 6 knots through the water but you may only be making 5.1 knots towards Bimini thanks to the Stream. Never forget that there are built in inaccuracies in figuring your course. Wind and wave conditions, your own ability to maintain a consistent speed, and the strength of the Stream itself all combine to give slight errors to even the best calculations but you should be "in the neighborhood" so to speak. For example, a vessel leaving Port Everglades would find its course to Bimini to be 121°. After solving the vector problem the skipper might find that he must now steer 143° to reach Bimini on the shortest and straightest route.

Even if you have a GPS aboard you must still solve the vector problem for your course. If you allow the GPS to steer to your waypoint and correct for the current you will be constantly changing course and covering more miles in a highly inefficient manner that is sometimes called a "dog curve." If you have ever seen a dog trying to swim across a river you will understand how inefficient this type of course is. A dog will always keep his nose pointed to his destination even as the river's current pushes him downstream. If a dog is heading east towards a certain tree and the current is pushing him south he will keep his nose pointed at that tree even as he gets pushed downstream and finally has to swim north-northeast to his destination. If the pup had simply swam more northeast to begin with or moved upstream before crossing he would have a had a far easier passage.

A final word on crossing the Gulf Stream. This narrow passage is very busy and getting busier every year. Keep a sharp lookout for other vessels and take the proper precautions to avoid collisions well ahead of time. If you don't know the "Rules of the Road," learn them.

COURSES FROM SOUTH FLORIDA ACROSS THE GULF STREAM

I will not endeavor to give the reader the proper courses to steer because all boats travel at different speeds through the water and make more or less leeway than other boats. However I will give you the bearings and distances from different locations in south Florida to the Biminis and the reader may plot his or her own course using the aforementioned vector method. In other words, I will not do your homework for you as it won't hurt you to do it yourself, and besides, many skippers have forgotten how to plot a course across a current. So with that in mind (and I do hope that not everyone is mad at me!) the following table will give you bearings and distances from south Florida to the Biminis. All courses are magnetic and corrections for the set and drift of the Gulf Stream must be applied to these bearings to arrive at your course to steer.

FROM	NORTH BIMINI	GUN CAY
Hillsboro Inlet	133° - 53.0 nm	139° - 58.3 nm
Port Everglades	124° - 48.3 nm	131° - 52.7 nm
Government Cut-R2	093° - 42.8 nm	109° - 44.5 nm
Cape Florida	090° - 44.5 nm	100° - 45.0 nm
Angelfish Creek	069° - 53.9 nm	077° - 51.6 nm

MAKING LANDFALL

As you leave south Florida in your wake you will find yourself alone on a big ocean. You will be traveling approximately 46-50 plus miles depending on your departure point and most of those miles (25-40) will be out of sight of land and any type of navigational aids. First timers will likely have feelings of apprehension. Don't panic! Even veteran skippers have those same feelings, it is quite natural when leaving port. You might be fortunate and find other cruisers going the same way and most don't mind the company. It usually increases the safety margin a little for all involved.

If you are bound for Bimini or Gun Cay you will be heading for a small set of islands barely visible until you get within 7-10 miles from their shores. This is no problem for GPS or LORAN but those who don't have a *boxed navigator* can still use other sources for directions. First, the high-rise buildings along the south Florida coast will stay within view for at least 10-15 miles from shore depending on their height and your own height of eye. Remember, if you have trouble or get lost you can always turn towards the west (that's where the sun sets) and sooner or later you will find Florida. Important: make sure your compass is correct and learn to trust it.

The prudent skipper uses as many navigational sources as he can muster. For confirmation of your heading keep your eyes on what is going on around you. Pan Am runs seaplanes into North Bimini on a daily basis. These planes are relatively small and don't fly too high so if you see one heading on a similar bearing it is a good clue that you are on course. Other boats passing you may also be headed to Bimini, although some may be headed for Gun Cay approximately 9 miles farther south. I once used a cruise ship's course to enable me to find Bimini when my LORAN went out. I was approaching Bimini from Ft. Lauderdale and I surmised that since the ship was heading generally northeast to east that he was either going to Freeport or around Great Isaac to the Berrys. Bimini then had to be off his starboard side just where I was hoping it was. Use caution here though, some cruise ships schedule runs to Bimini and anchor just outside the harbour entrance to the northwest. If you attempt to steer to their starboard you may get a little confused as to where to make landfall. As of this writing (June, 1997) the primary way to spot the Biminis **was** the radio tower on South Bimini, there's nothing else that you could confuse it with along this stretch of islands. It was 281' tall and painted orange and white. It flashed Morse code letter "B" (- . . .) in red every 20 seconds and was reportedly visible for 23 miles although I had never seen it at anywhere near that distance. You will notice that I used the past tense verb "was." The radio tower was removed in 1996 to be rebuilt. Nobody seems to know when it will be back up or what its characteristics will be. Keep an eye out and listen to reports of other cruisers to this area for the latest news. There was a DEA tower on the south end of Gun Cay which was destroyed by Hurricane Andrew and if the U.S. and Bahamian governments ever decide to rebuild it (it is still down) care must be taken not to confuse it with the tower on South Bimini.

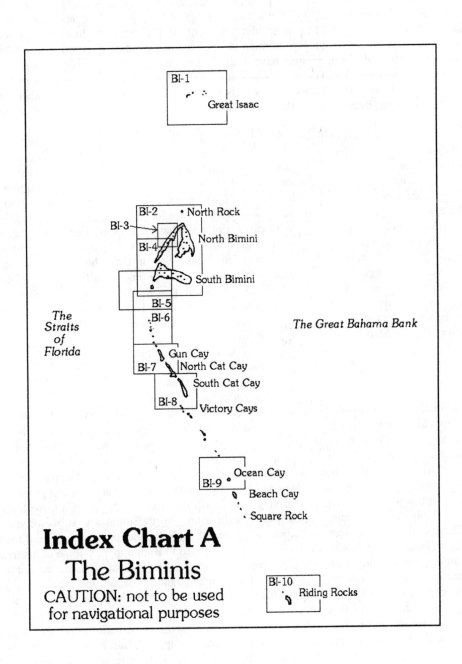

BI-1
Great Isaac

BI-2   • North Rock
BI-3
North Bimini
BI-4
South Bimini
BI-5
BI-6

The
Straits
of
Florida

The Great Bahama Bank

Gun Cay
BI-7   North Cat Cay
South Cat Cay
BI-8
Victory Cays

Ocean Cay
BI-9
Beach Cay
Square Rock

Index Chart A
The Biminis
CAUTION: not to be used
for navigational purposes

BI-10
Riding Rocks

THE BIMINIS

The Biminees, where there is a Harbour for Sloops...

Report to The Crown, Governor Phenney, 1721

"My greatest discovery was Bimini."

Ernest "Papa" Hemingway

"Bimini" — the name conjures up many images, most notably big game fishing, rum running, and Hemingway. North Bimini is home to over a dozen big game fishing tournaments each year and boasts World Class fishing just offshore in the deep blue waters of the Gulf Stream. Just south of South Bimini lies the wreck of the *Sapona* which brings to mind the rum running era during America's prohibition years. The islands of North and South Bimini have hosted numerous colorful characters, rogues, and other celebrities over the years. The likes of Martin Luther King, Adam Clayton Powell, Gary Hart, Johnny Cash, and George Albert Lyon all strode the streets of Alice Town at one time or another but the most popular, bar none, was Ernest "Papa" Hemingway whose "Islands In The Stream" was inspired by the Biminis.

Talk to any local who lived on Bimini during the Hemingway years and they will likely have a favorite "Papa" story to tell. Ernest Hemingway loved hard living, he thrived upon challenge and competition, it was no wonder he was a boxer. Hemingway once offered $50 to any Bahamian who could stay in the ring with him for three minutes but no one ever collected on the wager. Papa then offered $250 to anyone who could last three three-minute rounds with him using 6 oz. gloves. Now $250 was a lot of money in those days and Papa finally got a taker. His name was Willard Saunders, a muscular, 170 pound, bull-necked fisherman who is said to have been able to carry a piano balanced atop his unusually large skull. He approached Hemingway one day as he returned from fishing aboard his 38' *Pilar* and Hemingway offered to go get the gloves. Saunders said no, he intended to take him on right then and there, on the dock, without gloves. Hemingway knocked him out in about a minute and a half but not before Saunders paralyzed the side of Papa's face for half an hour with one punch. Hemingway and Saunders became friends and fought many times after that, not for money but for fun. Hemingway even built a ring to teach boxing to the youngsters of Bimini. His boxing and brawling exploits along the Bimini waterfront inspired songs such as *Big Fat Slob In The Harbour* with lines like:

> *He call Mistah Hemingway a big fat slob.*
> *Mistah Hemingway ball his fist and give him a nob.*
> *Big fat slob in the harbour.*
> *Tonight's the night we have fun.*

The Biminis, North and South, are situated at the northern end of a gently curving chain of small islands and cays stretching from North Bimini southward past South Cat Cay. These cays lie at the edge of the shallow waters of the Great Bahama Bank where the drop off to the deep water of the Straits of Florida offers fantastic fishing and diving opportunities. The island of North Bimini, and in particular the main settlement of Alice Town, is the traditional center of activity in this island chain. The island itself is a long thin strip of land approximately 7 miles long and only about 700 yards wide at its widest point. In the early days South Bimini was better suited to farming than North Bimini. But North Bimini with its reefs and access to the Gulf Stream became a prime site for habitation. North Bimini was at one time a refuge for pirates. Early settlers had to clear the harbour of pirate debris, hulls, muskets, cannons, and the like. It is said that Capt. Henry Morgan, after raiding Porto Bello, hurried to Bimini to bury some of his treasure.

The waters of the Biminis were so rich in wrecks that wreckers from Grand Bahama moved to Bimini to take advantage of the sea's bounty. Bimini's five founding families settled the area in 1835 and were licensed to engage in wrecking. In later years Biminites lived off the sea in one form or another, either harvesting shells, conch, and fish, or using Bimini's prime location off the eastern coast of the United States to run blockades during the Civil War and once again during the American Prohibition years. It has been said that the prohibition years actually "built" Bimini. "Pappy" Chalk built up a seaplane service to Bimini in 1919 which still operates today as the Pan Am Bridge (take care not to anchor in the "runway" that begins just off the seaplane ramp in the harbour and stretches northeast towards the anchorage).

APPROACHES TO THE BIMINIS

The routes across the Gulf Stream to the Biminis from South Florida are magnetic and should not be used without applying corrections for the strength of the Gulf Stream as described in the section *Crossing The Gulf Stream*. With the exception of the courses across the Great Bahama Banks from the Berry Islands and the courses across the Gulf Stream from Angelfish Creek, you will find that you must steer quite a bit higher than the bearings given from Hillsboro Inlet to Cape Florida to allow for the Gulf Stream.

From Hillsboro Inlet, the waypoint off North Bimini bears 133° at a distance of 53 nautical miles while Gun Cay lies on a bearing of 139° at 58.3 nautical miles.

From the sea buoy at Port Everglades, North Bimini bears 124° at a distance of 48.3 nautical miles while Gun Cay bears 131° at a distance of 52.7 nautical miles.

From the sea buoy at Government Cut in Miami, North Bimini bears 93° at a distance of 42.8 nautical miles while Gun Cay bears 109° at a distance of 44.5 nautical miles.

From the seaward entrance to the channel at Cape Florida on the southern end of Key Biscayne, North Bimini bears 90° at a distance of 44.5 nautical miles while Gun Cay bears 100° at a distance of 45 nautical miles.

From the eastern entrance to Angelfish Creek at Key Largo, North Bimini bears 69° at a distance of 53.9 nautical miles while Gun Cay bears 77° at a distance of 51.6 nautical miles.

From Great Stirrup Cay at the northern tip of the Berry Islands, North Rock bears 274° at a distance of 71 nautical miles. From "R2," the first tripod marker leading to Bullock's Harbour and *the Great Harbour Cay Marina*, North Rock bears 277° at a distance of 71.2 nautical miles while Gun Cay bears 266° at 74.6 nautical miles.

From Northwest Channel light, Gun Cay bears 281° at 62.1 nautical miles.

From a position two miles east of North Rock at 25° 48.06, 79° 13.50' W, Mackie Light bears 106° at 31.7 nautical miles, and from there Northwest Channel Light bears 123° at 29.7 nautical miles.

GREAT ISAAC

Standing sentinel at the northwest corner of the Great Bahama Bank, some 55 miles east of Ft. Lauderdale and about 20 miles north of North Bimini, at the convergence of the Gulf Stream in the Straits of Florida and the Northwest Providence Channel, is the white lighthouse of Great Isaac Light (FL ev 15 sec, 152 ft, 23m) on Great Isaac Island shown on Chart BI-1. This chart is included as a reference to those mariners wishing to pass safely within sight of Great Isaac on their way to or from Grand Bahama, the Berry Islands, or Nassau. It is possible to anchor in the lee of Great Isaac in an emergency but it is not recommended as an overnight stop as the area is very rolly. The waters shoal to the southwest and east of Great Isaac and mariners heading for the Berrys and Nassau should give the waters here a wide berth. Especially to be avoided is the area shown on DMA charts and known as The Gingerbread Ground. The area is home to scattered reefs and rocks with numerous wrecks about, a diver's delight.

Photo by Kelly Becker

Author's vessel at anchor, Bimini.

Great Isaac Light, the 152' tall structure, once known as Victoria Light in honor of the Queen, has quite a unique history. The light's structure was once a landmark in London. The Great Exposition of London in 1851, similar to a World's Fair, was held in Hyde Park. The centerpiece of the Exposition was a 152' tall iron structure which was to become Great Isaac Light. The structure remained for several years after the Exposition closed until it was finally removed, coded piece by coded piece, and packed away on three ships to be reassembled on Great Isaac Island in 1859. A powerful light was placed atop the structure and red and white stripes were painted around the new lighthouse.

The reconstruction, mostly done by the same workers who disassembled the structure, was plagued with accidents, deaths, and sightings of the ghost of the "Gray Lady." It seems that several years before the reconstruction began a British square-rigger was dashed to pieces on Great Isaac and the only survivor was a tiny infant who had been washed ashore and found a few days later by salvers. The baby was sent to Bimini for medical care and eventually reunited with relatives in England. The story did not end there however. Before each full moon the ghost of the baby's mother was said to walk the length of the ¾ mile long cay weeping and searching for her baby. A number of lightkeepers resigned their positions after only a month on the job after seeing "The Gray Lady of Great Isaac's Light." The ghostly visits went on until after the turn of the century when a headstrong lightkeeper, who was also a layman in his church, performed a religious rite to convince the Gray Lady that her child was safe and had survived. The story goes that she never returned although some say that she can still be heard wailing on Great Isaac Island just before a full moon. In another eerie occurrence, two lighthouse keepers, Ivan Major and B. Mollings, disappeared on August 4, 1969, never to be seen again.

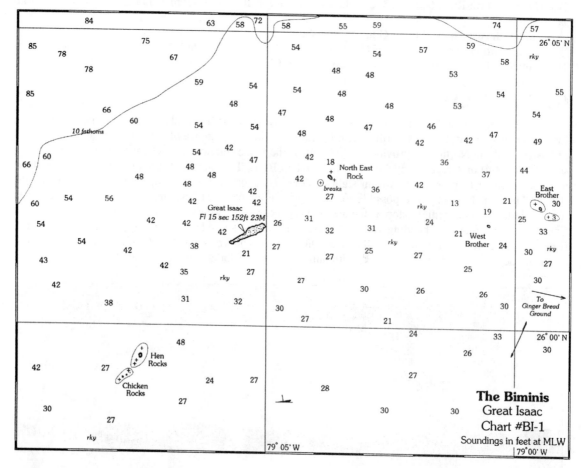

NORTH BIMINI

When approaching from Florida, North and South Bimini tend to blend together when visual contact is first made. A good daymark for the entrance to the harbour was the large (281') orange and white radio tower on South Bimini. As of this writing in June 1997 the tower is down and being rebuilt. Information about the tower's completion date and characteristics are sketchy so keep a good lookout. Until the tower is rebuilt try to look for the long stand of casaurinas with a few smaller patches just to their north. This will be North Bimini. As shown on Chart BI-4, a GPS waypoint at 25° 42.07' N, 79° 18.56' W will place you approximately ½ mile west of the harbour entrance between North and South Bimini in about 16' of water. Never attempt this entrance in strong onshore winds and seas or at night unless you are very, very familiar with the area. If you are caught in strong onshore conditions anchor behind South Bimini in Nixon's Harbour and await better conditions.

Finding the entrance is easy in good light. As you make out South Bimini you will see that it has a rather long beach on its western shore. Towards the beach's northern end is a very conspicuous group of salmon colored condos. Approximately 2/3 of the way south from the condos to the southern end of the beach lies the range just in front of a small clump of casaurinas. The range consists of a pair of orange and white poles. Line these poles up and follow the course in between the two sandbars on an approximate heading of 82°. Here the heading is not as important as following the range so keep the poles lined up and pay more attention to the range than your compass. Once inside the clearly visible sandbar turn to the north (to port) and pass between the sandbar and South Bimini in 6'-9' of water at MLW. When you approach the harbour favor the North Bimini side of the channel. The anchorage is north of the *Bimini Big Game Fishing Club*, the last marina to port. Do not anchor off the other marinas as this is the runway for *Pan Am* airlines.

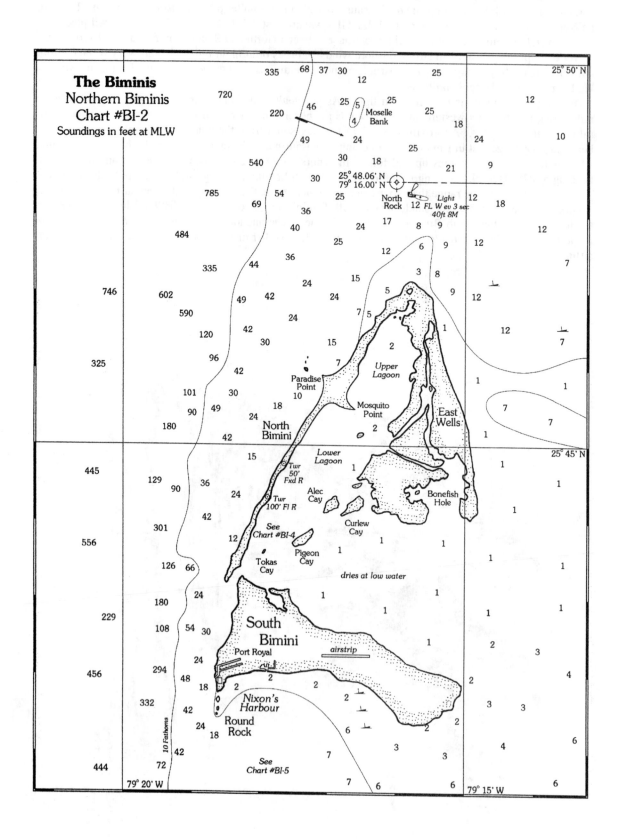

The Biminis
Northern Biminis
Chart #BI-2
Soundings in feet at MLW

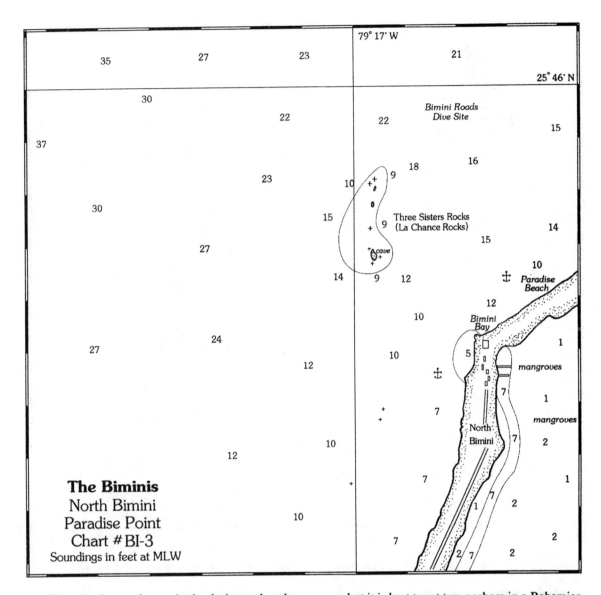

The Biminis
North Bimini
Paradise Point
Chart # BI-3
Soundings in feet at MLW

There is plenty of room in the designated anchorage area but it is best to set two anchors in a Bahamian Moor, one anchor up current and one anchor down current. The current flow parallels the shoreline here and it is quite strong so make sure your anchors are set properly. The bottom is very rocky hereabouts and holding ranges from poor to good (if you find a nice sandy spot). Use extra care when setting your anchors here. Dive on them if you can. It is a pleasant enough anchorage as long as you don't mind the local skippers flying past you in small fast boats (remember your anchor light) and a noisy power plant on shore. You can dinghy in to the dock across the street from the Government Complex or ask one of the marinas if you can use their facilities. Just off Entrance Point is a dinghy channel lying south of a set of rocks that are awash at low water. Thirty years ago this was the dredged entrance channel into Bimini Harbour but now it is only used for dinghies and small boat traffic.

The anchorage area narrows down to a small channel heading northeastward paralleling the shore of North Bimini. In places it is marked with stakes and the ability to read the water depth by its color is necessary to navigate this very conspicuous channel. A vessel with a draft of 6' or less can follow this channel all the way to the Bimini Bay Resort at Paradise Point. Tying up between the mangroves and the wreck or seawall on the upper end would offer fair hurricane protection for no more than two or three vessels.

Skippers wishing to clear in must tie up at one of the marinas along the waterfront most of which monitor ch. 16 or 68. The dockmaster will provide you with the proper Customs and Immigration forms. The skipper, after filling out the forms must then walk to the large pink Customs building to clear in and

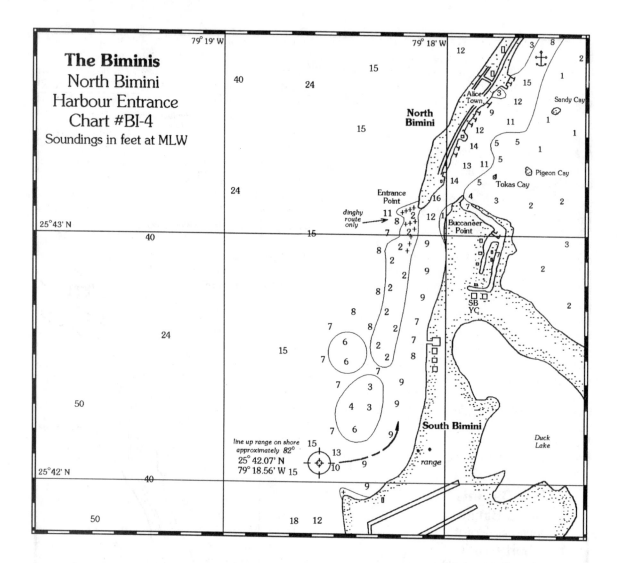

The Biminis
North Bimini
Harbour Entrance
Chart #BI-4
Soundings in feet at MLW

then to Immigration which is housed in the pink police station just north of the *Bimini Big Game Club and Marina.*

Vessels wishing to cross the banks to the Berry's or Nassau (see: *Crossing The Great Bahama Bank*) must pass north of North Rock. A GPS waypoint at 25° 48.06' N, 79° 16.00' W (Chart BI-2) will place you approximately ½ mile west of North Rock. Once you pass North Rock abeam, if you draw 6' or less you can immediately lay your course for Chub Cay, Great Stirrup, or *Great Harbour Marina* in the Berrys. If your draft is over 6' you should continue due east of North Rock for approximately three miles to avoid the shallow (6' at lw) sandbank to the northeast of North Bimini. It is possible to anchor east of North Bimini and East Wells to avoid westerly weather, but it is no place to be in winds from north-northwest through east to south. Mariners wishing to clear North Rock may anchor just west of the northern tip of North Bimini for a quick, early departure. This anchorage is usually rolly even though you are in the lee of the land.

The main harbour at North Bimini sits along the shore of Alice Town, and is what most visitors simply refer to as "Bimini." To the west of town lies a seemingly endless curving, and in some places rocky, beach, excellent for a day of, swimming, fun and games, or just catching rays. Most amenities on North Bimini can be found along the King's Highway in Alice Town. Bars, restaurants, marinas, and gift shops line the road between the Chalk's terminal and the Government Office Complex just north of the harbour. Unless you prefer to walk or bicycle, I highly recommend renting a golf cart to see the island, it's a very comfortable and efficient way to travel. You can find golf cart rentals all over town at such places as the *Compleat Angler* or *Sun Crest Marina.*

Starting at the southern terminus of the Queen's Highway at the *Pan Am Bridge*, formerly the *Chalk's Airline Terminal*, and heading northward you'll find the *Fisherman's Paradise Bar and Grill* serving breakfast, lunch and dinner. Next is the famous, or infamous, *Sand Bar*, once known as the *End of the World Bar*. Here is a must stop for party-goers but with a warning. The tradition is to leave your underwear hanging on the wall or ceiling. Try to pick out the celebrity underwear.

The first marina you will come to is the late *Capt. Harcourt Brown's Dock and Hotel* followed next by *Freddie Weech's Bimini Dock* which also houses the *Bimini General Store and Marine Supplies*, an amply stocked marine supply and hardware store. *Weech's* also has 6 rooms for rent, see Hank Weech. *Weech's* has a dinghy landing (for a fee) and fax service. Across the street from *Weech's* is Bill and Nowdla Keefe's *Bimini Undersea Adventures*, a well run dive shop where SCUBA enthusiasts can get all the latest info on dive sites. Just up the road is *CJ's Deli* serving delicious breakfast, lunch, dinner, ice cream and pastries. The next marina you come to north of the Custom's House is *Sun Crest Hotel and Marina* and the *Bimini Bluewater Resort Ltd*. *The Sea Crest Hotel* is the large three story yellow building with an excellent view from each room. *Bimini Bluewater Resort* has a guest house, cottages, and two bedroom suites for rent. Across the street from *Bimini Bluewater* are the late Ossie Brown's *The Compleat Angler Hotel and Bar*, probably the most popular stop for tourists in Bimini. *The Compleat Angler* was one of the first fishing clubs in Bimini and dates back to the 1930's. Here you can get a drink, see or be seen, or watch satellite TV to while away the time. The deep dark wood of its interior creates an ambiance of its own, this was Hemingway's favorite place and you can feel it as you enter. You can almost picture him there, sipping a drink and carousing with his friends after a long day of fishing on his beloved *Pilar*. There is a special room in his honor just off the entrance to the bar replete with photographs of Hemingway and some samples of his writing. The photos document many of Papa's greatest catches and show him boxing with some local fighters.

Next to *The Compleat Angler* you will find *The Royal Bank of Canada* and *Capt. Bob's Restaurant* (breakfast, lunch, and dinner). Capt. Bob's is the "in" place for breakfast. Capt. Bob is a native Biminite and has fished the waters of his home for over 50 years. Just north of *The Compleat Angler* is the newly reopened *All My Children Hotel* named after the owner's children and not the TV soap opera. The hotel has 50 rooms and two penthouses for rent as well as two bars and the *Le Sheriff Disco* on the second floor that is only open on weekends. The last marina to the north is *The Bimini Big Game Fishing Club and Anchorage Inn* situated along the narrow streets in the northernmost section of Alice Town. The *Inn* itself sits atop the hill in the center of the island with views of both the harbour and the ocean, a fantastic spot for dining. Here you will find two penthouses, 35 rooms, and 12 cottages for rent. The marina boasts the elegant *Gulf Stream Restaurant,* and for lunch there is the *Big Game Sports Bar* upstairs. There is also a swimming pool and small gift shop on the premises. Just north of the gate to the marina is the *Bimini Breeze Bar* where you may meet Yama Bahama, the Middleweight Boxing Champion of The Bahamas. It seems only fitting that the Champ should hail from Bimini.

Here in town you will also find the *Red Lion Pub* (closed on Mondays) serving drinks and delicious lunch and dinners (their *Shrimp Delight* has been recommended by *Esquire Magazine*), *Jontra's Food Store*, and Manny Rolle's *Bait and Tackle, Deli,* and *Supermarket*. At the corner of Sherman and King's Highway you will find *The Burger Queen* and *Opal's* which sits just up Sherman and serves excellent Bahamian and American dishes. Just north of *Bimini Big Game* is the *Bimini Breeze Restaurant, The Wee Wee Hours Club*, and the *Government Office Complex* with Immigration, the Police Station, and a Post Office. The *Government Office Complex* was once the *Lerner Marine Laboratory*. Just north of the *Government Office Complex* is a new coin laundry between the Police Station and *Roberts Grocery*.

As the road passes northward to Bayley Town, where most Biminites live, you will pass numerous small stores and shops, some appearing to do business out of the owner's living room. Across from the large *Batelco* complex (look for the big satellite dish) and the *Bahamas Electricity Corp.* (the noisy building) is the *Bimini Clinic*. Along this stretch of the King's Highway you'll find places such as *Tootsie's Groceries, Dun's Florists,* and *King Brown's Food and General Supplies*, a well stocked supermarket and hardware store. The local dentist, Dr. Larry Bain's office is just south of *Brown's*. On the Queen's Highway; the road running atop the hill, to the west of and parallel to King's Highway, is *Atlantis Spring,* which sells bottled water. Or you can bring your own container to their 24 hour self-serve window as long as you have plenty of quarters, their dollar bill changer never seems to work. For pickup and delivery service call 242-347-2245 or 2787; *Atlantis Springs* will deliver to any marina.

Just past Porgy Bay the pavement ends and turns left to the beach and here you will find one of the most beautiful spots on the island lying just past the cemetery known as *Spook Hill*. As you top the rise the long curving beach and vivid watercolors are a perfect backdrop for the shaded picnic tables under the casuarinas atop the beach. Local residents have a picnic here each day of Easter week.

North of Porgy Bay there are only a few tranquil villas. If you follow the dirt road northward you will wind up at the huge art-deco structure that George Albert Lyon (the inventor of the hubcap) built and which is often called the Rockwell House. It is a large multi-tiered yellow structure reminding one of the deckhouse of a ship sitting atop the hill. Located on a beautiful beach called Paradise Point, the house and surrounding buildings is now the *Bimini Bay Resort* and offers all amenities in beautiful surroundings. Their restaurant serves breakfast, lunch, and dinner, and they have a dinghy dock, tennis court, and pool. If you make reservations for dinner you can call the owners, Basil or Antoinette Rolle on VHF 68 (*Bimini Bay*) and they will arrange transportation for you from Alice Town.

To the east of North Bimini lies a mangrove island named East Wells. East Wells is very reminiscent of Shroud Cay in the Exumas. It is a maze of mangrove lined tidal creeks leading into a large lake in the center. If you approach the island from Bimini Harbour and wind your way up the creeks you may be lucky enough to find the *Healing Hole*, a spring that is said to have curative powers. Any bonefishing guide can take you here as well as the creek where Dr. Martin Luther King Jr. wrote his Nobel Prize acceptance speech. The waters of the lagoon between North Bimini, East Wells, and South Bimini is an excellent marine nursery and bonefishing location.

Fishermen hoping to test the Bimini waters will find themselves in some of the most productive fishing grounds of the world boasting numerous world record catches. These waters are home to marlin, sailfish, dolphin, wahoo, mackerel, shark, grouper, and snapper. Conch and bonefish can be found on the flats surrounding North Bimini, East Wells, and South Bimini. Lobster are normally found outside the harbour around the reefs, rocks, and drop-offs. Deep sea, reef fishing, and bonefishing guides are so plentiful in Bimini that we cannot list them all, it is best to inquire at any of the marinas. If you wish to rent a boat call Charlie Weech at 242-347-3290.

There are some super dive sites off of North Bimini that can pique the interest of anyone, diver or not. A good place to start is at La Chance Rocks, the offlying rocks just to the west of North Bimini. There is a cave in the southeasternmost rock that is 10' deep and excellent for those pursuing underwater photography. Probably the most popular dive site in this area is known as *Atlantis Rocks*, or *Bimini Roads*, lying approximately ¼ mile northeast of *Three Sister's Rocks*, also called *La Chance Rocks* in 15' of water. The site was discovered by Dimitri Rebikoff, the inventor of the Pegasus submarine. To find this exciting locale line up the northern tip of North Bimini on a heading of 60° and put the Rockwell House on a bearing of 164° and you are there (for those who wish to cheat there is a GPS waypoint for the site in *Appendix A*). On the bottom you will see a number of large rocks, some up to 16' square and weighing 25 tons, that resemble a road. Some say it is the remains of the ancient lost continent of Atlantis. Although this is purely speculation one thing is certain: radioactive dating of fossils found in the area show that this structure was above water 5,000 years ago and the rock formations themselves are shown to be between 5,000 and 10,000 years old.

The *English Wreck* lies 1¼ miles northwest of North Rock Light and is found when the light bears 155° and Rockwell House bears 190°. The ribs of this wreck can be found in 17' of water at the edge of the Moselle Bank. There is little left these days but pottery and other debris have been found in the general area.

Moray Alley can be found to the west of *La Chance Rocks* when Rockwell House bears 80° and the South Bimini Radio Tower bears 155°. The reef system is composed of numerous coral heads 10'-15' tall in an area about 150 yards wide and extending for ½ mile. Here you'll find a lot of canyons, passages, crevices, gorgonians, sea fans, and large fish including a few sharks.

Hawksbill Reef lies on a slope to the west of *Moray Alley* on the edge of the Gulf Stream. If you line up Rockwell House on a bearing of 75° and the South Bimini Radio Tower on a bearing of 145° you will be on top of it. The sloping bottom is covered with scattered coral heads and barrel sponges and descends to about 50' where it levels off to a sand bottom with more scattered heads.

There are quite a few sunken planes off the eastern and southern shores of North and South Bimini for snorkelers to enjoy.

SOUTH BIMINI

South Bimini, the largest of the Bimini chain, was once the agricultural center of the area and is now home to the only airport. Currently there are two airlines servicing South Bimini, Bimini Island Air and

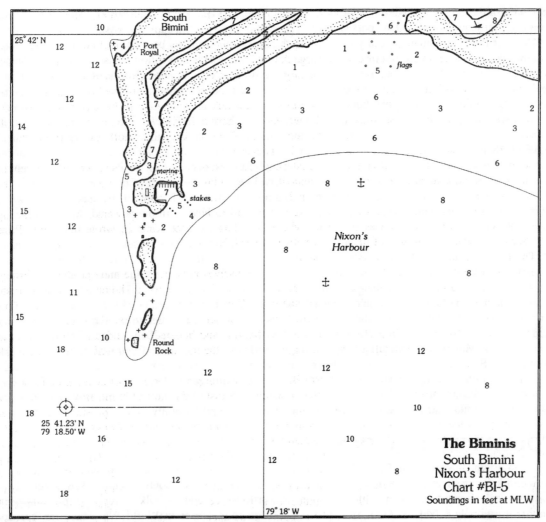

The Biminis
South Bimini
Nixon's Harbour
Chart #BI-5
Soundings in feet at MLW

Island Air Charters both out of Fort Lauderdale. Visitors arriving or departing by air from South Bimini can take a ferry from Alice Town to the landing at Buccaneer Point where taxis will take you to the airstrip.

Juan Ponce de Leon is credited with being the first European to set foot in the Biminis in 1513. Ponce de Leon was the Governor of Puerto Rico when he heard of a magical spring on Bimini. He left in search of the legendary Fountain of Youth, and some say he found it on the island of South Bimini. That site has been restored, and is now a tourist attraction although it is little more than a dry hole in the ground surrounded by a crumbling plaster and rock wall. In more recent years U.S. Congressman Adam Clayton Powell built several homes on South Bimini.

Deep inside the canals on the northwestern shore of South Bimini, just east of the ferry landing at Buccaneer Point, lies the *South Bimini Yacht Club*. You can inquire here about available dockage and check on the small hotel and restaurant, *The First Floor Bar*. If you need to rent one of their 10 rooms, see the manager Percy. There is a sandbar at the entrance to the canals with approximately 4' over it at low water. These canals could be considered as a possible hurricane hole although adequate protection is questionable due to the very low height of the surrounding land.

Sitting on the beach along the western shore of South Bimini is a group of conspicuous salmon colored condos. This is the *Bimini Sands* complex. The condos are for sale, and more are being built as of this writing. There is a small dredged channel and marina on the northern side of the complex. The marina is scheduled to open in 1998/1999.

Cruisers arriving at the entrance to the harbour at North Bimini in strong westerly weather are advised to take refuge in Nixon's Harbour on the south shore of South Bimini and await better conditions. The harbour is deep and has good holding in sand. It offers protection from west through north to northeast winds, but it can be very rolly. A GPS waypoint at 25° 41.23 N, 79° 18.50 W places you approximately ¼ mile west of the entrance to Nixon's Harbour as shown on Chart BI-5. From this position steer 90°-95° and pass south of Round Rock. Once past Round Rock simply head for the spot you wish to anchor. Vessels heading for the marina must give a wide berth to the rocks and shallows between Round Rock and South Bimini. Next, line up on the staked entrance channel into the marina and follow the stakes into the deeper water of the marina. The channel will take 7' at high water. A note about Round Rock, this is a nice shallow water snorkeling site amid rocks and corals. If you need the services of *Offshore Marine Towing*, contact *Ricky J* on VHF ch. 16. He acts as their relay in these waters.

The southwestern tip of South Bimini is the site of the *Bimini Beach Club and Marina*; with its restaurant, 50 slip marina, and 40 room hotel. Emil, the manager, invites all boaters to give him a call on VHF ch.68 for reservations and entrance details. The marina has no repair facilities or fuel, but can accommodate vessels up to 50 feet with a 7' draft though Emil boasts 8' to 10' of draft can make it into the marina. The marina complex is also the home of *SCUBA Bimini*. Just north of the marina is a small "F" shaped canal whose only entrance is along the western shore of South Bimini. The canal area, known as Port Royal, is dotted with homes, mostly owned by Americans who fly in on weekends and holidays. A five foot draft can make it over the bar at the entrance and into the 7'-9' water inside in the event of bad weather. Here you can tie to the mangroves or anchor in a stretch between houses.

The finest hurricane hole in the Biminis is up the creek along the northern shore of Nixon's Harbour. One skipper I know of took his 67' sailboat drawing 7'4" in there on the high tide and had plenty of water where he tied to the mangroves though he did bump a few times on the way in. The channel is easy to see with its flagged markers on each side. Follow the flags in and anchor in any of the three pockets. The creek to the east is the deepest and longest with the best protection. The creek to the left leads to the Shark Lab. Actually called the Bimini Biological Field Station, this is where Dr. Samuel Gruber from the University of Miami and his staff carry on lemon shark research. The shallow waters between North Bimini and South Bimini is a lemon shark nursery with adults mating every April and May. Juvenile lemons live in the lagoon for years until they are old enough to leave. Dr. Gruber and his staff capture specimens in the lagoon to tag and release. Some specimens are fitted with transponders which allow the researchers to follow the shark on its travels through the waters in the vicinity.

SOUTH BIMINI TO GUN CAY

From South Bimini to Gun Cay (Chart BI-6) there is little for the cruiser but there is quite a bit for the avid snorkeler or diver. There are some intriguing dive sites south of South Bimini. The wreck of the *Sapona* lies just south of South Bimini and east of Turtle Rocks and its bulk is very conspicuous. The *Sapona*, originally called the *Lone Star*, was a 2700 ton rock carrier in World War I and ran aground between South Bimini and Gun Cay in a hurricane in 1929. The hull served as a bootleg liquor warehouse during the rum running days of the American prohibition years, then a private club, and during the World War II years it was a bombing target for fliers, in fact, some bombs are still found on the bottom. Hurricane Betsy in 1965 split her stern, and left her pretty much as she is seen today. The hull lies in about 15' of water and is called home by a multitude of marine creatures. You can anchor off the wreck in 9'-15' of water. Pass south of Round Rock and head straight for the wreck keeping an eye out for the shallows to the east of Turtle Rocks and the small sandbar north of the *Sapona*. There is a 5' at MLW spot on this route so keep an eye on the depthsounder. You can also head straight for the wreck from the anchorage that lies to the east of Gun Cay with the only obstruction being a shallow area with 6' depths at MLW lying just northeast of the Gun Cay anchorage. Vessels may enter Barnett Harbour and head for the wreck.

North and South Turtle Rocks lie just south of South Bimini, and boast some interesting dive sites. The northernmost cay is known as *Grouper Hideaway*. This reef begins at 25' with some low profile coral and rock ledges, while a set of engines from a wreck lies off its northern tip. A site called *Fish Haven* is the best diving in the area. It lies between the third and fourth cays. This reef slopes down to about 40' with a canyon leading southward.

Vessels heading along the western shores of these cays between Bimini and Gun Cay will have deep water all the way, but take care that the strong, rising tide does not push you onto the rocks themselves. The shallowest areas are just to the east and northeast of Gun Cay and the sandbars just to the west of Turtle Rocks in the area of the Sapona. Do not head too far east as you can run up on some very shallow water very quickly along this route.

Piquet Rocks, just south of the entrance to Barnett Harbour, are named after Captain Piquet, a pirate who was a frequent visitor to these waters.

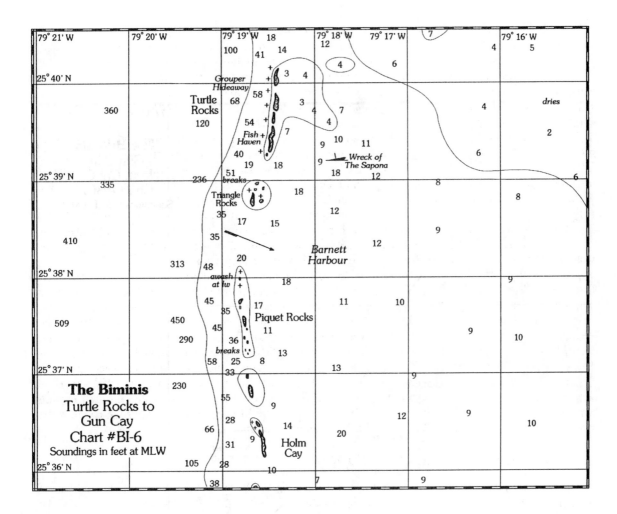

The Biminis
Turtle Rocks to
Gun Cay
Chart #BI-6
Soundings in feet at MLW

GUN CAY

Gun Cay, Chart BI-7, is a popular jump off spot for all cruisers, those with only a week to spare, or those heading north or south to or from distant islands. The very conspicuous Gun Cay Light (resembles an orange and white lighthouse-FL W ev 10 sec) easily marks this cay from offshore day or night. In winds from east to south most vessels will anchor in Honeymoon Harbour on the northern tip of the island. Enter this anchorage from the west between the northwestern tip of Gun Cay and the first small unnamed cay to its northwest in about 7'-8' at low water. Find a sandy spot inside to drop the hook away from the rocks in 6'-12' of water. The anchorage boasts a beautiful beach, but the wreckage of the sailboat *Nola* on shore reminds one that this is not a good spot in bad weather. It is possible to enter this anchorage from the east but you must skirt a long rocky bar stretching northwestward from Gun Cay all the way to the first set of rocks to the north.

Another popular anchoring spot is along the western shore of Gun Cay just south of the northern tip of the island. There is good holding here in sand but a swell usually runs through the anchorage and a second anchor or bridle is advised to keep your boat pointed into the swell unless you like rolling all night. In westerly or very light east to south winds, most vessels anchor on the eastern shore in 7'-10' of water. To anchor on the eastern shore, or to continue on to Chub Cay in the Berrys you must negotiate Gun Cay Pass between Gun Cay and Cat Cay.

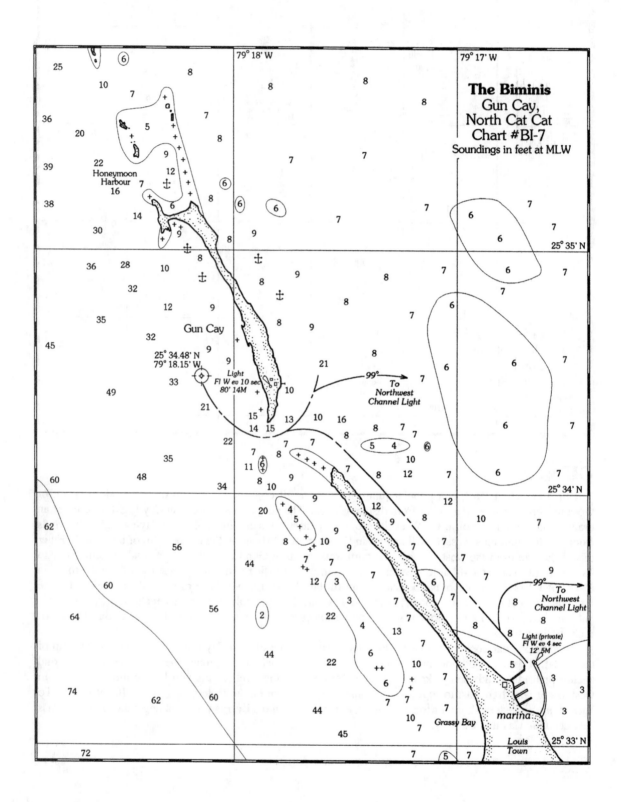

The Biminis
Gun Cay,
North Cat Cat
Chart #BI-7
Soundings in feet at MLW

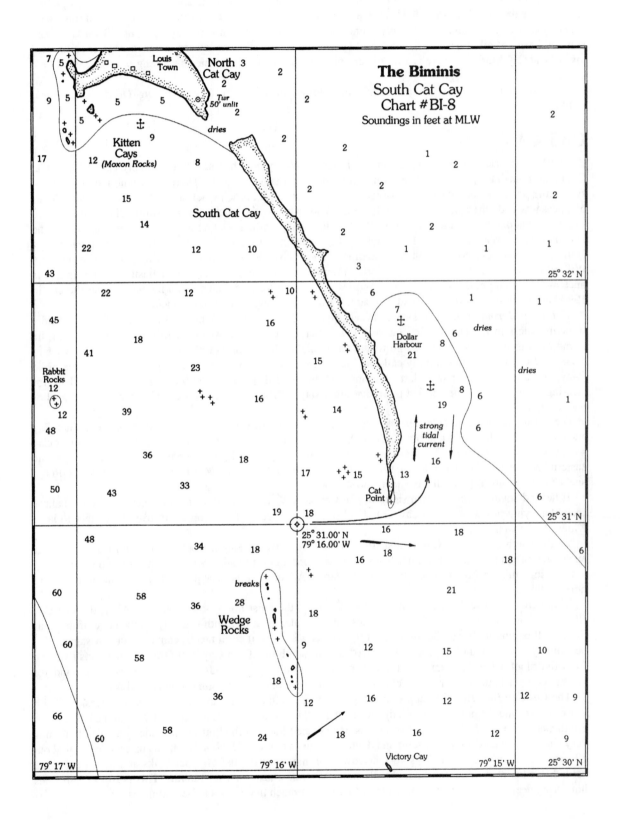

The Biminis
South Cat Cay
Chart #BI-8
Soundings in feet at MLW

A GPS waypoint at 25° 34.48' N, 79° 18.15' W will place you approximately ¼ mile NW of Gun Cay Pass in about 20'-25' of water. Head generally southeastward around the southern tip of Gun Cay being sure to favor the Gun Cay shore. There is a large rocky bar working out from Cat Cay and you must pass between Gun Cay and this bar. Simply round the southern tip of Gun Cay staying about 50 yards off and you will have 15' all the way in. Once inside you may head northward toward the anchorage or southward toward Cat Cay Marina. There is a lot of current in this cut and when it meets a strong opposing wind Gun Cay Pass can get a bit rough.

It is from here that most skippers begin their long banks passage (see: *Crossing The Great Bahama Bank*).

CAT CAY

In 1931, American Advertising executive Louis R. Wasey bought Cat Cay (originally called North Cat Cay) and immediately poured $1 million into it creating a lavish retreat. There were nine tennis courts, a swimming pool, a beauty parlor, a masseuse, and wine cellar, a French Chef, a skeet shoot, a casino, flocks of pheasants and turkeys, and over 250 servants to cater to the guests every whim. The club was so exclusive that one was not allowed to set foot on the island without an engraved invitation from one of the 100 members. Wasey died in 1961 and his heirs declined to subsidize the club. The following year Hurricane Betsy leveled the club and marina. The club was purchased following this catastrophe by Willard F. Rockwell, Jr., chairman of North American Rockwell and twenty-four business partners and is once again a going concern. Hurricane Andrew did quite a lot of damage when he passed over the cay in 1992 but rebuilding efforts have paid off and Cat Cay is once again lush and tropical.

Cat Cay Marina, selling gas and diesel, boasts 75 slips with a minimum depth of 8' dockside, sometimes less in the channel in places at low water. Cruisers are welcome to spend the night but the island itself is off-limits. There is a store and restaurant on the premises for your enjoyment. If you wish to clear in *at Cat Cay Marina* simply call them just prior to your arrival, say when you are still a mile or so away, and the dockmaster will alert Customs. At this time there is a $25.00 charge to use their dock for clearing in but this may be applied to an overnight stay. There is a clinic on Cat Cay for those in need of medical attention.

The marina is located inside a breakwater on the east side of Cat Cay. As you pass between Gun Cay and Cat Cay give the bar extending northward from Cat Cay a wide berth then parallel the shore of Cat Cay southward to the *Marina*. The *Marina* maintains a flashing white light (once every four seconds) on the eastern breakwater. The Cat Cay airstrip runs south of the light and the Marina requests that boaters do not anchor north of this light as this is an air traffic zone.

If headed south on the western shore of Cat Cay keep well east of the island as there is a long shallow rocky bar lying just west of Cat cay with 4'-6' over it in places. If heading south from here steer to keep Kitten Rocks well to port.

At the south end of Cat Cay is a shallow little cove between Kitten Rocks and South Cat Cay. This anchorage offers protection from northwest through north to east winds. Strong southeast winds will bring a swell into this anchorage from the Gulf Stream. All in all this is a pretty fair spot in northwest to northeast winds.

There are some excellent dive sites around Cat Cay, the most noteworthy are *Tuna Alley*, the *Cat Cay Blue Hole*, and *Victory Reef*. *Tuna Alley* lies some 2 miles west of South Cat Cay on the edge of the Gulf Stream. It begins at 40' and bottoms out at 90' and is wall to wall coral heads, canyons, and passages. The best diving is when Gun Cay Light bears 010° and the south tip of Cat Cay is at 60°. The reef gets its name from the bluefin tuna that migrate through the area heading north in July. It is a breeding ground for Nassau grouper in the January and February. You are very likely to see some sharks on this dive.

The *Cat Cay Blue Hole* lies approximately 3½ miles south of Gun Cay Light and ¼ mile west of South Cat Cay. To find the hole line up Wedge Rock at 150°, the south tip of Cat Cay at 007°, and the south tip of South Cat Cay at 105°. Previous dive groups have placed lines on the bottom to guide you. The bottom is very silty so take care not to stir it up and decrease your visibility. The bottom opens up at a depth of about 12' and the entrance to the hole is very narrow, you may have to take off your tanks and pull them along behind you to enter. You will undoubtedly notice a strange taste in your mouth. This is from a sulfurous hot spring deep below. The hole drops to 45' with one branch that is said to be bottomless.

SOUTH CAT CAY

South Cat Cay offers little for the cruising skipper except a pleasant anchorage and some offshore reefs to investigate. The cay itself has a beach on the western shore that, although it looks inviting, is littered with rocks and dead trees. There is an anchorage called Dollar Harbour off the southeastern shore of South Cat Cay that offers good protection from southwest through west to northwest. The anchorage is deep and has a strong tidal current flowing through it so be sure your anchors are set well.

A GPS waypoint at 25° 31.00' N, 79° 16.00' W (Chart BI-8) will place you approximately ½ nm west of the entrance to Dollar Harbour. Head east and around the southern tip of South Cat Cay keeping Cat Point to port and round up northward in the deep (19') water. Try to work your way northward into the anchorage as far as you can get to avoid any swells affecting you as they work their way around Cat Point. The shallow water to the east and southeast offer protection from seas in moderate east to southeast winds. It is possible in the event of a frontal passage to lie in Dollar Harbour during the pre-frontal southwest to north winds and then pass around Cat Point and work your way up into the small cove on the south end of Cat Cay for protection from the northwest to northeast winds to follow.

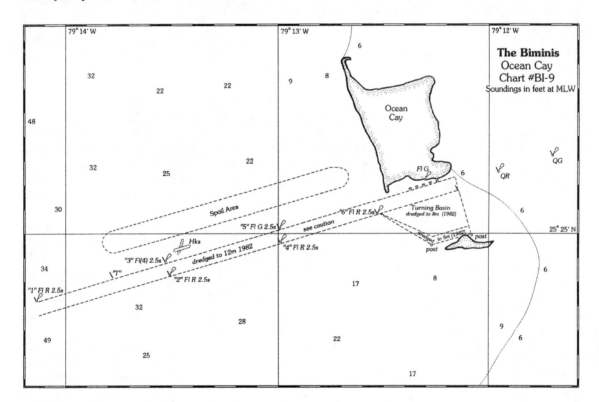

SOUTH CAT CAY TO OCEAN CAY

South of South Cat Cay there is little to offer cruisers except those bent on exploring where few have gone before. As always there is excellent fishing at the drop off and a few scattered reefs for the avid snorkeler. The best snorkeling is around the scattered rocks along the edge of the bank.

Victory Reef lies off of Victory Cay and Barren Rocks. To find it line up the northern tip of Barren Rocks at 60° and the southern tip of South Cat Cay at Cat Point at 25°. The reef system stretches some 2 miles to the south and begins at about 40' and drops off to around 90'. The reef is home to a multitude of fish life and is honeycombed with caves, canyons, and grottoes.

Ocean Cay is a man made island, a multi-million dollar aragonite mining operation. Aragonite, a type of limestone, is used in the manufacture of such products as glass, soda, cement, and fertilizer. Bahamian aragonite is extremely pure, containing 97% calcium carbonate. Ocean Cay is private and has no accommodations for visiting cruisers although the turning basin can be used in an emergency. The channel is well marked with a sea buoy (Qk FL W). Ocean Cay presents a very high profile (for this stretch of islands) when first seen from a distance. What you actually are seeing are the high mounds of sand dredged from the surrounding waters and the system of cranes that are often confused for towers or masts.

From Ocean Cay southward to Riding Rocks are a few scattered reefs and cays such as Brown's Cay, Beach Cay, and Square Rock. Riding Rocks, or Orange Cay farther south, is a good entrance to the banks for skippers coming from the lower cays.

It is possible to reach Northwest Channel Light from South Riding Rock. A vessel can enter the banks one-half mile south of South Riding Rock and head east until one-half mile south of Castle Rock. From there a heading of 80° for 56.6 nautical miles will bring you to Northwest Channel Light.

For those heading south from Orange Cay, the Great Bahama Bank curves gently southeastward and parallels the Cuban coastline. Its edge is littered with shoals, reefs, and wrecks so use extreme caution. The banks here shallow considerably the closer eastward you get to Andros.

The Biminis
South Riding Rock
Chart # BI-10
Soundings in feet at MLW

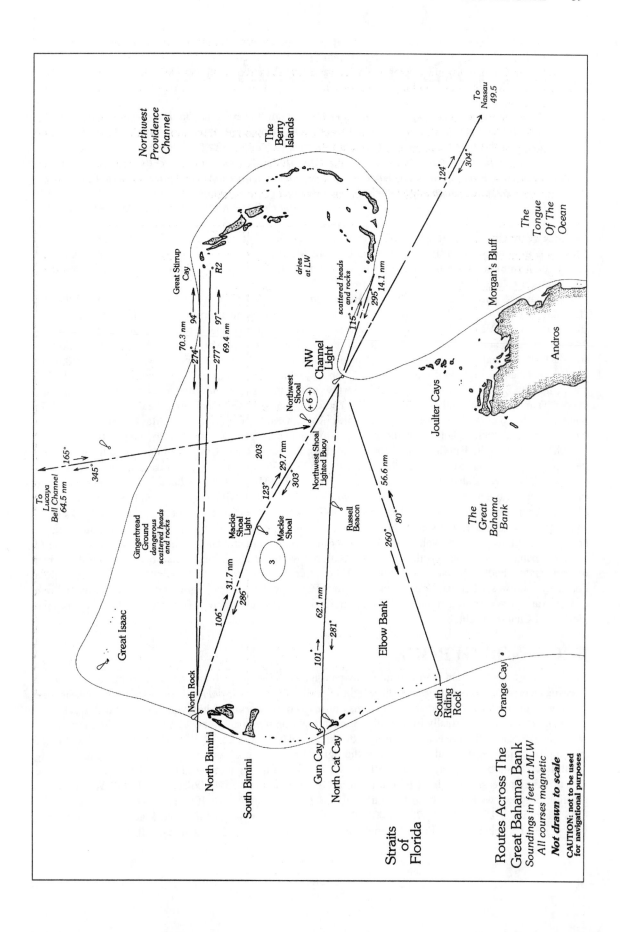

Straits
of
Florida

Routes Across The
Great Bahama Bank
Soundings in feet at MLW
All courses magnetic
Not drawn to scale
CAUTION: not to be used
for navigational purposes

CROSSING THE

GREAT BAHAMA BANK

Note: Navigators should be cautious, while crossing the Bahama Bank, never to follow vessels, if they alter course often, as the New Providence Wreckers have frequently decoyed them for the purpose of plunder; a crime which the most barbarous nation would punish with the greatest severity. This is not published to give offense to anyone, but it applies to some of the Providence Navigators, and it is our duty to point out danger to Mariners, from which the Editor will never deviate, or hide from investigation.

from *Blunt's* **THE AMERICAN COAST PILOT**, 1812

Things have changed quite a bit on the Bahama Banks since that pilot was published over 185 years ago. About the only dangers lurking about nowadays are Mackie Shoal and the remains of the NW Channel Light which still rise above the waters and are only marked by a floating light a few yards to the north of the structure.

Your passage across The Great Bahama Bank from Bimini or Gun Cay to Great Stirrup Cay, Bullock's Harbour, or Chub Cay will likely be the longest, and sometimes most boring, that you will face in your Bahamas cruise. Vessels heading to the northern Berry Islands will have relatively deeper water all the way. Starting at North Rock the water will get progressively deeper the closer you get to the Little Stirrup, from 20' to 40' and sometimes over 200' in places just west of Little Stirrup Cay. Vessels heading to Northwest Channel Light and then to either Chub Cay, Andros, or Nassau, will generally be in shallower water, usually 20' or less until they round Northwest Channel Light and cross over the drop off into the deeper water lying just southeast of the light. There are scattered reefs and small heads all over the banks but except for the shallows southeast of North Rock, west of Gun Cay, the Mackie Shoal area, and Northwest Shoal, there is nothing shallow enough to create a danger for a vessel drawing less than 7'.

When departing the Biminis bound for the northern Berrys or Chub Cay, weather plays a huge factor in determining when you leave. Your cruise across The Gulf Stream behind, you now must face the shallow waters of The Great Bahama Bank (see Chart: *Crossing The Great Bahama Bank*). Here you won't face the larger ocean swells of the Gulf Stream but you will have to deal with a strong wind blown chop. Winds of 15-20 knots from the east or southeast for a consistent period will often create waves on the banks up to five feet, close together, and steep. For sailors this can make your passage a very uncomfortable beat in choppy conditions, trawlers won't like these conditions much either. Unlike the Gulf Stream it is fine to cross the banks in moderate northerly winds. Sailors love those conditions. Also bear in mind that when transiting this body of water that you will be affected by tidal currents that normally flow in a northeast/southwest direction. These currents are affected by the wind strength, and their direction and rate of flow vary as you approach the Biminis, the northern Berrys, and the tip of the Tongue Of The Ocean at Northwest Channel Light.

FROM NORTH ROCK

Vessels proceeding from North Bimini may pass north of North Rock and enter the banks to begin their crossing. North Rock is equipped with a light (*FL W ev 3 sec, 40', 8M*) but, as with most lights in The Bahamas, consider it unreliable at best as it may or may not be working when you pass it. North Rock is so small and low that it is virtually impossible to see at night until you are almost on top of it. Of course radar would help but not all vessels are so equipped. A GPS waypoint at 25° 48.06' N, 79° 16.00' W will place you approximately ½ nautical mile west of the light. From this position steer 90° onto the banks keeping North Rock to starboard. Stay at least 150-100 yards north of the light to avoid the rocks close in and to the east of it. Head east for at least two miles to a GPS waypoint at 25°48.06' N, 79° 13.50' W. From this position Skippers wishing to head to Chub Cay can take up a course of 106° for 31.7 nautical miles to a GPS waypoint at 25° 42.00' N, 78° 39.00' W. This position lies just north of the Mackie Shoal light and well north of Mackie Shoal. From here take up a course of 123° for 29.7 nautical miles to bring you to a

GPS waypoint at 25° 28.40, 78° 09.80' W, or just north of Northwest Channel Light. Just two miles northwest of Northwest Channel Light on this route you will see the Northwest Shoal Lighted Buoy (*FL W ev 2 sec*). This marks a reef strewn shoal area with depths less than 6' over some of the heads. Make sure you pass to the south and west of this buoy but be advised that it is frequently off station and the light either not working or showing the wrong characteristics. From this position you can probably see the remains of the old Northwest Channel Light jutting up out of the water and a new lighted buoy placed approximately 200 yards north of these wreckage. Pass the Northwest Channel Lighted Buoy (usually just called Northwest Channel Light) on its north side and you may then take up your course for Chub Cay (115° for 14.1 nautical miles) or Nassau (124° for 49.5 nautical miles).

From the waypoint two miles east of North Rock, skippers wishing to head to Great Stirrup Cay can take up a course of 94° for a distance of 70.3 nautical miles. Those mariners wishing to head to *Great Harbour Cay Marina* at Bullock's Harbour can steer 97° for 69.4 nautical miles to pick up the tripod marker R2 at 25° 46.11' N, 77° 56.59' W.

FROM GUN CAY

Vessels departing from the eastern shore of Gun Cay and bound for the northern Berrys should be advised that the first 4-5 miles of their passage will be over some shallow sandbanks that barely carry 5' at MLW. If you attempt this route do it on a mid tide or better and make sure the tide is rising. From the eastern shore of Gun Cay a course of 86° for 74.6 nautical miles will bring you to R2, the tripod marker marking the entrance to the channel to Bullock's Harbour. Vessels wishing to make Great Stirrup Cay should proceed northward from this position and then eastward around the northern shore of Little Harbour Cay. Skippers wishing to make Northwest Channel Light can take up a course of 101° for 62.1 nautical miles. This will bring you well north of the remains of the old Russell Beacon. There is a lighted buoy that has taken the place of the old Russel Beacon. A GPS waypoint at 25° 29.00' N, 78° 25.54' W, will place you ½ mile north of the buoy.

Skippers leaving the *Cat Cay Marina* must clear the very visible shallow sandbank lying north and east of the marina. Once past this take up a course of 101° for 62.1 nautical miles and you will find yourself at Northwest Channel Light.

FROM LUCAYA

From the seaward entrance to Bell Channel at Lucaya it is possible for boaters to cross the Northwest Providence Channel and then the Great Bahama Bank to arrive at Northwest Channel Light. From Lucaya take up a course of 165° for 64.5 nautical miles. This will place you to the west of Northwest Shoal Lighted Buoy. Round the buoy to the south and take up a course of 123° for the final two miles or so to Northwest Channel Light.

FROM SOUTH RIDING ROCK

Entering the banks south of South Riding Rocks skippers can take up a course for Northwest Channel Light after passing Castle Rock on the port beam. From this position take up a course of 80° for 56.6 nautical miles to bring you to Northwest Channel Light. As you approach the light be sure to keep the buoy on your starboard side as you round it. This route takes you across the southeastern extremity of the Elbow Bank, lying about 10-20 miles along the course line from South Riding Rock. Here you will encounter some depths in the 6'-10' range at low water.

There is an old route from Orange Cay to Russell Beacon (53° for 51.2 nautical miles) and thence to Northwest Channel Light. I do not recommend this route as the waters in the area have shoaled considerably and can barely take 6' at low water in places. Scattered heads and small patch reefs are frequent the closer you get to Russell Beacon on this course.

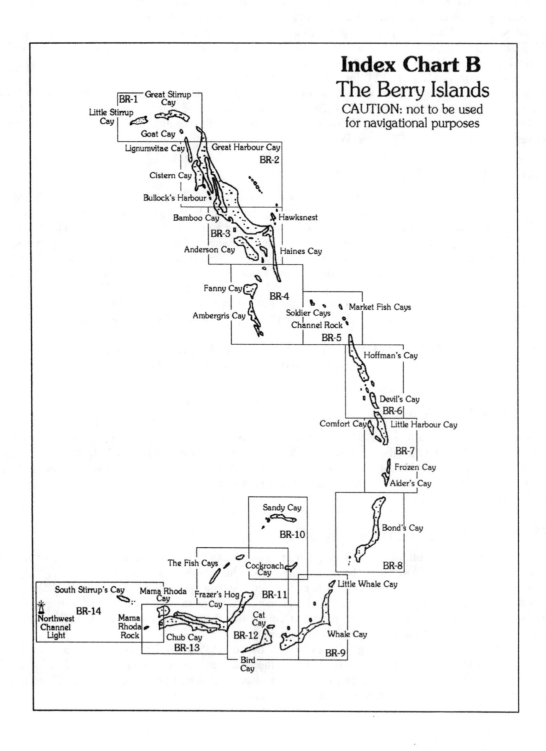

Index Chart B
The Berry Islands
CAUTION: not to be used
for navigational purposes

BR-1

Great Stirrup
Cay

Little Stirrup
Cay

Goat Cay

Lignumvitae Cay

Great Harbour Cay

BR-2

Cistern Cay

Bullock's Harbour

Bamboo Cay

Hawksnest

BR-3

Anderson Cay

Haines Cay

Fanny Cay

BR-4

Ambergris Cay

Soldier Cays

Market Fish Cays

Channel Rock

BR-5

Hoffman's Cay

Devil's Cay

BR-6

Comfort Cay

Little Harbour Cay

BR-7

Frozen Cay

Alder's Cay

Sandy Cay

BR-10

Bond's Cay

Cockroach
Cay

BR-8

The Fish Cays

Little Whale Cay

South Stirrup's Cay

Mama Rhoda
Cay

Frazer's Hog
Cay

BR-11

BR-14

Mama
Rhoda
Rock

Cat
Cay

Whale Cay

Northwest
Channel
Light

Chub Cay

BR-12

BR-13

Bird
Cay

BR-9

THE BERRY ISLANDS

East of the Biminis and approximately two-thirds of the distance to Nassau lie the Berry Islands. The Berrys form a crescent along the northeastern edge of the Great Bahama Bank near where it drops off into the deep waters of the Northwest Providence Channel. The entire bight on the western side of the crescent is very shallow with many sand bores and areas that dry at low water. Along the eastern shore of the Berry Islands the drop off into the deeper waters lies miles offshore in some places and in others, such as Chub Cay, just a few hundred yards off.

There are few true all weather harbours amongst the 30 some-odd cays which make up the Berry Islands although quite a few lee anchorages can be found from almost any wind direction. Most of the lee side anchorages offer good protection from seas but some swell seems to work its way in at times. The deep waters of the Northwest Providence channel and the Tongue Of The Ocean offer fantastic fishing opportunities and make the Berrys an ideal staging area for the fishing tournaments out of Chub Cay. The shallow grassy banks are teeming with conch while the rocks and reefs along the cays are home to lobster, grouper and snapper just waiting to hop into your frying pan. These shallow waters are tailor made for shallow draft monohulls, multihulls, and small outboard powered boats, offering many opportunities to explore where few others can go.

APPROACHES TO THE BERRYS

From North Rock in the Biminis a course of 94° for 71 nautical miles will bring you to the northwestern tip of the Berry Islands. Here a waypoint at 25° 49.64' N, 77° 57.41' W marks the beginning of the channel to Great Harbour Marina while a waypoint at 25° 49.60' N, 77° 55.66' W opens up the entrance to Slaughter Harbour just southwest of Great Stirrup Cay. Just past Great Stirrup Cay a waypoint at 25° 49.40' N, 77° 53.30' W will open up the anchorage at Great Harbour including Panton Cove and Goat Cay. Those mariners wishing to head directly for Great Harbour Cay Marina at Bullock's Harbour from North Rock can steer 97° for 71.2 nautical miles to arrive at the first tripod on the route to Bullock's Harbour at 25° 46.11' N, 77° 56.59' W.

From Freeport a course of 137° for 61.2 nautical miles will bring you to the Great Stirrup Cay/Slaughter Harbour waypoint while from Lucaya the course is 143° for 55 nautical miles. From the seaward entrance to Bell Channel at Lucaya it is possible for boaters to cross the Northwest Providence Channel and then the Great Bahama Bank to arrive at Northwest Channel Light. From Lucaya take up a course of 165° for 64.5 nautical miles. This will place you to the west of Northwest Shoal Lighted Buoy. Pass the buoy to the south and take up a course of 123° for the final two miles or so to Northwest Channel Light (see also *Crossing The Great Bahama Bank*).

From the western entrance of Nassau Harbour a course of 308° for 35.7 nautical miles will bring you to the Chub Cay waypoint. A course of 321° for 30.4 nautical miles from Nassau brings to a point just ¼ nautical mile east of the entrance to the anchorage at Little Whale Cay while a course of 333° for 34.4 nautical miles will bring you to the waypoint off the Frozen-Alder/Little Harbour Cay anchorage. Just a little further north lies the Devil's Hoffman anchorage where a course of 334° for 37 nautical miles from Nassau Harbour will place you approximately ¼ nautical mile off the entrance to the anchorage.

LITTLE STIRRUP AND GREAT STIRRUP CAY

The Stirrups (Chart #BR-1) lie at the northern corner of the Berry Islands where the Northwest Providence Channel bends to the west and towards America. Their unique location has kept these waters quite busy over the years. A wrecker named Captain Cameron once practiced his art in these waters using Little Stirrup Cay as his home while notorious pirates such as the infamous Blackbeard often passed here on their way from Nassau to the eastern shores of America. The reign of William IV saw the settlement of Williams Town laid out on Great Stirrup Cay and a Customs house built but with the death of William IV, so went the town. During the American Civil War Federal gun boats regularly patrolled the waters surrounding Little and Great Stirrup Cay to catch gun runners rounding the corner from Nassau bound for

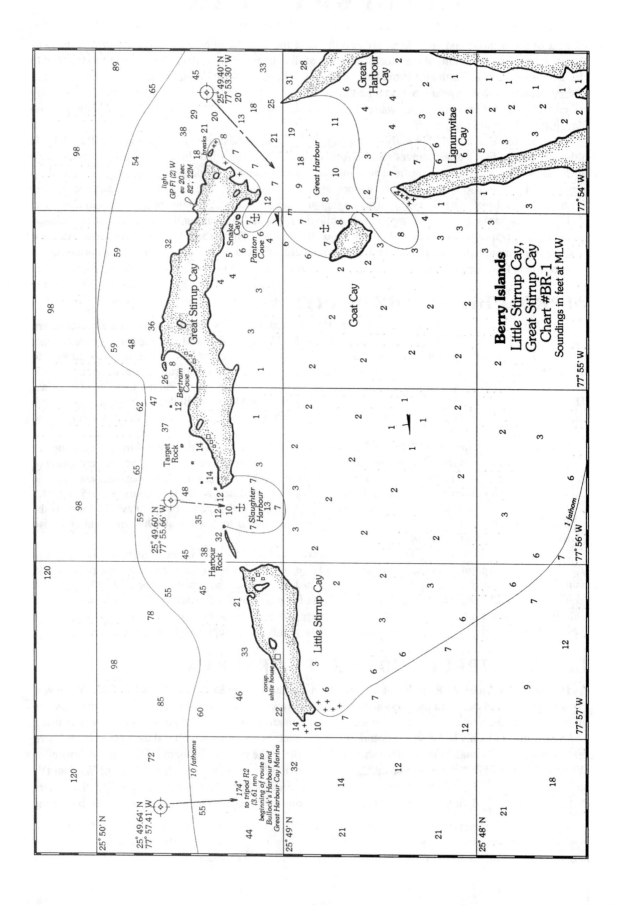

Berry Islands
Little Stirrup Cay,
Great Stirrup Cay
Chart #BR-1
Soundings in feet at MLW

the southern U. S. Coast. Federal agents again patrolled this area looking for rum runners during the American Prohibition years and for drug runners in more recent times. Definitely a popular spot.

The 92 acre Little Stirrup Cay was named after a former owner named Sterrup. Both Little Stirrup and Great Stirrup Cay are private, a cruise line has leased the cays and built facilities ashore for its guests. The cruise ships anchor just north of Great Stirrup and ferry passengers ashore to enjoy a sample of the "Bahamian Out-Island lifestyle." The manager of Little Stirrup Cay says that they don't mind if visiting yachtsmen wish to come ashore and look around as long as there are no guests ashore (this means no cruise ships anchored offshore) and that visitors contact Little Stirrup Cay on VHF ch. 16 first to ask permission. Cruisers in Panton Cove are welcome to come ashore on the western end of Great Stirrup Cay to explore the lighthouse (built in 1863, GP Fl W ev 20 sec, 82' 22M), or the remains of the U.S. missile tracking station. In years past cruisers anchored in Slaughter Harbour or Panton Cove dinghied ashore on Great Stirrup Cay and crossed the island on foot to mingle with cruise ship guests and help themselves to the free buffet. It didn't take long for the cruise ship crews to get wise and realize that the cruisers were very tanned compared to the comparatively pale liners guests. So much for the free buffets. Today, ship's guests wear plastic bracelets to take advantage of the buffet. Now if the cruisers could only get a couple of those and store them on the island. . . just kidding folks!

Bertram's Cove, where the cruise ship passengers alight, is named after a Commander Manuel Bertram of H.M.S. *Tweed* who died and was buried here by his crew on July 20, 1834. There is a plaque commemorating Commander Bertram that was left by the crew of the *Tweed*. Commander Bertram's survey work is the foundation of some of the charts of The Bahamas now being used.

Approaching the northern Berry Islands from Bimini or Grand Bahama your first sign of the Berry's will probably be the very conspicuous white house on Little Stirrup Cay (see Chart #BR-1). There is a small anchorage between Little Stirrup Cay and Great Stirrup Cay called Slaughter Harbour which has 8'-10' inside and is good for the winds of east through southeast but is not to be considered in a frontal passage as it is wide open to the southwest and the north. A GPS waypoint at 25° 49.60' N, 77° 55.66' W will place you approximately ½ nm north of the entrance. The entrance is fairly straightforward passing between Great Stirrup Cay to port and the unnamed rocks lying off Little Stirrup Cay. Once inside watch out for the long line of buoys to starboard which mark a private swimming area and don't travel too far south as the water shoals quickly.

Just east of Great Stirrup Cay lies the entrance to Great Harbour, a much better anchorage than Slaughter Harbour but a little uncomfortable in the prelude to a norther or in strong southeast winds. A GPS waypoint at 25° 49.40' N, 77° 53.30' W places you approximately ½ nm northeast of the entrance to Great Harbour. Head in between the rocks just off the eastern point of Great Stirrup Cay and the northern tip of Great Harbour Cay in 7-13' of water. The shallower water will be close in to the Great Stirrup shore. Vessels seeking refuge from west winds can go straight over to Goat Cay and anchor in the lee along its eastern shore. The most frequented anchorage is at Panton Cove just inside the southeastern tip of Great Stirrup Cay. Here you can anchor in 5-8' close in to Snake Cay. You'll find good protection in northwest to east winds but this is no place to be in strong east-southeast winds as the swells come right in the entrance.

From Great Harbour dinghies can follow the channel between Great Harbour Cay and Cistern Cay which will bring you near the entrance to Bullock's Harbour and Great Harbour Cay Marina. There used to be a lot of honeysuckle growing on Cistern Cay but where it is today is anybody's guess.

GREAT HARBOUR CAY, BULLOCK'S HARBOUR, GREAT HARBOUR CAY MARINA

Great Harbour Cay (see Chart #'s BR-2 and BR-3) is the largest cay in the Berry Islands being over 7 miles long and 3/4 mile wide in spots. The southernmost portion was once called Merryman and the northern portion Tiger Bay. This northernmost section was even later subdivided into areas known as Grape Tree and Sistare. Some five hundred people live in the Berry Islands and most of them reside here at Great Harbour Cay. Many are wealthy foreigners with splendid villas or condos overlooking the eastern shore of Great Harbour Cay with its beautiful, long, curving Queen's Beach.

The route to the entrance to *Great Harbour Cay Marina* and Bullock's Harbour (see Chart #BR-2) begins at the western tip of Little Stirrup Cay and bends its way southeastward across the banks in 9'-12' of water until you arrive at the entrance to Bullock's Harbour and Great Harbour Cay Marina. From a GPS

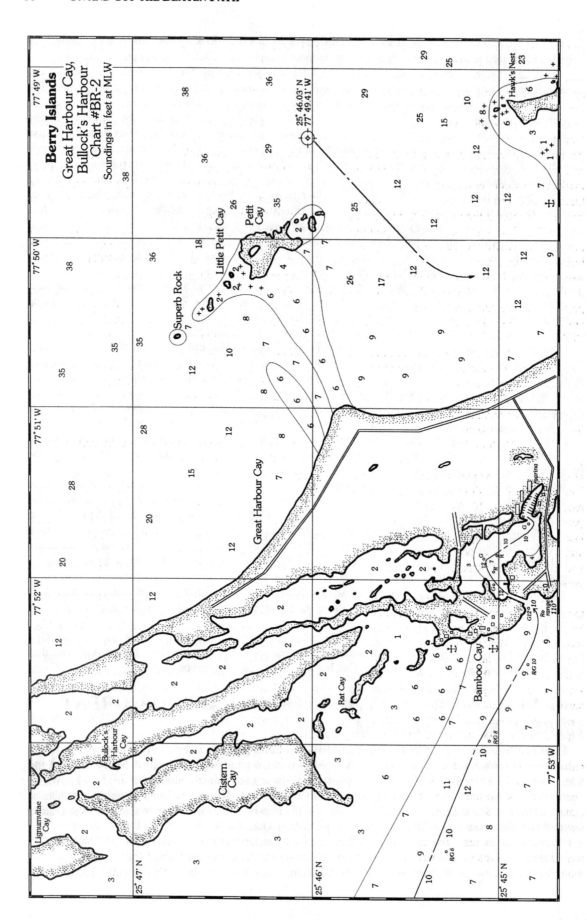

Berry Islands
Great Harbour Cay,
Bullock's Harbour
Chart #BR-2
Soundings in feet at MLW

waypoint northwest of Little Stirrup Cay (see Chart #BR-1) at 25° 49.64'N, 77° 57.41' W take up a course of 174° for the tripod marker "RG2" (Red/Green #2) that will sit on the horizon about 3.61 miles south of you. Once you clear the shallows along the southwestern tip of Little Stirrup Cay you will have deep water on both sides of your course all the way to the marker. In fact, to the west the deep water extends all the way to Bimini. A GPS waypoint at 25° 46.11' N, 77° 56.59' W places you approximately 200 yards east of "RG2." As previously stated there is deep water all around this marker, you may pass it to either side though it is painted red and should be taken to starboard when approaching from seaward. Once abeam of the tripod marker take up a course of 111° (for reference see chart *Approaches to the Berry Islands*). This will put the conspicuous Batelco Tower at Bullock's Harbour just off your port bow. The next three markers are single poles and marked red/green. They can be taken on either side though it is best to take them to starboard when approaching Bullock's Harbour. From "RG2" you will have no less than 9' to the final marker (for a listing of GPS waypoints on these markers see *Appendix D*). Keep all the markers to starboard and you will not have a problem. Simply steering approximately 110° and looking for the markers is usually the best way to enter but for those skippers who need waypoints and courses the following course can be steered. From the tripod RG2 it is 111° for 1.52 nautical miles to RG4, from RG4 steer 115° for 1.28 nautical miles to R6, and from RG6 steer 118° for .65 nautical miles to RG8, and from RG8 steer 125° for .46 nautical miles to reach RG10. From RG10, the fifth marker in, look just off your port bow ashore and you will see a house on the ridge with a 110° range. The range is designed to bring you in to the last red marker, a red diamond, where you will turn to port and line up on the entrance cut to Bullock's Harbour. There will be a green marker "G12" just outside the cut to lead you in. At this point you will travel through a narrow cut blasted through the rolling hills to a lake inside and *Great Harbour Cay Marina*. The cut is approximately 80' wide and has 8' at low water. Once inside follow the marked channel as it winds around to the marina or, if you need fuel, pull up to the Shell fuel dock just to starboard inside the entrance. You will have at least 7' here at low water. The marina is tucked into the eastern corner and is surrounded by a nice condo development. It looks almost as if it belongs in south Florida instead of The Bahamas.

Bullock's Harbour is the hub of the Berry Islands in that it is the largest settlement and the only one with a Government Administration Office with a Post Office and Clinic. *Great Harbour Cay Marina* offers all amenities and is the perfect place to ride out the fiercest frontal passage or even a hurricane. It is entirely landlocked and is situated in a tight "L" shape and well protected. Here dockmaster Rufus Pritchard monitors VHF ch. 16, 68, and 14, and is happy to welcome you to the Berry Islands and take care of all your needs while you enjoy your stay at the marina. The marina boasts 86 slips which will accommodate boats up to 150' long with drafts of 9'. It is possible to arrange for a mechanic or even someone to clean and wax your vessel here, but there is no propane available. Great Harbour Cay is a Port Of Entry and if you inform Mr. Pritchard upon your arrival he will arrange for Customs and Immigration to visit your vessel.

There are a dozen restaurants and bars in the vicinity including *The Wharf*, which is situated right next to the marina property. *The Warf* monitors VHF ch.16 and is open Wednesday through Saturday for dinner by reservation only. There's also the *Backside Inn* with cold beverages and cocktails, *Coolie Mae's Take Away* serving Bahamian dishes for lunch Monday through Saturday. Near the beach you will find *The Graveyard Inn*, a favorite spot for many, is closed now due to fire damage in the Spring of 1998, its future is uncertain. The *White Water Restaurant* will pick you up at the marina, ask the dockmaster about it. Also worth investigating is *The Pool Bar* at the *Marina*, the *Watergate Chicken Shack* which is open daily serving light snacks of chicken and fish. Here also you'll find gift shops, ice, laundry facilities, a dive shop, and scooter and bicycle rentals. Those skippers wishing to fly in guests should contact *Island Express Airlines* which services the Great Harbour Cay.

There is a little known, and little used route from Great Harbour Cay to Northwest Channel Light but it requires good visibility, the ability to read the water's depth, a good weather forecast, and the help of the tide. From RG4 a vessel of less than 6' draft, can take up an approximate heading of 240° and work her way around the western edge of the shallow banks that lie to the west of the Berry Islands. You should make Northwest Shoal Light, which lies about 3-4 miles northwest of Northwest Channel Light, your waypoint for this route. You will skirt the edge of shallow banks that lie west of the Berrys and are strewn with shallow sandbores. You can anchor in the lee of these sandbores in prevailing winds if needed. Once past these sandbores you will once again be in deeper water. If you wish to avoid these sandbores, steer more westerly from Great Harbour Cay before turning southwards to Northwest Shoal Light. When

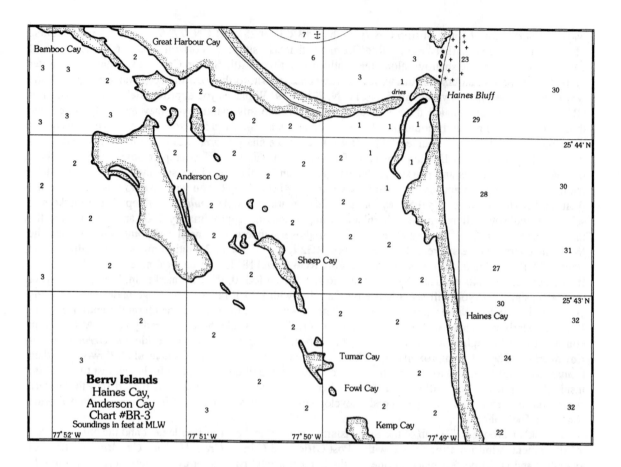

Berry Islands
Haines Cay,
Anderson Cay
Chart #BR-3
Soundings in feet at MLW

approaching Northwest Shoal Light try not to run up on Northwest Shoal. Pass to the west of the shoal and light.

The eastern shore of Great Harbour Cay offers an excellent lee in winds from southeast to almost northwest. The anchorage is beautiful and the holding is good. To enter (see Chart #'s BR-2 and BR-3) from the east you must pass well north of Hawk's Nest which lies at the northern tip of Haines Cay and Petit Cay which lies approximately midway along the eastern shore of Great Harbour Cay. A GPS waypoint at 25° 46.03' N, 77°49.41' W is an excellent place to enter from. Steer roughly southwest passing well south of Petit Cay and well north of Hawk's Nest in 25' of water and work your way inside along the shore to the southern most end of the small bay where you can anchor in 8'-10'. Keep well clear of the shallows between Petit Cay and Great Harbour Cay and the shallows lying southwest of Hawk's Nest and the southern tip of the bay.

Bamboo Cay (Chart #BR-3), lying just west of Great Harbour Cay, was once thought to be the most politically and commercially important cay in the Berrys. Sandy patches on the north side were once a burial ground but the soil is so shallow that the coffins often floated on the salt water. The Cay once had a few fruit trees along its shores. When asked why the island had such few trees, the residents of the Bullocks Harbour area said that *"They did not plan for posterity and what they themselves may not live to reap—posterity must look out for itself."* The residents at that time (1920's) were primarily involved with sponging and boat building. Just north of Bamboo Cay is a small unnamed cay ¼ mile long and 200' wide. It has a creek with a mouth about 50' wide known as the "waterfall." The strong tidal flow through here overturned and caused the sinking of several small unskillfully handled boats by the early residents.

Anderson Cay (Chart #BR-3), lying approximately ½ mile west of the southern end of Great Harbour Cay is very high with a cliff dropping right down to the water's edge The northern end is swampy with an old coconut orchard on the northwestern tip. There is an old well on the western side that is very brackish and filthy now but was of some use when cattle were raised on the cay in the late 1800's to early 1900's. Anderson Cay can only be explored by dinghy as the waters surrounding it are very shallow.

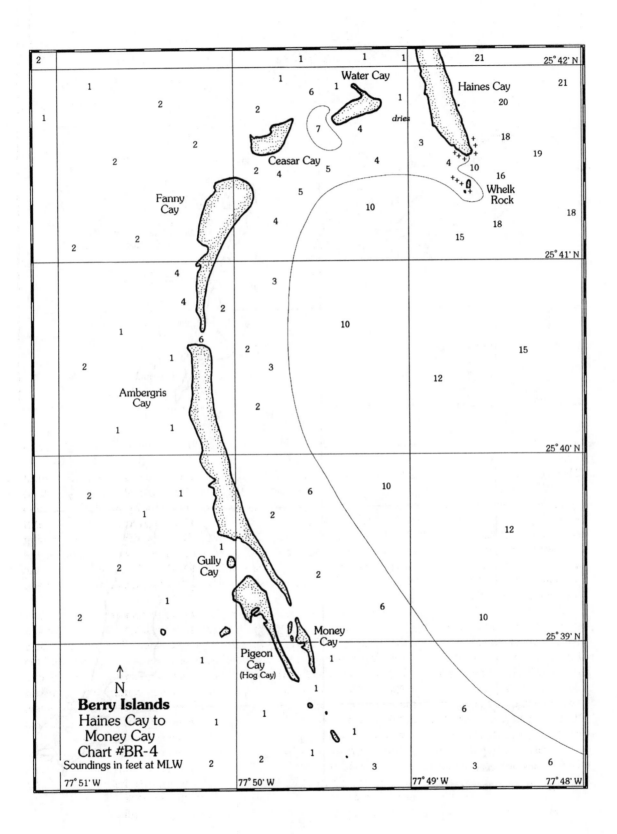

Water Cay

Haines Cay

Ceasar Cay

dries

Whelk
Rock

Fanny
Cay

Ambergris
Cay

Gully
Cay

Money
Cay

Pigeon
Cay
(Hog Cay)

↑
N

Berry Islands
Haines Cay to
Money Cay
Chart #BR-4
Soundings in feet at MLW

25° 42' N

25° 41' N

25° 40' N

25° 39' N

77° 51' W   77° 50' W   77° 49' W   77° 48' W

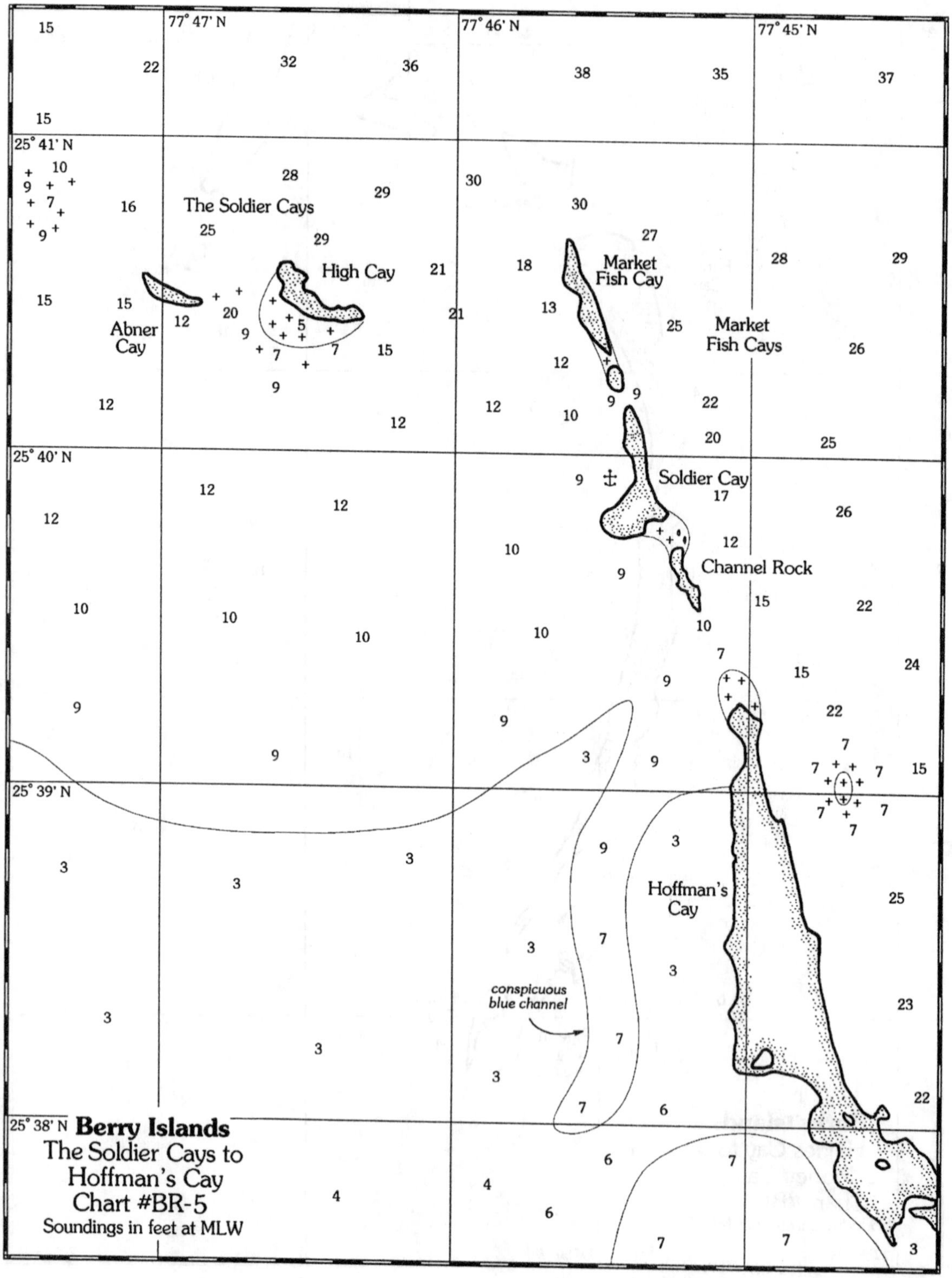

77° 47' N   77° 46' N   77° 45' N

15
22   32   36   38   35   37
15

25° 41' N
10
9 + +
+ 7 +   16   The Soldier Cays   30   30
+   9 +   25   29   18   Market   28   29
9 +   29   Fish Cay
High Cay   21   27
15   15   + +   25   Market
Abner   12   20   +   21   13   Fish Cays   26
Cay   9   + 5 +   12
+ 7 + 7   15   12   25
9   10   9 9   22
12   12   20   25

25° 40' N
12   12   9   Soldier Cay
12   17
12   10   26
10   9   Channel Rock
10   10   10   12
15   22
10   10   15   10
7
9   15   24
9   22
9
7
9   9   3   9   7 + + 7 7   15
+ (+) +
25° 39' N   7 + + 7
7   7
9   3   25
3   3   Hoffman's
3   7   Cay
3
3
3   *conspicuous*
blue channel   7   23
3
3   7   6   22

Berry Islands
The Soldier Cays to   6   7
Hoffman's Cay   4   4   6   7
Chart #BR-5
Soundings in feet at MLW   6   7   7   3

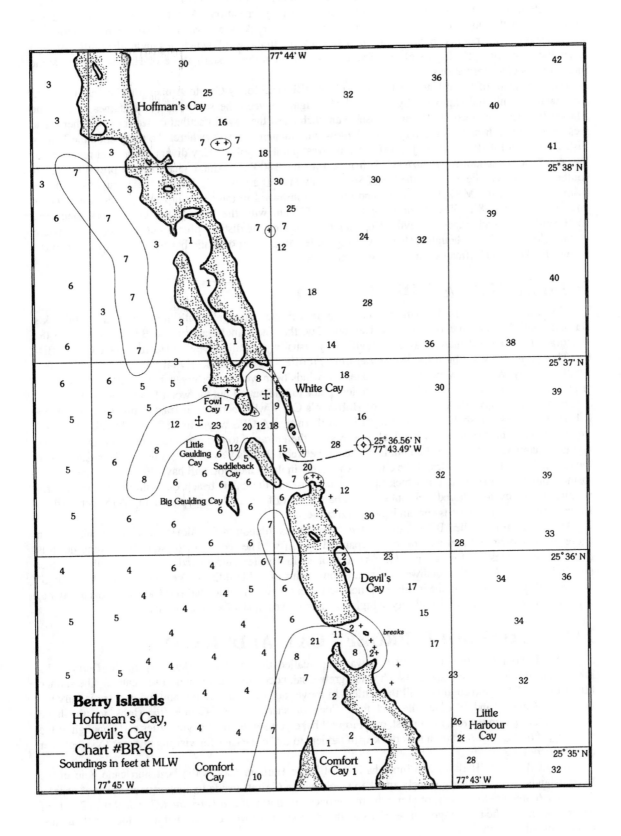

77° 44' W

30

3

36   42

Hoffman's Cay   32   40

25

16   25° 38' N

7 (+ +) 7   30   30

3   7   39

7 (+) 7   25

12   24   32

1   40

3   18

1   28

14   36   38   25° 37' N

3   6   7   18

6   8   White Cay   30   39

Fowl   7   9   16

Cay   28   ⊕ 25° 36.56' N
77° 43.49' W

12   23   20 12 18

Little   12   15   39

Gaulding   5

Cay   Saddleback   20

Cay   7   12

Big Gaulding Cay   6   30   32

28   33   25° 36' N

4   7   23

6   Devil's   34   36

Cay   17

5   15   34

6   breaks

11   2   17

21   8   2   23   32

Little   26 Harbour   Cay
28

Berry Islands
Hoffman's Cay,
Devil's Cay
Chart #BR-6
Soundings in feet at MLW   Comfort   Comfort Cay 1   28   25° 35' N
Cay   10   32

77° 45' W   77° 43' W

Hawksnest Cay at the northern tip of Haines Cay was named after ospreys that nested among the bluffs on its eastern shore. Under one of the bluffs is an interesting formation. About a hundred feet inland and surrounded on the northern, eastern and southern sides by rock is a small pool with a beach along its western shore. This pool is connected to the sea by a "hole in the wall" which lies under the bluff. At high water the archway is 18' high with 4' of water under it. On the western shore of Haines Cay are some interesting boulder formations.

The cays south of Great Harbour Cay (see Chart #BR-4), Money Cay to Ambergris Cay, are excellent for beachcombing and exploring by dinghy. The bight between the southern tip of Haines Cay to the Market Fish Cays is deep, 9'-18' and vessels can anchor off the cays in settled or westerly weather. The western shores of these cays are very, very shallow with mangroves everywhere. To the east lie the Market Fish Cays (Chart #BR-5), where just off the southwest point of Soldier Cay divers might find remnants of the wreck of the schooner "*Beatrice*," dating back to the 1800's. A nice anchorage in prevailing (east-southeast) winds can be found in the lee of Soldier Cay just off a low lying but very beautiful beach. Enter from the north of the Market Fish Cays and proceed southward in their lee until just off the beach where you can anchor in 8'. Vessels drawing less than 5' can, with the help of the tides, work their way southward to the anchorages at Devil's Hoffman by following the distinct blue water that curves westward around Hoffman Cay. Though it shallows, a high tide can get you over the bar into the deep water to the west of the Devil's Hoffman anchorage (see next section).

HOFFMAN'S CAY, DEVIL'S CAY

If you are looking for all around protection as in a frontal passage. With the exception of Bullock's Harbour, and the inner harbour at Little Harbour Cay, the finest anchorage in the Berry's, has to be the anchorage between Hoffman's Cay and Devil's Cay, usually just called Devil's Hoffman (see Chart #BR-6). Though it may get a bit rolly or surgy at times, it offers a lee from nearly all wind directions. A few small seas may work their way in from the banks in winds from west to northwest but nothing to fear if you are anchored properly. All in all it is an excellent place to ride out all but the worst frontal passages.

From seaward, give the eastern shore of Hoffman's Cay a wide berth of at least a mile to a mile and a half as there are some shallow reefs well off its northern tip. A GPS waypoint at 25° 36.56' N, 77° 43.49' W, places you approximately ¼ nautical mile east of the entrance to the anchorage between Devil's Cay and Hoffman's Cay. Steer for the middle of the cut between Devil's Cay to the south and the small rock to the north. Reefs line both sides of the cut but if you stay in the center you will have 20' at low water. Once inside, round up to starboard and tuck up to anchor just off the small beach on White Cay. In easterly weather I have even anchored well out onto the banks west of the anchorage proper in 12-15 feet north of Little Gaulding Cay. There is current here but no surge.

Devil's Cay (once called Bird Cay), has two hilly ranges to about 40'. Along the southern and eastern shore of the cay are several nice beaches separated by cliffs. The second of these cliffs coming north is home to an interesting formation. Here is a pool at low water surrounded by a low wall, a perfect swimming pool. Along the southwest shore are some ruins of old buildings. Vessels drawing less than 5' can work their way south on the inside from here to the cut between Little Harbour Cay and Frozen Cay but the ability to read water, good visibility, a high tide, and nerves of steel are a necessity.

LITTLE HARBOUR, FROZEN CAY, ALDER CAY

Little Harbour Cay (see Chart #BR-7) was once called the most important cay in the Berrys. Its inhabitants at this time were spongers who also grew sisal, coconuts, guava, and raised cattle. The sponge blight in the 1930's forced almost all the settlers to move, but some stayed on, and today there is only the family of Chester and Flo Darville and their flock of sheep. *Flo's Conch Bar* (look for the huge WELCOME sign on the roof) is a must, and Flo will bake you some bread if you order early enough in the morning. *Flo's Conch Bar* has a new dock with ladders to make it easier for visiting cruisers to sample her excellent cooking.

Next to Bullock's Harbour, the inner harbour at Little Harbour Cay is the best hurricane hole in the Berry Islands. The entrance channel can take vessels with a 6' draft inside to anchor in a pocket of water a little over 6' deep at low water, or along the mangroves just north of *Flo Darville's Conch Bar* in 7'-11' of water. Getting in the anchorage can be tricky as the channel is not well defined but a six foot draft can just make it in before high tide.

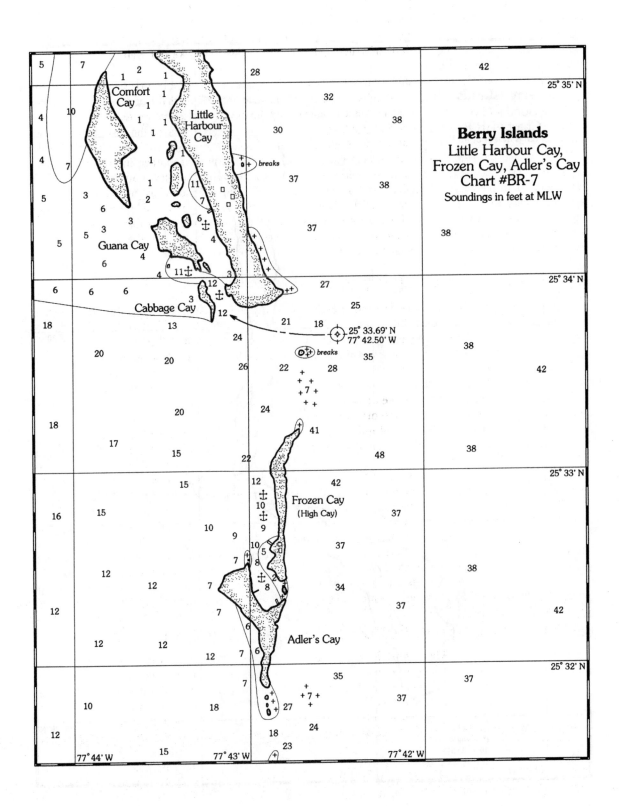

Berry Islands
Little Harbour Cay,
Frozen Cay, Adler's Cay
Chart #BR-7
Soundings in feet at MLW

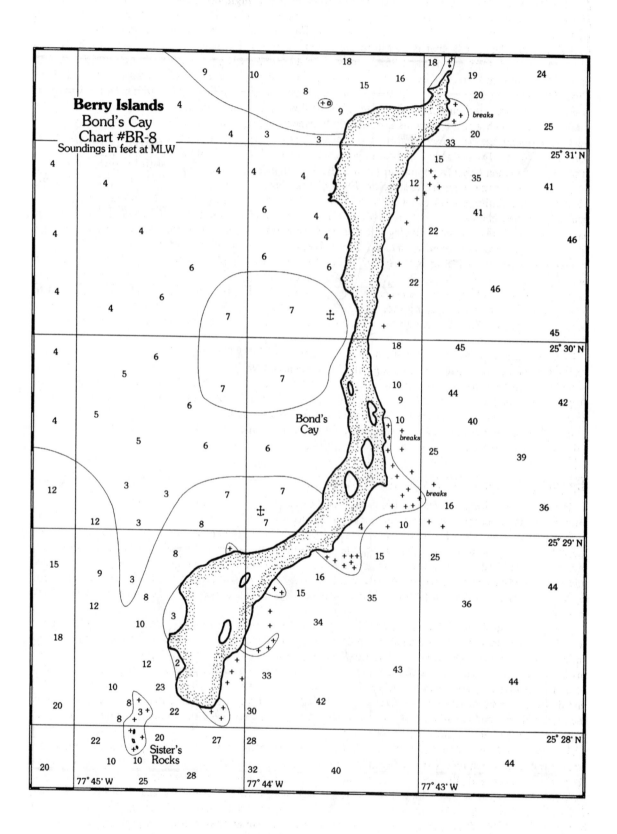

Berry Islands
Bond's Cay
Chart #BR-8
Soundings in feet at MLW

Little Harbour Cay is fairly easy to spot from offshore as it is high, bold, and has a distinctive spread of palm trees along its central ridge. To gain the anchorages at Little Harbour Cay you must enter from seaward between the southern tip of Little Harbour Cay and the northern tip of Frozen Cay. The only obstruction is a large rock that is awash in the center of the cut but it is very visible as almost any sea breaks upon it. A GPS waypoint at 25° 33.69' N, 77° 42.50' W will put your vessel approximately ½ nm east of the entrance. Steer between the partially submerged rock and the southern tip of Little Harbour Cay. The rock can be passed on either side but the deeper water is on the Little Harbour side. Round the south end of Little Harbour Cay and just to the west lies a small rocky island called Cabbage Cay. Most vessels tend to anchor just east of its northern tip between Cabbage Cay and Little Harbour Cay. This is a very good anchorage but it can get quite rough when a strong wind is blowing in through the cut from the southeast. When that happens it is best to go around the north end of Cabbage Cay and anchor in its lee just south of Guana Cay but be sure to double check your holding here. Vessels with less than a 6' draft who wish to enter the inner harbour below *Flo's Conch Bar* should only do so on a rising tide with good visibility. The ability to read the water is a necessity here if you wish to keep from going aground. The entrance channel begins just north of Cabbage Cay to the east of the small unnamed rock and proceeds in towards Flo's. It takes a small dogleg left and then to the right before the deeper water opens up near the dock. Use two anchors here, bow and stern if possible, as there is no swinging room.

Skippers wishing to anchor in the lee of Frozen Cay or farther south at Alder's Cay should turn to port once they enter the cut between Little Harbour Cay and the partially submerged rock. Vessels can anchor in the lee of Frozen Cay almost anywhere along its length but in strong east and southeast winds a large surge works its way in and along the shore. The rolliest night I ever spent in The Bahamas was spent behind Frozen Cay. At the southern tip of Frozen Cay is a bonefish camp currently under construction, and its distinctive green roofs are visible from well out to sea.

A good anchorage lies in the bight between Frozen Cay and Alder Cay in 7'-9' over a grassy bottom with a reputation for being poor holding. It is well sheltered from all directions except north with a reef protecting you from the swells coming in from seaward. The entrance lies close to the Alder Cay shore. Approach the anchorage heading south from the cut and keep west a little until you can line up the entrance channel on a northwest/southeast line. There is 5' in the entrance at low water.

Both Frozen and Alder Cays are private and visits ashore must be by invitation only. Vessels drawing less than 7' can go around Alder Cay to the west to make the northern tip of Bond's Cay.

BOND'S CAY TO BIRD CAY

Bonds Cay is a long slender cay lying just south of Alder Cay. The cay is steep to on the eastern shore with a few small beaches on the western side. Coconut orchard, sisal, and guava trees once flourished here and previous settlers raised some cattle here in the late 1800's. In the center of the cay are an old salt pond and the ruins of pasture walls. This cay was once covered in "honeysuckle" weed. A plant that cattle often ate, which would fatten them for 6-9 months and then rapidly kill them. Today Bond's Cay is uninhabited and may stay that way for a while. A couple of years ago a cruise line attempted to buy the cay to develop a resort similar to the one on Little and Great Stirrup Cays in the northern Berry Islands but the deal fell through.

If approaching Bond's Cay (see Chart #BR-8) from the Northwest Providence Channel give the cay a wide berth of at least a mile and a half to avoid the shallow reefs lying off its eastern shore. If approaching from the south, vessels drawing less than five feet can anchor along the western shore of Bond's Cay. The inside passage from the north has shoaled and is tricky unless you are very good at reading the water or have a local pilot. If you wish to anchor behind Bond's Cay enter through the cut between Sisters Rocks and the southern tip of Bond's Cay favoring the Bond's Cay shore and avoiding the shallow reefs between the Sisters Rocks and Bond's Cay. Then simply steer northward staying close in to shore and anchor as far north as your draft will allow.

Just south of Bond's Cay lies Little Whale Cay (see Chart #BR-9) with its very conspicuous light atop a stone tower that resembles a small lighthouse from offshore. Vessels may anchor along its northwestern shore but the area is shallow, rocky, surgy, and the entrance around the northern tip of Little Whale Cay is riddled with shallow reefs. The better anchorage is between Little Whale Cay and Whale Cay, but the entrance can be rough when a strong northeast to southeast wind opposes the outgoing tide. A GPS waypoint at 25° 26.77' N, 77° 45.13' W will place you approximately ¼ nm east of the cut. To enter the anchorage you must pass north of a small reef that lies just off the northern tip of Whale Cay so favor the

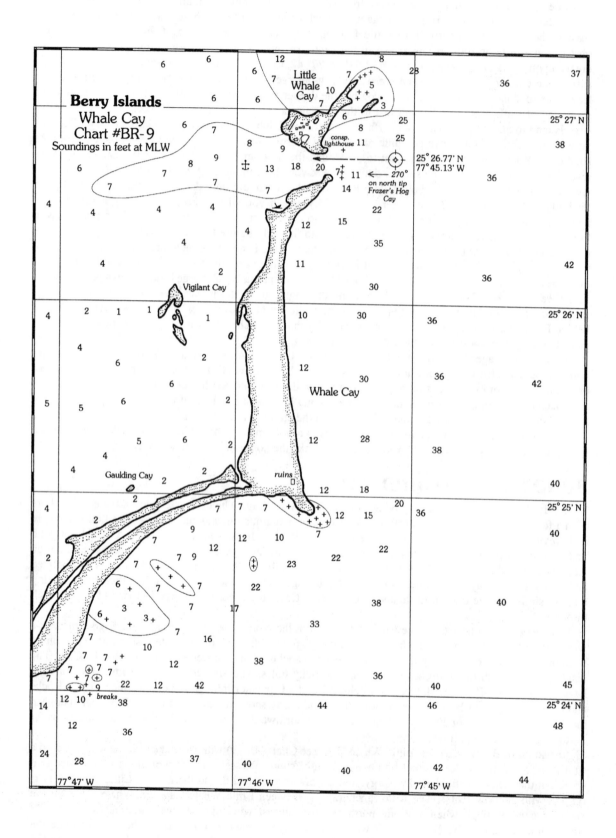

Berry Islands

Whale Cay
Chart #BR-9
Soundings in feet at MLW

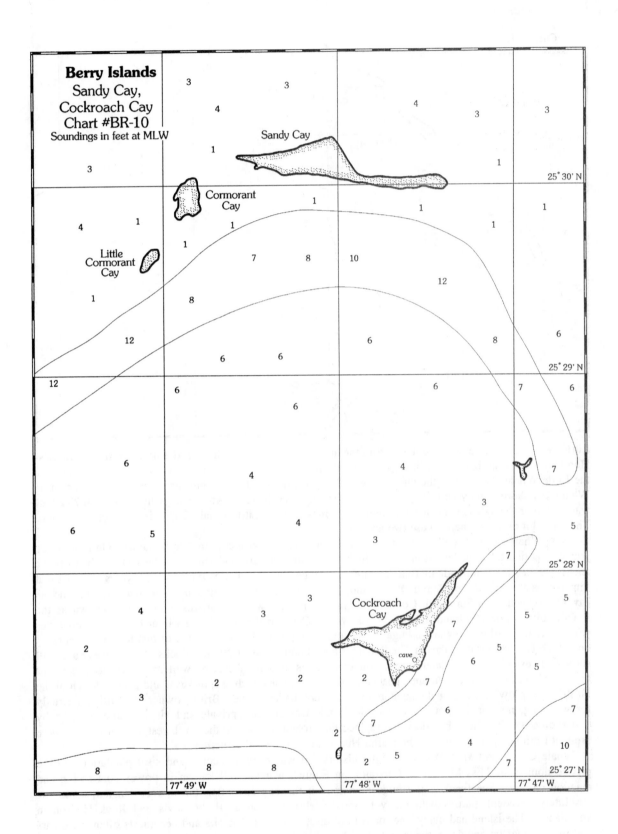

Berry Islands
Sandy Cay,
Cockroach Cay
Chart #BR-10
Soundings in feet at MLW

Berry Islands
The Fish Cays
Chart #BR-11
Soundings in feet at MLW

Little Whale Cay shore as you enter. From the area of your waypoint line up the northern tip of Frazer's-Hog Cay (on the horizon about three miles west) on your bow and steer in on a heading of 270° favoring the Little Whale Cay side of the cut. If the 270° course does not look right ignore it and favor the Little Whale Cay shore using your eyes to tell you if you can clear the reef. Anchor anywhere inside in 7'-20' of water. Favor the Whale Cay side for southeast winds and the Little Whale Cay side for northeast winds. There is a lot of current here so use two anchors.

Little Whale Cay is one of the prettiest and best managed private cays in The Bahamas. On first glance you will notice the excellent stone work in the seawall that surrounds most of the island. Just off the anchorage lies the man made marina (private) and stone church that was built over 50 years ago. At that time is was a parish of the Church Of England and was named *Our Lady Star of the Sea*. At that time the cay was owned by a Stamford, Connecticut yankee named Wallace Groves who is also known as the founder of Freeport on Grand Bahama. Little Whale Cay was developed as a winter home for the Groves with many terraced gardens and a huge aviary and duck pond. The inland lake of just less than 5 acres is one of the few fresh water lakes in The Bahamas and is home to over 200 teal ducks. Mr. Groves raised all sorts of livestock on the island, cows, donkeys, mules, and monkeys, as well as numerous species of birdlife such as chickens, pheasants, peacocks, flamingos, parrots, ducks, turkeys, and geese. Much of the birdlife was grown for personal consumption but today, under the new British owner, the birds are strictly for watching, not for the pot. Today Little Whale Cay remains private and visits ashore must be by invitation only. The huge boulders that replace the broken seawall on the northwest side of the cay were brought from Freeport and placed there after Hurricane Andrew's destruction.

Whale Cay (Chart #BR-9) has a unique history. It was once a coconut and sisal plantation and the private domain of Miss Marion B. Carstairs, an English woman well known in power boat racing and aviation circles. She lived in the huge mansion on the cay and often threw very elegant, some say absolutely decadent, parties with many famous celebrities such as Betty Davis and Rock Hudson in attendance. The island had many fine roads built on it and Miss Carstairs and her guests often raced cars and motorcycles up and down the island at all hours of the day and night. Miss Carstairs actually owned the entire Berry Island chain at one time. She had purchased the entire group of islands and immediately sold all save Bird Cay, Whale Cay, and Little Whale Cay.

If passing Whale Cay to seaward give the island a wide berth of at least 1½ miles to seaward to avoid the extensive shallow reefs lying off its eastern shore. Whale Cay Light on the southeast side of the island was destroyed in Andrew and may not be rebuilt any time soon so consider it not functioning at the present time. There is a fair lee anchorage under the lighthouse at the southwestern end of the cay good in north to east winds although some surge works its way in around the point here. To gain the anchorage pass between Bird Cay and Whale Point and anchor just off the little beach wherever your draft allows. There is the hull of a wrecked sailboat on the pretty little beach and a submerged barge near the center of the cove. Watch out for snakes if you check out the lighthouse, but remember, there are no poisonous snakes in The Bahamas. Whale Cay is private and visits ashore are by invitation only.

Divers will want to check out *Whale Point Reef* lying just a quarter of a mile off Whale Point. Here scattered heads begin sloping off to a sandy bottom with huge coral heads in 60' of water. Some of the heads are 15' high and the structure is home to an abundance of sea life. A little further out a drop off to 300' supports just a few solitary heads. Start your dive with Whale Point Light bearing 300° and the conspicuous white house bearing 50°.

Bird Cay (Chart BR-12), the most southern of the Berry Islands, is often mistakenly called Frazer's-Hog Cay which is actually the eastern half of the cay now more commonly called just Chub Cay (see next section *Chub Cay, Frazer's Hog Cay*). Bird Cay is approximately 130 acres and has several small ponds and groves of citrus and coconut. In the 1920's spongers lived here and also grew sisal on the island. Today the island is private with many elegant homes scattered about the cay. There is a lee side anchorage just off the southwestern tip of the cay but it gets very rolly in there when the surge works its way around the southern tip in east to southeast winds. The anchorage is just off the very conspicuous stone quarry near the tip of the cay. To enter the anchorage a GPS waypoint at 25° 23.45' N, 77° 51.05' W, will place you just southwest of the southwestern tip of Bird Cay. Head up into the lee of the cay along its western shore and anchor where your draft will allow. The anchorage shallows quickly the further north you head along the cay's lee shore. Bird Cay light was destroyed in Andrew and may not be rebuilt for some time so don't expect it to be there when you are.

Bird Cay is private and visits ashore must be by invitation only. The island is the home of Lady Francis, widow of the late Sir Francis Francis who also owned Bonds Cay. The beautiful mansion and surrounding houses offer a hint of the English countryside. There is a small village on the cay where the workers who keep everything working on the Cay live.

CHUB CAY, FRAZER'S HOG CAY

Chub Cay (see Chart #BR-13) is the most visited island in the Berry chain, due to its prime location on the route from Nassau to Bimini across the Banks. Lying approximately 35 nautical miles from Nassau, Chub Cay is the popular stopping place for cruisers seeking to unwind after the long Banks run or, if heading north, to prepare for the stretch to Bimini or Gun Cay. Devastated by Hurricane Andrew, *Chub Cay Marina and Hotel* has now been rebuilt for the better. Chub Cay is a Port Of Entry and skippers can clear Customs and Immigration at the *Chub Cay Marina*. There is a $25.00 fee for using the marina dock to clear but if you stay overnight the fee is applied to your dockage.

To find your way into the marina and anchorage a GPS waypoint at 25° 23.90' N 77° 55.08' W will place you approximately one nautical mile south of the entrance to the marina and anchorage and on the 35° range. The range is two small daymarks that are lit red at night. If approaching at night look for the bright lights of the power station ashore lying well to the west of the Batelco Tower with its flashing red light. The range is just a little west of the brightly lit power station showing one red light over the other. Take up a course of 35° on the range and remember that the deeper water will be to your starboard. If you must stray, by all means stray east as the principal danger, and one that must definitely be reckoned with, is Mama Rhoda Reef lying east and southeast of Mama Rhoda Rock. You can keep Chub Point Light close to starboard as there is deep water within 50 yards of the light. The light is sectored showing red in the dangerous sectors. Of course this light is like all lights in The Bahamas which is to say it is unreliable at best and subject to change. If you are approaching Chub Cay from the east it is best to stay outside (south of) Diamond Rocks as there are some shallow reefs closer into the Chub Cay shore.

The Chub Cay anchorage, lying just west of the light on Chub Point offers good protection from north through east but it can get very rolly in anything from east to southeast, even in light winds a swell seems to work around Chub Point. Cruisers often complain of a scoured bottom and poor holding here. A better anchorage for boats drawing 5' or less lies between Crab Cay and Chub Cay. This is where the fishing boats go to ride out fronts as the shallow bar (1' at low water) to the north of it breaks all northerly seas. In northerly winds you can move east of Chub Point (but WATCH OUT for the shallow reefs) just off the beach for a beautiful, calm anchorage but be prepared to move back when the winds begin to come out of the east.

Another anchorage is along the eastern shore of Frazer's-Hog Cay, the easternmost of the two islands that are usually called simply Chub Cay. From a GPS waypoint at 25° 23.45' N, 77° 51.05' W, work your way northward up the eastern shore in 7'-12' until you are off the marina. Keep a lookout for the very visible shallow bar to the east between Frazer's-Hog Cay and Bird Cay. The bottom is scoured in places and holding is iffy at best so take the proper precautions when setting your anchor. This is no place to be in strong north or northeast winds but most of the seas created by strong easterlies are usually broken by the shallow bar between Frazer's-Hog Cay and Bird Cay to the east. You can anchor north or south of the *Berry Island Club* dock or pick up one of their moorings. The *Berry Island Club* predates the *Chub Cay Marina* (which was built in 1962), and takes its name from the original club that was built by the *Stamford Conn. Yacht Club*. The bar, which serves excellent Cajun dinners and is a happening place to go, was originally the first house built on Chub Cay over fifty years ago. They even have a huge swamp buggy in which they will pick you up at Chub Cay Marina for dinner. The owners of the Berry Island Club have revamped the moorings and welcome visitors with open arms.

On the other side of the island *Chub Cay Marina* has 80 slips with a least depth of 10'. Three new computer controlled generators work hard to insure you of uninterrupted 115v-30 amp to 220v-3 phase-100 amp power available at daily or metered rates. RO water is available at each slip and laundry and shower facilities are located on shore. There are two telephones located on site, copy and fax service available, and cable TV at each slip. You can rent a bicycle and ride around the island where access to the Hotel's swimming pool, beach, and tennis courts is now available for guests of the marina. The *Harbour House Restaurant and Lounge* serves breakfast, lunch, and dinner in a relaxed and informal atmosphere. Those not arriving by boat can fly in on the nearby 5,000' runway.

Photo by Kelly Becker

Little Whale Cay, The Berrys.

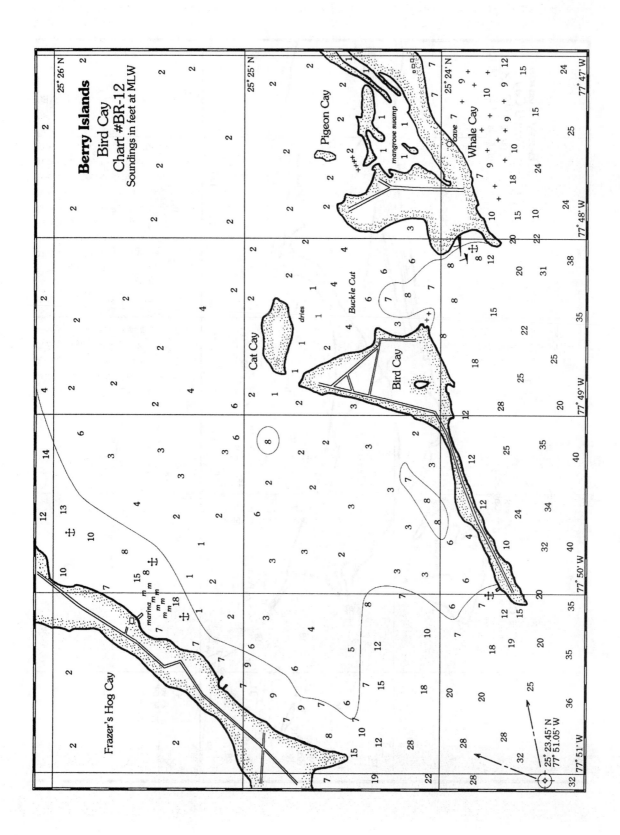

Berry Islands
Bird Cay
Chart #BR-12
Soundings in feet at MLW

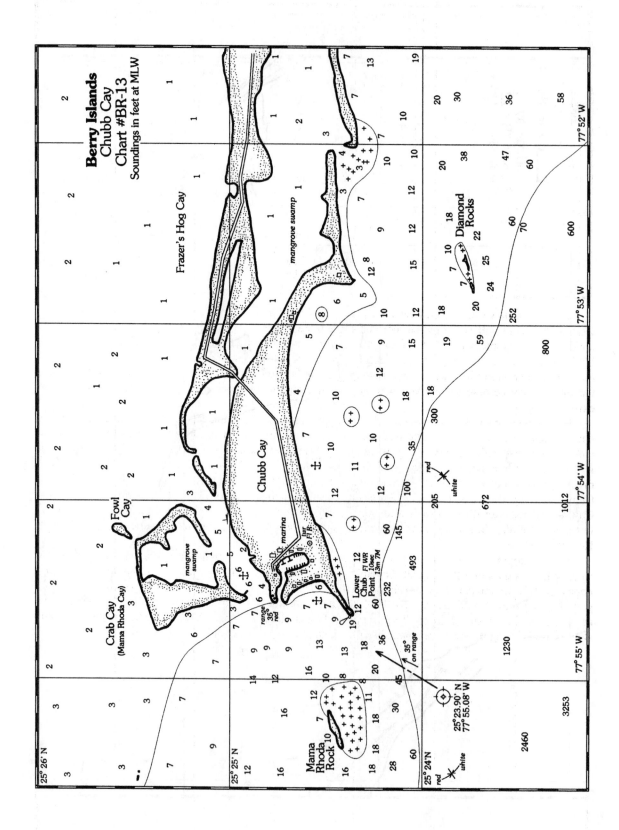

Berry Islands
Chubb Cay
Chart #BR-13
Soundings in feet at MLW

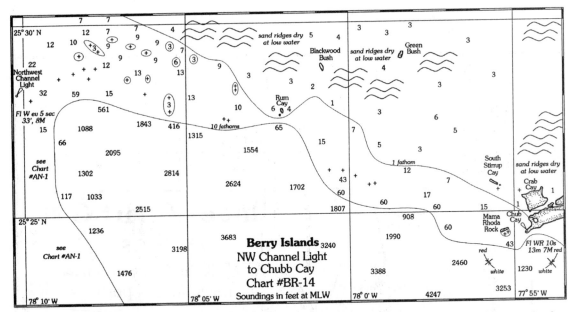

New owners have just taken over the operation of the *Chub Cay Marina*, and big changes are in the works. The store will now become more of a true store, a welcome delight to cruisers. The dive shop is under new management also, but you can still visit the excellent wall drop-offs at Rum Cay, or the reefs of Bird Cay on a diving charter. If you need diesel or outboard repairs, contact Randy, the dockmaster, and ask him to put you in touch with Anthony Martin, the local wrench. Mr Oliver, the chief of maintenance at the marina may be able to help you with any wiring, plumbing, or refrigeration problems you might be experiencing.

A great dive or snorkel is *Mama Rhoda Reef* lying just south of Mama Rhoda Rock. The reef begins in about 10' of water with scattered heads forming a huge reef structure of coral mounds and crevices down to a depth of almost 80'. Parallel walls rise some 10' high, and span 30' wide to a depth of about 75'. The reef gives way to a sandy shelf followed by a deep water drop off with just a few scattered heads. Best diving begins about ½ mile south of Mama Rhoda Rock with the Chub Cay water tower bearing 355° and Chub Point Light bearing about 75°. For those interested in the names of places such as this, Mama Rhoda Cay was named after Rhoda Morris who lived on what is now known as Crab Cay (then Mama Rhoda Cay) in the late 1800's. She lived off the generosity of the local spongers, but died a pauper in an asylum on New Providence.

Shellers should ask about Sanddollar Hill, a spit of sand that is only an island at low water and lies to the west of Chub Cay along the edge of the banks. Here shelling is great after a blow. Cockroach Cay, lying approximately 2½ miles northeast of Frazer's-Hog Cay has a large duck pond in the center that was once a good hunting spot. The mangrove creeks along in the interior of Chub Cay/Frazer's-Hog Cay are ideal for exploration. The entrance is north of Diamond Rocks along the Frazer's-Hog shore. There are some shallow reefs lining the entrance channel into the tidal creeks so be careful in your dinghy.

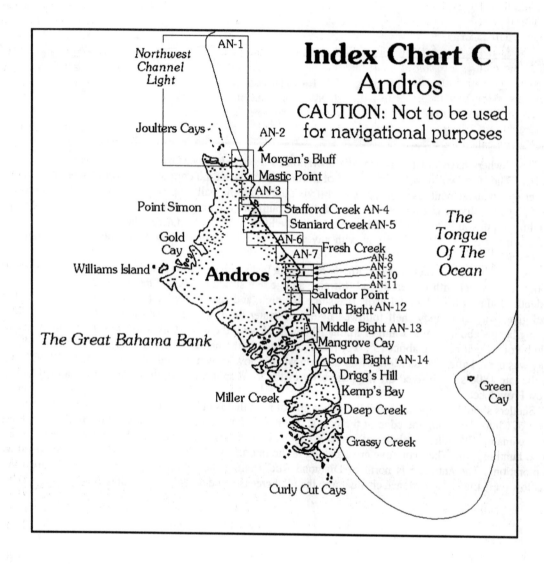

ANDROS

Andros is the largest of all Bahamian Islands with over 2300 square miles of land area lying about 20 miles from New Providence at its closest point. The approximately 105 mile by 40 mile island resembles a huge jigsaw puzzle separated by hundreds of creeks creating a massive swampy interior, a home to numerous birds and ducks that is best explored by small boat or dinghy. There are three "rivers" which divide the pine forested island into three distinct sections at North, Middle, and South Bight, while Mangrove Cay serves to separate the northern from the southern part of Andros. Andros is widely known for its vast mangrove creeks which offer some of the finest, if not the best, bonefishing in the world as well as some of the finest duck hunting in The Bahamas in years past. Offshore the island is home to the world's third largest barrier reef along its eastern shore at the Tongue of the Ocean. There is spectacular diving anywhere along its 145 mile length where it drops some 6,000' to the canyon-like bottom of the Tongue of the Ocean.

The island was originally called *Espirtu Santo* by the early Spaniards on early charts around 1550. There are quite a few stories as to how the island received its name. There is an Andros Island in the Aegean Sea with little, save a temple dedicated to Bacchus, to set it apart from any other island in the Aegean. A popular theory is that the island was named after Sir Edmund Andros, Commander of the Forces in Barbados from 1672-1674. From 1674 onward he was successively Governor of New York, Massachusetts, Virginia, and Maryland. In a map of 1872 the island is called *San Andreas* and in 1806 is once again called *Andreas Island*. The island most likely received its name in 1787 when Andros was selected as a haven by over 150 beleaguered residents of *St. Andro* on the Mosquito Coast of Nicaragua. The islanders requested to be moved to Andros after a treaty with Spain in 1783 led to their evacuation. The Bahamas provided transportation and deeded several parcels of land to some 70 men of British descent.

After the Siboneys and Lucayans left the island the first permanent settlers are believed to be Seminole Indians who paddled their canoes across the Straits of Florida. Bahamian wreckers and Privateers told the Seminoles that there was a free land to the east. Fleeing what they thought was to be a life of slavery at the hands of southern plantation owners, some 40-50 Seminoles and a party of escaped black slaves paddled their canoes across the Gulf Stream to Andros and settled on the deserted western shore between 1821 and 1840. The settlement was called Red Bay after the color of the sands in the area and here the settlers found the peace and quiet they were seeking. The government of The Bahamas didn't even know about them until the hurricane of 1866 wiped out the settlement. The Seminoles contacted the government representative and told him of their plight, offering to buy land to become citizens. In 1879 the government resettled the Seminoles 10 miles farther south at Lewis Coppice and renamed it Red Bay. Today if you visit Red Bay you will find that the residents create some of the most delightful basketry to be found in The Bahamas. Quite a few of the people you meet in Red Bay are direct descendants of these same Seminole warriors.

The legend of the Chickcharnie, sometimes written as Chick Charnie or Chickcharnee, the red-eyed creature who lives in pine trees, is said to have a basis in a Seminole Indian story. The Chickcharnie, as the legend says, is an elf-like creature resembling a bird with red eyes, three fingers, and three toes. In some versions they have a tail which they use to hang from trees. The Chickcharnie builds its nest between the heads of three pine trees which it binds together in the form of a tripod. The Chickcharnie is generally peaceful when left unmolested. The legend states that the Chickcharnies adopted and trained Billy Bowleg, the great Seminole medicine man who was able to cure any disease. Taking young Billy at the age of 14, they kept him for five years and when he returned to his people his reputation as a healer spread throughout The Bahamas.

One source of the story of the "little red men" originated with Hilton Albury, a successful sponge merchant and sportsman who lived on Andros at the beginning of the 20th century. He spent a lot of his time hunting birds in the interior of Andros which had incredible numbers of ducks in the winter. To keep his fertile hunting ground secret it is said that he began the tale of a band of pygmies who lived in the interior of the island and shot intruders with poisoned arrows. His tale and the Chickcharnie legend were somehow merged and corrupted in the retelling.

Many people felt the wrath of the Chickcharnies when they began to destroy their beloved forest. A story is told of a preacher who cut down all the trees on his land because he believed they were occupied by Chickcharnies. It is said that if you see a Chickcharnie that you will have good luck for the rest of your life. If you are harboring any bad thoughts about the Chickcharnie, or if you try to harm it, then your life will be filled with bad luck, they may even turn your head around backwards. A perfect example of being struck with bad luck by a Chickcharnie may be Neville Chamberlain, the former Prime Minister of England who grew up on Andros managing his father's sisal plantation. Against the advice of his foreman he cut down one of their favorite trees. The Chickcharnies worked their hoodoo on him which stayed with him to Munich and may have changed the course of history.

Today researchers believe that the residents of Andros actually mistook the Giant Barn Owl, which once inhabited the island but is now extinct, for the legendary Chickcharnie. If you happen across a Chickcharnie remember not to laugh or turn your head. The island is also said to have a Loch Ness-type monster, a sea dragon called the *Lusca*. Other mythological Androsian creatures are the *Bosee Anansee*, and the *Yahoo*.

A very real creature that you may spy is the rare great lizard cuckoo. Barely able to fly, this docile creature will allow you to come within a few feet of it before it hops or waddles away. Up until World War II there were flocks of pink flamingos on the island. Bored pilots on training missions out of Nassau would often fly over the vast flocks of pink birds to stir them up and set them in flight. After a few years of these types of disturbances the flamingos fled for quieter waters. Although there are quite a few cays throughout The Bahamas that have colonies of small iguanas growing up to three feet, there have been reports of iguanas on Andros growing to six feet. One creature that you will find in great numbers here are buzzards. Yes, that's right. Buzzards! You'll rarely find them on other Bahamian islands but on Andros they are everywhere. Some people jokingly refer to them as the Bahamian Air Force.

The western shore of Andros is undeveloped and the settlement of Red Bays on the northwestern tip of the island is the only inhabited area on the entire western shore. The very shallow waters off the western shore of Andros are known as *The Mud*, a fantastic, rich, 20 mile wide sponging ground running from South Bight to the northern tip of Andros. Over the last few decades the western shore of Andros has gained notoriety for the drug smuggling activity in the area. For the better part of the late 1970's through the mid to late 1980's, Andros was a very popular spot with those who sought fortune by running cocaine and marijuana to the United States (Please note that this is **not** the case today). Most of the local areas had their own "groups" of young people who were often involved with illegal activities, some would now call them gangs. Each group had their own "turfs," for example, there might be a group called, say, the Mastic Point Boys, or the Nicoll's Town Boys, or the Lowe Point Boys (all fictitious names mind you!). They even had a bar where they partied and that each group treated as neutral territory. At about this time pilots were warned not to fly low over Andros. It seems that planes that were flying low over Andros were considered drug runners and certain roguish characters would shoot at the wings or wing tanks hoping that they would blow up and the plane would crash and not burn up on landing saving the precious cargo for the shooters. A modern version of the old Bahamian art of wrecking. I've heard of tales of two pilots who were found deep within the pine barrens of Andros hanging from a tree with their throats cut. One person I know of lived on Andros during this time and decided to visit Mars Bay one day. On the road to Mars Bay he was met by two locals on motorcycles with automatic weapons who suggested that my friend did not wish to visit Mars Bay that particular day. Of course my friend agreed and went elsewhere, thankful for the sound advice. Mariners during these years were advised by the U.S. Coast Guard to avoid the waters to the west of Andros. Many rumors and stories of boats being hijacked surfaced during this era. Most of the boats hijacked were fishing boats that plied the local waters. It is said that the "pirates" would come out in small boats at night to sneak aboard their intended victim and kill those aboard. I heard a tale of an American boat with Bahamian owners called *Blue Jean* that was said to have been hijacked in just this way. In defense of the good people of Andros who are probably irritated by this account, you must understand that hijackings were also occurring in the Biminis and in the Freeport area at this time also.

The eastern shore of Andros is home to the third largest barrier reef in the world and has few entrances for vessels of any draft, all of which are impassable in a rage. The Tongue Of The Ocean just offshore is a huge canyon in the sea with soundings up to one thousand fathoms.

Andros is the only Bahamian island where fresh water meets sea water. There are several fresh water ponds and creeks stemming from springs in the interior of the island. The inland waterways of Andros offer a spectacular opportunity for dinghy exploration and fishing. Just pick a creek and head upstream, you'll find something along the way to pique your interest, but bring plenty of bug spray.

Andros is virtually honeycombed with blue holes, over 400 are scattered throughout the island and its surrounding waters. While these blue holes extend vertically to great depths in some places, most extend horizontally also. These blue holes are said to have formed over 15,000 years ago when the sea level was approximately 300' less than it is today. Some of these blue holes are home to a centipede-like crustacean, *Remepedia*, that is found nowhere else and whose closest relatives are fossils over 450 million years old.

In the 1960's, a Toronto research chemist by the name of George Benjamin began exploring the blue holes in and around Andros. Benjamin believed that these blue holes were actually part of a system of underwater caves that had once been above water. In South Bight he found a cave, now called *Benjamin's Blue Hole*, that is called one of the world's greatest underwater caves. In 1970, George Benjamin, and his son Peter, proved that these caves had actually at one time been above sea level. They discovered a spectacular cave absolutely bristling with stalactites and stalagmites. For those of you unfamiliar with spelunking, stalactites and stalagmites are deposits formed from dripping water. Water cannot drip in a submerged cave. Jacques Cousteau later visited Andros and with Benjamin's help filmed the cave and renamed it *The Grotto*. *The National Geographic Magazine* published a story about George Benjamin's exploits in 1970.

In September of 1996, deep in an inland blue hole called *Stargate*, divers excavated an ancient Lucayan canoe. The 6' long canoe, which may be as much as 500-800 years old and carved from a single log, was discovered by Rob Palmer about 60' down in the 300' deep blue hole. Palmer, who first dove Stargate in 1985 when he filmed it for the *National Geographic Society*, had actually been working in the deeper levels of the hole when he made his discovery. Palmer, who has been diving on blue holes for 15 years, had previously discovered 16 Lucayan skeletons in another nearby blue hole on Andros.

Why the canoe was placed on a ledge in the blue hole remains a mystery. Gail Saunders, the director of the *Bahamian Department of Archives*, speculates that the canoe was actually too small to have been used at sea and that it may have been placed there as part of a burial custom. Lucayan myths of creation centered around an underground world. They believed that their race, as well as the sun and the moon, arose from the center of the earth. As a burial custom it may have meaning as a spiritual return to the place of their origin. The canoe is slated to become an exhibit at the soon to open Bahamas National Museum.

APPROACHES TO ANDROS

Andros lies "down to leeward" from Nassau making it easy to get to for sailors but hard to return from against the prevailing winds. From the western entrance of Nassau Harbour, the waypoint off Morgan's Bluff bears 295° at a distance of 36.3 nautical miles. From the waypoint off Chubb Cay, Morgan's Bluff bears 208° at a distance of 13.6 nautical miles.

The entrance to Fresh Creek bears 214° from Golding Cay at the western end of New Providence at a distance of 20.2 miles. From Chub Cay, Fresh Creek bears 174° at a distance of 40.4 miles. From the northern Exumas, Fresh Creek is a straight shot in hazard free waters. From Warderick Wells, Fresh Creek bears approximately 298° at a distance of 62.1 nautical miles.

From Gun Cay in the Biminis, the waypoint at the northern tip of the Joulters bears 105° at 62.5 miles.

The barrier reef that stretches along the eastern shore of Andros has only a few navigable breaks. The narrow waterway between the reef and Andros is very shallow and strewn with numerous shallow heads and patch reefs. The inside route from Morgan's Bluff to Fresh Creek should only be attempted by vessels drawing 6' or less with good visibility and a rising, almost high tide in some places. The inside route from Fresh Creek southward to South Bight should only be attempted by vessels drawing less than 5'.

THE JOULTER'S CAYS

Off the northern tip of Andros, stretching from just north of Morgan's Bluff to just south of Northwest Channel Light, lie the Joulters Cays. To the north and west of the Joulters lies an enormous shallow bank, some of which is high and dry at low tide while other areas are overgrown with mangroves. Coming from Gun Cay, there is a route that passes north and then east of the Joulters bringing you to Morgan's Bluff by a passage inside the reef. This route will bring you around and through several shallow areas with quite a few shallow heads and small patch reefs to steer around. If you wish to head south from Morgan's Bluff to Fresh Creek inside the reef, this passage will give you a small inkling of what to expect on that route. The Joulters boasts one very nice, but tricky to enter anchorage that we will discuss in a moment. The Joulters are noteworthy for their unique sand, one of only three places in the world where this type of sand is found.

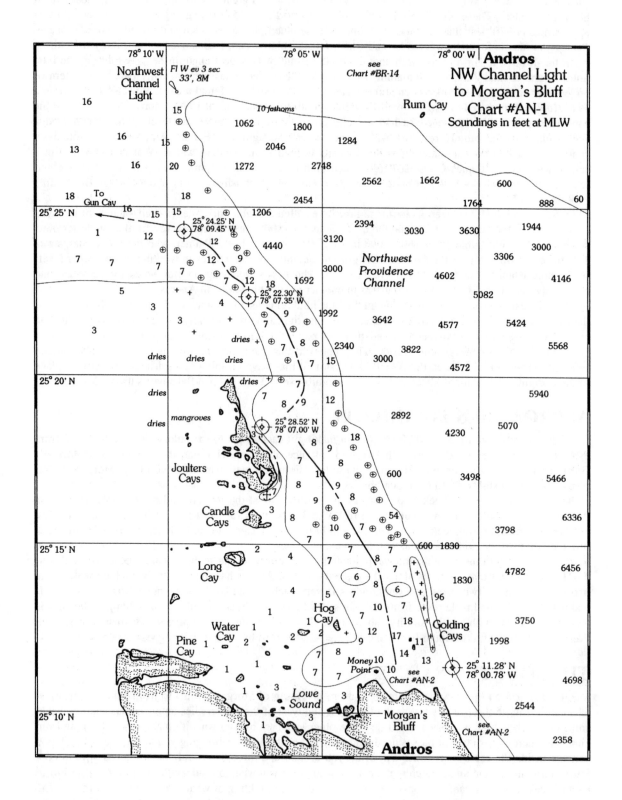

Andros
NW Channel Light
to Morgan's Bluff
Chart #AN-1
Soundings in feet at MLW

Vessels heading east from Gun Cay can steer approximatley 105° for 62.5 miles to a GPS waypoint at 25° 24.25' N, 78° 09.45' W. This will place you in about 15' of water well north of the bank that surrounds the Joulters to the north and west as shown on Chart #AN-1. From this position you must really begin piloting by eye as you begin to head in a generally southeast direction to a waypoint at 25° 22.30' N, 78° 07.35' W, which places you near the edge of the Great Bahama Bank, well east of the worst shallows and sandbores. Vessels with drafts of less than 5' can turn more south and work their way through this maze and avoid the small detour to the east but the detour is not that far out of the way for all the trouble it saves. Once at this easternmost waypoint, you may begin to steer a little more south to southwest to close the shore of the Joulters about ½-1 mile off. Keep a sharp lookout for shallows and reefs, there are still a few you will have to pilot your way around. To your east there is no barrier reef yet, it really doesn't begin until after Morgan's Bluff though there is a long reef just east of the Golding Cays. There are quite a few shallow heads and small patch reefs along the edge of the bank and the deeper water so use caution if you plan to proceed to the east into deeper water.

As you approach the long white beach on the eastern shore of the cays to your starboard side, you may wish to enter the lovely anchorage that lies off its southern point. Vessels with drafts of 5' or less can enter but only on high tide. There is a shallow bar with almost 3' over it at low water that you must cross before you get into the deeper channel which has 6'-7' along the beach. The anchorage area at the southern tip has 8' at low tide. A GPS waypoint at 25° 18.52' N, 78° 07.00' W, will place you approximately ¼ mile east of the shallow bar. From this waypoint follow the darker water in towards the rocky bluff with the old house that is partly hidden by casuarinas. Well off your port bow, just east of the long white beach, you will see a very obvious yellow/white shallow bar that parallels the beach. You will want to follow the darker water across the 3' area and pass between the obvious yellow/white bar and the beach where you will pick up the deeper water. Follow the shoreline around to the southern tip of the cay and anchor wherever your draft will allow and prepare for bugs if the weather is hot and windless.

Vessels heading south from here can steer to pass between the Golding Cays and Hog Cay but you will have a few small patch reefs and shallow bars to avoid as you head south. Once abeam of the Golding Cays you will have no obstructions into Morgan's Bluff save the buoys at the entrance channel.

MORGAN'S BLUFF, NICOLL'S TOWN

Morgan's Bluff is the northernmost settlement on the island of Andros and also the busiest. Andros produces so much fresh water that tankers and water barges come to Morgan's Bluff to take on some 6,000,000 gallons a day to help Nassau meet her water needs. The dock on the inside of the jetty is kept busy with tankers like the *Titas* or barges like the *Black Point*. The small inner harbour and the large concrete dock just inside the jetty are used by the smaller freighters and mailboats. For many years there has been some concern about yachtsmen using the inner harbour in bad weather. Many people said that you cannot use the harbour, that it was prohibited, that the locals would tell you to leave. It may have been that way at one time, but today cruisers are welcome. The inner harbour is now open to cruising boats if needed. This is a dredged harbour and the holding is fair to good inside but you'll be better off with one anchor down and another line tied off ashore to a bollard. Do not block the docks. Visitors are welcome to tie off to the freight boats if needed during bad weather, they usually don't mind but ask first.

A GPS waypoint at 25° 11.28' N, 78° 00.78' W will place you approximately ¼ mile west of the buoyed entrance channel as shown on Chart #AN-2. Enter the well marked channel (the first and third pairs of buoys are lit and the channel is easy to use at night) and follow the channel westward past the rock jetty into Pleasant Bay. There is a large range set up inland but it is really only necessary for larger ships, small boats will have no problem in this wide, 25' deep channel (watch out for large ship traffic whenever entering or leaving by this channel). Once past the jetty turn to port and tuck up into the cove at the southeast end of the bay, be sure not to anchor in the channel leading to the inner harbour or in the vicinity of the large concrete dock on the western side of the jetty. Always run an anchor light when anchored here, don't even think of staying overnight without one, there may be large vessels moving in and out at all hours of the day and night so practice safe anchoring, you'll sleep better. Holding in the anchorage ranges from poor to good in 7'-11' of water, you just have to find the right spot. Pick one of the lighter patches of sand close in to shore. Don't anchor west of the channel as the bottom is very rocky and difficult to set an anchor in.

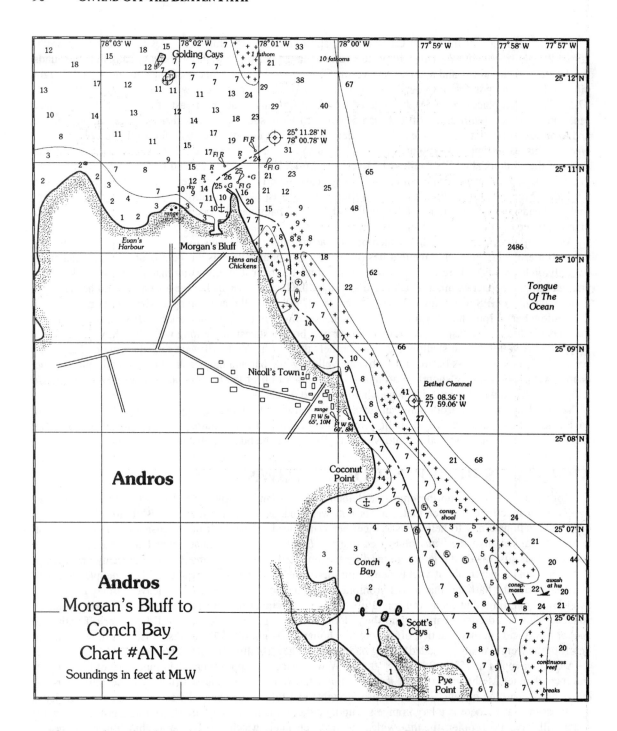

Andros

Andros
Morgan's Bluff to
Conch Bay
Chart #AN-2

Soundings in feet at MLW

If you tuck up inside the bay, you will be protected in winds from almost northeast through east to southwest and almost west. If threatened by a frontal passage and northerly winds, you can anchor in the inner harbour as previously mentioned or, as some suggest, you can anchor in the lee of Hog Cay in 6'-7' of water in northerly winds. Having done just that, I find that this anchorage leaves much to be desired, I'd rather be in the inner harbour, at Fresh Creek, or in Nassau.

About a mile west of Morgan's Bluff and just inside Money Point lies Evans Harbour. This is a good harbour, but only if you draw less than 3'. Another possibility is to anchor inside shallow Lowe Sound. Here the entrance carries just under 3' at low water with 4' and more inside in places and you will have to eyeball your way in here, never attempt it at night, or in poor visibility.

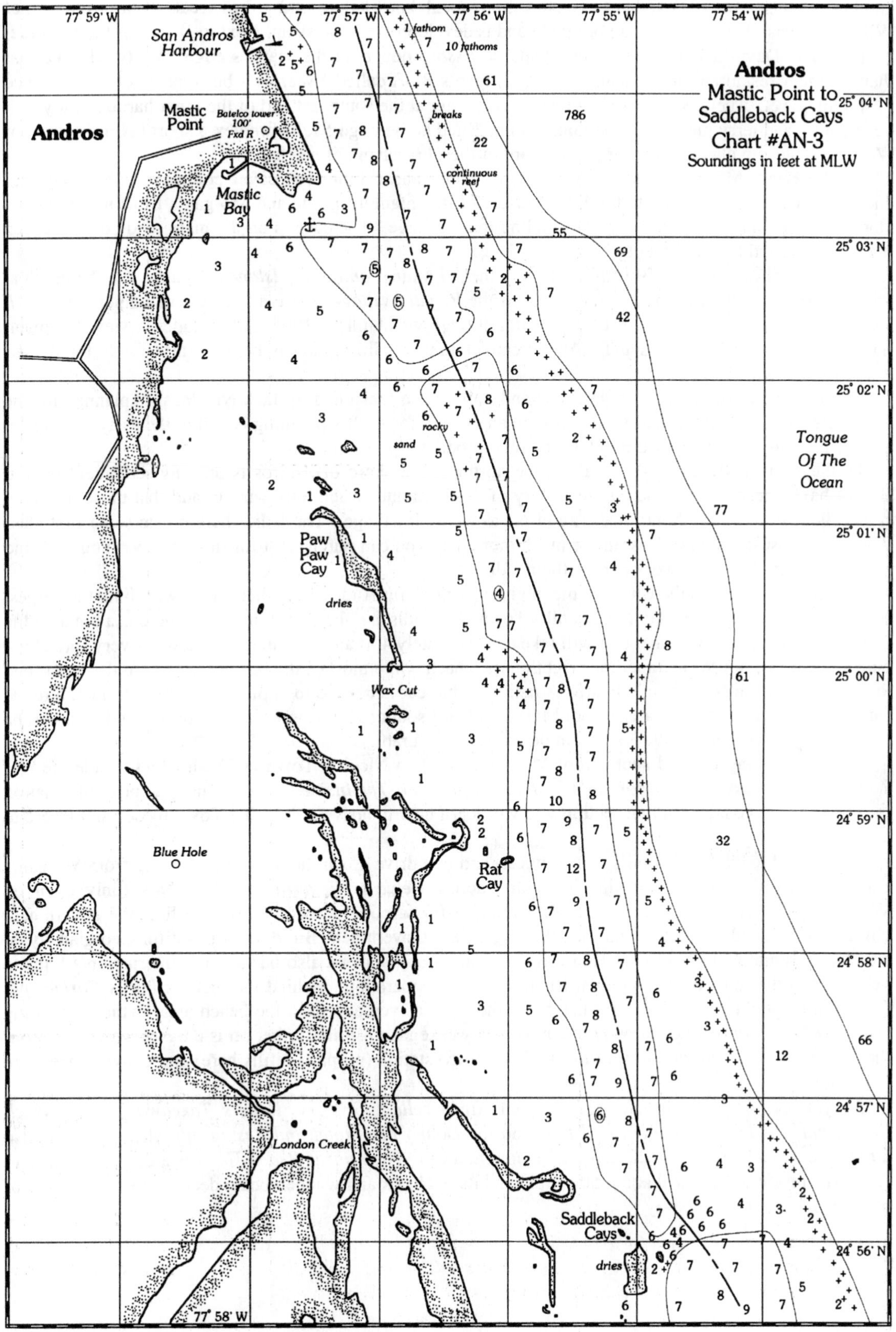

77° 59' W 77° 57' W 77° 56' W 77° 55' W 77° 54' W

San Andros Harbour

1 fathom
10 fathoms

Andros
Mastic Point to
Saddleback Cays
Chart #AN-3
Soundings in feet at MLW

25° 04' N

Andros

Mastic Point

Batelco tower
100'
Fxd R

breaks

continuous reef

Mastic Bay

25° 03' N

25° 02' N

Tongue Of The Ocean

rocky

sand

Paw Paw Cay

dries

25° 01' N

25° 00' N

Wax Cut

Blue Hole

Rat Cay

24° 59' N

24° 58' N

24° 57' N

London Creek

Saddleback Cays

dries

24° 56' N

77° 58' W

On the southwest side of the inner harbour at Morgan's Bluff is *Willy's Water Lounge* where you can get lunch, dinner, cold beverages, conversation, local knowledge, and even a car rental from owner Wilmore Lewis. Willy also has a pool table and is developing a book swap. Next to *Willy's* is the *Esso* fuel center where David and Patrick Romer dispense *Esso* products at the water's edge. Willy tells me that there is a new restaurant on the main road at Morgan's Bluff called *Sweeting's* but I have not had a chance to stop there yet. There is free, fresh, great tasting water at the southeast end of the inner harbour but you'll need a hose and jerry jugs. Propane tanks can be filled at the huge *Shell* complex a short taxi ride south of *Willy's*. Willy can also arrange for an outboard or diesel mechanic if needed.

Nearby Henry Morgan's Cave is a system of subterranean limestone caves complete with stalagmites and stalactites. They are said to hold the treasure of the infamous pirate and Morgan's Bluff namesake Sir Henry Morgan but nobody has reported finding treasure here. The cave is on the main road north between the jetty dock and the settlement of Morgan's Bluff.

In late October Morgan's Bluff plays host to the *All Andros and Berry Islands Regatta*. On the beach at the southeast side of Pleasant Bay is the site of the *Regatta Village* where a plaque commemorates the *All Andros Regatta* and Morgan's Bluff. *Regatta Village* was built in 1994 and includes a viewing tower, numerous stalls, and a grandstand. At the end of June a mini-regatta is held to raise funds for the *All Andros Regatta*.

I have been informed that a large resort and golf course (designed by Jack Nicklaus) is planned for the Morgan's Bluff area in the near future so keep an eye out for it. It's planning is still in the early stages so it may or may not work its way through to the final product.

To the west of Morgan's Bluff, along the northwestern shore of Andros is the tiny settlement of Red Bay. I have already given you a little history of this community and only wish to add that those in search of excellent straw work should make an effort to visit this village. The ladies here create some first class work that is usually sold in Nassau for much more than you can purchase it for in Red Bay. You will find some great deals on straw work here without a doubt.

Just south of Morgan's Bluff is the highest section of Andros and here you will find the largest settlement (600 people) on Andros, Nicoll's Town. The hills are about 100' high and there is a break in the reef here called Bethel Channel that will take approximately 4.5' at low water. The town is very spread out with some of the houses and facilities right on the beach while most of the businesses are on the main road that stretches towards Morgan's Bluff. A taxi or rental car is needed to explore this area. In fact, a rental car is the best way to see the areas from Morgan's Bluff south to Behring Point (be forewarned, you will be dodging some very large potholes and an occasional land crab).

Cruisers wishing to head south from Morgan's Bluff to Nicoll's Town or Fresh Creek inside the reef should read the next section, *Morgan's Bluff to Fresh Creek, The Inside Route*, for navigational information concerning that passage. In that section you will learn how to arrive at Nicoll's Town by sea and where to anchor.

If you elect to explore Nicoll's Town by car, and you drive down the main road leading from Morgan's Bluff to Nicoll's Town, you will first come across *Zelda's Restaurant*, *CIBC Bank* (only open on Wednesdays from 10:00 A.M. to 2:00 P.M.), an *Androsia* outlet store, a *Batelco* office, the government clinic with its resident doctor, and then the huge, pink Government Building, a beautiful Georgian-styled structure resembling Government House in Nassau. Nicoll's Town also has a small International Square, dedicated to the spirit of international friendship and cooperation. Behind the bank is *Lori's Cornucopia Deli* with its pool table. A little further down the road, as you approach the beach area, is the noteworthy *Rumours Restaurant and Disco* with live music on weekends. A little further on is the *Pinewood Cafeteria*, the *Green Windows Inn and Restaurant* with a *Texaco* station (propane refills here) and convenience store next door.

As you approach the beach area you will find *Welle's Grocery*, *Rolle's Takeaway*, the *Dayshell Restaurant*, *Hunter's Restaurant and Bar*, and the *Donna Lee Motel and Restaurant* where you can also arrange for diving or fishing charters and even rent a car. The *Andros Beach Hotel* is a delightful place to stay. The restaurant can seat about 50 people and its red brick and wooden beam decor seems almost out of place in an out island getaway.

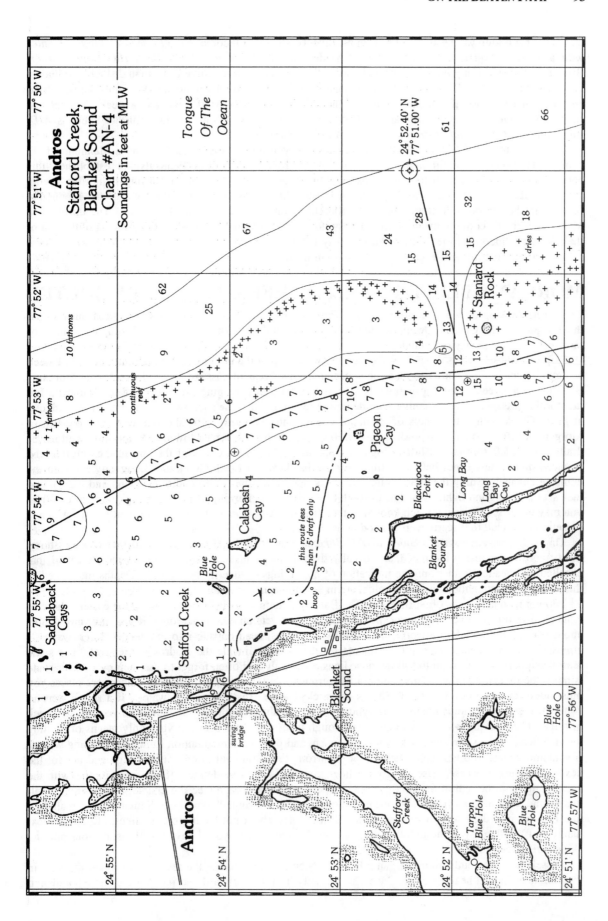

Andros
Stafford Creek,
Blanket Sound
Chart #AN-4
Soundings in feet at MLW

Tongue Of The Ocean

On the main highway headed south from Nicoll's Town you will come to the *Pineyard Shopping Center* with a grocery, liquor, and variety store. A pleasant attraction here *is Brinka's Hallelujah Corner*. Brinka's small stall is a great spot for lunch with two or three different native Bahamian dishes every day at very reasonable prices. This is real "native" Bahamian cooking at its finest, conch stew, crab and rice, fried chicken, chicken souse, if you can name it, chances are that Brinka serves it one day a week. You can eat right at her stall, pull up a chair and have a seat, or take it with you. A little further south is *AID*, *Automotive and Industrial Distributors*, a *NAPA* auto parts store.

Heading south from Nicoll's Town past the airport, you might be surprised to find a Mennonite farm community along the main highway. A group of Mennonites from Pennsylvania established this community in 1983 and their neat orchards full of rich, green, fruit trees are a startling sight after driving past mile after mile of pine woods and scrub brush. Almost as startling is the sight of the Mennonite families in their traditional dress, quite the difference from the average islanders attire. The thirty or so Mennonites in this community are a true success story. They produce almost as much as most of the rest of the island's farmers and their garage keeps many local cars in top running condition. Most of the local resorts serve their fruits and vegetables with all their meals.

MORGAN'S BLUFF TO FRESH CREEK-THE INSIDE ROUTE

Vessels drawing over 6' that are headed to Fresh Creek from Morgan's Bluff should head outside into the Tongue Of The Ocean. Once outside keep at least a mile east of the barrier reef, roughly 3 miles or more offshore, try to stay off soundings.

Skippers whose vessels draw 6' or less can, with the help of the tide, excellent visibility, nerves of steel, and confidence in their ability to read the water, make a successful passage inside the reef from Morgan's Bluff to Fresh Creek. This trip is roughly 30 miles and a boat averaging 5-6 knots will take almost a full tide for the passage. When planning your departure remember that the shallowest spots are at the south end at Fresh Creek with a few spots off Staniard Creek, and one rocky spot about a mile or two south of Morgan's Bluff. I usually leave Morgan's Bluff anywhere from just past low tide to mid-tide with my 5' draft. I have left Morgan's Bluff at high tide and arrived at Fresh Creek at the end of the ebb tide and bounced quite a few times before getting over the bar between Fresh Creek and Long Cay and into the entrance channel. Study the charts, allow for your speed and the local conditions (wind and wave), and then set out with good light. Never head south too early in the morning as the sun is right in your eyes and you may never see the rocky patch known as the *Hens and Chickens* just south of Morgan's Bluff which is sometimes difficult to discern even in good light.

The venerable *Yachtsmen's Guide to The Bahamas*, the "Bible" of cruisers for so many years, shows much more water inside the reef than is really there is many places. This is not an indictment of that excellent publication, rather only an indication of how things change in the islands. Depths mentioned in this section, as throughout this entire guide, are in feet at mean low water.

I do not recommend that first timers to The Bahamas attempt the inside route along the eastern shore of Andros. It can make even the most experienced Bahamas veteran a little nervous. If you have any doubts about your ability to safely traverse this area, by all means, head outside into the deeper, safer, water. I almost deleted the course lines on the Charts for the passages inside the Andros barrier reef. For some reason skippers seem to want to follow those lines religiously and often forget to use their eyes. This route is not to be treated like that. This can be a dangerous route in some circumstances. There are places you must pilot your way between sandy shoals and rocky patches that dry at low water. If a squall were to come through at that moment and reduce your visibility to almost nothing you could find yourself in a heck of a fix. There are no waypoints to get you through this one. Your eyes are your only means of piloting through here. Take your time, keep your eyes open, and pay constant attention to the surrounding waters. If something were to divert your attention at the wrong time you could find yourself high and dry for the next 6-12 hours or worse. Use the course lines given only as a guideline. If you are familiar with the passage through the reef at Samana into the Propeller Cay anchorage (see the chapter *Samana*), you will understand what my first mate Kelly means when she calls this route "30 miles of Samana." It's really not that bad but it is definitely to be respected. Don't worry about not having course lines. Keep this text handy and I will talk you through this route section by section and you'll have a real test of your piloting skills. OK, ready to go?

Vessels heading south from Morgan's Bluff to Nicoll's Town inside the reef should round the jetty in the entrance channel heading east. Once past the jetty, turn to starboard and parallel the shore southward towards Nicoll's Town as shown on Chart #AN-2. The water is still fairly deep here and the barrier reef does not reappear until about 1¼ miles south of the entrance channel to Morgan's Bluff. You can head in as close as 50-100 yards from shore here. On the first hill south of the jetty you will see the settlement of Morgan's Bluff. South of that hill, just east of the second hill and the small coconut palm trees, is a shallow rocky patch known as the *Hens and Chickens*, sometimes shown on some charts as the *Devil's Backbone*. There are two ways to pass this reef. Some publications suggest that you pass 50 yards off the rocky shoreline between the shoal and the shore in 9' of water. This would be fine if there really was that much water there. The truth is that there is 6' through here in places at low water over a rocky bottom. I prefer to head out into the slightly deeper water to the east of the rocky bar and pass it to the east, between the rocky bar and the outer barrier reef, angling back in towards shore at the north end of the long white beach that leads to Nicoll's Town. Here you will pass between the *Hens and Chickens* off your starboard beam, some small patch reefs off the north end of the beach, and a dark line of rocky ledges and heads that you should keep to port. Pass between the dark line and the small patch reefs off the beach in 7'-9' of water at low tide. It would help to have someone on the bow through here.

Paralleling the beach southeastward the water will get progressively deeper the further south you go towards Nicoll's Town, anywhere from 9'-13' at low water. Follow the shore staying a hundred yards or so off and you will come to the small point at Nicoll's Town with a dock at the *Andros Beach Hotel*. You can anchor here in settled weather or light southeast winds. This spot is also good for winds from south to west. The small anchorage shoals quickly in towards shore.

Heading south from Nicoll's Town give the point of land and its offlying shallow bar a fair berth and you will be in about 13' of water. On the hill to your starboard side you will soon see the lighted range (247°) for the Bethel Channel. The Bethel Channel is narrow and shallow and not recommended for the average cruiser. The channel barely carries 4½' at low tide. A GPS waypoint at 25° 08.36' N, 77° 59.06' W, will place you approximately ½ mile east/northeast of the eastern entrance of the Bethel Channel. Line up on the range and strictly follow it in. The range sits on the side of a hill without any trees on it. As you approach the shore do not turn north or south until less than 150 yards east of the shore. This is to avoid the shallow reefs which line both sides of the channel, especially the northern side.

Once past Bethel Channel you must give Coconut Point a wide berth as shown on Chart #AN-2. There is a shallow rocky bar that juts out eastward from the point and even as you head around it in water from 7'-10' deep you will be passing over scattered rocks. You can anchor just south of Coconut Point about 200-250 yards off shore in winds from northwest to north. You can also anchor in Conch Bay about ¼ mile off the beach, shallow draft vessels can work much farther in for better anchoring.

Heading southeast from Coconut Point you will see a very conspicuous, bright green sandbar. Keep this sandbar to your port side as you head for Mastic Point, the easternmost point of land on the horizon. From Coconut Point you will be steering approximately 150°-155° for Mastic Point. You will have 6'-7' at low water through here, in some places as much as 8' or 9'. As you approach Pye Point as shown on Chart #AN-2, you will see what appears to be a pair of small pilings to port. Give these a wide berth, they are actually the masts of a sunken freighter that lies in a large break in the reef. About 100 yards east of these masts is the sunken wreck of another, smaller vessel whose mast is awash at high water. Good diving but hazards to navigation. You can actually take a 6' draft through the break in the reef or around the bright green sandbar mentioned above, but you will be threading through some shallows and then some heads in the vicinity of the wrecks themselves.

South of Pye Point watch out for some shallow reefs, stay at least 150 yards or more offshore. Between Pye Point and Mastic Point, as shown on Chart #AN-3, is San Andros Harbour, once home to the *Mastic Point Field Station*. The field station has closed and the harbour is unused except by small local craft. Give the conspicuous jetties that mark this harbour a wide berth in at least 7' at low water. There is a submerged barge just off the entrance that is awash at high water, and several shallow patch reefs in the same general vicinity. Tiny San Andros Harbour is not a good refuge unless absolutely necessary. The shoreline is littered with wrecks and the holding is iffy at best. The settlement south of the harbour is called New Town and no facilities are available. Mastic Point, Chart #AN-4, and the New Town area was once home to a 20,000 acre sisal plantation owned by Neville Chamberlain's father. The plantation was a failure since sisal does not grow well in the Andros pine barrens, or perhaps it was the work of a Chickcharnie. It is possible to anchor south of Mastic Point as shown on Chart #AN-4 but you really can't get in too close to shore unless you draw less than 3'.

Heading southeast from Mastic Point as shown on Chart #AN-4, keep Paw Paw Cay well to starboard and you will have 7' most of the way with an occasional 5' or 6' spot at low water. You will see a small casaurina covered cay to starboard, this is one of the small cays just north of Paw Paw Cay. Keep it also well to starboard, about ¼–½ mile. The coves and bays between Paw Paw Cay and the mainland of Andros are beautiful and a delight to explore by dinghy but they are too shallow for big boats unless you draw less than 3'. From Mastic Point southeastward you will still be maintaining an approximate course of 150°. You are now aiming for the eastern end of a conspicuous flat island on the horizon with a slightly higher hump on its eastern end. This is Rat Cay. Don't plan on steering a straight course of Rat Cay though, you'll find some shoals and other obstructions to steer around but the water will get progressively deeper as you approach Rat Cay, in places 10'-12' at low tide. As I mentioned before, head for the eastern end of Rat Cay keeping Paw Paw Cay a good ¼–½ mile to starboard to avoid the green sandbank that lies just to the east of Paw Paw Cay. Off Paw Paw Cay you will see several dark grassy areas that, though they may look deeper, may not actually be deeper than the green areas you are going across. The grass makes the water depth difficult to determine by eye at times. Watch out for the 3'-4' rocky bar southeast of Paw Paw Cay and east of Wax Cut. Keep Rat Cay to starboard heading south and you can pass within ¼ mile of the eastern end of Rat Cay.

From Rat Cay you can begin steering to pass east of the Saddleback Cays as shown on Chart #AN-3. On the horizon you will see a point of land with a small beach. To the east of it is a fair sized cay with two smaller cays to its east. This fair sized cay and the two smaller ones are the Saddleback Cays. You will actually be steering a curving course towards them, first heading for the larger of the cays and then steering to pass east of the two smaller cays. As you get close to the Saddleback Cays you will notice a large green sandbank closing in on your port side towards the larger of the Saddleback Cays. This sandbank has some 4' spots at low tide with two 6' channels (at low tide also) through it. The first is just off the larger of the Saddleback Cays, and the other channel lies about ¼ mile off in the darker strip that splits the sandbank. When you get close you will see the two channels if you have good visibility.

Once past the Saddleback Cays you can begin to steer for the next island on the horizon, Pigeon Cay, as shown on Chart #AN-4. As you head for Pigeon Cay, northeast of Calabash Cay you will have to steer around some 4'-5' sandy spots in only 6' at low water. Having fun yet? Stay about ½ mile east of Calabash Cay as you head towards Pigeon Cay keeping the large green sandbank to port and you will once again find yourself in 7' at low water. You can anchor just north of Pigeon Cay in 5'-6' at low water. There is a green sandbank just off Pigeon Cay that, although it looks shallow, actually has 7'-10' over it in places at low water. Vessels drawing less than 5' can anchor south of Calabash Cay.

From Pigeon Cay, vessels drawing 4' or less can head northwest to Stafford Creek but only with a good high tide and excellent visibility. Pass north of Pigeon Cay and head in on the conspicuous white schoolhouse that is obscured by casaurinas just west of the small beach at the northern end of the Blanket Sound settlement. Head in on this schoolhouse on a course of 287° until you see the small orange buoy in the water just offshore. At one time this buoy was a stake, now it is a buoy that moves around with each blow. If you get confused and can't find your way in call the *Forfar Field Station* on VHF ch. 16 and they can talk you in, they'll be happy to help. Ask for Pete or Ricardo. If the buoy is there, keep it to port and proceed northward paralleling the shore and staying between the shallows off the shore and the shallow bank north of the buoy and south of the conspicuous wreck. Round the last of the small cays to port between it and the very obvious sandbank to their north and head into Stafford Creek. The creek has a lot of current and anchoring is tricky at best. A good spot in bad weather, even a minimal hurricane, is tucked up into the small pocket north of the bridge but you must watch out for the current on the south side of the creek by the bridge. Located just off the southeastern end of the bridge is a small blue hole that creates a whirlpool effect that at times can slam a small boat into the bridge or shore before you realize it. At slack tide the hole is a good dive but only during the 20 minute slack period. Use caution if diving the hole because as soon as the current begins to flow again, it does so with a vengeance.

Stafford Creek has no facilities and the only site of real interest is the Forfar Field Station, an educational and research center for high school and college students and educators. The station is owned by International Field Studies of Columbus, Ohio, a non-profit educational organization. The station has two sailboats that they use to teach a combined sailing, marine biology, and botanical program. For more information about their educational opportunities call (in the U.S.) 800-962-3805 or write to International Field Studies, 709 College Ave., Columbus, Ohio.

The *Forfar Field Station*, once known as the *Andros Reef Inn*, was constructed of local materials by Archie Forfar. Archie and his wife Toni were stranded on nearby Rat Cay on December 22, 1959 when their 40' schooner *Able Lady* ran up on the barrier reef. On Boxing Day the couple swam to the mainland where they were rescued and put on a plane to Nassau and then back to Canada. Their brief interlude in

Andros inspired Archie to return and return he did. He began construction of the *Andros Reef Inn* while living ashore in a tent. Later he explored numerous dive sites and blue holes with George Benjamin. After Archie and his wife Toni drifted apart, Archie took up with a young dive instructor name Anne Gunderson. Together they began exploring more and more dive sites and became determined to set a world record dive, to 500'. Even though backed up by four safety divers, Archie and Anne never returned from the depths. Under mysterious circumstances some suggest that it was a disappearance stunt although one safety diver said he briefly saw the couple at 500' with no movement or bubbles just before he had to come up suffering from tunnel vision. *International Field Studies* was operating next to the *Andros Reef Inn* and Archie had taken a personal interest in their concerns. The *Andros Reef Inn* was made available to *IFS* and was soon purchased and renamed the Forfar Field Station after Archie Forfar.

In the mid 1900's oil companies explored the Stafford Creek area and drilled down 14,000' but could not get their drills up again and had to abandon their entire rig. The old swing bridge once opened for boaters seeking refuge during hurricanes but hasn't opened in years and probably never will again. If you dinghy up the creek about 11 miles upstream you will come to the old Owens-Illinois docks. When this lumberyard was in full swing some 30 years ago, Stafford Creek was kept dredged. Today the creek hasn't seen a dredge in over 2 decades and it, and the waters around the settlement of Stafford Creek and Staniard Creek are silting in again.

Heading south from Pigeon Cay and Stafford Creek, you will notice Staniard Rock on your port side. Steer approximately 170°, about halfway between Staniard Rock and the conspicuous white roof on shore keeping Staniard Rock well to port as there are shallow rocky bars both north and south of it. Staniard Rock lies south of a well used but not well marked channel. Vessels wishing to enter from seaward are advised to eyeball their way through here. A GPS waypoint at 24° 52.40' N, 77° 51.00' W, will place you approximately ¼ mile east of the cut in the reef. From this position take up a course of approximately 230°-250° to steer between the reefs. This course is not that important, what is important is staying between the reefs (easily seen in good light) and then avoiding the shallow bar on the inside. The cut lies approximately 300-400 yards north of Staniard Rock. The light on the Staniard Rock has been destroyed and no plans are in the works for its replacement. The barrier reef comes in very close on your port side between Pigeon Cay and Staniard Rock, you'll see it breaking.

Vessels wishing to explore Staniard Creek have new opportunities opening for them in the near future, possibly even by the time this Guide comes out. At the south end of Long Bay Cay, a gentleman by the name of Daniel Hughes has built a resort called *Gumelemi Cove* aimed at attracting a very wealthy clientele. The harbour and entrance channel are being dredged even as I write these words and a marina is scheduled for construction, however the marina may or may not be open to the public. You can anchor just inside the point in the basin west of *Gumelemi Cove*. From a position southwest of Staniard Rock, steer approximately west/southwest for the point of land at the end of the long white beach. This is the northern end of Staniard Creek and inside is a new spoil island and the *Gumelemi Cove* harbour as shown on Chart #'s AN-4 and AN-5. You will have to eyeball your way into the harbour as dredging is currently going on and the depths may have changed by the time you read this. Before dredging 5' could make it inside on a very high tide and I have been told that the new channel will accommodate 6' at low water. If the entrance channel has not been dredged then you will need to wait for a high tide for help getting over the shallow bar that lies north of Staniard Creek, at the mouth to Gumelemi Cove. This shifting bar has only 2' over it at low tide. Inside Gumelemi Cove you will find 6' and more for anchoring. South of *Gumelemi Cove* is the settlement of Staniard Creek with its *Central Andros Inn and Restaurant*.

As I mentioned before, vessels heading south from Pigeon Cay should steer approximately 170°, heading roughly about halfway between Staniard Rock and the conspicuous white roof on shore keeping Staniard Rock well to port. Once past the area of *Gumelemi Cove* you may begin to parallel the shoreline again. This next stretch of the passage is possibly the trickiest part of the entire route. This can be a nerve-wracking stretch of water, not for the faint of heart or the deep of draft. The water gets very shallow here, anywhere from 5'-6' at low water in places with a few 4' spots thrown in just to keep you on your toes (as if you weren't already on the edge of your seat, right?). Very soon, off to starboard, you will begin to see a large curving and very shallow, white sandbank stretching southeastward from the shore. There is a small dark channel between the northwestern tip of the sandbank and the eastern shore of Andros that may look inviting from offshore but don't attempt to pass between the sandbank and the shore. The water between them is very rocky and shallow though it looks deeper from a mile away. As shown on Chart #AN-5, you can head southeastward past the shallow bar along its eastern edge but you will have to negotiate an area of numerous shallow, breaking, awash at high water reefs between the sandbank and the offshore barrier reef.

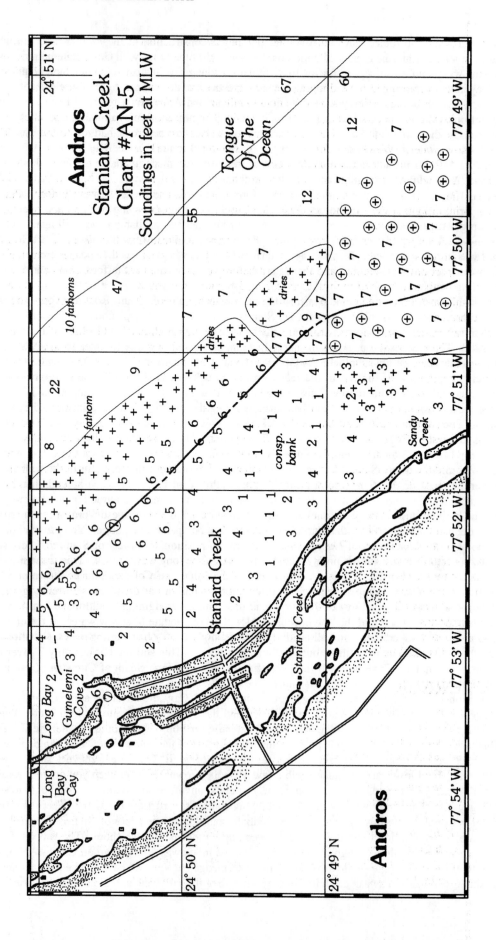

Andros
Staniard Creek
Chart #AN-5
Soundings in feet at MLW

These reefs and ledges are easily seen and avoided and the good new is that the water begins to get back to 7' depths at low tide. Once past the shallow bank you can angle back in towards shore somewhat as shown on Chart #'s AN-5 and AN-6 where you will have fewer reefs and shoals to avoid in depths of 7'-9' at low water. Closer in to shore you'll be dodging shallow green sandbars instead of the brown reefs that lie further offshore. You'll notice that you're still about ½ mile offshore through here.

Your next obstacle is the conspicuous and easily avoided Lightborn Bank just off the beaches to your starboard side as shown on Chart #AN-6. You will have plenty of deep water to pass it to the east, 7'-11' in places at low water. Watch out for a couple of shallow bars off Love Hill. You'll be steering approximately 140° through here towards the point of land off your starboard bow that is the entrance to Fresh Creek. You will see a large green sandbank in front of you will lead you to believe that Lightborn Bank extends far out to the east, almost to the reef. Don't panic, this green bank is fairly deep. Put your bow on the point of land at the entrance to Fresh Creek and steer approximately 140° and you will find 7'-8' across the bank the whole way.

Well, now you've got the AUTEC towers and the entrance to Fresh Creek in sight. I bet you think you're almost home now, right? Sorry to burst your bubble but you could not be further from the truth. The shallowest part of this route lies just ahead, just before you enter the Fresh Creek channel. If you left Morgan's Bluff within an hour of high tide, averaging 5-6 knots, and you draw over 5', you might as well anchor for awhile and let the tide come up, you ain't getting through here. If you draw 5' or less you might try to sneak through on a low tide but you'll likely bump.

There are two routes from offshore Small Hope Bay to the entrance channel at Fresh Creek as shown on Chart #AN-7. The eastern route, along the shore of Goat Cay and Long Cay, will just carry 5½' at high tide. The western route that parallels the Andros shoreline is good for over 6' at high tide. At low tide only the western route, along the Andros shoreline is good for 5', and like I said, you'll bump, maybe even run aground if you can't steer around some shallow sandy spots.

First we'll look at the eastern route that lies along the western shore of Goat Cay and Long Cay. When abeam of the dock at the *Small Hope Bay Lodge* (Chart #AN-7), head towards Goat Cay. At high tide you can pass to the west of Goat Cay and Long Cay, passing close in to the southern end of Long Cay. You'll have to steer between Long Cay and the large shallow bank to its west. Once past Long Cay keep the AUTEC tower and the shallow bank to starboard to enter the Fresh Creek entrance channel. This route has a controlling depth of 3' at low water just off the southern third of Long Cay, 5½' can make it through here on a high tide.

The western route from Small Hope Bay to Fresh Creek parallels the shoreline of Andros much closer in as shown on Chart #AN-7. When abeam of Goat Cay in 7' at low water, take up a course for the point at the northern end of the entrance to Fresh Creek. You will have almost 5' through here at mean low water, in some places slightly more but you will probably have to weave your way through some shallow patches and bump your way across the bar that runs parallel to the northern side of the entrance channel to Fresh Creek. Once in the channel keep to the northern side until just inside and then head towards the docks at the *Lighthouse Marina* off your port bow. Six feet of draft can make it through this western route at high tide with no problems.

Now you can take a deep breath, relax your white knuckle grip on your wheel or tiller, and prepare to unwind in Fresh Creek. You've earned it!

FRESH CREEK

Fresh Creek is probably the most frequented harbour by cruising boats visiting Andros. Fresh Creek gets its name from the fresh water creek that runs back into the wilderness of Andros for some forty miles, there joining up with some small fresh water lakes. Some of the locals say that if you head upstream far enough that you can drink the water surrounding your boat. At one time a hurricane raised the level of the creek over 10' and some vessels that were tied off in the creeks for protection were swept inland as much as five miles where some still sit today.

Though the area is called Fresh Creek, the creek actually separates two towns. On the north shore is the much larger Coakely Town while on the south side of the Creek sits Andros Town. A GPS waypoint at 24° 44.25' N, 77° 45.65' W, will place you approximately ¼ mile east/northeast of the well marked entrance channel into Fresh Creek as shown on Chart #AN-7 (at night, the loom of the lights of the AUTEC Base and Coakely town, coupled with the flashing amber lights of the AUTEC towers will give you a good idea of whether you're in the right vicinity or not). Immediately in front of you as you begin to steer down the

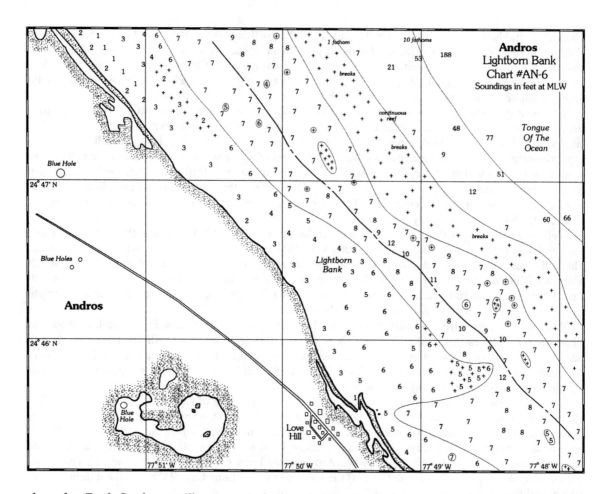

channel to Fresh Creek you will see two steel pilings just southeast of the small rock lying south of Long Cay. Keep these pilings to starboard. Next you will see an amber lighted AUTEC tower, keep it also to starboard passing south of it. Head straight in to the entrance channel from here avoiding the shallow sandbank to starboard between the AUTEC tower and shore. I found two shallow bars at the entrance to Fresh Creek that carry between 5' and 5½' at low water and can be entered at half-tide or more by drafts over 6'. One lies approximately 200 yards east of the entrance, and the second lies only about 100 yards east of the entrance. When approaching the entrance keep halfway between the center and the northern shore of the entrance, this is where the deeper water is and keeps you off the rocky shoal north of the southern jetty. Once inside, head for the east end of *Lighthouse Marina's* eastern dock keeping close to the dock, only the southern side of the entrance channel was dredged, the northern side is very shallow. Once past this dock you can anchor just past the marina but not too far past the marina as it shoals rapidly. The deepest water and the best holding is in the northwestern side of the harbour towards the bridge but the entire anchorage area is littered with old engine blocks and other debris so use caution when setting your anchors. The use of two anchors is recommended here as there is little swinging room if it's crowded and there's a lot of current here. Some cruisers head to the commercial dock on the north side near the bridge and tie off to the freighter *Lady Magic*, that is berthed there and hasn't moved in two years. There is a *Shell* gas station just a few yards from the commercial dock.

On the south side of the harbour is the *Lighthouse Hotel and Marina*, an excellent place to stop. They have a fine restaurant and bar, copy and fax service, and the front desk or the Dockmaster can arrange a car rental for you. The hotel itself is a great place to unwind even if you don't rent a room. You can dine on the verandah or just pull up a chair and relax, or perhaps you'd like to take a swim in their fresh water pool. Whatever suits your mood, they aim to please. The marina has a burger grill on Fridays at their outside *Shipwreck Bar*. With good food and good prices, don't miss this affair. This is a great place to meet other cruisers and some of the people who live aboard here and work at the nearby AUTEC base. Dockmaster Hank Roberts is one of the best guides to this area. He also owns a very nice restaurant across the harbour in Coakely Town. He will arrange transportation for you if you wish to dine at his establishment. Hank

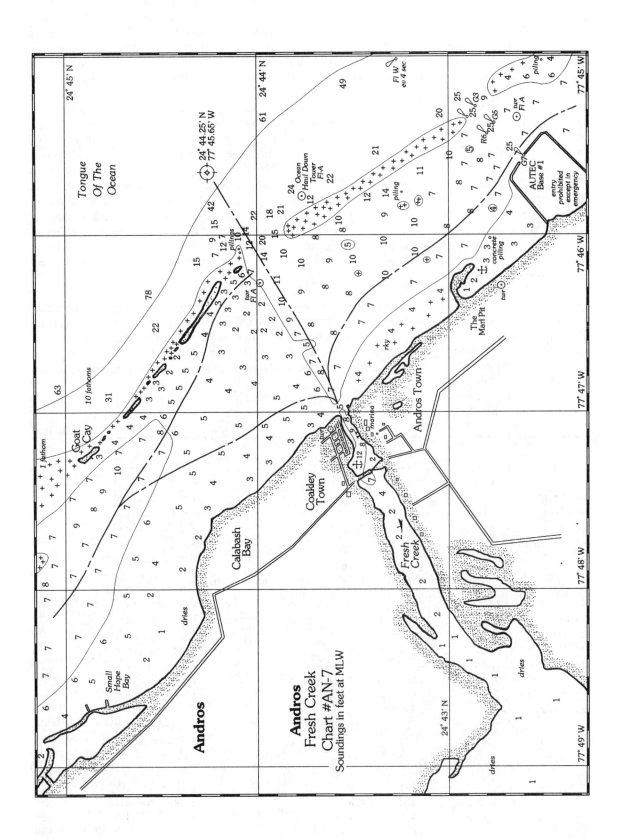

Andros
Fresh Creek
Chart #AN-7
Soundings in feet at MLW

can also help you arrange a propane fill with the truck that comes through on Thursdays from the *Shell* complex at Morgan's Bluff. The marina itself has 18 slips that can accommodate boats of 100' LOA and 9' draft. There is ample fresh water at the dock with 50 amp and 15 amp electrical service. Fresh Creek is a Port Of Entry and vessels wishing to clear Customs and Immigration should contact Lighthouse Marina on VHF ch. 16. The Dockmaster will supply you with the proper forms and call the officials for you. It may take a while to clear as the officers will have to travel from the airport and they might assess you a $10 travel charge.

Just a hundred yards up from the Dockmaster's office is a branch of the *Royal Bank Of Canada*. As of the fall of 1997 the bank is only open on Wednesdays for four hours so plan ahead if you need their services. Sometime over the late fall to early winter the bank is scheduled to begin 5 day work weeks, so maybe it will be open all week by the time you visit. Outside the entrance to the marina, a short five minute walk away, is the *Androsia Boutique*. You've probably seen the batik *Androsia* for sale throughout The Bahamas. It is manufactured and sold here on Andros and this boutique, a sort of factory outlet store, has some great deals waiting for you, they take all major credit cards. Nearby is the *Androsia Factory*, check in the outlet store for a self-guided tour of the factory. If you're stuck in Fresh Creek waiting on weather, you might want to take advantage of the batik classes offered by the *Androsia Factory*. Check at the *Androsia Boutique*, that's where they post information on the classes. The price of the class is $10 and that covers a piece of cloth that you will design and prepare. The factory staff then dyes the material and you get to take it home with you.

Across the harbour from the *Lighthouse Marina* is Coakely Town. You can walk across the bridge or dinghy over to the landing at the commercial dock or you can tie up to the concrete dock at Papa Gay's *Chickcharnies Hotel*, the large, yellow, two story hotel that dominates the waterfront on the northern shore. Papa Gay says that he will rent out dock space but it's rarely available. The dock itself is a rough concrete wall with barely 5' at low water, you'll need plenty of good, fat, fenders. The hotel has a very nice restaurant serving breakfast, lunch, and dinner, a bar, a well stocked grocery store, and the hotel can also arrange for car rentals.

In town along the eastern shore you'll find *Skinny's Landmark Restaurant and Lodge* with *Donny's Sweet Sugar Lounge* also on the premises. Across the street are the Government Offices, a *Batelco* office, Police Station, and a Post Office. On the side streets north of the *Chickcharnies Hotel* you fill find *Adderly's Grocery*, a well stocked grocery store with a laundromat next door. At the corner is the *Square Deal Restaurant and Bar*, and nearby is *Gaitor's Variety Store*, and *Treats*, a small bar with a pool table.

A mile north of Coakely Town is the small hillside community of Calabash Bay where you will find a small gift shop and the *Sunshine Cafe* serving Bahamian and American dishes. A mile or so north of Calabash Bay is the small community of Love Hill. Here is an *Esso* station, liquor store, and the *Quick Wash Laundromat*. Still further to the north is Small Hope Bay with it's extremely laid back *Small Hope Bay Lodge*. Small Hope Bay is said to have been named by the legendary pirate Sir Henry Morgan who decided that there was "small hope" that anyone could find his buried treasure here. He might have been right as no reports of treasure finds have surfaced in the area.

Calling *Small Hope Bay Lodge* "laid back" is not just an advertiser's tool, this place is just that. Founded by Canadian Dick Birch in 1960, the Birch family has created and maintained a true out island getaway that I cannot help but recommend. There are no phones, no TV's, and no keys for the rooms. The only rule seems to be that you must enjoy yourself and have fun. The lodge specializes in SCUBA and snorkeling trips to the nearby reefs and blue holes and they also cater to bonefishing or sportfishing enthusiasts. The lodge offers 20 cottages built of coral and Andros pine set among a beautiful shoreline of casuarinas and palm trees. On its beach is a bar that is famous for its conch fritters and its rum laced sundowners. The restaurant offers excellent breakfasts, lunches, and dinners with reservations. Children under 12 can dine in a separate dining room with a chaperone to allow the adults a little "adult time." There is a lovely beach and the Lodge gives free snorkeling lessons. They have a huge library and book trade, a game room for checkers and chess enthusiasts, and a very nice gift shop. Manager Peter Douglas, a local government official who is a delight to converse with, is a native Androsian who is extremely proud of his Island and his heritage. The Bahamas needs more government officials who are as concerned about their country as Peter. On the main highway at the entrance to the Lodge is a small grocery store and *Rolle's Variety Store*.

If you dinghy up Fresh Creek past the bridge you will come to an area of very nice homes on the southern shore of the creek. Locals say that if you go far enough upstream the water is so fresh you can drink it. The wreck of an old Staten Island Ferry lies mid-stream about ½ mile west of the bridge. The ferry was brought to Andros many years ago, before the bridge was built. The ferry's job was to run between Nassau and Fresh Creek bringing freight and passengers. She only made one run before she wound up where she now lies.

At the southern point of the entrance channel to Fresh Creek you will see the remains of a lighthouse that dates back over a century. The two cannon you see mounted there are said to have come off the wreck of a British Man Of War that sank in the channel just off the point. Cannonballs are still being found at the site in about 12'-15' of water.

Just south of the entrance channel to Fresh Creek is the main AUTEC (*Atlantic Undersea Testing and Evaluation Center*) base (#1) on Andros. There are three other smaller bases up and down the island's eastern shore at Salvador Point (#2) just north of Cargill Creek, the southern end of Big Wood Cay (#3), and at Golding Cay (#4) at South Bight It's not unusual to see a U.S. Navy Warship or Submarine in these waters. The U.S. Navy conducts test on Submarine and Anti-Submarine Weapons in the 6000' deep Tongue Of The Ocean. Farther south in the Tongue Of The Ocean the Navy also conducts preparedness tests of surface ships. The AUTEC base is run by a private contractor with only a few Naval personnel on hand. If you happen to be in the area during testing you won't even know it. You will not be warned by radio, the Navy will simply wait for you to pass before resuming testing. AUTEC wants all boaters to understand that all AUTEC bases are U.S. Navy Installations and entrance is prohibited except in real emergencies. A summer squall, running out of gas, or just stopping for lunch are not real emergencies. AUTEC Base #1, Fresh Creek, monitors VHF ch. 16 and answers to *Snapper Base* if you have any questions. South of Fresh Creek AUTEC maintains several towers and buoys, all flash amber at night. Some of the smaller buoys are hard to see even at night. Use caution when transiting this area at night.

If you take the road a few miles south of Fresh Creek you will come to a "T" intersection. The road to the left leads you to the entrance to the AUTEC base and the road to the right continues south to Behring Point. Just a couple of miles south of this intersection is Bowen Sound whose only facility is *Kell's Grocery & Takeaway Snacks*.

FRESH CREEK TO NORTH BIGHT-THE INSIDE ROUTE

Leaving Fresh Creek and heading south you will have another test of nerves. Feel like playing again? If not, head outside, it's much safer and easier on the blood pressure. This next section, from Fresh Creek south to North Bight on the inside is shallower and strewn with more heads than the inside route from Morgan's Bluff to Fresh Creek and you remember how much fun that was. I recommend that vessels drawing more than 5' go outside at Fresh Creek if headed south to Cargill Creek or South Bight. The inside route is long, winding, and shallow, there are many 4'-6' spots at low water that must be avoided. There are no real anchorages between Fresh Creek and North Bight (with the exception of lying in the lee of Long Rock, or Green Cay) and the entire trip takes at least one full tide for vessels maintaining a speed of 5-6 knots which only adds to the problem. Once again, unless you adamant about using this route, I suggest going outside. Piloting by eye is the only way you're going to get through here, don't leave too early in the morning as the sun will be right in your eyes.

If you are headed outside (Chart #AN-7) you must give the amber lighted AUTEC tower that sits outside the reef about ¼ mile south of the entrance channel to Fresh Creek a wide berth, AUTEC suggests two miles to the east. There is a 1½" cable that heads down from the tower at about a 30°-45° angle, it's called the *Ocean Haul Down Cable*, and it is dangerous to be in its vicinity. The cable is used to haul equipment, targets, shapes, anything the Navy needs, down to the floor of the Tongue Of The Ocean where there is a huge base and sheave. The cable is not so much a danger as is the possibility that you may hit what it is being hauled up or down. If you pass this way at night and you see a lot of lights about, keep well clear as lights mean activity and the cable is being used.

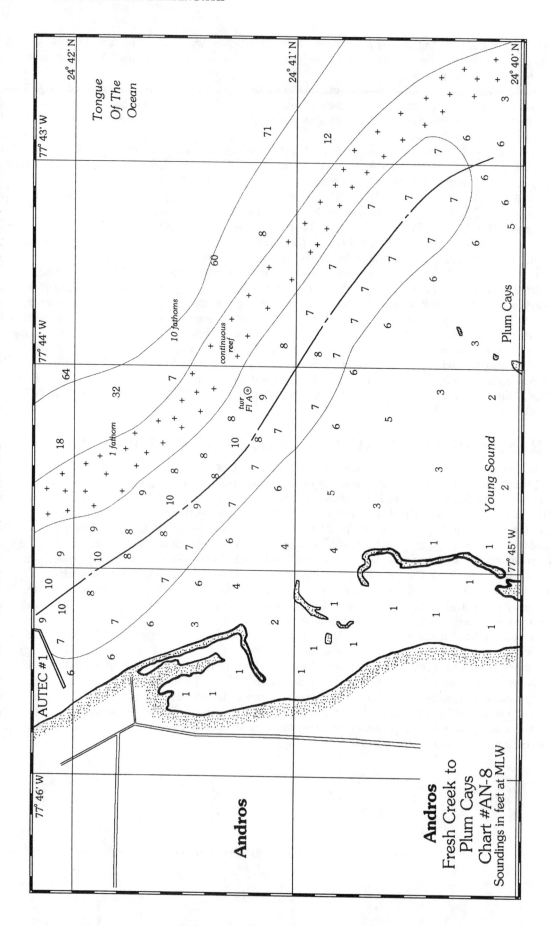

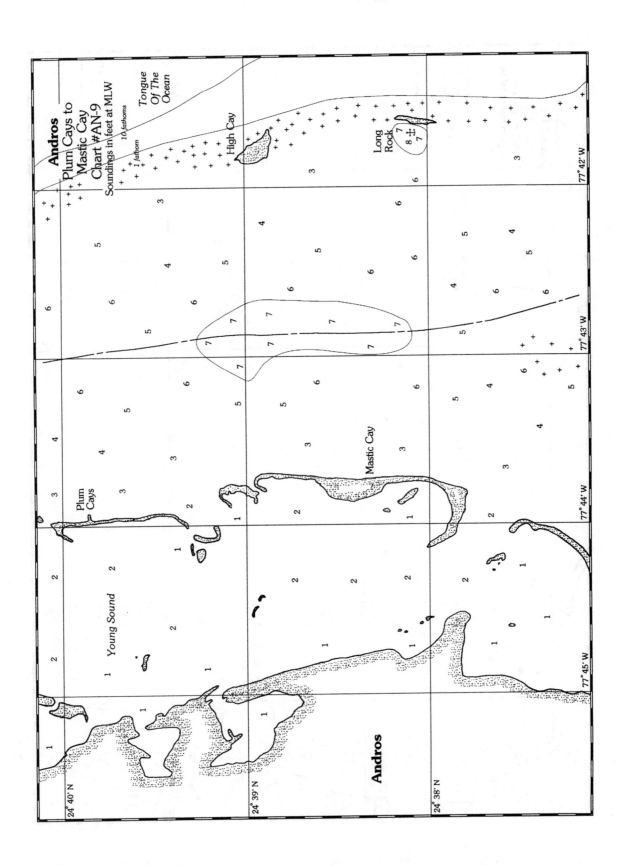

Andros
Plum Cays to
Mastic Cay
Chart #AN-9
Soundings in feet at MLW

Tongue
Of The
Ocean

10 fathoms

1 fathom

High Cay

Long
Rock

Plum
Cays

Mastic Cay

Young Sound

Andros

24° 40' N

24° 39' N

24° 38' N

77° 45' W   77° 44' W   77° 43' W   77° 42' W

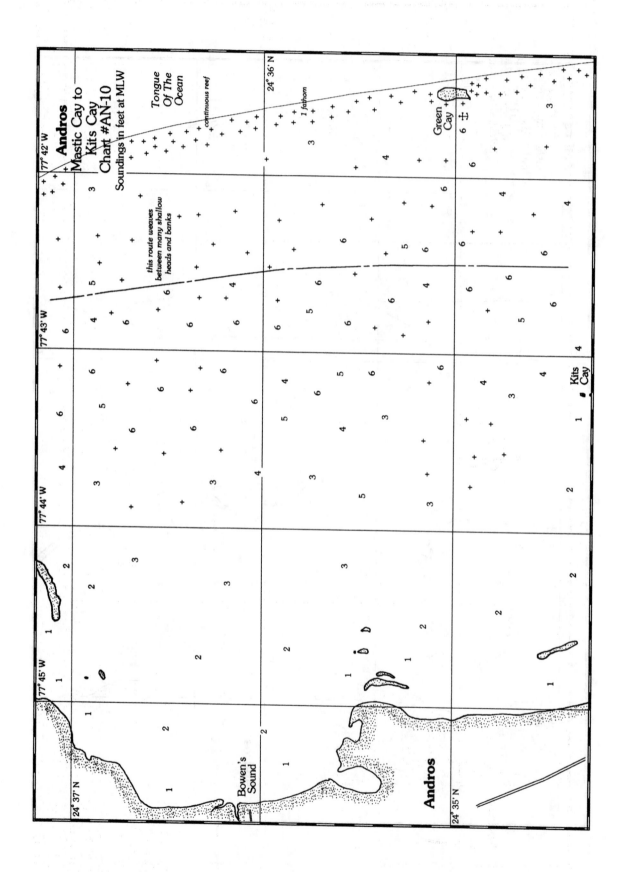

Andros
Mastic Cay to
Kits Cay
Chart #AN-10
Soundings in feet at MLW

*Tongue
Of The
Ocean*

continuous reef

*this route weaves
between many shallow
heads and banks*

1 fathom

Green
Cay

Kits
Cay

Bowen's
Sound

Andros

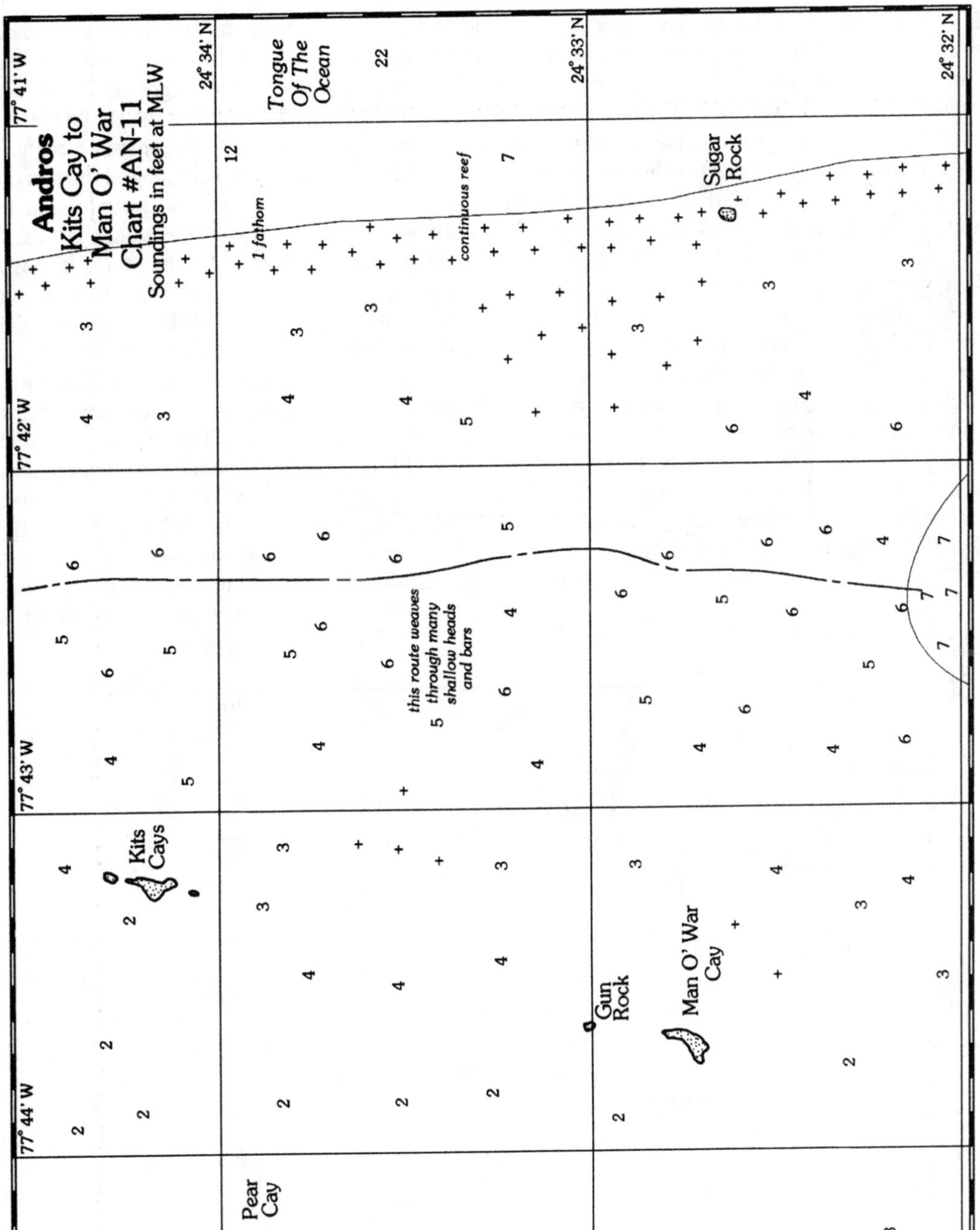

Andros
Kits Cay to
Man O' War
Chart #AN-11
Soundings in feet at MLW

Tongue
Of The
Ocean

continuous reef

1 fathom

this route weaves
through many
shallow heads
and bars

Kits
Cays

Gun
Rock

Man O' War
Cay

Sugar
Rock

Pear
Cay

Man O' War

Andros

77° 41' W
77° 42' W
77° 43' W
77° 44' W
77° 45' W

24° 34' N
24° 33' N
24° 32' N

If you are headed south from Fresh Creek inside the reef; head out the entrance channel until you are at least 200 yards east of the southern jetty. To avoid the shallows that lie along the eastern shore of Andros between Fresh Creek and the Marl Pit, turn to starboard and take up a course for roughly the middle of the northern breakwater of the AUTEC base as shown on Chart #AN-7. This is to avoid the shallow reefs just west of the piling that lies inside the reef and about halfway between the Fresh Creek entrance channel and the AUTEC base. On the eastern shore of Andros is a small hook of land that juts out and creates a basin that is locally called the Marl Pit. At one time it was an excellent anchorage and refuge from frontal passages. Today it has filled in to the point that only vessels with drafts of less than 3' can avail themselves of its protection. You will notice a concrete piling inshore just south of the Marl Pit, stay away from it, it sits in less than 6' of water at low tide. As you pass that conspicuous steel piling to port you may begin to work your way to pass just outside the eastern breakwaters of the AUTEC base. Parallel the eastern breakwater crossing the entrance channel until abeam of the southern breakwater.

Once past the entrance to the AUTEC Base as shown on Chart #AN-8, set your bow generally pointing to High Cay on the horizon. Follow the curve of 7' deep water staying closer to the reef than to the shore. Soon you will be in water less than 6' deep at low water. Get used to it. You will be in water less than one fathom deep at low tide for the next 10-12 miles. Keep the Plum Cays to starboard as you approach High Cay as shown on Chart #AN-9. Just west of High Cay is a small pocket of water 7' deep at low tide. Offshore High Cay is a deep reef that comes up from the depths of the Tongue Of The Ocean called the *Dallas Reef*. The reef was named after the U.S. Navy Submarine *Dallas* after she ran aground and stayed there three days. Passing south of High Cay is much like turning the corner, the waters south of High Cay are often much rougher than those north of High Cay. In prevailing winds you can anchor in the lee of Long Rock in approximately 7'-8' at low water.

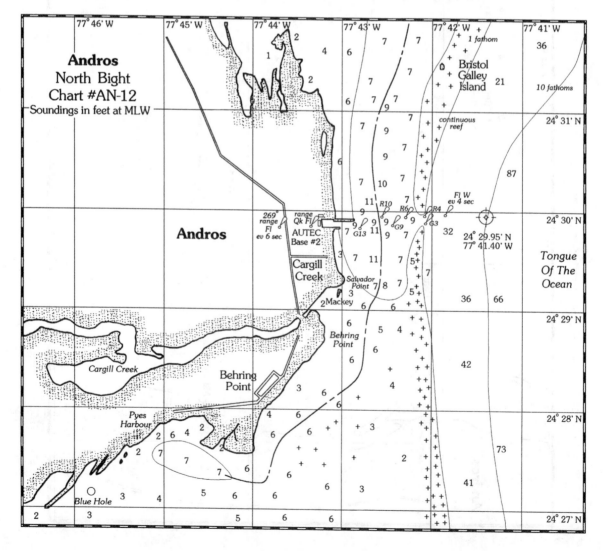

Heading south from Long Rock pass well off the eastern shore Andros in 4'-6' at low water as shown on Chart #AN-10. Through here you will be weaving your way through numerous reefs and shallow bars especially in the area north of Green Cay. In prevailing conditions you can anchor in the lee of Green Cay in 5'-6' at low water. Heading south from Green Cay as shown on Chart #AN-11, stay between the visible barrier reef and the eastern shore of Andros leaving Kits Cays and Man Of War Cay well to starboard. Once again, you will have to eyeball your way through here, between many shallow bars and heads. Are you wishing that you were outside yet?

NORTH BIGHT

As you approach Salvador Point, Cargill Creek, and North Bight as shown on Chart #AN-12, you will find yourself temporarily free of the many heads and shoals that plagued you over the last few miles. Heading south, pass about halfway between Andros and Bristol Galley Island in 7'-9' of water. Directly ahead of you lies AUTEC Base #2 at Salvador Point. You will likely notice its large tower, jetty, buildings, and marked entrance channel. Cross the channel and continue heading southward to Behring Point.

If you are outside and wish to enter by the AUTEC channel, a GPS waypoint at 24° 29.95' N, 77° 41.40' W, will place you approximately ½ mile east of the sea buoy that marks the 9' deep channel. AUTEC does not mind if cruisers use their channel as long as you do not block any of their vessels or attempt to enter their bases. There is a large, unmistakable range ashore that leads you in on a heading of approximately 269°. Follow the channel markers until well inside the reef and then turn north or south as you wish.

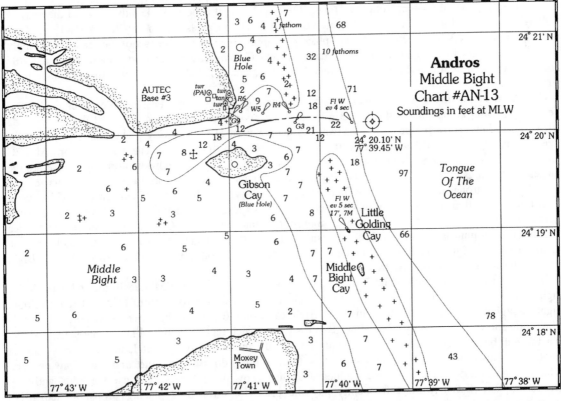

Heading south, on your starboard side is the settlement of Cargill Creek. Continue on past Behring Point and the settlement of Behring Point keeping an eye out for the rocky bar that you will want to keep to port heading south. Round up inside Pye's Harbour and you can anchor in 4'-7' at low tide if you pick your spot right. You will be open to prevailing winds here but if it's not blowing too bad, you'll be comfortable enough.

Next to Pye's Harbour is the dock at Behring Point, where, just about 200 yards from the end of the road, you'll find the *Tranquillity Hill Fishing Lodge* with 10 rooms, satellite TV, and a fine restaurant. If you take the dinghy north to Cargill Creek, just north of the bridge, you'll find a *Batelco* office, *Gateway Liquors*, an excellent restaurant *Dig Dig's Bahamian-American Cuisine* (dinner by reservation please-368-

5097), *Carter's Convenience Store*, and two very nice bonefishing lodges. The *Andros Island Bonefish Club* and the *Cargill Creek Fishing Lodge* both have bars and restaurants and are right next to each other just north of the bridge. Both provide dinner with reservations but only *Cargill Creek Fishing Lodge* monitors VHF ch. 16. Just south of the bridge is a liquor store and the *Sea View Restaurant and Bar* serving breakfast, lunch, and dinner.

MIDDLE BIGHT AND MANGROVE CAY

The route from North Bight to Middle Bight will not be discussed in great detail and not charted in this edition of this guide (if there is enough interest it may be included in a later edition). The route is very shallow and literally strewn with shallow heads and patch reefs. So difficult is this route that all boats, even locals frequently, must pass outside the reef at the AUTEC tower that sits north of Middle Bight. If you are headed to Middle Bight from North Bight, I suggest heading out the AUTEC channel at Salvador Point, turning south well outside the reef, and heading inside at the AUTEC channel at Middle Bight. AUTEC has so generously marked these channels for us, it's a shame that we don't use them. The passage from North Bight to South Bight and further is extremely difficult for vessels with drafts over 4'. A draft of 5' could make it through with a high tide, 5½' with the right tide, but the route is strictly piloting by eye. Your attention on this route will be so concentrated on piloting by eye that you will have little room for error. If you happen to be one small patch reef off to one side or the other you might find yourself inside a cul-de-sac at best. Use extreme caution if you decide to pilot your way through here. If you would like the help of a pilot, contact Hank Roberts, the Dockmaster at Lighthouse Marina at Fresh Creek.

When entering Middle Bight from the Tongue Of The Ocean, it is best to take advantage of the marked AUTEC channel for Base #3 at the southeastern tip of Big Wood Cay as shown on Chart #AN-13. A GPS waypoint at 24° 20.10' N, 77° 39.45' W, will place you approximately ¼ mile east of the sea buoy. Simply follow the markers in keeping the reef to starboard and Gibson Cay off to port. Farther south, Little Golding Cay has a light that flashes white every 5 seconds, stands 17' above the water, and is visible for 7 nautical miles.

One of the most popular anchorages in Andros lies west of Gibson Cay. Pass between Gibson Cay and the AUTEC base on the southeast tip of Big Wood Cay, giving the rocky shoal south of the base a wide berth, and follow the deep blue water westward to anchor west of Gibson Cay. There is a lot of current here so use caution. You'll see some white buoys on your way through the channel, these are AUTEC buoys, not channel markers. On the west side of Gibson Cay are several more white buoys, these are the hurricane moorings for the AUTEC boats. If you choose to anchor here be sure to set two anchors so you can ride to the strong current properly. There is deep water even further west of Gibson Cay with several areas to anchor, all exposed more or less to the prevailing winds. Keep an eye out for several small patch reefs through here. There is an oceanic blue hole in the center of Gibson Cay that is connected to the sea by subterranean tunnels teeming with ocean fish. In the mid-1900's the 222' *Vagabondia* was a frequent visitor to Middle Bight. She drew 12' and her owner, William Mellon, even put a mooring in Middle Bight to which he could lay when in Andros.

Vessels wishing to head to South Bight should once again go outside at Middle Bight and enter South Bight via the unmarked but wide, deep entrance channel. The inside route from Middle Bight to South Bight, though easier than the route from North Bight to Middle Bight, still has areas where the water is 4' at low tide and there are plenty of coral heads and shallow patch reefs to avoid. I know that some will say that the mailboats use this route, why shouldn't I. You can use the route, but I, in all honesty, cannot recommend this route for a 6' draft vessel. Yes, the mailboats do use this route, and they draw six feet. What one must understand is that the mailboat Captains know these waters, they use the tides, and they accept the fact that they must frequently pay the price for error by replacing props, an expensive proposition. Many carry extra props with them. Do you?

South of Middle Bight lies Mangrove Cay, an island to itself in some manners. Some residents deny being from Andros—they want it to be made clear that they are from Mangrove Cay! Mangrove Cay is a picturesque settlement of nodding coconut palms. In a cave near Mangrove Cay an ancient Lucayan canoe and paddles were found. Mangrove Cay is said to be the bonefishing center of Andros. The adult bonefish mate in North Bight and South Bight and their young mature in the calm waters of the interior of Andros. This has led to the construction of many fish camps in the interior.

The eastern shore of Mangrove Cay has a number of small communities that are rarely visited. The northernmost settlement is Moxey Town, just across the Middle Bight from AUTEC Base #3. Moxey

Town is sometimes called Little Harbour and is the site of the three day August Monday Regatta. In town there is a *Shell* service station and fuel can be delivered to the town dock but you will have to dinghy it out to the big boat. For fuel call Hubert King at 369-0478 or ask in town. In town you will find a laundromat, a small hardware store, and the *Travelers Rest Restaurant* for lunch and dinner with reservation. Moxey Town also offers *Lundies Restaurant* and *Terry's Apartments*. Nearby is the 60' high Crow Hill. On the top are many caves where crows have constructed unique multi-tiered communities to hatch their young.

South of Moxey Town, small villages like Swains, Dorsetts, Grants, Burnt Rock, and Pinders line the shoreline amid groves of coconut palms face the Tongue Of The Ocean. In Dorsett you'll find Nelson Thompson's *Swain's Wholesale and Retail Bar* which probably should be in Swain's judging by the name. The *Mangrove Cay Inn* at Pinder's lies about a two minute walk away from the beach. This is a good location to begin an exploration of the islands blue holes. The inn has eight rooms, each with a bath and paddle fan. The hotel dining room and lounge serves breakfast, lunch and dinner at reasonable prices. If a guest gets lucky and catches some fish, the restaurant will gladly prepare your catch for you.

SOUTH BIGHT

The creek system that makes up South Bight is very extensive and quite deep is some places. With the help of a high tide it is possible to take a 4' draft through South Bight from the Tongue Of The Ocean to the vast flats that lie on the western shore of Andros. The entrance to South Bight is wide and deep, no need to use an AUTEC channel here.

A GPS waypoint at 24° 14.25' N, 77° 35.50' W, will place you approximately 1 mile northeast of the entrance channel to South Bight. From this position take up an approximate course of 248° on the southernmost of the two Channel Rocks. Eyeball your way through and as you approach Channel Rocks swing to port to avoid them. Once inside, between Channel Rocks and Golding Cay, where the AUTEC base is, watch out for the shallow Channel Shoal about mid-channel south of Channel Rocks.

At the southern end of Mangrove Cay, Chart #AN-14, lies the small settlement of Victoria Point, sometimes called Bastion Point. The settlement is rich in fresh water, there are wells almost everywhere. In town you'll find *Cool Breezes Cottages* available year round.

A mile inland from Victoria Point lies the settlement of Lisbon Creek. Lisbon Creek was, and still is, the center of boat building activities on the island of Andros with a few Family Island Regatta winners constructed here. You can work your way into the mouth of the creek with 6' at low water. About 300 yards from the creek a dredged channel is very visible in all but the late afternoon sun. The creek was dredged about two years ago and will now take a 6' draft a considerable distance inside where you can get excellent protection even in strong east winds. It has been suggested that boaters can anchor in Drigg's Hill Harbour to await the tide to go up the creek. I do not recommend it. The local AUTEC people often moor their boats in the harbour and there are numerous reports of theft and vandalism to their vessels. You're better off anchoring behind Golding Cay or off Forsyth Point.

In Lisbon Creek, Sylvia Bannister has a unique guest house appropriately named the *Bannister's House*. Sylvia and her husband Henry have collected pet turtles for over 25 years and their restaurant, the *Aquamarine Club*, has a turtle pen which connects to the sea right from the dining room. When I was last there Sylvia had nine hawksbill turtles that she would feed lettuce daily. The Bannisters do not eat or serve turtle on their menu. Henry is an excellent guide to this area and knows of several blue holes in the immediate area. Ask him about the three divers lost in one of the blue holes a few years ago. Accommodations can also be found at the *Longley Guest House*. Leroy Bannister is a guide for diving and fishing and has lived hereabouts fishing, farming, and racing sailboats all his life. His bar, *Leroy's Harbour Bay* is the most popular spot in town. Leroy can arrange to have diesel and gas delivered to the dock for boaters. Leroy is one of the premier boat builders in this area, but Ralph Moxey in Moxey town will tell you that Leroy has never beat him. *Elliott and Pat's Inn* will pick you up for dinner in their taxi as groceries and restaurants are all but out of walking range for even the hardiest trekkers.

Driggs Hill lies at the northern tip of south Andros on the southern side of South Bight. They have a new dredged harbour that was at one time said to be a future home to cruise ships but this has never come about. Just south of Sirius Cay is a pile marking the northern side of the harbour. The green piling is halfway in. A day range is inside but hard to see from outside the channel. You can tie to the tires along the eastern wall but use caution as it is no place to be in a strong easterly wind. Bear in mind what the AUTEC people have to say about this harbour and use your own judgment.

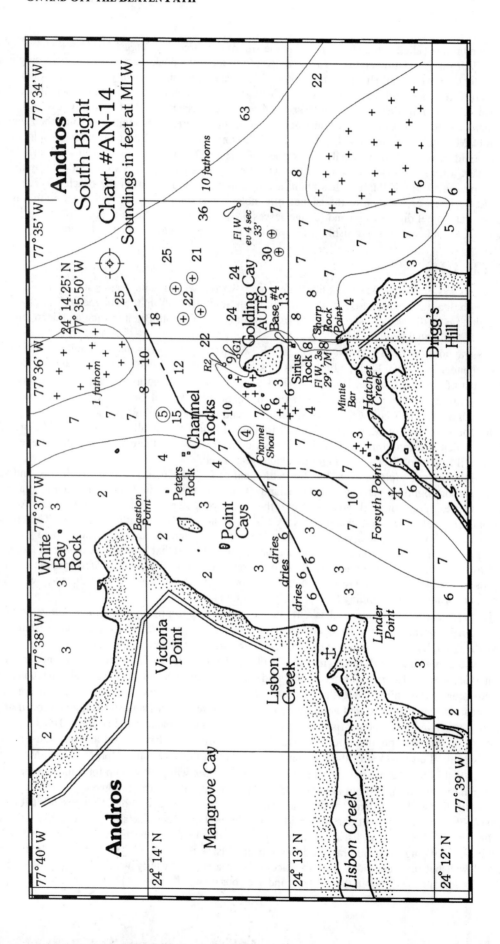

Andros
South Bight
Chart #AN-14
Soundings in feet at MLW

Photo by Kelly Becker

Cannons from a sunken man of war, Fresh Creek, Andros.

About two miles south of Driggs Hill is the *Emerald Palms By-The-Sea* resort. Not far from the airport at Congo Town, this seaside resort has it all, palm trees, a swimming pool, 20 air-conditioned rooms with ceiling fans, TV, VCR, refrigerators, and, last but not least, romantic four poster double or king size beds. Dinners are by reservation and the *Emerald Palms* will provide transportation. The resort can also arrange diving and fishing charters for you. One mile further south lies another fine resort, the *Congo Beach Club* with its restaurant right on the beach.

Congo Town is a Port of Entry for The Bahamas and a main waypoint for incoming flights to clear in. It has a 5,000' airstrip between High Rock and Congo Town itself. Although spread over a few square miles, the actual center of Congo Town is a place known as The Jungle. *The Jungle Club* run by Babar Paul and her mother is an excellent restaurant situated right on the beach. *The Congo Beach Hotel Restaurant and Bar* even offers satellite TV. The manager, Jerry Davis, also has a grocery store with very good prices. Two miles north on the water at the border of Congo Town and Long Bay is the *Las Palmas Beach Hotel*. It is the only truly modern resort in South Andros with a large swimming pool, tennis court, and offering world class deep sea and bonefishing charters.

Kemp's Bay is a popular spot for visitors to Andros. Here you'll find Norward Rahming whose diversified holdings include an grocery store, a resort, a shipping company, a lumberyard, and a school bus system. One of his newest enterprises is the *Royal Palm Beach Lodge* in town by the beach. Here you can purchase groceries, diesel, gas, kerosene, or rent a car for an island excursion. In town you'll find a branch of the *Bank of The Bahamas*. Just north of town is the *Kemp's Bay Club*, a wonderful little tropical paradise for tourists seeking a private getaway. The *Kemp's Bay Club* can organize bonefishing trips for interested parties. There is an old AUTEC base in Kemp's Bay that was returned to the Bahamian government and I understand that Norward Rahming is planning to build a marina there. The entrance channel, the only way in to Kemp's Bay, is a narrow but marked dogleg channel. The markers may or may not be there as they are no longer maintained.

From Kemp's Bay to The Bluff are many deserted beaches, numerous coconut groves, one after another, and some very shallow water. The Bluff is home to the local government complex which includes a government Clinic, the fishing co-op processing plant, and the main *Bahamas Electricity Corporation* (*BEC*) station for Andros.

About three miles south of Deep Creek is the small settlement of Little Creek where you will find *M & S Takeaway*. South of Little Creek and just north of High Point is Pleasant Bay. A good landmark to the area is the plane stranded along the shore. High Point is home to an AUTEC Base, the smallest one on Andros.

Mars Bay is the southernmost settlement on Andros. Small boats only can enter at high tide and anchor in its harbor which is nothing more than a blue hole. It is a shame that only small boats can get in here as this is one of the prettiest harbors in The Bahamas with palm trees growing along the shaded beach. The settlement of Mars Bay lies a few hundred yards inland with a few very clean, if not modern, homes. In town you will find Mrs. Wilbur Smith who has given birth to 24 children. It is interesting to note that many people in Mars Bay hail from the Exumas, the Staniel Cay area in particular.

South from Mars Bay, around the southern tip of Andros the fishing and diving is fantastic but the piloting is murderous, shoals and shallow reefs abound. You will certainly have to work your way in to find any sort of shelter and then if a blow built up overnight, you could not leave until daylight.

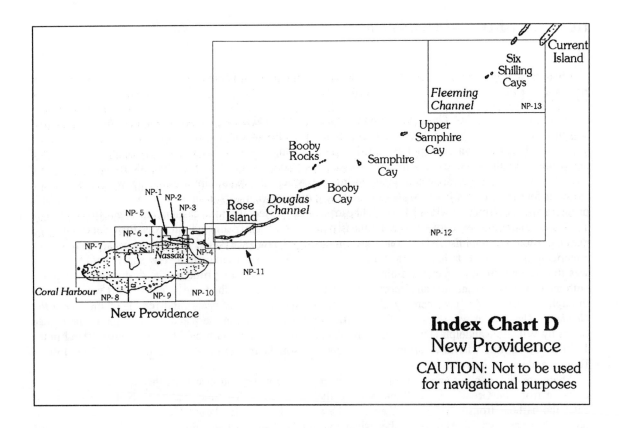

Index Chart D
New Providence
CAUTION: Not to be used
for navigational purposes

NEW PROVIDENCE

The island of New Providence lies on a corner of The Great Bahama Bank and is bounded to the west by the deep water of the Tongue Of The Ocean and along its northern and northeastern shores by the Northwest and Northeast Providence Channels. The southern shore is relatively shallow and one must pass a fair distance offshore to pass south of New Providence if bound for The Exumas. The 147 square miles of New Providence is home to over half the population of The Bahamas owing that distinction to the fact that its major city, Nassau, the capital of The Bahamas, lies along its northeastern shore. New Providence was once known as *Nequa* in Lucayan.

APPROACHES TO NEW PROVIDENCE

New Providence can be reached by a variety of shallow and deep water routes. From the Caribbean skippers can travel northward up Exuma Sound to cross the banks from Exuma. From the east vessels can approach the island from Eleuthera via the banks or in the deeper water of the Northeast Providence Channel along with vessels heading south from Abaco. From the U.S. coast most skippers take either the traditional Bimini-Chubb-Nassau route or they may pass north of Great Isaac and round the northern Berry Islands to make landfall at Nassau. This same route can be utilized by boats heading south from Grand Bahama.

From Andros it is but a short hop across the Tongue Of The Ocean to the western edge of New Providence. The only obstruction is the Autec buoy located at 24° 57.36' N, 77° 43.94' W, roughly 12.5 nautical miles from Andros and 12.5 nautical miles from Goulding Cay. The buoy was not originally in this position, it broke loose once and was replaced at its current location bearing approximately 245° from Goulding Cay.

NASSAU

Nassau is the capitol of The Bahamas and has a very long and active history in the New World. The city was originally a haven for pirates such as Henry Morgan, Edward Teach (aka Blackbeard), Charles Vane, and Calico Jack Rackham. Originally called Charles Town, Nassau was burned and looted by the Spanish and captured by the Americans in its day. Nassau has also served as home to blockade runners during the American Civil War years, rum runners during the American Prohibition years, and was quite often a stopover for drug runners from the more recent drug running years. Nassau is now touted world wide as a prime vacation destination with its beautiful beaches, near perfect weather, casinos, and nightlife.

Nassau Harbour lies between the northeastern shore of the mainland of New Providence and the extremely touristy Paradise Island, once known as Hog Island. In 1961, Hog Island was purchased by American millionaire Huntington Hartford and renamed Paradise Island. In a few short years the island was transformed from a quiet Bahamian cay into one of the world's prime tourist destinations complete with major hotels, restaurants, an airport, a golf course, marinas, and the huge *Atlantis* resort with its walk-through aquarium. An 11th century cloister was transported to the island and rebuilt in the *Versailles Gardens*. The cloister was originally from a 14th century French monastery and was brought to the United States by William Randolph Hearst. Hartford acquired the cloister and brought it to Paradise Island in the 1960's. Celebrities who have at one time or another sought refuge on Paradise Island include Howard Hughes and the Shah of Iran.

There are only two entrances to Nassau Harbour, a deep water entrance from the west and a shallower entrance from the Great Bahama Bank lying to the east. Most first time visitors to Nassau will usually enter the harbour from the west (be sure to keep a good lookout for large ship traffic; Nassau is a busy port). There are two things to remember when entering Nassau Harbour. First, all boats must call *Nassau Harbour Control* on VHF ch. 16 to request permission to enter the harbour from either the western or the eastern entrance. The controller will ask you to switch to VHF ch. 9 and proceed to inquire as to your destination, last port of call, documentation number, and destination within the harbour, whether you plan to anchor or tie up at one of Nassau's many fine marinas. Second, you must also call *Harbour Control* when leaving the harbour. *Nassau Harbour Control* is very proud of the records they maintain concerning ship traffic so don't blow off calling them in the mistaken assumption that they won't miss you. The records *Nassau Harbour Control* keeps are primarily aimed at commercial vessels. For private vessels, it is a courtesy for you to call and check in, so don't forget to do so.

Approaching Nassau at night from the north, either from the Abacos or the Berrys, your first sight will probably be the flashing white light atop the water tower at Fort Fincastle. This revolving light flashes approximately once every 5 seconds. A GPS waypoint at 25° 05.33' N, 77° 21.35' W, will place you approximately ½ nautical mile north-northwest of the harbour's western entrance. The entrance to the harbour is very straightforward and wide, lying between two rocky breakwaters. On the shore of the eastern breakwater lies the Paradise Island Lighthouse with its flashing light. At night you can of course use the red and green lights on the buoys or the range lights ashore to come in on a heading of 151°. Remember that The Bahamas use the Lateral Buoyage System-Region B, more commonly known as the three **R**'s, **Red, Right, Returning**. It is absolutely imperative that when approaching the western entrance to Nassau Harbour, you **do not mistake** the small arched bridge leading to the *Coral World* attraction on Silver Cay (1 mile east of the actual harbour entrance) for the Paradise Island Bridge. In 1996 a 45' catamaran did just that and in attempting to enter what the fatigued skipper thought to be Nassau Harbour ran aground, holed his boat, and lost her on a reef. This one incident was not the first and will most likely not be the last. The skipper who takes this for the entrance has no idea until it is too late that he is actually coming in over a reef.

The entrance to Nassau harbour during winter frontal passages can be absolutely impassable. With large northerly swells a rage will build up across the entrance closing the entrance. When this occurs the light on Paradise Island will change to red. If in doubt call *Nassau Harbour Control*.

Entering Nassau Harbour from the east, usually for vessels arriving from Exuma or Eleuthera, is also easy. A waypoint at 25° 03.50' N, 77° 14.55' W, will place you approximately 500 yards south of Porgee Rocks. From this position you should parallel the southern shore of Athol Island and Paradise Island working your way into the eastern entrance. Be careful that the bright lights on the southeastern tip of Paradise Island belonging to the Airport do not ruin your night vision and cause you to run aground on the

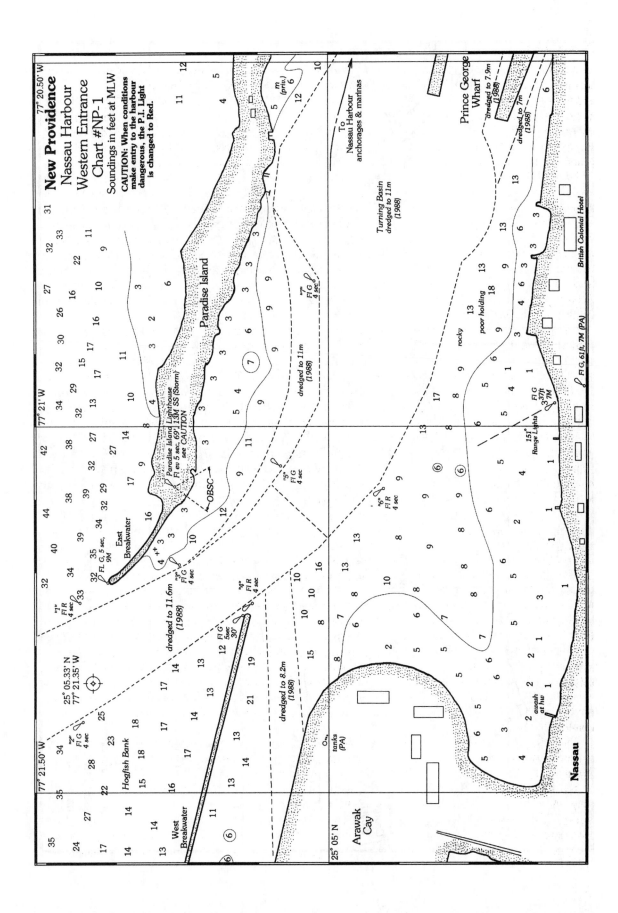

New Providence
Nassau Harbour
Western Entrance
Chart #NP-1
Soundings in feet at MLW
CAUTION: When conditions
make entry to the harbour
dangerous, the P.I. Light
is changed to Red.

Paradise Island

Paradise Island Lighthouse
Fl ev 5 sec, 69', 13M SS (Storm)
see CAUTION

OBSC

East
Breakwater

Fl G, 5 sec,
9M

"7"
Fl R
4 sec

"5"
Fl G
4 sec

"5"
Fl G
4 sec

Fl G
4 sec

dredged to 11m
(1988)

"6"
Fl R
4 sec

Prince George
Wharf

To
Nassau Harbour
anchorages & marinas

Turning Basin
dredged to 11m
(1988)

dredged to 7.9m
(1988)

dredged to 7m
(1988)

poor holding

rocky

151°
Range Lights

Fl G
37ft
7M

Fl G, 61ft, 7M (PA)

British Colonial Hotel

Nassau

"3"
Fl G
4 sec

"4"
Fl R
4 sec

"2"
Fl G
4 sec

12 Fl G
5sec
30'

dredged to 11.6m
(1988)

dredged to 8.2m
(1988)

tanks
(PA)

Arawak
Cay

awash
at hw

West
Breakwater

Hogfish Bank

25° 05.33' N
77° 21.35' W

25° 05' N

77° 21.50' W   77° 21' W   77° 20.50' W

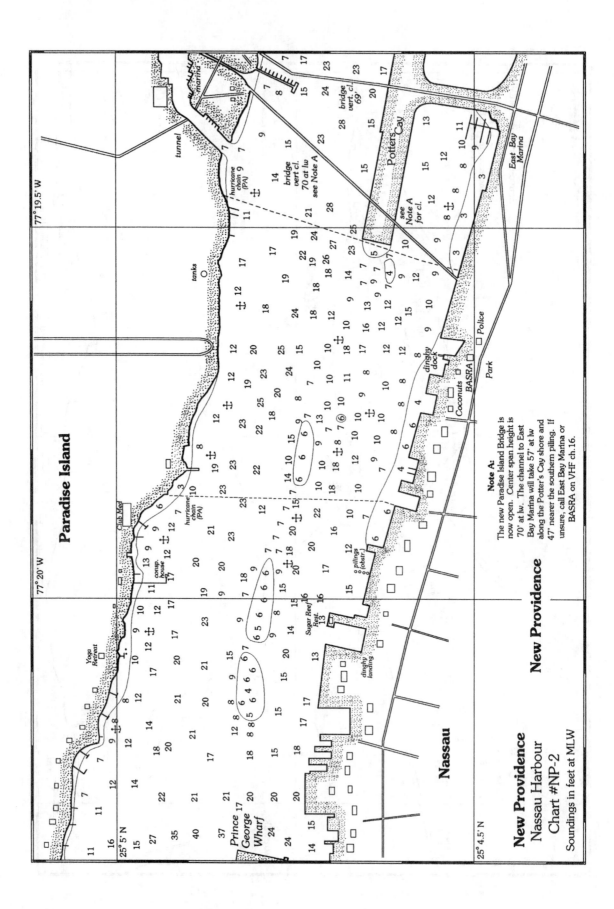

Paradise Island

New Providence

Nassau

New Providence
Nassau Harbour
Chart #NP-2
Soundings in feet at MLW

Note A:
The new Paradise Island Bridge is now open. Center span height is 70' at lw. The channel to East Bay Marina will take 57' at lw along the Potter's Cay shore and 47' nearer the southern piling. If unsure, call East Bay Marina or BASRA on VHF ch.16.

bar in *The Narrows* between Paradise Island and Athol Island. This bar is marked with a light flashing red every 5 seconds, standing 12' high and visible for 2 miles. Parallel the southern shore of Paradise Island and either head west under the bridge or south between Potter's Cay and the light which marks the rocky bar just to the east of Potters Cay. Vessels may also head for the marinas along the northern shore of New Providence east of the bridge by steering straight towards the *Nassau Harbour Club* as soon as they come abeam of the eastern point by the *Nassau Yacht Club*.

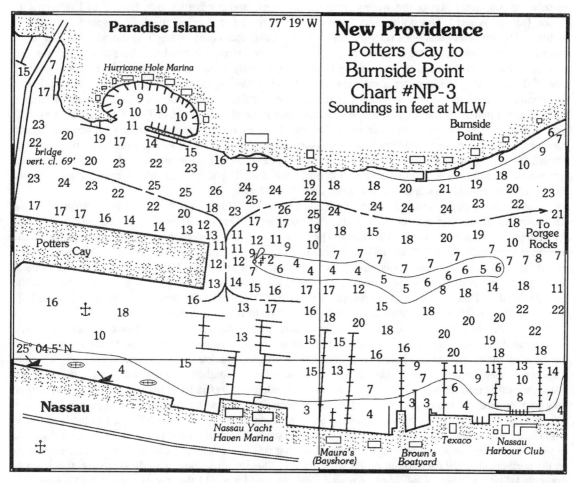

The old Paradise Island Bridge, the eastern most of the pair of bridges has a center span height of 69' at low water. The new Paradise Island Bridge, the westernmost of the pair, has a center height of 70' at its center at low water. The entrance into East Bay Marina will take 57' along the Potter's Cay shore and 47' closer to the southern piling at low water. If in doubt, contact BASRA or East Bay Marina on VHF ch. 16.

After you have entered the harbour you may wish to anchor directly off the beach at the *British Colonial Hotel,* the large pink building directly west of the cruise ship dock, but bear in mind that this is not the place to be in bad weather. The holding is poor here, only a little sand over coral, its better to anchor inside the harbour proper just past Prince George Wharf. After entering bear to port to pass Prince George Wharf and its cruise ships to starboard and head towards the conspicuous Paradise Island Bridge. Most vessels will anchor south of the center of the harbour between Potter's Cay and *Marine Diesel*. Due to the increased ship traffic in Nassau Harbour over the last couple of years, vessels anchoring west of Marine Diesel towards *Sugar Reef Restaurant* may be asked to move. Large ships come in and out of the harbour 24 hours a day to load and unload their cargo along the docks east of *Sugar Reef Restaurant* and small boats anchored in this area are definitely in danger. If you are anchored in an unsafe place *Nassau Harbour Patrol* or the *Defence Force* will most likely remind you to move.

Vessels anchoring near the western edge of Potter's Cay should be advised that large shallow draft vessels are now using the western tip of Potter's Cay for loading and unloading supplies. Also, all vessels must leave open a channel for the tug and sand barge that operates off the southern shore of the harbour just west of Potter's Cay. If you are attempting to head to *East Bay Marina*, which lies at the southwestern foot of the Paradise Island Bridge, you must give the southwest corner of Potter's Cay a wide berth. There is a shallow spot here, (4') that usually grounds a boat every week during the season. Vessels drawing over 6' should be aware of the bar of shallow water lying in the center of the harbour lying east/west.

A final word on anchoring in Nassau Harbour. Nassau Harbour is a <u>working harbour</u>. Although there is now a 5 knot speed limit in the harbour, do not expect the harbour to be a no wake zone. Large and small vessels are constantly plying the waters from east to west, and north to south, from Paradise Island to Prince George Wharf. The police and Defence Force are also enforcing the 5 knot speed limit in the harbour. Unfortunately this does not deter many of the boats that come through here, and there is a lot of wake along the channel. Some skippers may choose to anchor along the northern shore of the harbour, but you are a little more exposed to wake along there. There really is no place in the harbour where you are free of the wake of passing water taxis, jet skis, and tourist hauling drink/dive party boats. If you do not feel comfortable where you are anchored, or if the large ships are just a little too close, you should move, the sooner the better. If the tug and barge is turning down the channel west of Potter's Cay and is just off your bow, then it is time to move your vessel. Even if you are damaged, you will be hard pressed to gain compensation. There are virtually no such things as lawsuits in The Bahamas. By the way, the bottom of Nassau Harbour is littered with all kinds of junk such as car frames, refrigerators, steel cables, all matter of construction debris, a few anchors, and who knows what else. If you have problems bringing your anchor aboard you've probably hooked something or other. Good luck!

Nassau is in the early stages of privatizing Nassau Harbour. This means that a private company will one day in the near future take over control of Harbour operations. This translates to increased patrols, citations for littering, speeding, and other violations. The construction and placement of 50 large 40 ton hurricane moorings is now underway. These moorings will be placed on the bottom at certain GPS waypoints for the use of large fishing boats, mailboats, and even yachts during hurricanes. There will be no marker balls to tie to. In the event of a hurricane, one will need to get the postions of the moorings from BASRA or the Port Authority. There are also plans for yacht moorings throughout the harbour to be rented on a daily basis. Don't look for these yacht moorings until at least the turn of the century.

Nassau has just gotten over a year of steady construction of its new Paradise Island Bridge. The new bridge was designed to be a feeder to Paradise Island and its new, huge *Atlantis Resort*, and to greatly ease the flow of traffic on and off Paradise Island that so clogged the old Paradise Island Bridge. The city planners, in their infinite wisdom, have planned that each bridge handles only one way traffic, one onto the island, the other leading off. This has created some monumental traffic jams over the last year that will be long remembered. It was originally thought that the *East Bay Marina* would be cut off for sailboats of any size, but the marina will once again be hosting sailboats with masts of less than 57'. Just as the land traffic in Nassau has gotten thicker, you will notice that the water traffic will mirror that a bit. Expect an increase in water traffic and anchor accordingly. Remember that this is a working harbour. There is a new marina on the northern shore of the harbour on Paradise Island. There is also a newly dredged channel that leads to the new *Atlantis Marina*. One word of note on the marina, I am told that they charge $3.00 a foot! To further add to the confusion in the harbour, is the new Miami-Nassau ferry. This 300' futuristic, high-speed vessel (50 knots – Miami to Nassau in five hours!) can carry 700 passengers and 240 cars. Watch out for this vessel on the high seas my friends.

The large pink building on the southern shore of Paradise Island just east of the Prince George Wharf is now *Club Med*. You can anchor off its shore in 8'-12', as long as you don't mind Karaoke nights, and live entertainment most evenings. The building was once known as the *Porcupine Club*, a very exclusive retreat for millionaires, membership was limited to 125 and you had to be worth a minimum of one million dollars. It was built in 1912 on seven acres on Paradise Island by a group of American millionaires who belonged to a club in Philadelphia by the same name.

Once past the Paradise Island Bridge, some skippers seek to anchor along the southern shore of Paradise Island. Watch out for traffic here, and stay out of the channel. Some vessels pass between the Potter's Cay and the light which marks a shoal area just 100 yards to its east. This shoal area continues some ways east in the center of the harbour. After you pass between the light and Potter's Cay, steer to port and pass the rows of marinas where you may find anchorage between the last marina on your right (*Nassau Harbor Club*) and the *Nassau Yacht Club* at the extreme eastern end of the harbour. The only traffic problems you will encounter here are a few high speed boats and scores of jet skis. The *Nassau Yacht Club* is considering placing moorings off the club for visiting boaters so check with someone in the harbour to see if they are available in late 1997.

Nassau hosts quite a few marinas along its shores. On the Paradise Island side is the upscale *Hurricane Hole Marina,* catering primarily to mega-yachts on the outside and smaller vessels inside its protected cove, and the new *Paradise Harbour Club. Hurricane Hole* has 64 slips and can accommodate vessels of 7' draft inside and 11½' draft on the outside. Propane refills are available if you leave the dockmaster your tank. *Hurricane Hole* also hosts the annual *Charter Boat Show* which attracts luxury yachts from around the world. The *Hurricane Hole Fuel Dock* is situated just on the western side of Paradise Island Bridge along the southern shore of Paradise Island. They offer diesel, gas, and some dockage. Farther east lies the *Paradise Island Harbour Club.* What may seem to be a private marina is actually open to the public though they have no fuel sales. They do have a hot tub, the *Columbus Tavern,* and plans are in the works for a saltwater pool and swim-up bar.

On the other side of the harbour you may choose from *Nassau Harbour Club* where Peter the dockmaster will welcome you and make your stay as pleasant as possible. Use of the hotel's pool is included in dockage and there is a laundry on site and a shopping center with grocery, bank, and hardware directly across the street. Two fine restaurants are also on the premises, *Cuda Bay* and *Passin' Jack's. Nassau Yacht Haven* lies closest to the Paradise Island Bridge on Marina Row and boasts the *Poop Deck,* arguably the most popular restaurant and watering hole in Nassau. There is a dive shop and laundry on site and liquor stores, restaurants and shopping nearby, and propane refills are available. Vessels can have their mail forwarded to *Yacht Haven* and have it await their arrival. Send your mail to you on your boat at *Nassau Yacht Haven Marina,* East Bay Street, P.O. Box SS 5693, Nassau, New Providence, Bahamas. Between *Nassau Harbour Club and Nassau Yacht Haven* lies *Brown's Boat Basin* (where you can get hauled out), *Bayshore Marina,* and the *Texaco* fuel dock (with its dinghy dock, telephone, and small store).

East Bay Marina, lying southwest of the Paradise Island Bridge between Potter's Cay and the mainland, offers the budget minded skipper an alternative to the higher priced marinas east of the bridge but sometimes at the expense of space. During the busy part of the season the marina will be so crowded some boats must raft off another boat to fit everyone in safely. Dockmaster Alfred Dorsett is your genial host and no one is better at getting everybody tucked in comfortably and safely. *East Bay* also sells ice and RO water. Some of the docks are a little rough so be sure to have some fenders or a fenderboard handy.

Nearby is a new laundromat that everyone is raving about. *The Pondwash* on Alice Street opened up in early 1997, and is within easy walking distance of *East Bay Marina.* For more info call 393-2399.

Just west of *East Bay Marina,* west of the huge sand unloading area, lies the BASRA (**B**ahamas **A**ir **S**ea **R**escue **A**ssociation) headquarters. Their dinghy dock is available for cruisers, but remember to chain your dink; but please don't chain it up so that others are denied access to the dock, use courtesy (you remember *courtesy* don't you?). Cruisers can use the dinghy dock at BASRA for no charge except perhaps to stop in and say hello. Chris Lloyd is on duty from 9A.M. to 5P.M., five days a week and welcomes all visitors to come in and look around. Even if you can't stop, look in the window and wave, he'll appreciate it a lot more than if you pass by and treat him like a stranger. This is not New York City, people are quite a bit friendlier here. Those with a more generous bone may wish to join BASRA or donate to the dock fund to improve the dock by installing a ladder and lights. BASRA also sells charts for those in need. You can have your mail delivered to BASRA to await your arrival, but be sure to include your boat name on it so Chris can contact you and tell you that it has arrived. The address is BASRA, P.O. Box SS 6247, Nassau, Bahamas. For UPS or Fed-X packages, address it to BASRA, East Bay Street, Nassau, Bahamas, and add your cruising permit number to the package label. Besides monitoring VHF ch. 16, BASRA also monitors 2182 and 4125 on single sideband. Most of the Bahamian fishing fleet uses 4125 and this is why BASRA monitors that frequency. BASRA also has a book trade for cruisers needing new reading material. If you have some extra dog food aboard bring it with you as there are always a half-dozen or so potcakes (Bahamian dogs) hanging out around BASRA. For those cruisers who elect to anchor out, garbage may be deposited in the containers in front of the green colored Police station situated just east of BASRA. Those wanting water should cross the street at BASRA and walk 60 yards west to the small spigot and concrete tub. Do not use the faucet in front of the police station as the Police are charged for it.

Cruisers can also have mail sent either to *Sugar Reef Restaurant, Luden's Liquors,* or *Harbour Bay Liquors,* and they will gladly hold it for your arrival. *Luden's Liquors* is quite a unique place and a must stop. Owner Dennis Knowles not only has the lowest liquor prices in town but an amazing collection of knickknacks, old artifacts, tools, bottles, and an amazing collection of mounted insects along with some live birds and bees. He also has a barn owl as a security guard in his warehouse. *Luden's* is on Dowdeswell St. just one block up from Bay St. If you want your mail waiting on your arrival, have it sent to *Luden's Ltd.,* Dowdeswell St., P.O. Box 5649, Nassau, Bahamas. There is also a laundromat on

Photo by Author

All sorts of vessels call at Nassau.

premises. *Harbour Bay Liquors* sits directly across the street from the *Nassau Harbour Club*. They will hold mail for your arrival, deliver your order of liquor to your boat, and accept faxes for you. Their address is *Harbour Bay Liquors*, P.O. Box SS 6218, Nassau, Bahamas. Their fax number is 242-394-0632.

Everybody has probably heard the tales of theft in Nassau Harbour. They are true, there was quite a bit of theft over the last few years leading to an increased police presence in 1996. Perhaps this will bring this problem to an end soon. Until then however, lock up your dinghy. Also watch out for hustlers ashore, especially in the area of the roundabout, at the intersection of Mackey Street and Bay Street at the foot of the Paradise Island Bridge at Potters Cay. If you take your bicycles ashore, lock them up, even if you leave them for only a minute or two. It doesn't take long at all for someone to hop aboard one and pedal off.

Nassau offers those in need whatever they want; if it's not available locally, it can be shipped in. You will find diesel and outboard mechanics, car rentals, *UPS*, sail repair, a haulout yard, electronic repair, dive shops, shopping centers, and chandlers just as you would in any major metropolitan area. See *Appendix C* for services available.

One could write a book strictly on Nassau, what to do and what to see. The best thing to do is pick up one of the tourist guides in any of the local marinas or shoreside shops for the latest scoop on land life and night life in Nassau. Most cruisers take advantage of the excellent bus system on New Providence that covers most of the island and Paradise Island as well. And speaking of bus rides, or jitneys as they are sometimes called, you must experience them. Take a ride downtown from the marinas on any of the buses heading west on Bay Street. Each bus is different according to the driver's preference. One bus might have loud reggae blasting out of its speakers while roaring down the road pell mell to who knows where, while the next bus may have gospel or opera on its sound system and its driver more laid back in his approach to driving. All bus rides are $.75 and all have some sort of music to entertain the riders. It is actually quite pleasant to see a well mannered Bahamian board the bus and wish everyone a "Good afternoon!" as they climb aboard. Downtown is a shoppers delight with all sorts of small shops offering the usual tourists goodies plus fine gems, quality cameras, tapes and CD's, and all sorts of electronic equipment. When the cruise ships are in, downtown can be a madhouse with tourists everywhere and Bahamians trying to sell them something or braid their hair. Young people will still try to sell you drugs on the street corners but this is changing due to the increased police presence.

Nassau is a city steeped in history, from the historic over-the-hill-section with its small shops and neighborhood atmosphere, to the three forts built to protect Nassau from all sorts of rampaging rogues, Fort Montague to the east, Fort Charlotte to the west, and Fort Fincastle above the city. An interesting stop is the *Queen's Staircase*, a 102' staircase built to celebrate the 65 year reign of Queen Victoria. The 65 steps are said to be carved out of stone by slaves in the late 1700's to provide an escape from Ft. Fincastle to town without exposing the troops to fire from ships in the harbour.

There's *Blackbeard's Tower*, the Government House, Parliament, and the *Straw Market* on Bay Street. Bay Street becomes quite alive during Junkanoo with costumed dancers and musicians vying in heated competition (see *The Basics: Junkanoo*). You might want to check out the *Junkanoo Museum* with its large display of intricate Junkanoo masks and costumes. There are even some handicrafts for sale. Beware: you may not be allowed to leave the museum unless you can perform the Junkanoo dance.

There's Potter's Cay with its mailboats and fishermen selling their catch. The yellow *Produce House* is a good spot to pick up a deal on veggies in season. *Coral World's* 100' tower and the *Coral Island Observatory* is an excellent place to visit to see reef life in its natural habitat without getting wet. One of my personal favorites is the tour given by *Bacardi and Co*. You may tour the plant and check out samples of rum during Hospitality Hours, Monday through Thursday from 9 A.M. until 4 P.M. and on Fridays from 9:30 A.M. until 3:30 P.M.

The *Ardastra Gardens*, a lush tropical park, is home to 300 birds, mammals, and reptiles including a marching band of pink flamingos. It boasts 18 acres of Botanical Gardens with 600 species of flowering shrubs and trees and a equally impressive cactus garden. Equally beautiful is *The Retreat*, the home of The Bahamas National Trust (BNT). Here the BNT has preserved 11 acres of tropical gardens with tours available.

West of downtown Nassau and the *Ardastra Gardens* lies Cable Beach, named after the first cable transmission that was received in The Bahamas. Cable Beach offers fine hotels, casino gambling, and the party animal hangout in the area named *The Zoo*, just a short bus ride from town.

Southeast of Nassau is the *St. Augustine Monastery*. Designed in Romanesque style by Father Jerome of Cat Island and Long Island fame, the monastery was originally built in 1945 as a boy's school.

If you wish to rent an outboard powered boat that allows you to explore the waters around Nassau in a day, contact *Coral Reef Boat Rentals* at 242-362-2058. Owner Jeffrey Stubbs will gladly put you into one of his 90 hp outboard powered boats and tell you just where to go and where not to go to enjoy your stay in Nassau.

Photo by Kelly Becker

Paradise Island Light, Nassau.

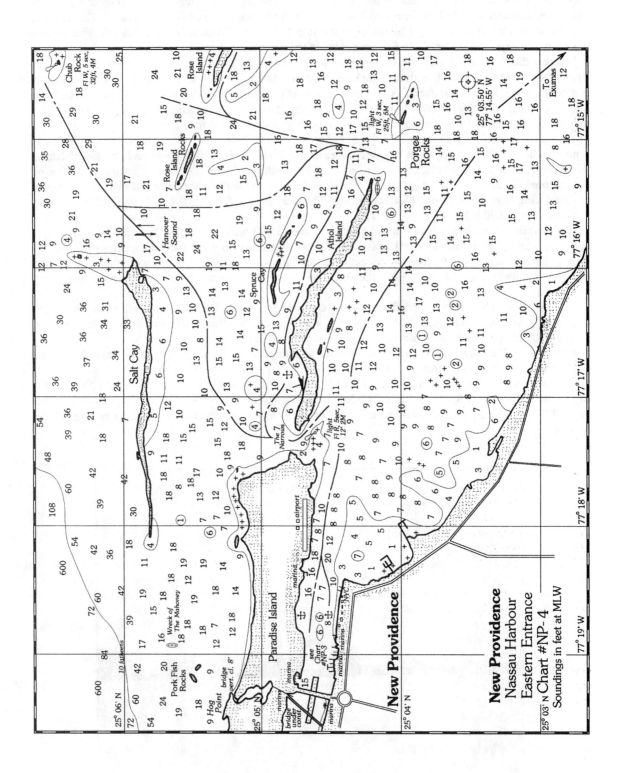

New Providence
Nassau Harbour
Eastern Entrance
Chart #NP-4
Soundings in feet at MLW

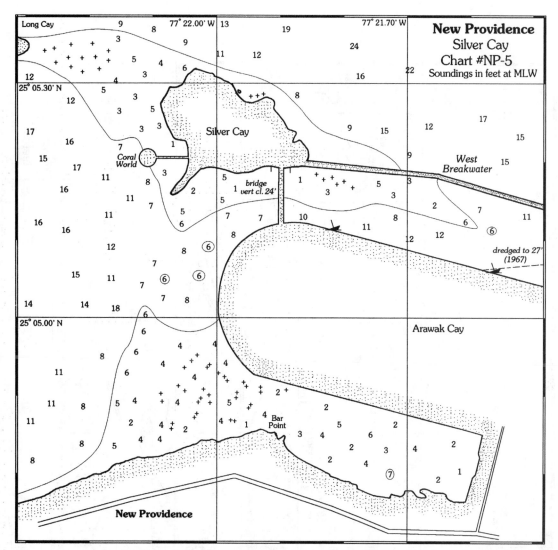

The waters surrounding New Providence are teeming with dives sites, many of which were featured in films such as *Thunderball, Never Say Never, Dr. No, Wet Gold, Splash, Cocoon, Day of the Dolphin*, and the TV series *Flipper*. Divers wanting a guided tour or simply diving information should *contact Diver's Haven* (242-393-3285), *Bahamas Divers* (242-323-2644), *Sun Divers* (242-322-3301), *Underwater Tours* (242-322-3285), or *Coral Harbour Divers* (242-326-4171). *Coral Harbour Divers* leans toward longer, deeper reef dives for more experienced divers. Stuart Coves and the Nassau SCUBA Center offer an exciting shark dive that gives divers the chance to swim up close and personal with sharks in complete safety. For a professional diving experience in the waters around New Providence, the Exumas, or Eleuthera, call *Custom Aquatics I* at 242-362-1492. Capt. Francis Young has over 20 years of experience in these waters and offers diving as well as instruction.

North of Paradise Island and Porkfish Rocks lies the wreck of the *Mahoney*. The *Mahoney* was a beautiful 212' steel hulled steam powered yacht that was once known as *Candance, Firequeen, Firebird*, and the *Bahamian*, but was never actually called the *Mahoney*. I could find no one who actually knew how it came to be called the *Mahoney*. Some say she broke in two and went down in the hurricane of 1929 while others have said that she broke her tow line on the way to being scuttled, and chose her own resting spot for eternity. Either way the hull was dynamited to prevent it from being a navigational hazard. The boiler is still intact though encrusted with fire coral. The *Mahoney* lies approximately one mile west of Salt Cay when the East Breakwater light bears 255° and the *Holiday Inn* on Paradise Island bears 210°. This is a slack water dive due to the amount of tidal action.

Just north of the *Club Med* beach on Paradise Island and in about 45' of water lies the *Trinity Caves*. This site consists of three caves with two smaller ones a few hundred feet to the west of the main group.

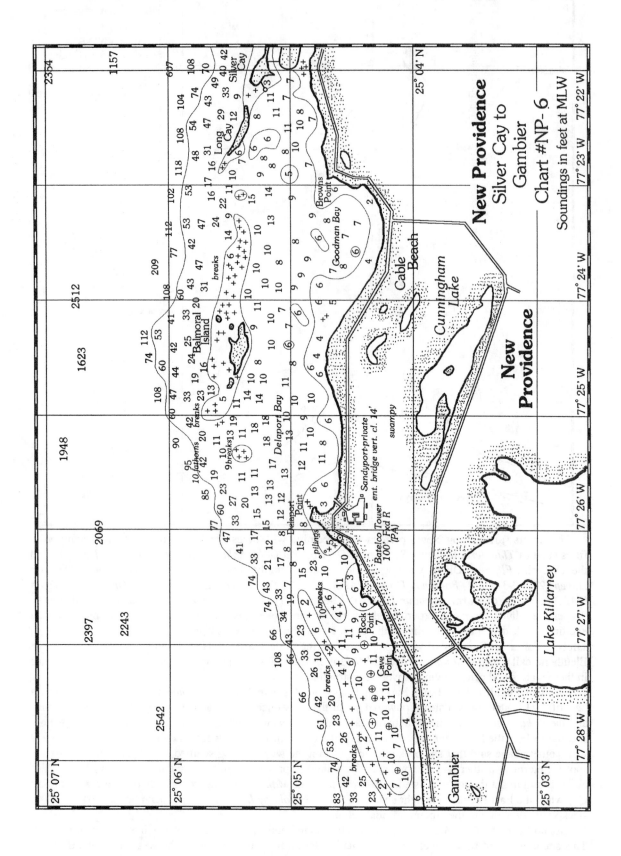

The reef consists mostly of soft corals with one stand of pillar coral. *Trinity Caves* is a protected area, no fishing is allowed at this site. This entire area along the northern shore of Paradise Island, from the tip of the eastern breakwater to north of the *Club Med* beach offers exciting diving with many deep reefs, holes, and crevices. One of the favorite dive sites around Nassau is the *Nassau Blue Hole* lying just east of New Providence. A GPS waypoint at 25° 01.7' N, 77° 08.5' W will place you virtually on top of it. Be careful anchoring and enjoy the dive.

One last word on Nassau. You may see some security officials or Police on duty with dogs or even armed with submachine guns outside many business establishments. In fact many businesses must buzz you in before you can open the door to enter. This is just part of life in Nassau: don't feel threatened, you'll get used to it. Walking downtown around the straw market you will often be accosted by Bahamians who want to braid your hair, hustle up a cab for you, give you directions for a dollar, sell you drugs, or even sing you a song for a dollar. Everyone must survive on the tourist dollars. If you are not interested simply tell them no and keep walking, they usually get the message.

NASSAU HARBOUR TO CORAL HARBOUR

Arawak Cay, lying just south of the western entrance to Nassau Harbour (Chart #NP-1 and NP-5), houses some old buildings that were once used as a Customs office and bonded warehouses. Today Arawak Cay is a prime commercial dock with many of the Nassau water barges that ply the waters between Morgan's Bluff, Andros and New Providence docking here. You will likely see a colorful Haitian sailboat anchored off the eastern tip of Arawak Cay awaiting cargo to carry back to Haiti. These stout wooden vessels pass out the eastern entrance to Nassau Harbour and work their way south through the Exumas via the mailboat route and out into Crooked Island Passage and beyond.

On DMA Chart #26309, New Providence and Nassau Harbour, a channel is shown around the southern shore of Arawak Cay with a small bridge. This channel is no longer there, it has been filled in from the bridge eastward almost to the tip of Arawak Cay. To the west of the bridge a deep channel is sometimes shown along the southern shore of Arawak Cay. If this was ever there it must have been a long time ago. The only vessels that can transit this area now are small outboard powered boats as there are numerous rocky patches along the southern shore, see Chart #NP-5.

Silver Cay, accessible from the arched footbridge leading from Arawak Cay, is home to one of Nassau's most popular attractions, *Coral World*. Here visitors can descend into the submarine world of the reef environment while staying entirely dry. Through *Coral World's* glass viewing windows one can get up close and personal with all sorts of marine creatures that inhabit the reef lying 15' below the surface along the western shore of Silver Cay. If approaching by dinghy don't expect to get close to the Coral World tower, about 100 yards out from the tower is an encircling rope and buoy network.

Long Cay lies just west of Silver Cay and is private. Though some plans were in the works in 1996-1997 to open a nightclub/restaurant with some room rentals, the owners are said to have changed direction and the island is likely to remain private for some time to come.

Balmoral Island, sometimes called Discovery Island and shown on most navigational charts as North Cay, is a private island lying just west of Long Cay and north of Cable Beach at the mouth of Goodman's Bay. The island is the private property of the *Sandals* resort on the mainland of New Providence and is used as a nude beach for its guests. Cable Beach is the home to resorts, casinos, fine restaurants, and numerous smaller hotels.

Silver Cay, Long Cay, and Balmoral Island make up a line of barrier islands that run along the outer reef just north of New Providence. The best snorkeling is along the reef in 10' on the northern shore of the island so choose a day with settled weather for your exploring. The reef is very shallow, 1'-2' in many places and there are only a few breaks. A cruising vessel should stay well offshore and not venture inside the reef as there is very little inside that is of interest to a cruising boat, unless one wishes to run aground on any of the many small, shallow heads and patch reefs strewn hereabouts. Dinghy trips should be considered instead with the mother vessel anchored in Nassau or in Old Fort Bay.

Just east of Delaport Point is the entrance channel leading into the *Sandyport Development*, a private time-share and condo community. The entrance channel takes only 1½' at low water and is often blocked by a chain. The security guard in the small shack just under the bridge (14' vert. cl.) is your contact if you wish to enter. There is nothing of interest inside unless you wish to check out the time shares for sale.

A little further west lies Gambier Village which one might mistake for an out-island town, similar in looks to Cat Island. Just offshore lies *Gambier Reef*, about one mile off the beach when Delaport Radio

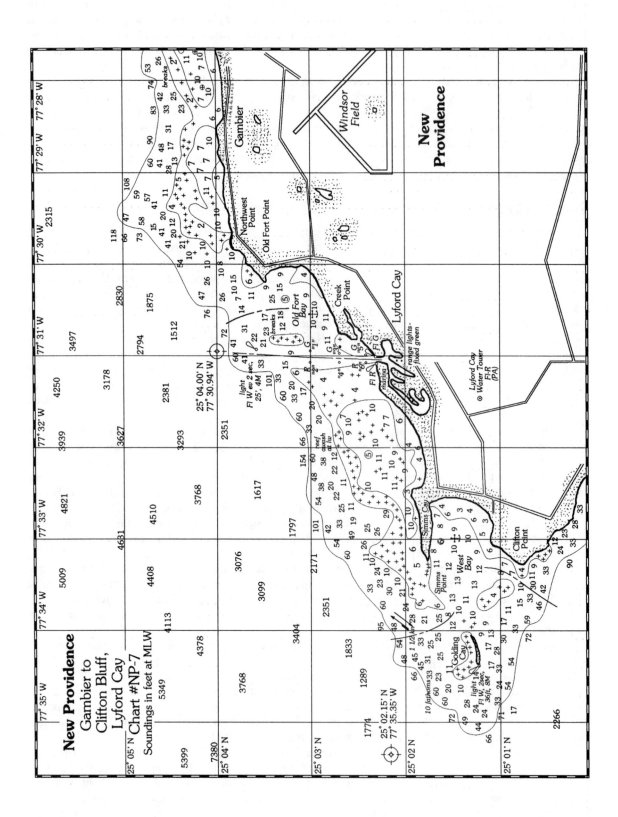

Mast bears 90° and *Gambier Cut*, a conspicuous ravine, bears 190°. The drop-off begins at about 80' with much star coral and other scattered heads before thinning out after 100'.

Just around the point lies Old Fort Bay where dolphins and mantas frolic in its harbour. Old Fort Bay is sometimes shown on charts as *Charlottesville Bay* and is a very pretty beach lined cove, excellent in easterly winds. Although Old Fort Bay offers excellent natural protection in prevailing winds it is seldom used by the cruising skipper. It's a shame, that most yachts carry on to Nassau and bypass this wonderful place. The entrance can be rather tricky and should only be attempted in good light, never at night. One must pass between the shallows off Old Fort Point and the shallows lying just east of the well-marked Lyford Cay channel.

Just a little further west lies Lyford Cay, one of the most exclusive and wealthiest residential areas in the world. *Lyford Cay Marina* is private but yachtsmen are invited to refuel (diesel and gas) and pick up whatever they may need from the nearby grocery, hardware, liquor stores and bank. Some minor repairs are available. You can contact the Asst. Harbourmaster, Gino Rahming, who is standing by on VHF ch. 16 to assist you in any way possible. During the winter season the marina is open only to members and their guests, however during the less crowded summer months it may be possible to acquire a transient slip. Inquire as to availability on VHF.

The well marked entrance channel to *Lyford Cay Marina* (see Chart #NP-7) will allow vessels of 9½' draft to enter the marina. Vessels with drafts of 11' may tie up inside solely at their own risk. A GPS waypoint at 25° 04.00' N, 77° 30.94' W, will place you approximately ¼ mile north of the light (Fl W) that marks the entrance channel to *Lyford Cay Marina*. Start steering south staying west of the light. Be sure to stay a little west of the light (if entering the marina channel keep the light to port) to avoid the shallows and breaking reefs to the east. There is a range ashore consisting of twin green lights at the marina, and a higher set of twin green lights on the hill above the marina. These lights stay on day and night. As you begin your passage south down the channel you will notice that there are three pairs of red and green daymarks, keep between these and finally you will come to the entrance jetties which have red and green lights on their respective sides. Just inside, before the marina, white floodlights shine across the opening. The fuel dock is to port immediately inside.

Divers will enjoy *Lyford Cay Reef*, a gorgeous blue-toned wall dive starting at about 80' and dropping straight down to the bottom of the Tongue Of The Ocean. The cliff begins at about 115' when the eastern tip of Goulding Cay bears 225° and the Lyford Cay Water Tower bears 150°. This area can be very rough due to the current so try to time your dive on an incoming tide. It is suggested by the pros to start your dive at the deepest depth and work your way up. You will see coral and caves with a very distinct bluish tone with a lot of sponges, sea fans, and soft corals.

Another popular dive site in the area is *Lambton Wall*. *Lambton Wall* lies about 2 miles west-northwest of Lyford Cay when the Lyford Cay Water Tower bears 125° and Simms Point bears 190°. Here a sandy slope begins at about 30' of water with scattered coral heads at a 70° angle to about 40'. At around 50' there is a 90° drop which joins another sandy slope at 115' creating an underwater range of small mountains and valleys.

Leaving Lyford Cay and heading south cruising vessels should stay well outside the fringing reef as shown on Chart #NP-7. A nice anchorage is shown in West Bay and it accessible from two directions, neither of which should be attempted at night or in poor visibility. Small shallow heads and patch reefs abound. It is possible to pass between Goulding Cay and the reefs off Simms Point in 8'-10' of water. I prefer to pass south of Goulding Cay and enter from the south, between Clifton Point and the small shallow reef strewn area to its west. This route usually gives better visibility but you are limited to 7' at low water. Never remain anchored here overnight if bad weather threatens. First, the holding is fair at best in shallow sand over a rock base. Second, if you had to leave at night you would not be able to see your way out and you would stand a better than good chance of going up on a reef or rock.

Marking the western extremity of New Providence is Goulding Cay, sometimes shown on charts as Golding Cay. Goulding Cay is a bird sanctuary and nesting area and is protected by The Bahamas National Trust. Divers will want to check out *Goulding Cay Reef* which lies just north of Goulding Cay when Clifton Point bears 130° and Goulding Cay Light bears 230°. The elkhorn coral reef begins in about 25'-30' of water about 500' north of Goulding Cay. Some of the coral comes to within 6'-7' of the surface. The reef is about 600' long in a northeast-southwest direction and vanishing into the abyss of the Tongue Of The Ocean. The reef strewn waters around Goulding Cay were once used by wreckers to lure ships to their end. A GPS waypoint at 25° 02.15' N, 77 ° 35.35' W, will place you 1¼ miles northwest of Golding Cay in deep water. From this waypoint you can head to Fresh Creek or southern Andros, or if approaching from Andros, alter your heading to parallel the northern shore of New Providence on your way to the western entrance to Nassau Harbour. Caution: Do not attempt to steer directly for the waypoint off the western entrance to Nassau Harbour from the waypoint northwest of Golding Cay, you will run hard aground. Instead, follow the charts and stay well offshore avoiding the fringing reefs west of Nassau.

SCUBA enthusiasts may wish to dive the *Porpoise Pen* which is situated on *Clifton Wall*. The *Pen* lies approximately one mile south of Clifton Point when Clifton Point bears 345° and the eastern edge of Goulding Cay bears 320°. The reef was used in the movie *Day of the Dolphin* and the TV series *Flipper*.

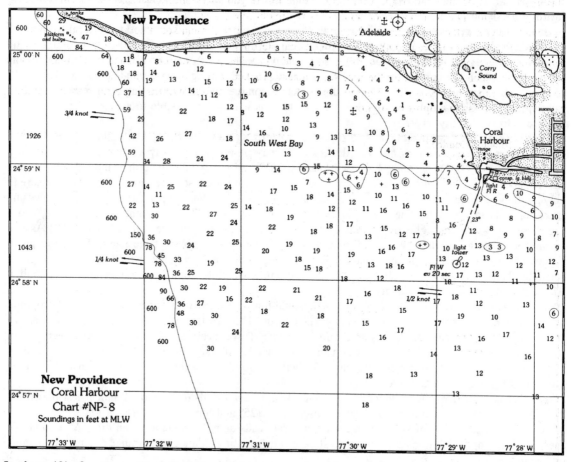

In about 40' of water scattered heads begin to appear on a sandy bottom and slope down at a 70° angle to about 80'-90' before dropping off vertically into, you guessed it, the Tongue Of The Ocean. The *Porpoise Pen* is noted for its variety and abundance of sea life including the occasional pelagic species. Along *Clifton Wall* is a site called *The Chute* a huge crevasse in the wall with sand spilling through. *The Chute* sits in about 40' of water and is itself 20' wide and 20' tall before spilling over the lip of the wall. There is also a cave and chimney at the site but these are only for the experienced diver.

From Goulding Cay around to Coral Harbour the western shore begins to take on a rocky, barren, bluff sided appearance until you round the point past Clifton Pier. The caves in the bluffs were once shelter for Lucayan Indians and later on pirates. Just off Clifton Point you will see two large platforms and numerous large buoys. These are for the large fuel ships to tie to when they offload their cargoes to the New Providence fuel companies. Give this area a wide berth.

Once past the fuel platforms you will make out the point at Coral Harbour, Chart #NP-8. It will look like a very large, square sided bluff. In reality it is a low jetty with a large abandoned concrete high rise just south of it that from a few miles off resembles a large cliff. Ashore between Clifton Point and Coral Harbour lies the town of Adelaide. Adelaide has the distinction of being one of the first black settlements established in New Providence after the abolition of slavery. Southwest Bay can be used as a sheltered anchorage in strong north-northeast winds.

As you approach the entrance to Coral Harbour you will notice the large light tower lying about a mile offshore. This is shown on current DMA charts as being abandoned. It is far from abandoned. It flashes white approximately every 20 seconds to direct the Royal Bahamas Defence Force vessels to their base inside Coral Harbour. The best approach into Coral Harbour is to steer toward the light to avoid the shallows just offshore between Clifton Point and Coral Harbour. Pass on either side of the light and take up a course of approximately 23° for the entrance. The entrance channel is very conspicuous, lying between two rock jetties just north of the abandoned concrete high rise. The easternmost jetty has a red flashing light, remember red, right, returning. Once inside you will notice the large Defence Force base just to starboard. The base was once an elegant marina before it folded in 1972. As you work your way past the base you will come to the canals that make up the small, palm-clad community of Coral Harbour.

Vessels transiting the area south and west of Coral Harbour must be aware of the Defence Force firing range that stretches approximately 9 miles west and 8½ miles south of the entrance to Coral Harbour. When the Defence Force is using the area for gunnery practice they will make an announcement on VHF ch. 16 to all concerned mariners. Vessels engaged in gunnery practice will display a red flag by day and red fixed or red flashing lights by night.

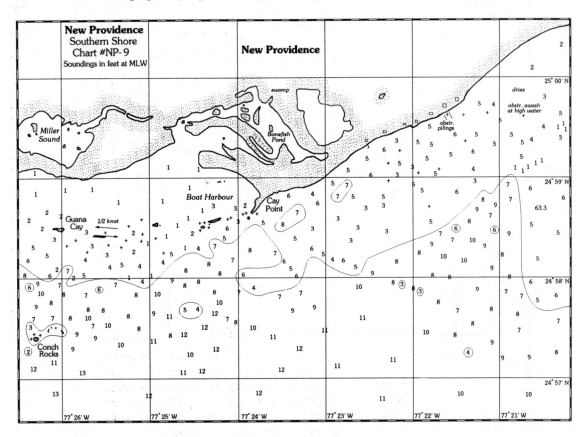

THE SOUTHERN SHORE OF NEW PROVIDENCE

There is really not much to say about the southern shore of New Providence, Chart #'s NP-10, and NP-9. The shore is generally low-lying and fringed with many stands of casaurinas. There are absolutely no facilities hereabouts. The only thing the southern shore has to offer is some good bonefishing in places like Malcolm Creek and the Bonefish Pond inside Cay Point. The waters inshore dry at low water in many places as far as ¼ mile or more out from shore. There are many scattered heads, patch reefs, shallow bars, and the wreckage of a few old boats to maneuver around. Ashore you will see a few scattered houses and one small community.

Vessels wishing to pass south of New Providence, say perhaps from Andros to Exuma, should give the southern shore of New Providence a wide berth. As a very minimum I would suggest passing 2½ nautical

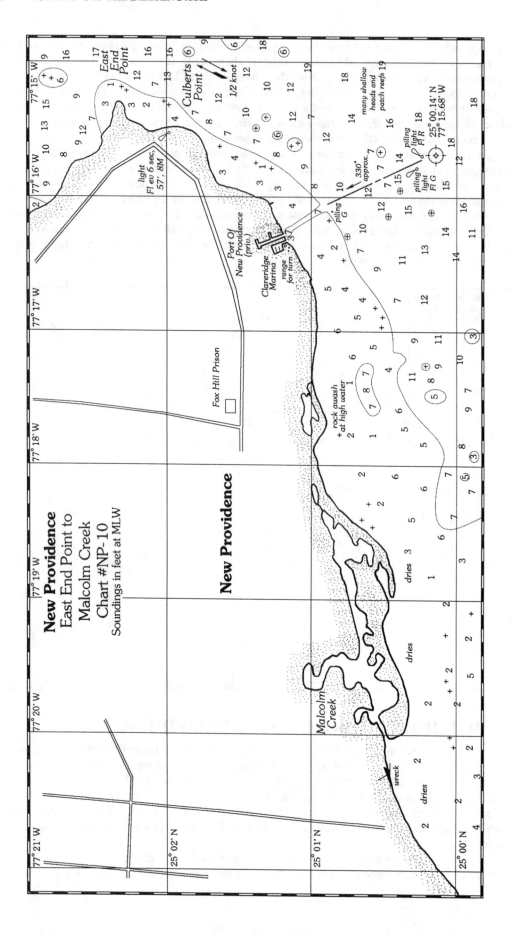

New Providence
East End Point to
Malcolm Creek
Chart #NP-10
Soundings in feet at MLW

New Providence

Fox Hill Prison

Malcolm Creek

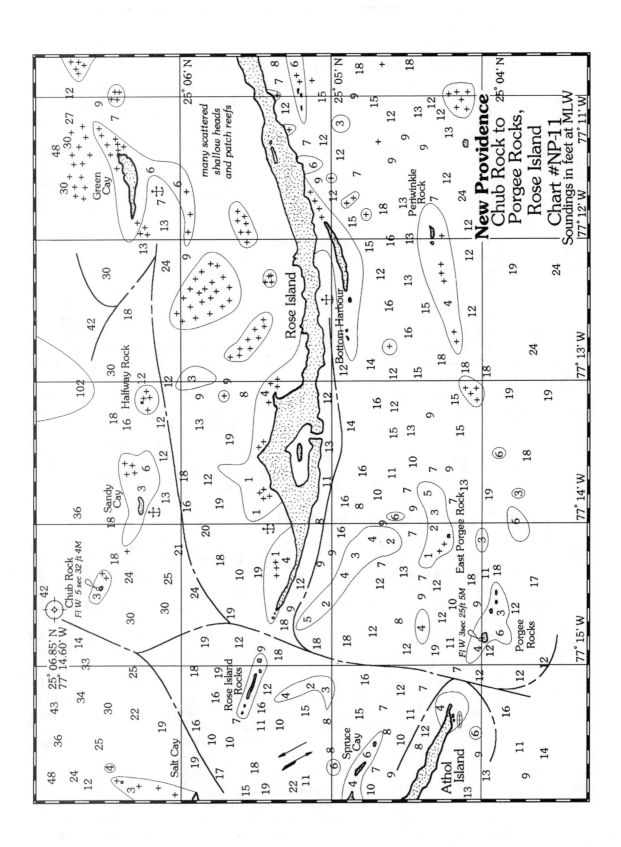

miles south of any land masses. If leaving Coral Harbour pass well south of the offlying rocks just south of Coral Harbour as well as Conch Rocks (Chart #NP-9).

THE EASTERN SHORE OF NEW PROVIDENCE

The eastern shore of New Providence (Chart #'s NP-4 and NP-10) is shallow close to shore while the deeper waters are strewn with reefs, some with less than six feet over them at low water. The only places of interest to visiting yachtsmen along this shore are the Port of New Providence, a very nice canal community and Clareridge Marina with its full service haulout facility.

The entrance channel to the Port of New Providence (Chart #NP-10) serves both facilities. Some folks say that navigating from the eastern entrance to Nassau Harbour around the eastern tip to the *Port of New Providence* is akin to stumbling through a minefield, in fact some call the area "the minefield." There are definitely some shallow heads on the way, even lining the edges of the entrance channel itself, but with good visibility it should be no problem. Do not attempt this at night unless you are extremely familiar with these waters; even then I cannot recommend transiting this area.

A GPS waypoint at 25° 00.14' N, 77° 15.68' W, will place you approximately ¼ nautical mile southeast of the first set of markers that define the entrance channel. The markers flash red and green at night. Line up between the first set of markers and steer towards the entrance to the complex on a course of 330°. Ashore you will see some large light pink condos that look white from offshore. The entrance is just to the west of these buildings. A little further down the channel you will come to a pair of daymarks, stay between these and soon you will be upon the jettied entrance channel to the Port of New Providence. Boaters wishing to visit *Clareridge Marina* should look to port and pick up the two metal poles ashore and use them as a range. Currently they are rust colored but are slated to be painted orange in 1997. The route into *Clareridge Marina* will take 3½' at low water and just over 6' at most highs. The route into the *Port of New Providence* can handle 6' at low water.

Clareridge Marina is basically a small boat marina. They are often overlooked but have a lot to offer. Besides selling diesel and gas, they are a full service boat yard. They have a travel-lift and can haul out boats to 40 tons and 55'; longer boats must call with details if needing a haulout. Here you can get a bottom job, all sorts of hull repair, even have your hull Awl-Gripped. No mechanical repairs are performed here unless you can get a mechanic to drive over from Nassau. A couple of cruisers leave their boat on the hard here during the off-season and the rates are very competitive for that service. The marina does not really cater to transients as they have no showers, laundry, and no stores closer than a mile and a half.

ST. PETER, THE TURTLE MAN OF NASSAU

Kelly and I were sailing along on the Great Bahamas Banks one fall day when we saw what we thought was a man in the water, his head bobbing along just above the surface, miles from anywhere. On approaching we discovered it was a huge loggerhead sea turtle the size of a car hood. Nothing out of the ordinary until you realize that these magnificent animals are getting scarce and harder to find. When Columbus first sailed in these waters he noticed some areas where there were scores and scores of turtles which the great explorer mistook for rocks in the water.

Throughout The Bahamas, Bahamians have been catching and raising turtles for centuries. Deep holes along the shores of some of these rocky cays were used as turtle kraals (pens) and owners built up walls around their lips while other kraals were carved out of the native limestone to farm the animals. Then, as today, the turtles were highly prized for their tasty meat and for the beauty of their shell, which is used for making jewelry and other items. Sailing ships once kept turtles aboard as a source of fresh meat. The turtles would be kept on their backs so their weight would not crush their lungs and they were kept constantly wet. Turtles could last indefinitely like this as long as they were fed and kept wet.

Today's ships stock huge freezers to the brim before departure guaranteeing the crew and passengers a steady supply of meat for their voyage. Only a few islanders, mostly in the more remote areas still eat sea turtles and that will always be. It's a matter of survival. Unfortunately some trendy restaurants throughout the cays still have turtle on their menu, turtle steaks and turtle soup. Tasty? Absolutely! Pricey? You bet! Politically correct? That depends on public opinion which, like the weather, is subject to change. Apparently enough tourists shell out the bucks to experience this unique gastronomic delight to keep turtle on the menu. When they return home, will they go to their local supermarket and buy a few turtle steaks?

No. Will they put it on their weekly menu? No. Will they petition their schools to put it on the lunch menu? Of course not. It's only an island t'ing mon!

Have you ever gotten close to one of these large pelagic turtles? Have you ever swam with one? Have you ever touched one, looked in their gentle, doe-like eyes? They are quite graceful in their movements and inspiring to watch. By now some readers are probably comparing me to a child who has named a pet pig and refuses to allow it to become an entree. Get real! I love bacon but turtles were not raised for slaughter. They are majestic ocean roamers who suffer enough from eating all the plastic that we humans throw overboard to clog up their digestive systems. I am told that some of the larger turtles can be over 200 years old. So old that they may have witnessed the coming of the Loyalists in 1783. Now they are fast going the way of the whales, all for a positive cash flow in some dingy tourist dive with sticky salt and pepper shakers, dirty tablecloths, surly help, and a 15% gratuity (Gratuity? What for?) added to the check.

Nassau is the capitol of The Bahamas, both politically and culturally. Like all major metropolitan areas, Nassau has always had, and still has, more than its share of shysters and heisters, shucksters and hucksters, con-men and thieves, and all sorts of other rogues whose only intention is making a buck and damn all the rules. Amidst all this survives a saint with a heart as big as all The Bahamas; Saint Peter, the turtle man of Nassau.

Peter Attaloglou was born in Athens, Greece, and shortly after his marriage to a Bahamian woman of Greek descent he moved to Nassau where he is now the dockmaster of the Nassau Harbour Club. One day in Nassau Peter witnessed the slaughtering of a large Hawksbill turtle, a protected sea turtle highly valued for its meat and shell. If you have ever witnessed the butchering of a large sea turtle you may understand, if you haven't then I will spare you the gory details. The needless butchering of this peaceful, gentle animal set Peter on a course that has been spiritually rewarding yet financially draining. Peter now goes far out of his way to save the large sea turtles that fishermen often bring in to the dock.

In Nassau the local fishermen can sell turtle meat for $4 a pound to the restaurants that still keep it on their menu. Somewhere else they can then scrounge another $50 or more for the shell and maybe a little extra change for the head. For a 175 pound turtle a fisherman can reap $400-$500 selling it this way. Peter on the other hand cannot afford to compete with the prices the restaurants pay. He can only afford at most, $1 a pound, but that way fishermen get quick, easy money and don't have to bother with cleaning up the mess of butchering the creature. In 1994, Peter spent over $1,000 of his own money just on purchasing turtles, not to mention spending $50 or more a week per turtle for food.

Peter's turtles are well cared for. Peter keeps them in a 60' x 20' x 4' deep pen at the Nassau Harbour Club. Peter has a marine biologist friend who takes blood samples of each one to find out where they are from and then tags the turtles. When his charges grow strong enough Peter turns them over to Ray Darville, the Park Warden at The Exuma Cays Land and Sea Park, who releases them within the protected confines of the Park. Until Peter and Ray joined forces Peter would release his turtles in the waters surrounding New Providence.

Most turtles come to Peter in fairly good shape, but thoroughly exhausted and very scared. Fishermen, after spotting the turtle, will swim with it, chasing it sometimes for hours until the creature tires and can be wrestled into the boat. After a week or so in its new surroundings the turtle will begin to settle down and eat again. Once Peter bought a large Hawksbill turtle that had been speared through the neck. Peter tended to his wounds as best he could, but the turtle was unable to dive to eat, it could only eat what was on the surface. So Peter, who usually feeds a turtle 50 pounds of conch a week, packed conch meat inside lettuce so that it would float. This Hawksbill turtle is now a resident of Exuma Park. Peter soon picked up another large Hawksbill that had a huge chunk bitten out of its side by a shark. Local turtle experts were "too busy" to help so Peter took it upon himself to find some antibiotics and treat the turtle himself. He would slice open conch meat and place the antibiotics inside. The wound healed and the turtle is free once more roaming the waters of the Exumas. Peter cannot save every turtle that is brought into Nassau Harbour, but what he does is certainly a start. Peter sadly admits that the larger turtles are getting fewer and fewer. He cannot even remember the last time he saw a leatherback.

Peter has done all this of his own accord and asks nothing in return. His satisfaction comes on the day of their release, that's Peter's payoff. Personally I believe there should be a fund to ease Peter's self-sacrifice but Peter does not see it that way, the burden is his and his alone, he asks for no help. So if you're sailing through the New Providence area or the northern Exumas, and you should have the opportunity to see a large sea turtle in the wild you can thank the saints above, primarily St. Peter over in Nassau.

NEW PROVIDENCE TO ELEUTHERA

The cays stretching from New Providence to the northern tip of Eleuthera offer good diving and although there is no true all-weather anchorage, there are several lee-side anchorages available. In northerly winds it is possible to traverse the waters to Eleuthera on the southern side of the cays while in southerly winds you can pass to the north of the cays for a slightly calmer ride. In strong easterlies it will be tough going either way.

NASSAU TO ROSE ISLAND

Athol Island lies just east of Paradise Island and was once, and still is, used as a quarantine island. In fact some of the older charts show the quarantine buildings. The last time Athol Island was used in this capacity was during the Haitian influx to The Bahamas in the early 1990's. Many refugees were quarantined on Athol Island and some lost their lives trying to swim *The Narrows* to freedom. *The Narrows* will accommodate a vessel with of 7½' draft at low water. The channel lies along the Athol Island shore between The Narrows Light and Athol Island and is situated in a southeast-northwest direction. Do not attempt to pass west of the light, unless you have a very shallow draft, as all you will find are rocks. This can be a tricky area, there is a lot of current here. If heading north through The Narrows (see Chart #NP-4) head east past The Narrows Light and then turn and head back to the west/northwest staying halfway between the light and Athol Island. Watch out for the shallows just south and southeast of the light. Once through The Narrows you can take up a course to a settled weather anchorage that lies off the northern shore of Athol Island just off the small beach. Holding is fair at best so make sure your anchor is set well here. Just northeast of this anchorage lies the new Spruce Cay complex which you can't miss. Its landmark lighthouse resembles the real thing. Spruce Cay is slated to open up in 1997-1998 as a nightclub and restaurant complex. Just off the western tip of Spruce Cay are some isolated reefs that snorkelers will enjoy. Vessels can transit either north or south of Spruce Cay as there is deep water off both shores.

Salt Cay, also called Blue Lagoon Island and lying north/northwest of Athol Island, is an enormous tourist draw in the Nassau area. It is home to 12 beaches as well as a huge entertainment center that seats 1,000 people. Other popular tourist stops on Salt Cay are *Sting Ray City* where you can dive with numerous manta rays, *Blue Lagoon*, and the *Dolphin Encounter* where you can swim with their playful dolphins. The island is for rent when there are no cruise ships due in the harbour and the owners discourage any visits by dinghy, they request that you take one of their boats over from Nassau.

Chub Rock, as shown on Chart #'s NP-4 and NP-12, is an important little piece of real estate in the New Providence area. Smaller than a large truck, this low, flat, rock's only redeeming quality is its light which marks the heavily traveled passage between the banks and the Northeast Providence Channel. Boats leaving the banks pass between Salt Cay and Chub Rock keeping Chub Rock to starboard to head out into the deeper water. From here you can take up your course to Abaco, the Berry Islands, Grand Bahama, Royal Island, or Spanish Wells. To leave by Chub Rock from Nassau you must first pass through The Narrows between Paradise Island and Athol Island. Once through The Narrows, head to a position halfway between Salt Cay and Rose Island Rocks. Watch out for the shallow rocky areas shown on Chart #NP-4 on this route. Once past Salt Cay and Rose Island Rocks head for a position northwest of Chub Rock giving Chub Rock a wide berth to avoid the reef just off its western end. One can also head to Porgee Rock and then take up a northerly course to pass between the western tip of Rose Island and Rose Island Rocks. From this position you can then steer approximately northwest to round Chub Rock well off. A GPS waypoint at 25° 06.85' N, 77° 14.60' W, will place you approximately 200 yards north of Chub Rock.

Athol Island has some nice diving just off its shores. Off the southeastern tip of Athol Island is the *LCT* wreck which is visited on a regular basis by dive boats from Nassau. It is the wreckage of a landing craft that was used as the scene for an underwater fight in the James Bond thriller *Thunderball*. The bow sits in 5' of water while the stern lies in 13'. To find the *LCT* wreck line up Porgee Rock Light on a bearing of 110° and the eastern tip of Athol Island at 30°. Along the northern shore are some isolated reefs that some of the local dive boats frequent near the anchorage shown on Chart #NP-4.

At the southeastern end of Athol Island is the *LCT Wreck* which is visited on a regular basis by dive boats from Nassau. It is the wreckage of a World War II vintage landing craft that was used to ferry freight to Exuma after the war years. She was purposely ran aground at her present location by her crew who could wanted to salvage her cargo as she left Nassau and began taking on water. The wreck was used as the scene for an underwater fight in the James Bond thriller *Thunderball*. The bow sits in 5' of water while the stern lies in 13'. To find the *LCT Wreck* line up Porgee Rock Light on a bearing of 110° and the eastern tip of Athol Island at 30°.

ROSE ISLAND TO CURRENT ISLAND

Rose Island is a popular anchorage for both visiting cruisers and local boaters. The cay can get quite crowded on weekends and holidays. The most popular anchorage is on the south side of Rose Island at Bottom Harbour as shown on Chart #NP-11. Vessels heading to this anchorage from Nassau should head east to Porgee Rock and head northward between Athol Island and Porgee Rock towards the western tip of Rose Island. Once you arrive at the western tip of Rose Island follow the shoreline eastward to anchor in Bottom Harbour.

Another fine anchorage is just off the nice beach on the northern side of Rose Island just east of its western tip. From Nassau you can head for a position between Salt Cay and Rose Island Rocks. Pass between them and head east to work your way in to the Rose Island shore as shown on Chart #NP-11. You can also use the route from Porgee Rocks to the western end of Rose Island. Once at the western tip of Rose Island, pass between Rose Island and Rose Island Rocks and turn to starboard to work your way into the anchorage as shown on Chart #NP-11. Watch out for the reefs at the western tip of Rose Island.

North of Rose Island lies Sandy Cay, sometimes called Gilligan's Island. Truth be known, Sandy Cay had nothing to do with the popular TV show, it seems the story was told and grew with the retelling. All the better for Sandy Cay perhaps. There is a nice anchorage off the southern shore of Sandy Cay that is good in north to northeast winds or settled weather.

North of Rose Island and east of Sandy Cay lies Green Cay and *Green Cay Reef*. There is an excellent anchorage on the southern shore of Green Cay. There are two routes to access this anchorage from Nassau. The first is to go outside at Chub Rock and steer east until you can enter the anchorage at Green Cay as shown on Chart #NP-11. A shorter route is to head east from Sandy Cay passing just south of Halfway Rock avoiding its reefs and the large reef south of it. Never try to head east from Green Cay along the shoreline of Rose Island, the area is foul with scattered shallow heads and reefs. Small outboard powered boats even have trouble here at times. Green Cay itself has a nice reef a bit off its northern shore with huge coral heads in 35'-50' of water. The heads themselves rise up some 25'-30' off the bottom. *Green Cay Reef*, a beautiful pillar coral reef lies southwest of Green Cay when the southern edge of Green Cay bears 80° and the western tip of Green Cay bears 45°.

The cays from Rose Island to Current Island have little to offer to cruising boats though some offer a lee anchorage in settled weather. Fishing and diving on the numerous reefs is superb. There are two deep water channels, Douglas Channel and Fleeming Channel, from the Northeast Providence Channel and the banks south of the cays. Douglas Channel lies between the eastern end of Rose Island and Booby Cay as shown on Chart #NP-12. A GPS waypoint at 25° 10.00' N, 77° 05.50' W, will place you approximately 1 mile northwest of the channel while a GPS waypoint at 25° 07.80' N, 77° 03.00' W, will place you approximately 1 mile southeast of the channel. Pass between Rose Island and Booby Cay giving the reefs off the eastern end of Rose Island a wide berth. Fleeming Channel is used far more by cruising boats wishing to traverse the waters between the Abacos and the Exuma or northern Eleuthera and the northern Exumas. A GPS waypoint at 25° 16.00' N, 76° 55.30' W, will place you ¼ mile north of the entrance to Fleeming Channel while a GPS waypoint at 25° 15.50' N, 25° 15.50' W, will place you approximately ¼ mile south of the channel entrance as shown on Chart #NP-13. Fleeming Channel is wide, deep, obstruction free, and marked by lights on both sides.

Further northward, near Current Island, a GPS waypoint at 25° 18.10' N, 76° 53.60' W, will place you approximately ½ mile southwest of Little Pimlico Island as shown on Chart #NP-13. This waypoint will allow you to pass south of Little Pimlico Island to access the southern tip of Current Island, or to parallel the eastern shore of Little Pimlico and Pimlico Island, or the western shore of Current Island to head to Current Cut. For more information on this route see the chapter *Eleuthera: The Current and Current Cut*.

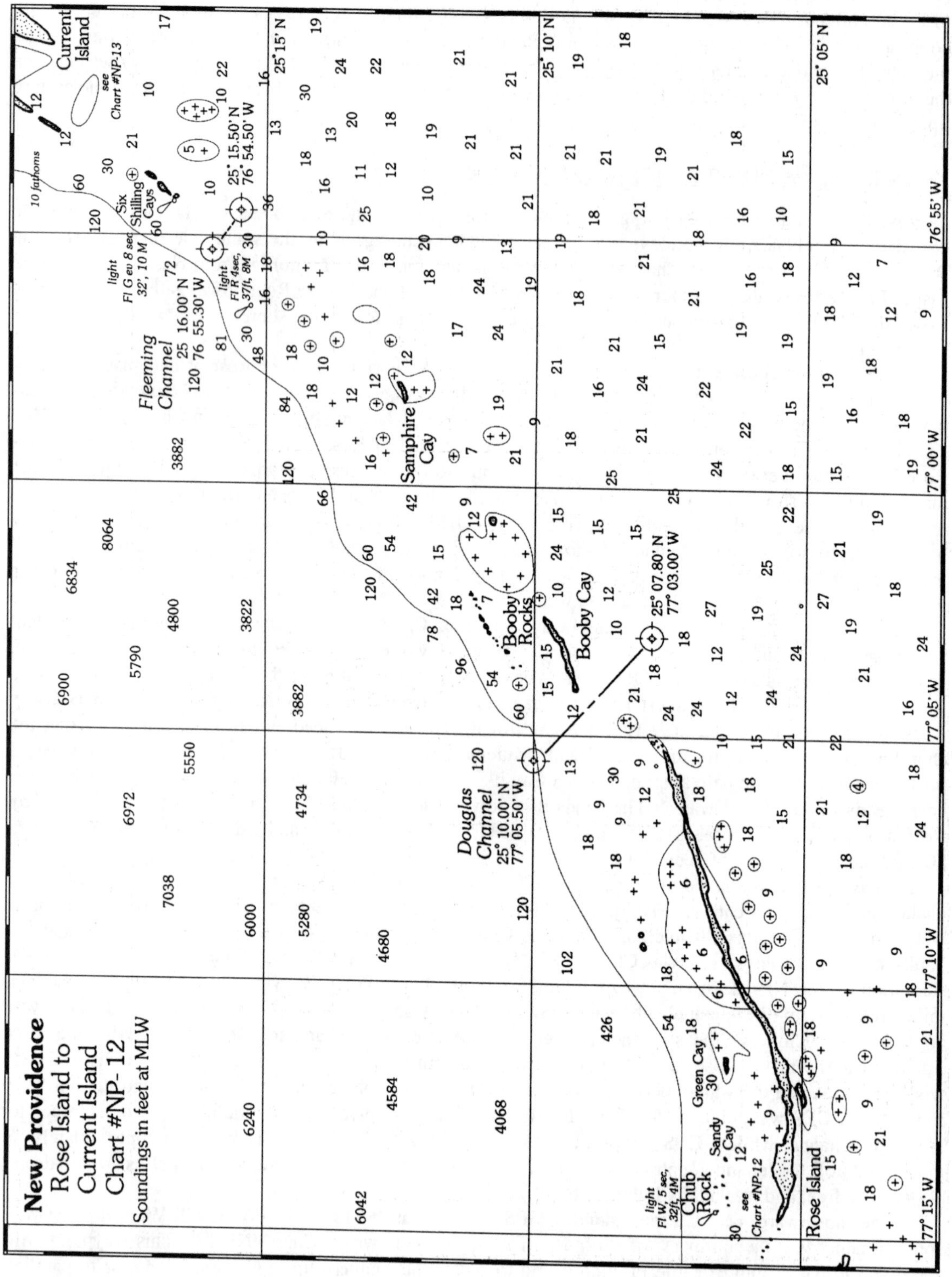

New Providence
Rose Island to
Current Island
Chart #NP-12
Soundings in feet at MLW

Current Island

see Chart #NP-13

10 fathoms

Six Shilling Cays

60 Cays

light Fl G ev 8 sec, 32', 10 M

light Fl R 4sec, 37ft, 8M

Fleeming Channel
25 16.00' N
76 55.30' W

25° 15.50' N
76° 54.50' W

Samphire Cay

Booby Rocks

Booby Cay

25° 07.80' N
77° 03.00' W

Douglas Channel
25° 10.00' N
77° 05.50' W

Green Cay

Sandy Cay

Chub Rock

light Fl W, 5 sec, 32ft, 4M

see Chart #NP-12

Rose Island

25° 15' N
25° 10' N
25° 05' N

77° 15' W   77° 10' W   77° 05' W   77° 00' W   76° 55' W

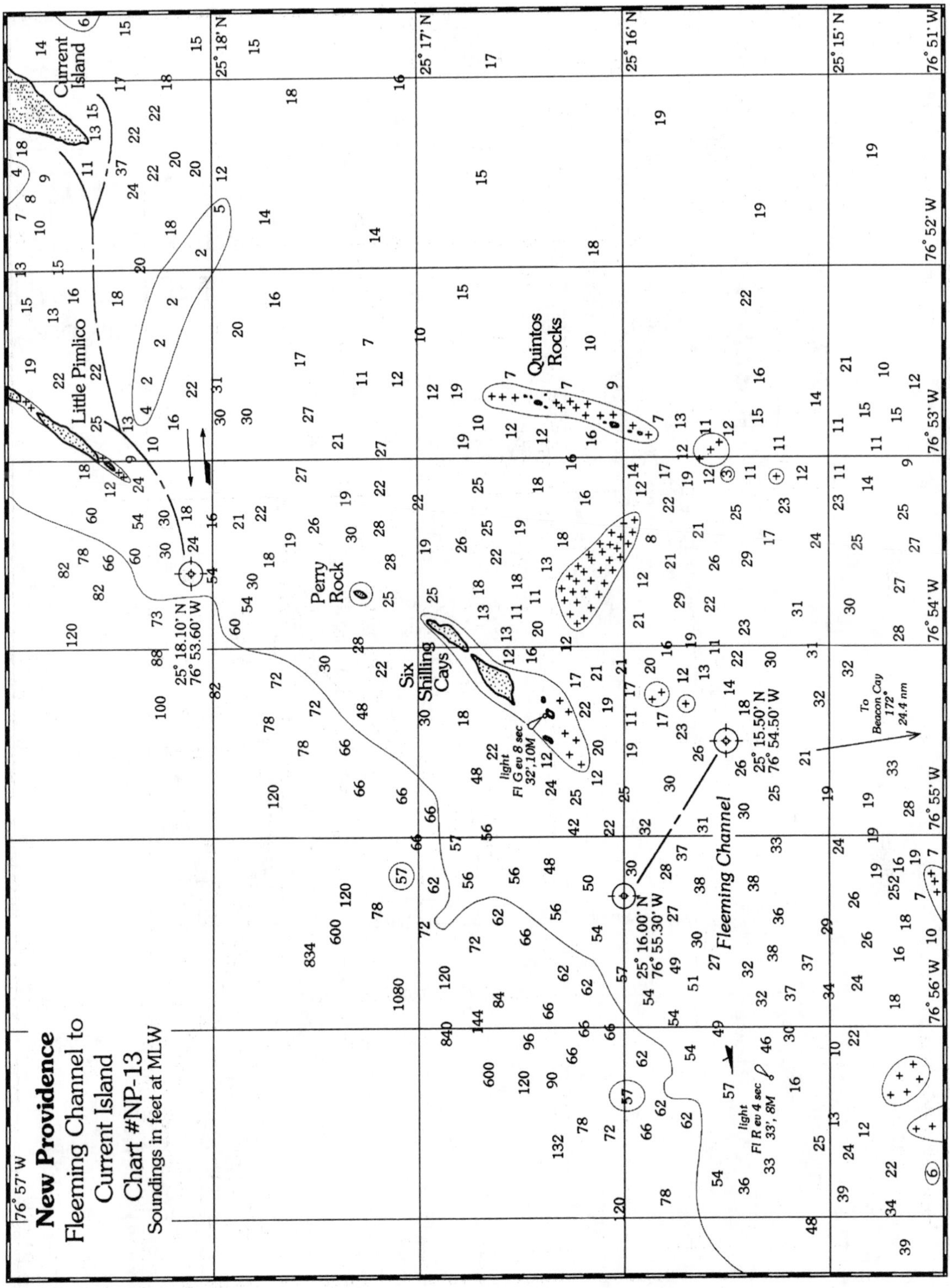

76° 57' W

New Providence
Fleeming Channel to
Current Island
Chart #NP-13
Soundings in feet at MLW

Current Island

Little Pimlico

Perry Rock

Six Shilling Cays

Quintos Rocks

light
Fl G ev 8 sec
32', 10M

25° 18.10' N
76° 53.60' W

25° 15.50' N
76° 54.50' W

25° 16.00' N
76° 55.30' W

Fleeming Channel

To
Beacon Cay
172°
24.4 nm

light
Fl R ev 4 sec
33', 8M

25° 18' N
25° 17' N
25° 16' N
25° 15' N

76° 51' W
76° 52' W
76° 53' W
76° 54' W
76° 55' W
76° 56' W

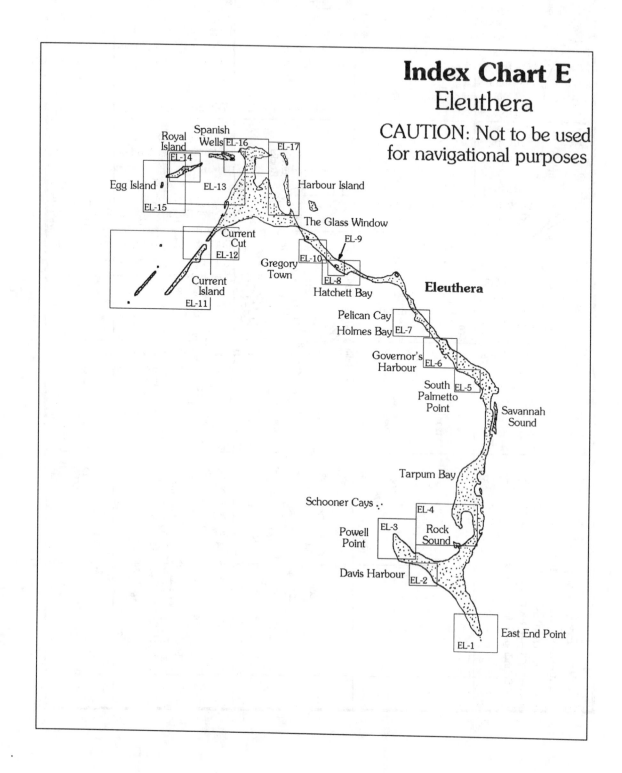

Index Chart E
Eleuthera
CAUTION: Not to be used
for navigational purposes

Royal Island
Spanish Wells   EL-16   EL-17
EL-14
Egg Island   EL-13   Harbour Island
EL-15
The Glass Window
Current Cut   EL-9
EL-12   Gregory Town   EL-10
Current Island   EL-8
EL-11   Hatchett Bay

Eleuthera

Pelican Cay
Holmes Bay   EL-7

Governor's Harbour   EL-6

South Palmetto Point   EL-5

Savannah Sound

Tarpum Bay

Schooner Cays   EL-4
Powell Point   EL-3   Rock Sound

Davis Harbour   EL-2

East End Point
EL-1

ELEUTHERA

Eleuthera is an island of firsts. It was the first republic in the New World with the first Constitution, and the first Parliament. The first inhabitants of Eleuthera of which there is proof were the peaceful Lucayan Indians who were enslaved by the marauding Spanish in the early 1500's. The Spaniards put the Lucayans to work in their mines in Cuba and Hispaniola and sold them as divers for the rich pearl beds off Venezuela. The island was originally shown on charts as *Cigateo* although it had many variations such as *Ziguateo*, *Ciguateo*, *Guateo*, *Sygateo*, *Segatoo*, and *Sigatoo*. Early maps and charts show the island as *Ilathera* and *Islathera*, thought to be corruptions of the Spanish *Isla de Tierra*. In one instance it is called *Alabaster Island*. The 70 settlers in William Sayle's Eleutheran Adventures, who you shall learn of in the next paragraph, named her *Eleutheria* for the Greek word for freedom, *eleuthros*. Today the name has dropped the "*i*" and is simply known as Eleuthera.

The first attempt at actual colonization of the island was in 1649. William Sayle, a former Governor of Bermuda, and several merchants in London formed a company called the Company of Eleutherian Adventures with the object of settling this and adjacent islands. An Act of Parliament was passed in response to their petition and they were granted the whole area to be known as Eleuthera and off they sailed. Each Adventurer was required to pay into the public fund £100 and was guaranteed 300 acres to begin with and later 2,000 acres. The waters of The Bahamas at that time were teeming with seals and Sayle was enthusiastic about the commercial possibilities. He was intent on establishing a seal oil trade with Barbados. Whether he did this or not is not known although he and the seals are both now long gone.

Sayle and his Adventurers wrecked their two vessels somewhere along the northern shore of Eleuthera and took shelter in a huge cave known today as Preacher's Cave along the northern shore between Spanish Wells and Harbour Island. Although they only lost one crewman, the group lost all their provisions. They had a hard struggle to survive even with a relief ship sent from Boston. The colonists spread out throughout Eleuthera with some building homes at Governor's Harbour. Many early settlers returned to Bermuda while others were driven from Eleuthera by the Spanish in 1680 and emigrated to Boston and in particular North Yarmouth near Portland.

This island has a little bit of everything that The Bahamas has to offer. Sunny beaches, deep water, shallow banks, grassy rolling hills, rocky cliffs, and a healthy agricultural, fisheries and tourism oriented economic base. The island is laid out like a ribbon, almost 100 miles long and barely 2 miles wide.

Tides along the eastern and northern shores of Eleuthera including Harbour Island, Spanish Wells, Royal Island, and the waters north of Current Cut are the same time as Nassau. Tides in the Bight of Eleuthera along the western shore of the island and including Davis Channel, Powell Point, Rock Sound, Governor's Harbour, and Hatchet Bay are approximately 2:17 later than Nassau tides and are generally .2' less.

APPROACHES TO ELEUTHERA

Most boats headed to north Eleuthera arrive from Abaco, leaving Little Harbour Bar and making landfall somewhere in the vicinity of Royal Island or Spanish Wells. From Little Harbour Bar in Abaco (GPS waypoint 26° 19.30' N, 76° 59.32' W) it is approximately 49.2 nautical miles on a course of 179° to the waypoint lying 1½ nautical mile WNW of the cut between Egg Island and Little Egg Island (GPS waypoint 25° 29.60'N, 76° 54.75' W) where you can pilot your way in by eye to the anchorage at Royal Island.

If leaving Little Harbour and bound for Spanish Wells via Ridley Head Channel, the pilot pickup waypoint lies 46.7 nautical miles away on a course of 170°.

From Nassau to Royal Island there are a few different routes to take. If you leave the eastern entrance to Nassau Harbour bound for Royal Island you can pass between Paradise Island and Athol Island passing south of Blue Lagoon Island (Salt Cay) and enter the Northeast Providence Channel at Chub Rock Light (GPS waypoint 25° 06.61' N, 77° 14.38' W). The wreck of the *Arimora* (GPS waypoint 25° 27.87' N, 76° 53.75' W) is approximately 28.3 nautical miles on a course of 49° on this route. Once in sight of the wreck pass around its remains on the south side and take up a course of 55° for the final 3.4 nautical miles to the entrance to the anchorage at Royal Island (GPS waypoint 25° 30.60' N, 76° 51.73'W). If you wish you can

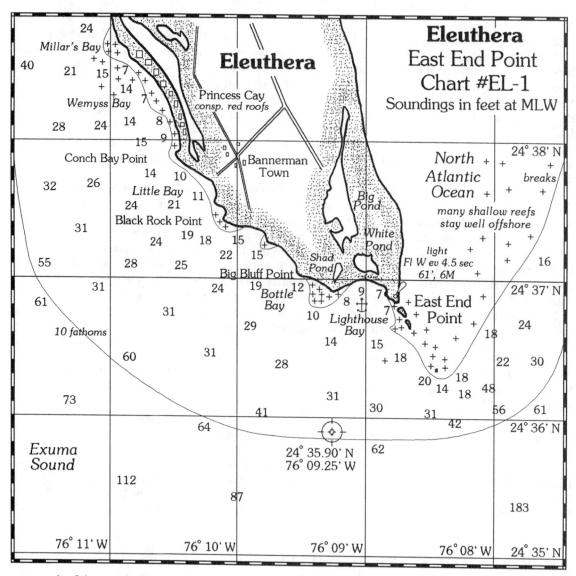

pass north of the wreck, between Egg Island and Little Egg and parallel the shore of Royal Island until you arrive at the mouth of the anchorage. If taking this route, give the reef at the southern end of Little Egg a wide berth. Vessels leaving Nassau may also opt for the route lying south of Athol Island and Rose Island.

There are virtually no dangers from the eastern end of Davis Channel all the way to Current Cut along the eastern shore of Eleuthera. You can coast along the shore all the way northward past Gregory Town, almost to the Glass Window. The entire eastern shore of Eleuthera is basically a lee shore in the prevailing winds and is seldom cruised except in passing.

Vessels heading to or from the Exumas have several different routes. The most northerly route begins at Beacon Cay (GPS waypoint at 24° 52.82' N, 76° 49.50' W, approximately 500 yards northwest of Beacon Cay) and bears 003° for approximately 25.6 nautical miles to the southern tip of Current Island (GPS waypoint at 25° 18.45' N, 76° 51.29' W approximately ½ nautical mile southwest of the southwestern tip) from which point skippers can parallel the eastern shore of Current Island headed to the settlement of The Current, or, pass along the western shore of Current Island and head to either Royal Island or Spanish Wells. Also beginning at Beacon Cay it is possible to steer 352° and pass into the Northeast Providence Channel via Fleeming Channel. Here a GPS waypoint at 25° 16.00' N, 76° 55.30' W, will place you approximately ¼ mile north of the entrance to Fleeming Channel. This is a good jumping off spot for Hole In The Wall or Sandy Point, Abaco, Nassau, or even Royal Island. Cruisers leaving Beacon Cay may also pass north of Finley Cay to head towards Hatchet Bay, Governor's Harbour, or Rock Sound. All skippers leaving Beacon Cay for any of these routes should only do so in daylight and with good visibility. Just

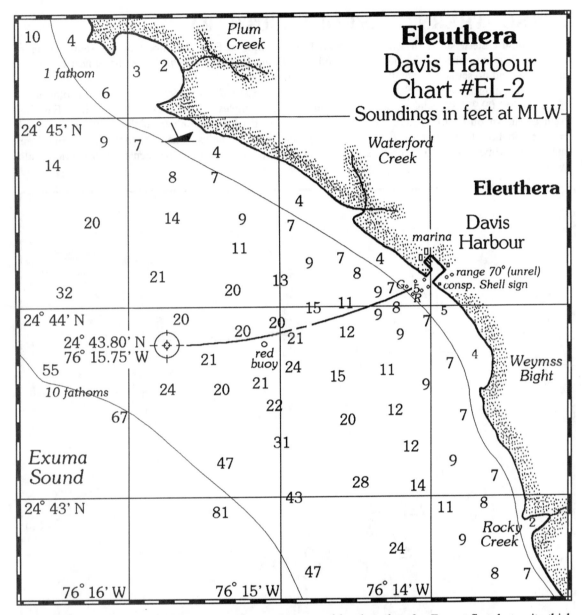

Eleuthera
Davis Harbour
Chart #EL-2
Soundings in feet at MLW

Plum Creek

Waterford Creek

Eleuthera

Davis Harbour

marina

range 70° (unrel)
consp. Shell sign

Weymss Bight

Exuma Sound

Rocky Creek

10   4
1 fathom
3   2
6
24° 45' N   9   7   4
14   8   7
20   14   9   7   4
11
21   20   13   9   7   4
32   15   11   9   8
24° 44' N   20   20   20   21   12   9   5
24° 43.80' N   21   red buoy   24   15   11   7   4
76° 15.75' W
55   24   20   21   22   9
10 fathoms   31   20   12   7
67   47   12
47   28   14   9   7
24° 43' N   81   43   11   8
24   9   2
47   8   7

76° 16' W   76° 15' W   76° 14' W

north of Beacon Cay you will begin to encounter large coral heads and reefs. Few at first, but quite thick about 6½ to 10 nautical miles north of Beacon Cay. Some are very shallow, less that 6', but there is plenty of deep water from 7'-22' between them so steering around them is not a problem.

Vessels heading for Powell Point from the northern Exumas have only one obstruction to worry about, the TMB2 buoy that lies approximately 15 nautical miles southwest of Powell Point, Eleuthera (this buoy is scheduled to be removed in the near future so it may or may not be there, until you are sure it is no longer in place, act as if it was still in position at 24° 38.20' N, 76° 31.30' W). From Warderick Wells, Powell Point bears 36° at a distance of 36.0 nautical miles. From Highborne Cay you can steer 76° for 26.5 miles to arrive at Powell Point.

Although many cruisers visiting Eleuthera do so as part of their journey from Abaco to points south, and a few head over from Nassau, the vast majority of cruising boats travel Eleuthera from south to north. For these vessels Eleuthera is usually part of a Cat Island, Little San Salvador, Abaco route that is popular with boats returning from George Town to the U.S. and often for those who are returning from the Caribbean northwards and wish to sample something other than deep water passages. For these reasons we will visit Eleuthera from the south to the north.

THE SOUTHERN COAST OF ELEUTHERA

The southwestern shore of Eluethera, from Powell Point to East End Point at the southern tip of Eleuthera, has only one facility but it is a good one, *Davis Harbour Marina*. The shoreline has few lee anchorages and no settlements on the shore itself, all are inland.

If approaching from Little San Salvador, steer approximately 285° for 9.8 miles to a waypoint at 24° 35.90' N, 76° 09.25' W, which places you about 1 mile southwest of the rocks lying south of East End Point as shown on Chart #EL-1. Give the point a wide berth if coming from the north as the shoals extended offshore to the east and northeast of the point for over 2 miles. There is a light at East End Point that flashes white every 4½ seconds, stands 65' above the water, and can be seen from 6 nautical miles away.

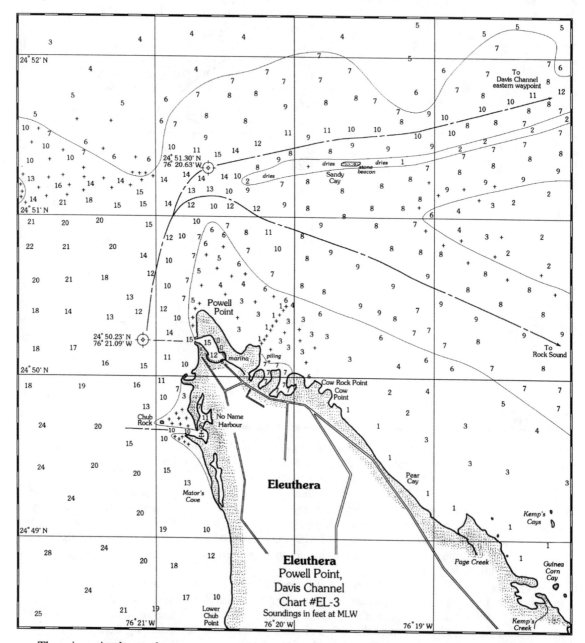

Eleuthera
Powell Point,
Davis Channel
Chart #EL-3
Soundings in feet at MLW

There is a nice lee anchorage at coconut palm framed Lighthouse Bay that is good in winds from north to east but not southeast as some seem to think. The bottom is sand and rock but it's not hard to find a sandy spot to drop your anchor. Just north of Lighthouse Bay near Black Rock Point is an old graveyard just under the line of casuarinas at the top of the beach. These graves are very old, most of the dates on the rocks used as headstones are weathered to nothing. This area can also be reached by road from Bannerman Town. Bannerman Town is little more than a few houses these days, most people have moved away. On the road north of the cemetery are the ruins of a very old church. Bannerman Town was named after the former Governor of The Bahamas, Sir Alexander Bannerman. The few settlements at the southern end of Eleuthera are best visited by road. South of Bannerman Town, at the end of the dirt track that is used as a road, lies the wind swept cliffs at the southern tip of Eleuthera. Here you can gaze out to sea and view the outline of Little San Salvador 10 miles away, and on a clear day, Cat Island.

Vessels heading northwards along the southwestern shore of Eleuthera towards Davis Harbour or Powell Point should give the shoreline a berth of at least one mile. Although it is possible to follow the shoreline closer in, dodging the shallows, banks and reefs, some of the shoals stretch westward almost a mile while in other places the 10 fathom line lies very close to shore.

Along the coast north of Black Rock Point and Bannerman Town you will see the bright red roofs of the Princess Cay area at Wemyss Bay. This facility and beach is manmade and was constructed by the *Princess Cruise Line* for their passengers to use when their ships pass through this area in the fall and winter. During late spring and summer the place is almost deserted as the liners go elsewhere.

North of Princess Cay you will come to Wemyss Bight and the entrance to *Davis Harbour Marina* as shown on Chart #EL-2. The entrance to the marina sits in a tall stand of causarinas about 2 miles south of the very conspicuous wreck of the rusty freighter. A GPS waypoint at 24° 43.80' N, 76° 15.75' W, will place you approximately ¾ mile west of the red buoy (sometimes it's difficult to see) that marks the entrance channel to *Davis Harbour Marina*. Take the red buoy to starboard when entering the marina and head in on a bearing of 70° on the range which consists of a very visible white cross in the rear and a much less visible short white pole in the foreground. A good landmark is the cross and the *Shell* sign. Take up an approximate course of 70° on the white cross and you will soon make out the three pairs of channel markers in front of you. Take the red ones on the right and head in making a dogleg to port to enter the marina proper after the last pair of poles. The controlling depth for this channel is 5' at low tide. If you are in doubt as to the state of the tide call the Dockmaster, Delroy Richards, on VHF ch. 16.

Until *Cape Eleuthera Marina* opened, *Davis Harbour Marina* had a lock on the boating facilities in southern Eleuthera. Nowadays it remains busy primarily catering to sportfishing vessels trying their luck in the very productive surrounding waters. *Davis Harbour Marina* can accommodate 8 boats with drafts up to 7½'. This very protected marina sells diesel, gas, and RO water and takes major credit cards. The marina is no longer associated with the elegant *Cotton Bay Club* on southern Eleuthera as the club has, for now anyway, closed down.

The nearby town of Wemyss's Bight was named after the early Scottish proprietor who deeded this land to his heirs. In town you will find *Kell's Take Away* which also sells *Shell* gas and a has a laundromat on site. You're also near the *R & W Restaurant and Bar*, *Mary's Restaurant*, and *Tropicana's*.

POWELL POINT

Powell Point is a popular jumping off spot for cruisers bound for the Exumas and points south or those bound from Exuma northward along the shore of Eleuthera to Abaco. *Cape Eleuthera Marina* is an excellent and inexpensive place to hang out and wait for weather or whatever. The marina is a Port Of Entry for The Bahamas, ask for the forms when you arrive.

A GPS waypoint at 24° 50.23' N, 76° 21.09' W, places you approximately ¼ mile west of the entrance to *Cape Eleuthera Marina* which sits almost ¼ mile south of Powell Point as shown on Chart #EL-3. The entrance is straightforward, simple, and deep, a draft of 12' can enter here at low water. There is a hole at the entrance that I have sounded to a depth of 49' that it is full of big fish awaiting the chance to offer themselves up to your dinner plate-there are some similar holes just off the beach lying south of the marina entrance. To enter the marina, pass between the entrance jetties and follow the water around to the south where the marina opens up. There is an unlighted range at the entrance on a bearing of approximately 90° but the entrance is so easy as to make the range unnecessary. The fuel dock sits at the southeastern end of the harbour by the small bridge. *Cape Eleuthera Marina* sells diesel, gas, and water and takes major credit cards. The marina is scheduled to install a washer and dryer on the premises in the fall of 1997 so perhaps we will all be able to do our laundry there also. If you need assistance in entering the marina you can call the *Cape Eleuthera Marina* on VHF ch. 16 and marina operators Kenny Thompson and Monique Wright will do everything in their power to help you in and make your stay as enjoyable as possible. These two ladies are excellent hosts and a wealth of information. Kenny is a like a breath of fresh air. Sometimes when you call a marina you get someone on the radio who is less than enthusiastic about answering your call or someone who treats all yachts as gold-platers (and some of us are far from that!). Not our dear Kenny. Call *Cape Eleuthera Marina* (*Cape E* as Kenny sometimes calls it) and you'll be warmly welcomed with a hearty "What's happening?" Don't ever change Kenny!

In late 1970 work began at Powell Point on the $35 million development that came to be called *Cape Eleuthera*. Originally seen as a 20 year project it was originally owned by *Avon Harbour Ltd.* and included 5,000 half-acre residential lots, a hotel and marina complex, beach club, and a golf course. Today a few condos and houses are privately owned, some on a time share basis, and the rest of the facilities lie dormant. Hopefully now that the marina is up and running again these things will change and the current owners will invest a little more money into the project and turn the marina area into the bustling complex it was meant to be.

Just south of the entrance to the marina is No Name Harbour as shown on Chart #EL-3. To enter take Chub Rock well to port and steer generally eastward staying in the deeper water between the shallow rocky bars to your port and starboard. The entrance is not easily made out from Chub Rock, you'll probably have to pick it out with the binoculars. Once inside you can anchor well up any of the fingers, some of which have 13'-25' in them with only 6'-7' between the deeper parts. No Name Harbour was dredged out by the owners of the Cape Eleuthera project and the harbor is in essence owned by them. This means that they can (and do) charge to anchor here, the same rate as at the marina. No Name Harbour offers excellent protection and could even be considered as a possible hurricane hole. The only problem with the harbor is the fact that it is dredged out. This creates some sheer rock walls and less than ideal holding. The best spot in a hurricane would be in the upper northeastern finger. Skippers will have to tie to trees and probably set an anchor or two ashore on the land to be secure in here and even then a major storm surge could decimate the place. Bugs are definitely a problem here as at *Cape Eleuthera Marina* and *Davis Harbour Marina*.

On the northeastern shore of the Cape Eleuthera property, east of Powell Point (Chart #EL-3), are some more dredged harbours that face north and east. These have 7'-9' of water inside but the entrance is guarded by shallows that restrict entry only to vessels of less than 6' and then only at high tide. I do not recommend anchoring in here and only mention them as alternatives. I believe No Name Harbour and *Cape Eleuthera Marina* offer better protection.

Just inland from Powell Point is the community of Deep Creek. Deep Creek sits on the edge of Deep Creek which is definitely not deep. Initially hurt by the closing of the Cape Eleuthera resort, Deep Creekers (Creekites? Creekians?) now have a stable economy again. If you want to visit Deep Creek, or any place in Eleuthera for that matter, you can call *Friendly Bob* on VHF ch. 16 (Bob rents cars and has a taxi service as well as a liquor store in Deep Creek). At the top of the hill as you come into town from Powell Point is *Pinder's Marine*. Here owner Trevor Pinder repairs outboard engines and has a nice supply of marine supplies and necessities. Next to Pinder's is *Hilltop Liquors*. At the bottom of the hill on the right is *Shiril's Restaurant* with some of the best cracked conch you've ever had. Across the street from *Shiril's*, in the concrete building with no sign, is *Friendly Bob's Liquor Store, Car Rental, and Taxi*. Just past Bob's on the left is *Bertha's Go-Go Ribs*. *Bertha's* is associated with the chain of the same name on New Providence and is simply an out-island version of the Nassau locations. Past *Bertha's* is *Thompson's Food Store*, a *Shell* gas station, and *BB's Drugs and Notions*. The new hot spot in town is *Arthur's* (with satellite TV) at the top of the hill just off the main road.

Between Deep Creek and Rock Sound lies Green Castle, the largest and oldest of the communities on the southern end of the island. Some of the inhabitants of Green Castle are the descendants of freed slaves from the Rock Sound and Gregory Town areas. The name of the town comes from a house that looks like a castle and is painted green and yellow and once served as the school (usually schools in The Bahamas are painted yellow with green doors and windows). In town you'll find *Freddie's Convenience Store*, a *Shell* gas station, *Brown's Superior Food Store*, the *Club 9000*, *Breeze's Restaurant, Bar, and Liquor Store*, and a Batelco office. The Batelco tower at Green Castle flashes red from its top.

DAVIS CHANNEL

The Davis Channel is a deep (8'-12' at MLW) passage from Powell Point northeastward to the western shore of Eleuthera. The channel passes between the shoals that lie southeast and east of the Schooner Cays and a long shallow sandbar that parallels the shoreline of Eleuthera northeast of Powell Point.

From Powell Point, as shown on Chart #EL-3, work your way northward to the GPS waypoint at 24° 51.30' N, 76° 20.63' W, which marks the western end of the Davis Channel (watch out for the shallow reefs to the west of the waypoint). To starboard you will clearly see the long sandbar that is marked by the 22' tall stone beacon on Sandy Cay. To port you will see what looks like deep water for a great distance, don't try heading that way, it will shallow quickly. Take up a course of approximately 80° for 4.12 miles to the waypoint at 24° 52.25' N, 76° 16.30' W, which lies at the eastern end of the Davis Channel. Do not just set this course and put the boat on autopilot. Keep a sharp lookout, the channel narrows in a couple of places. The general idea is to parallel the very obvious sandbank on the southern side of the Davis Channel until past its eastern end if heading northward or to Rock Sound.

Vessels heading northward from Davis Channel to Governor's Harbour or Hatchet Bay can take up their course for those destinations after reaching the eastern waypoint for Davis Channel at 24° 52.50' N, 76° 16.30' W. Vessels wishing to enter Rock Sound without having to dodge coral heads can head straight east for the mainland of Eleuthera from the eastern waypoint of the Davis Channel and then turn south to parallel the shoreline ½ mile off until at the waypoint for Rock Sound.

Boats heading to Rock Sound and drawing 6' or less can bypass Davis Channel and head directly to Rock Sound at low tide. That's right, I said 6' or less-I know that "other" publications say only 5' but there is actually more water here than what is shown in the "other" publications). From the waypoint at the western end of Davis Channel pass south of the conspicuous sandbar that is marked by the beacon on Sandy Cay and head generally southeast past the second large sandbank that lies south of the one marked by the beacon as shown on Chart #EL-3. Once clear of this second sandbank you can head east for the waypoint at the entrance to Rock Sound at 24° 50.30' N, 75° 11.70' W. As shown on Chart #EL-3 and #EL-4 you will have good water all the way. Further east you will begin to pick up some scattered shallow heads and small patch reefs but these are easily seen and avoided. Never attempt this route in the early morning when the sun is in your eyes.

Vessels can also bypass Davis Channel from Rock Sound to Powell Point by following the above directions in reverse. From the waypoint at the entrance to Rock Sound head directly west (270°) for the northern tip of land on the horizon. That tip of land is Powell Point. As shown on Chart #EL-3 and #EL-4, you will have deep water all the way with only a few heads to dodge and the two sandbars. The heads and sandbars are easily seen in good visibility. Don't attempt to head to Powell Point on this route in the late afternoon when the sun is in your eyes.

Northwest of Powell Point and the Davis Channel lie the Schooner Cays, a very popular place for local fishermen. The Wild Bird Act has declared the Schooner Cays, and the more northerly Finley Cay, a protected area and off limits for bird hunting. Wood Cay is home to a large population of White Crowned Pigeons who were once hunted for their eggs. Fishermen from Eleuthera once inhabited Wood Cay for periods of time and evidence of their tenure is the fresh water well they built. The Schooner Cays lie along the northern edge of Exuma Sound. The area is very shallow and sand bores abound. Some of the deep blue channels leading in between the sandbores from Exuma Sound run through to deeper water in the Bight of Eleuthera but most of them are dead ends. The locals number the channels, and can tell you which number will take you through. This area has not been surveyed, and if you attempt to investigate the surrounding waters you must have good visibility. The ability to read water, as you would guess, is necessary here.

ROCK SOUND

Rock Sound is the largest settlement on Eleuthera as well as the commercial center. In old documents Rock Sound is shown as Wreck Sound owing to the major source of income for its inhabitants. A changing of the nature of the economy led to a changing of the name over the years. The anchorage in Rock Sound has good holding and can be a refuge from a frontal passage in winter. When winds come out of the southwest and west, boats should tuck up under the lee at the northwestern end of Rock Sound. When the wind goes northeast it's time to head back over to the eastern side of the sound.

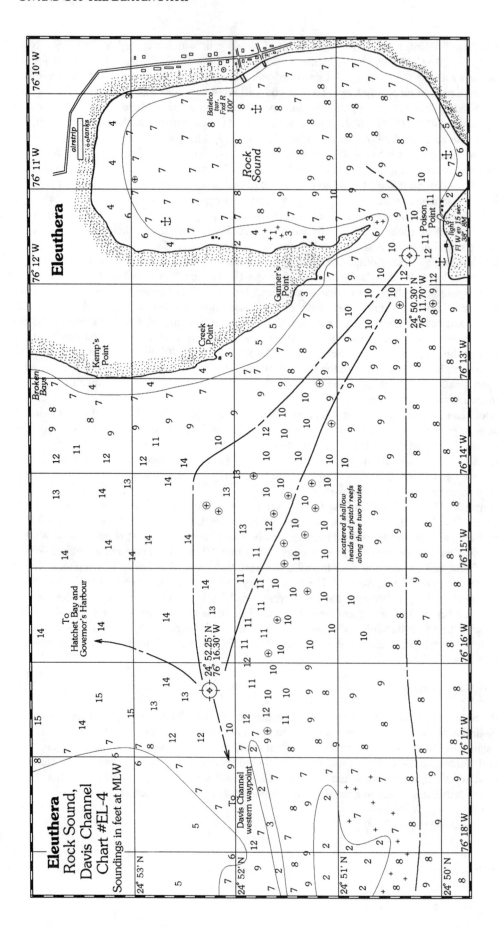

Eleuthera
Rock Sound,
Davis Channel
Chart #EL-4
Soundings in feet at MLW

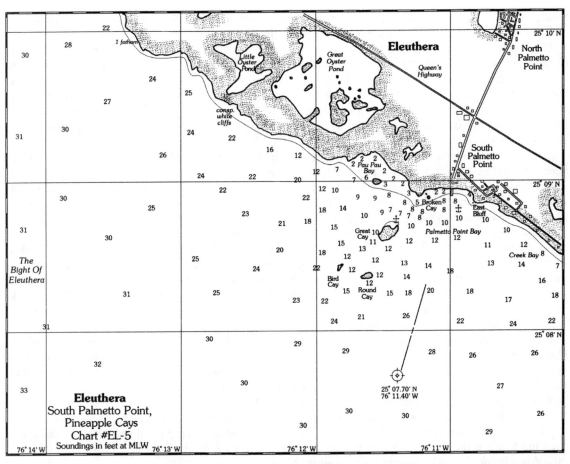

A GPS waypoint at 24° 50.30' N, 75° 11.70' W, will place you approximately ½ mile west of the entrance to Rock Sound as shown on Chart #EL-4. Give Sound Point a wide berth as you head east and once clear of the shallows off the point you can steer towards the large white church to the northeast. Anchor anywhere you like off the town, the holding is excellent here. If a frontal passage threatens the best place to avoid southwest through northwest to northerly winds is in the northwestern corner of Rock Sound tucked in as close as you can get. For shelter from southeast to southwest winds the southern shore of Rock Sound is excellent. A 6' draft can enter and tuck in very well at the entrance to Starve Creek at the south end of Rock Sound east of Poison Point. The light on Poison Point flashes white every 15 seconds, stands 24' above the water, and is visible for 7 miles. A good shelter in southeast to south/southwest winds lies just west of Poison Point with a nice little beach to cavort on while awaiting better weather. The bluffs on the southern shore of Rock Sound offer some nice overhangs and small cave holes for exploring.

Rock Sound is a Port of Entry for The Bahamas and skippers seeking clearance should anchor off the concrete dock by the large pink building which houses the Customs and Immigration Offices. Don't block this dock unless Customs instructs you to as the mailboat lands here. A faucet on the western wall of the Customs building delivers good water at no charge but be sure to bring a short length of hose with your jerry jugs. Inshore from the Customs building is the *CC Super Wash*, the local laundromat, *Gem's*, *Ron's Marine and Auto Parts*, *PK's Auto Rentals*, and *Eleuthera Stationary* with its copy/fax service.

South of Customs, north of the white church, is the long towns dock, where most cruisers like to anchor. At the head of the dock is the *Harbour View Restaurant and Bar*, I haven.t been back to Rock Sound since late Spring of 1998, but I am told this excellent land mark and restaurant has sadly closed. In the vicinity of the main road are a couple of clothing boutiques, a tailor shop, and an *Esso* gas station. North of the town dock, across from the *Esso* station, in a large pink building is the government clinic. Nearby, are a couple of gift shops. At the base of the Batelco tower is the local Batelco office where phone calls can be made and phone cards purchased. Across the Queen's Highway from the Batelco office and up the side streets you will find *Sammy's Place*, the local hangout serving breakfast, lunch, and dinner. Proprietors

Sammy and Kathleen Culmer also have rooms for rent with satellite TV. Nearby are *Lita's Blue Diamond Restaurant* and *D & N's Down Home Pizza*, a bit of a walk, but well worth it.

North of the Customs building on the main road is *Discount Liquors*, and across the street *Cairey's Garage and Service Station*. On the left just past *Cairey's* is a small shopping center that will likely be the center of your shopping activity while in Rock Sound. Here you will find *Rock Sound Hardware* with its huge selection of tools and supplies. You can get your propane bottles filled here also. Next door is the best stocked grocery store on the island, the *Rock Sound Grocery* which also runs the gas pumps outside. Next to the grocery is a small liquor store and a *NAPA* auto parts Across the side street from *NAPA* is a branch of *Barclay's Bank* open five days a week till 5:00 P.M. The rear of the mall can be accessed by dinghy. A little over ¼ mile north of the Customs dock you will see the silver/white roof of a long building. This building is the mall. You will have to drop someone off here as the shoreline is rocky close in and it is not a place to leave an inflatable. There is a small beach a few hundred yards north of the mall where you might land but the houses around it are private, you might want to ask permission before tying up there for any length of time. Just past *Barclay's Bank* on the east side of the road is *Eleuthera Fish and Farm Supplies* with all sorts of fishing gear, anchors, and first aid kits.

At the northern end of Rock Sound itself is the Rock Sound International Airport with regular flights from *Bahamasair* and *Island Express*. The road northward, the Queen's Highway, is an absolute thrill to travel on. Winding its way through rolling hills, one minute you'll have the western shore on your flank, the next you'll be up on a hill overlooking the eastern shore and the Atlantic Ocean. Just north of Rock Sound Airport the road goes through an area where huge tree limbs arc over the road creating a shaded canopy to several sections of the highway.

Just outside town to the east is the famous Rock Sound Water Hole Park, a semi-fresh water hole. Much like a blue hole, researchers are unsure of its depth and whether or not it connects with the sea through a system of caves. There is a lot of sea life in the 360' diameter hole but some locals say they are placed there by local fisherman who often donate a couple of groupers or snappers from their catch. One time a gentleman decided to play a trick on his neighbors and he put a small shark in the hole. Well, being a small town, the culprit was soon discovered and taken to court. His was sentenced to staying by the hole until he caught the shark and removed it. Three days later he finally found the right bait and removed the shark from the hole and the local inhabitants could once again go for a swim in the hole The walls of the hole drop down about 15' and from there they fall away sharply.

Vessels heading north from Rock Sound can parallel the shoreline staying at ½ mile off to avoid the shallows and a few scattered heads. North of Rock Sound lies Tarpum Bay, a small settlement stretching for over a mile just along the western shore. It was originally called Glenelg after Lord Glenelg, a former Secretary of State for the Colonies. The current name came from the tarpon that once inhabited the waters of the area. The only approach is by dinghy as the water is very shallow up to ½ mile offshore by the conspicuous rocky bar. The holding here is fair in sand but only in calm weather. The town is an art colony of sorts with a couple of art galleries gracing the settlement (and how often does one find an art gallery in the out-islands?). As you approach Tarpum Bay by road you will see the signs for the *Ventaclub*, the local resort with dive and sailing charters for guests. Next to the entrance to the hotel is a small strip mall with a building supply center, hardware store, meat shoppe, and *Shell* station. As you enter Tarpum Bay you will find *Pop's Welding*, *DD's Variety*, *Barbies Food Store*, *Bert's for the Best Food Store*, *Kinky's Korner Shell Service Station and Auto Parts*, and *Audrey's Boutique*. On the waterfront you'll find *Shines Famous Seafood*. Next door you'll find *Ethyl's Cottages and Car Rentals*, *Bayside Liquors*, *Bayshore Snacks and Cold Drinks*, and *Carey's Buywise Hardware and Grocery*. Just to the north you'll find the *Hilltop Haven Restaurant and Bar* and *Ingraham's Beach Inn*.

Well north of Tarpum Bay is a small road leading to the eastern shore of Eleuthera and a tiny bridge leading to the very, very, ritzy Windemere Island. This was a favorite spot of the British Royal Family, especially Charles and Di when they were still news.

North of Tarpum Bay along the western shore of Eleuthera lies the small beachside settlement of South Palmetto Point where a large concrete and wooden dock marks the town. North Palmetto Point lies north of the Queen's Highway though most cruisers call South Palmetto Point simply Palmetto Point. As shown on Chart #EL-5, a GPS waypoint at 25° 07.70' N, 76° 11.40' W, will place you approximately 1 mile southwest of the town. The best holding lies off the town dock and is good in winds from north/northwest to northeast. A slight lee in southwest to west winds can be found in the small casuarina lined cove on the eastern side of Great Cay, the largest of the Pineapple Cays, for shallow draft vessels only (less than 3'). The great white scar in the rolling green hills of Eleuthera is a good landmark for Palmetto Point. Atop the

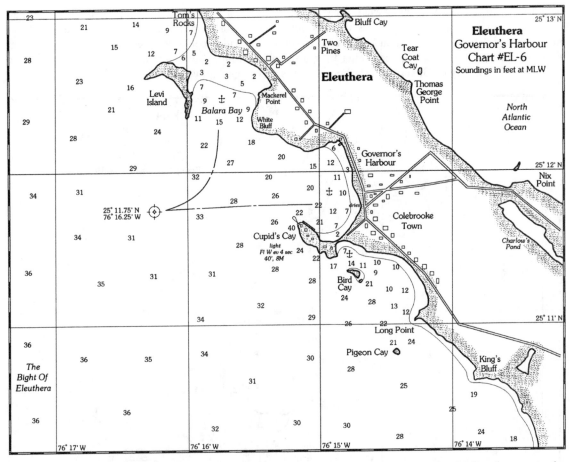

Eleuthera
Governor's Harbour
Chart #EL-6
Soundings in feet at MLW

cliff at Palmetto Point once stood a resort that was gutted by a fire in 1975. On the beach area to the southeast of Palmetto Point on Creek Bay lie several very nice villas.

Just up from the dock is the *Palmetto Beach Inn* with its restaurant and bar. Nearby is *Thompson's Seaside Convenience Store* and *Millard's Variety Store*. The principal hangout is *Mate and Jenny's Pizza*, a don't miss stop sitting just up the road from the dock towards the Queen's Highway. Visit Palmetto Point if for no other reason than to visit *Mate and Jenny's*. Just inland from *Mate and Jenny's* is the Queen's Highway where you'll find *Pinder's Meats and Fruits*, a *Shell* station, a laundromat, *Unique Hardware and Building Supplies*, and the *Eleuthera Dental Centre*. *Sand's Enterprises* on the Queen's Highway has it all, food, clothes, auto accessories, hardware, and gifts. South of Palmetto Point on the main road is *Big Sally's Restaurant*.

In the summer of 1997 the government of The Bahamas announced a new resort/condominium complex to be built in the area of Palmetto Point. Constuction is slated to begin in the fall of 1997 and completion is set for the fall/winter of 1998. I do not have the exact location of this project as of this writing, it may or may not be on the western shore at South Palmetto Point, so keep your eyes open as you travel through this area.

GOVERNOR'S HARBOUR

Governor's Harbour, like so many towns throughout The Bahamas, was once a prosperous trading center that suffered an economic setback. Located about midway up (or down depending on which way you're headed) the island of Eleuthera, the town today is enjoying a new prosperity, in part due to the opening of a *Club Med* nearby on the Atlantic side. The town is lovely to look at with the colorful houses and buildings spread over the hillsides overlooking the harbor.

Just north of Palmetto Point and around the corner lies the entrance to Governor's Harbour. A GPS waypoint at 25° 11.75' N, 76° 16.25' W, will place you approximately 1 mile west of the entrance to Governor's Harbour as shown on Chart #EL-6. From this position head eastward taking the northern tip of

Cupid's Cay to starboard. Anchor wherever your draft will allow. The anchorage is good only in moderate prevailing winds or settled weather as there is notoriously poor holding here (grassy with a lot of old moorings and debris scattered about). Governor's Harbour is wide open to the westerly prelude to a frontal passage although it does give some shelter from a southwest wind. Never attempt to pick up any mooring you see in the vicinity of Governor's Harbour. All the moorings that were once in the harbour and south of

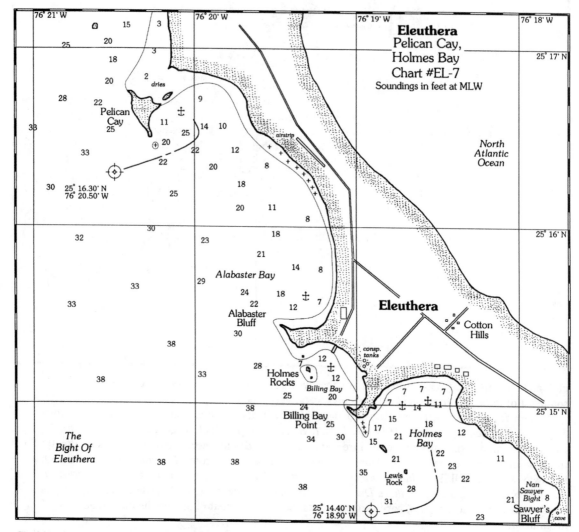

Cupid's Cay earned a bad reputation for neglect. Practice safe anchoring instead.

    Just south of Cupid's Cay is a small anchorage that offers good protection in strong northwest through north to east winds if you can get your anchor to set in the grassy, rocky bottom in the lee of Laughing Bird Cay, usually just called and shown as Bird Cay on most charts. When entering this anchorage you can pass either side of Bird Cay. This anchorage is usually taken over by local boats and is very rough in anything from a southeast to southwest wind. Balara Bay to the north offers fair protection in the lee of Levi Island but this entire area is no place to be in a frontal passage, it would be much safer to head to Pelican Cay, Hatchet Bay, or Rock Sound. Besides, many locals are hip to putting their boats in Balara Bay for protection and they'll likely get there before you.

    Ashore, at the curve in the road in the center of the town frontage, is *Eleuthera Supply Limited*, the local grocery and hardware store and gas station. *Eleuthera Supply* can also fill your propane tank. This is the center of the commercial district and here you will find the *Clear Water Dive Shop, Barclay's Bank, Rolle's Ice Cream Parlour, Tasty Treats Ice Cream, Daiquiris, and Deli,* and several gift and T-shirt shops. To the north lie the *LeClair Food Centre,* the *Buccaneer Club Restaurant and Bar,* and the *Club Med La Marina.* This is the dock in the northeastern end of the harbour where *Club Med* brings its guests to ride jet skis, water ski, and sail their small cats and sloops. This can make for an uneasy anchorage, far from calm for the weary traveler.

On the Queen's Highway just south of the main part of town but an easy walk up from the water's edge, is Eleuthera's only movie house, *The Globe Princess Theater*, with movies every evening. Next door is *Rolle's Auto Parts* and a *Royal Bank of Canada*. If you need a car call *Griffin's Car Rentals* at 332-2077/9 located at the *Griffin's Auto Repair and Esso Service Station* just south of the theater. Here too you'll find *Sawyer's Food Store* and *Pammy's Restaurant and Bar*. For car rentals you can also try *Nixon-Pinder Car Rentals* at 332-2568.

Cupid's Cay, that small plot of land that sits at the outer edge of Governor's Harbour, houses the Customs office and the government dock. The cay received its name when someone said that the curving piece of land resembled the bow of Cupid. The first inhabitants could only walk across to the cay at low tide carrying whatever supplies they could handle. Over the years a wooden bridge was built that was later destroyed in the hurricane of 1929. Finally, when the current causeway was built, people flocked to Cupid's Cay, now home to over a hundred souls. Most of the quaint, pastel colored buildings on Cupid's Cay are very old and all are very close together, the roads being very narrow. The main stop on Cupid's Cay is the *Hi-D-Way Satellite Lounge*.

North of Governor's Harbour the water is deep very close to shore with no obstructions save a few offlying rocks which we shall now discuss. A few miles north of Governor's Harbour are several nice anchorages in the vicinity of Governor's Harbour International Airport. As shown on Chart #EL-7, a GPS waypoint at 25° 14.40' N, 76° 18.90' W, will place you approximately ½ mile southwest of the entrance to the anchorage in beautiful Holmes Bay. This is an excellent anchorage in winds from northwest to east. From the waypoint steer south of the southernmost rock called Lewis Rock. Once past Lewis Rock head northward to anchor off the beach, once the site of the *Tranquillity Bay Club*. You can also enter the anchorage by passing between Billing Bay Point and the first rock to its south but there is a large rock south of the point that is awash at high water. The deeper water lies south of the rock that is awash and the northernmost of the two offlying cays.

Just north of Holmes Bay is Billing Bay. This anchorage is fine in north to east winds but there is no beach and the bay is mainly used by fuel tankers supplying fuel to the airport, you will be happier anchored at Holmes Bay.

North of Billing Bay lies Pelican Cay which offers excellent protection in winds from the northwest to the northeast. As shown on Chart #EL-7, a GPS waypoint at 25° 16.30' N, 76° 20.50' W, will place you approximately ½ mile southwest of Pelican Cay. From the waypoint head south of Pelican Cay to anchor off its western shore. When the wind starts heading back into the east you will probably want to move over and tuck in against the western shore of Eleuthera. In winds from east to southeast you can anchor north of Pelican Cay in the lee of the very shallow bank that stretches between Pelican Cay and the mainland of Eleuthera.

North of Pelican Cay sits the village of James Cistern along the western shore of Eleuthera. As at Tarpum Bay you'll find that you can't get in closer than ¼ mile from shore and you will have to anchor out a little to gain access to the settlement. The spectacular view from the top of the hill at James Cistern offers the Atlantic Ocean to the east and the Bight of Eleuthera to the west.

James Cistern was named after a former Governor of The Bahamas, Sir James, while he was serving at Governor's Harbour. It seems that Sir James left on horseback in search of water and discovered a natural water hole in the area where the town is now. The cistern was built up and people began to drift in and settle nearby. The best way to visit this community is by car. When approaching from the south you will find several eating establishments, *Savory Snacks*, *Mom's Snack Shop*, and *Kell D's Restaurant and Bar*. There is a small gas station with a phone booth in town and the *Halfway Laundromat*. North of James Cistern on the main road is the very well stocked *Big Rock General Store* with its gas pumps, hardware, appliances, building supply outlet and car rentals. *Big Rock* offers delivery for yachtsmen to James Cistern or Hatchet Bay with a minimum purchase. North of *Big Rock*, and about 2½ miles south of Hatchet Bay, is the *Rainbow Inn and Restaurant*. The restaurant and bar has a good view of the Bight of Eleuthera as well as good dining and live music and cottages to rent. This is an absolutely beautiful place to have dinner and watch the sun set. Ask about transportation from Hatchet Bay.

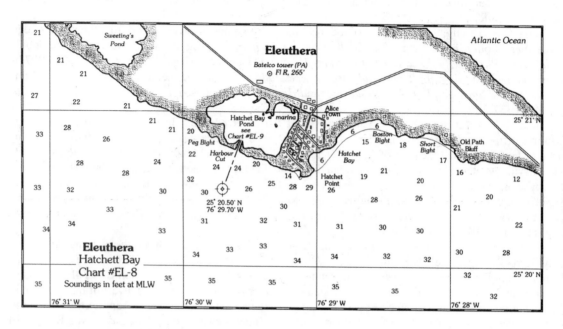

HATCHET BAY

As shown on Chart #EL-8, Hatchet Bay is actually a small bay southeast of the small inland cove that most call Hatchet Bay but which is really named Hatchet Bay Pond. For our purposes in this section whenever we refer to Hatchet Bay we will be talking about Hatchet Bay Pond as shown in detail on Chart #EL-9. The entrance to Hatchet Bay (Chart #EL-8 and EL-9) is sometimes difficult to distinguish from offshore. It is a narrow pass (90' wide) called Harbour Cut that was blasted through sheer rock with two small jetties stretching inwards from the Bight of Eleuthera. The light atop the bluff on the western side of the entrance flashes white twice in four seconds and repeats that characteristic every 10 seconds. The light is 57' above the water and is visible for 8 miles. The easiest landmarks for this area are the large white silos, once part of a large plantation, standing like silent sentinels up and down this stretch of coast, and the 265' Batelco tower with its flashing red light. A GPS waypoint at 25° 20.50' N, 076° 29.70' W, will place you approximately ¼ mile south of the pass into Hatchet Bay. From this position head straight in and anchor wherever you choose.

The holding in Hatchet Bay is pretty good in some places, worse in others, although it may be a fine spot to ride out a norther it is definitely no place to be in a hurricane as many found out in Hurricane Andrew (you will still see the wrecks along the shore from that catastrophe). The anchorage on the west side of the bay is grassy with a few rocks while the anchorage in front of the marina is mud. By no means anchor off the dock at Alice Town on the eastern side of the harbour as mailboats and propane tankers come in here at all hours of the day and night. *Marine Services of Eleuthera* offers moorings for rent at $5.00 per night on both sides of the bay on a first come-first serve basis. Just pick up a mooring and then dinghy in to pay. They tell me that they have old diesel engines and tractors down for the moorings but be advised that you use them at your own risk. There is a very nice cave at the water's edge just below the bluffs at Alice Town that is definitely worth checking out.

Marine Services of Eleuthera is the closest thing to a full service marina you will find on Eleuthera. There is 600' of dock space with 12' depths alongside. The marina offers diesel, water, parts, marine diesel repairs, woodworking, car rentals, and they have a 50 ton crane that can haul out a 46 footer. Ask about propane as a local company picks up empty bottles on Fridays and returns them the same day. The marina also charters a group of *Cabo Rico* sailboats and a few catamarans through their *Charter Cats of Eleuthera* division. They can be reached in the US at 800-446-9441, or in The Bahamas at 242-335-0186, or if you're in the area, see Pat at the office. Hatchet Bay is also a Port of Entry for The Bahamas, call the marina as you enter and they will assist you with the clearance process.

Across the street from the marina is *Marilyn's Take Out* serving good local cuisine. At the end of the marina you will find the *Harbour View Restaurant* serving breakfast, lunch, and dinner with music on the

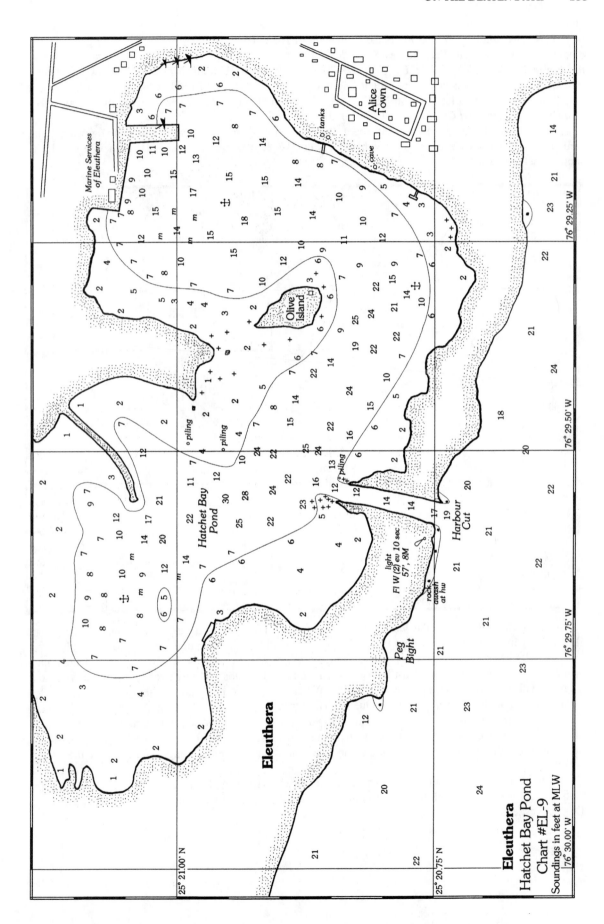

Eleuthera

Hatchet Bay Pond
Chart #EL-9
Soundings in feet at MLW

weekends. Just south of the marina is the settlement of Alice Town where you can jerry can gas for your dinghy. In town you will find the *Sea Side Club* serving cold beverages, *Assories Ice Cream and Drinks*, the *Forget-Me-Not Club*, *Triple T's Groceries*, and the *Red Dirt Laundromat, Snack Shack and Game Room*. If you need a taxi driver you might find one hanging out at the Sea Side Club although the easiest way to reach a taxi is to hail one on VHF ch. 16. You can also get a car rental or Taxi by calling *Larry Dean's Taxi Service and Car Rentals* at 335-0059 or 332-2568.

Across the street from the marina and about two hundred yards north along the Queen's Highway, is the well stocked *Sawyer's Grocery Store* with fresh fruits, vegetables, and meats. Next door is a small gift shop and a liquor store.

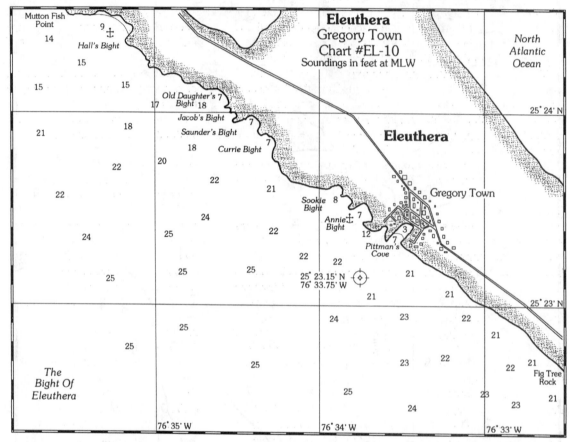

North of Hatchet Bay on the west side of the Queen's Highway is a large inland pond, larger than Hatchet Bay itself, called Sweeting's Pond. A small dirt road leads to the pond which is said to be haunted and allegedly has a Loch Ness type creature living within its waters. Just north of this pond is the entrance to the huge Hatchet Bay cave. Turn left on the dirt road by the silos and just over the rise you will see a clearing with the cave's entrance on your right. Watch out for the bats and the bat guano. Three miles north of town, on the eastern side of the Queen's Highway, you will come to a sign and a dirt road leading across the hills towards the Atlantic Ocean and Surfer's Beach. This beach is famous among surfing aficionados the world over who have been coming here since the 1960's, some even moving here permanently. With a good swell running some awesome waves come barreling in daring only the best to ride them.

North of the beach along the eastern side of the Queen's Highway at Eleuthera Shores is a great night club called *Cush's Place* with live music sometimes supplied by the owner, the well known Calypso artist, Dr. Seabreeze.

GREGORY TOWN

About five miles north of Hatchet Bay you will come to the small settlement of Gregory Town as shown on Chart #EL-10. The water between Hatchet Bay and Gregory Town is deep close in to shore with no offlying dangers. This picturesque little settlement of pastel painted houses is nestled among several hillsides overlooking the Bight of Eleuthera and Pittman's Cove, just an opening in between two steep cliffs which leads to the town dock. It is advisable to visit Gregory Town by car. Only in settled weather should you attempt to anchor off and dinghy in between the cliffs to the town dock due to the surge bouncing back and forth off the cliffs. There is a small cove less than ½ mile north of town that would be an adequate anchorage for a visit to town in settled weather. A GPS waypoint at 25° 23.15' N, 76° 33.75' W, will place you approximately ¼ mile southwest of the entrance to the cove at Gregory Town as shown on Chart #EL-8. The best places to anchor are in the small coves northwest of Gregory Town, Annie Bight or Sookie Bight, but only in settled weather. Another good spot to anchor is about 3 miles northwest of Gregory Town in Hall's Bight, just below Mutton Fish Point.

The scenery here will remind one of someplace other than The Bahamas. Perhaps New England, Spain, or maybe Scotland. The town was originally called Pittman's Cove but was renamed after James Gregory who was appointed Governor of The Bahamas in 1849. Gregory Town's biggest claim to fame is its pineapple industry and the pineapple wine and rum produced on the Thompson Brothers plantation just north of town. The first weekend of June Gregory Town becomes a small city when thousands of visitors pack in for the annual Pineapple Festival.

If you choose to visit Gregory Town the time spent will be well worth it. At the heart of town *Thompson Brothers Super Market* has fresh fruits and vegetables as well as excellent prices on fresh and frozen meats. You can also purchase gas here and you will find film, batteries, and a few other sundry items inside. About 100 yards east of the store and behind it is the *Dr. Bones Liquor Store*. In the immediate area of the super market are several small gift shops. Across the street is *Jay's Laundromat* and just up the hill is *Thompson's Bakery*, known far and wide for their delicious treats and baked goods (they also serve hamburgers). For meals try the *Driftwood Cafe* and *Elvina's Restaurant* (excellent) which boasts a pool table, satellite TV, and also rents cars and bicycles. Nest door is *Gem's Laundromat*. North of town on the Queen's Highway is *The Cove Eleuthera* with its excellent restaurant/bar and 26 comfortable air-conditioned rooms. At *Eleuthera Island Shores* you will find *Cush's Place* serving lunch and dinner with music on the weekends.

Gregory Town is THE place for pineapples in Eleuthera. Check with Joe Darville who lives just up the hill from the store, you'll see the sign that says "Darville Residence." If anyone in town has pineapples, Joe will. Thompson Brothers make an excellent pineapple rum in Gregory Town but it is extremely hard to come by these days.

The biggest event to ever happen to Gregory Town never even happened. It was the International World Peace Festival, a proposed 1970 rock concert scheduled to take place in Gregory Town which was canceled by the Bahamian Government. The festival's promoter told the world in an interview on ZNS radio that The Bahamas ". . . grows the best grade of marijuana in the world." A ZNS broadcaster took up the issue on her radio program and even visited Gregory Town in her attempt to thwart promoters. The festival never came off and today the closest Gregory Town gets to mainline rock music is the home owned by rock star Lenny Kravitz.

From Gregory Town northward to the Glass Window, the western shore of Eleuthera has some scattered cliffs which drop right down to the water and a few small coves good for settled weather anchoring only. The water is deep close in to shore except in the vicinity of the Glass Window.

THE GLASS WINDOW

Between Upper and Lower Bogue and Gregory Town along the Queen's Highway sits a remarkable sight, The Glass Window. The Glass Window, once the subject of a painting by the American artist Winslow Homer, is a beautiful rock formation where the Bight of Eleuthera and The Atlantic Ocean almost meet. It was originally a natural rock bridge 85' above sea level which was washed away in a hurricane in 1926 and replaced by a bridge in 1960. The site was originally called the Narrow Passage and in 1872 an enormous wave rose without warning and washed over the arch and island carrying away several young couples who were picnicking there. To the east lies the cobalt blue water of the open Atlantic Ocean while to the west lies the Bight of Eleuthera in its myriad shades of emerald and turquoise. The Queen's

Highway crosses the span via a large concrete and steel bridge. A rage on Halloween Day of 1991 spawned a rogue wave that picked up the bridge and moved the northern end of it 7' westward. When you are atop the bridge and look down at the Atlantic Ocean your mind will reel as you realize the forces involved in moving such a structure. It is most likely a short time, geologically speaking, before the rock underneath the bridge is eroded and the Atlantic Ocean and the Bight of Eleuthera meet forever effectively cutting Eleuthera in two. In March of 1996, the huge seas of a severe northeasterly blow hit the bridge and washed away two people, one of whom survived. I have been told that a pilot actually flew under the

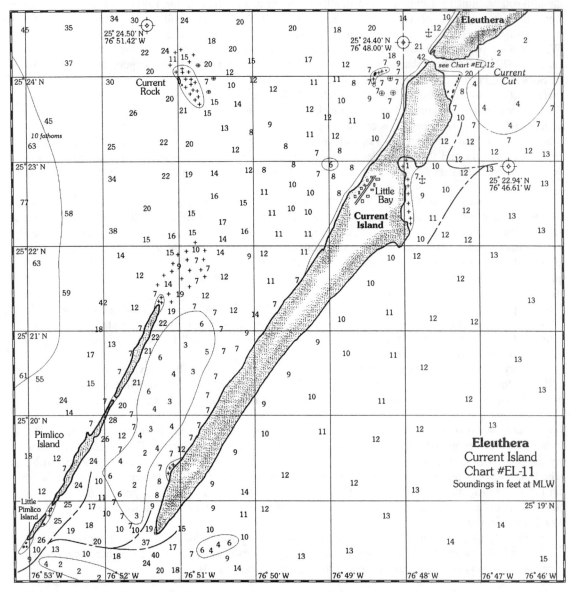

bridge in a single engine Piper Warrior II. This same pilot later died in a crash at nearby Lower Bogue. You can anchor your boat well west of the bridge and dinghy in but only in settled weather.

Along the northwestern shoreline of Eleuthera north of the Glass Window are the two communities of Upper Bogue and Lower Bogue. Access to these towns is best accomplished by road as the shoreline offers little lee except in north to northeast conditions. Some visitors ask what is the difference between Upper and Lower Bogue. Well, Upper Bogue sits on the upper road while Lower Bogue sits on the lower road. Simple, isn't it? The Bogues were once called Bog due to the characteristics of the surrounding land. The low marshes actually filled with fish during a hurricane in 1965 and some are still there in small ponds well inland. Lower Bogue seems to be the commercial center of the Bogues with a Batelco office, the *C & R Convenience Store*, *Juggie's Videos*, the *Seven Seas Restaurant and Bar*, *Johnson's Grocery*, *Eleuthera*

Meats and Convenience Store, and *Aggie's Bakery, Gullies Restaurant,* and last but certainly not least, *Lady B's Lifesaver Restaurant and Takeaway.*

THE CURRENT AND CURRENT CUT

At the northwestern tip of Eleuthera sits Current Cut and the small settlement of The Current. The Current is primarily a fishing town, the men staying gone for weeks at a time while the women raise their families and crank out some excellent straw work. The original settlers here came from Scotland and, like the Eleutheran Adventurers, they were shipwrecked on the Devil's Backbone. Some of The Current's 200 year old wooden clapboard houses were all but destroyed by Hurricane Andrew but after a few years of rebuilding the half-mile long town is as charming and picturesque as ever.

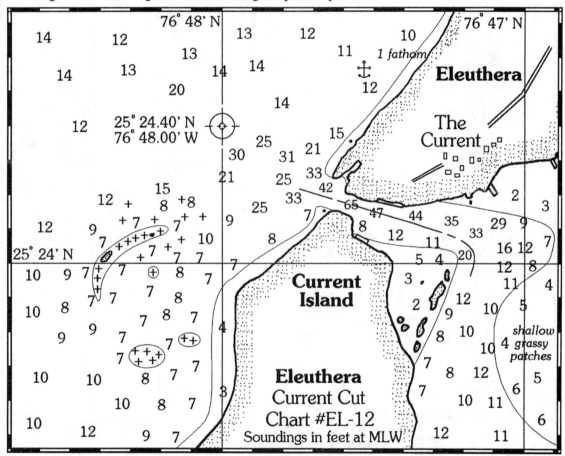

Approaching Current Cut from Hatchett Bay or Governor's Harbour, a GPS waypoint at 25° 22.94' N, 76° 46.61' W will place you approximately 1 mile south/southeast of the eastern entrance to Current Cut as shown on Chart #EL-11. From this position head approximately 270°-280° until you can turn to starboard and parallel the shoreline of Current Island northward to Current Cut (which is shown in greater detail on Chart #EL-12). There is a small cove west/southwest of the waypoint that offers good protection in winds from the west and northwest. In calm prevailing conditions you can anchor here to await the change of tide at Current Cut. Heading northward stay close to shore, about 50-150 yards off, and follow the coastline northward until you can round the last offlying rock to port giving it a wide berth. Then head straight through the cut to the other side. Try to time your passage at slack tide or when the tide is ebbing. Going east to west against a flood tide is very difficult as the current flows at speeds of over 5 knots at times. Once through you can take up your course to Royal Island or Meek's Patch and Spanish Wells as you choose.

Vessels wishing to pass through Current Cut from the west to the east should head for a GPS waypoint at 25° 24.40' N, 76° 48.00' W, which will put you about ½ mile northwest of the western entrance to the

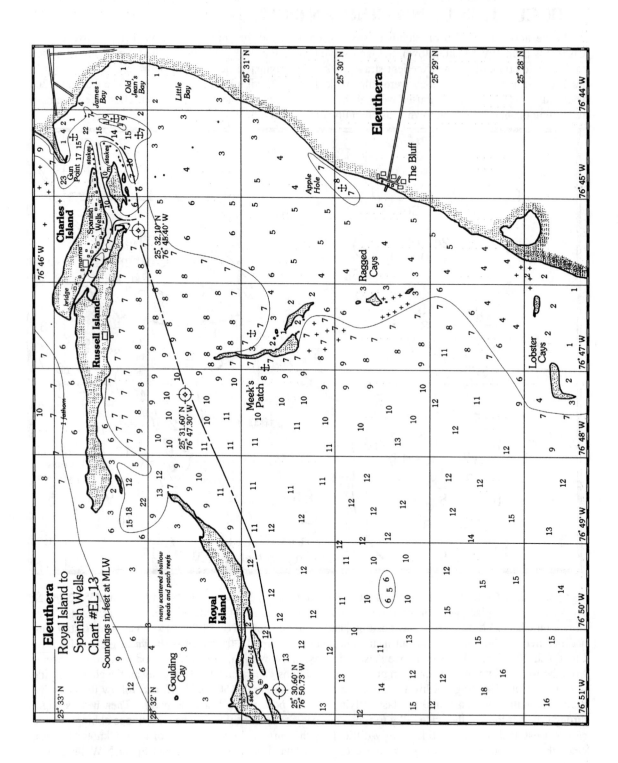

cut. In prevailing conditions you can anchor anywhere in the lee of Eleuthera or Current Island to await the tide. Try not to head east against an ebbing tide in Current Cut. I have motored against the tides in Current Cut many times and although it is safe in a boat with a good auxiliary, the prudent navigator will await a favorable tide. Quite often people run aground at Current Cut and it is usually after they pass through the cut from the west to the east. Their mistake is almost always not turning southward quick enough to parallel the shoreline and avoid the shallows east of Current Cut. These grassy bars are sometimes hard to see and often skippers are unaware that they are so shallow. Once past the offlying rock at the eastern end of Current Cut (be sure to give it a wide berth as you round it to the north), turn sharply to starboard and parallel the shoreline southward staying about 50-150 yards off until you come to the cove I mentioned in the last paragraph that lies almost 1 mile south/southwest of Current Cut. When abeam of the point at the north end of this cove you can turn to the west and take up your course for Hatchett Bay or Governor's Harbour.

On the northern bank of Current Cut is a dock where the mailboat *Current Pride* loads and unloads her cargos of peoples and supplies. On the south side of Current Cut, at the northern end of Current Island, is a small dock that is used by people from Little Bay and The Current as a landing for Current Island. On the northern shore of Current Cut, at the western end of the cut is a small concrete-lined canal that would make a good refuge but only for shallow draft boats. All the local boats head there at the first sign of threatening weather.

Vessels can pass along the shore of Current Island either north or south or pass to the east of Pimlico Island and Little Pimlico Island along the shore of those two islands. The eastern shore of Current Island is deep with few obstructions from Current Cut southward. The only other danger is a shallow sandbank east of the southern tip of Current Island as shown on Chart #EL-11.

Vessels can also coast along the western shore of Current Island from Current Cut southward but the channel gets narrow and shallow, 7' at low water, the further south you go. Just southwest of Current Cut are two small offlying cays with shallow reefs around them and east of them. Give these a berth of ¼ mile. I cannot recommend passing between these rocks and Current Island unless you have good visibility and you can read the water well. There are a few rocky bars here that are hard to see. The mailboat does come through here though and you might follow him if you draw less than 6' and the tide is high. Watch out for the shallow bar in the center of Bar Bay. The southern tip of Current Island has a fierce current (2-3 knots and more at times) just off the point, be careful here. There is a nice though sometimes rolly anchorage off the beach on the southwestern shore of Current Island. You will need two anchors here due to the srong current. From Current Cut you may also head southwest along the eastern shores of Pimlico and Little Pimlico Islands as shown on Chart #EL-11. This route is much deeper and wider than the one along the

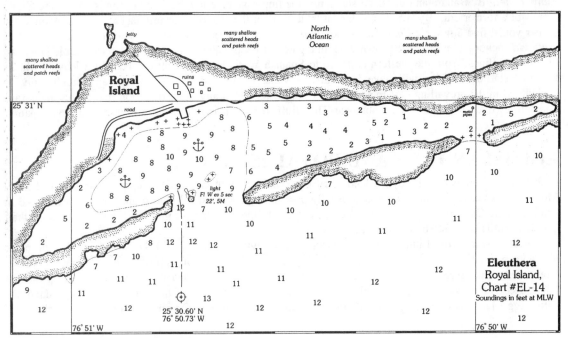

Eleuthera
Royal Island,
Chart #EL-14
Soundings in feet at MLW

western shore of Current Island though it too is affected by strong currents. Along the western shore of Current Island is the small village of Little Bay. Here you will find about 100 residents. Most of the men are fishermen who are gone for weeks at a time in search of lobster, conch, and scalefish. The chief point of interest in Little Bay is the cemetery. Sitting in an open field, there are several large limestone rocks that were carved out and used for tombs.

Vessels heading to Spanish Wells or Current Cut from Nassau have another route to choose from. A GPS waypoint at 25° 24.50' N, 76° 51.42' W, will place you approximately ½ mile northwest of Current Rock as shown on Chart #EL-11. The light that once stood on Current Rock was destroyed and nobody seems to know when or if it will be rebuilt. If heading north to Spanish Wells or over to Current Cut, keep Current Rock and its surrounding reefs to starboard. If heading to Current Cut, give the north end of Current Rock a berth of at least ½ mile. Keep an eye out for Southwest Reef which lies north/northwest of Current Rock.

If you choose to anchor off The Current and wish to dinghy in to town you will find the well stocked *Durham's Grocery*, *Griffin's Snack Bar*, a *Texaco* gas station, a Batelco office, and *L & M's Bakery and Takeaway*. Near the dock you'll find *Monica's Curio Shop* for those in need of cards or gifts.

Divers will want to take advantage of the unusual drift dive that Current Cut has to offer. The western end of the cut is 65' deep in places with sheer canyon-like walls rising vertically on both sides. Drifting by the scoured walls at 5 knots or more can be a thrilling experience for the avid SCUBA enthusiast wanting something just a little bit different. SCUBA divers can often drift through four times without exhausting a tank of air. The drift dive has been described as the closest thing to flying for the SCUBA diver.

There is a little known cave along the northern shore above The Current in which the suspected remains of a Lucayan Indian was found. He had apparently been murdered, shot in the head by the invading Spanish.

Three miles west of Current Cut on a heading for Egg Island lies *Mystery Reef* in the middle of a large sandy area in 25' of water. Six colorful, large, and imposing coral heads crop up 10'-20' with schools of fish darting in and out in abundance. This is an excellent spot for underwater photography.

On Current Island is the small, outlying community of Little Bay with its nearly 100 inhabitants. Rarely attracting visitors, the town's small store carries only the barest necessities. Most of the residents are fishermen.

North of The Current, almost as far as the landing for Spanish Wells, is the settlement of The Bluff lying about 5 miles south of Spanish Wells as shown on Chart #EL-13. The Bluff was originally a settlement of liberated slaves. The settlement contained many fine orange orchards at that time and shipped much of its product to the U.S. Here on the water's edge just above the dock you will find the huge, elegant *Miss Annie Hotel*. By Bahamian out-island standards, the impressive yellow building reminds one of the Grand Hotels of a former era. By American standards, it is about the size of your ordinary mansion. Around the corner you'll find *Sawyer's Food Store* and *Onassa's Snacks*. As shown on Chart #EL-13, a vessel of 6' draft can anchor just north of the town dock in a patch of deep water sometimes called the Apple Hole just off the shoreline. From the western entrance to Spanish Wells head straight for The Bluff leaving Meeks Patch to starboard. You will have 5'-6' at low water on this route. The anchorage should only be considered in the prevailing east to southeast winds, winds from any other direction makes this anchorage untenable. Even if you don't anchor near The Bluff, the town is only a long dinghy trip from Spanish Wells.

EGG ISLAND CUT AND ROYAL ISLAND

Just to the southwest of Royal Island lies Egg Island and Egg Island Cut as shown on Chart #EL-15. Most boaters headed south from Abaco usually pass through Egg Island Cut to anchor at Royal Island or head towards Current Cut or Spanish Wells. Boaters headed north pass through the cut to take up their course towards Little Harbour at Great Abaco.

If headed south from Little Harbour, Abaco, a GPS waypoint at 25° 29.60' N, 76° 54.75' W, will place you approximately 1½ mile west/northwest of Egg Island Cut. As you approach this waypoint and Egg Island Cut, make sure that the strong easterly current here does not push you to the east and up on Egg Island Reef. If headed south from this waypoint, head for the middle of the cut between Egg Island and Little Egg Island. Once through the cut you can head for Royal Island, Current Cut, or Spanish Wells.

If you are headed to Abaco head out Egg Island Cut and head for the waypoint mentioned above. Once at the waypoint you can take up your northerly heading to Little Harbour. Do not turn to the north too soon as you may find yourself fetching up on Egg Island Reef. Watch out for the strong easterly current here.

On the southwest shore of Egg Island in the cut between Egg and Little Egg is a picturesque little anchorage called Bimini Bay. This should be considered a daytime, settled weather anchorage only due to the surge that works through here. I knew one skipper that sought shelter in here in 25 knot northerly winds and wound up rolling gunnel to gunnel all night. Some skippers like to anchor on the western side of Great Egg Island off the small beach in prevailing winds. This spot has a good holding sandy bottom but you must pass over a rocky area with 8'-11' of water over it to get to this pleasant anchorage.

Due west and northwest of Egg Island Light is the *Egg Island Lighthouse Reef* lying in about 60' of water. Heads rise up some 35' from a sandy bottom and the proximity to the drop off brings a large variety of fish from large jewfish to jacks and even a few pompano to the reef.

Vessels headed to Royal Island or Spanish Wells from Nassau can head to a waypoint at 25° 27.87' N, 76° 53.75' W, which will place you approximately ¼ mile southwest of the very visible wreck of the *Arimora*. The 250' *Arimora* was a Lebanese freighter that caught fire and ran aground here on purpose. Pass south of the wreck in 20' of water and take up your course to Royal Island or Spanish Wells. There is

Eleuthera
Egg Island,
Egg Island Cut
Chart #EL-15
Soundings in feet at MLW

20' of water all around this wreck, you can even pass between the wreck and the reef off the southern tip of Little Egg Island. The wreck is a popular dive spot.

Royal Island is about 3½ miles long and very narrow with a good all weather harbour that is not the best of hurricane holes as those who attempted to ride out Andrew found out. Royal Island was originally named *Ryal*, after the Spanish coin, but this was corrupted to Royal, its present name. The island was purchased in the 1930's by a W.P. Stewart from Florida who built an extensive and very beautiful plantation upon the island. The conspicuous ruins of stone and intricate tile work are all that remain of a once elaborate estate. The huge blocks of stone used to construct the buildings were brought over from Eleuthera in small sailboats, 21 to a boat, and hand carried up the hill to their current place. In the early 1990's an attempt was made to acquire funds to rebuild the estate but no money ever materialized. If you want to find out more about the ruins or the history of Royal Island contact Edsel Roberts (*Dolphin*) at Spanish Wells. Edsel was the caretaker for the Island thirty years ago. Edsel told me in June of 1997 that he heard Royal Island was in the process of being sold. If this happens you can probably expect to see some changes. Keep an eye out.

As shown on the chart, there are actually three openings to the anchorage at Royal Island. The entrance to the northeast is navigable only by very small boats or dinghies. Even then use caution as there is only about a foot of water in places compounded by a small rocky bar just inside. The best landmarks are the two hills, the highest points on Royal Island, the entrance to Royal Island Harbour lies about ½ mile north of these hills. A GPS waypoint at 25° 30.60' N, 76° 50.73' W will place you approximately ¼ mile south of the entrance to the anchorage at Royal Island as shown on Chart #EL-14. In the middle of this pass sits a large rock (or a small cay) which is home to the Royal Island Light (FL W ev 5 sec, 22', 5m). The entrance to the anchorage lies through the narrower cut to the southwest of the light. Keep the rock with the light to starboard upon entering the anchorage. The cut that lies just to the northeast of the light has a large submerged rock lying approximately 50 yards inside and just barely under the surface. It is possible to pass on either side of the submerged rock but it is so hard to see and the passage on the other side of the light is so easy it is best to ignore this route no matter how inviting it appears.

Once inside the anchorage you may notice a few moorings still in the anchorage. These were once part of some 20 well kept moorings whose conditions have now degraded to the point that it is unsafe to pick one up. Over the winter and spring of 1997, word quickly spread about the danger of the moorings as boats broke loose and drifted away. The owner no longer charges for the use of the moorings and if you pick one up it is entirely at your own risk. Personally, I would forget the moorings, the holding is great here so don't be afraid to anchor in the white mud/sand/grass bottom. I once rode out a frontal passage here with my two CQR's buried, the wind blowing a sustained 50+ knot for six hours with gusts to 70, and if I did move, it was not enough to notice. The skippers and crews of the boats that rode out Hurricane Andrew here would probably tell you a different story though.

Ashore you will find plenty of ruins that testify to the once grand estate that flourished here over half a century ago. Be sure to check out the beautiful tile work in the buildings, some of which is painted over, and the intricate concrete finishing on the road that leads up the hill from the dock. Use caution as you approach the dock. There are some shallow heads just to the southwest of the dock. A huge section of the outer end of the dock is submerged due to hurricane damage and there are a few pieces of re-bar rising up to spear the errant dinghy. The western section of this submerged dock is above water at low tide.

At the dock you will find a faucet that runs from the cistern atop the hill. On warm days the water that is in the pipes and comes out first may serve as a short hot shower. Please, do not be so discourteous as some other cruisers in the past have been, do not leave your garbage ashore here. If you follow the road over the hill to the other side where you will find a paved road that used to stretch out to a small cay just offshore. Snorkelers will love diving this side of the island and checking out the reefs.

SPANISH WELLS

Spanish Wells was once called *Sigatoo* when the area was occupied by Lucayan Indians in pre-Columbian times. The Spanish slavers named the area Spanish Wells for the abundance of good water found thereabouts from which they could fill their casks. Some of today's inhabitants are descendants of the Loyalists who fled from the American Revolution while others are descended from William Sayles Eleuthera Adventurers, English Puritans who arrived in 1648 just off the northern tip of Eleuthera seeking freedom to work and worship their God as they saw fit. One hundred and fifty seven Eleutheran Adventurers came ashore after piling up their ship on the Devil's Backbone. They lived in caves on the northern tip of Eleuthera for almost two years before 57 went to Spanish Wells and 100 left for Harbour Island. They held religious services in these early years in what is now known as Preacher's Cave on the northern shore of Eleuthera just inland from the Devil's Backbone. During the War of 1812 Spanish Wells was plundered and partially burnt by an American vessel.

Although in most of the settlements in The Bahamas the principal religion is Anglican, Spanish Wells is Methodist, the only Methodist island in The Bahamas. This is because John and Charles Wesley, the founders of Methodism, landed in the area for several months on their way to Georgia in the New World.

Today's Spanish Wellsians have an unusual accent, not quite British, Bahamian, or American yet somewhere in between standing quite on its own in The Bahamas. Of an estimated 1500 Spanish Wellsians over 1480 are white, a very unusual ratio in The Bahamas. The black workers that you see in Spanish Wells are Bahamian or Haitian and live on Eleuthera commuting by boat daily.

Spanish Wells has a thriving seafood industry with a strong industrial base and does not rely on tourism for its economy. Agriculture plays a minor role in the economy of Spanish Wells. The hills of Russell Island contribute oranges and tangerines while local gardens boast tomatoes, lemons, cucumbers, and even pineapple. The town itself is crime-free, you can walk anywhere at anytime of the day or night without fear, but bring a flashlight as they shut down the city street lights at 9:00 P.M. The attractive houses, some dating back 150 years, are well kept and almost all are nicely landscaped. Every Christmas season the homeowners in Spanish Wells join in a Christmas lighting competition. The highly decorated houses vie for prizes and the entire island puts on a very festive air.

Although there is an excellent school on the island most young male Spanish Wellsians leave school at 14. Burdened by a lack of academic skills, 9 out of 10 boys become lobster fishermen. However a lobster fisherman can earn upwards of $40,000 for a four week trip making this a highly profitable line of work in anybody's book. During the off-season and between fishing trips Spanish Wells fishermen spend their time repairing their boats and preparing lobster traps for future use. The women outnumber the men in Spanish Wells and tend to marry quite young, usually between 15 and 20. If a girl hits 25 and is still single she is considered akin to an old maid. It is tradition on Spanish Wells to invite the entire island to your wedding.

Spanish Wellsians are very independent and quite proud of it. I will probably have a few of my Spanish Wells friends mad at me for including their lovely island in the same chapter with Eleuthera. They make it very clear that they are not from Eleuthera. . .they are from <u>Spanish Wells</u>!

Vessels heading to Spanish Wells from either Royal Island or Current Cut should head for a waypoint just off Meek's Patch at 25° 31.60' N, 76° 47.30' W, as shown on Chart #EL-13. From this waypoint head to a GPS waypoint at 25° 32.10' N, 76° 45.40' W, which will place you just south of the pilings that mark the western entrance to the harbour. Here you will see two large steel I beams about 8'-10' out of the water. The westernmost one is slightly leaning, probably due to a boat collision. Pass between the two and keep the inner I beam to starboard and you will enter the channel to the harbour. South of these entrance pilings are some scattered pilings painted orange that lead towards the mainland of Eleuthera. Ignore them, they mark a channel where a cable is buried.

Just a few hundred yards up the channel at the end of the jetty on your port side, another channel branches off to the west (to port) leading to *Spanish Wells Yacht Haven Marina*. The passage lies between the tip of the shoal bank to port and the piling that you must keep to starboard. Keep the shoal bank to port as you approach the marina and look for the large boat shed, you can't miss it. Between the spot where you turned to port from the main channel and the marina, almost where the stake marks the small boat channel to starboard, there is a 5' spot at low water, this is the controlling depth for this channel to the marina. If you need assistance call the marina on VHF ch. 16.

To venture into Spanish Wells Harbour proper simply continue up the main channel as it bears away to the east away from the marina entrance channel keeping the conspicuous piling to port, never venture north of that piling. There is a small anchorage and mooring area at the far eastern end of the harbour on the south side of the channel just before you enter the eastern entrance channel. For a mooring call Edsel Roberts, *Dolphin* on VHF ch. 16. Edsel also has moorings in town along the waterfront though you will be rocked quite constantly from passing boats. This is a commercial area, there is no speed limit and there are no "No Wake" restrictions. Wake is a part of life for boats tying up along the dock at Spanish Wells, be prepared.

The eastern entrance channel is easily seen in good visibility and well marked. There is a line of pilings that you need to keep to your port side as you head east. Vessels coming into Spanish Wells from Ridley Head Channel or Harbour Island should proceed to a waypoint at 25° 32.13' N, 76° 44.35' W, which will place you just east of the mouth of the eastern entrance. Keep the poles to starboard and follow the channel into the harbour and you will have 10' all the way in at low water. The poles have red reflectors on them to aid a nighttime approach.

If approaching from Meek's Patch, it is possible to pass south of Spanish Wells from the western entrance to the eastern entrance in the channel that rounds George's Cay. From the pilings south of the western entrance to the harbour, head east keeping just south of the offlying rocks. There is a small orange tipped piling between the channel pilings and the first small cay to port. Keep that piling to port as you head eastward. To starboard you will see a pair of these orange tipped markers and then a few more stretched out towards Eleuthera. Ignore them, they mark a pipeline channel that is too shallow for navigation. The shallowest part of this route is in the area of the orange tipped piling and the first rock that lies south of George's Cay. Here you will find 5'-6' at low water. Once you get past the first small rock the water begins to get progressively deeper from 7' to 15'. Keep the small offlying rocks close to port staying about 50 yards off and once past them you will begin to pick up three pilings. Keep these very conspicuous pilings to port as you head eastward. Some of these pilings are painted green but ignore the paint atop them If using the red-right-returning maxim these should be painted red and I have no idea how these came to be painted incorrectly. Personally, I don't know why someone would want to take this route to get to the eastern side of the harbour near Gun Point. By taking the channel through Spanish Wells Harbour you avoid the shallows, get to see a bit of the town, and only lengthen your trip by a few minutes, less than ½ mile.

If heading from the eastern entrance south to the western entrance, follow the above route in reverse. Keep the green painted pilings to starboard, then follow close in to the offlying rocks on your starboard side. As you approach the pilings at the western entrance to the harbour you will cross the shallowest part of this route, 5'-6' at low water. Once you arrive at the pilings the water gets progressively deeper from 7'-9' and more as you continue to head west. Keep the northernmost orange tipped piling to starboard and ignore the orange pilings that lie south of the western entrance, these mark a buried cable that leads to the mainland of Eleuthera.

There are some excellent settled weather anchorages just east of Spanish Wells off the eastern edge of the channel in some deep water pockets surrounded by steeply rising grassy topped sandbanks as shown on Chart #EL-13. There is 10'-20' in these pockets and holding is excellent although not a place to ride out a frontal passage. Another excellent anchorage east of Spanish Wells is in the bight just off the beach south of Gun Point on the mainland of Eleuthera. If a front is approaching it would be wise to head back into Spanish Wells or over to Royal Island.

There are three places in Spanish Wells to obtain diesel and gas. From the east along the shore the first business you come to is *Ronald's Marine and Service Center*. *Ronald's* is an *Evinrude-Johnson* dealer as well as a supplier of marine supplies and they also have a fuel dock for diesel and gas. Next as you head west you will come across the *Anchor Snack Bar* which serves some of the best food in town, reservations are suggested for dinner on the weekends as the locals tend to keep them quite busy Fridays and Saturdays. Next door is the purple building that used to be *Langousta's Restaurant and Bar*. The owner has passed away and the building is for sale. With the exception of the bar at *Yacht Haven Marina*, there is no other place in town to get a drink or purchase alcoholic beverages. Next along the road is *Marguerita's Dry Goods* and then *Pinder's Supermarket* where you can get free water right at the dock along with fuel. Next door is *R & B Boat Yard* where you can get your boat hauled out and the hull repaired or painted. Next is *Spanish Wells Marine and Hardware Ltd.* with a complete selection of marine goods, diesel and gas at their *Texaco Starport* fuel dock, *Mercury* repairs (some say they have the best *Merc* mechanic anywhere), some hull and electrical repair, and ice. Further west is the old building that once housed the *Sea View Restaurant* and which is now *Jack's Outback*. Jack serves excellent food but no alcohol although he doesn't mind if his customers bring their own. If you need a diesel mechanic, welding, or refrigeration repairs you can call *On Site Marine and Auto* at 333-4389. If you walk up the hill past *Pinder's Supermarket* you will come to a gift shop and a hardware store. If you take a left here and head towards the water tower you will come to the *Captain's Diner* with its laundromat in the back of the building.

Heading westward down the creek west of town lies *Spanish Wells Yacht Haven Marina* with 40 slips that can accommodate a 10' draft although the entrance channel will only allow 5'-6' at MLW. *Yacht Haven* has a restaurant and rooms for rent on premises and accepts major credit cards. There is also a Batelco phone booth on premises, diesel and gas, and RO water at 25¢ a gallon. Dockmaster Anthony Bethel wishes to remind boaters that *Yacht Haven Marina* is the only place to get gas on Sundays and Holidays at Spanish Wells. West of Yacht Haven is the recently rebuilt *Adventurers Paradise Hotel*. Over the hill from *Yacht Haven Marina* and slightly to the west lies the large *Food Fair* supermarket and

pharmacy with the best provisioning in the area, quite comparable to Nassau prices. A new g⸍
clinic is scheduled to open across the street from the *Food Fair* in 1998. If you find yourself w⸍
to do and want to catch the latest releases check out *Crazy Frank's Videos* which lies just up the⸍
east. There is not a local dentist although one visits weekly from the mainland of Eleuthera on Thursơays
and Fridays if your teeth are giving you problems while in the area. Dr. Pfeifer, formerly of Abaco, now
has a small practice in Spanish Wells.

Meek's Patch, as shown on Chart #EL-13, is a nice spot to anchor in some conditions. In easterly winds
you can anchor off the small beach on the western side, when the winds go southwest to west, you can
anchor off the even nicer beach on the eastern side of the cay. This cay is a popular picnic and swimming
spot for local boaters and on holidays and weekends it may get crowded.

For excellent guide service to this area, including fishing, diving, or navigating Ridley Head Channel or
the route to Harbour Island (along *The Devil's Backbone*), try Edsel Roberts (333-4209, VHF ch. 16-
Dolphin), Broadshad Pinder (333-4427, VHF ch.16-*A1 Broadshad*), Bradley Newbold (333-4079, VHF ch.
16-*Cinnabar*), Dave Roberts, John Roberts, or Preston Sands.

RIDLEY HEAD AND THE DEVIL'S BACKBONE

Harbour Island is one of the most popular vacation destinations for visitors to The Bahamas and getting
to Harbour Island may well be one of your greatest feats of piloting. I suggest that first timers, those new
to cruising these waters, hire a pilot from Spanish Wells to show you the way along the Devil's Backbone.
If you refuse to hire a pilot you should rethink your situation. This is not an easy run unless you are an
experienced Bahamas hand and are confident in your ability to read the water. This can truly be a
dangerous route, but almost all of them are in The Bahamas. Personally, I think the entrance into the
Propeller Cay anchorage at Samana is harder to see and almost as dangerous if you stray. The controlling
depth for the Devil's Backbone route is 6' at low water.

The Devil's Backbone should only be run on a fairly calm day (as in no large ocean swells) and with
good visibility. Any large swells or strong winds out of any northerly quadrant make this an extremely
risky route. I have run this route in 6'-8' leftover northeasterly swells from a low pressure system that was
hundreds of miles to the northeast and the passage was highly uncomfortable to say the least. To arrange
for a pilot see the last paragraph in the previous section on *Spanish Wells*. Vessels returning from Harbour
Island to Spanish Wells should follow these directions in reverse. If you hired a pilot when headed to
Harbour Island, you may feel confident enough to try the route by yourself on the return trip.

CAUTION: I am going to give you some waypoints that lie along this route. These waypoints are for
reference only or for entering or leaving by Ridley Head Channel or Bridge Point Channel. Never attempt
to run waypoint to waypoint on this route. Eyeball navigation is the only way through here unless you hire
a pilot. If you insist on using waypoints, I urge you to change your mind and hire a pilot.

When leaving Spanish Wells for The Devil's Backbone one must first negotiate the channel past Ridley
Head as shown on Chart #EL-16. Leaving the eastern entrance channel to Spanish Wells turn to port and
take Gun Point to starboard to take up your course for Ridley head as shown on Chart #EL-16. Once you
round Gun Point you will see Ridley Head towards the northeast and the huge steel I-beam that sits a little
to seaward of it. Take up a course to a position north of that I-beam. Just past Gun Point on this route you
will find some shallows with 7' over them at low tide. Do not attempt to pass between the I-beam and
Ridley Head as this area is foul with shallow rocks and heads. Watch out for the scattered reefs on your
port side as you approach Ridley Head. A GPS waypoint at 25° 33.54' N, 76° 44.33' W, will place you just
north of Ridley Head and is the southern waypoint for vessels entering Ridley Head Channel from seaward.
Let us pause here and discuss Ridley Head Channel. If you are heading east along the Devil's Backbone
you can skip the next paragraph.

Ridley Head Channel is a good but narrow passage from the Spanish Wells area to the North Atlantic
Ocean. Many boats bound to or from Abaco use it as it gives a better angle on the prevailing wind and a
slightly shorter distance than the course from Egg Island Cut. If you are not experienced at eyeball
navigation and are approaching this area from offshore wishing to use Ridley Head Channel to enter the
Spanish Wells area, I suggest calling for a pilot as mentioned in the last paragraph in the section on Spanish
Wells. A GPS waypoint at 25° 34.50' N, 76° 44.30' W is a good spot to await a pilot. If you wish to
negotiate Ridley Head Channel without the assistance of a pilot head to the northern waypoint for the
Ridley Head Channel route at 25° 34.00' N, 76° 44.30' W. This position is approximately ½ mile north of
Ridley Head and the southern waypoint at 25° 33.54' N, 76° 44.33' W. The course from the northern

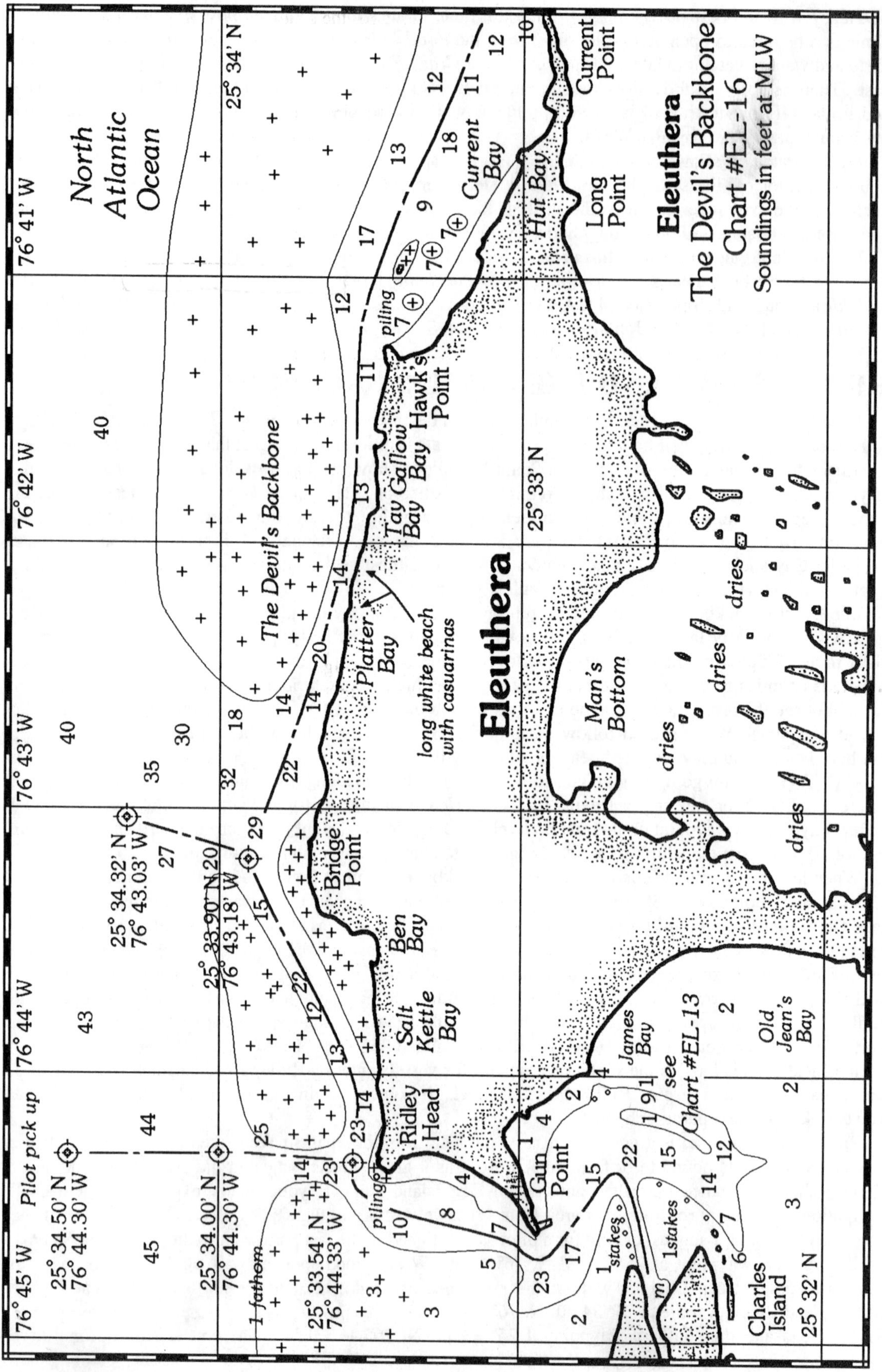

North
Atlantic
Ocean

25° 34' N

The Devil's Backbone

Current
Bay

Current
Point

Hut Bay

Long
Point

Eleuthera

The Devil's Backbone
Chart #EL-16
Soundings in feet at MLW

piling

Tay Gallow
Bay

Hawk's
Point

Bay Bay

Platter
Bay

long white beach
with casuarinas

Eleuthera

25° 33' N

Man's
Bottom

dries

dries

dries

dries

dries

25° 34.32' N
76° 43.03' W

25° 33.90' N
76° 43.18' W

Bridge
Point

Ben
Bay

Salt
Kettle
Bay

Ridley
Head

Pilot pick up

25° 34.50' N
76° 44.30' W

1 fathom

25° 34.00' N
76° 44.30' W

25° 33.54' N
76° 44.33' W

piling

James
Bay

Gun
Point

see
Chart #EL-13

Old
Jean's
Bay

stakes

stakes

Charles
Island

25° 32' N

waypoint to the southern waypoint is almost due south. Head for the southern waypoint but don't just steer that course until arrival. You must watch out for the reefs on both sides of the channel. Particularly dangerous is the very visible reef that will come up off your port bow just as you approach the southern waypoint. This was once marked by a steel I-beam which has since been knocked down to just under the surface of the water. It is almost awash at low water. The I-beam sits at the western edge of the reef so give it a wide berth. Once at the southern waypoint you can head around Gun Point to Spanish Wells or continue eastward to Harbour Island along the Devil's Backbone route.

Vessels continuing eastward from Ridley Head along the Devil's Backbone's route should proceed eastward from Ridley Head taking care to stay south of the reefs lying just east of Ridley Head Channel. Head generally east until abeam of the last palm trees in the grove on the shore on your starboard side. Once past these palm trees head for a point north of the next point of land which is called Bridge Point. Here you will be heading slightly more to seaward, passing between the offshore reefs on your port side, and the reefs that lie southwest of Bridge Point just off the shore of Eleuthera at Ben Bay. A GPS waypoint at 25° 33.90' N, 76° 43.18' W, will place you in good water north of the reefs that lie just off Bridge Point. This waypoint is also the southern waypoint for the Bridge Point Channel route. Let us once again pause while we discuss Bridge Point Channel. Vessels continuing along the Devil's Backbone route eastward can skip the next paragraph.

An open water entrance to the Devil's Backbone route lies just off Bridge Point with deep water all the way in from the ocean. It is an excellent entrance for boats bound for Harbour Island, or even for boats bound for Spanish Wells that do not want to negotiate Ridley Head Channel which is considerably narrower and quite a bit riskier. Bridge Point Channel is a deep, wide, obstruction free channel that is sometimes called the Wide Opening. Vessels entering from seaward should head to a waypoint at 25° 34.32' N, 76° 43.03' W, which lies about ½ mile north of the southern waypoint at Bridge Point. The passage from the northern waypoint to the southern waypoint at 25° 33.90' N, 76° 43.18' W, is wide, deep, and obstruction free. The closest reef lies a few hundred yards to the west and over ¼ mile or more to the east. Once at the southern waypoint you can turn and head to Ridley Channel and Spanish Wells or continue east along the Devil's Backbone route.

Okay, now back to the Devil's Backbone route. Once past Bridge Point you will enter the trickiest part of the entire route, the narrow passage between the Devil's Backbone Reef and the shoreline of Eleuthera. Once past Bridge Point you will begin heading in closer to the shoreline. Ahead of you is a long beach with an equally long stand of casaurinas behind it. Head in for this beach where you will pass between the Devil's Backbone Reef and the beach staying about 30-50 yards off the beach. Continue close in past the beach until you reach Hawk's Point. A GPS waypoint at 25° 33.53' N, 76° 40.85' W, lies just north of Hawk's Point. Continue east and once past Hawk's Point the channel gets a little wider. You can now breathe a sigh of relief. You have passed through the trickiest part. Just east of Hawk's Point is a rocky bar marked by a piling. Keep this bar and piling to starboard. Pass between the piling and the reefs to its north. The shoreline of Eleuthera can take 7' close in here but there are some shallow heads and bars between the piling and Eleuthera in Current Bay.

Continuing eastward past the piling head for the next point of land which is called Current Point. A GPS waypoint at 25° 33.05' N, 76° 39.88' W, lies just north of Current Point as shown on Chart EL-17. The waters on your port side will open up as you come abeam of Pierre Island. In olden days large sailing boats would anchor here because they could not get closer to Dunmore Town. As you pass Current Point you will see another steel I-beam to the east. Pass to the south of this piling within 50 yards or so. This is the shallowest part of the Devil's Backbone route and you will find 6' of water here at low tide. As you head southeast past this piling you will be steering approximately 140° and you will have to eyeball your way past the shallow bar to your starboard side. A GPS waypoint at 25° 32.26' N, 76° 39.17' W, is clear of the sandbar and a good reference for your southward turn. From this position head southward staying clear of the sandbars west of Harbour Island as you make your way south to the anchorage or marinas at Dunmore Town. Vessels heading to Spanish Wells along the Devil's Backbone from Harbour Island should head to this waypoint and then begin steering approximately 320° to pass south of the steel piling. Then follow the directions for the Devil's Backbone route in reverse.

For snorkelers and SCUBA divers alike there are some excellent dive opportunities in the waters surrounding the Devil's Backbone. Along the Devil's Backbone lies the *Train Wreck*, a wooden barge bearing a train that sank in 15' of water in 1865. It is said that it was a Union train captured by the Confederacy and sold to a Cuban sugar plantation owner to raise money for the war effort. Now overgrown with elkhorn and brain coral, the wreck consists of three sets of wheel trucks believed to be part of a locomotive and pieces of wooden beams lying half buried in the sandy sea floor.

A few hundred yards away from the *Train Wreck* lies the wreck of the *Cienfuegos* in 10'-35' of water. The *Cienfuegos*, a Ward Line passenger liner, sank in 1895 but not before saving all her passengers and even salvaging her cargo of rice. All that remains of the wreck is a twisted section of her 200' hull, two huge heat exchangers, a boiler, and the main shaft.

Aground on the Devil's Backbone, is the wreck of the *Cienfuegos*. A few feet away from the *Cienfuegos* lie the remains of the grain and passenger ship *Vanaheim*, an 86' coaster that hit the reef during a winter storm in 1969, and was pushed over the reef where she broke up in 15' of water. She was carrying a load of potatoes and onions and is now known as the *Potato and Onion Wreck*. Other wrecks along this treacherous reef system include the *Carnarvon*, a 186' steel freighter that sank in 30' of water in 1916 (I've also heard she sank in 1918) and a 76' shrimper that went down in 20' of water in 1969. For those wishing to visit these sites, check with *Valentines Yacht Club Dive Shop* on Harbour Island or with one of the guides listed above at Spanish Wells.

For those few who wish to see Harbour Island without the risk of running *The Devil's Backbone* you can catch a ferry from the mainland of Eleuthera. First take the ferry from Spanish Wells to the mainland and then just ask any taxi driver about it. Another option is the Friday morning mailboat. At precisely 6:00 A.M. on Friday mornings the mailboat *The Eleuthera Express II* leaves the dock at Spanish Wells for the trip to Harbour Island. *The Express* stays at Harbour Island for approximately three hours then heads back to Spanish Wells. Be sure to ask the Captain just how long his ship will stay at Harbour Island before you go roaming about. The price for this trip is only $10.00 per person. For those who wish to stay longer you can always take the ferry back to the mainland and then a taxi and ferry back to Spanish Wells. Ask the mailboat Captain if the mailboat *Yeocomico II* (sometimes just called the *Yoco*) is at Harbour Island. The *Yeocomico II* often leaves Harbour Island on Friday afternoons and stops at Spanish Wells, at no charge to passengers. This alternative might allow you a few extra hours at Harbour Island.

HARBOUR ISLAND

Well, we've discussed how hard it is to get there, now let's see what you're missing if you don't try. Harbour Island is one of the oldest settled islands in The Bahamas. It is occasionally called Briland (and its inhabitants Brilanders) which is a slurred corruption of Harbour Island. The 3 mile long island's only settlement, Dunmore Town, is named after the Earl Of Dunmore who was once the Governor of Virginia. The Earl later acquired a summer residence on Harbour Island when he was Governor of The Bahamas from 1786-1797. Prior to that Dunmore Town was primarily a military post with Barracks Hill and a few old guns being the only reminders of that age. Dunmore Town was a settlement before the United States was a nation and, until recently, the second city of The Bahamas next to Nassau. Dunmore Town was known as a shipbuilding center from the 1700's until World War II and the largest ship ever constructed in The Bahamas, the four-masted *Marie J. Thompson,* was built there in 1922. The famous pirate Calico Jack Rackham is said to have once raided Harbour Island and burnt a few fishing boats. Harbour Island was also once a sugar refinement center. The Brilander's skill in the refinement process gave them an important second industry. . . rum. With the advent of prohibition Harbour Island became quite a popular spot. Today the island is tourism oriented, the guests focusing on the three mile long pink sand beach. Reflective of the tourist industry here, prices are a little higher for most goods.

When skippers reach the last waypoint on the Devil's Backbone route, the one that places you well southeast of the last piling and east of the large sandbank at 25° 32.26' N, 76° 39.17' W, you can take up a route southward to the anchorage off Dunmore Town proper as shown on Chart #EL-17. Most boaters anchor off Dunmore Town simply because it offers easy access to shore. For those not so inclined there are other nice anchorages throughout the area. A good anchorage in northeast to southeast conditions lies at the southern end of Man Island as shown on the chart. In westerly weather you can head over to the mainland of Eleuthera at the ferry landing as shown on Chart #EL-17. Here you will find shelter in winds from southwest to northwest. For shelter from southeast to southwest winds you can head all the way to the southern end of the bay. Leave the sandbank off Dunmore Town to port and head towards Cistern Rock. Pass between Cistern Rock and the shallow bank to its east and you can anchor off the beach at the southern end of the bay in 7'-8' of water at low tide.

If you do intend to anchor off Dunmore Town proceed south from the waypoint and give the sandbank northwest of Dunmore Town a wide berth. After passing the sandbank head in to shore and anchor

Eleuthera
Harbour Island
Chart #EL-17
Soundings in feet at MLW

76° 40' W 76° 39' W 76° 38' W 76° 37' W

10 fathoms

25° 33' N
25° 32' N
25° 31' N
25° 30' N
25° 29' N
25° 28' N

Pierre Island

1 fathom

Current Point

Man Island

piling

25° 32.26' N
76° 39.17' W

Iron Sound Rock

Jacob's Island

North Atlantic Ocean

Little Pigeon Island

The Narrows

Pigeon Island

Centipede Cay

Eastmost Rock

Old Jean's Bay

Westmost Rock

Harbour Island

Nurse Creek

Girls Bank

Pear Rock

jetty

Dunmore Town

Three Islands

Round Head

Pond Rock

Maho Creek

Mastic Point

for instructions on these two routes see text

25° 28.70' N
76° 37.30' W

pilings

Whale Point

Eleuthera

Cistern Rock

Cistern Bay

Bottom Harbour

wherever you choose. If you prefer a less crowded and less busy anchorage, head south of the last marina (*Harbour Island Club*) and anchor in the small cove about ½ mile south of the marina. You can tie up to the beach around the town dock, the large concrete wharf with the yellow building on it, north of the marinas. Often the marinas will let you tie up for a few hours if you ask first.

There are two marinas on Harbour Island. South of the large sandbank (where Brilanders are building a new jetty) and the town dock is *Valentines Yacht Club*. *Valentines Yacht Club* is the largest marina (42 slips) in the area and has complete amenities including a dive site on premises. Dockmaster Marcus Pinder will make you feel right at home and wants boaters to know that even though the marina has only sold diesel, that they are installing new pumps and Valentine's will begin selling gas also in later 1997. Here you'll find *The Reach Restaurant and Bar* right on the water's edge. Across the street is *Valentines Yacht Club Inn* and its dining room, dinner with reservation. SCUBA divers will want to check out the dive operations here at *Valentines Dive Shop*, especially *Miller Reef* which lies just offshore. The reef is a maze of coral archways, canyons, and caves in waters from 50' to 100' deep. Ask them about *The Arch* also. The marina can arrange a laundry take out service for you.

About a mile south of Valentines is the *Harbour Island Club and Marina* nestled among beautiful shade trees on a grass covered hillside. The marina sells diesel and gas 7 days a week and is home to the *Devil's Backbone Bar and Restaurant*. Guests have access to a fresh water pool at the clubhouse. The marina can also arrange a laundry service and golf cart rental. Between the two marinas lies the swank *Romora Bay Club* which has absolutely one of the best views on the island. On site are *Sloppy Joe's Bar* and *Ludo's Restaurant*.

Dunmore Town is quite large and the shops spread out. For those not inclined to walking, the best way to see the town is to rent a golf cart from one of the local entrepreneurs. You can call *Sunshine Rentals* or *Ross Rentals* on VHF ch. 16. They will deliver the carts to wherever you are, preferably at one of the marinas. There are also a few other places around town that rent golf carts and scooters, ask at either of the marinas for more information. It is a real joy to hop in a golf cart and tool around the narrow streets where you get a close up view of Harbour Island life and architecture.

There are quite a lot of businesses on Harbour Island, too many to list here, so I will just give you a feel for the most important ones. Ask the golf cart rental agent or the marinas for a map of the town. In town is *Chaqaro's Hardware* where you can get your propane tanks filled. There are a lot of places to eat and drink and it would take a couple of weeks to sample them all. A great spot for lunch is the *Dunmore Deli* with great sandwiches and cold drinks and nice open air porch for dining. Next to the deli is the *Piggly Wiggly* food store, no relation to the American chain of stores. Around the corner is *J's Automotive Parts* and an ice cream shop.

On Bay Street at the government dock is a row of small gift booths under the shade trees. The one place on Harbour Island that remains unspoiled by too much exposure as a tourist center is the *Harbour Lodge* under the fig tree. Here Judy Bloodworth will be happy to chat all day but won't take *American Express* cards. Across the street is the *Pineapple Fruit and Veggies* store. Just up from Bay Street is a branch of *The Royal Bank of Canada*.

One of the most peculiar places in town is the *House of Assembly*. Just a block up and inland from Valentines is a large shady tree with all kinds of lights draped on its lower branches. But what catches your eye is the number of knick knacks and hand painted signs placed there by Brilanders and visitors. Clichés, jokes, Psalms, words to live by, you'll find them all here and perhaps a few local Brilanders in the chairs and hammocks around the place. This is a great spot to just relax and hang out.

Bahamians have a saying: "Meat for the man, bone for the dog." With that in mind Brilanders hold an annual Big Beautiful Doll contest at *Seagrapes Bar*. Here, Bahama Mamas strut their stuff to see which full figured woman will be crowned Miss Big Beautiful Doll for the year. Rubens would have had a ball here.

Dunmore Town is steeped in history and there are a few sites to pique the interest of history buffs. The *Hill Steps,* originally cut by prisoners, has a subterranean tunnel leading from the cove to *Rock House*, a nearby resort. *Titus Hole* is a cave overlooking the harbour and is said to be the first jail on Harbour Island. On Bay Street is the *Loyalist Cottage* which dates back to the 1790's.

Harbour Island is big with sportfishermen who use the southern entrance for speedy access to the deep waters off the shores of Eleuthera. There are two entrance channels south of Harbour Island, one I call the northern route and one I call the southern route, both are shallow and tricky. Although an experienced skipper could run these routes, the ability to read the water is a must, a guide is suggested if you insist on taking this route. These routes are a little trickier than the Devil's Backbone, it's harder to read the depths here, but they are less dangerous in general. The northern route will take a 5' draft at high tide. Vessels with drafts over 3½' should wait for high tide to attempt the northern route. The southern route can take a 5' draft at low tide but there is a narrow spot where you must thread between two shallow banks that are less than 100'-150' apart.

To exit via the northern channel, head south from the anchorage at Dunmore Town and round the first highly visible sandbar that stretches westward from the southwestern end of Harbour Island as shown on Chart #EL-17. You will notice a line of pilings stretching from Harbour Island to the mainland. These pilings mark the new water lines serving the community of Harbour Island. About midway along the line is a piling with a horizontal red marker atop, it is the fifth one to the west from Harbour Island. Round the shallow bank and head for this piling keeping it close (within 100') as you round it on either side. A GPS waypoint at 25° 28.32' N, 76° 38.52' W (the inner waypoint on the N route), will place you just south of the piling. Once around the piling and within a boat length or two of the piling take up a course of 80° which will bring you to the southwestern tip of Harbour Island. This will bring you over the deepest water to a GPS waypoint at the southern tip of Harbour Island at 25° 28.50' N, 76° 37.81' W (the outer waypoint on the northern route). A draft of 5' can go through here with no problem at high tide but be careful not to steer too far north or south of your course or you will find yourself in shallower water. A 6' draft could work its way through here with a good high tide but the first two hundred yards closest to the piling are the shallowest and you will have to zigzag and feel your way through here.

To head out the southern channel, head south from Dunmore Town and pass to the west of the highly visible sandbar, passing between it and Cistern Rock. Follow the curve of the sandbank around to the inner waypoint. You will have to eyeball this route. The curve of the route basically follows the curve of the bay. Steer between the two shallow banks staying over the green spot (the brown and dark areas are shallow grassy bars) that is marked by small white floats (one on either side) at the time of this writing, and head towards the outer waypoint and then out into the North Atlantic Ocean.

Vessels wishing to use the above mentioned entrances south of Harbour Island from the North Atlantic Ocean should head to a GPS waypoint at 25° 28.70' N, 76° 37.30' W, which will place you approximately ½ mile to the east/northeast of Whale Point as shown on Chart #EL-17. Enter the cut slightly favoring the Harbour Island shore to avoid the shallows stretching northward from Whale Point. Once inside you can head for the waypoint for either the northern or southern route. Run the above routes in reverse. For the northern routes, head approximately 260° from the outer waypoint towards the inner waypoint. When within a boat length or two of the piling round the piling to starboard and take up your course to clear the sandbar south of the Harbour Island anchorage. If running the southern route, take up a position at the outer waypoint and head for the inner waypoint. The inner waypoint lies between two shallow banks about 100'-150' apart. The ability to read the water is necessary here. From the inner waypoint follow the deeper water around to pass between Cistern Rock and the shallow bank to your starboard side. Once clear of Cistern Rock head for the anchorage of your choice.

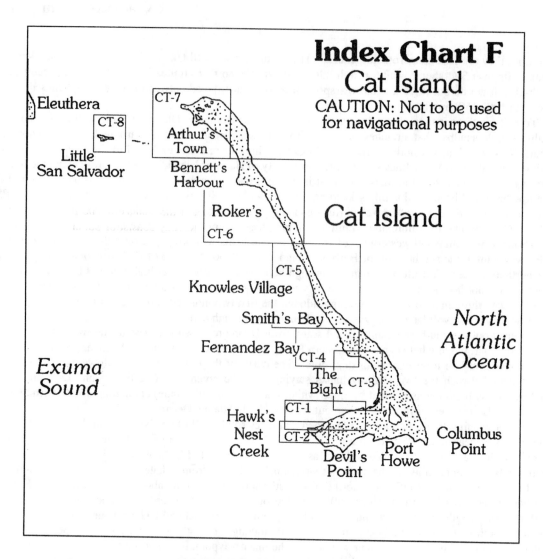

Index Chart F
Cat Island
CAUTION: Not to be used
for navigational purposes

Eleuthera

CT-8

Little
San Salvador

CT-7

Arthur's
Town

Bennett's
Harbour

Roker's

CT-6

Cat Island

CT-5

Knowles Village

Smith's Bay

Fernandez Bay

CT-4

The
Bight

CT-3

North
Atlantic
Ocean

Exuma
Sound

CT-1

Hawk's
Nest
Creek

CT-2

Devil's
Point

Port
Howe

Columbus
Point

CAT ISLAND

The original Lucayan name for Cat Island was *Guanima* but after the time of the Spanish explorers the island was called *San Salvador*. Some of the older families still retain land titles referring to the island by that name. Some of these same older residents insist that Columbus' first landfall was at Cat Island instead of the more widely accepted San Salvador. The island acquired the name Cat Island in the 18th century, some say the island was named after William Catt, a little known pirate or British sea captain depending on whose side you take. Another opinion is that the island was named after the hordes of feral cats that the English discovered on the island in the 1600's, descendants of tame cats orphaned by the Spanish in their quest for gold.

Cat Island, one of the finest agricultural producers in The Bahamas, is approximately 45 miles long from Orange Creek in the north to Port Howe in the south and averages about 4 miles wide. The island is akin to Eleuthera in that it is bordered by the North Atlantic Ocean along its windward eastern shore and shallow banks along its western shore with numerous possibilities for lee anchorages. In the 1700 and 1800's the island was home to many fairly successful Loyalist cotton plantations.

Cat Island's culture today is very traditional, some residents still cook in outside ovens. Cat Islanders are warm, friendly, and quite proud of their island. Tradition dictates that when the last of a generation dies his house is left for the spirit to reside in. Remaining family members gather stones from the site to construct a new dwelling. Elsewhere, particularly in the northern end of the island, homeowners place spindles atop their houses to keep harm from befalling anyone who resides there, a lightning rod for evil spirits of sorts. Many believe that the spirits of the dead still walk Cat Island. As I mentioned earlier, Obeah, a form of magic, is still practiced on Cat Island though most residents won't talk about it except in covert whispers and only if they know you. Many Cat Islanders are hesitant to enter the inland blue holes, possibly due to the stories of monsters lurking within or perhaps because things floating in the hole one week are found in the Atlantic the next week. Bush medicine is widely practiced and the people of Cat Island are known for their longevity, less so today than two centuries ago when a certain Daddy Sundown died in 1810 at the young age of 120.

One of the traditional types of music of Cat Island (as well as most of the islands of The Bahamas) that you will likely hear is the well known *Rake n' Scrape*. The instruments may consist of but are not limited to a bass, similar to an American washtub bass and made of a length of wood, an old tin tub, and a piece of fishing line, a rhythm section containing a conchshell horn, a harmonica which is a paper covered comb, a concertina, and a carpenter's saw scraped with a piece of metal. Setting the beat is the smoking drum made out of goatskin with a flame inside to heat it up.

Although far from remote, Cat Island is seldom visited mainly due to its lack of all weather harbours and protection from fierce northers, the only true protection being at Bennett's Harbour, Smith's Bay, and in Hawk's Nest Creek. Smaller, shoal draft vessels may find shelter in some of the extensive creek systems along Cat Island's western shore. In prevailing winds, cruising Cat Island's western shore is truly pleasurable. Even if the wind is blowing 20 knots or more, you can sail right in the lee of the land ½ mile offshore in most places and sometimes within 50 yards of the shoreline in 9' of water. There are only three large sandbars to avoid, one at Hawk's Nest Point, another at Bonefish Point, and the largest at Alligator Point.

There are no propane filling facilities on Cat Island, all tanks must be shipped to Nassau by mailboat for filling.

APPROACHES TO CAT ISLAND

From Calabash Bay, Long Island, Hawk's Nest Point bears 007° at a distance of 31.1 nautical miles. From Conch Cay Cut at George Town, Exuma, Hawk's Nest Point bears 34° at a distance of 38.8 miles. If approaching Hawk's Nest Point from Conception Island, beware of the reefs off the southern shore of Cat Island that lie some two miles off the land.

Vessels heading north along the western shore of Cat Island should be aware that the drop off to the deeper water of Exuma Sound lies just off Hawk's Nest Point in the south and follows the contour of Cat Island northward staying between 8 and 9 miles to the west of Cat Island. This area is unsurveyed and although deep reefs exist all along the drop off, there may be some shallow heads or reefs also. Likewise, there may be any number of shallow heads or reefs inshore of the drop off between the 10 fathom line and Cat Island's western shoreline. Caution is advised when traversing this area.

The vast majority of cruisers visiting Cat Island do so from south to north. We too shall visit Cat Island in that direction.

THE SOUTHERN COAST

The southern tip of the "foot" of Cat Island was a lair for pirates and wreckers. Stretching from Columbus Point at the "heel" to Devil's Point at the "toe," the southern coast was treacherous to shipping. Between Columbus Point and Devil's Point is the deceptively named Port Howe. It is not a port as the name implies, it is really no more than a mass of jagged coral where wreckers once lit fires to lure passing shipping into contributing to their economy. It is said that the buccaneer Arthur Catt used these same wreckers for his piratical schemes. Port Howe was named after Admiral James Howe, the first English Commander during the Revolutionary War. Today Port Howe has an airstrip and it is more noted for its coconut palms and lush pineapple fields. An interesting stop are the ruins of the Andrew Deveaux Plantation. Col. Andrew Deveaux was renowned for driving the Spanish from Nassau in 1783 and for this feat was rewarded with 1,000 acres on the southern end of Cat Island. Still intact is the mansion with its hand-pegged kitchen.

Columbus Point is believed to be where Columbus landed on Cat Island. At the roundabout, a landmark on the road that stretches the width of the foot of Cat Island, is a conch shell monument utilizing some 570 conch shells to commemorate that event. West of the roundabout lie McQueens, Hawk's Nest Creek, and Devil's Point. East of the roundabout lay Port Howe and Bain's Town, home of Cat Island's *Masonic Lodge* and *The Galleon Bar*. The reef offshore along the 12 mile front is very popular with SCUBA divers. Wall diving begins at 50' and drops to the bottom between 2,000 and 6,000' with a myriad of coral canyons, caves, and tunnels. Nearby Cutlass Bay is an adult's only resort with a nude beach.

In Greenwood, nine miles north of Port Howe, the *Greenwood Beach Resort* sits a hundred feet above the Atlantic Ocean and boasts an 8 mile long stretch of pink beach. The *Cat Island Dive Center* is also on premises and offers a full service dive shop facility for those wishing to explore the reefs of Cat Island. They conduct shore dives, night dives, and also provide boats for wall diving off the eastern shore and Port Howe. They accommodate all divers and certification is available with dive gear and accessories for rent. Greenwood is the only establishment of any type on the entire eastern shore of Cat Island.

North of the roundabout is Armbrister Creek where at one time a small railroad came from the other side of Cat Island bringing sisal to be shipped to Nassau. Little remains of it today, almost all the rail was sent to England during World War II for armament manufacture although a few lengths can be found supporting cauldrons in backyard kitchens. The nearby *Pilot Harbour Restaurant* offers Cat Island seafood and boasts a beautiful sunset view from its waterfront location. Dean's Wood, just east of the road contains what is left of a government forestation project from the 1930's. Madeira (mahogany) trees were planted to make furniture and some still remain in the wild.

Standing upon a crest above the Atlantic near the roundabout, about 500' off the road, are the remains of an octagonal fortress divided by a double-faced chimney. This was used to signal islanders when pirates were approaching so they could run to nearby caves to hide. It is also said that it was a pirate's lookout where they could scan the waters for passing prey. There are tales of pirate gold buried here.

South of Cat Island in the mouth of Exuma Sound lies the Tartar Bank. The Tartar Bank is a huge underwater mountain which rises to within 7 fathoms of the surface from the surrounding depths. The top of the bank is only a few hundred yards in diameter and the walls slope away from it like a cone. This creates some excellent diving opportunities for the SCUBA enthusiast but you must be wary of the currents. The tidal action in the mouth of Exuma Sound creates strong currents that swirl around and over the bank and even the most experienced divers should exercise the utmost caution when diving in this area. Skippers too should be alert as to dangerous sea conditions on the bank when wind and tide oppose. Needless to say that the fishing in this area is superb.

HAWK'S NEST CREEK

At the very toe of the "foot" of Cat Island, is Hawk's Nest Point and Hawk's Nest Creek. The creek will take 6' over the bar at low water but it shallows quickly once past the marina. As you approach McQueen's the water even gets too shallow for most dinghies. Hawk's Nest is one of the oldest British settlements on Cat Island, being originally settled in the 1600's but later destroyed by pirates in 1717.

Hawk's Nest Creek may well be an important stop on your Cat Island cruise. The creek and marina offer excellent protection from frontal passages and almost anything short of a hurricane but the holding in the creek is questionable. If really strong winds threaten, I would rather get a slip in the marina than try to anchor in the creek.

A GPS waypoint at 24° 08.55' N, 75° 32.45' W, will place you approximately ¾ mile west of the entrance to Hawk's Nest Creek as shown on Chart #CT-1. Contact the marina on VHF ch. 16 if you have any questions about entering their channel. The outer edge of the channel lies just north of the offlying rock and is marked by a red and a green floating buoy. Pass between the two, remember **Red, Right, Returning**, and head up the creek keeping the conspicuous jetty to port. There is a shallow spot at the mouth of the entrance channel with 6' at low water and another spot about 150 yards further in with the same depth. Once past the end of the jetty the marina's fuel dock will be immediately to port. Just past this dock the marina basin opens up to port with 10 slips accommodating drafts up to 7½'.

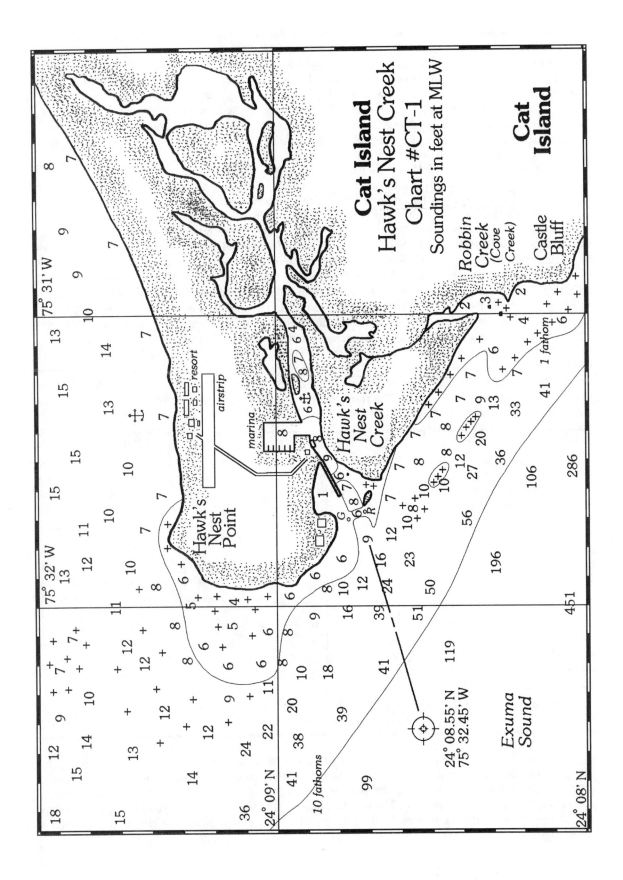

Cat Island
Hawk's Nest Creek
Chart #CT-1
Soundings in feet at MLW

**Cat
Island**

If you wish to anchor in the creek, head upstream past the marina and anchor wherever your draft will allow. A 5' draft can work up stream a good way and shallow draft vessels even further. Do not use the mooring that lies about 200 yards in from the marina. It's 20 years old and not in good shape. I must caution you about anchoring in Hawk's Nest Creek. The bottom is very, very rocky, and its hard to get an anchor to set in the thin sand. As if that was not enough, the strong current threatens to drag you along with it. There are countless stories of skippers who have dragged their anchors in this creek. The further up stream you go, the better the holding, but not much better. Make sure your anchor is well set, dive on it if you must, before you turn in for the night. Oh yes, don't forget the bug juice. This anchorage is notorious for those vile, biting insects we all love so much.

The Hawk's Nest Club and Marina is back in full swing under new management. New managers, Manny and Ora Mae Lacour, invite all boaters to stop in and sample their hospitality, and this Cajun couple really knows how to make you feel at home. They are absolutely sincere in their efforts to accommodate every guest, whether they arrive by boat or by air. The marina has 8 slips, diesel and gas, water, ice, showers, and full electric hookups. There is a washer and dryer at the resort but if you don't feel like doing your own laundry the staff can handle it for you for a small fee. Bicycles and golf carts are complimentary for marina or resort guests. The resort also rents cars and scooters. The office at the resort has a phone and fax for those who need to keep in touch. The dining room at the resort has a beautiful waterfront view and serves up some extraordinary cuisine. Folks come from all over the island, even from the other resorts to sample the dining at the *Hawk's Nest Resort*. The resort has 10 rooms and one 2 bedroom house for rent, all equipped with satellite TV. For more information call them on VHF ch. 16 or by phone at 242-357-7257. The resort does not have a store on premises but Manny and Ora Mae will sell limited grocery supplies to those in need if the resort can spare them. The resort has a fully equipped dive facility on site with a compressor and dive gear for rent. They also have a 26' boat (with Captain) available for dive or fishing charters. If you would like a fishing guide contact the marina office and ask for Nathaniel Gilbert or one of their other excellent guides. The resort can also handle your request for bait fish. Bonefishermen will love the upper reaches of Hawk's Nest Creek.

At the mouth of the entrance to Hawk's Nest Creek are two small houses on the northern shore. The old, gray, ramshackle, three story house is said to have hosted the ex-Panamanian dictator and convicted drug smuggler Manuel Noriega during the years when this part of Cat Island, due to its secluded airstrip, was heavily into a positive cash flow. The structure today is unsafe to enter but if you look inside you may see the false floors that were torn up by drug agents when they closed down this hive of activity over a decade ago.

THE BIGHT

Heading north and east from Hawk's Nest Creek, you must clear the small sand bar off the northwestern tip of Hawk's Nest Point (Chart #CT-1) to continue east. Once past the bar you can head directly for New Bight, Fernandez Bay, or continue along the coast to Old Bight staying ¼ mile offshore.

About 5 miles northeast of Hawk's Nest Point, situated on a hillside overlooking the long beach at the southern end of The Bight, is McQueen's as shown on Chart #CT-2. The homes are very traditional, stone and thatched roofs, and the inhabitants are primarily Rolles from Exuma. Lucayan cooking areas were found in the vicinity of McQueen's. You can tuck in close to anchor off the beach at McQueen's but watch out for the small patch reefs and shallow heads just offshore. They are easily seen and avoided. Never try to come in close to this shore at night.

At the south end of The Bight, in the crook of the "foot" of Cat Island, is the community of Old Bight. As shown on Chart #CT-3, a GPS waypoint at 24° 13.40' N, 75° 25.20' W, will place you approximately ¾ mile northwest of the anchorage area off Old Bight as shown on Chart #CT-3. Head in to the beach in prevailing winds as far as you can and drop the hook in excellent holding sand. Many cruisers heading northbound from George Town make this their first stop. Never anchor here in strong winds from southwest to northeast.

Old Bight is home to the old St. Francis of Assisi Catholic Church which was also built by Father Jerome who built *The Hermitage* at New Bight (read a little further in this section for more information on Father Jerome). The Church's Gothic facade, frescoes, and detailed interior sculptures are quite impressive. Old Bight is also home to the high school and a government clinic as well. For those wishing to spend money, Old Bight has a number of shops including *Peter Hill's Restaurant, Winniefred Dry Goods and Straw Mart, Pass-Me-Not Pool Parlour and Bar, Jade's Unisex Beauty Parlour, The Corner Drug, C.A. Rolle's Bar,* and the *Southern Food Fair.* The largest goat farm in The Bahamas, the *Mango Hill Ranch,* is located here in Old Bight. One mile south of the road to Greenwood, look up the Straw Lady of Cat Island for excellent straw work. Access to Old Bight is via Old Bight Landing.

New Bight is the capitol of Cat Island and sits at the northern end of The Bight. Most cruisers stay north of the town at Fernandez Bay but some anchor off the town which offers a good lee anchorage in winds from Northeast to southeast as shown on Chart #CT-3. Vessels heading northward from Hawk's Nest Point can head straight to New Bight once they clear the sandbar lying northwest of Hawk's Nest Point. Another alternative is to cruise the western coastline of Cat Island staying about ¼ mile offshore. A GPS waypoint at 24° 16.75' N, 75° 25.75' W will place you in The Bight approximately ¾ mile west/southwest of the Batelco Tower. Anchor wherever you choose off the town. There is no longer an active navigational light at The Bight, the Batelco Tower more than makes up for its loss though, it is a great landmark, day or night.

At the head of the dock, under the Batelco tower, is the Government Administration Building and the Batelco Office. Just south of the dock is the *Bluebird Restaurant and Bar.* Across the street are the ruins of the old Armbrister Plantation, easily seen from the waterfront. These are the ruins of the great house of Henry Hawkins Armbrister which was burned by slaves during those heady days prior to emancipation. The house was actually pre-Loyalist period, it was built in the 1760's.

The local hotel, *The Bridge Inn,* offers 12 rooms at reasonable rates and has a restaurant on premises. You can access town by using the town dock located by the Batelco tower. In town you will find the Commissioner's Office and Police Station in the Government Building and nearby, a *Shell* gas station. In town you can find plenty of places to spend your money such as the *New Bight Food Store* (the best grocery on the southern side of Cat Island), the *Honourable Harry Bethel's Wholesale Bar, Idelle Dorsete's Convenience Store, Virie McKinney's Convenience Store,* the *Sweet Things Confectionery,* and *Romer's Mini Mart.* Most of these places are on the main road a mile or two north of the Batelco Tower.

One of the most interesting places in The Bahamas, *The Hermitage,* is probably the most noted tourist attraction on Cat Island. *The Hermitage* is situated just outside of New Bight atop 206' high Mt. Comer (more often called Mt. Alverna) the highest point of land in The Bahamas. *The Hermitage* is a monument to the faith of one man, John Hawes, known as Father Jerome. Father Jerome, born in 1876, spent five years studying at the Royal Institute of British Architecture before entering Lincoln Theological College to become an Anglican Minister. In 1911, Father Jerome went to Rome to study three years for the Catholic Priesthood. He built both St. Paul's and St. Peter's Churches in Clarence Town, Long Island (see the chapter *Long Island, Clarence Town*). He later went to Australia to pursue the callings of his faith as a bush priest but when it came time to retire he chose Cat Island. Father Jerome received permission from the Catholic Bishop in Nassau to retire on Cat Island as a hermit and in 1939 he arrived and surveyed Mt.

Comer. In 1940 he began construction of *The Hermitage*, a miniature replica of a European Franciscan Monastery. Father Jerome built the entire structure by himself out of native rock including the Stations of the Cross. He chose a place where he could look to the east and see the cobalt blue of the Atlantic Ocean and to the west where he could gaze upon the emerald and turquoise waters of the banks. Father Jerome lived here until his death at age 80. He is buried beneath *The Hermitage* that he so lovingly built with his own hands. *The Hermitage* is only a 20 minute walk from town. After you pass the portal inscribed "Mount Alverna" take the path that bears off to the right and winds straight up the hill past the Stations of the Cross. You must signal your approach by striking a stone on a piece of scrap metal left hanging there for that purpose at the turnoff.

Just north of New Bight is Freetown, basically a suburb of New Bight (along with Pigeon Bay and Doud's), and where car rentals are available at the *New Bight Service Station*, the *Shell* station next to *Lorry's Fashion Store*. You can call them on VHF ch. 16 (*New Bight Service*), ask for Jason. You can also inquire about a mechanic here. Just north of Freetown is a straw market in the little blue wood store next to the *Last Chance Bar*. *The Bridge Inn*, famous for its Bahamian fare and Saturday night dances, has 12 rooms with private baths and television. The interior of the inn is decorated with handsome murals of fish and marine life and one panel depicts some Cat Island history. Freetown was settled by freed slaves, actually they were put on ships to be sold into slavery but were rescued enroute and they then settled on Cat Island, never really being sold into slavery. Just north of Freetown lies the Cat Island International Airport which is a Port Of Entry.

Vessels headed north must detour around Bonefish Point and its shallow bar that stretches about a mile southwest of the point. This bar actually starts well to the east at the north end of The Bight as shown on Chart #CT-3. A GPS waypoint at 24° 16.50' N, 75° 28.90' W, will place you approximately ¾ mile southwest of the southwestern tip of the bar. From here you can head straight to Fernandez Bay, Smith's Bay, or points north as you wish.

Photo by Kelly Becker

Hawks Nest Creek Marina, Cat Island.

Cat Island — Whale Creek to Fernandez Bay, Chart #CT-3. Soundings in feet at MLW.

FERNANDEZ BAY

Fernandez Bay is home to the *Fernandez Bay Village Resort* and has one of the most beautiful beaches on Cat Island. Fernandez Bay has been in the Armbrister family, one of the oldest families on Cat Island, since the 1780's although the resort has only been open about 25 years. Jacqueline Onassis once stayed aboard her yacht just offshore. The resort is a well laid out series of villas, each with a kitchen and maid service. Guests can take their choice of activities such as snorkeling, windsurfing, skiing, or sailing. A dive master on premises conducts SCUBA divers and snorkelers to deep water reefs some 7 miles west of Fernandez Bay. Among the features are coral heads 100 feet around and wall diving in water from 70-100' deep. Certifications and dive gear rentals are also available but only for guests of the resort. The restaurant offers fine dining serving breakfast, lunch, and dinner (with reservations by noon), an open-air beach tiki-bar is simple to use. It works on the honor system, make your drink, sign your name, and pay later.

The anchorage off the horseshoe shaped beach at the Fernandez Bay Village resort is easy to enter and offers good holding in 8' over a sandy bottom. As shown on Chart #CT-4, a GPS waypoint at 24° 19.10' N, 75° 29.55' W, will place you approximately ¾ mile west of the entrance to Fernandez Bay. Steer eastward between the northern tip of the bay and the small unnamed rock in the middle of the entrance. Slightly favor the north side of the channel. The best holding is in the northern end of the bay. If you head too far to the east the bottom gets rocky and the holding is poor. If your draft is not too deep, less than 6', you can tuck in close to the northern shore if west and northwest winds threaten. Although you can anchor in the southern part of Fernandez Bay to escape southerly winds, the Bay is not a pleasant place to be in the prelude to a frontal passage. If the wind is forecast to be strong out of the south to west, a better place to be would be north about a mile at Smith's Bay (See next section: *Smith's Bay*). If you have a draft of less than 3', and bad weather threatens, you might be able to work your way in over the bar at high tide into Armbrister Creek where some local fishing boats are moored. There are a couple of spots inside the creek where the depths are 3' at low water but the entrance is about 1' at low water. Sound the entrance carefully before attempting to enter.

Fernandez Bay Village Resort has gotten a bad reputation from cruisers over the years. If you've cruised these waters at all you've probably heard tales that the resort is unfriendly towards cruisers and that the management does not want cruisers to stop here. Actually they don't mind cruisers stopping here and taking advantage of the common area, restaurant, and bar, as long as the skippers and crews don't abuse what they use. The problem concerning their bad rap relates to those cruisers who have misused the facilities at Fernandez Bay, been rude to the staff, and been anything but honorable at the honor bar. Over the years this would tend to make anyone less than a Saint wince whenever a boat enters the anchorage. Perhaps that is why some members of the staff, a few of whom are former cruisers, are not exactly enthusiastic when greeting incoming boaters. I would like to take a moment to look at both sides of this sad state of affairs. The cruisers and the Resort need to take a few steps in each others sandals and perhaps all will walk away happier. I am not trying to repair the damage, let's just say I'm trying to make each side aware of the other's point of view. Let's start with the boaters. Okay boaters, let's pretend that you are the resort managers and look at this from their viewpoint. If you're not interested, skip the next two paragraphs.

When I first started cruising I was quite naive. I thought all cruisers lived in a sort of symbiosis with Mother Nature. To me it seemed like the logical way to live. Man, was I wrong! Many cruisers haven't a clue about living in sync with their surroundings. That seems to be one of the problems here at Fernandez Bay. The bay is small and really doesn't get a lot of flushing action. The resort asks that cruisers use their holding tanks when anchored in the bay as the waste washes up on shore if discharged overboard. Right on the resort's front yard so to speak. Some boaters throw all sorts of trash overboard which also washes up on their beach. On the other hand don't walk up on the beach and dump your garbage into a bin, the Resort will not dispose of boater's garbage. Once a cruiser asked to rinse off at the outside shower, used by guests to rinse off after swimming at the beach. The manager said yes. Later, when she looked down to the waterfront, the cruiser was soaping up and taking a full fledged shower. This is a resort. They have guests. Guests do not want to see this. The resort is not here for boaters. Their guests are their livelihood. Some cruisers tend to treat all people who work with the public as servants. More than a few times boaters have entered the office with no hellos, no good mornings, no introductions, and said that they needed to use the phone or fax, that it was important, and that it needed to be done now! The resort is a small, family run operation. "A little manners goes a long way!" as the staff says. The honor bar, it's a wonderful thing. Can you name any other place with one? I certainly can't. Yet some cruisers have sat there for hours, getting happier by the minute, and when it comes time to pay the bill claim that they only had a couple of beers. The resort has a common area under the casaurinas where all the deck chairs are. Boaters are welcome to use this area and relax. The hammocks are to be saved for guests and the guest areas off to either side of the common area are for guests only. Many boaters simply make themselves at home and wander aimlessly around the grounds. What must the resort do? Hire a security guard?

Now for the rest of the story (with apologies to Paul Harvey). I hope the resort staff can see fit to place themselves in the topsiders of the visiting yachtsmen for a moment. Not all cruisers have bad manners. Not all cruisers have evil intentions. No matter how much you have been abused, the resort must not indict all cruisers for the actions of a few. The innocent must be accorded the benefit of a doubt. Some of us would like to walk up to your establishment, hoping to make use of your bar and restaurant, and receive a genuine welcome. In 1991 I was treated well by all involved and had a great time. This changed gradually over the years and the last time I visited, in May of 1997, I also had a great time, but my reception was, well, lukewarm at best. I had the distinct feeling that I, being a visiting cruiser, was being tolerated. To be perfectly honest, this changed when the staff found out that I was completing the research for this section (add to that the fact that I had been lucky enough to have the way paved for me by a friend of the resort's managers). Once the staff realized who I was, I could not have been treated nicer. This too was improper. Should only cruising guide authors be welcomed? No, I am a cruiser before I am an author. I can see where some cruisers with thinner skins could sail away feeling unwelcome. I am not suggesting any answers. The problem exists and it is up to both the cruisers and the resort to work at it to satisfy each other, the resort is not going away and cruisers will always be stopping here.

If Fernandez Bay is not where you wish to stop, there is an excellent anchorage just south of Fernandez Bay called Kelley Bay. Here you'll have good protection from winds from the north/northeast to the east/southeast. The sandy bottom is excellent holding and the pretty beach is deserted, no one from the resort comes here.

The Fernandez Cays are home to many white crowned pigeons. Please don't disturb their fragile nesting sites.

SMITH'S BAY

This area of Cat Island is heavily agricultural and Smith's Bay is most noted for its government packing house. Prior to its construction in 1971, growers had to ship their produce to Nassau, a headache for all involved necessitating a middleman or family member in Nassau. Now growers receive a check from the packing house which handles everything involved with its shipment and sale. Smith's Bay residents make their living farming and fishing as do most of the people you will meet along this shoreline. Smith's Bay was once a much larger settlement, obvious when you notice the layout of the buildings. In town there is a tree called the Passion Tree because it is said to bleed a red liquid at Easter. Smith's Bay is a Port Of Entry and there is a Customs and Immigration office here.

A GPS waypoint at 24° 19.75' N, 75° 29.55' W, will place you approximately ¾ mile west of the entrance to the harbour at Smith's Bay in Culbert's Creek as shown on Chart #CT-4. Head generally eastward to pass between the opening between Cat Island and the small unnamed cay to the north. There is a lighted range (flashing red) to lead you in. The front range is a white pole topped with an orange daymark and a red light, and the rear range is an inverted triangle as a daymark. You'll have 9' at the entrance and it deepens inside to 11' just off the long concrete dock. If approaching from Fernandez Bay you can stay ¼ mile offshore and you'll be there before you have hardly a chance to warm up the engine or trim the sails.

The only place deep enough to anchor in Smith's Bay is between the dock and the entrance. Smith's Bay offers good protection in a frontal passage but a good size sea can work its way in with westerly winds. If you intend to anchor here to get out of bad weather don't block access to the dock as the mailboat calls in here on a weekly basis, usually on Wednesdays, and other freight boats are in and out at other times.

In town, well north of the town dock, you can have a cold one at *Hazel's Hideaway Bar*, sometimes called the *Sea Side Bar,* and other times simply called *Hazel Brown's Bar,* with its distinctive bright green exterior. Owner Hazel Brown offers cold drinks, the coldest beer in The Bahamas she claims, and pleasant company. Four miles to the east along the path is a surfer's beach on the Atlantic shoreline. There is a clinic in Smith's Bay with a resident doctor who resides in town. Shoppers can visit *The Heritage*

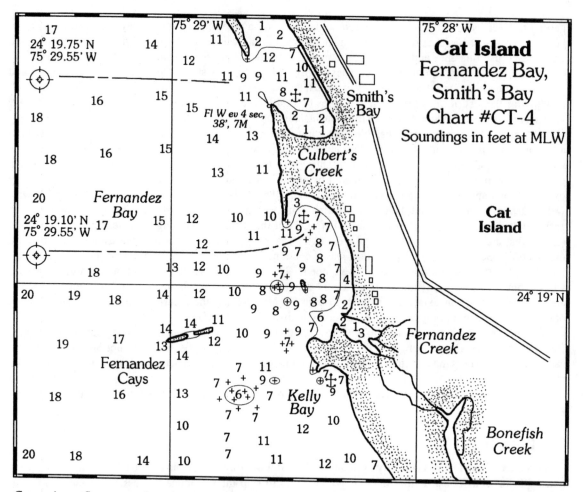

Convenience Store or perhaps have another cold one at *The Haulover Restaurant and Bar*. If you wish to stay in town, the *Little Bay Inn* has 6 rooms with private baths and shared kitchens.

Vessels heading north from Smith's Bay have no dangers if they stay at least ¼ mile offshore. This part of the coast is basically one long lee anchorage. Just tuck in close to shore in prevailing winds and drop the hook wherever you like. Just north of Smith's Bay are a small string of rocks lying about 200 yards or so offshore. They all sit on the edge of the one fathom line with the exception of a small break north of Smith's Bay. Here cruisers can head in towards the southern end of the first beach lying about ½ mile north of the entrance to Smith's Bay. Pass south of the large rock lying off the beach, you must eyeball your way in, good visibility is important. The area between the rocks has 7' at low water and there is up to 9' inside.

North of Smith's Bay lies friendly Tea Bay and Knowles Village, with its colorful primary school sitting just a few paces from the water's edge (see Chart #CT-5). Tea Bay got its name from the plantation owners who would meet daily in the shade of a large tree for tea. In Tea Bay you will find *Linnette's Convenience Store*, *The Liquor Store*, and the *Snack Counter and Vegetable Stand*. In Knowles Village you will find the *Bachelor's Restaurant and Bar* serving excellent Bahamian cuisine, *Moncur and Sons Grocery*, and the *Up and Down Bar*. A little further north, The Cove sits approximately midway down the western shore of Cat Island, the halfway point. The town was originally called Jesse Cove and was first inhabited by a Loyalist. Off The Cove on the Atlantic shore are the wrecks of the *Whisky* dating back to the last century and the S.S. *Modegard* which sank on the reef in 1910. On the western shore, partially hidden by the casaurinas, are some fuel tanks that feed the large power station just inland. The small antenna tower marks the power station.

Further north are the settlements of Stephenson, Industrious Hill, Cairey's, and Gaitor's. Stephenson has an area known as Poitier Village where the few residents claim kinship to their native son, the famous actor, Sydney Poitier. Inland of Stephenson are two caves that are home to a healthy population of bats. There is a small cave at the point just above Stephenson on the western shoreline. I have not investigated

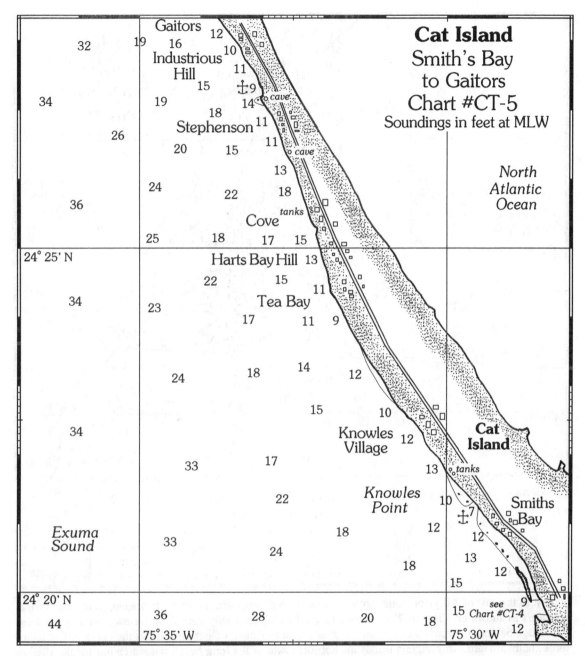

Cat Island
Smith's Bay
to Gaitors
Chart #CT-5
Soundings in feet at MLW

North
Atlantic
Ocean

Cat
Island

Smiths
Bay

Exuma
Sound

24° 25' N

24° 20' N

75° 35' W

75° 30' W

see
Chart #CT-4

this cave so I can tell you nothing about it. Perhaps you might check it out and tell me. Any takers? Industrious Hill is not so industrious, it is more agricultural than anything and it's the home of the multi-chambered *Bat Cave*, another dark hole in the ground spelunkers will want to climb into and explore. Cairey's was founded by Eleuthera pineapple farmers in the late 1800's when Cat Island and Eleuthera were the major pineapple growers in The Bahamas.

North of Gaitor's at Ben's Bluff, Chart #CT-6, is a small cave mouth on the western shore of Cat Island just above the water's edge. The cave consists of a main tunnel with a large chamber off to the left and an even larger one at the rear of the cave. The entire cave is only 50'-60' long, the largest chamber is about 20' x 40' x 15' high and is home to a large number of bats. You must check this one out, even if you're not a spelunker.

Another worthwhile stop is at he nearby village of The Bluff where you'll find Anita *Wilson's Triple X Restaurant and Bar, Mack's Restaurant,* and the *Island General Shopping Center. The Pigeon Cay Club* on the beach has 5 rooms and 8 cottage for rent.

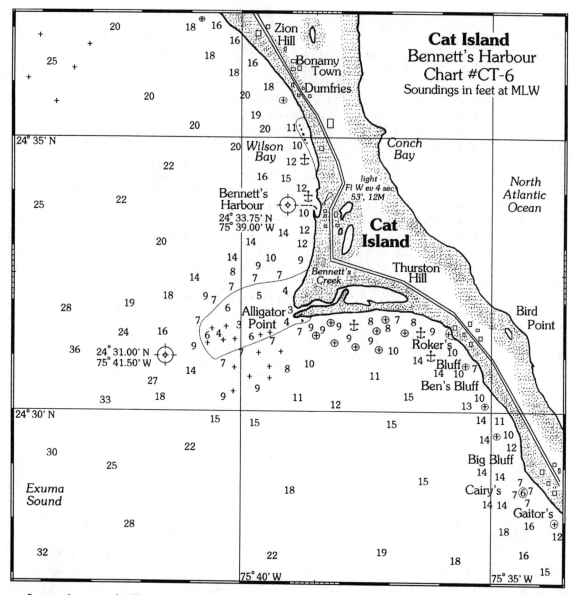

Just to the east of Alligator Point, around Roker's, is an excellent anchorage in winds from the north to northeast as shown on Chart #CT-6. Here a long white beach (easily seen from far away due to the white sand ridge behind it) stretches east from Alligator Point to Roker's where it follows the curve of Cat Island turns southeastward. In northerly winds anchor just south of the long beach but watch out for the shallow stray heads and small patch reefs that this area is strewn with. Never attempt this at night. In easterly winds anchor in the lee of Roker's.

BENNETT'S HARBOUR

Bennett's Harbour, Chart #CT-6, was originally settled by freed slaves. This community of some 400 is spread around a small harbour that is alleged to have hidden pirates in days of old. Today the only regular visitor is the Nassau mailboat, *The North Cat Island Special* which calls weekly for the fresh produce that can be found in season at the produce exchange. *The Ocean Spray Guest House* offers fine accommodations to the weary traveler. On the water's edge you will find the *Beverage Restaurant and Disco.* Also in town you might wish to stop at the *Remanda Inn Restaurant and Bar* and *Len's Grocery* with fresh bread and cakes.

Vessels heading north for Bennett's Harbour must first round Alligator Point with its long, shallow, rocky bar. A GPS waypoint at 24° 31.00' N, 75° 41.50' W, will place you approximately ½ mile southwest of the shoal's southwest tip. From here you can head generally northeast towards Bennett's Harbour. At Alligator Point, Bennett's Creek is alive with sealife (good bonefishing) and worth the time to explore by dinghy. The mouth of the creek is blocked by a bar with less than 3' a low water

A GPS waypoint at 24° 33.75' N, 75° 39.00' W, will place you approximately ½ mile west of the entrance to Bennett's Harbour. From this position steer generally east and round the spit of land and its offlying shoal and turn to starboard to anchor in the small harbour near the dock. This is a very small anchorage and there is no such thing as swinging room here if there is more than one boat present. Don't block the dock as the mailboat and other freight boats call here regularly. This is a good spot to ride out a front though it gets a little choppy inside when strong winds from the northwest to north push in the seas. There's also a lot of current here, two anchors are a must. Bennett's Harbour has room for two to three vessels of moderate draft, no more than 6' or so. On the eastern shore of the small harbour you will see some shallow ponds, the remnants of the days when the creek system was expanded during World War II to create salt pans. If the weather is settled or out of the northeast to southeast, you'll find a fine anchorage at the northern end of the little cove north of the dock at Bennett's Harbour.

With the upcoming construction slated for Little San Salvador (see the next chapter: *Little San Salvador*), there is some talk that Bennett's Harbour will be expanded to allow greater use of the facility for ferrying workers to and from Little San Salvador. By the time you visit Bennett's Harbour, the current chart may be obsolete.

North of Bennett's Harbour is Dumfries. Originally settled by Loyalists and once named Ways Green, Dumfries is home to the dramatic *Great Crown Cave*, said to stretch for over three miles and which should only be visited with the help of an experienced guide from Dumfries or Arthur's Town. Ask for Mr. Gaitor in Dumfries. This vast labyrinth and its chambers is a spelunkers delight. The path north of the *Gossip Bar* leads to this cave passing through a huge stretch of mangroves growing to upwards of 40'. After you visit to the earth's innards, you might like to stop at *The Turning Point Club* where the sign warns "Eat Before Drinking," sage advice that I can testify to. *The Turning Point Club* features the occasional rake and scrape band and their mutton souse is excellent. Here you'll also find the *Stubbs Grocery Store*, and *The Gossip Bar and Restaurant* which frequently has music.

ARTHUR'S TOWN AND ORANGE CREEK

North of Bennett's Harbour is Arthur's Town, the commercial center of Cat Island with an 8,000' long airstrip and commercial flights provided by Island Express. Arthur's Town was raided by the Spanish in the 1700's and later in that century was settled by Loyalists from America. It is said that Sydney Poitier lived here for a time as a child.

Boats heading to Arthur's Town from Alligator Point or Bennett's Harbour have deep water all the way with few obstructions save a few shallow heads very close inshore. The 200' Batelco tower makes an excellent landmark day or night. A GPS waypoint at 24° 36.80' N, 75° 41.20' W, will place you approximately ½ mile southwest of Arthur's Town. Vessels can anchor anywhere, north or south of Arthur's Town as shown on Chart #CT-7, the water is deep and the holding good. This is a lee anchorage, prevailing winds only.

At the head of the town dock is the Commissioner's Office and the Police Station. These buildings sit right on the large grassy town square called *Christie Park*. Surrounding the square you will also find the Post Office, Batelco office, the school, and a clinic. Nearby is the *Lover's Boulevard Disco and Satellite Lounge*, the *Hard Rock Cafe Restaurant and Bar*, *Boggy Pond Bar*, *Jabon Convenience Store and Car Rental*, *Campbell's Big Bull Food Store*, *E & K Takeaway*, *Dean's Inn*, and *In the Mud*. The pink building with concrete steps leading down to the waterfront just north of the town dock and the school is *Pat and Dell's Cookie Center Restaurant and Takeaway*. Owner Patrick Rolle also rents scooters. The first weekend in May finds Arthur's Town hosting the *Annual Heritage Festival,* an exhibit of historical artifacts while the first weekend in August you'll find the annual *Cat Island Regatta* in full swing.

The northernmost settlement on Cat Island is Orange Creek which received its name from the color of the creek when certain light and bottom conditions exist. You can anchor just off the mouth of the creek in 8'-14' of water as shown on Chart #CT-7. Some of this bottom is rocky so pick a good sandy spot to drop your hook. Just west of the mouth of Orange Creek is a beautiful long beach that makes for an excellent anchorage in northerly winds.

Orange Creek is important for cruisers because it has a gas station with one of the island's few mechanics. There are two new hotels in Orange Creek, the *Sea Spray Inn*, and the *Orange Creek Inn* and

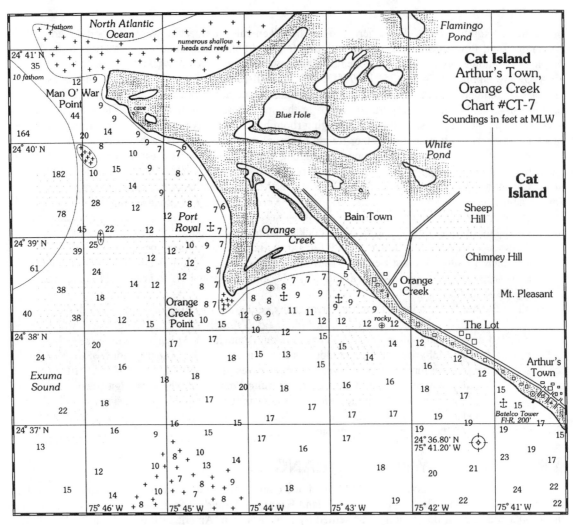

both sell groceries and ice and the *Orange Creek Inn* has a laundry. In town you'll also find a clinic, a post office, *Magnolia's Bar,* and *Seymore's Bayside Grocery.*

Many cruisers probably know a gentleman named Nicholas Cripps, the former owner of Marsh Harbour Marina in Marsh Harbour, Abaco. Well, today Nick lives at Orange Creek and has plans in the works to build a large marina in the Creek itself, and that will take a lot of dredging.

Orange Creek itself has waters that are in some places up to 6' deep but the bar at the entrance restricts entry to boats with drafts of less than 3' at high water. The creek has a few scattered wrecks along with some fishing boats anchored inside. As Orange Creek shallows, in return for the loss of depth one gains some excellent bonefishing grounds. Inland, Orange Creek boasts two blue holes whose levels rise and fall with the tide. Their most famous blue hole is known as the "Bad Blue Hole." This blue hole, off Dickies Road behind Orange Creek, is said to be home to a ferocious monster who likes to eat horses. It has been said that a man and his dog out hunting near this blue hole disappeared thus adding fuel to the fire of the legend. Orange Creek is also home to the Griffin Cave, another spelunker's delight. Northward, after the road runs out, sits a lonesome two story house at Man O' War Bluff. The structure looks as if it is haunted and it is said to be.

Vessels can round Orange Creek Point to anchor at Port Royal in 7'-10' of water with beautiful beaches and a good holding sand bottom as shown on Chart #CT-7. This spot is excellent in northeast to east winds. At Man of War Point is a large cave right at sea level, definitely worth a dinghy ride. North of Man Of War Point is one of Cat Islands most beautiful beaches. The beach is inaccessible by road but not by dinghy. About a mile from Man Of War Point you will see a coconut palm grove. Here you will find the Drip Cave, said to be a Lucayan cave.

At the extreme northwestern tip of Cat Island, north of Man Of War Point, is an extensive reef system that offers fantastic opportunities for fishing, snorkeling, and SCUBA diving. A word of warning, the locals say that there are a lot of sharks on the reef so use caution. I only dove on the reefs twice and neither time saw any sharks but that doesn't mean that they didn't see me.

Photo by Kelly Becker

Cave on western shore of Cat Island.

LITTLE SAN SALVADOR

Little San Salvador is an excellent stopover in anything but strong westerly weather between Cat Island and Eleuthera. It is uninhabited and was once farmed by residents of nearby Cat Island. If you wonder why the cay would be called "Little" San Salvador, being as it is so far from the island of San Salvador, you must remember that Cat Island was known as San Salvador for a long period of time.

APPROACHES TO LITTLE SAN SALVADOR

From anywhere in the Exumas it is a straight shot across Exuma Sound to Little San Salvador, the only obstruction being the TMB2 buoy that lies approximately 15 miles southwest of Powell Point, Eleuthera (this buoy is scheduled to be removed in the near future so it may or may not be there, until you are sure it is no longer in place, act as if it was still in position at 24° 38.20' N, 76° 31.30' W). If you are heading to Little San Salvador from anywhere south of Norman's Cay, Exuma, this buoy should not present a problem. From Conch Cut in Exuma Park, a bearing of 68° for 34.6 miles will bring you to the GPS waypoint approximately 1 nautical mile west of the West Bay anchorage at 24° 34.48' N, 75° 58.60' W. A vessel leaving the north anchorage at Warderick Wells should steer 82° for 37.7 miles while those departing Staniel Cay at Big Rock Cut will run 34.3 miles at a heading of 55°. From Joe Cay Cut in Pipe Creek, West Bay lies 35.0 miles distant on a course of 62°.

From Bennett's Harbour, Cat Island, a course of 93° for 15.6 miles will place you at the GPS waypoint at 24° 32.70' N, 75° 56.30' W, which lies approximately 1 mile south of the light. Vessels heading to Little San Salvador from Arthur's Town or Orange Creek should head to the area of Bennett's Harbour to take up the course for the waypoint south of Little San Salvador. I have traveled west/southwest from Orange Creek and there are a lot of shallow patch reefs lying west of the Long Rocks, especially in the area of 24° 36.00' N, 75° 44.60' W. These reefs are easily seen and avoided in good light. All vessels heading to Little San Salvador from Bennett's Harbour or points north must keep well south of the Long Rocks and Tea Cay. Between Tea Cay and the Long Rocks to its north and east are numerous shallow patch reefs and there are places where there are few if any passages between them. It's best to avoid this area unless you intend to dive on the reefs. Vessels heading to Little San Salvador from Fernandez Bay should steer 306° for 27 miles to reach the waypoint south of the light. From the waypoint south of Little San Salvador, boats can head generally northwest, parallel to the shoreline but not too close in to avoid the shallow patch reefs, and then make the turn into West Bay.

For those heading to Little San Salvador from Eleuthera, simply parallel the southwest shoreline of Eleuthera from Cape Eleuthera southward and once clear of East End Point take up a course of 105° for 9.8 miles to the anchorage at West Bay.

WEST BAY

As of this writing in June of 1997, there is no island in the central and southern Bahamas that will change over the next few years half as much as Little San Salvador. In early 1997, the *Holland America Cruise Line* purchased the island of Little San Salvador and has renamed it Half-Moon Cay (until it shows up with that name in the Nassau Land and Survey Department Topographical Maps I will still refer to it as Little San Salvador. . . I'll probably always call it Little San Salvador no matter what the maps say!). Plans include cruise ships stopping three times a week beginning in November 1997. There is to be a large jetty/dock at the southern end of the beach in West Bay for offloading passengers and three building groups, one at the southern end of the beach, one at the central section of the beach, and one on the northern shore of the beach. Once ashore the passengers are slated to find all sorts of toys like paddle boats and jet skis. There will also be a children's play area (I thought the whole beach was that!), and other recreational activities. Passengers wishing to spend money will find what is described as a shopping center with an art gallery and "native" crafts. There will be upwards of 15 full time employees from Cat Island and at least one management couple living on Little San Salvador. One bright spot is that the cruise ships will only stay overnight when they do stop. Plans also call for the dredging of the creek and the construction of a seaplane landing area. These facilities may well be in place shortly after this publication goes to market. Won't this island be fun soon! A loss of a beautiful, secluded treasure for all cruisers.

The managers of the facility say they do not wish to keep cruisers from anchoring in West Bay. There is

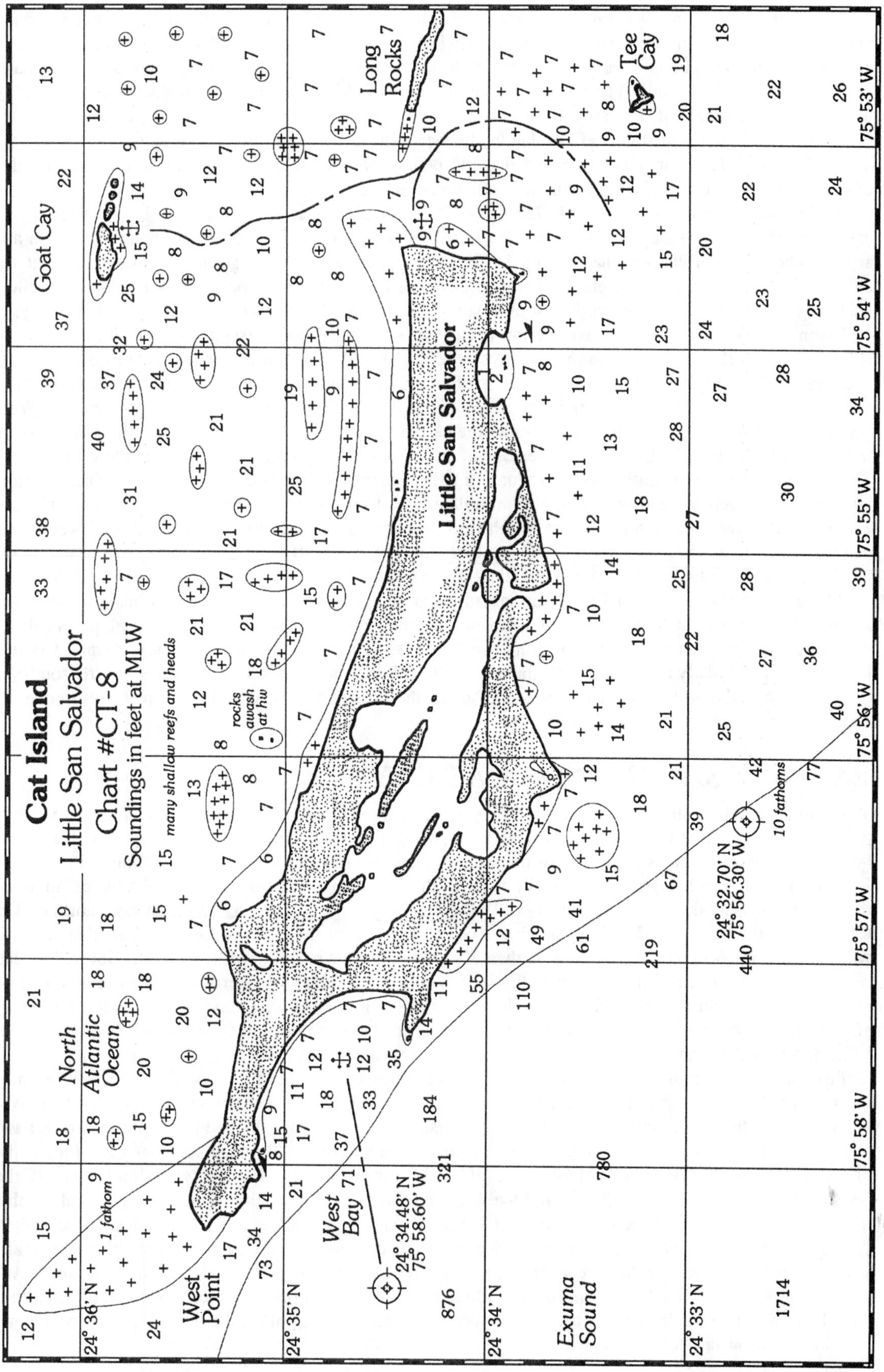

Cat Island
Little San Salvador
Chart #CT-8
Soundings in feet at MLW

Little San Salvador

Goat Cay

Long Rocks

Tee Cay

North Atlantic Ocean

West Point

West Bay

Exuma Sound

many shallow reefs and heads

rocks awash at hw

1 fathom

10 fathoms

24° 36' N

24° 35' N

24° 34' N

24° 33' N

24° 34.48' N
75° 58.60' W

24° 32.70' N
75° 56.30' W

75° 58' W

75° 57' W

75° 56' W

75° 55' W

75° 54' W

75° 53' W

some talk about installing moorings along the northern shore of the beach and charging cruisers $3.00 per night which is quite fair compared to some mooring prices. This would put all visiting boats in one area and away from the "public areas." The owners do not own the bottom and they cannot stop any boater from anchoring in West Bay. The owners also wish cruisers to know that they are welcome to make use of the beach to a distance of 3' above the high water mark but no further. This is in accordance with the Bahamian law which reads to the effect that landowners only own their land to "one cart width" above the high tide mark. This law was written so that the people of The Bahamas, who have always depended heavily on the sea for part if not all of their livelihood, would always have access to it.

A GPS waypoint at 24° 34.48' N, 75° 58.60' W, will place you approximately 1 mile west of the anchorage area at West Bay as shown on Chart #CT-8. From this waypoint simply head straight in and anchor wherever you choose, the holding is great throughout the anchorage area. Remember that the changes I mentioned may be in place when you arrive so keep your eyes open. West Bay is an excellent anchorage in even the strongest north to southeast winds but it is not the place to be in anything westerly.

I won't go into detail about what is here, it will all be changed soon, except to say that there is good fishing on the reefs off the rock at the southeastern tip of West Bay. At the northwestern tip of the bay, just west of the conspicuous rocks, is the wreck of an old barge in shallow water. There's usually a lot of fish around this one. Speaking of fish, the drop off lies just off West Bay. What does this mean? Well, besides good fishing, it means that sharks enter the harbour at night looking for food. It's not wise to swim in West Bay at night. The first shark I ever caught, a 7' lemon, I caught in West Bay just before sunset.

The northern shore of Little San Salvador is a fisherman's and diver's delight. There are many, many large and small reefs lying along the shoreline stretching eastward past Goat Cay and Long Rocks. There is a huge, shallow reef system that stretches northward for over a mile from West Point at the northwestern tip of Little San Salvador. I have seen some very large lobsters come off these reefs. The long beach on the northern shore of Little San Salvador is excellent for beachcombing, especially after a northerly blow.

Along the southern shore of Little San Salvador are quite a few shallow reefs. The main draw on the southern shore is the shallow entrance to the extensive creek system in the interior. As I said, plans call for the creek to be dredged, we shall all wait and see what will happen. East of the creek is a small bay that looks inviting but really isn't. It is very shallow, 1'-2' at low water, and very rocky. Just a little southeast of this beach is the wreck of a large vessel. Part of the bow of this upside down wreck juts above the surface at low tide as shown on Chart #CT-8.

EASTERN SHORE AND GOAT CAY

If caught at Little San Salvador with westerly weather threatening, skippers have the option of heading to Bennett's Harbour at Cat Island or moving to the eastern shore of Little San Salvador. (One could also head to Eleuthera but that is quite a bit further and to windward if westerly winds are blowing). From West Bay, head southward along the southern shore of Little San Salvador staying at least ½ mile off to avoid the shallow reefs as shown on Chart #CT-8. Work your way towards Tea Cay and then steer north of Tea Cay towards the western end of Long Rocks. Keep an eye out for the shallow reefs and bars that you will want to leave to port. You'll have no less than 7' of water on this route if you're careful. Never, I repeat, never attempt this route at night, even with waypoints it would be too dangerous, a small error could be disastrous (if you must leave at night head downwind to Bennett's Harbour staying well south of Tea Cay and the rocks that lie to its east and northeast). Once clear of the reefs you can work to the eastern shore of Little San Salvador where you can tuck in between the reefs and the shore in 6'-9' of water.

From this area one can head over to Goat Cay which lies a little over a mile north of the eastern tip of Little San Salvador. I think visiting Goat Cay by dinghy is the best idea but you can take the big boat over and anchor off the cay in settled weather if you so desire. The anchorage is open to the prevailing east and southeast winds though, only giving a little lee in northerly winds. To head to Goat Cay, follow the directions to arrive along the eastern shore of Little San Salvador. Pass between the reefs off the northeastern tip of Little San Salvador and the western tip of the Long Rocks. You will have 7' along this route at low tide. Once between the reefs steer towards Goat Cay, the larger and westernmost of the cays to your north. The water will get progressively deeper as you approach Goat Cay and you will have to zigzag your way through a few shallow reefs that are easily seen and avoided in good visibility. Again, never attempt this at night. Goat Cay is ringed by shallow reefs and the best place to anchor is south of its eastern end. Dinghy in to the small beach and you can snorkel the nice reefs right off the beach. Goat Cay is home to a flock of white crowned pigeons.

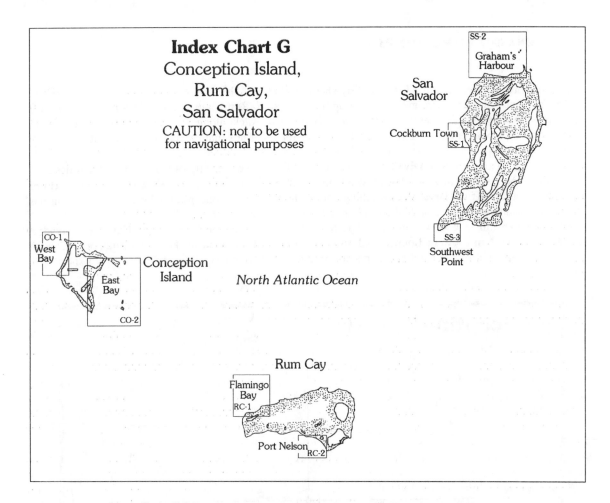

Index Chart G
Conception Island,
Rum Cay,
San Salvador
CAUTION: not to be used
for navigational purposes

North Atlantic Ocean

CONCEPTION ISLAND

Conception Island is the smallest of the three islands that lie just off the mouth of Exuma Sound where it meets the Atlantic Ocean. Rum Cay lies to the southeast of Conception with larger San Salvador lying to the northeast. These isles are a popular stop for cruisers heading to or from the Caribbean. They are most often visited by those skippers who are just spending a short time in George Town, Exuma and seek a little break from the hustle and bustle of Elizabeth Harbour.

Conception Island is a National Park and is under the protection of The Bahamas National Trust. Contrary to popular belief, Conception Island is not a land and sea park, only its land area is protected. This means that nothing on the island may be disturbed, removed, or damaged. You cannot take shells, you cannot have a fire, and most of all, you cannot leave any garbage. This also means that cruisers can fish on the rich surrounding reefs. Good news for cruisers indeed.

APPROACHES TO CONCEPTION ISLAND

The high wooded mass of Booby Cay will probably be the first thing you can make out when headed for Conception Island. The land mass of Conception Island is hilly and scrub covered and steep-to along the western shore. From the waypoint to clear Cape Santa Maria Reef at the northern end of Long Island it is approximately 15.4 nautical miles on a course of 62° to the GPS waypoint at 23° 51.00' N, 75° 08.00' W, ½ mile west of the anchorage at West Bay.

If approaching Conception from Rum Cay, from the waypoint north of the wreck north of Flamingo Bay, a course of 311° for 8.6 nautical miles will bring you to a GPS waypoint at 23° 47.25' N, 75° 04.66' W, which will allow you to clear the reefs that lie southeast of Conception Island. From this point keep the reefs well to starboard and round the southern point of Conception Island, Wedge Point, and parallel the shore about ¼ mile offshore until you arrive at the West Bay anchorage. Watch out for the reefs close in along the shore. Vessels heading for Rum Cay should sail around the southern shore of Conception Island to the waypoint just mentioned and then take up their course to Rum Cay. Watch out for small buoys off the southern shore of Conception Island that mark dive sites along the Conception Island Wall. Commercial dive boat operators use these small buoys for moorings that can easily get caught in the prop of the unwary skipper.

From Cockburn Town, San Salvador, the waypoint at the southeastern tip of Conception Island lies 33.1 miles distant on a course of 250° A GPS waypoint at 23° 55.18' N, 75° 05.40' W, will place you north of the wreck that lies off the large reef stretching out northwards from Conception Island. That position lies 30.8 miles distant on a course of 264° from Cockburn Town.

Skippers transiting the areas between Cape Santa Maria, Conception Island, Rum Cay, San Salvador, and the entire eastern shore of Long Island must be aware that a branch of the North Equatorial Current called the Antilles Current generally sets in a northwesterly direction through here from .5 to .75 knots.

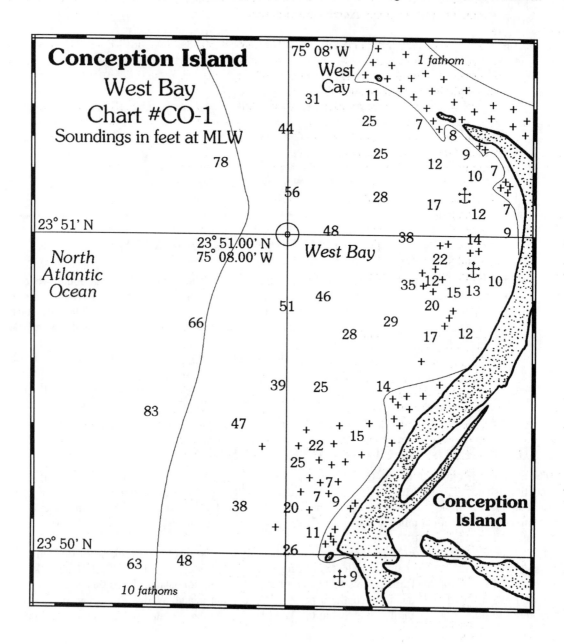

WEST BAY

Leaving Cape Santa Maria you will begin to see your first sight of the hills of Conception Island about 10 miles away depending on your height of eye. A GPS waypoint at 23° 51.00' N, 75° 08.00 W, will place you approximately ¾ mile southwest of the anchorage just off the beautiful long white beach as shown on Chart #CO-1. Boats can anchor just off the beach in 6'-25' over a beautiful, excellent holding, sandy bottom. This anchorage is good in winds from northeast to almost south but is not the place to be in the westerly prelude to a frontal passage. If a front threatens, round the south tip of Conception Island and Wedge Point (see next section: *East Bay*) and anchor in the lee of Conception Island or north near Booby Cay.

At the north end of the beach is a trail leading over a cliff with a rope attached to assist climbers. Another trail then leads to the northern beach which offers excellent beachcombing through its piles of flotsam and jetsam as well as some exciting camera shots of the reefs lying off Conception Island's northern shore.

A beautiful sight to see is the turtle in the creeks at Conception Island at high tide. Enter the creeks just before high tide and kill your engine. Row your dinghy if possible, trying not to use your engine so as not to frighten the turtles. Quite often you will see dozens of sea turtles cavorting in the shallows, the warm water making a delightful temperature controlled climate for them.

Along the south shore of Conception Island is a snug little anchorage in northerly winds as along as there is no surge. The anchorage is just off the small beach that lies west of the entrance to the creeks.

Divers will love the reefs to the north and south of the West Bay anchorage. You don't even have to leave the anchorage for some truly marvelous snorkeling.

Stretching northward from West Rock some four miles is *Southampton Reef*. At the northern end of *Southampton Reef* you can dive on the remains of a wrecked freighter which sank over 90 years ago. The 300' long hull lies amid elkhorn and staghorn corals in 25' of water with its very prominent engines, boilers, anchors, and props.

For diver's, one of the most beautiful reefs in The Bahamas is the *Conception Island Wall* which lies just 300' off the beach. Here gigantic coral heads climb from 90' depths to 50' and less. The wall drops in ladder-like steps and is covered with hard and soft corals and sponges. Some of the best spots are south of the island where you will find the small buoys placed there by the charter boat operators.

EAST BAY

Vessels caught at Conception Island when a frontal passage threatens have the option of heading around to the eastern side of the island to gain a lee in southwest through west to northwest winds. To gain access to the anchorages along the eastern shore of Conception Island, pass south of Conception Island, giving the southwest tip a wide berth to avoid the shallows along that shoreline. Head eastward along the southern shore of Conception Island at least 200 yards offshore taking Wedge Point, the conspicuous pointed bluff, to port as shown on Chart #CO-2. Watch out for the reef stretching east from Wedge Point, pass between the reef and Wedge Point. From here, head northward along the eastern shore of Conception Island and anchor wherever your draft allows and where you feel safe from the southwest to northwest winds. The best spots are north of the small unnamed point north of Wedge Point where you can get close in to the beach, and at the northeastern tip of Conception Island, just southeast of Booby Cay, between the reef and the shoreline. The anchorages on the eastern shore of Conception Island are only good in winds from south/southwest to north/northwest. When the wind moves into the north on its way eastward, it is time for you to move back around to the shelter of West Bay. One can also anchor just south of Booby Rock but there are a lot of shallow patch reefs around that you must avoid. This anchorage is only good in northerly winds, winds from any other direction make this anchorage uncomfortable at best. The beaches on the eastern and northern shores of Conception are excellent for beachcombing. Booby Cay, the conspicuous high island at the northern end of East Bay, is a protected bird sanctuary.

There is a light on the southern shore of Conception Island that is supposed to flash white every two seconds, stands 84' above the water, and is visible for 6 nautical miles. Don't expect this light to be working. It was not functioning as of June 1997, and had not been in operating condition in a long, long time. When it will be repaired is anybody's guess.

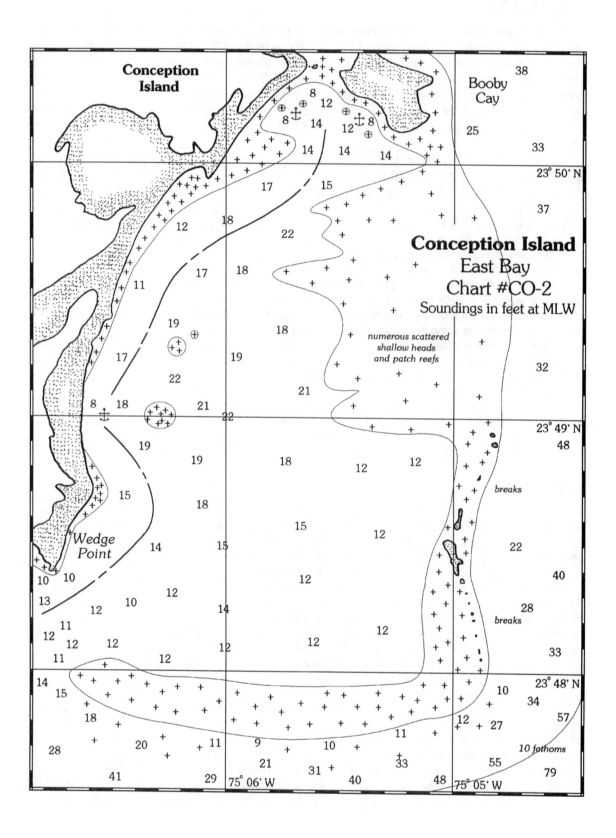

Conception Island

Booby Cay

38

8   12

8   14

12   8

25

33

14   14   14

23° 50' N

17   15

37

12   18

22

17   18

18   11

19

18

Conception Island
East Bay
Chart #CO-2
Soundings in feet at MLW

17

22

numerous scattered
shallow heads
and patch reefs

32

8   18   21   22

23° 49' N

48

19

19   18   12   12

breaks

15   18

15

22

Wedge
Point

14   15

12

40

10   10

28

breaks

13   12   10   14

33

12

11   12   12   12

23° 48' N

14

15   10   12

34

18

12   27

57

28   20   11   9   10   11

10 fathoms

41   29   21   31   33   48   55   79

75° 06' W   75° 05' W

RUM CAY

About twenty-five miles southwest of San Salvador and nearly the same distance southeast of Conception Island lies Rum Cay. Lucayan Indians named the cay *Mamana* and it is said to be the second island that Columbus visited on October 15, 1492. The great discoverer named the island *Santa Maria de la Concepcion* which was transferred over time to nearby Conception Island. The current name of this 30 square mile island allegedly came from an Indiaman with a cargo of rum which ran aground here. There also seems to be some speculation that the cay was named after the Isle of Rum in Scotland.

Once settled by Loyalists and later famous for its salt pond production, pineapples, and sisal, it now has only one settlement at Port Nelson. The local inhabitants are a very personable and friendly people. One gentleman, a former Commissioner for Andros, even offered free land on Rum Cay to the inhabitants of Tristan De Cunha a few decades ago when their volcano blew its top and displaced many islanders. The Tristanians, saying they were not acclimated to the colder English weather, declined the gracious offer and returned to their island home.

Rum Cay is a very popular jumping off spot for vessels southbound to the southern Bahamas and the Caribbean. The Island itself is generally low-lying and flat although there are a few small hills that run down to the shore to end up as white bluffs. A large reef system stretches northward for approximately two miles with a visible wreck on its northernmost tip.

Tides at Rum Cay run approximately 1 hour before Nassau.

APPROACHES TO RUM CAY

From the GPS waypoint that clears the reefs lying southeast of Conception Island a course of 131° for 8.6 nautical miles will bring you to a waypoint just north of the wrecked freighter lying north of Flamingo Bay. Rum Cay will be spotted very shortly after leaving Conception Island. A GPS waypoint at 23° 38.50' N, 74° 57.30' W, will place you approximately ½ nautical mile off Sandy Point, Rum Cay, and in very deep water. From this position skippers wishing to gain access to Port Nelson may take up an eastbound course staying at least ½ mile south of the shoreline of Rum Cay to avoid the shallow rocks and shoals close in.

From Cockburn Town, San Salvador, a course of 235° for 29.9 miles brings you to a point north of the wrecked freighter lying off the northwest tip of Rum Cay at Flamingo Bay. From Sandy Point at San Salvador, a course of 218° for 22.1 miles will bring you to a GPS waypoint at 23°37.00' N, 74° 47.0' W, which places you approximately 1½ miles southeast of Rum Cay and clear of its offlying reefs. From this waypoint stay at least 1 mile off the eastern and southern shore until you can work your way to Port Nelson and the waypoint which allows you to clear the reef lying south and west of Sumner Point.

From Clarence Town, Long Island, Port Nelson bears 019° at a distance of 31.1 nautical miles while from Little Harbour, Port Nelson bears 006° at a distance of 39.2 nautical miles. From Bird Rock at Crooked Island, Port Nelson bears 338° at a distance of 53.2 nautical miles.

Skippers transiting the areas between Cape Santa Maria, Conception Island, Rum Cay, San Salvador, and the entire eastern shore of Long Island must be aware that a branch of the North Equatorial Current called the Antilles Current generally sets in a northwesterly direction through here from .5 to .75 knots.

FLAMINGO BAY

There is a great anchorage at the northwestern tip of Rum Cay in Flamingo Bay that is good in east to almost southwest winds. If you are tired of the maddening roll at Port Nelson, and you want a great beach for swimming with plenty of shallow and deep reefs offering great snorkeling or diving, this is the spot for you. The entrance can only be done in daylight as you must steer between a lot of small patch reefs that are easily seen and avoided, there's plenty of room to go around and between them. Before entering, make sure your weather forecast doesn't call for any westerly to northerly winds overnight because you'll never safely find your way back out in the dark.

The entrance, as shown on Chart #RC-1, is gained by rounding the northern tip of the reef well north of the very visible wreck of an old Haitian freighter. A GPS waypoint at 23° 42.45' N, 74° 56.80' W, will place you approximately ¼ mile north of the conspicuous wreck of a Haitian freighter at the northern end

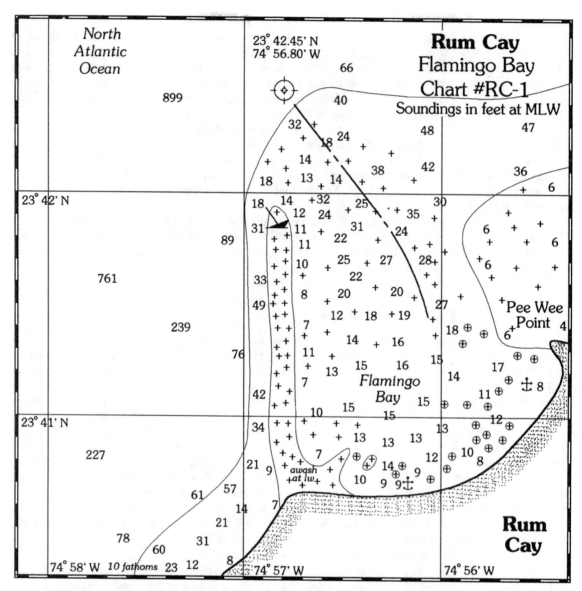

North
Atlantic
Ocean

23° 42.45' N
74° 56.80' W

Rum Cay
Flamingo Bay
Chart #RC-1
Soundings in feet at MLW

of the reef. Do not attempt to bring your big boat close to the freighter, use your dinghy for exploring as the shallows extend north of the freighter about 50-100 yards.

From the waypoint, steer well east of the wreck giving it a wide berth, and head in for the beach at Flamingo Bay. There are two narrow, twisting, turning, entrances through the reef south of the wreck but I cannot recommend them as viable passages. Better to enter the standard way north of the wreck. Just north and east of the wreck are some tremendous coral heads lying in 20'-30' of water but they are not hazards to navigation.   The dangerous heads lie inshore, mostly south of a line from Pee Wee Point to the northwestern tip of Flamingo Bay. The shallow heads and patch reefs are easily seen and avoided in good light and anchor anywhere you choose off the beach in 7'-12' of water and more in places. In strong easterly winds you will want to tuck up into the lee of Pee Wee Point.

At the northern end of the reef lying northwest of Rum Cay, just north of the wreck, is a dive site known as *Pinder's Pinnacle*. Here a spectacular coral pinnacle rises from the sandy bottom in 75'-110' of water. Fish life is prominent as are numerous colorful tube sponges. An occasional shark may visit the site.

A short distance east of Flamingo Bay, a dinghy ride in settled weather, is Hartford Cave. Hartford Cave was discovered by Rum Cay residents who would enter the cave to collect the bat guano for fertilizer. Sometimes the farmers would find utensils like plates, cups, and bowls underneath the rich carpet of guano.

Rum Cay
Port Nelson
Chart #RC-2
Soundings in feet at MLW

Batelco tower (PA)
⊙ 100' Fxd R

Fxd G
4 16', 5M

Port
Nelson

airstrip

consp. white house

Cotton
Field
Point

rocky and
dangerous

Fl WYR, 8s,
75', 10M

marina

Sumner
Point

buoy

stake

breaks

087° white
mag.
red
yellow

018°
mag.
red
white
yellow

red
white
yellow

23° 39' N
23° 38' N
23° 37.75' N
74° 51.20' W

74° 50' W
74° 51' W
74° 52' W

The items were found to be Lucayan in origin. The walls of the cave are decorated with ancient Lucayan drawings carved by these original inhabitants of Rum Cay.

PORT NELSON

Port Nelson, originally called Wellington Bay, is the only settlement on Rum Cay at the present time. In the past there were other communities all over the island with names like Port Boyd, Carmichael, Black Rock, Times Cove, The Village, and Gin Hill. The buildings that remain in these areas are now overgrown with vegetation. After you round Sandy Point on your approach to Port Nelson you can see the ruins of Black Rock on the southern shore of Rum Cay on a ridge approximately ½ mile east of Sandy Point. There are the remains of numerous slave built stone walls called "margins" all over the island.

As mentioned earlier, a GPS waypoint at 23° 38.50' N, 74° 57.30' W, will place you approximately ½ nm off Sandy Point in very deep water. Be advised that there is a westerly setting current around Sandy Point. Once you round Sandy Point take up an eastbound course towards Port Nelson staying at least ½ mile south of the southern shore of Rum Cay and passing south of Cottonfield Point. There is a privately maintained light atop Cottonfield Point (*Fl WYR, 10s, 23m, 10M*) sitting approximately 70' above MLW. The light flashes for two seconds every 10 seconds providing two safe white sectors bearing 018° and 087° magnetic to assist vessels wishing to gain access to Port Nelson. The area between 018° and 087° shows amber to warn of some scattered heads. Red shows in all other sectors.

Approach Port Nelson and St. George's Bay as described and you will be in 20'-30' of water almost the entire way until you come abeam of Cottonfield Point. Anchor just south of the town dock (Chart #RC-2) wherever your draft will allow staying well off the dock to avoid the shallows close in. Watch for scattered heads hereabouts. Some of the elkhorn coral rises out of the water at low tide as if reaching out to snag a passing boat or dinghy.

Photo by Kelly Becker

Port Nelson, Rum Cay.

Photo by Kelly Becker

Sumner Point Marina, Rum Cay.

Sumner Point Marina, whose entrance channel lies just north of Sumner Point, often uses buoys to mark their entrance channel but they are often missing after storms so do not expect them to be there when you are. If you wish to enter the marina call *Sumner Point Marina* on VHF ch. 16 and they will be happy to talk you in. Once again, watch out for all the coral heads that are awash at low water south of the town dock and especially near the entrance to Sumner Point Marina.

Heading to Port Nelson from the south, the conspicuous white cliffs just east of Sumner Point make an excellent landmark. Vessels approaching Port Nelson from the south can head to a GPS waypoint at 23° 37.75' N, 74° 51.20' W, which will place you safely south and west of the western tip of Sumner Point Reef. From this waypoint head north until well inside the reef and turn to starboard to anchor. Be careful, there are a lot of shallow, dry at low water, patch reefs in this area, especially along the northern edge of Sumner Point Reef. In good visibility, that means in daylight with the sun not in your eyes, they are easily seen and avoided.

Vessels wishing to gain access at night (not advised), should line up the white light on Cottonfield Point on a heading of 018° to bring their boats into the harbour. The waypoint I have given lies well east of the white sector of the light and is not advised for use at night. Skippers not comfortable with the waypoint given are advised to head in on the light on Cottonfield Point, day or night, on a heading of 018° as this route has been safely used for years. The waypoint given, although clear of all dangers, may place some skippers too close to the reef for their comfort. If this is the case, head in on Cottonfield Point and then head to the anchorage off the dock. There are some deeper pockets surrounding the docks and there's usually a catamaran or two occupying them. Be advised that Rum Cay, although touted as the best spot to wait for weather for southbound cruisers, has a reputation for being a rolly anchorage, a well deserved reputation.

At the southeastern end of St. George's Bay lies the entrance channel to the Sumner Point Marina. As mentioned earlier, the entrance channel is usually buoyed from the end of Sumner Point Reef into the marina. It is best to call the marina on VHF ch. 16 for directions. Once inside you will find 6'-9'. The marina is a well run family operation that had been open since 1992 and is currently expanding. As of this writing the marina has 12 slips but managers say that they are expanding to 30 by the end of 1997. The entrance channel is then to allow entry to a 9' draft, currently a 6' draft can enter without any problems.

Thirty and fifty amp power is available at the docks. The marina sells diesel, gas, and water and accepts credit cards. Skippers needing diesel or outboard repairs should contact the Dockmaster, John, the guys at the marina are very handy and have even replaced engines in visiting boats. A plane is available for medical emergencies. The marina has a wonderful bar and restaurant, both open every night and reservations are requested for dinner. The chef is a young man who studied for years under a Japanese chef and creates some truly elegant and memorable dishes. The restaurant also has a very nice book swap.

If you anchor out and wish to dinghy in to town you can beach your dinghy by the dock or tie your dinghy to the town dock and clamber up. If you choose to tie to the dock, bear in mind that at low tide your dinghy may be extremely hard to reach. There is a two foot lower ledge on the western side of the dock but there is a huge pile of conch shells in the water that are well above the level of low tide and that could possibly hole an inflatable. Fishermen also use this ledge to clean fish so watch out for a mess.

Port Nelson is situated in a beautiful setting of casaurinas and palm trees. At the head of the dock is a newly rebuilt wooden tower 16' feet high where a resident is supposed to place a light each night. Next to the tower is a trash dumpster of sorts, a large plywood box painted tan with wheels. Just place your garbage in the box. Once past the dumpster look to the right across the road and you will see a purple building. This is *Kay's Restaurant and Bar* and is a must stop for anybody visiting Port Nelson. Although, as in most places in the out islands, a little notice for a meal is necessary, Kay's proved quite the exception. I was there one day when 10 yachties showed up spontaneously and wanted lunch. Well, Kay and her mother, Doris Wilson, cooked a fantastic meal of salad, stewed cabbage, potatoes au gratin, johnny cake, fried conch, and baked grouper and the lunch bill for two people with two Kaliks and two sodas was only $22.00. Kay and Doris created this remarkable feast on a one burner stove and oven. Absolutely the best deal, and the best food, that I have found in The Bahamas, and I have eaten a lot of native cuisine in The Bahamas, all strictly in the name of research . The meal was unforgettable. Kay also has a nice book trade. Don't forget to sign Kay's guest book.

Walking west from Kay's you will come upon the *Last Chance Yacht Supply, Grocery, and Ice Cream Parlour*. This name is a little misleading as there are few if any "yacht supplies" and the ice cream is gone soon after the mail boat delivers it. However groceries and fresh veggies are no problem along with gifts, some clothes, and a video rental with quite a selection of some of the latest movies. Further up the road is the Batelco station if you wish to place a call. Sam Maycock runs the office and is open all day except during the lunch hour.

West of the town dock is Ted Bain's *Oceanview Bar*. Next door you'll find Reuben and Hermie Bain's *Variety Store*, and the *Oceanview Commissary*, where Hermie offers groceries, fresh eggs and vegetables, and wonderful conversation. Hermie is the closest thing to a doctor to be found on Rum Cay. Hermie has been the midwife on Rum Cay for almost 25 years now. Party Animals will want to visit *Toby's Bar* which is THE place to be on Friday nights. *Toby's,* located next to the school, boasts the coldest beer on the island. It should be, it's kept in the freezer. George Gaitor is proprietor of the *Two Sisters Take Away* and will deliver to Sumner Point marina if you wish.

Snorkelers and SCUBA divers alike will be thrilled at what awaits them at Rum Cay. South of Cottonfield Point lies *Cottonfields*. This is an excellent snorkel in calm weather in depths of 5'-18'. The reef is alive with fish and also makes for a unique night dive when the basket stars and red coral shrimp are on display.

The best diving at Rum Cay, and some say the entire Bahamas, lies along the reefs south and east of Sumner Point. The entire reef can be snorkeled and the fishing is outstanding in its waters.

Just south of Sandy Point lies a dive site known as *Snowfields* in 20'-40' of water. Here the currents feed countless small fish, invertebrates, and sponge encrusted corals.

At the western end of the Sumner Point reef lies a site called *The Chimney* in 75'-110' of water. *The Chimney* is a series of large tunnels, one ascending through the reef from about 100' to 75'. It is a narrow vertical tunnel but wide enough for a diver with camera gear.

Directly south of Sumner Point and in 20'-50' of water lies the *Grand Canyon*, with its deep coral canyons and a few tunnels. The fish are very tame here as divers from the old Rum Cay Club fed them on a regular basis. The divemasters even named a few such as Radar, a Nassau Grouper with the damaged dorsal fin, Klinger, a Queen Trigger who thinks she is a grouper, and Lady Di, who nibble food from the divemaster's hands.

About ½ mile off the centermost of the three prominent sandy bluffs east of Summer Point, and about 200 yards south of the reef, lying almost southeast of Signal Point, is the wreck of the H.M.S. *Conqueror* which sank here in 1861. This wreck, the first propeller driven British warship, lies amid a forest of coral in a gully almost 30' deep. The wreckage that remains today is scattered over the bottom but plainly visible are the main shaft, crankshaft, and the anchor chain. Quite often divers find small trinkets, cannon balls, and bullets at the site hiding in holes and under ledges. Divers are reminded not to take anything from the site and not to disturb it. The site is the property of the Government of The Bahamas and is a National Historic Site.

For a complete list of the dive sites stop in at *Last Chance*. They sell some of the leftover plastic coated place mats from the old Rum Cay Club which lists the dive sites and gives their approximate location. A valuable piece of information for only a buck.

Photo by Author

Columbus Monument, San Salvador.

SAN SALVADOR

By most people's consensus, Columbus' first landfall in 1492 was made on San Salvador and no less than four monuments will remind you of that although other islands have at one time claimed the honor. Ask different Bahamians and you will find claims that Columbus first landed on Samana or Cat Island, it almost depends on who you ask. Originally called *Guanahani* in pre-Columbian times, San Salvador was known as Watling's Island until 1925-1926. As Watling's Island it was named after the pirate George Watling who was noted for his strict observance of the Sabbath Day. He severely punished his crew if they so much as threw dice on a Sunday. In some old charts the island is spelled *Watland*. The ruins of what is known as Watling's "Castle" (some say the ruins date to a time later than the pirate's career) still stands some 85' above sea level at Sandy Point awaiting your exploration.

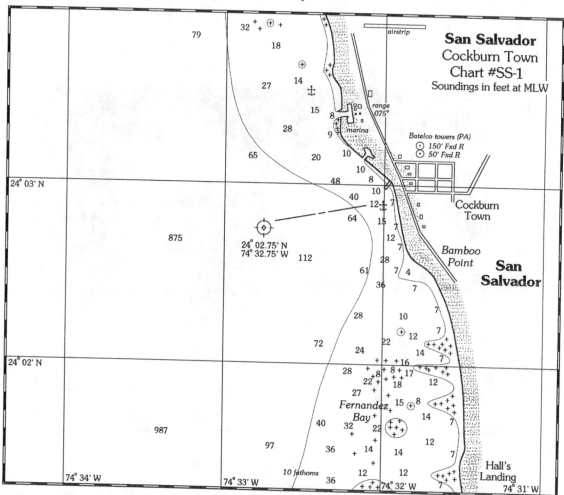

San Salvador is approximately 12 miles long and from 5-7 miles wide. It is surrounded by dangerous reefs and has no all weather anchorage. There is a beautiful lake in the interior that may be the one Columbus referred to saying that it would hold ". . . as many ships as there are in Christendom." If that is true he neglected to mention that a canal would have to be dug through the cay to the sea to accomplish this.

San Salvador was once noted for its breed of horses and other livestock, consignments of which were sent to Jamaica on a regular basis. The island once provided hardwoods such as Lignumvitae in abundance.

The U.S. Navy had a submarine tracking station on San Salvador for many years. Some local inhabitants feel that the base, as well as the U.S. Pan-American Base also on San Salvador, were in general bad for the economy. True, the Navy brought a boom to the economy when they were here, but they also caused a severe slump when they departed. For over twenty years the young sons and daughters of San Salvador forgot the ways of fishing and farming to earn their money in the employ of the military presence. When they left, the young San Salvadorans faced a decision, return to the ways of their ancestors, or move to Nassau or some other place where they could perhaps make better money and live a lifestyle that they had become accustomed to. Many left, few stayed. Now however, San Salvador has come into its own as a tourist destination and hopefully the sons and daughters will not have to leave the island in search of the almighty dollar.

APPROACHES TO SAN SALVADOR

Skippers transiting the areas between Cape Santa Maria, Conception Island, Rum Cay, San Salvador, and the entire eastern shore of Long Island must be aware that a branch of the North Equatorial Current called the Antilles Current generally sets in a northwesterly direction through here from .5 to .75 knots. Not only must you concern yourself with the current in the area of San Salvador, you must also be on the lookout for large ship traffic. San Salvador marks the northern end of the shipping lane that passes through the Crooked Island Passage and the area is heavily traveled so keep a good lookout and pay attention when sailing these waters, especially at night.

From the waypoint off the reefs that lie southeast of Conception Island, Cockburn Town bears 70° at a distance of 33.1 miles. From the waypoint north of the reef lying north of Conception Island, Cockburn Town bears 84° at a distance of 30.8 nautical miles.

From the waypoint southeast of Rum Cay, Sandy Point bears 38° at a distance of 22.1 nautical miles. From the waypoint north of the reef lying north of Flamingo Bay, Cockburn Town bears 55° at a distance of 29.9 nautical miles.

Sandy Point, San Salvador bears 358° at a distance of 65.1 nautical miles from Bird Rock at Crooked Island. Sandy Point also bears 41° at 52.9 nautical miles from Clarence Town, Long Island, and 59.0 miles on a course of 22° from Little Harbour, Long Island.

COCKBURN TOWN

Most cruisers approaching San Salvador will head north along its western shore in the vicinity of Fernandez Bay. Beginning two miles south of Fernandez Bay (sometimes shown on charts as Long Bay) there are a series of reefs close inshore that almost dry at low water. These reefs generally do not break giving little warning of their presence. In Fernandez Bay, about two miles south of Cockburn Town you will find the White Cross Monument, erected in 1956 to commemorate Columbus' first setting foot in the New World here. Of course, others say he stepped ashore on the eastern shore first (one cannot imagine why a seasoned seaman like old Chris would attempt to land on a windward shore, the leeward shore at Fernandez Bay makes much more sense). Nearby is the Olympic Monument which was erected to commemorate the transfer of the Olympic Flame from Greece to the New World for the 1968 Olympic Games in Mexico City.

At the northern end of Fernandez Bay is principal settlement of Cockburn Town, pronounced Co'burn Town, which was once called Riding Rock. Cockburn Town is a pretty, clean, friendly, and extremely busy (by out-island standards) community. Cars are constantly buzzing down the roads. There are a lot of cars here for such a small island. The economy here is in great shape primarily due to *Club Med*. There is almost 100% employment on San Salvador. Anybody who wants to work can find a job, some folks even manage to hold down two jobs.

The entrance to the anchorage in the bay at Cockburn Town is only to be approached from the west. Give the western shore of San Salvador a berth of at least 1 mile to avoid the many shallow reefs that abound in this area. Never attempt to parallel the shore close in from Sandy Point or southward from Green Cay. There are numerous shallow reefs inshore, particularly south of Cockburn Town. As shown on Chart #SS-1, a GPS waypoint at 24° 02.75' N, 74° 32.75' W, places you approximately 1 mile west of the anchorage of Cockburn Town. Head straight in on the Batelco tower and drop your hook off the town anywhere you like. You can also head south to anchor off the beach but if you head too far south you must dodge a few shallow reefs. Skippers can also anchor north of town near the *Riding Rock Inn*, the long motel-looking building just south of the sprawling, pastel colored, *Club Med* complex.

The town dock is pretty much falling apart these days but you can dinghy up to the beach south of the dock to land your dinghy. Just off the end of the town dock is the Batelco office and the Government Building which houses the Commissioners Office. The two story salmon colored building right on the waterfront is the *San Salvador Museum*. Here, history buffs will find Lucayan, pre-Columbian, Colombian, and post-Colombian artifacts from the San Salvador region. The upstairs of the building itself was the seat of government for San Salvador while the downstairs was the jail. If the museum is not open check at the Batelco office at the foot of the huge tower and dish that sit just a couple of hundred yards away. Garbage can be deposited in any of the trash cans located around town.

In and around Cockburn Town you will find three fine restaurants, the *Three Ships*, *Club Med*, and *The Driftwood Bar* at the *Riding Rock Inn*. If you're looking for groceries try *Jake Jones Grocery Store* and *Dorett's*. You'll have to shop both to find the best deals. For a night out in town try *Harlem Square* (across the street from the *Three Ships*) or the *Ocean View*, both serve food and drinks and *Ocean View* even has ice cream while *Harlem Square* boasts a pool table and fantastic Friday night buffets. There is a clinic with a resident doctor and nurse in town. The *Bank of the Bahamas* has a branch in Cockburn Town.

Photo by Author

Cockburn Town, San Salvador.

About ¼ mile north of the town dock is the entrance to the government marina. This is private, only for use by the mailboat and other commercial vessels. Approximately ½ mile north of the town dock is the jetty that marks the entrance to the *Riding Rock Marina*.

The *Riding Rock Inn Resort and Marina* is quite often the center of attention for cruising skippers. Once you locate the jetty (at approximately latitude of 24° 03.40' N) at the entrance you can come in on a heading of 75°. There is a range with green lights but the daymarks have been destroyed during the last hurricane. Stay in the center of the channel as the sides are rocky. If you need assistance upon entry call the marina on VHF ch. 06, they don't monitor ch. 16 (in fact most of the island monitors VHF ch. 06, if you need anything such as bread, simply place a call on ch. 06, ch.16 is unusually quiet at San Salvador). Skippers are advised that this is a good spot to ride out a front. Although the marina staff has doubled the length of the jetty, a little surge still makes it in during strong southwest to northwest winds. If you use plenty of fenders and tie off properly you won't have a problem. The marina has recently dredged out a new area south of the entrance channel and it gets very little surge. Ask the Dockmaster, Kevin, if you can tie up there if a front threatens. There is a small snack bar across the street from the marina that is open from 10 A.M. until 4 P.M.

The marina can handle 10 boats with drafts to 9' and offers 110v and 220v, 30 amp and 50 amp electric service. The marina also has diesel, gasoline, good well water, and ice. Trash disposal is $1.00 a bag unless you are a guest. Skippers in need of a mechanic can contact the marina to inquire about a diesel or outboard mechanic. If the job is not too serious the marina will be able to find someone to handle the repairs. Major repairs may require a mechanic flying into San Salvador. Steve, a local mechanic, has a small shop across from the marina behind the National Insurance Board office. The marina is open from 8 A.M. to 5 P.M., Sunday through Friday and is closed on Saturdays. If you need assistance outside those hours you can call *Riding Rock Inn* on VHF ch. 16 until 9 P.M. Plans are underway to purchase the equipment that will allow the marina to fill propane tanks. This would be a big help to cruisers as well as locals since all tanks must now go to Nassau by mailboat for refilling. The marina also has a washing machine and dryer that takes tokens that you can purchase at the marina office. The cost is $2.00 a load to wash and $2.00 a load to dry.

Cockburn Town is a Port Of Entry for The Bahamas and skippers wishing to clear in must tie up at the marina where Kevin will give you the forms you need and contact Customs for you. There is a fee of $10.00 for the use of the marina for this service but it allows you to drop off your garbage and spend a half a day touring the town if you like. If you wish to stay overnight, the fee will be applied to your dockage.

There is a quality dive center at the marina and SCUBA enthusiasts may want to sample some of the magnificent wall diving just off the resort. *Riding Rock Marina* is sorry to inform folks that they are unable at this time to handle private tank fills. The marina also has a photo lab on premises that attracts underwater photographers who frequent the nearby dive sites. The photo shop can develop slide film only, in at 1:30 P.M. and you'll have it back before 5 P.M. The wall dives along San Salvador are a diver's paradise, some areas are virtually unexplored and run for 12 miles along the leeward side of the island. Who knows, maybe if you take the time to explore you might get a reef named after you. There is also excellent wreck and reef diving at High Cay, Low Cay, and Middle Cay on the eastern shore of San Salvador. The dive shop at the *Riding Rock Marina* requests that visitors refrain from fishing on the reefs along the western shore of San Salvador. There are a lot of tame grouper on these reefs that the local SCUBA divers feed and do not wish to lose to your frying pan. Remember that Bahamian law prohibits spearfishing within 200 yards of any family island, a lot of the reefs along the western shore of San Salvador are within that limit.

At the *Riding Rock Inn*, *The Driftwood Bar* is an excellent place to stop and have a cold one and stare at the ceiling of driftwood where visitors have carved their names. *The Driftwood* also serves breakfast, lunch, and dinner. The resort has 42 rooms for those skippers whose crews are tired of bouncing around all the time and need a night ashore. If you wish to rent a car or scooter, the *Riding Rock Inn* can handle the arrangements for you, it's a lot easier to let them do the legwork for you. The *Inn* can also arrange a bus tour of the island if you are interested.

Just north of the *Riding Rock Inn* is the *Club Med* resort with its 300 rooms with all the bells and whistles a full service resort has to offer. This all inclusive resort offers the best in diving, fishing, sailing, snorkeling, swimming, or just plain relaxing on the beach.

Bahamasair has twice weekly flights to San Salvador.

GRAHAM'S HARBOUR

At the north end of the island is a nice little anchorage that gives good protection from southeast through southwest winds. The reefs on the northern side of San Salvador extend for over two miles forming a northward pointing triangle from Cut Cay in the east and Northwest Point in the west. Along the edge of the reefs lie White Cay (wait till you see it-this cay is WHITE!) and Green Cay which have been designated a National Park primarily due to their huge bird populations. White Cay, as one might guess from its name, has distinctive white cliffs which are often covered with brown boobies and red-footed boobies.

There is only one way in and one way out of this peaceful anchorage. Never attempt this route at night or with the sun in your eyes. As shown on Chart #SS-2, a GPS waypoint at 24° 08.15' N, 74° 31.60' W, will place you approximately 1 mile west of the entrance channel that lies just south of Green Cay. When heading for this waypoint come at it from the west. Never, I repeat, never try to head to this waypoint along the shore of San Salvador. Give the western shore of San Salvador a berth of at least 1 mile due to the numerous shallow reefs that abound in this area. Head east staying about 100 yards south of Green Cay bound for Goulding Cay. There is one small patch reef on this route that has less than 6' of water over it but it is easily seen and avoided. When you are abeam of Goulding Cay you will be in 15' of water or more and can then take up your course for the conspicuous dock at Graham's Harbour. There is one dark patch of water between Goulding Cay and the dock but it is grass. Don't try to head for the dock until you are abeam of Goulding Cay as there are some very shallow reefs that lie west of the dock as shown on the chart. Don't try to head to the rust and white checkerboard tower as the reefs are directly on that route, approach the tower from the dock. You can anchor off the dock in 7'-9' of water.

Cut Cay is a small cay just separated from the mainland of San Salvador. It is believed that a fort was once situated on the cay as evidenced by a cannon and cannon balls that were found nearby. This also implies that Cut Cay was once part of the mainland of San Salvador within the last 500 years and has only recently been a separate island.

Located in Graham's Harbour is the Bahamian Field Station of the College of the Finger Lakes in upstate New York. Here researchers study the island's biological and geological features. Part of the station was once the site of an old U.S. Navy base from the 1950's.

For those venturing inland, a road leads south from the dock and locals will usually give you a ride if you stick out your trusty thumb. A little ways south is Reckley Hill, a small but friendly community where you can find cold thirst quenchers at *Ed's First and Last Bar*. Further south is United Estates, or EU as it is often called, the second largest settlement on San Salvador. If you plan a short stop here, by all means stop by the *Club Short Stop*.

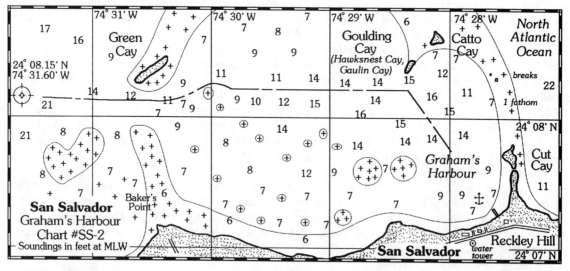

Dixon Hill is easy to find, just look for the lighthouse. Dixon Hill Lighthouse was built in 1887 by the Imperial Lighthouse Service. Here you can take a guided tour and climb 72' above ground level and 163' above sea level to get a beautiful view that is said to stretch for 21 miles. Dixon Hill Lighthouse is one of the few remaining manually operated lighthouses in the world. For another good lookout try Mt. Kerr, just east of the airport. At 140' Mr. Kerr gives you an excellent view of San Salvador and her creeks. Just south of Dixon Hill is Polly Hill where the Storr family dominate. If you need a few supplies try *Bernie's Grocery Storr*, (no pun intended folks, that's the name).

Along the eastern shore of San Salvador, about ½ mile southeast of Cut Cay, lies Manhead Cay. Here a small colony of iguanas rule over what was once an archeological dig signifying a Lucayan presence. Further south along the mainland shore is another monument to the discovery of the New World, erected in 1892 by the Chicago Herald and known as the Chicago Herald Monument.

You may wish to explore the Pigeon Creek area by dinghy. Here are a series of excavations offering evidence of Lucayan villages called the Pigeon Creek Sites. You can travel up the creek and visit places like South Victoria Hill with its small cement dock and the nearby and almost totally abandoned villages of Farquharson, Old Place, Trial Farm, Montreal, and Allen. Until recently these places were all visited by small boats on a regular basis. The ruins of the Farquharson Plantation are known locally as Blackbeard's Castle as it is said he once visited here. The remains include the great house, a kitchen, and a prison.

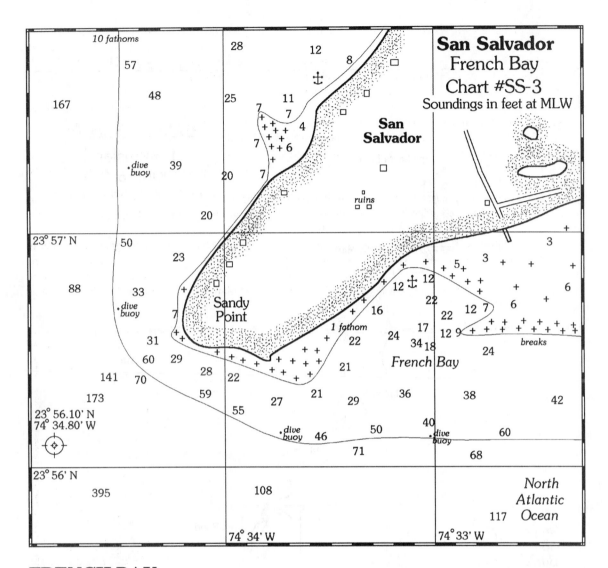

San Salvador
French Bay
Chart #SS-3
Soundings in feet at MLW

FRENCH BAY

If you need a shelter from northwest to almost northeast winds you might try anchoring in French Bay at the southern end of San Salvador. A GPS waypoint at 23° 56.10' N, 74° 34.80' W, will place you approximately ¾ mile southwest of Sandy Point as shown on Chart #SS-3. Pass well south of Sandy Point giving it, and the reefs lying off the point, a wide berth. Watch out for the many dive boat mooring buoys located in this area. Head into French Bay and anchor well west of the dock as close in as your draft will allow. There are a few coral heads about with plenty of sand between them where you can set your hook. When entering French Bay be careful to avoid the reef lying to the south and east of the dock.

This anchorage is not good for winds from east/northeast through south to west. In the event of a frontal passage you might avoid the southwest-west winds at Graham's Harbour but that anchorage is no place to be in northerly winds. Another option is to get a slip at the marina but beware of the surge in strong westerly winds and fender or tie off accordingly. The reefs south and east of French Bay offer excellent diving and fishing. In places, tremendous stands of elkhorn and staghorn coral rise from 30'-50' foot depths almost to the surface.

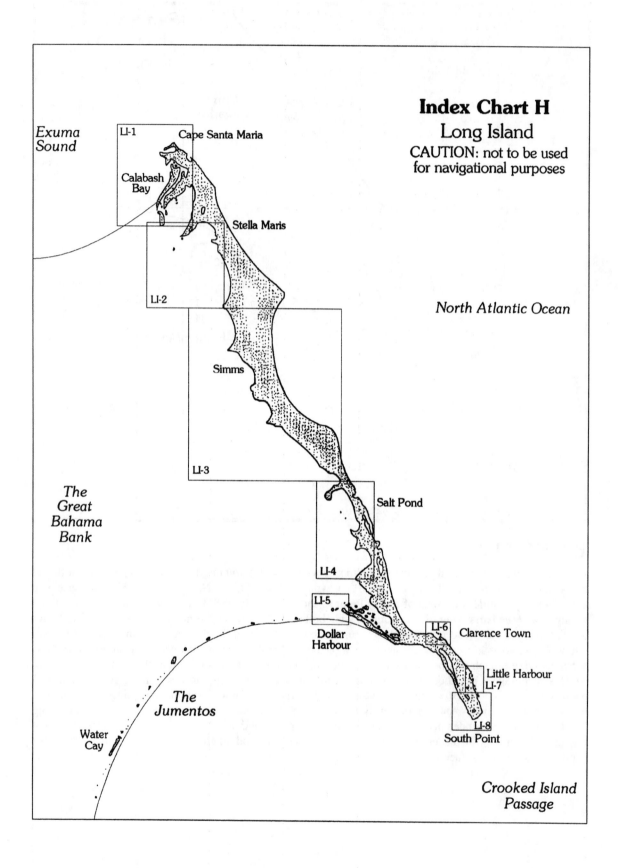

Index Chart H
Long Island
CAUTION: not to be used
for navigational purposes

LONG ISLAND

"Long" is quite likely the best description of this island. Long Island is 76 miles in length by 4 miles in width at its greatest breadth and stretches from the southern Exumas and Exuma Sound to the deep Crooked Island Passage. Long Island is similar to Eleuthera and Cat Island in that along its eastern shore (its northern shore according to Long Islanders) lies the Atlantic Ocean while to the west (the southern shore according to Long Islanders) lies the shallow waters of an arm of the Great Bahama Bank. Long Island has many natural caves with some having guided tours for visitors. A skeleton believed to be the remains of a Lucayan Indian was found in one of Long Island's caves.

In pre-Columbian times the island was known as *Yuma*, *Yumetta*, or *Yametta*, but the great discoverer, who landed there on October 16, 1492, renamed the island *Fernandina* after his King. Long Island was the third stop for Columbus in the New World after San Salvador and Rum Cay. In fact, Columbus's flagship, the *Santa Maria*, went aground on a reef off the northern tip of the island earning the area the name Cape Santa Maria.

Long Island has some 40 communities along its length (more than any other Bahamian island) with over 3,500 residents of very different ethnic backgrounds. Some of the most physically attractive people in The Bahamas come from Long Island. Here one can find descendants from many different peoples that have migrated to The Bahamas over the centuries from pirates and slaves to French missionaries and Greek sponge fishermen.

Long Island has always been known for its livestock, particularly Scottish "black face" sheep and thoroughbred horses, both introduced to the island over two hundred years ago. At one time there were numerous large estates on the island with extensive stone wall pastures the ruins of which can still be seen today. The islanders have always been big on raising sheep, mutton being an excellent local dish, and have long been known as "sheep runners." Many Long Islanders are still involved with the fishing and sponging industry. A curious note for those interested in tilling the soil. Long Island farmers, as many farmers throughout The Bahamas, plant their crops by the phases of the moon. Certain phases cause higher tides resulting in a higher water table. This brings the water closer to the plants roots.

Tides in Long Island are quite varied. Tides at Calabash Bay and Joe Sound tend to run approximately 45 minutes to 1 hour behind Nassau tides while Salt Pond tides are 2½ hours later than Nassau tides and tides in the vicinity of Newfound Harbour are approximately 1¾ hours after Nassau.

APPROACHES TO LONG ISLAND

From the Eastern Channel entrance to Elizabeth Harbour in the Exumas a course of 68° for approximately 22 nautical miles will bring you to the GPS waypoint west of Calabash Bay (those skippers wishing to detour around Cape Santa Maria may take up a heading of 60° to clear the Cape Santa Maria reef waypoint at 23° 42.00' N, 75° 21.50' W). From this position you may enter between the reefs (see Cape Santa Maria and Calabash Bay, Chart #LI-1) to anchor just off the beach at Calabash Bay. Those wishing to anchor just below Cape Santa Maria may proceed another mile northeast to the waypoint marking the anchorage off the beach just below the light and beacon. From Conch Cay Cut, the western entrance to Elizabeth Harbour, a course of 78° will bring you to the waypoint to clear the reefs at Cape Santa Maria. From Conception Island, a course of 242° for 15.4 nautical miles will also bring you to the waypoint to clear the reefs at Cape Santa Maria. Dollar Harbour lies 90° at 5.62 nautical miles from Nuevitas Rocks.

Clarence Town bears 199° at 31.1 miles from Port Nelson at Rum Cay while Little Harbour bears 186° at a distance of 39.2 miles. The southern point of Long Island bears lies at a distance of approximately 47.5 miles on a generally south/southwest heading but use caution if running this route as you need to parallel the southeastern shore of Long Island. Don't head directly for that waypoint from Port Nelson as you will run aground on Long Island, that's something you probably won't want to do.

From Bird Rock at Crooked Island, Clarence Town bears 303° at a distance of 36.3 miles, Little Harbour lies on a course of 293°, 26.9 miles distant, and the southern tip of Long Island bears 275° at 27.4 nautical miles distant. From French Wells, Clarence Town bears 314° at a distance of 44.1 miles, Little Harbour lies on a course of 309°, 33.7 miles distant, and the southern tip of Long Island bears 294° at 31.6 nautical miles distant.

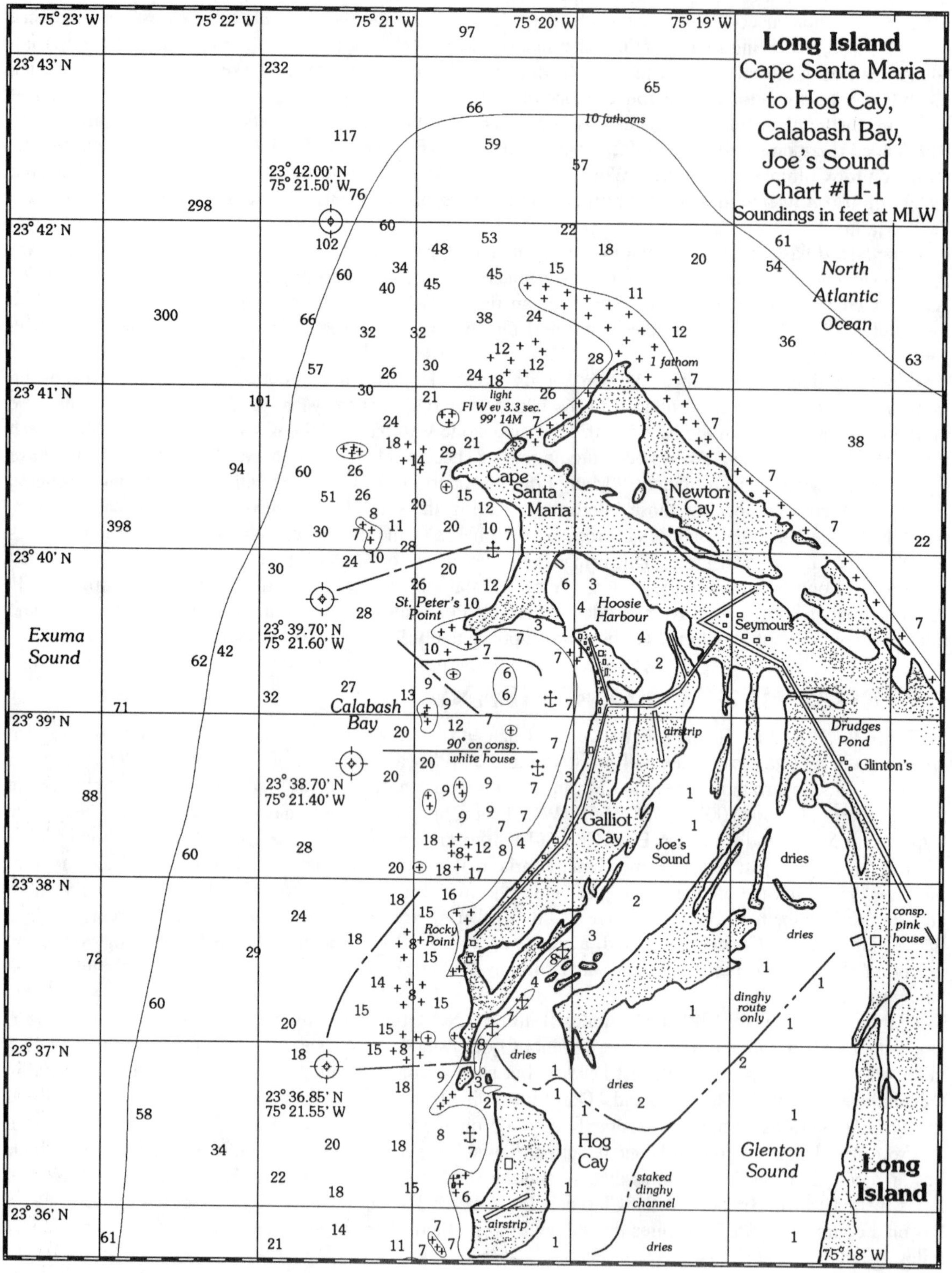

75° 23' W · 75° 22' W · 75° 21' W · 97 · 75° 20' W · 75° 19' W

Long Island
Cape Santa Maria
to Hog Cay,
Calabash Bay,
Joe's Sound
Chart #LI-1
Soundings in feet at MLW

23° 43' N · 232

66 · 65

10 fathoms

117 · 59

23° 42.00' N
75° 21.50' W 76

298 · 102 · 60 · 53 · 22 · 61 · North
23° 42' N · 48 · 18 · 54 · Atlantic

34 · 45 · 15 · 20 · Ocean
60 · 40 · 45 · 24 · 11

300 · 38 · 12
66 · 32 · 32 · 28 · 1 fathom · 36 · 63
57 · 26 · 30 · 12 · 12
24 · 18

23° 41' N · 101 · 30 · 21 · light · 26
Fl W ev 3.3 sec. · 7 · 38
24 · 99' 14M
18 · 29 · 21
14 · 7
94 · 60 · 26 · Cape · Newton · 7
51 · 26 · 15 · Santa · Cay
8 · Maria · 12
398 · 30 · 11 · 20 · 10 7 · 7 · 22
28

23° 40' N · 30 · 20 · 6
26 · 12 · 4 · Hoosie · 4
28 · St. Peter's 10 · Harbour · 4 · Seymours
Point · 3 · 2 · 7
Exuma · 23° 39.70' N · 7 · 7
Sound · 62 42 · 75° 21.60' W · 10 · 7
71 · 32 · 27 · 13 · 9 · 6
Calabash · 9 · 6 · 7
23° 39' N · Bay · 20 · 12 · 7 · airstrip · Drudges
90° on consp. · Pond
white house · 7 · Glinton's
20 · 20 · 3
88 · 20 · 9 9 · 1
23° 38.70' N · 9 · Galliot · 1
60 · 75° 21.40' W · 9 7 · Cay · Joe's · dries
28 · 7 · Sound
18 8 12 8 · 2 · consp.
20 18 17 · pink
23° 38' N · 18 · 16 · 2 · dries · house
24 · 15 · 1
72 · 18 · Rocky · 3 · dries · 1
29 · Point · 1 · dinghy
14 · 15 · route
60 · 15 · 15 · 4 · only · 1
20 · 15 · 1
23° 37' N · 18 · 15 8 · dries · 2
18 · 9 3 · 1 · dries · 1
23° 36.85' N · 2 · 2
58 · 75° 21.55' W · 8 · Hog · Long
34 · 20 · 18 · 7 · Cay · Glenton · Island
22 · staked · Sound
18 · 15 · 6 · dinghy · 1
23° 36' N · 14 · 7 · channel
61 · 21 · 11 7 7 · airstrip · 1 · dries · 1
75° 18' W

Skippers transiting the areas between Cape Santa Maria, Conception Island, Rum Cay, San Salvador, and the entire eastern shore of Long Island must be aware that a branch of the North Equatorial Current called the Antilles Current generally sets in a northwesterly direction through here from .5 to .75 knots.

A special note for vessels transiting the waters between the Jumentos, Long Island, and the Crooked/Acklins District in the vicinity of the Crooked Island Passage. At an approximate position at 22° 50' N, 74° 48' W, lies the center of the Diana Bank. The approximately 100 square miles of Diana Bank lies west of the southern tip of Long Cay, south/southeast of the southern tip of Long Island, and west of Nurse Channel. Here is a shallow bank, 35'-600' deep, lying in the midst of much deeper water, 1800'-6000' deep. With a strong swell in any direction the seas on top of the bank can get very rough as the water is pushed up the sides of this underwater obstruction. If you are experiencing rough seas in your transit of this area, by all means avoid the area of Diana Bank. If the seas are calm try fishing on the bank.

CAPE SANTA MARIA AND CALABASH BAY

At the northern tip of Long Island is Cape Santa Maria, named after Columbus' Flagship which allegedly ran aground on the reefs hereabouts. The cape is a beautiful headland where stunning white cliffs with a series of caves and a beautiful white sand beach lie to leeward. Off the point an immense reef system marks the meeting place of Exuma Sound and the Atlantic Ocean. The reef structure to the northwest of the Cape is awash at low water and almost always breaking. There is a passage through the reefs just north of Cape Santa Maria but it is not recommended except for shallow draft vessels, with experienced pilots, in excellent visibility, and with very settled weather. Calabash Bay is the usual anchorage for boats bound south from George Town who wish to wait a day or so to round Cape Santa Maria. The bay, with its beautiful 2 mile beach, is best as a lee anchorage with good protection from east to south although some swell works its way in around the Cape.

Approaching from George Town, Exuma, your first sight of this area will likely be the high headlands of Newton Cay (see Chart #LI-1). On the northern tip of Galliot Cay you will soon spot the neat rows of buildings that make up the *Cape Santa Maria Resort*. A GPS waypoint at 23° 38.70' N, 75° 21.40' W, will place you approximately ½ nautical mile west of the entrance through the reefs off Galliot Cay and the anchorage at Calabash Bay. From this waypoint line up the conspicuous white house with the peaked-roof on a course of 90° and follow it in leaving the very conspicuous brown bar to port. The entrance is very wide and the only obstruction is the shallow brown bar just to the north. The white house lies approximately 1/2 mile south of the *Cape Santa Maria Resort* and sits by itself under some casuarinas. It has a flagpole on its north side and a windmill on its southside. You can anchor about 100-150 yards off the beach in 6'-10' of water over one of the prettiest white sand bottoms you will ever see. You can anchor quite a ways south of the white house (actually anywhere along Galliot Cay south of the house) or you can anchor almost as far north as the resort before the water shoals. The anchorage just under Cape Santa Maria Light also offers good holding over a sandy bottom. To enter this anchorage proceed northeast another mile to a waypoint at 23° 39.70' N, 75° 21.60' W. From this waypoint eyeball your way in to the anchorage off the beach keeping the conspicuous brown reef well off your port side and staying north of St. Peter's Point. Both of these anchorages tend to be surgy and are no place to be in a norther. Even in strong east or southeast winds these two anchorages may get too uncomfortable for you. If that happens, or if bad weather threatens, you should round the southern tip of Galliot Cay and enter Joe Sound.

The entrance to Joe Sound is through a very narrow cut that is hard to see except from straight on. A GPS waypoint at 23° 36.85' N, 75° 21.55' W will place you approximately ¾ mile southwest of the cut. Vessels anchored in Calabash Bay wishing to gain access to Joe Sound may coast south between Galliot Cay and the outlying shallow reefs being careful to avoid the shallow bar just off Rocky Point. The entrance lies about ¼ mile south of the very distinctive angular white houses. Never attempt this cut at night unless you are very familiar with it. As I mentioned earlier the cut is extremely narrow, a catamaran with a beam of 16' such as a Prout 37 Snowgoose will have a very nervous entry. Enter the cut (7' at high tide) being careful to avoid the rocks on the southern side of cut. Once in the channel, slightly favoring the southern side, follow the slight curve until you pass into the deeper water (7'-9') on the other side. When you are through the cut you may turn to port and anchor wherever your draft will allow. Shallow draft vessels can go further up into Joe Sound, really nothing more than a creek. The sides dry at low water with about 6'-9' in the deep water passage. A small anchorage also sits just to the south of the entrance channel. About ½ mile north of the entrance, after crossing a 5' bar and between the two groups of mangroves, vessels will find 9' at low water before the creek shoals. A dozen boats can sit comfortably in here and ride out even the fiercest frontal passage, safe from the fury of the seas but open to the wind. Just south of Galliot Cay is a fine anchorage in the lee of Hog Cay with room for four to six boats. A nice, calm anchorage even in very strong north/northeast to south/southeast winds. Here you can anchor in 7'-8' at low water but be prepared for some surge, not always, but sometimes. Hog Cay is privately owned and visits ashore must be by invitation only. Hog Cay is home to one of the largest, if not the largest, flock of West Indian Whistling Ducks in The Bahamas. The owners, I am told, leave out food for their feathered, quacking, friends.

When you are ready to depart Joe Sound, simply head west to avoid the reefs lying west off the Cape and Galliot Cay. Those skippers leaving from Calabash Bay and wishing to round Cape Santa Maria may pass through the reefs just south of St. Peter's Point but only with good visibility. The shallow reefs are clearly defined and there is plenty of deep water between them. If in doubt use the traditional way out, put the white house with the flagpole on your stern and steer 270° until you are clear of the reefs. Then head for the waypoint to clear Cape Santa Maria reefs making sure you are keeping the reefs west of the Cape well to starboard.

About ¼ mile north of the white cliffs below Cape Santa Maria light are some caves and one very beautiful grotto which you can take your dinghy into if there is no surge. A hole in the roof allows sunlight in and creates a very dramatic effect. Watch out for submerged rocks upon entering this grotto and never attempt it with a surge running.

Ashore, the *Cape Santa Maria Beach Resort and Fishing Center* boasts 12 beachfront cottages and excellent dining Boaters can make lunch or dinner reservations on VHF ch. 16 by calling *Cape Santa Maria*. The resort also has small sailboat rentals, windsurfers, snorkeling gear, and deep-sea and bonefishing packages. Just north of the resort a dirt road leads over to Cape Santa Maria light and the Columbus Monument which looks like a day beacon from the water.

Just south of Cape Santa Maria and north of Galliot Cay is the very attractive settlement of Seymours where many of the inhabitants have their houses built on high ground. Some residents say that from this vantage point you can see Conception Island and Rum Cay on the horizon (on a clear day). There is a lady in Seymours who has transformed her front porch into a telephone booth. She will allow you to make calls and charge them to your card for a small fee. You can gain access to Seymours via the small dock that lies north of Galliot Cay facing Hoosie Harbour.

Just south of Seymours lies Glinton's where the remains of a Lucayan village was found which enabled archeologists to once and for all establish Lucayan occupation on Long Island. The all age school for the nearby communities is also located in Glinton's as well as a clinic when the doctor visits. Also in Glinton's is *Williams Car Rentals* (338-5002), *The Rose Haven Meat Market*, and the brand new *Barbie's Ice Cream Shoppe* which also serves food and drink.

Just a little further south lies the settlement of Burnt Ground, home to the ruins of a 200 year old building, a two story structure which is one of the oldest structures on Long Island. Most of the people in Burnt Ground work in Stella Maris, just south along the main highway. Skippers anchored at Joe Sound can easily access Burnt Ground by dinghy. From Joe Sound, follow the deep blue creek just off the small house with the wrecked dock, on a rising mid-tide or better, eastward until the blue water begins to shallow. Here, keep the offlying rocks to port and pass over the shallow bar until you are in the deeper water (3') of Glenton Sound. From this point steer straight for the large bright pink house on the northern end of Glenton Sound. Dinghy skippers can also round the southern tip of Hog Cay and follow the blue dinghy channel as it snakes between shallow sandbanks that dry at low water. The channel is marked with stakes by local fishermen but is very easy to see in good visibility. Once at the pink house you will find a large concrete dock where you can safely leave your dink (sometimes you can purchase fish or lobster from the local fishermen here). This area almost dries at low water so be sure you don't get caught by the tide. From the dock, walk to the road and take a right. Just a few hundred yards down you will come to Burnt Ground where you will find a *Adderly's Supply and Gas Station*, a small but well stocked grocery store that even sells kerosene and some hardware supplies. Here you will also find a Post Office, *Taylor's Garage*, the *B.G. Convenience Store*, the *Sabrina Bar and Grill*, the *MGS Food Store*, *Pratt's Restaurant and Bar*, *Burt's Dry Goods* and *Idealla's Strawworks* for some excellent plait work, and *The Everglades Shell Shop*.

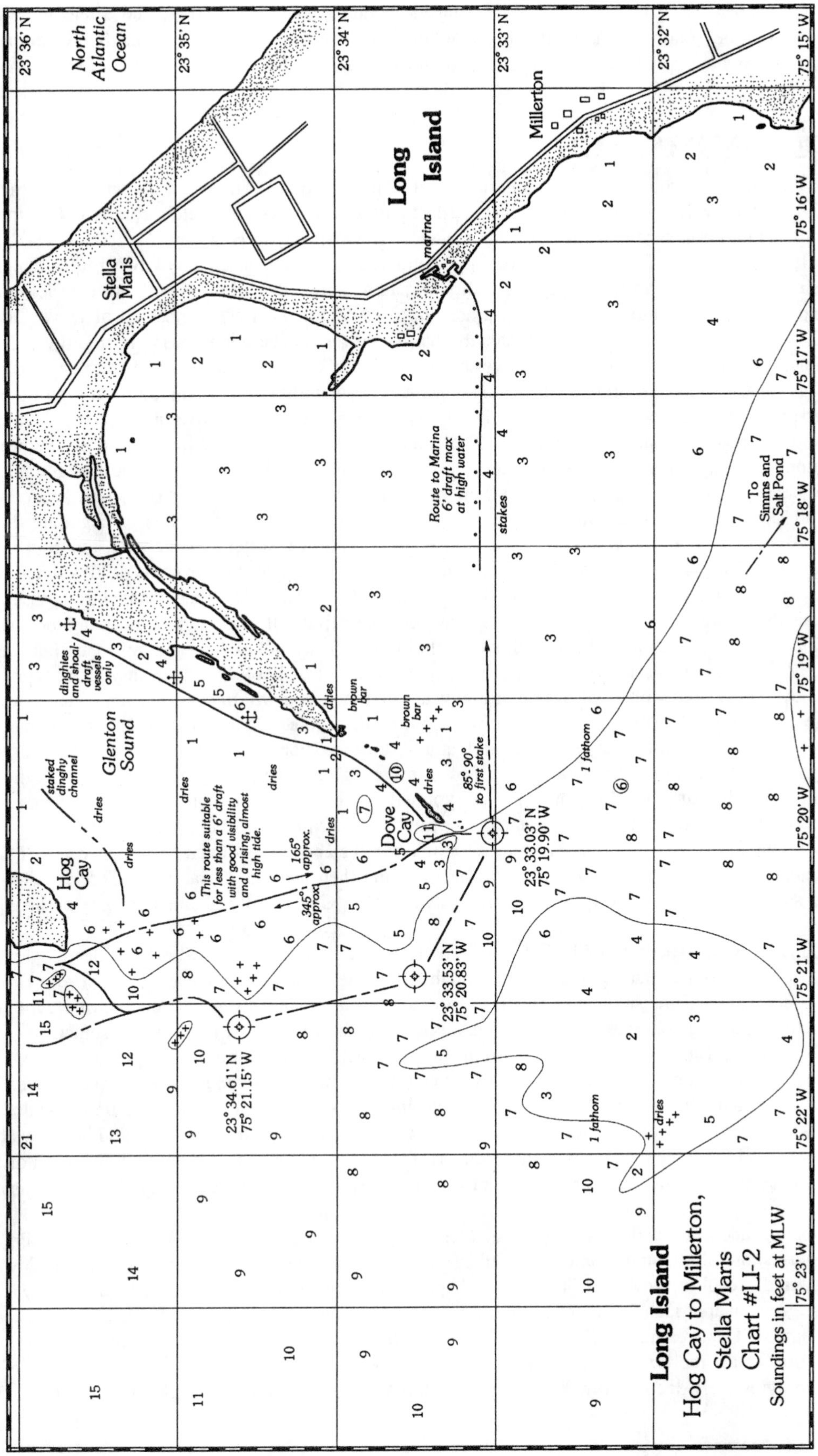

23° 36' N
North Atlantic Ocean
23° 35' N
23° 34' N
23° 33' N
23° 32' N
75° 15' W

Long Island

Stella Maris

Millerton

marina

Route to Marina
6' draft max
at high water

stakes

To Simms and Salt Pond

Glenton Sound

staked dinghy channel

dinghies and shoal-draft vessels only

Hog Cay

This route suitable for less than a 6' draft with good visibility and a rising, almost high tide.

165° approx.

345° approx.

85°-90° to first stake

brown bar
brown bar

Dove Cay

dries

1 fathom

23° 33.03' N
75° 19.90' W

23° 33.53' N
75° 20.83' W

23° 34.61' N
75° 21.15' W

1 fathom

dries

Long Island
Hog Cay to Millerton,
Stella Maris
Chart #LI-2
Soundings in feet at MLW

75° 16' W
75° 17' W
75° 18' W
75° 19' W
75° 20' W
75° 21' W
75° 22' W
75° 23' W

If you were to turn to the left at the road up from the concrete dock, you would find a telephone booth sitting in the middle of nowhere about two miles up the road. For some reason telephone booths often sit in the middle of nowhere up and down the main road on Long Island. For car rentals try *Taylor's Garage* on VHF.

DOVE CAY PASSAGE

From Calabash Bay you can sail south in the lee of Long Island past Simms all the way to Thompson's Bay and Salt Pond with few obstructions. The hardest part will be the short stretch from Hog Cay to Dove Cay, or if heading northward in the lee of Long Island, from Dove Cay to Hog Cay.

Vessels heading south from Hog Cay or Joe Sound can choose from either of two routes depending upon their draft, visibility, and the skipper's ability to read water depths. Vessels with drafts of less than 6' can round Hog Cay very close and take up a heading of 165° for the westernmost tip of Dove Cay (see Chart #LI-2). Watch your leeway and make sure that the current or the wind does not set you west of this route. Put Hog Cay on your stern and the western tip of Dove Cay on your bow and steer approximately 165°. This route is good for drafts of less than 6' with good visibility and a rising, almost high tide. The helmsperson must have good visibility and the ability to read water depths to run this route. Once you round Hog Cay heading south you will be in 12' of water that will begin to shallow to 5'-6' at low water in places along this stretch, particularly off Dove Cay. Just south of Hog Cay you must negotiate some scattered heads for a few hundred yards and then the bottom remains sandy. The tricky part awaits you as you round Dove Cay and you will need good light (as in NOT IN YOUR EYES) to negotiate this last section. As you approach Dove Cay you will notice some shallower water to your west, ignore it, it does not effect you. Pass close to the western tip of Dove Cay in water that goes from 4' at low water to 12'. You will see the small offlying rocks just southwest of Dove Cay. There is a deep channel that passes very, very close to the western end of those rocks that you must find. It is a slightly deeper blue than the surrounding shallows. To the east is a shallow bar, to the west is a shallow bar, you must pass between the two close enough to the westernmost of the small rocks to toss this book onto it from your cockpit. You will pass over a bar here with 3'-5' over it at low water and then you will once again be in deeper water in the range of 7' at MLW. This bar is the shallowest spot on this route. On a good high tide 6' can pass over it easily but I cannot in all honesty recommend that a 6' draft attempt this route. Shoaling can occur which would make this route impassable for drafts of 6' or more. This route is very difficult to run in the early morning light as the sun is right in your eyes and you will not be able to pick out the deeper water, even an experienced pilot who can read the water may have trouble discerning where to go the first time.

Vessels heading northward around Dove Cay should run the above mentioned route in reverse. Take the westernmost of the Dove Cay rocks close to starboard and then take up a heading of 345° for Hog Cay. Pass the southern tip of Hog Cay to starboard between Hog Cay and the distinctive brown shoal to its southwest.

Captains who have been scared off by my description of this route, or who have deeper drafts, or possibly just more sense, may take a more roundabout course as shown on Chart #LI-2. From Hog Cay follow the curvature of the sandbank around towards Dove Cay. I have shown a couple of waypoints on the chart to help navigators with their job if the banks become indistinct. Strong winds sometimes stir up silt in the water and make eyeball navigation all but impossible. Please do not simply steer waypoint to waypoint. You may run across an arm of the sandbank I have misrepresented or one that has moved. Use your eyes. If you don't have good visibility, by all means, consider postponing your trip until you do.

You will notice by the chart that there is a large, shallow sandbank with some scattered heads well west of Dove Cay. This bank extends south and southeast for quite a few miles with only a few breaks of water over 6'. Take care if you find yourself west of this bank. It has not been accurately charted for its entire length.

Catamarans and shallow draft vessels, 3' and less, may find a comfortable secluded anchorage along the southeastern shore of Glenton Sound just northeast of Dove Cay in 4'-6' of water. From Dove Cay, steer northeastward, keeping Dove Cay to starboard, paralleling the line of Dove Cay and the cays to its northeast. As you approach the mainland of Long Island you must negotiate a narrow passage between two shallow banks. This area has 1'-2' at low water. To your port you will notice that vast areas are dry at low water so don't stray too far that way. Eyeball your way between the shoals and you will be back in water that gets progressively deeper from 2' to 6' as you approach the marked anchorages on Chart #LI-2. There is a lot of vegetation along this shore so be prepared for bugs. Also, don't forget to use an anchor light as some fishermen use this route to and from the dock west of Burnt Ground.

STELLA MARIS

Stella Maris, *Star of the Sea*, is a huge resort complex lying about halfway between Dove Cay and Simms along Long Island's western shore. The resort is home to a full service marina, the last before the Turks and Caicos. The airstrip has regular flights via Island Express and Bahamasair from south Florida. Stella Maris is a port of entry and yachts can clear Customs and Immigration at the marina.

The marina cannot be seen from the normal routes of boats passing around Dove Cay as shown on Chart #LI-2. If bound north or south along the western shore, a GPS waypoint at 23° 33.03' N, 75° 19.90' W will place you approximately ½ mile southwest of Dove Cay and approximately 3½ miles west of the entrance to the marina. From this waypoint steer 85°-90° for a few hundred yards and you will begin to pick up the first of 12 PVC stakes that lead into the marina. Except for the very first one, all the stakes will be topped with an orange Styrofoam float but they do not show up well on radar. Although you can take these stakes to either side, the deeper water lies south of the stakes, take the stakes to port when entering *Stella Maris Marina* and you will have at least 4' of water at MLW the entire way in on an approximate course of 90°-95°. At the last stake you will turn to port to enter the marina complex. A draft of 6' can easily make it into Stella Maris at high tide while vessels with drafts over 6' may wish to call the marina for advice although the marina tries to discourage drafts of over 6' from entering the channel. Either way, be sure you call the marina on VHF prior to your arrival and to secure accommodations. As you enter the marina, the fuel dock (gas and diesel) will be to starboard, and the slips directly in front and to port of you. Well to port is a narrow "S" shaped canal that works its way around the marina and is an excellent hurricane hole where several local boats rode out hurricane Lili with no damage. The canal is 6'-7' deep at low water.

Stella Maris Marina is a full service marina and offers some very fine work or you can do your own. The marina has a railway that has hauled boats up to 86' long and displacing 48 tons. Dockmaster Gerd Fuhrmann tells me that the marina will have a new 40 ton travel-lift in use by the end of 1997. Boaters wishing to do their own bottom jobs are welcome to bring their paint and supplies and have at it although the marina requests that they do all serious underwater repairs for safety's sake. The marina has a full service machine shop where they build and rebuild engines, transmissions, and manufacture specialty metal parts for the commercial fishing boats of Long Island (including TIG welding). The marina can repair gas and diesel engines, outboards motors, as well as do fiberglass repairs and painting. There is a local dealer on the island at *Harding's Supply Centre* in Thompson Bay for outboards and parts can be flown directly into the resort complex on a daily basis. The marina's alternator and starter shop is as good as any anywhere and better than most. The marina also offers dry storage of small boats. If you have a faulty refrigeration system it can also be brought back to working order here at *Stella Maris Marina*. Propane tanks that need refilling can also be handled though the marina. The marina and resort take all the major credit cards. *Sally's Bar and Restaurant* on the second floor at the marina is closed due to damage from Lili and its future is uncertain.

The dive shop at the marina offers excellent snorkeling and reef dive trips as well as a fantastic shark dive where the dive masters hand feed what are described as "friendly" bull sharks. The dive shop has free snorkeling gear for hotel guests as well as two complimentary boat trips per week. The shop is able to fill and test your tank for you and they have a concrete SCUBA training pool (saltwater) 15' deep for those who need a refresher course or wish to take advantage of their PADI open water course. The dive operators can take you to dive sites like the wreck of the *M.S. Comberbach*, a 103' steel freighter which had been prepared for safe diving before being sunk, one mile offshore on Cape Santa Maria Reef. Another popular spot is *Flamingo Tongue Reef* where thousands of flamingo tongue shells litter the bottom here hence the name. This reef lies some 6 miles from Stella Maris about ½ mile offshore in 25' of water. *The West Bar* is a very primitive coral garden in the shape of a bar 600' long and 300' wide lying within ½ mile of 2 beautiful beaches. Here you will spy a variety of brain, staghorn, and towering pillar corals in 15' of water. *Poseidon's Pint* lies just a few minutes from Stella Maris and boasts massive brain corals, elkhorn and staghorn coral in water from 3'-30' deep. The dive shop can also arrange for trips to *Southhampton Reef* at Conception Island where you can dive on the remains of a wrecked freighter which sank over 90 years ago.

If you walk to the road from the marina and take a right you will see a small grocery store across the street with some meats and limited groceries. Next to the marina to the south is *Potcakes*, a bar and grill serving sandwiches and pizza. Dining is also available at the resort with courtesy transportation provided.

Laundry service is available through some local ladies but you can also send your laundry to the resort (quite expensive). The marina also has freshwater showers, cistern water available at the dock, and can handle all you garbage needs. RO water is available at the resort if you bring your own containers, the marina is not yet hooked up to the *Stella Maris Resort* water system. There is regular bus service into Seymours and Simms with buses leaving the marina at approximately 7 A.M., 9 A.M., noon, and again at about 4 P.M. This is an excellent way for boaters on a budget to get to town to shop and spend some time. Taxis are also available at all hours. Car rentals are available through the hotel desk, contact Gerd at the marina for information.

Stella Maris Resort Club is often described in brochures and guides as a plantation style resort. This is actually quite a fitting description since the resort sits on what was once Adderley's Plantation, a Loyalist cotton plantation now residing in ruin. There are three buildings that are left intact to the roofline situated just to the north of the resort complex right off the main road. The resort offers several different packages from honeymoon specials to bonefishing and diving packages. The resort spans Long Island from the western shore on the Great Bahama Bank to the eastern shore on the Atlantic Ocean with beaches on both shores. For information contact the front desk or call 800-426-0466 in the U.S. or 242-336-2106 locally. Fax numbers are 954-359-8238 in the U.S. and 242-338-2052 locally. Accommodations (60) range from rooms to apartments, cottages, and townhouses and from two bedroom villas to bungalows.

The resort has a large cave that is home to the weekly Cave Party with open fires, great food, live music and dancing. Spelunkers may wish to check it out at a less crowded moment. Signs at the resort will direct you to the Cave. Also on the resort property is the *Stella Maris General Store*, *The New Watering Hole Liquor Store*, two tennis courts, *The Bank of Nova Scotia*, the *MGM Food Store*, *Tingum's Boutique*, *The Tennis Club Restaurant*, a Post Office, the Stella Maris Police Station, and Customs and Immigration officers.

There are some excellent snorkeling sights just off the eastern shore of Long Island at the resort. *Coral Gardens* lies in 3'-25' of water just at the northern end of the resort with signs to direct you. Almost at the southern end is the *Eagle Ray Reef* lying in 3' to 30' of water, also with signs to direct you.

Photo by Author

Blue Hole, Long Island.

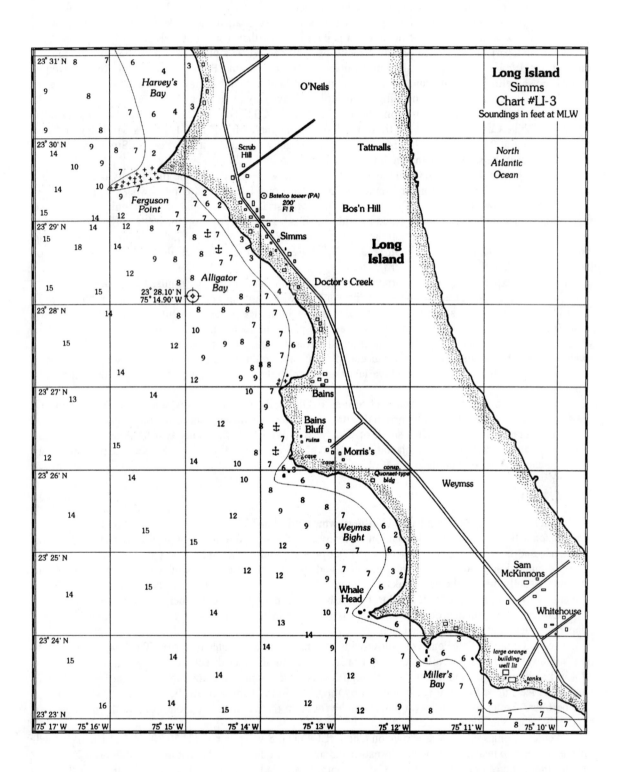

STELLA MARIS TO THOMPSON'S BAY

From the waypoint at Dove Cay it is possible for a cruising boat to sail directly for Thompson Bay and the GPS waypoint off Indian Hole Point in water that gets progressively deeper, 7' at Dove Cay to over 16' in places as you approach Thompson Bay. It is also possible for boats to sail close to shore in the lee of the land in 7' at low water. The major obstruction is the rocky bar that works out well west of Ferguson Point as shown on Chart #LI-3. Once past this rocky bar you can cruise right past Simms heading southward staying just a few hundred yards offshore in places, even less around Bain's Bluff. From Simms simply follow the shoreline, basically running from one point of land to the next staying about 200 yards off each point. When leaving Simms and heading northward for Dove Cay remember to give Ferguson Point a wide berth. Vessels heading to Simms from the waypoint (23° 24.93' N, 75° 21.62' W) at Sandy Cay (also known as White Cay) at the southern tip of the Exumas, a course of 70° for 11.2 miles will bring you to a GPS waypoint at 23° 28.10' N, 75° 14.90' W, approximately ¾ mile southwest of the Simms settlement. Head in towards the settlement and anchor wherever you prefer in 7' at low water.

Simms is one of the oldest settlements on the island and was named after the first family that settled the area in the 1700's. The government center for northern Long Island is in Simms where you will find a Police Station, Post Office, a Batelco office, the Magistrate's office and a community clinic. An agricultural packing house is also located in Simms and is a good spot to shop for fresh veggies where once a week the mail boat arrives to pick up the fresh produce. Here you will also find the wonderful *Blue Chip Restaurant and Bar*, the *MGS Food Store*, and *Tyre King Auto Parts*. There is also a community outlet for local straw work at the *Simms Handicraft Outlet*.

If you are experiencing uncomfortable conditions while anchored off Simms, say perhaps that it is blowing east to southeast at 20 knots and the water is whitecapping and you are just miserable, there is some relief. Head south about a mile or so and anchor in the lee of Bain's Bluff, the bold headland just south of Simms. Here you will find two or three nice places to anchor in calm water with good holding in 7'-9'. The shore around the bluff is full of small caves and cave holes awaiting your exploration as you wait for the winds to subside. From your cockpit you can see the ruins of some pasture walls, sometimes called "margins" that were built by slave labor and date to the Loyalist days of the late 1700's and early 1800's.

The first inhabited settlement south of Simms is Old Neils, one of the few settlements located on the eastern shore of Long Island. The original settlers preferred the western shore for its accessibility and for protection against hurricanes. Just south of Old Neils is Wemyss where only two families remain, living amidst the ruins of a 200 year old plantation. South of Weymss are Miller's and McKann's, predominantly farming and fishing communities.

SALT POND

Further south lies Salt Pond and Hardings which are considered one town. Salt Pond, lying along Thompson's Bay, is a favorite destination of many cruisers who venture through the Exumas and central Bahamas and is named for the numerous old salt ponds found in the area. Many cruisers make this area their primary destination in their yearly cruise and use it as a base from which to explore surrounding waters. Usually, when a boater speaks of Thompson's Bay or Salt Pond they are considered to be one and the same. One would judge Salt Pond to be a fishing community by the number of fishing boats anchored in Thompson's Bay in the off-season. This is reflected in the economy of Salt Pond which is heavily dependent upon the richness of the catch.

The anchorage at Salt Pond is shallow with less than 6' at low water in spots. The harbour is open to the southwest and west but offers excellent protection from all other directions. I have anchored there in 25-30 knots out of the southwest and although it was quite choppy, the anchorage provides good holding and some lee can be found, if it is not taken by the Long Island fishing boats, behind the two small cays in the harbour. Relief from northwest winds can be found in the lee of Indian Hole Point at the northwestern end of Thompson's Bay.

To enter Thompson's Bay as shown on Chart #LI-4, a GPS waypoint at 23° 20.70' N, 75° 10.30' W, will place you approximately ½ mile southwest of Indian Hole Point. Vessels heading to Thompson Bay from the northern end of Long Island, Dove Cay or Simms, can head directly for this waypoint in water that gets deeper the closer you get to Salt Pond. Vessels heading to Salt Pond from Exuma can head directly to this waypoint from the waypoint (23° 24.93' N, 75° 21.62' W) off Sandy Cay, also known as White Cay, at the southern tip of the Exumas. The only obstruction may be a small arm of the Sandy Cay shoal that juts into your path and is easily seen and rounded. From the Indian Hole waypoint head east into Thompson's Bay. Most cruisers tend to anchor in the northeastern end of Thompson's Bay in 6'-8' at low water. Dinghy in to the beach and a short walk will enable you to gain access to the main highway. Land your dinghy by the tree with the large orange float hanging from its branches. Here you will find a conch shell lined path leading past a fresh water well with excellent water. A short trek of a few more yards through the woods and you will come out onto a dirt road. Take a right on the dirt road and walk 100 yards to the main highway. A few hundred yards to your left will be the *Thompson's Bay Inn* with its 9 rooms. Here Tryphena Bowe Knowles holds court and serves up excellent Bahamian dishes. She requests that you make reservations for lunch or dinner. Tryphena also rents cars for island exploration.

The public dock is about a mile south of this anchorage and some cruisers like to anchor off that area in 5'-6'. The commercial fishing boats tend to anchor in the vicinity of the town dock, for obvious reasons. South of town is a small bay known as The Bight with areas of water that are 6'-7' deep at low water. The best way to reach this anchorage is by going out and around the small cays in the middle of Thompson's Bay and head in on the beach staying just north of the point. Vessels seeking shelter from southwest winds can find some protection in the lee of Salt Pond Cay and Eva's Cay. If you plan to anchor in the lee of Eva's Cay watch out for the submerged wreck of an old Haitian boat that lies approximately 200-300 yards northeast of the grounded wreck of the old mailboat *Seaker* lying close in behind Eva's Cay. The submerged Haitian boat sits in about 3½'-5' of water and has a metal pipe that juts out above water at low tide. Near Salt Pond Cay lies the *boiling hole* at approximately 23° 20.20' N, 75° 07.69' W. This hole is small and deep and water just *boils* out of it when the tide is running strong. South of the town dock and just north of The Crossing is a nice anchorage with depths of 7'-8' in places. The best way to gain access to this anchorage is by heading west around the offlying cays in the center of Thompson's Bay. A draft of 6' can be taken from just off the town dock at high water to the anchorage also. There are a few small, deep holes in this anchorage that are good for snapper fishing.

Just across the street from the main dock is *Harding's Supply Centre*. Here owner Roy Harding stocks groceries, meats, some marine supplies, paints, hardware and is also a Johnson and Evinrude dealer. This is the most complete grocery and hardware store in the southeastern Bahamas and some groceries are often cheaper here than at George Town. Roy Harding also owns *Harding's Realty* across the street. Just south of Harding's is an *Esso* gas station but you'll have to jerry jug it to your dinghy as there is no fuel dock. Right next door to *Harding's* is *JVC Electronics*. Here you can get your TV, VCR, or VHF radio repaired and even purchase some film and rent or buy a video. Next to the *Esso* Station is Hardings Seafood where you can purchase fresh fish, conch, or lobster when available. North of town, approximately halfway between *Harding's* and the *Thompson's Bay Inn* three miles to the north, is the Thompson's Bay Post Office. South of Salt Pond is The Bight where you will find the *Midway Inn Club and Restaurant*.

Just north of *Harding's Supply Center* you can visit Salt Pond's extensive cave system. To find the caves go north along the main road from *Harding's Supply Centre* about ¼-½ mile to the top of the next rise. By the house along the road you will find a path through the bush that leads west to Thompson's Bay. Follow the path for the two minute walk to the water's edge, turn south (left), and walk about 10 yards, then walk back into the bush and there will be the entrance. A flashlight is necessary to enjoy the caves. If you take the road leading east from *Harding's Supply Centre* you will come to a beautiful double bay with great scenery, shelling, and sheltered swimming.

In late May or early June Salt Pond hosts the Long Island Regatta. The week long party is a homecoming of sorts for native sons and daughters and is highlighted by four days of Bahamian sloop racing, partying, dancing, and marathon Gin and Coconut Water drinking. It has been said that after regatta there is not a single coconut left on Long Island. Some of the greatest Bahamian sloops were built right here on Long Island by the late Rupert Knowles. Rupert built the famous *Tida Wave* and the *Lady Muriel*, although she has been rebuilt many times at her current home on Staniel Cay in the Exumas.

Skippers heading south will want to meet John McKie, *Sunseeker*, who lives on the ridge above Thompson's Bay. John and his wife have sailed these islands for years and are a treasure trove of information about them. It would behoove the cruiser headed south to seek the benefit of John's years of experience.

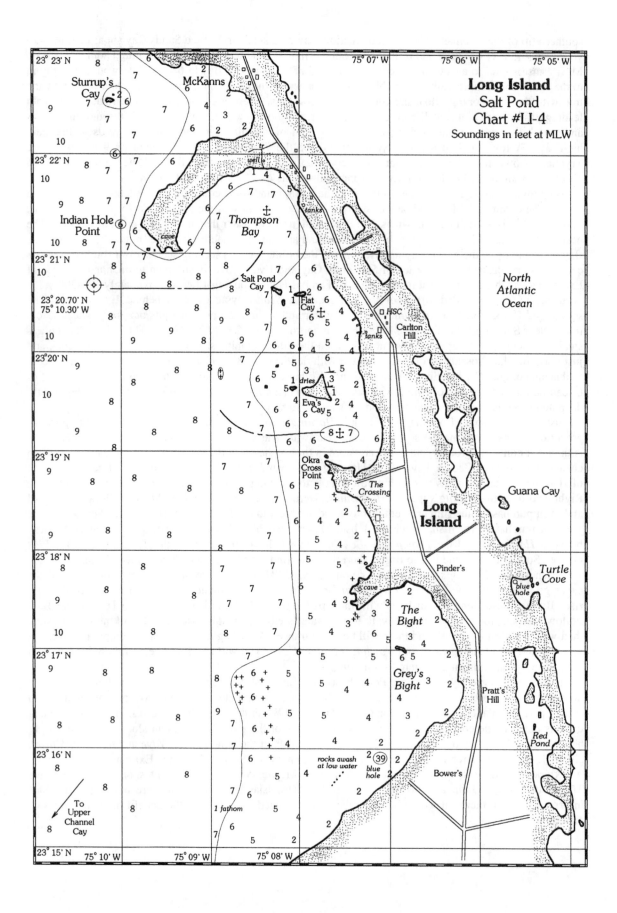

Long Island
Salt Pond
Chart #LI-4
Soundings in feet at MLW

A couple of final words about the Thompson's Bay area. First, the settlement known as Thompson's Bay actually is in the area of the *Thompson's Bay Inn*. Salt Pond is just about 1½ miles further south in the general vicinity of the school. *Harding's Supply Centre*, the hub of activity in the area, is actually in Carlton Hill. If you ask a local for directions to Salt Pond they will direct you to the school. Second, most experienced cruisers to the Thompson's Bay area usually will not run their watermakers in the bay. The bottom of Thompson's Bay is great holding but the top layer is very fine silt. A little wind and the silt gets very stirred up. This can clog filters and damage pumps.

THOMPSON'S BAY TO SOUTH END

Much of the land south of Salt Pond is generation land, title being owned by various families. The primary names to be found here are Darville, Dean, Cartwright, Burrows, and Knowles. They all seem to be related and there is much truth to their saying that "Everyone on Long Island is related." The best way to visit these communities is by renting a car or hitchhiking, you won't have to wait long for a ride. Although the communities may be spread apart, they are all along the island's main road. The best way to see the island is to rent a car and take your time exploring each and every community. By the way, as you drive along keep a sharp eye out for the numerous goats and sheep that will wander in front of your vehicle causing you to slam on the brakes to avoid the little bleating critters.

South of Salt Pond lies a large bay known as The Bight as shown on Chart #LI-4. Here you will find a very large blue hole lying just offshore and approximately 100 yards long and perhaps half that wide. I sounded it again and again and found depths of 39' a low water but local fishermen tell me there is a small hole in the center that is very, very deep. Ashore, right off the main highway, are the ruins of St. Mary's Anglican Church, said to be the oldest church building on Long Island. It is said that the church was built by the Spaniards.

Just south of Salt Pond, at Pinder's, there is a road leading eastward across the island to the Atlantic side where you will find Guana Cay. There is no safe anchorage along the eastern shore in the area so the only access you will have to Guana Cay is by land. Here you will find a beautiful protected shallow bay perfect for snorkeling and shelling along the long beach. A short swim over to Guana Cay will reveal a palm grove, a pretty little beach, and an abandoned hut. Here you can hand feed the small iguanas that populate the cay giving it its name. On the oceanside you can snorkel the old wreck of a steel freighter that came to rest on the rocks off Guana Cay in 15' of water.

Six miles south of Salt Pond and well inland lies Gray's. Here you will find a branch of the *Royal Bank Of Canada* as wells as the *Falcon's Rest Bar and Liquor Store*. Some of the local inhabitants are involved with the raising of sheep for market. Here you will find the ruins of three houses that once were part of Gray's Plantation. Between Gray's and Clarence Town, some 20 miles to the southeast are a number of small communities. Places like Andersons, Old Grays, Lower Deadman's Cay, Scrub Hill (yes there is also one north of Simms), and Stevens are home to only a few families each. In lower Deadman's Cay you will find the *J. B. Supermarket, Furniture, and Gas Station* with groceries, hardware, and fresh produce. Here you will also find the *Twilight Club* and *Cartwright's Garage and Auto Parts*.

The larger communities such as Deadman's Cay, Buckleys, Mangrove Bush, and Cartwright are all located in a small area within a five mile radius. All these settlements are located in an area of shallow water well south of Salt Pond only suitable for dinghies and small outboard powered boats. The Junkers and Jerry Wells Landing, located just north of Deadman's Cay are the only places where boats can unload supplies and fish.

South of Salt Pond along the highway sits Deadman's Cay, the top producer of sugar bananas for Nassau. Besides sugar bananas the area produces some very tasty mangoes. Long Island's main airport, other than the one at Stella Maris, is in Deadman's Cay with service from Bahamasair and some local charter companies. Also at the airport is the *Sierra Club* with food, drinks, and dancing. Also in Deadman's Cay you'll find the *J&M Food Store*, a branch of *Scotia Bank*, and a community Clinic. Spelunkers may want to visit the nearby Deadman's Cay Cave where stalagmites and stalactites abound. The cave goes in two directions, one branch heading directly for the ocean has never been completely explored. Why the area is called Deadman's Cay is up in the air. One version is that pirates marooned somebody or bodies on one of the local cays. Another story says that a cholera epidemic in the late 1700's to the early 1800's killed a number of the local inhabitants. They were buried on the offlying Upper Channel Cay. Some old timers will say that they won't set foot on Upper Channel Cay.

Buckleys lies just south of Deadman's Cay and is home to the only high school on the island. Buses travel the entire island bringing students here on a daily basis. The main Batelco station is located here. Buckley's is also home to a branch of the *Royal Bank Of Canada, The Long Island Historical Museum and Library*, the *Queen's Highway Liquor Store* and the only available laundromat. Near Buckleys is Cartwright known for its pineapple and sugar cane crops. Just beyond Cartwright is Hamilton's where a series of limestone caves were discovered with Lucayan carvings on the walls. Hamilton's is also home to the *Pharr-More Pharmacy, Long Island Wholesale Groceries*, and *Summer Seafood* where you can purchase conch, grouper, and lobster in season. Here too you will find the very well stocked *Sea Winds Super Market* and *Treco's Supermarket*. Between Petty and Mangrove Bush is the *Hillside Tavern Bar and Restaurant* where you can sample some of the best mutton you will find anywhere. Quite often there are few clues as to which settlement you are actually in, there are very few town signs in southern Long Island.

The next stop south is Mangrove Bush. Here you will find *The Long Island Historical Museum, A & M Electrical Supplies, Kooter's* serving breakfast, lunch, dinner, and ice cream, and *Under The Sea Marine Supplies*, a well stocked marine supply store that also sells Yamaha outboards. In nearby McKenzie's you will find *Knowles Supply*. Also near Mangrove Bush is the important town of Petty. Important because the only movie theater on Long Island is located there.

Further south you will come to a place that I consider a must see, especially before access is denied due to construction. As you drive south from Mangrove Bush you will pass a pink wall with white trim. Here you will see a nice road leading east over the ridge. The signs will tell you that this is the Turtle Cove development and plans include housing, a hotel, golf course, and a marina. If the chain is not blocking the drive follow it eastward over the ridge where you will come to a picturesque little cove. This is not Turtle Cove but the small cove north of it. Follow the road as it curves past the house and it will take you to a small gazebo with a picnic table on the southern end of this cove. Just before the gazebo another road leads off to the right. Follow this one about ¼ mile for a superb sight. When the road ends walk about another 100 yards and you will be standing on the beautiful beach at Turtle Cove, originally called Eastern Harbour. Look to your left and you will see a rocky cliff and a stunning deep blue pocket of calm water. This is touted as the *World's Deepest Blue Hole* and the *8th Largest Underwater Cavern*. Divers have penetrated it to 220' and sounded it with lead lines at over 660'. Bring your snorkeling or SCUBA gear and check it out. You must visit this place, it is absolutely gorgeous (I'm running out of adjectives for some of these places).

The next community is Clarence Town which is covered in the next section on the eastern shore of Long Island.

South is the town of Dunmore, named after Lord Dunmore. The shining white church on the hilltop is an excellent landmark in the rough surrounding terrain. Near Dunmore are the ruins of an old Loyalist plantation, some walls and two large hexagonal pillars that may have been part of a gate. Some of the ruins of the old Dunmore Plantation are still standing including parts of the main house with a fireplace, chimney, and sketches of sailboats on the walls. Just to the right of the pillars are some open holes that are usually fill with water during rising tides. These seem to indicate that Long Island may have an extensive cave system connected to the sea and running all through the island. Locals say that when the tide is running you can hear "a rumbling noise." Long Islanders call these phenomena "Beaten Holes" and they are found in many places on Long Island. Speaking of caves, here you will find *Dunmore's Cave* which was used by Lucayan Indians and Pirates. In Dunmore you can stop at the *Sweet P Restaurant and Bar* for food and/or drink. Further south are some smaller settlements such as Taits, Molly Well, Berrys, Cabbage Point, and Ford.

A little further along the road you will come to Hard Bargain where there is a road leading to the abandoned Diamond Crystal Salt Pans. Here salt was big business until recently. Now you will only find fish and shrimp farms with the harbour being off-limits to cruisers except in an emergency, and even then the owners are not too thrilled about your being there.

Further south is the village of Mortimer's. Most of the fishermen in southern Long Island live in Mortimer's and Gordon's. In Mortimer's the fishermen bring their small boats two miles up the creek at day's end. There are approximately 120 people living here, three churches, a school, *Mortimer's Grocery*, and the *Mid Way Bar*. The fishermen here have easy access to the large schools of grouper that inhabit the waters of southern Long Island. Mortimer's is home to Cartwright's Cave, once inhabited by Lucayan Indians. It is sometimes referred to as Duho Cave, duhos being ceremonial stools use by the Lucayan Indians. You can inquire about guided tours in town.

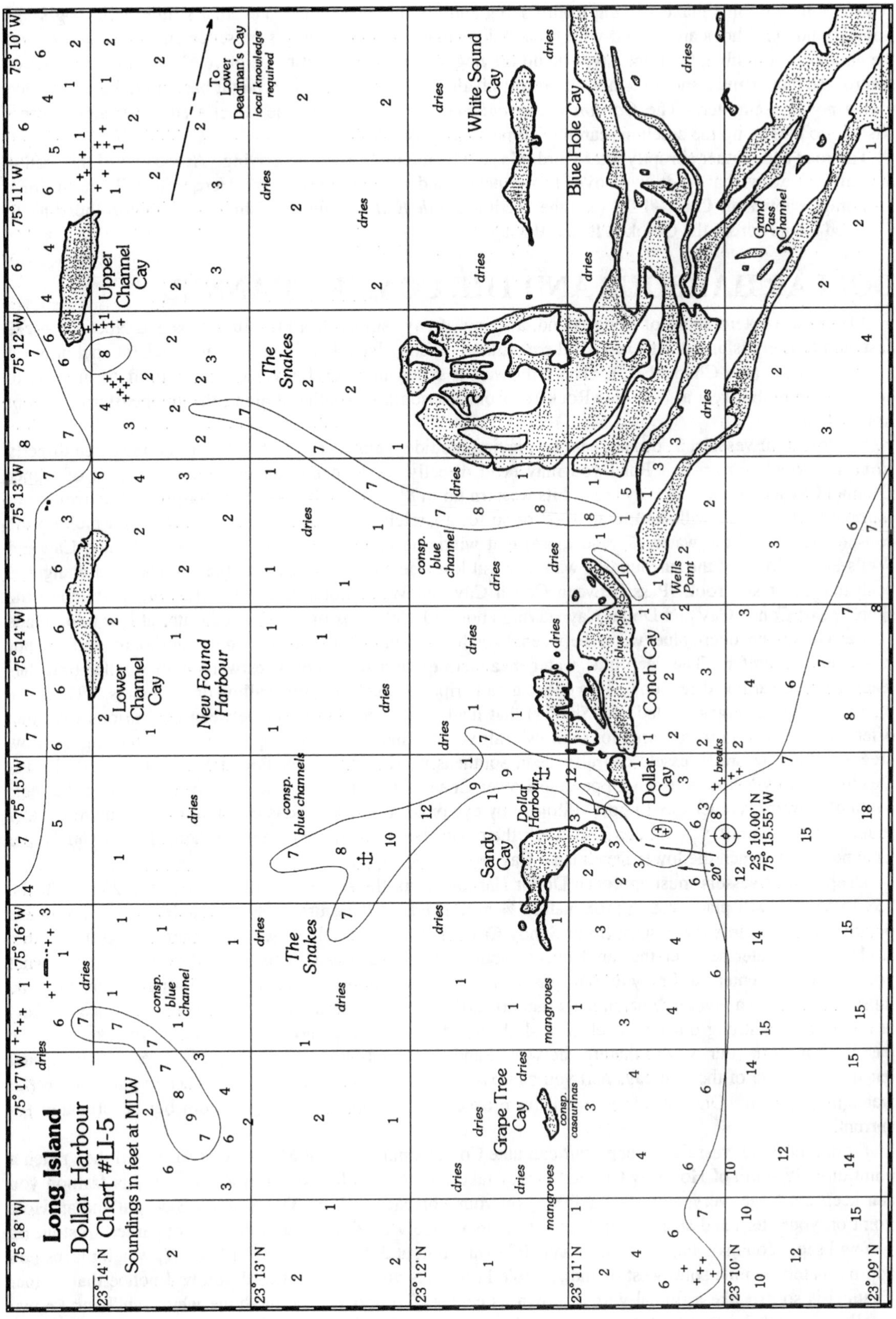

Long Island
Dollar Harbour
23° 14' N   Chart #LI-5
Soundings in feet at MLW

Upper Channel Cay

The Snakes

Lower Channel Cay

New Found Harbour

consp. blue channel

Grape Tree Cay
consp. casaurinas

mangroves

dries

Sandy Cay

Dollar Harbour

consp. blue channels

Dollar Cay

Conch Cay

Wells Point

blue hole

breaks

23° 10.00' N
75° 15.55' W

White Sound Cay

Blue Hole Cay

Grand Pass Channel

To Lower Deadman's Cay
local knowledge required

75° 18' W   75° 17' W   75° 16' W   75° 15' W   75° 14' W   75° 13' W   75° 12' W   75° 11' W   75° 10' W

23° 14' N   23° 13' N   23° 12' N   23° 11' N   23° 10' N   23° 09' N

Gordon's should probably be called "Watsonville" as the only family living there is named Watson. The Watson's in Gordon's make a living from fishing and hunting wild hogs. Yes, that's right, wild hog's. In Long Island, wild hogs are hunted with trained dogs that can sense a hog's presence and chase and corner the animal. If possible, the hunter will tie up the hog's feet and bring it home alive. If the animal is out of control the hunter must shoot the hog to protect his dogs. If the animal is brought back alive he will be fed until ripe for slaughter. The *Gordon's Convenience Store* is next to the water's edge for any cruisers wishing to dinghy up the creek in search of some small groceries.

The road ends rather abruptly after Gordon's so pay attention if you're driving. At the end of the road is a small causeway that leads west over to the beach and it is worth a view. Here you will see the nice anchorage shown on Chart #LI-8 (see the section *South End*) for those wishing a lee before heading to Crooked Island across the Crooked Island Passage.

DOLLAR HARBOUR AND THE COMER CHANNEL

Along the western shore of Long Island, a string of cays stretch from the Jumentos and Nuevitas rocks eastward to Long Island itself. Just off the mainland of Long Island can be found an excellent anchorage at Dollar Harbour (see Chart #LI-5). The only way to reach the area for vessels of 3' draft or more is to approach from the west at Nuevitas Rocks or from the south or southeast along the southeastern shore of Long Island.

Shallow draft vessels, 3' or less, can, by playing the tide, gain access to the Dollar Harbour area directly from Salt Pond. From Salt Pond you may head directly for Upper Channel Cay. Pass west of Upper Channel Cay and work your way around its western tip in 8' of water keeping the conspicuous brown bar to starboard. The water will shallow to 1'-2' or so for a stretch of half a mile or more until you pick up the conspicuous deep blue water, (7' and more) that winds its way to the small cut between Conch Cay and Wells Point. Most of the surrounding waters dry at low tide and every now and then you'll see a mangrove bush that has taken root. Pass between Conch Cay and Wells Point and head westward paralleling the shoreline of Conch Cay and Dollar Cay staying about 50-100 yards off in 2'-3' of water at low tide. Once you arrive at the deep blue water between Conch Cay and Dollar Cay turn to starboard and anchor wherever you prefer. The deep blue water meanders quite a ways northwestward with smaller branches leading off in various directions. This entire area is ripe for exploring by shallow draft vessels. There are many shallow passages (called *The Snakes*) that lead to deeper blue water between the various cays that offer good protection from fronts for shallow draft vessels that can venture up the twisting, turning, shallow creeks. Shallow draft vessels can also head southeastward across New Found Harbour towards Lower Deadman's Cay. Pass between Upper and Lower Channel Cay and head southeastward keeping the reefs south of Lower Channel Cay to port. Pilotage by eye or local knowledge is essential on this shallow water route. Shallow draft vessels can also work their way between the mainland of Long Island and Upper Channel Cay to reach the lower Deadman's Cay area.

Deeper draft vessels must approach Dollar Harbour from the south. A GPS waypoint at 23° 10.00' N, 75° 15.55' W, will place you approximately ¾ mile south of the entrance to Dollar Harbour. From this position steer towards the eastern tip of Sandy Cay. You will be able to see a channel of slightly deeper, slightly bluer water between the sandbanks to your port and starboard. This channel of blue water is what you will want to enter but first you must pass over a bar with almost 5' over it at low water. After that you must steer around a few large patch reefs that are easily seen. Never attempt this passage in poor visibility, at night, or in a strong onshore swell as a slight miscalculation may not be forgiving to your keel. Once past the bar work your way to the area between Sandy Cay and Dollar Cay. There is a very obvious sand bar in the middle of the two cays and you can pass it on either side in 5' at low water to gain the deeper water just beyond. Once inside you will have excellent holding in a sandy bottom but be prepared for current.

From Salt Pond, vessels of deep draft can take Comer Channel, 7' at MLW, westward until they reach a point directly south of Hog Cay Cut and thence take up a course for Nuevitas Rocks. In this fashion you can keep the large, very obvious sandbank, on your port side. From Thompson's Bay, put Indian Hole Point on your stern and steer generally west, approximately 270° but that course is not carved in stone as you will see. You may begin at the Indian Hole waypoint at 23° 20.70' N, 75° 10.30' W, which places you approximately ½ mile southwest of Indian Hole Point. As you head westward you will notice that Comer Channel is sort of like a funnel with 7' down its center. To port will be the huge white sandbank known locally as South Pointa Bank. As you head westward you will see Sandy Cay (AKA White Cay, the southernmost of the Exumas) appear on the horizon. Keep it to starboard. If you drift too far south you will notice you are getting in the shallower water of the South Pointa Bank. If you are too far north of the channel you will also be getting into shallow water or even going up on the conspicuous brown bar known as Red Bar. A good clue that you are in the Comer Channel is the sea fans under your keel. They are harmless to your vessel and if they lean west you will know that the tide is going out and if they lean east you will know that the tide is rising. When you are south of Hog Cay in the Exumas you will notice that Hog Cay and Little Exuma Island appear as one cay. As Hog Cay Cut opens, look for the conspicuous palm tree on O'Brien's Cay, you will notice the blue water on the other side of the cut. Once Hog Cay Cut closes, you may begin to steer southwest for approximately one mile. Keep a sharp lookout to port to keep off the South Pointa Bank. From this point you may steer south for approximately four miles to clear the bank. From this position you can take up an approximate course of southeast for Nuevitas Rocks taking the cays and light to starboard. From Nuevitas you can steer generally east to the waypoint off Dollar Harbour keeping off the bank (if you stay south of 23° 09.90' N you will be south of the extent of the one fathom line). If you wish to anchor for the night while on this route simply head east or south in the lee of the bank and anchor where your draft permits. If you get a chance you may wish to look for the wreck of the old Haitian power vessel that went aground on South Pointa Bank. For years its superstructure was above low water but storms and hurricanes have destroyed it and only its hulk remains. A final note on Comer Channel. Over the years the channel has seemed to silt in somewhat. Many yachts claim they have found less than 7' in its center, more like 5' at MLW. I have personally found less than 7' in areas of the Comer Channel. This may be that I, like other skippers, was simply off course or it may be an indication of shoaling. If in doubt about whether to use it or not ask some of the fishing boats that anchor in Salt Pond, if anybody would know the current condition of Comer Channel it would be them. For those of you who are in need of waypoints to stay in the Comer Channel here they are. From the Indian Hole waypoint you may head generally west to the Comer Channel #1 waypoint at 23° 20.82' N, 75° 19.95' W. From here steer a little south of west to the Comer Channel #2 waypoint at 23° 19.53' N, 75° 24.00' W. From this position steer a little north of west to reach Comer Channel #3 waypoint at 23° 20.30' N, 75° 32.00' W which lies a little over three miles south of Hog Cay Cut and is the western end of the Comer Channel. Vessels heading to Salt Pond via the Comer Channel from the Jumentos should use this as their starting waypoint. Vessels heading south to the Jumentos can also use this as their starting waypoint.

This entire area, known as Newfound Harbour is a haven for birdwatchers. You may wonder why this area is called a "harbour," it dries in so many places and mangroves are currently sprouting up in the shallows that are filling in west of Grape Tree Cay and between Grape Tree Cay and Sandy Cay. Up until a decade or so ago the harbour was deeper and vessels of 5' draft could pass through it but various storms left their mark and it is now a vast shallow bonefish marl. The Spanish were some of the first visitors to the Newfound Harbour area and on one of the cays (I am told it is near Wells Point though I have not found it) is said to be a well with stone around it and Spanish writing. Conch Cay was once farmed by the local population from the mainland.

THE EASTERN SHORE

The eastern shore of Long Island is rarely visited by cruising yachts due to its lack of good harbours. Most simply pass it by on their way to and from the southern islands. The only two places for refuge on Long Island's rugged, inhospitable, windward shore is at Clarence Town and a little further south at Little Harbour. It is a long haul, approximately 41 miles, from Cape Santa Maria, along the eastern shore to Clarence Town, and even longer for cruisers bound for Crooked Island. Some skippers heading for points south opt to take the back side of Exuma and Long Island, along the mailboat route thereby avoiding the area to windward of Long Island. The problem with the eastern shore is the Atlantic Ocean ground swell. When it is running it can make coming into port nerve wracking to say the least. If a significant ground swell is running your safest port on the eastern shore is at Clarence Town. I have been told that north of Clarence Town vessels can anchor behind Guana Cay passing either south or north of Guana Cay but never attempt it with a ground swell running. I have never anchored behind Guana Cay and therefore cannot recommend it as an anchorage, I would rather suggest you anchor at Clarence Town, but I merely mention it for your knowledge in case of emergency. I will endeavor to sound this harbour for a future edition.

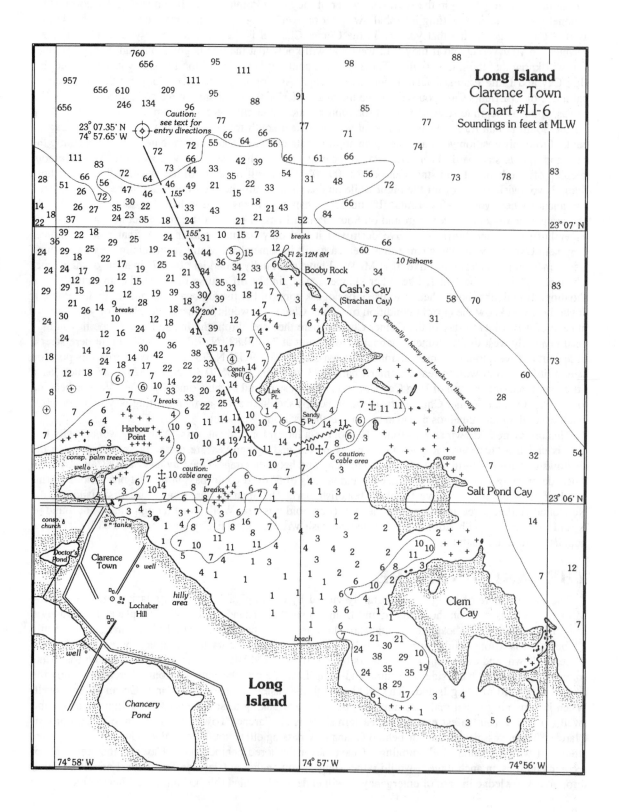

Long Island
Clarence Town
Chart #LI-6
Soundings in feet at MLW

CLARENCE TOWN

The spires of the two churches in Clarence Town can be seen from far out at sea makin_ landmark to home in on. The two churches are definitely worth seeing and were built by the same man, Father Jerome, who built the Hermitage on Cat Island. When he was known as Jerome Hawes, an Anglican missionary, he built St. Paul's Church. Later he converted to Catholicism and became Father Jerome. He returned to Long Island and in an effort to outdo his earlier construction he built the stunning, white, St. Peter's Church (for more information on Father Jerome, see the chapter and section: *Cat Island, New Bight*).

Photo by Author

Chuch in Clarence Town, Long Island.

The entrance to the harbour at Clarence Town is not too complicated. As shown on Chart #LI-6, a GPS waypoint at 23° 07.35' N, 74° 57.65' W, will place you approximately ¼ mile northwest of the entrance proper. As you can see by the chart, a good skipper can work his way into the anchorage in other ways than by the standard route that people have been using for years. This is fine, it may be easier for you to do that. But if you get confused and have to call someone ashore and ask for directions they will only be able to relate to the usual route for the entrance. From the waypoint, line up the southwestern tip of Cash's Cay, formerly Strachan's Cay but now named after its new owner, and head towards it on a course of 155°. When the white stand that used to be Harbour Point Light (east of the prominent stand of palm trees) bears 200° take up that heading to avoid Conch Spit which lies southwest of Cash's Cay. You will notice the seas breaking in the vicinity of Harbour Point so don't get too close to it, there are a lot of rocks and heads just off this point. When you can clear Conch Spit, take up a heading of 155° again on the southeastern point of the long beach. When you are abeam of the town dock and Sandy Point on Cash's Cay, you can turn to starboard to anchor off the town dock or turn to port to anchor past Sandy Point south of Cash's Cay in the lee of the reef. If you decide to anchor south of Cash's Cay use extreme caution, there is a submarine cable leading to Cash's Cay that lies across the anchorage as shown on the chart. Sometimes you can see it from your deck, most times not. Take care when setting your anchor here.

In settled weather you may wish to anchor just off the mailboat dock in grass and sand keeping an eye out for the submarine cable. If winds are strong out of the east you will probably be better off just south of Cash's Cay and east of Sandy Point. Here the reef breaks the seas and they don't have a chance to build very much before they reach this anchorage with its good holding sand/grass bottom. If you choose to anchor at the mailboat dock in strong easterly winds you will find the small fetch allows the seas to build slightly making for a lot of movement at anchor. You'll find that it's a little calmer if you anchor south of Cash's Cay.

If you wish to ride out a front at the mailboat dock you will have good protection except from strong north/northeast to east winds. The best anchorage for a frontal passage is south of Cash's Cay. My personal preference, if I have a window, is to head south about 10 miles to Little Harbour (see the next section *Little Harbour*).

Ashore, fuel and water can be obtained from Henry Major and groceries from his wife at prices that compete and often beat prices in Nassau. Clarence Town is your last chance for fuel until you reach Landrail Point, Crooked Island, Matthew Town, Inagua, Abraham's Bay, Mayaguana, or Provo in the Turks and Caicos Island group. The town dock carries 10' of water at low tide.

Just up from the town dock is the *Agricultural Packing House* where you can purchase fresh produce and fish when available. Don't expect to find a lot of the sugar bananas that Deadman's Cay is so famous for as most of the crops were destroyed by Hurricane Lili in 1996 and it takes a couple of years for the new plants to produce. Next door is the *Harbour Rest Restaurant and Satellite Lounge*, the place in town for dining. Also on the main road is the Government Complex and Community Clinic, the *Oasis Bakery and Restaurant, Harbour Grocery, Skieta OK Bar, True Value Food Store*, and *Milander's Auto, Marine, and Industrial Parts and Service*.

LITTLE HARBOUR

Not enough can be said about this small anchorage. Little Harbour offers excellent protection in all wind directions and you can ride out even the fiercest frontal passage here. The anchorage lies about 10 miles southeast of Clarence Town. You'll know you're getting close when you see the conspicuous long house sitting atop a ridge about seven miles south of Clarence Town. Little Harbour lies a little over two miles south of that house, the entrance being just south of the very visible rusty remains of an old freighter wrecked on Long Island's eastern shore. The entrance to this picturesque harbour as shown on Chart #LI-7 is easy to enter even with 6' following seas. To enter take the southernmost of the two openings, between the unnamed cay and the mainland of Long Island favoring the northern side of the entrance between the two. There were once two rock cairns ashore that you would pass between, nowadays they've been torn down and a couple of white stakes take their place, one on the small cay to the north, and two stakes on the

Photo by Author

Fisherman near Cape Santa Maria, Long Island.

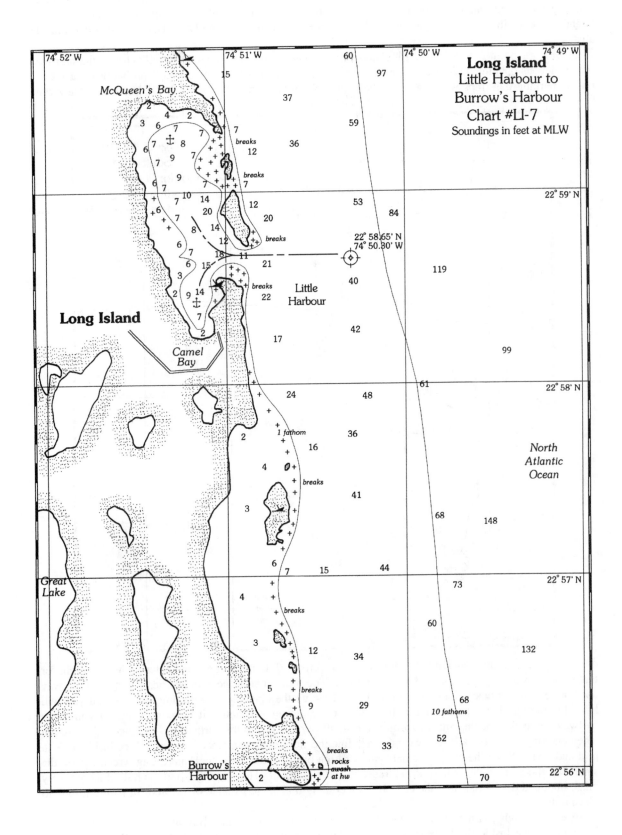

Long Island
Little Harbour to
Burrow's Harbour
Chart #LI-7
Soundings in feet at MLW

mainland to the south of the entrance. Do not attempt this entrance in strong easterly weather or with a heavy ground swell running, instead head north to Clarence Town or south around the southern tip of Long Island to anchor in its lee. If a ground swell is running and you are inside Little Harbour, stay put until it abates.

A GPS waypoint 22° 58.65' N, 74° 50.30 W, will place you approximately ½ mile east of the narrow, inconspicuous opening. Little Harbour is used by Long Island fishermen so you'll probably see a lot of buoys marking fish traps within a few miles north or south of the entrance to Little Harbour. They can

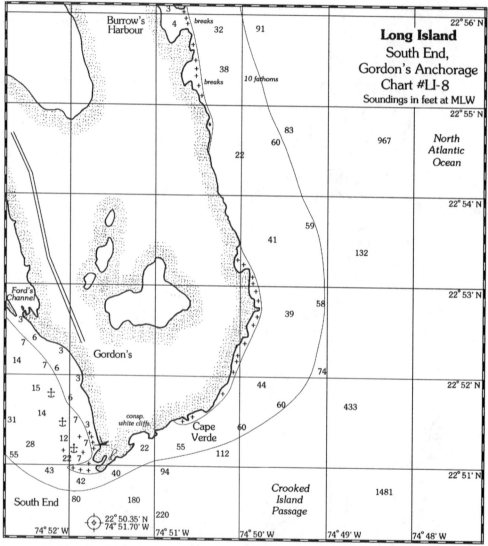

often be quite a nuisance and at times downright dangerous. I do not recommend entering here at night for that reason. Keep a good lookout for these buoys. The best water at the entrance lies about ¾ of the way north across the entrance from the mainland tip. Line up the opening on a heading of 270° and you will have 11' through here at low water. If a sea is running you will notice it breaking south of you about halfway across the opening and also around the small cay that lies to the north of the entrance. Use caution when entering as some rocky ledges and heads line the sides of the entrance channel. Once inside look to port and you will see the hull of a small sailboat high on the rocks. Another interesting wreck lies on the small cay about one mile south of the entrance to Little Harbour. Here you will find the hull of a boat, very much high and dry, sitting atop the cay. It will certainly make you wonder what forces of nature it took to place it there.

In east through south to west winds the best anchorage is in Camel Bay at the south end of Little Harbour. Once inside the harbour, turn to port and tuck in wherever your draft will allow. In strong easterly winds the harbour can get a little rolly, just a little uncomfortable, but nothing a bridle won't cure. In the event of a frontal passage you can tuck in at the north end of the harbour at McQueen's Bay and enjoy the calm while anchored in a good holding sandy bottom. Once the wind comes into the east you must move south to Camel Bay to get out of the incoming swell. To access McQueen's Bay, once inside steer northward keeping an eye out for the shallow reef area northwest of the cay at the entrance and a few scattered heads that are easily seen and avoided.

There are no communities in Little Harbour although some local fisherman often leave their boats there. There is a picturesque cactus and wildflower lined trail leading to the nearby community of Roses as well as a road from Camel Bay. At William Darville's *Carpenter Arms* you find good conversation as well as fresh bread. You are likely to see some wild goats ashore, especially around Camel Bay. The waters of Little Harbour itself are home to a lot of large and small sea turtles.

South of Little Harbour are two more small harbours that are only viable in settled weather and if your draft is 4' or less. In any type of seas their entrances break all the way across. Local knowledge, or the ability to read the water, coupled with good visibility, calm waters, and nerves of steel will get you inside. Little Harbour is a much better anchorage, easier to enter and leave, and good protection.

SOUTH END

Many vessels, mine included, if headed for Crooked Island and points south, sometimes opt to take the route in the lee of Long Island instead of the usual Conception-Rum-Mayaguana route so favored by those in a hurry. I will usually leave George Town, pass through Hog Cay Cut, take Nuevitas Rocks to starboard, and anchor overnight in Dollar Harbour. I leave the next morning and work my way southeastward in the lee of Long Island to anchor just north of South End. Bear in mind that this is only to be done with a weather window of two days or more (although Dollar Harbour and French Wells are both good harbours in any wind, you will be completely exposed from south through west to northwest at South End). Allow one day to get to South End, one more day to get to French Wells at Crooked Island. I have gone from Dollar Harbour, around South End, and on to French Wells in 12 hours but it is a trip of about 60 or so miles. It may be easier for some skippers to break that down into two shorter legs. Many fishing boats and Haitian vessels use South End as a waiting spot for good weather to cross the Crooked Island Passage. If heading south from Dollar Harbour to South End you can always turn east to anchor in the lee of Long Island at any time. In some places the shallows stretch out a mile to the west of the shore and you must always keep an eye out for the occasional head, never attempt this at night though. A favorite spot is at Calloway Landing where there used to be a light. Once, all sorts of sailing vessels from Nassau called here, now hardly anyone stops.

From Crooked Island or points south, a GPS waypoint at 22° 50.35' N, 74° 51.70' W, will place you approximately ½ mile south of the southwest point of Long Island as shown on Chart #LI-8. From this position head northwest around the southwest tip of Long Island giving the shallow, very visible reef a good berth. Once past the reef turn to starboard and tuck in behind the reef wherever your draft will allow. This is called the Gordon's Anchorage and is a good spot in the prevailing east and southeast winds although you may get some roll from strong southeast seas bending around the reef which breaks most of these seas. If that happens you'll probably want to rig a bridle.

If you are approaching from the north, say from Dollar Harbour, head for the above mentioned waypoint and about a mile before you reach it you will see the long beach and anchorage off the southwest tip of Long Island. If headed to this area from Dollar Harbour, keep a good watch out for Comer Rock, West Comer Rock, and Long Rocks lying about two miles west of Long Island and about half the distance from Dollar Harbour to South End.

There are some creeks in the area, just off the anchorage area and about 1½ miles north that are worth exploring. The upper creek leads to Gordon's and Mortimer's. For a description of what little is available see the earlier section *Thompson's Bay To South End*. If you dinghy into the long beach you will see a table ashore where the local fishermen clean their catch. Just north of this table is the end of the Long Island highway. A short walk will bring you to a couple of residences and you may be able to bum a ride north if someone is headed that way.

When you leave South End headed across the Crooked Island Passage, bear in mind that conditions may moderate once you get out a couple of miles or so. Often the seas "hump" up on the southern end of Long Island sometimes creating a false sense of what sea conditions are really like in the Crooked Island Passage.

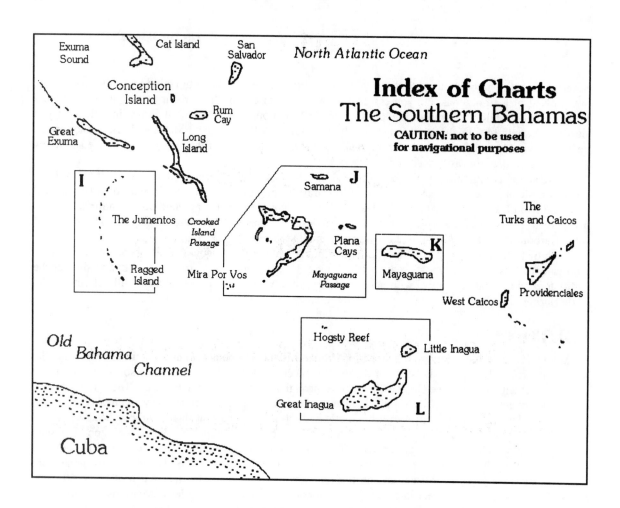

Index of Charts
The Southern Bahamas
CAUTION: not to be used
for navigational purposes

Index Chart	Region	Page
I	Jumentos Ragged Island	238
J	Crooked Islands Samana Plana Cays Mira por Vos	266
K	Mayaguana	291
L	Great Inagua Little Inagua Hogsty Reef	299

Part II

Off the Beaten Path

The Southern Bahamas

The Jumentos to the Turks and Caicos

Part II
Off The Beaten Path
THE SOUTHERN BAHAMAS

The Jumentos To The Turks And Caicos

Two roads diverged in a wood, and I-
I took the one less traveled by,
And that has made all the difference.
Robert Frost

. . . to boldly go where no man has gone before.
Capt. James T. Kirk

These islands, lying well off the beaten path taken by so many cruisers, are rarely visited by yachts. Those that do stop in are usually in transit southward from The Bahamas to the Caribbean or northward from the Caribbean to the U.S. Some of these areas are extremely isolated and if you get weathered in you may find yourself the only boat in the anchorage for days, and sometimes, weeks at a time.

The cruiser in these waters definitely needs to be as self-sufficient as possible. Extra jerry cans of fuel are a good idea, a necessity if you have a small fuel tank and motor a lot. In places like The Jumentos, the residents get their fuel in 55 gallon drums from Nassau and there may be little if any to spare for visiting yachtsmen as most of it must go to fuel their fishing boats. Adequate medical supplies and the knowledge to use them properly are a necessity. One time at Samana Cay, my first mate Kelly severely injured her hand while attempting to disengage our *Windbugger*, an altogether too uncommon occurrence amongst boaters. Luckily I had the proper medical supplies aboard to take care of her and make her comfortable. If the situation had been worse, or if I did not have a well stocked medical kit, an air-evac would probably have been required as conditions were too rough for travel.

A well stocked pantry is a prime consideration. If leaving George Town or Long Island, make sure you provision well. Some of the stores in the outer islands, although they might carry a few staples, often lack a lot of the luxuries that you may be used to such as cigarettes, fresh milk, eggs, veggies, meat, and even alcoholic beverages which are not sold at Landrail Point on Crooked Island. You may become like the islanders themselves, waiting on a mailboat that is late or that may not even arrive at all for weeks. However, if you can fish, you can eat, so sharpen your hooks and spears, and grab a line to string some conch up and have at it! The fishing is superb. If you are used to conch such as are found in the Exumas, you will find that the conch in the outer islands are plentiful and much larger.

Here in these outer islands, with their many open lee-side anchorages, you will learn a new dance, "The "Out-Island Roll," and no matter how hard you try, you will not escape performing it somewhere down the line. Usually a bridle arrangement, or a stern anchor, setting your bow into the swell is your only salvation, and that may not be enough if the wind picks up. I have rolled for days at a time at Abraham's Bay, Mayaguana with 25 knot easterly winds and southeasterly swells working their way around Guano Point and over the reef. If I adjusted my bridle to meet the swells, I rolled with the wind waves, if I adjusted my bridle to ride the wind waves, I rolled from the swells coming in over the reef. It was not a dangerous situation by any means, but highly uncomfortable and it makes for poor sleeping, at least aboard *IV Play*.

But all these things are minor. The provisioning and medical supply situations can, and should, be thought out well ahead of time. The roll, well, you'll get used to it, and when you find a peaceful harbour such as Attwood or Samana, you will be all the more grateful for it. As for fuel, usually someone will come to your assistance and let you have a few gallons, enough to get you to someplace where you can purchase fuel. With a little preparation, determination, and a definite desire to have fun, you will succeed in doing just that. These outer islands are not to be missed. The people are some of the friendliest in The Bahamas and you may even learn some new tricks from them. For instance, people on Crooked Island are very aware of the moon's influence on our lives. They tell the tide not by the height of the water, but rather by the position of the moon. Some can even predict the kind of a day they are going to have by whether or not the moon is "on the right or on the left." Enjoy. Open your mind and your heart and you'll have an unforgettable time here.

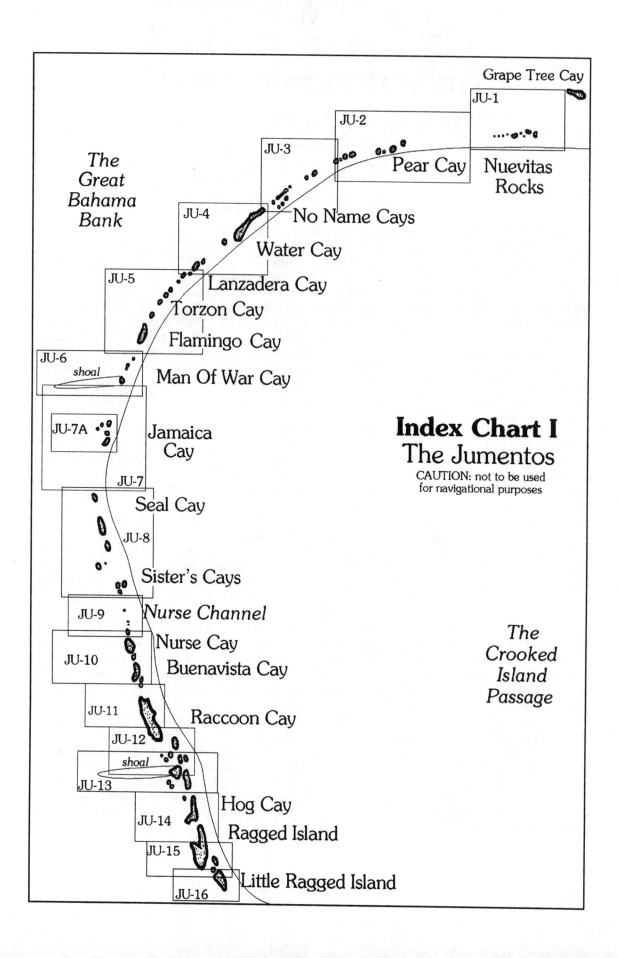

Grape Tree Cay

JU-1

JU-2

JU-3

Pear Cay

Nuevitas
Rocks

*The
Great
Bahama
Bank*

JU-4

No Name Cays

Water Cay

JU-5

Lanzadera Cay

Torzon Cay

Flamingo Cay

JU-6   *shoal*

Man Of War Cay

JU-7A

Jamaica
Cay

Index Chart I
The Jumentos
CAUTION: not to be used
for navigational purposes

JU-7

Seal Cay

JU-8

Sister's Cays

JU-9   *Nurse Channel*

Nurse Cay

JU-10   Buenavista Cay

*The
Crooked
Island
Passage*

JU-11   Raccoon Cay

JU-12

shoal

JU-13

Hog Cay

JU-14   Ragged Island

JU-15

Little Ragged Island

JU-16

THE JUMENTOS

AND RAGGED ISLAND

I have a nagging feeling deep down that I shouldn't tell anyone how to get to this lovely, unspoiled island chain. I really want to keep this one for myself. The Jumentos have all the flavor of the most pristine islands of the Exumas Cays but without all the hordes of cruisers, and yet, if needed, George Town is only a day or two away. Here is solitude. Here is natural beauty. Here you can relax, enjoy life at your own pace, and rarely see another human being except for the local fishermen who frequent these islands in great numbers. This is my favorite island chain in the entire Bahamas. Giving away the navigational information to allow cruisers to have a safe, enjoyable, memorable cruise through these cays is like giving away my daughter. Please take care of her.

When you are cruising The Bahamas you will often meet people who will give you the impression that they are old and knowledgeable Bahamas veterans. In fact, this is the very impression that they enjoy giving. Unfortunately, quite a few people dole out misleading information with an air of authenticity whose only purpose is not so much to assist you as it is to boost their status in your eyes. Be careful, these types can be outright dangerous if not simply ludicrous. One couple I know spend their summers in Abaco and their winters in George Town and have been doing this regularly for years. I have known them to shake their heads and tell cruisers headed for the Jumentos ". . . tsk, tsk, the water is too shallow for you there." You may also hear that there are no safe anchorages in which to weather a front in the winter cruising season. These people that have been encouraging these misplaced notions only show their ignorance of this beautiful island chain. Many of the passages between the islands are over 30'-40' deep and there are two excellent spots for riding out fronts, more if you have a shallow draft vessel. True Bahamas veterans are out cruising and enjoying the islands, not growing a reef on their anchor chains as they confuse other skippers who seek the benefit of their experience. Read on and you will soon see the myths exploded and the truth laid bare. The next time you see these so-called experts holding court on Volleyball Beach or at the Two Turtles, tell them where to go. Tell them to go to the Jumentos. On second thought, maybe you shouldn't tell them to come here. Maybe you should tell them that they are correct, it is too shallow and there are no places to weather a front. Then slip through Hog Cay Cut and head back to paradise.

The Jumentos, once called the *Yumettos*, are a croissant shaped chain of islands approximately 110 miles long that lie at the southeastern edge of the Great Bahama Bank at the Crooked Island Passage. The entire island chain is often called the Ragged Island Range although they are most often referred to as the Jumentos with the Ragged Island Range sometimes spoken of as a separate entity. With the exception of Jamaica Cay where a new resort is being planned, the only inhabitants of the cays reside in the Ragged Island area at its only settlement of Duncan Town. As a side note, *jumento* in my Spanish dictionary means donkey.

The Jumentos are an ideal place for cruisers wishing to get off the beaten path, to visit unspoiled islands free from commercial development, and to enjoy superb fishing, diving, and beachcombing. When cruising the Jumentos you will rarely see another cruising boat although this will surely change as more and more visitors to George Town, Exuma begin to venture in that direction. During lobster season, from August 1 through April 1, you will probably only see fishing boats from Long Island. Nassau, or Exuma, in the anchorages up and down the cays. There are a few large cays in the northern Jumentos with the majority of the larger cays lying in the southern Jumentos in the area of Ragged Island and northwards. Many of the passages in between are wide open to the deep water of the Crooked Island Passage with a few small cays spread over a very large area. These areas are prone to heavy seas in strong winds, even well out onto the banks you may experience large seas. Strong currents and tides abound in all the cuts from the banks out to the Crooked Island Passage. Do not take this warning lightly. If you think a rage in Exuma can be rough, you haven't seen one in the Jumentos. Wind against tide in some of these cuts sometimes makes for some truly awesome waves. A ground swell against the tide, even with little or no wind, can do the same.

From George Town it is possible to pass through Hog Cay Cut and head southward, cruise the Jumentos to Ragged Island and then go offshore across the Crooked Island Passage to Long Cay or Castle Island in the Crooked/Acklins group. Another possibility is to head down island to Ragged Island, then return along the string of cays past Nuevitas Rocks and further east along the western shore of Long Island to anchor at Dollar Harbour or off Long Island's southern tip. From here it is only 30 some odd miles or so to Landrail Point or French Wells in the Crooked/Acklins group.

Tides in the central and southern Jumentos and the Ragged Island area are approximately 15 minutes later than Nassau. Tides in the area of Nuevitas Rocks are approximately ¾ hour later than Nassau.

A words about fishing in the Jumentos. You will find grouper, hogfish, and conch quite easily. Lobster on the other hand may be quite scarce. I don't know why, perhaps the area is fished so thoroughly by the commercial boats during the season that few are left for the cruisers. This is not to say that lobsters cannot be found, you just have to look harder, longer, and maybe even deeper, either that or look where the commercial guys don't go.

APPROACHES TO THE JUMENTOS

From a waypoint just south of Hog Cay Cut in the Exumas, it is approximately 15.7 nautical miles on a course of 156° to Nuevitas Rocks, 14.8 nautical miles on a course of 188° for Pear Cay, and 24.6 nautical miles on a course of 216° to the waypoint west of Water Cay. Along these routes you will find water that progressively gets deeper, from 4'-6' just south and west of Hog Cay Cut, to 25'-35' and more as you approach the islands themselves. These routes are relatively free from navigational hazards for the first 10-15 miles from Hog Cay Cut, however, as you approach the northern Jumentos you will begin to see deep water patch reefs and scattered heads. Initially these heads and reefs are not a threat but as you approach the cays they begin to get closer and closer to the surface. For instance, if heading to Water Cay, straying east of your courseline may put you on the shallow bank that lies just north of the No Name Cays (see Chart #JU-3). Although I have made every endeavor to chart the waters correctly in the vicinity of the cays themselves, I cannot chart every bit of water between the Jumentos and Exuma. There may well be shallow areas along and on either side of the course lines mentioned that I have missed. The prudent navigator will keep a sharp lookout for scattered shallow reefs, heads, and sandbanks, and steer around them.

One final note on Hog Cay Cut. Ideally, when headed to the Jumentos from George Town, Exuma, you should plan to anchor just north of Hog Cay Cut between West Rock and Little Exuma Island, and pass through the cut on a rising tide early the next morning (unless you draw less than 3'). This allows you to make landfall in the Jumentos about midday or later depending on the speed of your vessel. Unfortunately high tide is not always so gracious, often making its appearance later in the day (tides at Hog Cay Cut usually run 30 minutes to an hour later than George Town). If this is the case, you may wish to pass through Hog Cay Cut and anchor on the other side. NEVER ATTEMPT TO TRAVEL THE BANKS FROM HOG CAY CUT TO THE NORTHERN JUMENTOS AT NIGHT. In calm winds, vessels with a 5'-6' draft would have to proceed about two miles on their courseline to find water deep enough in which to anchor safely (9'-11' at high tide). If the wind is blowing, say 12 to 15 knots or more, anchoring on the banks can be a real experience, one I prefer to avoid. If you feel the same you may consider passing through Hog Cay Cut and heading northwestward along the shoreline of Little Exuma Island past the Ferry, approximately 10 miles or so from Hog Cay Cut. Here you can find shelter from the prevailing east to southeast winds behind the small cays north of The Ferry. If headed to Water Cay or Flamingo Cay the next morning, this delay will add about five miles to your trip but it is a fair exchange for a pleasant night's sleep. (For more information on Hog Cay Cut and the cays north of The Ferry, see *The Exuma Guide, 2nd Edition*, Stephen J. Pavlidis, Seaworthy Publications, ISBN 0-9639566-7-1).

Vessels wishing to gain access to the Jumentos from the central Exumas can pass west of Galliot Bank and take the mailboat route past Hawksbill Rock to either Water Cay, Flamingo Cay, or Nuevitas Rocks. If headed for Nuevitas Rocks it would be shorter to head inside Jewfish Cut off the western shore of Great Exuma. Nuevitas Rocks bears approximately 270° at a distance from 5.62 miles from Dollar Harbour at Long Island (for information concerning routes from Long Island via the Comer Channel, see the chapter *Long Island, Dollar Harbour and the Comer Channel*).

Vessels bound to the Jumentos or Ragged Island from the southern islands of The Bahamas will find them usually downwind. For instance, from French Wells at Crooked Island, Raccoon Cut bears 264° at a distance of 84 nautical miles.

A special note for vessels transiting the Crooked Island Passage between the Jumentos and the Crooked/Acklins District. At an approximate position at 22° 50' N, 74° 48' W, lies the center of the Diana Bank. The approximately 100 square miles of Diana Bank lies west of the southern tip of Long Cay, south/southeast of the southern tip of Long Island, and west of Nurse Channel. Here is a shallow bank, 35'-600' deep, lying in the midst of much deeper water, 1800'-6000' deep. With a strong swell in any direction the seas on top of the bank can get very rough as the water is pushed up the sides of this underwater obstruction. If you are experiencing rough seas in your transit of this area, by all means avoid the area of Diana Bank. If the seas are calm, quite unusual hereabouts, try fishing on the bank.

NUEVITAS ROCKS TO WATER CAY

We will begin our tour of the Jumentos from north to south. From Hog Cay Cut it is approximately 15.7 nautical miles to Nuevitas Rocks (Chart #JU-1) on a course of 156°. If you are enroute past Nuevitas from the Comer Channel, Hog Cay Cut, or Hawksbill Rock, to the southern tip of Long Island or across the Crooked Island Passage to the Crooked/Acklins group, a GPS waypoint at 23° 10.00' N, 75° 22.10' W will place you approximately ½ mile northeast of the light on Nuevitas Rocks. Keep Nuevitas Rocks to starboard until out in the deeper water and then take up the course to your destination. If approaching from the Crooked Island Passage, a waypoint at 23° 09.30' N, 75° 21.60' W will place you approximately ½ mile southeast of Nuevitas Rocks. In northbound towards Hog Cay Cut keep Nuevitas Rocks to port.

From Nuevitas Rocks westward lie a string of small cays and rocks leading to Water Cay (Chart #'s JU-2 and JU-3). There is little to attract cruisers except some lee anchorages at Pear Cay and Stony Cay, as well as excellent diving and fishing. You may see some Long Island fishermen working this area during lobster season. Their usual routine is for the big boat to head west down Comer Channel and then south to Water Cay while the divers head straight across in their small Whalers and dive the reefs along the way. This way they don't waste a day in transit.

Pear Cay lies west/southwest of Nuevitas Rocks some 9 miles. If approaching from Hog Cay Cut, a GPS waypoint at 23° 08.65' N, 75° 31.20' W will place you approximately ½ mile north of Pear Cay Pass and north/northeast of Pear Cay. If headed for deeper water keep Pear Cay to starboard and head out Pear Cay Pass between Pear Cay and the unnamed cay to its east. If approaching from the Crooked Island Passage towards Hog Cay Cut or other points north, a GPS waypoint at 23° 07.80' N, 75° 30.65' W, will place you approximately ½ mile southeast of Pear Cay Pass. Keep Pear Cay to port and pass between Pear Cay and the unnamed cay to its east.

The southernmost of the No Name Cays (Chart #JU-3) lies just north of Little Water Cay and slightly to seaward of its neighbors. This cay is ringed by the ruins of an old pasture wall that dates to Loyalist days. Along its northern shore are the ruins of an old building, all that is left are the footings.

The Jumentos
Pear Cay to
Stony Cay
Chart #JU-2
Soundings in feet at MLW

Just south of the No Name Cays is a deep water cut that allows access to the Water Cay anchorages from offshore. A GPS waypoint at 23° 02.20' N 75° 40.35' W, will place you approximately ¼ mile southeast of the cut. Pass between the southernmost of the No Name Cays as shown on Chart #JU-3 and the northernmost of the small cays lying north of Little Water Cay. Head roughly northwest through the center of this cut until you pass the last of the small cays to port. At that point you may turn to port to parallel the string of small rocks to Little Water Cay and Water Cay.

Just north of Water Cay sits Little Water Cay. On its western shore is a small cove known as Moxey Harbour. Here a small creek leads eastward into a small lake. This cove and lake were once used as a hurricane hole. About fifty years ago you could take a 6' draft into a 10' deep mangrove lined pond. The renowned Capt. Henry Moxey once spent 15 stormbound days in this harbour that Linton Rigg named after him. Moxey Harbour has now filled in to the east with mangroves and they have all but closed off the entrance to the lake save for a narrow, shallow creek. There is still enough room for one small, shallow draft vessel, say perhaps a small sloop or catamaran, to anchor in 3'-7' of water in the prevailing winds just before you reach the mangroves. Watch your swing room as there are rocky shallows on both sides of you.

As a first stop on your southbound cruise through the Jumentos you should definitely consider Water Cay. Although Pear Cay and Stony Cay offer adequate lee anchorages that are very nice in calm weather, Water Cay's anchorage is the first truly comfortable anchorage in strong north to almost south winds that you will find in your cruise southward through these islands. Along the shore of Water Cay are some very prominent white cliffs that make up three distinct hills which are easily seen from offshore, sometimes from as far as 10 miles away.

A GPS waypoint at 23° 02.00' N, 75° 44.00 W, will place you approximately 1 nautical mile northwest of the anchorage at Water Cay as shown on Chart #JU-4. From here, head in towards the shore of Little Water Cay or the northern end of Water Cay, you will have deep water (15'-17') right up to the shoreline. Pass the point off Water Cay and anchor anywhere along the shore of Water Cay. The best spot is just inside the northern cove, inside the point. This offers the best protection and the least surge. The Water Cay anchorage is excellent for the prevailing east/southeast winds as well as north and northeast, but this is no place to be in a frontal passage. If a front threatens you need to get your vessel to Buena Vista Cay (37 nautical miles south of Water Cay) or Raccoon Cay (5 nautical miles south of Buena Vista Cay) for excellent protection. If caught out in oncoming westerly weather your only option is to do what some of the local fishing boats do, tuck in along the eastern shore of some of these cays wherever your draft will allow and expect a somewhat rolly time until the westerly winds calm the seas in the Crooked Island

The Jumentos
No Name Cays
Chart #JU-3
Soundings in feet at MLW

Passage and give you a more comfortable lee. As soon as the winds begin to approach the north, shoot around to the southern or western side of your chosen refuge and tuck in wherever possible.

The holding along the entire length of Water Cay is fair to good. The sand is very hard and you must dive your anchor, especially if you expect any sort of a blow. One can also gain access from the southern end of Water Cay but the entrances there are narrow and only 7'-9' deep at MLW. It is safer to head northward up the western shore of Water Cay about ½ mile off, staying clear of the offlying shallow reefs and enter the anchorage from the west as shown on Chart #JU-4.

You can also enter the anchorages at Water Cay from offshore via the cut lying south of Water Cay between Water Cay and Melita Cay. Pass between the two and parallel the shoreline of Water Cay northeastward staying clear of the reefs that lie off its southwestern shore. If this entrance to the banks does not interest you, it is possible to enter the wide and deep cut lying south of Melita Cay to Lanzadera

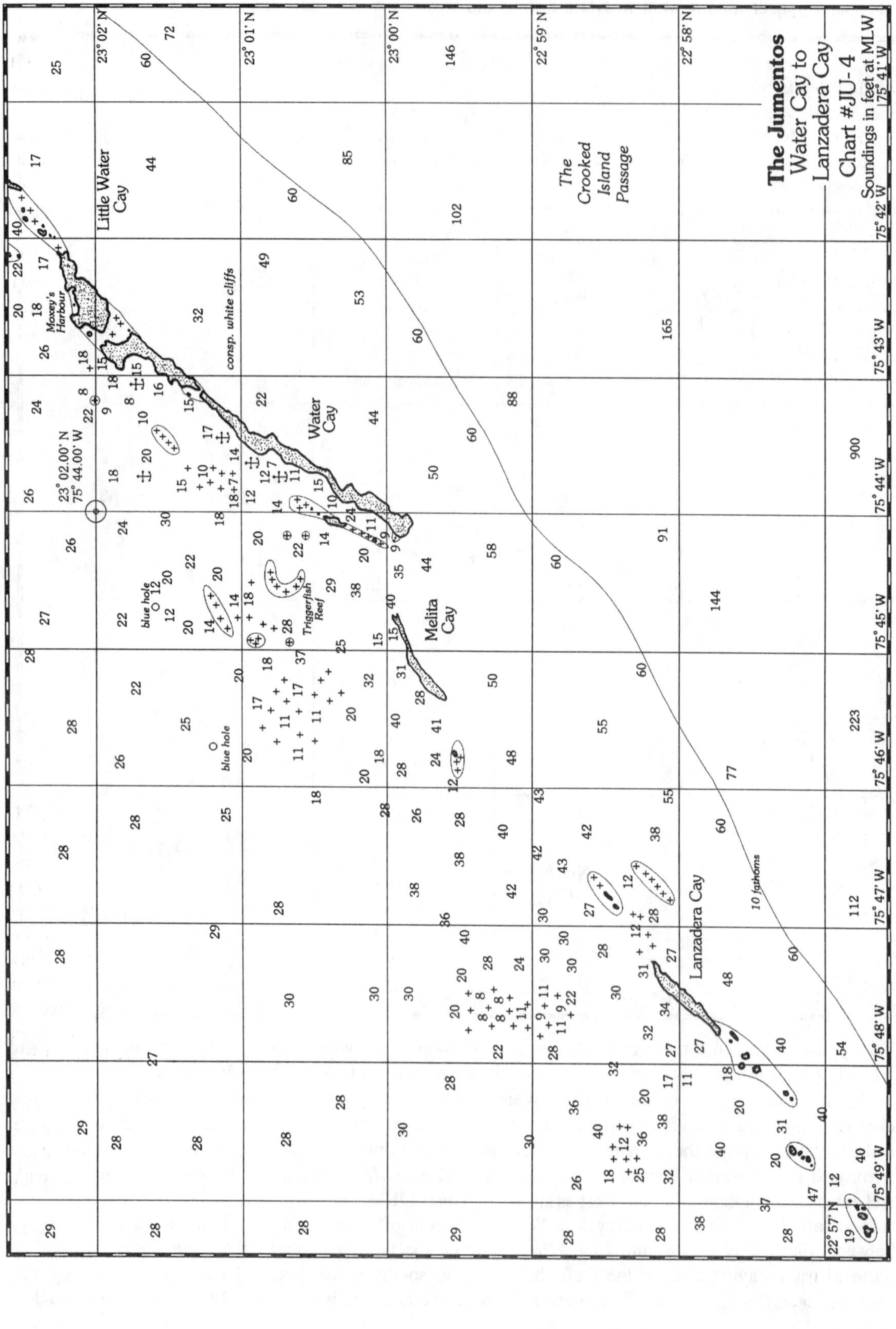

Little Water Cay

Moxey's Harbour

23° 02.00' N
75° 44.00' W

Water Cay

consp. white cliffs

blue hole

blue hole

Triggerfish Reef

Melita Cay

The Crooked Island Passage

Lanzadera Cay

10 fathoms

The Jumentos
Water Cay to
Lanzadera Cay
Chart #JU- 4
Soundings in feet at MLW

23° 02' N
23° 01' N
23° 00' N
22° 59' N
22° 58' N
22° 57' N

75° 41' W
75° 42' W
75° 43' W
75° 44' W
75° 45' W
75° 46' W
75° 47' W
75° 48' W
75° 49' W

Cay. This cut is over 40' deep and a mile wide with only a small reef area lying just southwest of Melita Cay as a hazard.

Water Cay is actually two cays separated by a narrow creek. The water in this creek flows strongly in and out with the tide and is excellent just to sit in and enjoy the flow. In extremely heavy weather seas break over the low lying land just to the north of the creek and one should not anchor in its vicinity if a strong blow is forecast. South of the last hill is a very small beach. Here you will find a path that leads over the island and also up along the ridge of the cliffs giving you a spectacular view in all directions.

Water Cay offers some excellent diving easily accessible by dinghy from the anchorage. Off the western shore of Water Cay are a few shallow reefs, excellent for snorkeling and fishing. One in particular, *Triggerfish Reef* abounds in large trigger fish. There are a lot of reefs in the deeper waters (12'-20') surrounding Little Water Cay and Water Cay that make for excellent spearfishing and the banks are home to a plentiful supply of conch.

SCUBA enthusiasts will want to check out the two blue holes in the area, both within about three miles of the anchorage as shown on Chart #JU-4. In March of 1997 I hooked up with Dive Instructors Andy Lowe and Star Droshine (and their dog *Chief* who unfortunately is not PADI certified) aboard their ketch *Moria*, and with their professional help we began exploring these blue holes. The first hole lies at 23° 01.59' N, 75° 44.68' W, about 1½ nautical miles west of the anchorage. This hole, the smaller of the two, is only about 48' deep with a sandy bottom. This hole is surrounded by reefs about 12' deep and the walls of the hole itself are vertical reef structure with many small holes and tunnels. There is no noticeable current in the hole itself. The hole is full of large grouper and snapper. The hole also has a small population of sharks which is probably why there are so many grouper and snapper present as they prevent divers from annihilating the groupers.

The second blue hole at 23° 01.20' N, 75° 45.73' W, lies just about one nautical mile west/southwest of the first blue hole. This hole is truly spectacular having almost vertical walls plunging to 122' with many holes, tunnels, and crevices to hide the numerous large groupers, permits, and other marine life that inhabit it. Watch out for sharks here also. At the southeastern end of the hole there is a ledge where the hole heads even deeper downward. A handline and some conch for bait would probably bring up enough for a few meals at either of these two holes.

WATER CAY TO FLAMINGO CAY

Just south of Water Cay lies Melita Cay. Anchored at Water Cay in moderate to strong easterly winds, you can watch waves crash into the eastern shore of Melita Cay and shoot skyward to fantastic heights. Southward of Melita Cay lie Lanzadera Cay (Chart #JU-4), and Torzon Cay (Chart #JU-5). These cays offer little to visiting cruisers except a lee if caught out in heavy east/southeast winds.

South of Torzon Cay lies Flamingo Cay, largest of the northern cays of the Jumentos and a must stop on your Jumentos cruise. Flamingo Cay, sometimes called *Fillimingo* by the locals, is easily recognized by its high bluffs. From Water Cay there are several different routes from which to choose to gain Flamingo Cay. Your choice will depend upon sea and wind conditions, and your own personal preference. From Water Cay you can pass outside into deeper water at any of the deep cuts south of Water Cay. There are no hazards on this route except the cuts themselves which, though deep, have a lot of current. Another choice is to parallel the inside of the small cays southwest of Water Cay to Flamingo Cay. Here again, all the cuts have a lot of current that can sweep you off your courseline before you know it. If you choose to sail down on the banks you can head west of Water Cay about 1½-2 miles before taking up a course to parallel the cays southwestward to Flamingo Cay. This is a better route if the wind is kicking up. The only hazards when leaving Water Cay are the reefs just southwest and west of Water Cay and a small reef (6' at MLW) not shown on the charts in this guide, at 22° 57.00' N, 75° 50.56' W.

For skippers using the banks route, a GPS waypoint at 22° 54.30' N, 75° 53.10' W, will place you just northwest of the anchorages that lie along the western shore of Flamingo Cay. If paralleling the western shore of the cays from Water Cay southwestward, watch out for the large reef that lies just north of the small cays that stretch northwest of Flamingo Cay as shown on Chart #JU-5. From this waypoint pass south of those same offlying cays and enter the anchorage area proper.

From offshore, a GPS waypoint at 22° 54.30' N, 75° 51.00' W, will place you approximately ½ mile to seaward of Flamingo Cut. The only obstruction is the two large rocks that are awash at low water in the center of the cut as shown on Chart #JU-5. These rocks usually break in any seas and can be taken on

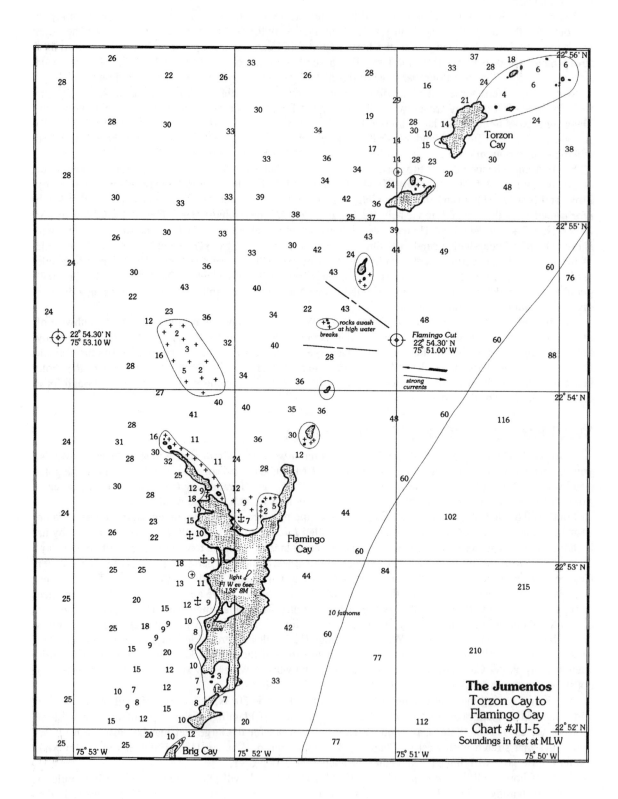

The Jumentos
Torzon Cay to
Flamingo Cay
Chart #JU-5
Soundings in feet at MLW

either side. Once past these rocks head northwest until you can clear the reef system lying northwest of Flamingo Cay. Then turn and head southward until you can make your turn towards the anchorages in the lee of Flamingo Cay.

You can anchor anywhere along the western shore of Flamingo Cay in winds of any strength out of the northeast to southeast. At the northern end there is a small cove which would be suitable for a small, shallow draft vessel, say perhaps a catamaran, to enjoy. In the cove south of it is the wreck of the *John Davis*. Just south of the *John Davis* is a pretty cove, my favorite, with a trio of palm trees ashore, and deep water very close in to the beach. This anchorage has good holding (it's still a good idea to dive on your anchor folks) and is the least prone to surge along this western shore. Ashore and to the north you will find the ruins of small house, a dry well, and a burial site. Just behind the well is a small cave that leads down about 10' to a small room that has enough room for four or five people to enjoy a sit down dinner. There are some other ruins in the area including some grave sites but one must cut a trail to them and the area is thick with poisonwood.

South of this beach is another large cove, just north of the cave, that is just a little shallower than the one just mentioned. Here you will find a trail leading up the hill to the light (Fl W ev 6 sec, 138', 8M-the light is in such a state of disrepair as of May, 1997, that only a complete overhaul or replacement will get it back in working order again-don't plan on that happening any time in the near future). Just south of this anchorage sits a very special cave that can be entered by dinghy. Three natural holes in the roof of the cave allow streams of light to enter the cave making this a very peaceful little grotto. Along the back wall is another window leading out onto the back side of a hill overlooking a lake. This window can be reached from the beach just north of the cave and from here you can climb right down onto the conch shell floor of the cave.

At the northern end of Flamingo Cay is a beautiful beach and a good anchorage in winds from southeast to southwest. In strong winds from east to southeast there can be a bit of surge. You will obviously not want to be here in any northerly wind. To enter the anchorage you can turn to port as you come in Flamingo Cut and steer right up to the beach to anchor in 6'-9'. From the west you can pass north of the offlying reef northwest of Flamingo Cay or pass between it and the small rocks stretching northwest of Flamingo Cay. There is a dinghy channel between Flamingo Cay and the first rock leading off to the northwest. On the beach at this anchorage you will find the wreckage of a small, single engine amphibious plane.

At the southern end of Flamingo Cay lie two very conspicuous, large dome shaped rocks. Between them and Flamingo Cay is a pocket of water 15' deep at the end of the creek that separates Flamingo Cay from its southern tip. Between these rocks and Flamingo Cay a shallow draft vessel of 2'-3' draft could find protection from a frontal passage in about 3' of water. Care must be used if you attempt to tie up in here. The anchorage shoals quickly to the north and is quite rocky. Check it out by dinghy first or head south to Buena Vista Cay if a front threatens. This area is a breeding ground and nursery for nurse sharks that frequent the area in May and June.

Divers will want to check out the numerous small heads lying along the western shore of Flamingo Cay well out into the anchorage area. Just northeast of the small cays lying northwest of Flamingo Cay is a beautiful elkhorn and staghorn coral reef whose top dries at low water.

FLAMINGO CAY TO BUENA VISTA CAY

South of Flamingo Cay to Man Of War Cay (as shown on Chart #JU-6) are a small string of cays with narrow but deep cuts between most. I do not recommend these cuts for use if you wish to gain access to Flamingo Cay unless you have absolutely calm conditions and good visibility. It is far safer to use Flamingo Cut.

The first cay immediately south of Flamingo Cay is called Brigantine Cay, or more often Brig Cay, and the cleft in it is called Brig Cay Cut. Many years ago a brigantine was caught off Brig Cay in a gale and was unable to claw her way to windward. Flirting with disaster the Captain spied the narrow opening in the cay and estimated it to be just a few yards wider than his spars. He squared away and sailed right through the cut to a safe anchorage in the lee along the western shore.

Man Of War Cay offers some small lee in strong east to southeast winds just off the rocky beach on its southwestern shore. There is a small cave in the cliff to the north of the beach and the wreckage of some small boats ashore.

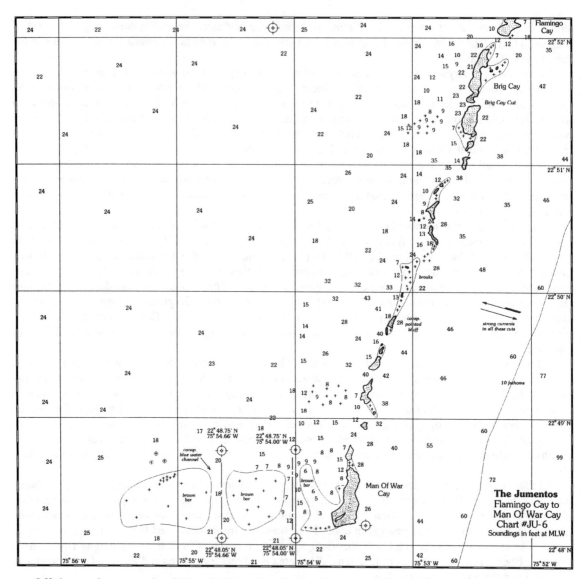

Off the southwestern tip of Man Of War Cay is a reef that stretches westward out onto the banks for approximately two miles. Vessels headed south to Jamaica Cay, your next recommended stop, can pass either out into deep water to avoid this shallow brown bar or head out onto the banks to bypass the shallows or go right through them the way the Mailboats do. If you wish to head out onto the banks to bypass the reef you must go to at least 75° 56'.00 W to clear the western tip of the reef before you head southwards to Jamaica Cay. If you wish to act like a mailboat, then read on.

There are two passages through this reef that you can take to avoid having to detour further west onto the bank. If you wish to parallel the string of cays as you head north or south you can take the inside route, just off Man Of War Cay. Approximately ¼ mile west of the southwest tip of Man Of War Cay is a small break in the reef and a deep blue channel that leads through it. From the south the channel is much easier to discern. If you stay in the center of the channel you will have 9' at low water all the way through. The northern end is much harder to distinguish, especially if the light is in your eyes. The northern end of the channel lies between two brown bars just west of the northern tip of Man Of War Cay. A GPS waypoint at 22° 48.75' N, 75° 54.00' W will place you in the approximate area to search for the deep channel by eye, approximately ¼ mile north of it. As you look southward you will see the deep blue water of the channel and you must line up with that and steer between the two brown bars in 9' at MLW. I have run right down 75° 54.00' W keeping an eye on the two brown bars. From the south a GPS waypoint at 22° 48.04' N, 75° 54.00' W, will place you just south of the southern end of the channel where you should easily pick up the deeper blue water by eye in good visibility. If you cannot read the water that well (and how did you get this far if you can't?), you may wish to try the other break in the reef that lies approximately 1 mile west of Man Of War Cay. This break is a much more conspicuous deep blue channel with 17'-22' throughout. A GPS waypoint at 22° 48.75' N, 75° 54.66' W, will place you approximately ¼ mile north of the cut. Head southward in the middle of the deep, wide, dark blue channel and you will soon be back in deep water. If you are approaching from the south, a GPS waypoint at 22° 48.05' N, 75° 54.66' W, will place you approximately ¼ mile south of the cut. From this position head north through the cut and you will soon be back in deep water. There, that wasn't so hard was it? You can now qualify to take the exam to drive a mailboat.

Man Of War Cay has what appears to be a very pretty beach on its southwestern shore but as you approach you will notice that it is extremely rocky and may not be worth the trouble to land. There is a small cave hole on the small hill north of the beach and the wreckage of some small boats ashore.

Man Of War Channel (Chart #JU-7), deep and wide, lies just south of Man Of War Cay, and stretches southward some three miles or so to Jamaica Cay. There are no hazards except rough conditions when strong winds or swells oppose the tide, but you can say that about all the cuts in The Bahamas.

A GPS waypoint at 22° 44.55' N, 75° 55.10' W, will place you approximately ½ mile west of Jamaica Cay. To enter the anchorage at Jamaica Cay as shown on Chart #JU-7A, you can pass either north or south of the small rock that lies just northwest of the house on Jamaica Cay. You can anchor off the northwestern shore of Jamaica Cay or just below the house in the small cove in 13' (see next paragraph about moorings). Both anchorages are subject to swell and have a grass/sand bottom. There is a small cove on the southern side of the island where you can tuck in during northerly/northeasterly weather. Although some protection from west/southwest winds can be found in the lee of the large rocks lying just to the west of the cay, this anchorage is not recommended for a frontal passage, better to head south to Buena Vista Cay or preferably, Raccoon Cay.

Jamaica Cay is the only cay north of Ragged Island that is inhabited. Here you will find Perseus ("Everybody calls me Percy!") Wilson. Percy is in the midst of transforming Jamaica Cay into what will some day soon be quite a resort. He is building 15 one bedroom cottages, 5 two bedroom cottages, and a fuel dock. In the near future he will be placing moorings west of his house in that anchorage area between his house and the small cay to the west. This he says, will save whatever reef is left. If you do plan to anchor at Jamaica Cay, you may want to anchor out of the reef area. **CAUTION:** In 1998, Percy stretched a thick steel cable between Jamaica Cay and it's neighboring cay (see Chart #JU-7A). This cable lies about a foot underwater and is intended for snorkelers, but it is a tremendous hazard to navigation. Percy currently has two large tanker trucks on shore for diesel and gasoline. If you need fuel, he may be able to help you even though his fuel dock is not yet open. Percy also owns *Percy's Eagle's Nest*, the famous bar built into an airplane body just south of Duncan Town, (you will read more on that in the section on Duncan Town and Ragged Island).

Photo by Kelly Becker

Flamingo Cay, Jumentos.

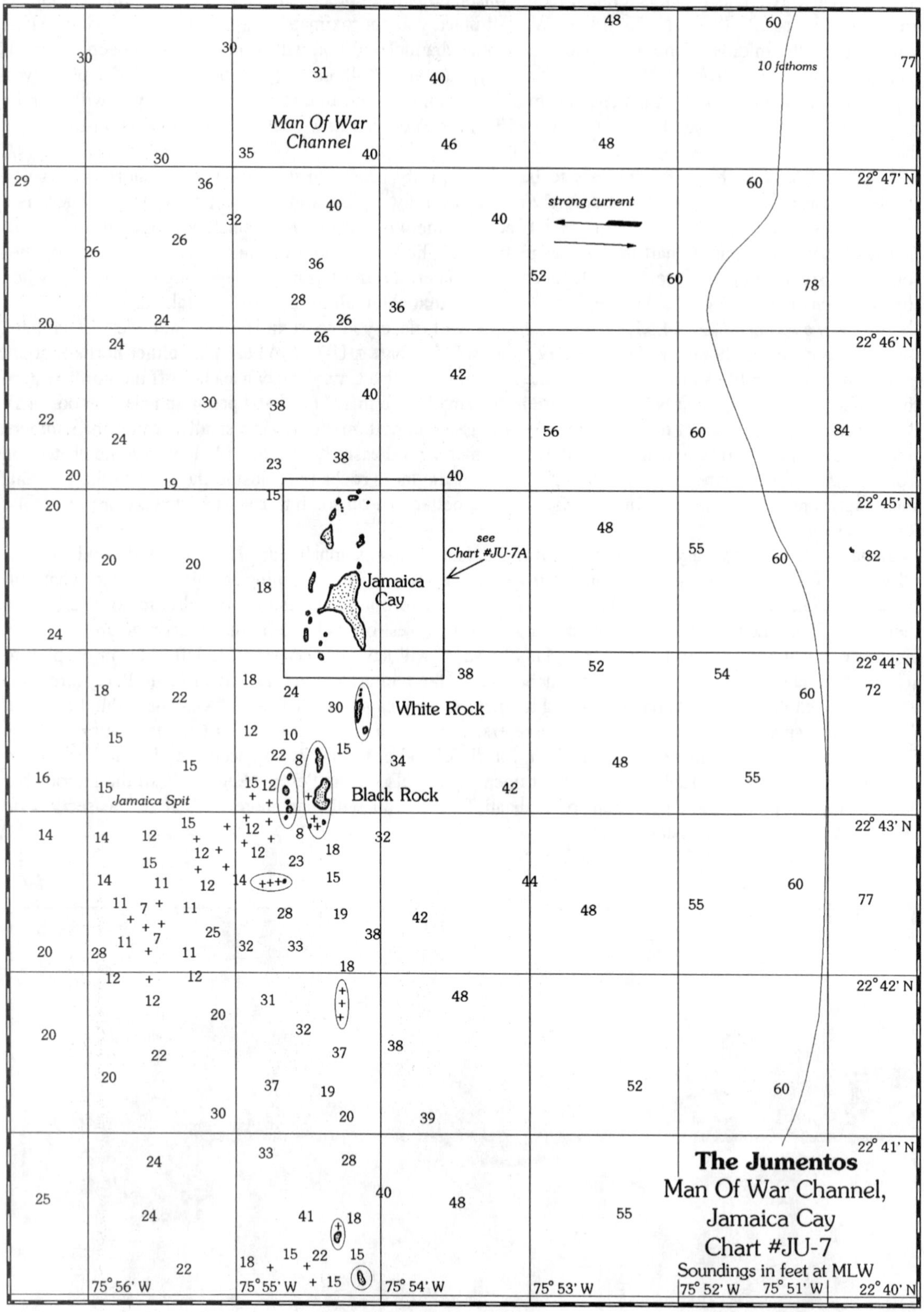

Man Of War Channel
10 fathoms
strong current
see Chart #JU-7A
Jamaica Cay
White Rock
Black Rock
Jamaica Spit
22° 47' N
22° 46' N
22° 45' N
22° 44' N
22° 43' N
22° 42' N
22° 41' N
22° 40' N
75° 56' W
75° 55' W
75° 54' W
75° 53' W
75° 52' W
75° 51' W
The Jumentos
Man Of War Channel,
Jamaica Cay
Chart #JU-7
Soundings in feet at MLW

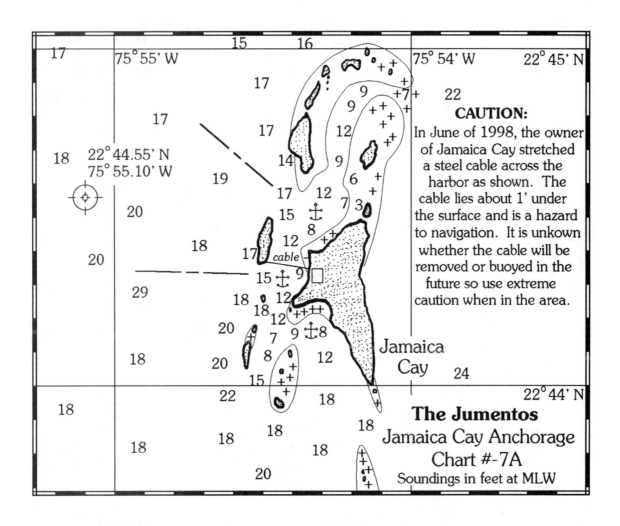

17

15   16

75° 55' W   75° 54' W   22° 45' N

17

17   9   +7+   22

17   17   9   +++   **CAUTION:**
                                        +   +   In June of 1998, the owner
18   22° 44.55' N   12   + +   of Jamaica Cay stretched
      75° 55.10' W   14   9   +   a steel cable across the
                19   6   +   harbor as shown. The
            17   12   +   cable lies about 1' under
20   15   ⚓   7 3   the surface and is a hazard
                    8   to navigation. It is unkown
18   12   +   whether the cable will be
20   17   cable   removed or buoyed in the
            15 ⚓ 9 ▢   future so use extreme
29   18 ø 12   caution when in the area.
            18 12 +++++
20   7   9 ⚓ 8
            +   **Jamaica**
18   20   8 ø 12   **Cay**   24
            15 +
                            22° 44' N
      22   18
18   18   **The Jumentos**
      18   18   Jamaica Cay Anchorage
18   18   Chart #-7A
      20   Soundings in feet at MLW

Photo by Author

Cave at Flamingo Cay, Jumentos.

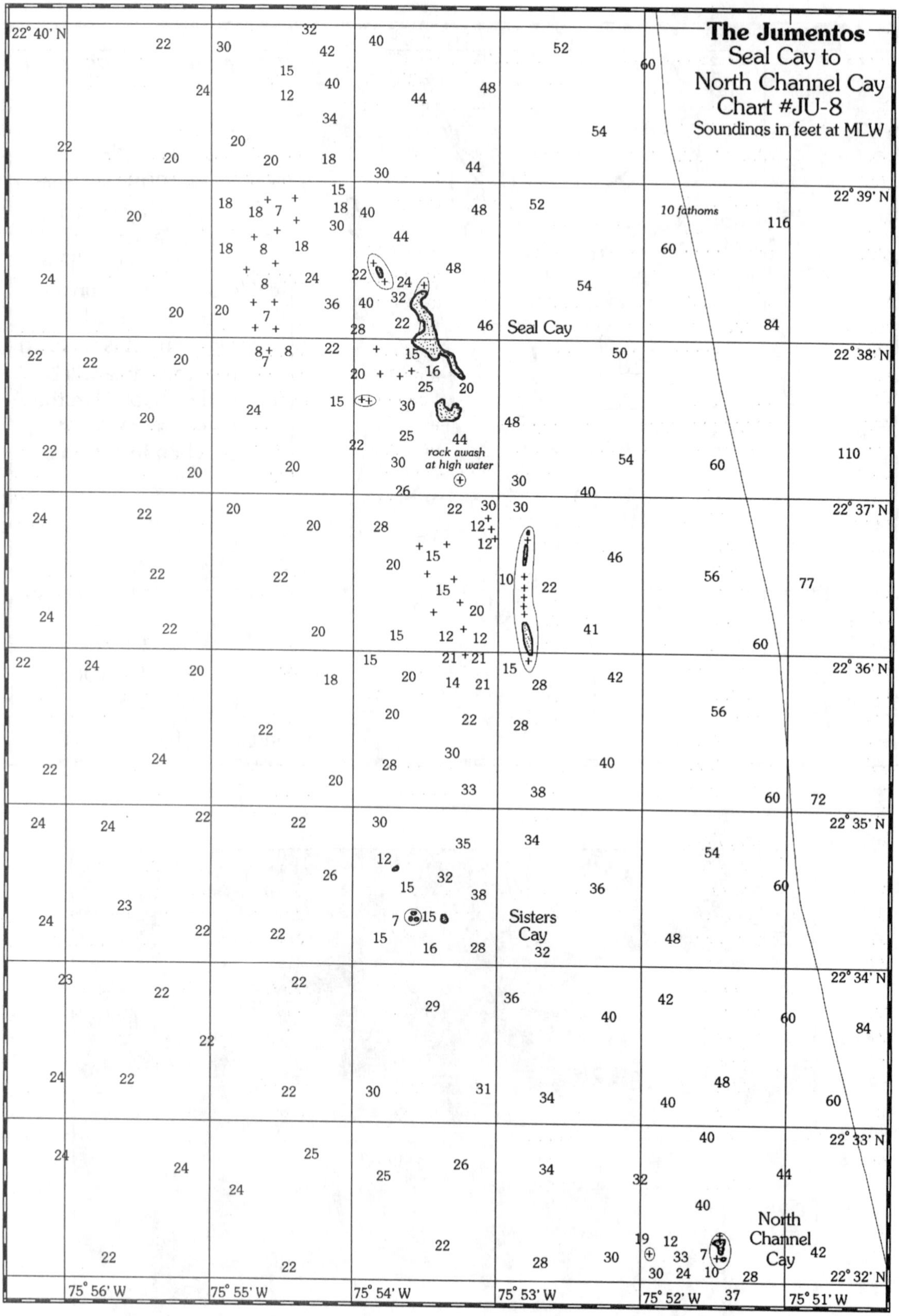

The Jumentos
Seal Cay to
North Channel Cay
Chart #JU-8
Soundings in feet at MLW

22° 40' N

22° 39' N

22° 38' N

22° 37' N

22° 36' N

22° 35' N

22° 34' N

22° 33' N

22° 32' N

22
30
32
42
40
52
60
22
24
15
12
40
44
48
54
22
20
20
18
34
20
30
44
20
18
15
18
18
7
18
40
48
52
10 fathoms
116
20
30
44
60
18
8
18
24
8
24
22
24
48
54
84
40
32
20
20
7
36
28
22
46
Seal Cay
22
22
20
8
7
8
22
15
50
20
16
20
25
20
22
20
24
15
30
48
22
20
20
25
44
54
60
110
20
30
rock awash
at high water
26
22
30
40
24
22
20
20
28
22
30
30
30
12
20
15
46
56
77
22
22
22
20
15
10
22
15
24
22
22
20
15
12
12
41
60
22
24
20
15
21 21
15
42
18
20
14
21
28
56
20
22
28
22
24
30
40
22
20
28
33
38
60
72
24
24
22
22
30
35
34
54
12
32
60
26
15
38
36
23
7
15
Sisters
24
22
22
15
16
28
Cay
48
32
23
22
22
29
36
42
60
22
24
36
40
84
24
22
22
30
31
34
48
40
60
24
25
26
40
24
24
25
25
34
32
44
24
40
North
Channel
22
22
22
28
19
12
7
Cay
42
33
28
30
30
24
10
28
37

rock awash
at high water

75° 56' W   75° 55' W   75° 54' W   75° 53' W   75° 52' W   75° 51' W

From Jamaica Cay southward it is a long haul, approximately 15 miles, over very exposed water until you reach the lee of Nurse Cay. Between Jamaica Cay and Nurse Cay are a lot of very small cays and rocks with the only decent lee available at Seal Cay (Chart #JU-8). One can go south from Jamaica Cay either on the inside in water ranging form 7' to over 40' or outside in the deeper waters of the Crooked Island Passage. If you plan to parallel the lie of the cays be sure to keep an eye out for small rocks as shown on Chart #'s JU-7 and JU-8, especially in the vicinity of Jamaica Spit, south of Jamaica Cay and southwest of Black Rock. Here depths range from 7' to 30' with scattered patch reefs. Farther south as you parallel the lie of the cays you will find some rocks that are barely out of the water at high tide but are easily seen in good visibility. The anchorage in the lee of Seal Cay can be a little surgy in strong winds. There is a small cove on the southern end of Seal Cay that is good for northeast winds. Watch out for the shallows northwest and west of Seal Cay as shown on Chart #JU-8.

South of North Channel Cay and north of Nurse Cay lies the deep and wide Nurse Channel (Chart #JU-9). The channel is easily seen by the large pointed stone beacon on Channel Cay. From afar it may look like a sailboat mast. You can pass either north or south of Channel Cay in deep water. The DMA and BA charts for Nurse Channel mention something about "ripples" in the channel north and south of Channel Cay. Ripples make me think of a pebble thrown into a mill pond. What you see north or south of Channel Cay in the right, or should I say, wrong conditions is certainly not ripples. As in most of the cuts in the Jumentos, a strong wind opposing an outgoing tide makes for some truly horrendous seas in the cuts. You can have the same conditions with little or no wind but a strong ground swell running. Seas in the cuts in these conditions can be anywhere from 6'-10' high and very close together. These are definitely not ripples. Use caution in these conditions. When such seas are in evidence you can still head north or south out on the banks. These "ripples" are confined to the areas of the cuts only. Don't forget that a strong easterly wind can create 6' seas well out onto the banks.

Once you reach the lee of Nurse Cay (Chart #JU-10) you will once again have smooth, calm seas in which to sail. A GPS waypoint at 22° 28.60' N, 75° 51.70' W will place you approximately one mile west of Nurse Cay. Nurse Cay is named after the nurse sharks that once frequented the small creek on its southern shores in May and June to mate. That creek has since filled in and its mouth is now a beach. Nurse Cay is a beautiful cay that upon closer examination looks a bit out of place here. No scrub covered bush cay this, its shores are rather steep-to and covered with tall silver buttonwoods. The western shore offers some excellent small coves in which to anchor, one in particular has a beautiful small beach at its eastern end. Nurse Cay is home to Loyalist ruins (many pasture walls) as well as a family of wild goats. All the cays in the Jumentos offer excellent beachcombing on their weather shores and Nurse Cay is no exception. On the eastern shore of Nurse Cay is a beautiful beach where Bob Rader and Anita Martinec on the M/V *Janice L* found a glass fishing float that had been buried in a hole for many years, as you may well know, glass fishing floats are extremely rare.

South of Nurse Cay sits Little Nurse Cay. The waters between Nurse Cay and Little Nurse Cay are home to numerous small patch reefs and isolated heads, good for fishing. The area between Nurse Cay and Little Nurse Cay offers good protection from northerly winds but ideal protection lies further south at Buena Vista and especially at Raccoon Cay. Little Nurse Cay is home to hundreds of tiny bananaquits, in fact, the entire Jumentos offer excellent birdwatching.

Just south of Nurse Cay sits Buena Vista Cay with one of the prettiest beaches in the Jumentos. You can anchor anywhere off its 1½ mile length in 6'-12' of water. The best holding is at the north end and around the central and southern section just north of the shallow rocky bar which lies off the southern end of the beach. There are a few patches where the holding is tricky due to rocks and small coral heads but with a little searching you will soon find a nice plot of sand to set your anchor in. Holding is good though its still a good idea to dive on your anchor. This anchorage is excellent even in strong east winds. Strong northeast or southeast winds, above 20 knots, causes a small surge to work its way around the points to roll you, not dangerously mind you, but sometimes very uncomfortably.

Buena Vista is home to goats, chickens, and I am told, a wild horse although I have not seen it or any sign of it, although I have seen a trio of pink flamingos off the point at the north end of the anchorage and many tropic birds performing their Springtime aerial mating rituals off the windward shore. Ashore you will find a trail marked by a white steel pipe about halfway down the beach that leads to a tiny cavern in the small hill.

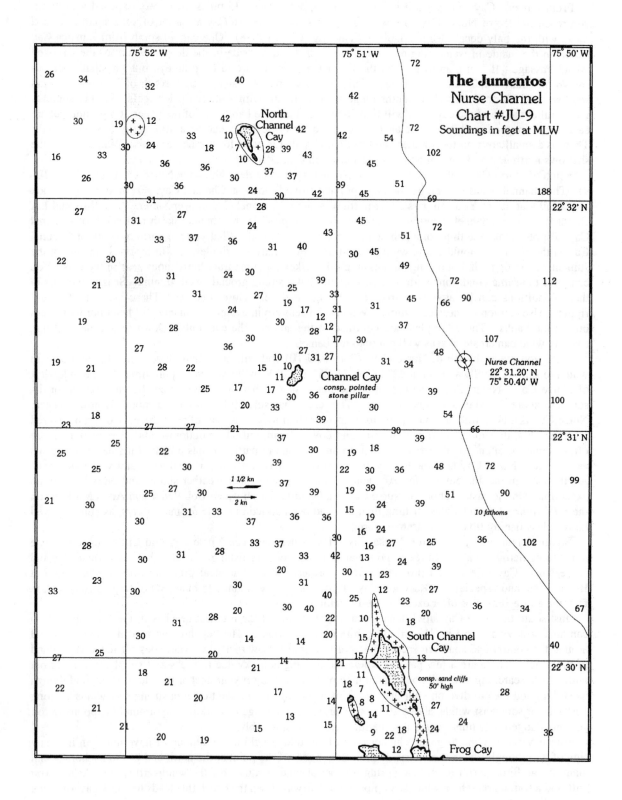

75° 52' W

75° 51' W

75° 50' W

72

The Jumentos
Nurse Channel
Chart #JU-9
Soundings in feet at MLW

26   34
32   40
42
30   19 + + 12   42   North   72
+ +   Channel 42   42   54   72
33   + + 33   10   Cay   102
30   24   18   7 + 28 39   43   45
16   33   36   10   37   37   51   188
26   30   36   30   24   30   42   39   45   69

22° 32' N

27   28   45
31   27   24   43   72
33   37   36   31   40   51
22   30   30   45   49
21   20   31   24   30   39   72   112
31   27   25   33   45   66   90
19   24   19   17   31   37   107
28   30   28 12   30
27   36   30   17   48   Nurse Channel
19   10 27 31 27   31   34   22° 31.20' N
21   28   22   15 10   Channel Cay   39   75° 50.40' W
25   17   11   consp. pointed   100
18   17   30   36   stone pillar   30
23   20   33   39   54
27   27   21   39   30   66

22° 31' N

25   37   30   19 18   39
25   22   30   30   22 30 36   48   72
25   30   39   19 39   51   99
1 1/2 kn   19   24   39   90
21   25   27 30   37   39   15   19   10 fathoms
30   2 kn   36   36   16 24   36   102
28   31 33   37   30   16 27   25
30   33 37   42   13   24   39
31   28   20   30 11 23   24
23   30   31   12   27
33   30   40   25   23   36   34   67
28   20   30 40   22   20   10   18
31   20   15   South Channel   40
30   14   14   15   Cay   13
27   25   20   21   11   consp. sand cliffs
21   14   18   7   50' high   28

22° 30' N

22   18   21   17   18   8   27
21   20   14   7 8 11
21   13   15   14   24
21   15   9 22 18   24   36
20   19   12   Frog Cay

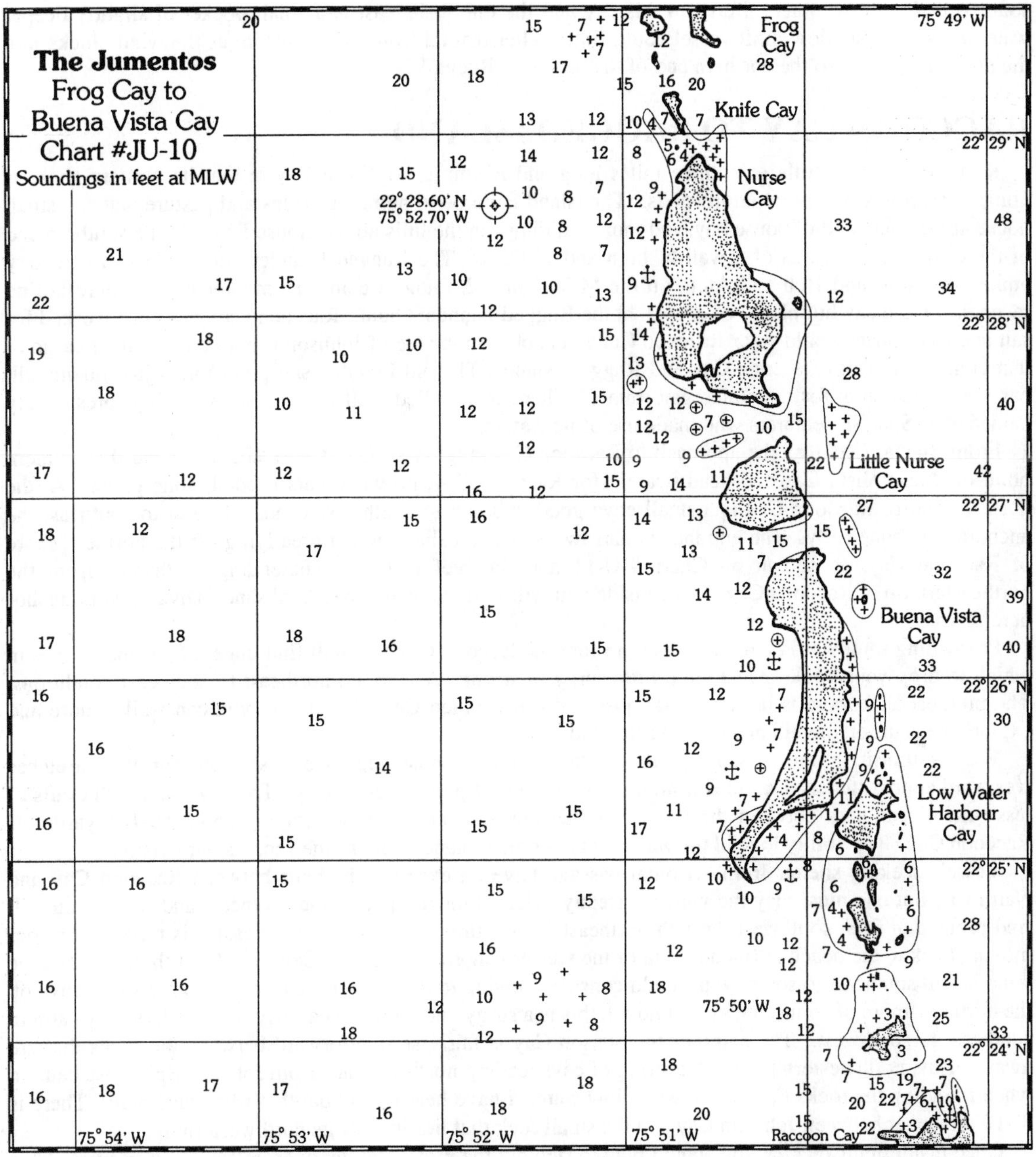

The Jumentos
Frog Cay to
Buena Vista Cay
Chart #JU-10
Soundings in feet at MLW

Frog Cay
Knife Cay
Nurse Cay
Little Nurse Cay
Buena Vista Cay
Low Water Harbour Cay
Raccoon Cay

22° 28.60' N
75° 52.70' W

75° 49' W
22° 29' N
22° 28' N
22° 27' N
22° 26' N
22° 25' N
22° 24' N

75° 54' W
75° 53' W
75° 52' W
75° 51' W
75° 50' W

Vessels seeking shelter from a frontal passage can pass south of Buena Vista Cay and anchor in the deep water channel between Low Water Harbour Cay and Buena Vista Cay (see Chart #JU-10). This area is open somewhat to the southwest but once the wind is into the west and northwest you are protected. When the wind shifts to the northeast you should immediately head back around to the western shore of Buena Vista and tuck into the calm pocket at the northern end of the beach. Just south of Low Water Harbour Cay is a series of small unnamed cays. There is a pass between Low Water Harbour Cay and the first cay to its south with 6' at low water. Between this cay and the one to its east is a small pocket of slightly deeper water where one shallow draft vessel could find shelter from a front. Once again, as the wind clocks into the north, head back to the northern end of the beach on Buena Vista.

RACCOON CAY TO RAGGED ISLAND

Raccoon Cay is a little over three miles long and is similar to Nurse Cay in that its western shore is home to a growth of silver buttonwoods. The island is home to numerous ruins and pasture walls, a small house at the south end of house bay, and more buildings on the hills above House Bay. At the southern end of the cay are some ruins of a wall 6' high and 7' thick. The Ragged Islanders say there is a cemetery amidst the ruins and Bob and Anita on the M/V *Janice L* found a cemetery marker here. There are no raccoons on the cay but plenty of goats that the Ragged Islanders hunt. Raccoon Cay was once worked for salt and large boats would enter Raccoon Cut and anchor in the lee of Johnson Cay to take on their cargo of that commodity from Raccoon Cay and Ragged Island. The old Loyalist salt pond found just inland still has the walled slots for the sluice gate intact. There is a walled well at Spanish Well Bay, presumably named after Spanish seafarers who made use of its waters.

From Buena Vista Cay the approach to Raccoon Cay is fairly simple (Chart #JU-11), clear the southern point of Buena Vista Cay and head straight for Raccoon Cay, no waypoints needed, none given. At the northern end of Raccoon Cay is a small cove good in south to southwest winds. In east to southeast the anchorage is quite rolly. The entrance is narrow, between a shallow reef area lying off the northern shore of Raccoon Cay, as shown on Chart #JU-11 and the reef and rocks extending northward from the northeastern tip of Raccoon Cay. Once inside you will find about 10' over hard sand. Dive on your anchor here!

Proceeding southward along the western shore of Raccoon Cay you will find quite a few small coves in which to drop your hook. Most are a little surgy in strong (20+ knots) northeast to southeast conditions. The prettiest anchorage is in House Bay just north of Pimlico Cay. From here you can walk ashore and explore the ruins on the hill and the old salt pond.

Vessels transiting the western shore of Raccoon Cay must negotiate a shallow bar that stretches westward approximately 1½ miles from the southwestern tip of Raccoon Cay. Those vessels with drafts of less than 8' can pass between the shoal and Raccoon Cay at low water staying about 50-100 yards off Raccoon Cay. The ability to read the water would come in handy here as the shoal is very visible.

Vessels seeking shelter from a frontal passage have an excellent harbour between Raccoon Cay and Nairn Cay but one must play the winds correctly. Here, though open to the southeast and south, you will find protection from southwest through northeast. Once the wind is in the northeast it is time to consider moving back to the beach at Buena Vista or the western shore of Raccoon Cay. If a front threatens and the wind is still southeast to south, you should consider moving to the beautiful anchorage in the small cove on the northern shore of Johnson Cay. Although this is a surgy anchorage in easterly weather it is very calm in southeast to southwest. The entrance to Johnson Cay is fairly straightforward between the rocks that are awash off its northwestern tip and the string of cays leading northeastward from Johnson Spit. Use caution when rounding the rocks that are awash at low water, I have heard of a boat that was holed here. There is 8'-10' however between Johnson Cay and the small rock that lies just off its northwestern tip.

Once inside Johnson Cay you should plan to ride out the prefrontal winds from southeast to west. This is exactly when the anchorage at Nairn Cay is the roughest. Once the wind comes into the southwest to west, preferably west, grit your teeth and tough it out for the one mile run to the anchorage between Raccoon Cay and Nairn Cay, **but not at night**. Once safely inside (watch out for the rocky bar in the middle of the entrance as shown on Chart #JU-12), you will once again be in calm water. The reason you should sit at Johnson Cay is because Nairn can be very rough in southeast through just southwest winds. If sitting at Nairn Cay during those conditions appeals to you more than crossing Raccoon Cut in westerly weather, (for the most part Ben's Cay will give you a slight lee), by all means make yourself at home. I

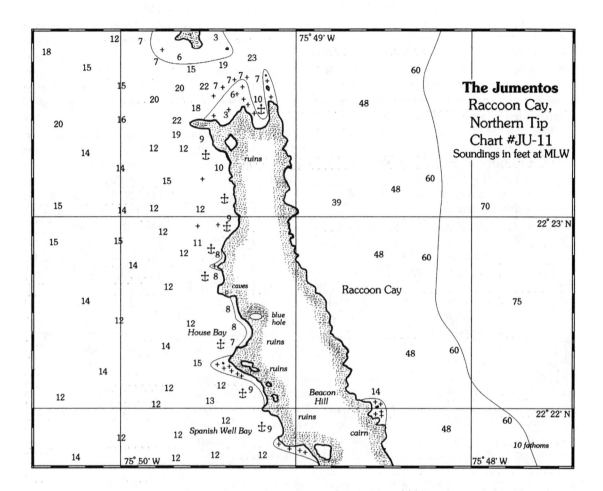

only offer these suggestions, it is up to each skipper to make the correct decisions concerning the safety of his or her own vessel.

Boats wishing to gain entry to the banks through Raccoon Cut will find it fairly easy and deep. A GPS waypoint at 22° 21.40' N, 75° 46.90' W, will place you approximately ½ mile northeast of the cut and well north of Johnson Spit, the shallow breaking area that lies northward of Johnson Cay as shown on Chart #JU-12. Steer southwestward between Nairn Cay and Johnson Cay. You can then take Ben's Cay on either side, to the north if you wish to head up to the anchorages off the western shore of Raccoon Cay, or to the south if you plan to head around Margaret Shoal and southward. Keep an eye out for the shallow area just north and east of Ben's Cay, in an easterly sea rollers will heap up and break upon it.

South of Johnson Cay sits Double Breasted Cay where you will find a small and surgy anchorage between its northern tip and Loggerhead Cay. This anchorage is protected from southeast to west but not the place to be in any northerly wind. Another nice anchorage in settled weather is south of Loggerhead Cay in the bight between Big Pigeon Cay, sometimes called Golding Cay, and Double Breasted Cay.

Shallow draft vessels can of course explore the waters much closer to Double Breasted Cay and find better shelter in its lee. This anchorage offers a little lee from west winds in the shelter of Big Pigeon Cay. Wild goats can be found roaming the shores of Double Breasted Cay. Good beachcombing abounds on the windward side of all the cays in the Jumentos and Double Breasted Cay is no exception. I have heard of people finding bales of marijuana on the eastern beach of Double Breasted Cay (no joke intended here folks).

Margaret Cay, sometimes called Ishmael Cay, lies south of Raccoon Cut and west of Double Breasted Cay and stretches in an east/west direction. It is home to a family of goats, numerous mosquitoes, caves, large stands of lignumvitae, and ruins on the southeastern tip, accessible only by dinghy.

Vessels heading south from Raccoon Cut to Hog Cay, Ragged Island, or Little Ragged Island must negotiate the large, westward stretching Margaret Shoal, a huge shallow sandbank stretching almost three miles out onto the banks. Shallow draft vessels, 3' or less, can shorten their trip by using the tide and cutting across the narrow bank at least ½ mile west of Margaret Cay. I draw 5' and I cross the bank at high tide anywhere west of 75° 48.50' W by steering south down that longitude but only a rising, almost high tide. A six foot draft vessel can cross Margaret Shoal at 75° 49.00' W. If you are a skipper of great wisdom and don't wish to gamble on a shortcut you must go to 75° 50.00' W where you can head south in relative comfort just west of the shoal.

Once past the western end of Margaret Shoal you can begin steering southeast towards Hog Cay. Margaret Shoal will parallel your course on your port side. The shoal edges out near Darville Cay and the unnamed rocks lying between Darville Cay and Hog Cay. Once past the shoal it is best to steer to the southern end of Hog Cay. You will see some large whitish cliffs in the center of Hog Cay, don't steer for those, steer for the second beach south of the cliffs. A GPS waypoint at 22° 14.60' N, 75° 45.50' W, sits almost a half mile west of the beach at Hog Cay and is as good a spot as any to head for. Use caution when headed for this spot though. Make sure the currents don't sweep you north towards the southern edge of Margaret Shoal or south towards the shallow area that lies southwest of Hog Cay. You can anchor off either of the two beaches or under the white cliffs at Hog Cay. Do not head straight for the cliffs, head for the beach and then when just off Hog Cay, steer northward in the deeper water between Margaret Shoal and Hog Cay towards the cliff. The beaches offer the least surge and good holding in soft grass/sand. The anchorages off Hog Cay offer better protection in prevailing conditions than Ragged Island Harbour and they are but a short dinghy ride from the entrance to Duncan Town.

Hog Cay is covered in a dense growth and was used for raising cattle, primarily Brahma bulls in the 1970's and 1980's. One Ragged Islander told me a story of a Defence Force vessel that landed on Hog Cay whose crew killed a Brahma Bull and only took the hindquarters. The owner was furious when he found out and he filed a claim with the Government asking for $50,000 saying the unfortunate creature was his prime breeding bull. I was told he received some compensation but no amount was mentioned. There are still some wild goats on the cay. There are quite a few ruins on the southern shore of Hog Cay just east of Hog Point. At the north end of the second beach to the north are the ruins of a pasture wall. Follow this wall to an old salt pond, from there you can follow the trail to the eastern shore where you will find some offlying reefs that form some sheltered pools ideal for snorkeling.

RAGGED ISLAND AND LITTLE RAGGED ISLAND

South of Hog Cay lies Ragged Island Harbour and the entrance to Duncan Town as shown on Chart #JU-14. I do not recommend the cut between Hog Cay and Ragged Island unless you are familiar with the waters of this area or are adept at reading the water's depth by its color. There are three reefs guarding the entrance to this cut, two at the eastern end that make up what is called the Outer Bar Reef, and one inside directly between Hog Cay and Ragged Island called the Inner Bar Reef. If entering from offshore come in on a southwesterly course passing southeast of the rock beacon on Black Rock Reef. This course takes you inside the Outer Bar Reefs. Southwest of the beacon lies the dangerous and extensive Inner Bar Reef which is easily seen as it breaks with almost any sea. Although the northern side is best, you can pass to either side of it. Watch our for the shallow spot, 5' at low water, lying southwest of the reef and north of Gun Point.

A lee anchorage, and quite often a bit surgy, can be found just west of the northwestern tip of Ragged Island in Ragged Island Harbour, just below the conspicuous diesel tank that fuels the power generator and Batelco office in Duncan Town. This is also where the mailboat anchors. Duncan Towners must come out in small boats to ferry goods and passengers ashore as the channel is too shallow for the mailboat to enter (more on that later).

Ragged Island is approximately 4 miles long lying in a NW/SSE direction. Duncan Town, the only settlement, lies at the south end of a natural bay of shallow water. The settlement was named after Duncan Taylor, a Loyalist who discovered the island's charms in the early 18th century. Taylor, with his brother's help, built the salt ponds in the town's vicinity based on slave labor. Many of the inhabitants of Duncan Town are direct descendants of the first settlers and bear their names. Here you will find names like Lockhart, Munroe, Curling, Wilson, Moxey, and Maycock. Ragged Islanders are not dependent on the tourist trade, some still work the salt ponds in the area and of course many fish. From the abolition of slavery up until the 1960's, Ragged Island relied heavily on the salt trade with Cuba and Haiti. Ragged

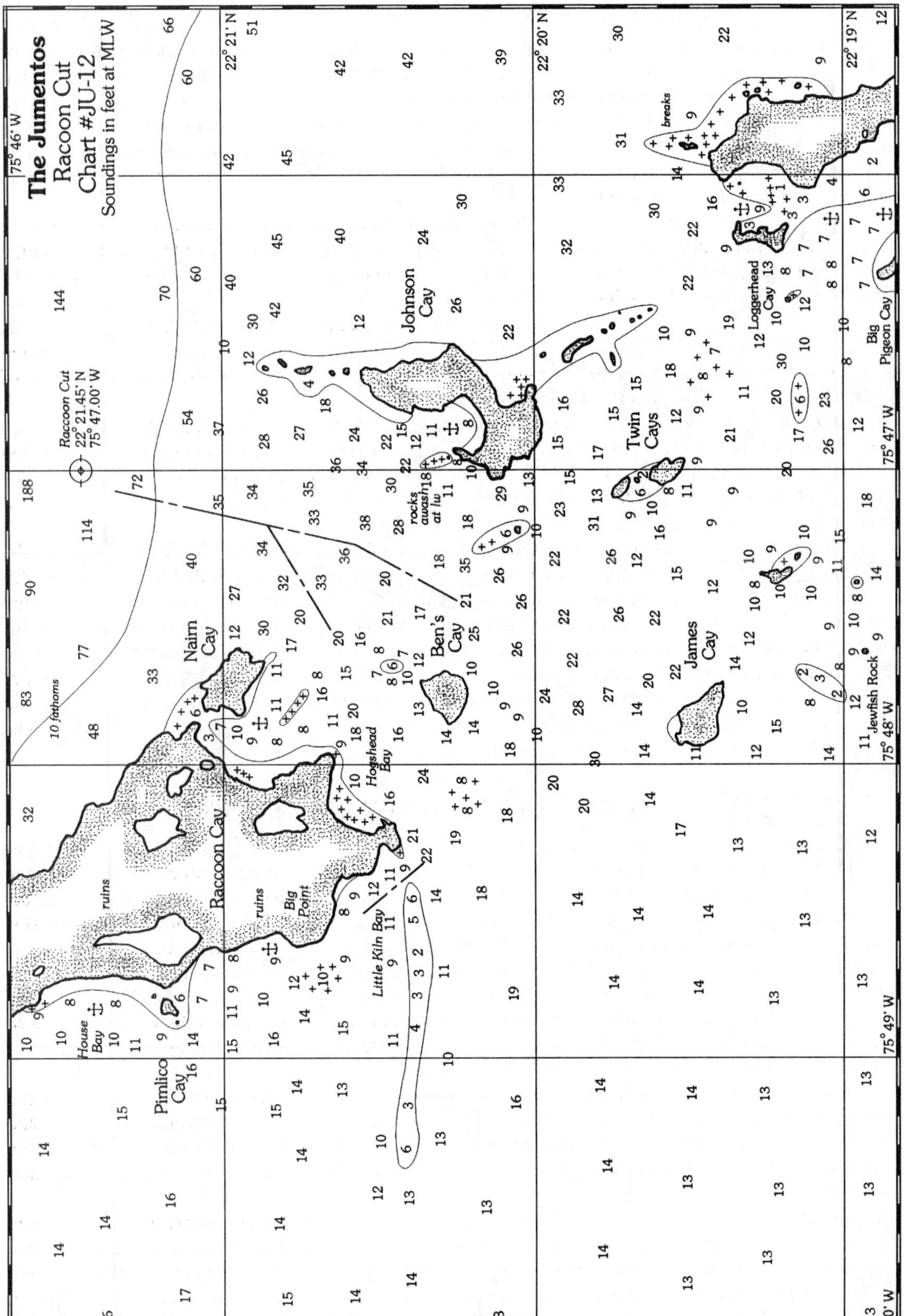

The Jumentos
Racoon Cut
Chart #JU-12
Soundings in feet at MLW

75° 46' W

Raccoon Cut
22° 21.45' N
75° 47.00' W

10 fathoms

Naim Cay

Johnson Cay

Ben's Cay

Twin Cays

Raccoon Cay

ruins

ruins

Big Point

Little Kiln Bay

Hogshead Bay

House Bay

Pimlico Cay

James Cay

Jewish Rock

Loggerhead Cay

Big Pigeon Cay

breaks

rocks awash at lw

22° 21' N

22° 20' N

22° 19' N

75° 47' W

75° 48' W

75° 49' W

75° 50' W

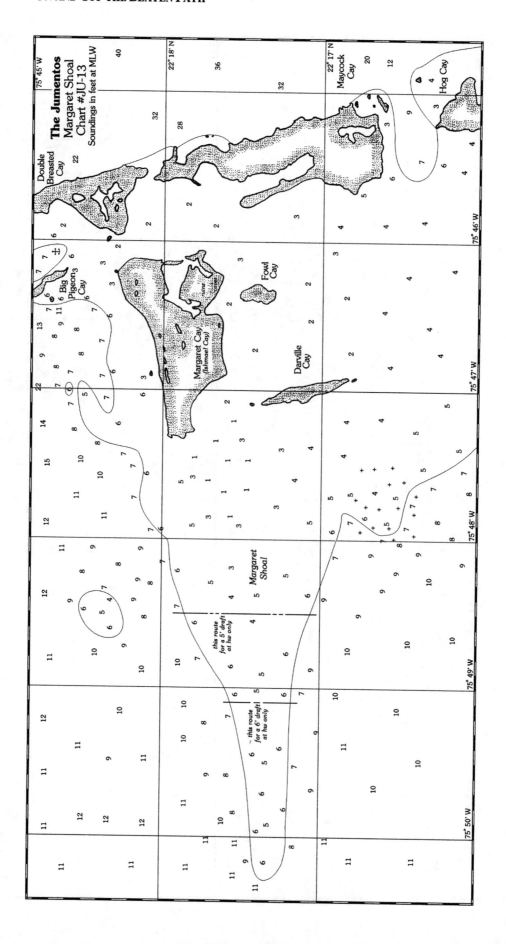

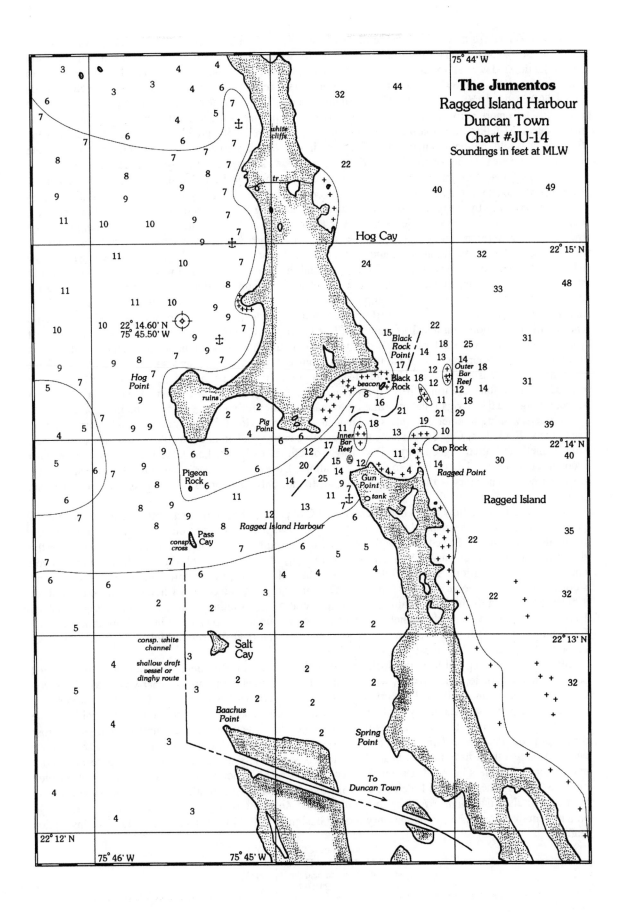

The Jumentos
Ragged Island Harbour
Duncan Town
Chart #JU-14
Soundings in feet at MLW

Islanders received fruits, vegetables, and other goods that they could not produce in exchange for their salt and fish. After Castro came to power the salt industry went into decline to the point that there is virtually no production today at all except for personal consumption. Part of the reason is that there is no access to Duncan Town due to the shallowness of the waters. As a result the islands population has declined from about 500 in the 1950's to about 100 inhabitants today. The amount of uninhabited houses give silent testimony to a more active past. Today their economy is primarily based on the richness of the sealife in their waters. I talked to a marine biologist who was involved with grouper studies in Nassau and the Exumas who told me that the majority of groupers in the Nassau markets come from the Jumentos and the Ragged Island areas. The last monk seal seen in The Bahamas was spotted off Ragged Island in 1957.

Ragged Islanders are quite a different breed altogether than can be found in the rest of The Bahamas. Here people talk to you as equals, neither up or down, and are extremely friendly and helpful. Duncan Towners have been by themselves so long, so very few cruising boats as wells as Bahamians visit this area, that they have become fiercely independent. The Ragged Islanders have a strong feeling of being forgotten by their own government, they received no assistance after Hurricane Kate in 1985. Nevertheless, they are determined to restore the island to some semblance of its former glory. They are confident with a new harbour, trade could be revived, new jobs created, and the youth of the island would be more interested in staying put and working towards a revitalization of the community. Plans are now in the works to re-dredge the entrance channel to accommodate the mailboat (which now has to anchor in the lee of the northern tip of Ragged Island) and an RO plant. Duncan Towners look forward to increased yacht traffic and the financial boom that it will bring. It will be up to you, the cruiser that visits this cay, to insure that you hold up your end of the bargain and don't become a burden as some thoughtless cruisers in other areas have done. Drop your trash off at the town dock, someone will pick it up and take it to the dump. Don't play the ugly, insensitive, tourist. Ragged Islanders are truly warm people, respect shown will be respect returned. These folks are truly different than any other Bahamians you will meet. Please don't make me regret giving you the navigational information to make it easier for you to get here in the first place.

Skippers wishing to enter the waters of Duncan Town from Hog Cay should head south from Hog Cay past Pigeon Rock, Pass Cay, (with its conspicuous large cross), and enter the shallow bank just west of Salt Cay, sometimes called Pigeon Cay. Pass Cay, sometimes called Bishop Cay, has a very conspicuous wooden cross on it. I have been told that a Catholic Bishop, some say a Church Of England Bishop, drowned here. The story is that his body was not found, only his clothes. The cross was erected in his memory.

As you enter the shallow banks northwest of Salt Cay you will begin to see a white channel between two grassy shoals. This is the channel to follow, it has been swept clean by the constant outboard traffic hence the white sand bottom. The channel begins to bend to the southeast at Baachus Point and you will enter the dredged portion of the channel. You may see the remains of the old channel heading off to the east as you enter the dredged portion. Do not follow the old channel, it will just shallow out. In years past, small sloops would sail into town down this channel. Old timers can tell you of days when there were upwards of 100 small sloops in the harbour awaiting salt to carry out to ships waiting at Raccoon Cut or Ragged Island Harbour. Follow the dredged channel into the basin and tie up to the town dock but be sure to leave room for fishing boats. There are spots in the channel that are well over 6' deep at high water while the inner harbour barely carries 5'-6', mostly 3'-4' at high water.

Straight up the steep hill from the dock sits the pink Government Building. This may well be your first stop. Lovely Charlene, the secretary, will be happy to tell you where to go for what you need. Here you may also see the Duncan Town Jail, little more than a jail cell that has been so little used that it is now a storage room, a pleasant testimony for Duncan Town. If you walk up the hill to the right you will find the clinic just on your right, the nurse comes in the afternoon but if you need her ask anyone you see. Across the street is the *Ponderosa Bar and Grill* where owner Cephas Maycock also sells fresh fruits and veggies when he can get them from the mailboat. Next door is *Maxine's*, a small but well stocked grocery and dry goods store. Maxine's husband, Daniel Wallace, is the Chief Councilor, the highest government position on the island. To the left of the Batelco Tower is *Louie's Sweet Shop* with great bread and pies to order.

You will also find *Sheila's Fisherman's Lounge* and *Angie's Grocery* located on the main road. High on a hill south of town is a simple masonry mound designed with thirteen steps all around. The inscription reads:

In memory of ICELY, LLOYD
and one seaman of H.M.S. THUNDER,
who were drowned near the Brothers Rocks.
23/1/31.

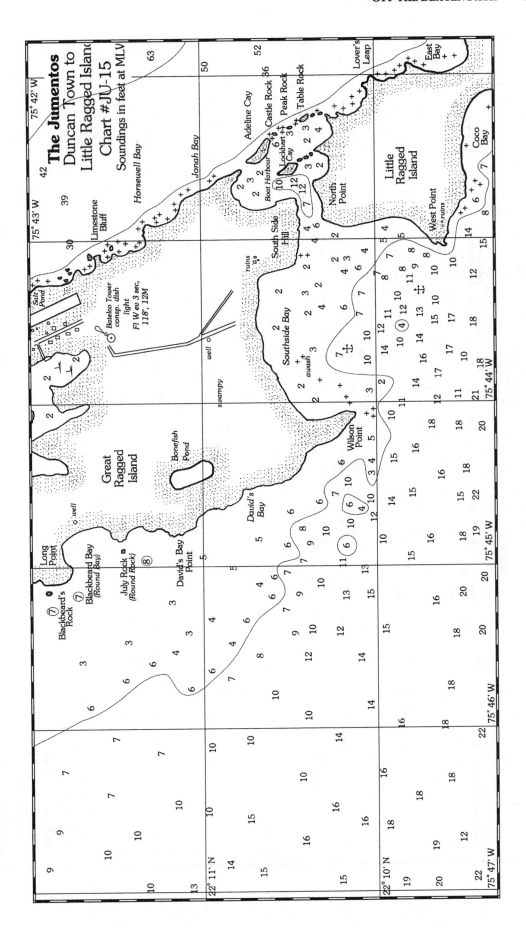

The Jumentos
Duncan Town to
Little Ragged Island
Chart #JU-15
Soundings in feet at MLV

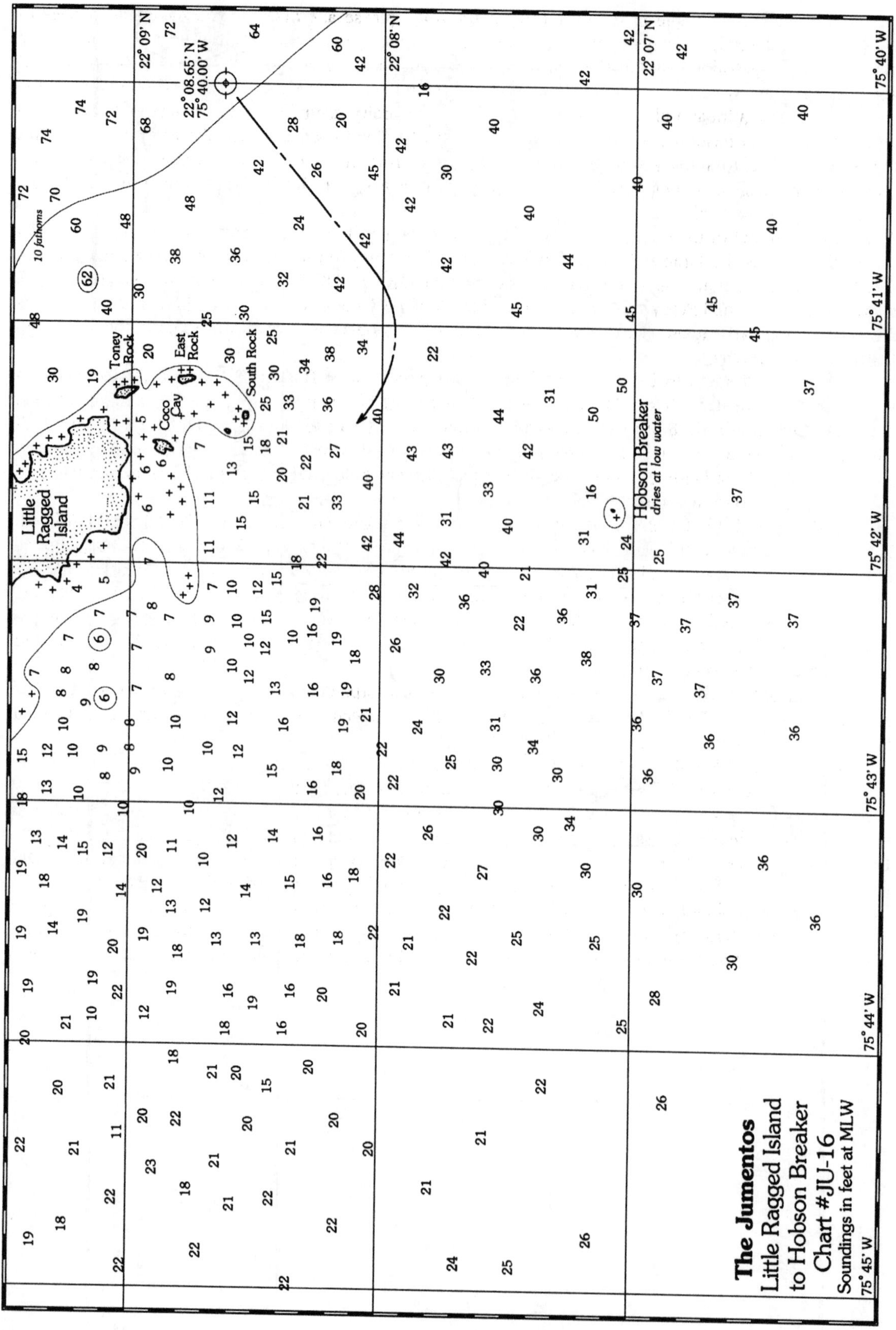

22° 09' N

22° 08.65' N
75° 40.00' W

22° 08' N

22° 07' N

10 fathoms

Little Ragged Island

Toney Rock

East Rock

South Rock

Coco Cay

Hobson Breaker
dries at low water

75° 45' W 75° 44' W 75° 43' W 75° 42' W 75° 41' W 75° 40' W

The Jumentos
Little Ragged Island
to Hobson Breaker
Chart #JU-16
Soundings in feet at MLW

Cistern water is available at the Government Building, please ask first. If you have sealed bags of garbage, leave them at the concrete dock and someone will take them away. There is no propane available but if you need gasoline, ask Charlene at the Government Building or Maxine Wallace if they know of anybody who can let you have a few gallons. Bear in mind that everybody here gets their fuel in 55 gallon drums from the mailboat and it is a rare and valuable commodity, their fishing boats depend upon having an ample supply of gasoline. If you need diesel you may be able to persuade Leander Maycock, who runs the Batelco office, to allow you to purchase a few gallons from their supply. If you need a repairman for your outboard engine, contact Alpheas Nespitt, known as *Fish*, or Derek Carter, who uses the handle *Monkey Man* on the VHF.

A short walk out of town, though easily accessible by dinghy if you land on the beach at Southside Bay (Chart #JU-15), is the famous *Percy's Eagle's Nest*. Here Percy Wilson (remember Percy from Jamaica Cay?), owns and operates the unique bar that is constructed using a DC-3 as its focal point. The bar is open sporadically at best and Percy explained to me in March of 1997 that it would be a while before the *Eagle's Nest* is open regularly again. Currently it houses building materials that Percy hopes to use to build 15 one-bedroom villas nearby.

Vessels headed south to Little Ragged Island must pass west of Ragged Island to clear the shallows lying just off the western shore. There is a pleasant anchorage off the northwest tip of Little Ragged Island and another in Southside Bay in settled weather as shown on Chart #JU-15. Lockhart Cay, just north of Little Ragged Island, was once the home to a boat building facility many years ago. The small harbour to its west is called Boat Harbour and is often used as a hurricane hole. Ask any Ragged Islander how to find the twisting route into its semi-safe water.

If approaching Little Ragged Island from offshore a GPS waypoint at 22° 08.65' N, 75° 40.00' W, will place you a little over a mile southeast of Little Ragged Island. From here head southwest and pass around the small rocks lying south of Little Ragged Island and head up the western shore at least a quarter mile off. Watch out for the reef off the southwest tip of Little Ragged Island as shown on Chart #JU-16. If passing south of Little Ragged Island keep a sharp lookout for Hobson Breaker. A dangerous rock that dries at low water, Hobson Breaker lies approximately two miles south of Little Ragged Island. By the way, you're only about 60 miles from Cuba here.

Little Ragged Island is privately owned as plans for a resort/cottages complex are in the works. For more information ask Percy. Off the eastern shore of Little Ragged Island is a white limestone cliff called Lover's Leap. A perfect spot for distraught lovers.

Approximately 35 miles east/southeast of Little Ragged Island across the Columbus Bank, at the southeast tip of the Great Bahama Bank and West Channel (the channel that lies to the west of the Mira Por Vos Cays) lies Cay Verde. Cay Verde is a surgy anchorage at best but is a fair lee for vessels headed to Inagua or the Windward Passage. Approximately 30 miles south of Little Ragged Island lies Santa Domingo Cay at the southern tip of the Great Bahama Bank at its junction with the western end of the Old Bahama Channel. The fishing around these cays is outstanding as evidenced by the amount of illegal Cuban and Hispaniolian fishermen who frequent this area. The Royal Bahamas Defence Force has regular patrols in the southern waters of The Bahamas to fight poaching by non-Bahamian fishing vessels. From Ragged Island southeastward to Inagua the VHF is often filled with Cuban, Dominican, and Haitian voices.

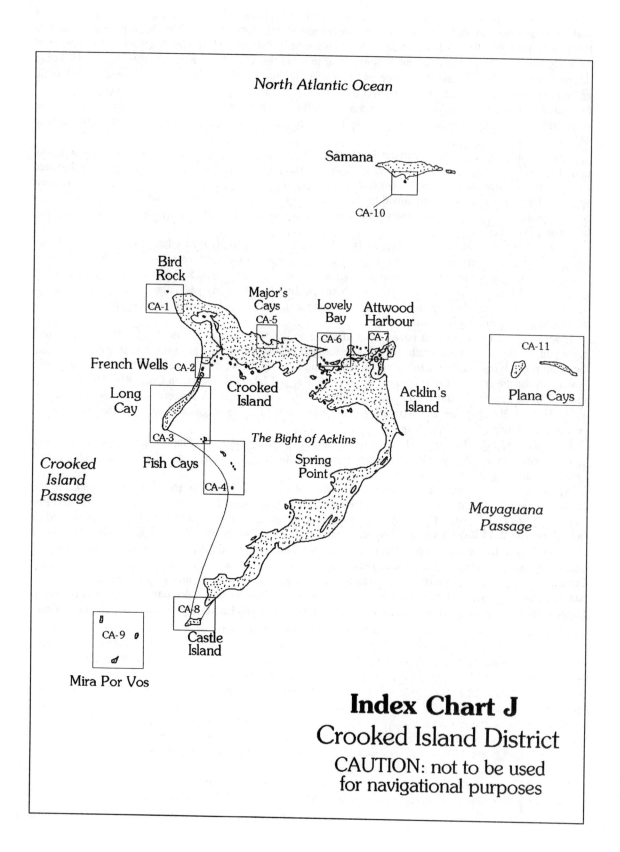

North Atlantic Ocean

Samana

CA-10

Bird
Rock

CA-1

Major's
Cays

CA-5

Lovely
Bay

CA-6

Attwood
Harbour

CA-7

French Wells   CA-2

CA-11

Plana Cays

Long
Cay

CA-3

Crooked
Island

Acklin's
Island

*Crooked
Island
Passage*

Fish Cays

CA-4

The Bight of Acklins

Spring
Point

*Mayaguana
Passage*

CA-8

CA-9

Castle
Island

Mira Por Vos

Index Chart J
Crooked Island District
CAUTION: not to be used
for navigational purposes

THE CROOKED ISLAND DISTRICT

Though all the others we had seen were beautiful, green and fertile, this was even more so. It has large and very green trees, and great lagoons, around which theses trees stand in marvelous groves. Here and there throughout the island the trees and plants are as green as Andalusia in April. The singing of small birds is so sweet that no one could ever wish to leave this place. Flocks of parrots darken the sun and there is a marvelous variety of large and small birds.

Christopher Columbus (Describing Crooked Island.)

The Crooked Island District is composed of three major islands, Crooked Island, Acklins Island, and Long Cay, which together encompass approximately 260 square miles of land lying inside twice that amount of shallow water. On some old charts the cays are called *The Fragrant Islands*. When Columbus visited the island group on October 21, 1492, the rich aroma of the Cascarilla bark caused him to think that he had discovered the Spice Islands of the Indies. Columbus was directed to Crooked Island by Lucayan Indians who spoke of an island called *Samoete* and of gold being found there. Finding no such island or gold, Columbus continued on toward Cuba. Columbus christened Crooked Island "Isabella" after his Queen and named Portland Harbour "Cabo Hermoso" or "Beautiful Cape."

The islands and cays that make up the Crooked/Acklins group are still untouched by large developments and retain much of their natural flavor. Acklins is a very peaceful, undisturbed, quiet island where the residents say you have to ". . . make your own sunshine," in other words you are on your own. The cays are home for flocks of pink flamingos, osprey, egrets, and herons and the shallow waters in some of the interior sections are excellent for bonefishing. The Bight of Acklins is home to some enormous conch.

In the 1800's the Crooked Island District was more populated than any other Bahamian Islands. Albert Town on Long Cay was a Port of Entry and was heavily visited by commercial vessels. At this time Crooked Island had a population of 3,000-4,000, Acklins boasted 3,000-4,000, and Long Cay was home to almost 2,000 people. When steam replaced sail power as the principal means of ship propulsion and the shipping routes changed accordingly, the huge population of the district quickly dissipated, almost overnight, to other economically healthier areas. Today's population of over 1,200 Crooked/Acklins Islanders is far less than the original inhabitants, the Lucayan Indians. Over 30 Lucayan Indian sites have been found on Acklins Island and over 10 on Crooked Island.

Spelunkers will note that Crooked Island is noted for its extensive cave system. The Ocean Den in the Bight of Acklins, more than a mile long, is one of the most impressive marine caves in The Bahamas. Divers may tour and study the cave system by making prior arrangements with The Bahamas Blue Holes Foundation, tel. (242) 373-4483.

APPROACHES TO THE CROOKED ISLAND DISTRICT

The Crooked Island District lies approximately 300 nautical miles southeast of Nassau. If approaching from the northwest the first sight you will likely see is the 112' tall white lighthouse on Bird Rock lying off the northwest tip of Crooked Island, or the high bluffs on the northern end of Crooked Island.

From Clarence Town, Long Island a course of 123° for 36.3 nautical miles will bring you to the waypoint north of Bird Rock. From Clarence Town, French Wells bears 134° at a distance of 44.1 miles. Bird Rock lies 26.9 miles from Little Harbour, Long Island on a course of 113°, while French Well bears 129° at a distance of 33.7 miles from Little Harbour. A course of 114° for 31.6 nautical miles will bring you from the southern tip of Long Island to French Wells while a course of 95° for 27.4 miles places you at the waypoint north of Bird Rock. The southern tip of Long Cay lies 32.6 nautical miles distant on a course of 132° from South End, Long Island. French Wells lies 84.0 nautical miles from Raccoon Cut in the Jumentos on a course of 264°. Bird Rock bears 158° at 53.2 miles from Port Nelson, Rum Cay. The waypoint north of the northwestern tip of Bird Rock is 36.6 miles from the Propeller Cay anchorage at Samana Cay on a course of 260° and 27.4 miles from Attwood Harbour on a course of 113°.

Castle Island bears 338° at a distance of 75.2 miles from Matthew Town, Great Inagua and 319° at a distance of 38.9 nautical miles from Hogsty Reef.

A special note for vessels transiting the waters between the Jumentos, Long Island, and the Crooked/Acklins District. At an approximate position at 22° 50' N, 74° 48' W, lies the center of the Diana

Bank. The approximately 100 square miles of Diana Bank lies west of the southern tip of Long Cay, south/southeast of the southern tip of Long Island, and west of Nurse Channel. Here is a shallow bank, 35'-600' deep, lying in the midst of much deeper water, 1800'-6000' deep. With a strong swell in any direction the seas on top of the bank can get very rough as the water is pushed up the sides of this underwater obstruction. If you are experiencing rough seas in your transit of this area, by all means avoid the area of Diana Bank. If the seas are calm, quite unusual hereabouts, try fishing on the bank.

CONCERNING THE CROOKED ISLAND AND MIRA POR VOS PASSAGES

The Crooked Island Passage is a deep and very busy thoroughfare that funnels vessels from the open Atlantic to the Ragged Islands, Cuba, and Hispaniola. Vessels wishing to transit Crooked Island Passage southward are advised to steer 188° from a position 10 miles due east of San Salvador. On this route you will pass Bird Rock abeam at 6½ nautical miles. As you come abeam of Windsor Light, 7 nautical miles off, alter your course to 169° for 26 nautical miles to pass between Mira Por Vos and Castle Island through the Mira Por Vos Passage. When you are abeam of Castle Island Light, at 4 nautical miles off, you can alter your course once again to 165° to pass west of Cabo Maisi, Cuba.

There is an area north and northwest of Bird Rock where the Antilles Current meets the currents flowing through the Crooked Island Passage. Natural factors such as the wind, the tide, and the moon act on this area with unpredictable results. The normally northwest flowing Antilles Current may sometimes not flow northwest, and sea conditions can get downright nasty compared to other waters just a few miles away. If you are in this general area and note an odd current, cross-sea, or unusually suspect rough waters you might be in this very active zone. Don't panic, you'll soon pass through it.

Use caution when transiting the Mira Por Vos Passage. The currents generally set in a southwesterly direction directly onto the Mira Pro Vos reefs. The prudent navigator should favor the steep-to Castle Island shore. If the currents should happen to be setting in a northeasterly direction (this is rare but it does happen) favor the Mira Por Vos side of the Passage.

CROOKED ISLAND

Crooked Island takes its name from the land's twisted shape over hills and cliffs and through creeks and lakes. Although its 92 square miles make it larger than New Providence it only has a population of around 650. The shores of Crooked Island offer three different cruising grounds. To the north lies the reef protected windward side of the island. There are few natural harbours on this route for vessels of any draft and reef entrances are few and far between. The leeward or western shore of Crooked Island is where most cruisers visit. The eastern shore edges the Bight Of Acklins and only shoal draft vessels and dinghies transit this area except for some vessels seeking a safe lee in westerly winds off Long Cay and those transiting eastward towards the western shore of Acklins Island. Let's begin our exploration of Crooked Island along its western shore, from Bird Rock to Long Cay.

BIRD ROCK TO LANDRAIL POINT

The first landfall most southbound vessels make is Bird Rock which lies just northwest of Portland Harbour and Pittstown. The reef encircled basin of Portland Harbour (Chart #CA-1) is a fair anchorage but there is a very uncomfortable surge which works its way through here at times. This anchorage is well protected in winds from south/southeast through south to west/southwest. Is has been said that Columbus' three ships anchored here in 1492. If you wish to enter Portland Harbour a GPS waypoint at 22° 50.40' N, 74° 21.90' W, will place you approximately ½ mile west of the entrance. The best water is approximately two-thirds of the distance from Pittstown to Bird Rock. Favor the Bird Rock side of the channel heading eastward. Once inside turn to starboard and anchor wherever your draft will allow making sure to avoid the scattered reefs. Never attempt this entry at night or in poor visibility.

A better anchorage for today's skipper lies just south at Pittstown or 2½ miles further south at Landrail Point in sand and grass The best anchorage, and with the easiest access, is about halfway down the long beach that lies just south of Pittstown. This is a lee side anchorage only and skippers should beware that they must move in the event of a frontal passage when the wind comes around to south of east. A GPS

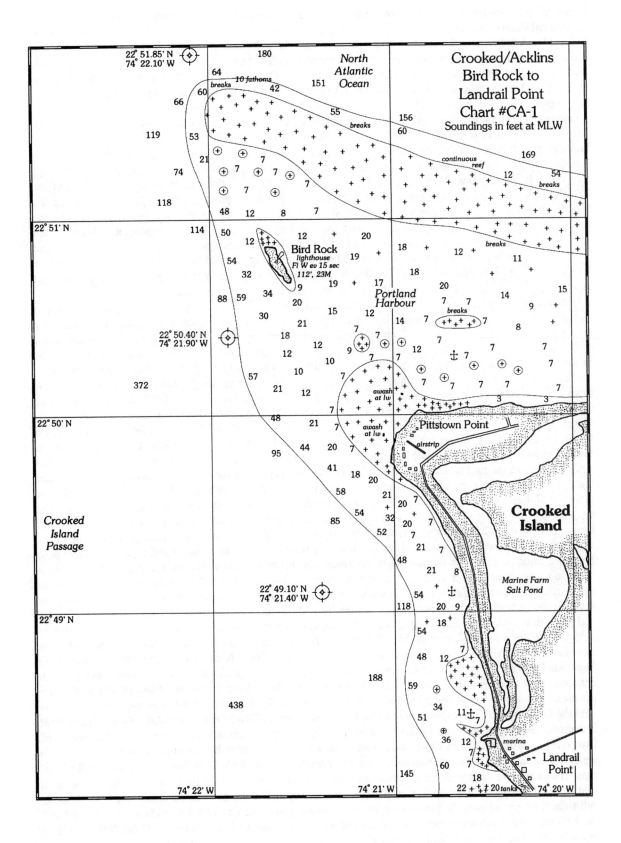

22° 51.85' N
74° 22.10' W

180

*North
Atlantic
Ocean*

**Crooked/Acklins
Bird Rock to
Landrail Point
Chart #CA-1**
Soundings in feet at MLW

64

breaks

10 fathoms

60

42

151

66

55

156
60

119

53

breaks

169

74

21

continuous reef

54

7

12

breaks

118

48

12

8

7

22° 51' N

114

50

12

12

20

18

12

breaks

11

54

Bird Rock
*lighthouse
Fl W ev 15 sec
112', 23M*

19

18

32

19

19

17

20

14

15

88

59

34

9

*Portland
Harbour*

7

9

30

20

15

12

14

breaks

8

21

18

12

10

14

7

22° 50.40' N
74° 21.90' W

12

9

12

57

10

7

7

7

7

372

21

12

*awash
at lw*

3

3

22° 50' N

48

21

7

*awash
at lw*

Pittstown Point

95

44

20

7

airstrip

41

18

20

**Crooked
Island**

58

21

20

7

*Crooked
Island
Passage*

85

54

32

20

7

52

21

7

48

21

8

*Marine Farm
Salt Pond*

22° 49.10' N
74° 21.40' W

54

20

9

118

22° 49' N

18

54

48

12

7

188

59

438

34

11

7

51

36

12

marina

145

60

7

**Landrail
Point**

18

22

20 *tanks*

74° 22' W

74° 21' W

74° 20' W

waypoint at 22° 49.10' N, 74° 21.40' W, will place you approximately ½ mile west of the beach just north of Landrail Point

Bird Rock is home to the bright white lighthouse simply known as Bird Rock Light. Standing 112' tall and constructed of native limestone mined just behind Gun Bluff on the northern shore of Crooked Island, Bird Rock Light may appear to be a sailboat from far off. The light flashes white every 15 seconds and is visible for 23 nautical miles. When I last visited the area in March of 1997 the light was not working and, as you probably know quite well by now, it may be a while before it is repaired.

Pittstown is home to a large group of primarily Canadian snow birds and pilots as there is a large airstrip nearby. The first Post Office in The Bahamas was built here when William Pitt was Prime Minister of England and the remains of its walls are now part of the Pittstown Landings which offers very nice accommodations with 12 rooms available. For more information contact *Pittstown* on VHF ch. 16. During the era of the Napoleonic Wars this Post Office served to deliver mail to the West India Squadron of the British Fleet. This area was once surrounded by some 40 cotton plantations of 3,000 acres during the Loyalist years of 1783-1835 when some 1,200 slaves worked the local land. Gun Bluff, just beyond the hotel at Pittstown, was once a pirate's lookout and local residents have found cannon thereabouts which gave the area its name. These guns served to protect the plantations against the raids by privateers and pirates. The northern entrance to the Crooked Island Passage was guarded by a fort here called The Marine Farm. The U.S. Privateer *Saucy Jack* raided Marine Farm during the War Of 1812. Later she attacked again only to be driven off by newer and larger guns brought down from Nassau.

Between the northern shore of Crooked Island, from Gun Bluff westward to Pittstown, and then south to Landrail Point, there is a large inland lake that serves little or no current purpose. Plans are being hotly discussed to dredge a channel to it from the northern shore just west of Gun Bluff, and then another south of Pittstown to flush out all the debris, thus creating a deep water inland lake with good access. This would make a large marina a real possibility as well as offering good hurricane protection for boats and boaters.

Landrail Point sells no alcohol or tobacco as most of the residents are Seventh Day Adventists. The town is the commercial center of Crooked Island and has the usual Government Dock where the mailboat calls once a week, a church, a food store, a gas station, and a restaurant. Earl Scavella's gas station sells diesel, gas, and kerosene as well as a few basic food items. For fuel call *Early Bird* on the VHF. Except for Mayaguana, this is the last fuel stop before the Turks and Caicos if you are headed southeast. If you are headed south you can find fuel at Matthew Town, Great Inagua. If you wish to tie up at the fuel dock that sits just south of the fuel tanks, not a good idea as it is very rusty and dangerous, you should med-moor and back in towards it. Kenneth Scavella will pass a long hose out to your boat by rope so you can fill your tanks. Another option is to dinghy into the small marina where Kenneth can bring the truck to you. The very narrow entrance to the marina lies about ¼ mile north of the fuel tanks and winds back into the small basin. A boat up to 25' long can maneuver its way in here with 4' at low water inside and 3' at the bar at the entrance. The walls are rock and fenders are required. If you wish to tie up overnight call *Early Bird* for more information. The marina offers no amenities, no power, no cable, no running water, simply a place to tie up to the land if needed. For obvious reasons don't ask Kenneth to bring the fuel truck over to the marina for 10 or 15 gallons, instead walk the few yards to the gas station and jerry can it back to your boat. It won't be long and someone will happen by and be glad to give you and your jerry jugs of water and gas a ride back to the marina or beach. The gas station has a faucet for well water, some may say it is salty but we use it for washing and find it excellent. The price is right also, free. Just east of the fuel tanks is a phone booth sitting about 200 yards south of the gas station. Next to the gas station is *Scavella's Supermarket* for your grocery needs. Not as well stocked as George Town or Long Island, but you can certainly get a few basics and frozen meats (best to wait until the day after the mailboat, the *Lady Matilda*, arrives). You can dine out nearby at *Gibson's Lunch Room* which sits under the huge sapodilla tree along with the Gibson house, it sits just south of the fuel dock. Marina Gibson runs the place and serves excellent Bahamian dishes and delicious home-baked bread in an "at home" atmosphere. You haven't experienced Crooked Island if you haven't met Marina and had a meal with her at her Lunch Room. Be sure to call ahead if you intend to dine out, Marina answers to *Lunch Room* or *BASRA* as she and her son are the local reps. You can have your mail sent to you care of Gibson's but expect a wait of 3-4 weeks. Have your mail sent C/O Gibson's Lunch Room, Landrail Point, Crooked Island, Bahamas. You can also place a telephone call from the *Lunch Room*. If you need a diesel mechanic you can contact Timothy Thompson, *Cold Front* on the VHF, and if you are in need of an outboard mechanic contact Clinton Scavella whose VHF handle is *Snow White*. There is a clinic at Landrail Point.

The Crooked Island/Acklins Island area is fast becoming a prime bonefishing destination. For an excellent diving, tarpon fishing, and bonefishing guide contact Junior McKinney, *Ocean View* on VHF ch. 16 or his brother Elton McKinney, *Blue Thunder* on the VHF. If deep sea fishing interests you more, you can contact Robbie Gibson, *Thunderbird* on the VHF to help you with your deep sea angling for dolphin, wahoo, tuna, and marlin. Flyfishing Charters operates a 47' Catamaran in the Bight of Acklins where up to three couples can stay for a week or two and enjoy bonefishing or tarpon fishing on a daily basis. The anglers will stay aboard the luxurious Catamaran *Blue Lagoon* for their stay. For more information call 410-280-0859 in the United States.

History buffs will want to visit the Hope Great House, the centerpiece of the ruins of an old plantation which are now protected by the Bahamas National Trust.

Just about a half mile south of Landrail Point are some small bluffs which are deeply undercut. These are full of small cave-like openings for diving and exploration. Never bring the big boat in here, there are far too many shallow reefs. When heading south along the shore of Crooked Island south of Landrail Point give the land a berth of at least a mile to avoid the shallow reefs and sandbars which lie well to the west in places.

FRENCH WELLS

Off the southern tip of Crooked Island, between Crooked Island and Long Cay, is French Wells, obviously named for its fresh water supply. Here you will find the ruins of an old fortification including an old cannon. A lovely sight, if you are fortunate, is to wake up and see a flock of thirty or more pink flamingos wading in the shallows on the north side of the anchorage.

A GPS waypoint at 22° 41.40' N, 74° 18.90' W, will place you approximately 1 nautical mile west of the entrance to the anchorage at French Wells as shown on Chart #CA-2. This entrance should only be attempted in good visibility, never at night, and never with a heavy following sea. If you are caught in strong westerly conditions do not attempt to enter French Wells as any small mistake may put you up on a shallow bank or rocks. In strong westerlies it is better to head around the southern end of Long Cay and anchor in the calm lee off its eastern shore to await better conditions.

From the waypoint steer towards the northern tip of Goat Cay which lies just south of the anchorage at French Wells (bear in mind that there is a very strong current that flows in and out of this cut so be prepared for it). To port you will see a shallow sandbar that looks very yellow, almost white. East of this sandbar is a narrow channel of slightly deeper and bluer water that arcs around north and northeastward towards the southern shore of Crooked Island. Here you will also see a brown bar that lies just south of the deeper water and arcs in the same direction. Turn to port after you pass the shallow sandbar and use the brown bar as a guide keeping it to starboard, the deeper water lies just along its northern side although you can steer directly on top of the brown (grassy) bar. Follow the darker water and the curve of the bar around until you are in the anchorage area.

The western end of the anchorage area is a bit rocky, you will find much better holding at the eastern end of the anchorage, near or east of the bend as shown on Chart #CA-2 As I have mentioned, there is a very strong current through here so use two anchors in a Bahamian moor. The current is so strong (2½-3½ knots or more) that even in winds of 25-30 knots you may be turned beam to or even stern to the wind. Even in strong winds from the east the banks offer little protection and you can get some small wind-blown seas in here, nothing dangerous as long as your anchors are set well, though they can be uncomfortable. During any period of strong winds you will spend approximately 12 hours out of every 24 on an outgoing tide. This means that when the winds opposed the tidal flow you may find yourself sailing around and around, spinning around your anchor and tangling your lines. Linton Rigg in his *Cruising the Bahamas*, the first cruising guide of its kind to The Bahamas, calls French Wells "a perfect ocean locked harbour." As nasty and miserable as all this may sound, this is the best protection you will find in all around conditions unless you have a shallow draft vessel and can gunkhole your way up the small creeks that abound in the Crooked/Acklins area. Keep an eye on your anchor lines and keep them from fouling each other and don't cuss too much. This is a very beautiful anchorage during periods of calm to moderate winds. Some locals prefer Portland Harbour for frontal passages. I consider Portland Harbour unacceptable in anything north of west, it is wide open to the northwest through northeast except for the protection that the reefs provide which is downright little.

There is a small creek that winds its way through the mangroves along the western shore of Crooked Island from the anchorage at French Wells northward. This is an excellent dinghy trip and shallow draft

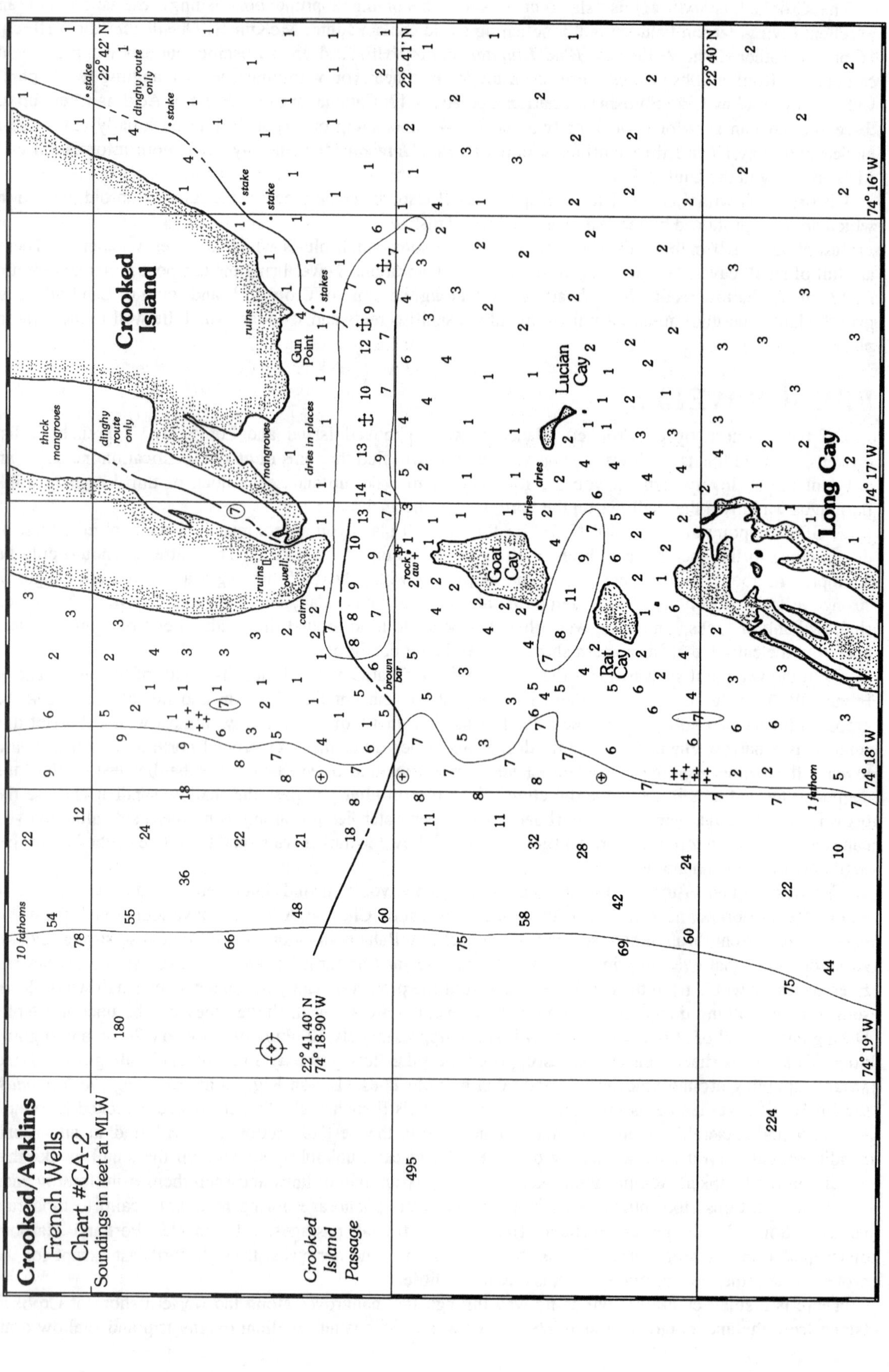

Crooked/Acklins
French Wells
Chart #CA-2
Soundings in feet at MLW

Crooked Island

Gun Point

ruins

thick mangroves

dinghy route only

mangroves

dries in places

ruins

swell

cairn

brown bar

rock
aw

Goat Cay

Rat Cay

Lucian Cay

dries

dries

Long Cay

dinghy route only

stake

stakes

Crooked Island Passage

10 fathoms

1 fathom

22° 42' N

22° 41' N

22° 40' N

74° 16' W

74° 17' W

74° 18' W

74° 19' W

22° 41.40' N
74° 18.90' W

vessels could have a field day if they could work their way up into the waters of Turtle Sound. There are some small trees used as marker stakes to lead you up the creek from French Wells. The water taxi uses this creek on Tuesdays and Saturdays to ferry passengers between Albert Town to Church Grove Landing on the days the Bahamasair plane lands at the airstrip. If you are so inclined, you can follow the taxi and acquaint yourself with the route if you are having trouble finding it. This creek leads up past Church Grove Landing where you can get ashore and hoof it over about 2 miles to a road that leads from Landrail eastward through Church Grove where you'll find the *Tiger Bar*. The terrain is rough on your shoes, it's much easier to dinghy up to Landrail on a good day and try to hitch a ride. Further up the creek you will find Turtle Sound, a gunkholer's delight. Divers will want to investigate the blue holes and fishermen will want to tangle with the large tarpon that inhabit these shallow waters. Even in French Wells you may see tarpon frolicking about the anchorage.

On the southwest tip of Crooked Island as shown on Chart #CA-2 is a small cairn. If you follow the sandy trail that leads inland for about 100 yards you will come to two more cairns with a stone arrow in the ground pointing in the direction of a fresh water well about 50 yards away. The well has plenty of fresh water that, while it may not be potable, it certainly is suitable for washing. There is even a clothes line that someone has strung up in the trees surrounding it. If you wash your laundry or dishes here take care not to let soapy water re-enter the well. If you walk, or dinghy, northward along the beach past the cairn you will discover what is one of my absolute favorite beaches in all The Bahamas. Once the large, flat, slabs of limestone run out, you will find a beautiful, curving, white sand beach stretching northward for a couple of miles. The few patches of casaurinas dotting the shore offer shade while the fine sandy bottom makes for excellent swimming. This is as pretty a beach as you could expect to find in the islands, possibly all it needs to be perfect would be a few palm trees, but not being a perfect world, it's certainly close enough for this beach bum.

Just inside the entrance to French Wells on northern side is a narrow, mangrove lined creek that you can follow northwards into the interior of Crooked Island for a couple of miles. The creek is over 6' deep in places and can get quite narrow. A wonderful place to explore, you will find plenty of sealife, and bugs so bring some repellent on warm, windless days.

LONG CAY

Long Cay was once known as Fortune Island and the name fit it very well indeed as in the early years of its history is was a rendezvous for the windward wreckers. Albert Town was a Port of Entry and the island's most prosperous settlement in the heyday of the early 1800's before the coming of steam power. Long Cay served as a clearing house for sailing ships in those days. The water is very deep and the ships could just anchor right off shore in the lee of the island. The commercial shipping activity created a very healthy economy and the town had street lights for the carriages of its residents. Long Cay itself even had a railway system to assist in moving shipments. Great steamers of the Hamburg-American line stopped at Albert Town to engage laborers to help with their cargoes in South American ports.

The island became a ghost town of sorts almost overnight when steam power became the prevalent means of propulsion and the population of almost 2,000 in the mid-1800's is now less than 30 today. The eastern part of Long Cay is a sanctuary for pink flamingos which can also be seen at French Wells on the southern tip of Crooked Island. Long Cay is also host to a fresh water pond, one of the few in The Bahamas.

Heading south from French Wells keep at least 1½ miles off Long Cay to avoid the shallows and reefs lying just to the west of the land as shown on Chart #CA-3. These shallows stretch out almost a mile in places and reach as far south as two miles south of Albert Town. A GPS waypoint at 22° 36.35' N, 74° 21.50' W will place you approximately ½ mile northwest of Albert Town. Albert Town sits amid a long grove of palm trees easily seen from offshore. Another landmark is the prominent Fortune Hill, easily seen from over 10 miles away. I wish I could brag about the anchorage off Albert Town and tell you how safe it is but it would be a lie. The waters off Albert Town are strewn with shallow reefs and heads that stretch westward for over ¼ mile. If you wish to anchor off Albert Town do it well offshore and dinghy in. Better yet, anchor off the eastern shore and walk across or dinghy down from French Wells. There is almost always a surge off Albert Town.

As you approach Albert Town there is a small concrete wharf you can tie up to. (Use extreme caution here), and walk up the path to the settlement. The first thing you will notice is the old cemetery on the hill overlooking the Crooked Island Passage. There is a good freshwater well just up the road that you are

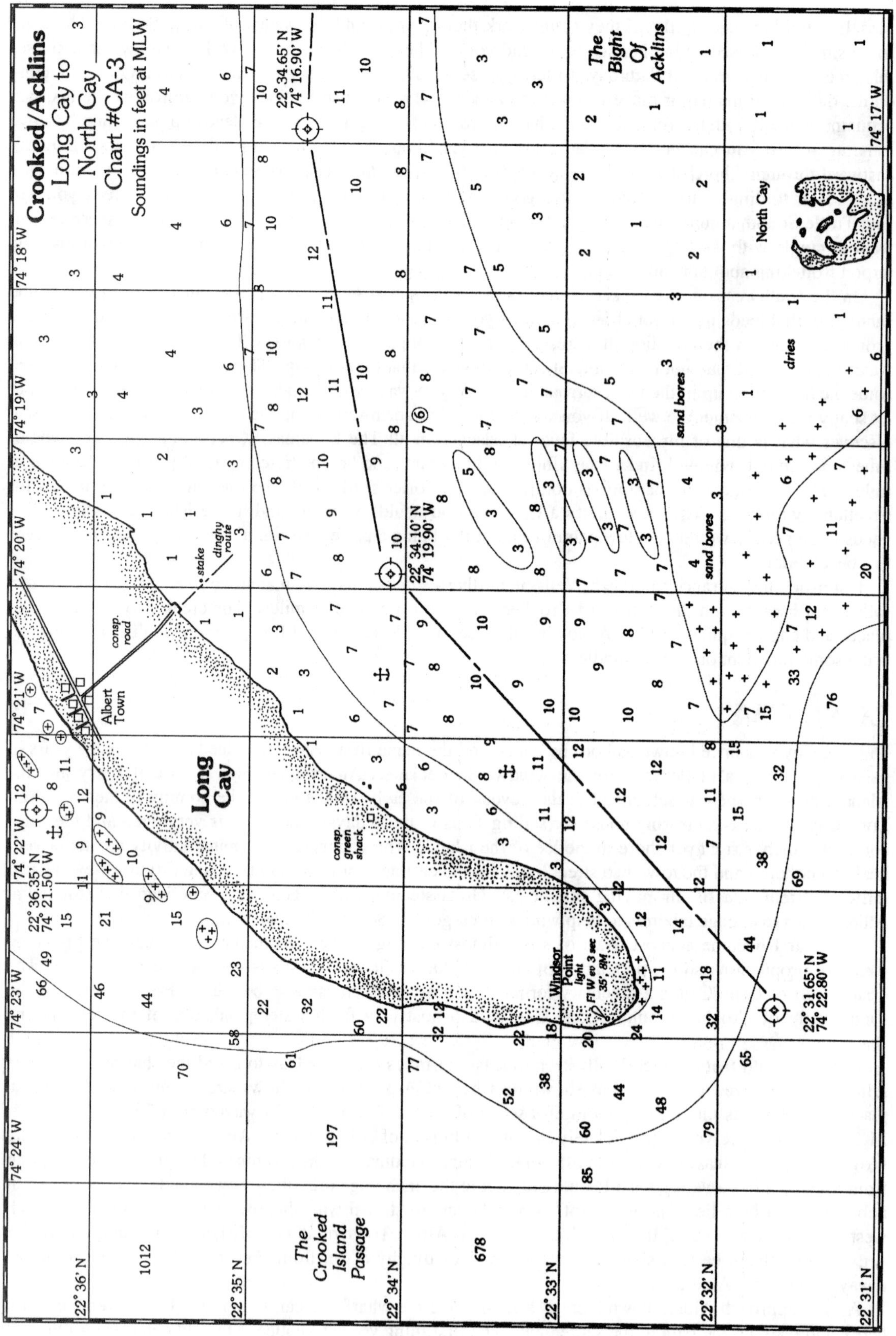

Crooked/Acklins
Long Cay to North Cay
Chart #CA-3
Soundings in feet at MLW
Long Cay
Albert Town
consp. road
stake
dinghy route
consp. green shack
Windsor Point
light
Fl W ev 3 sec 35' 8M
The Crooked Island Passage
The Bight Of Acklins
North Cay
sand bores
dries
22° 36.35' N 74° 21.50' W
22° 34.65' N 74° 16.90' W
22° 34.10' N 74° 19.90 W
22° 31.65' N 74° 22.80' W
74° 17' W
74° 18' W
74° 19' W
74° 20' W
74° 21' W
74° 22' W
74° 23' W
74° 24' W
22° 31' N
22° 32' N
22° 33' N
22° 34' N
22° 35' N
22° 36' N

welcome to use. The only store is Stephen Rose's *Ready Money Store* just up from the dock a ways. Stephen is a former mailboat owner and Captain and is an excellent source of information about these waters. At his store you will find a limited selection of supplies but you can purchase beer, unavailable at Landrail Point. The Batelco office is open every day from 9:00 A.M. to 5:00 P.M. There is a small fish processing plant here that ships directly to Nassau on the mailboat.

If you are headed southward from Albert Town the reefs stop about two miles south of Albert Town. From there southward the coast is steep sided, about 30-40' high, with many undercuts and small cave holes ideal for dinghy exploration. On the southern point of Long Cay at Windsor Point is Long Cay Light which flashes white every 3 seconds, is 35' high, and is visible for 8 miles. If you are intending to round the southern tip of Long Cay to anchor off its eastern shore give Windsor Point a wide berth, at least ½ mile as there is a shallow, reef strewn area just off its southern tip.

A very good anchorage in westerly conditions, or even in light prevailing winds, is off the eastern shore of Long Cay. There is a lot of current here so be sure to set your anchors well. Large conch abound and you may even see some of the pink flamingos that inhabit the eastern shore of Long Cay. A GPS waypoint at 22° 31.65' N, 74° 22.80' W, places you approximately ¾ mile south of Windsor Point and in a position to head northeast along the eastern shore of Long Cay. Parallel the eastern shore of Long Cay and anchor wherever your draft and the sea conditions allow. In the vicinity of a small green shack on shore you will see three small islands. These are man-made in the sense that they are nothing more than large piles of conch shells with mangroves now growing out of them. North of the conch shell islands you will see a very conspicuous road that cuts over the ridge and leads down to a tiny dock with a very shallow small boat channel marked by a stake. You can tie your dinghy up here and hike the road across to Albert Town. On the way you will pass the ruins of Douglas Town, the old railroad, and the ruins of the old Catholic Church atop a hill to the south.

THE FISH CAYS

Southeast of Long Cay lies a string of small islands called the Fish Cays as shown on Chart #CA-4. The waters to their east are shallow with many sand bores and are virtually impassable except for small boats. Some of the areas between the cays, east of the cays, and to seaward of the cays to the one fathom line dry at low water. These shallow waters are teeming with sea fans and you may even find some conch. Along the western shores of these cays the drop off offers excellent trolling and diving opportunities for the adventure loving SCUBA diver. There are numerous shallow water reefs with abundant marine life waiting to become your dinner. Just southeast of Long Cay lies North Cay with its large reef/sandbar off its northwest tip. Give it a wide berth.

South of North Cay, the larger Fish Cay is home to a large population of small iguanas. One would think that the Guana Cays (which actually does have a small colony of iguanas), which lie just to the south of Fish Cay, would be their home instead. Rather, the better fishing is around the Guana Cays. Doesn't quite make sense does it? Perhaps someone misnamed the cays?

The only viable anchorage in the area lies between Fish Cay and the Guana Cays in 8'-12' of water as shown on Chart #CA-4. A GPS waypoint at 22° 28.00' N, 74° 16.20' W, will place you ¼ mile southwest of the entrance to the dark blue channel that leads to the anchorage. From this position you can head generally northeast-east/northeast across a bar with 7' at low water. Once past the bar, and the sea fans that inhabit it, you will find the depths getting progressively deeper to about 12' between the cays. This is not a good spot in southerly to northwesterly winds and there's a lot of current here, so use two anchors. Fish Cay's western shore has an absolutely gorgeous beach, good for beachcombing, sunbathing, swimming, or whatever other recreational diversions you can think of.

The waters south of Fish Cay, between Guana Cays and South Cay are very shallow and strewn with sand bores as are the waters to the east of these cays. There is little here for the cruising vessel but plenty for dinghy exploration, lots of sea fans, conch, and marine life.

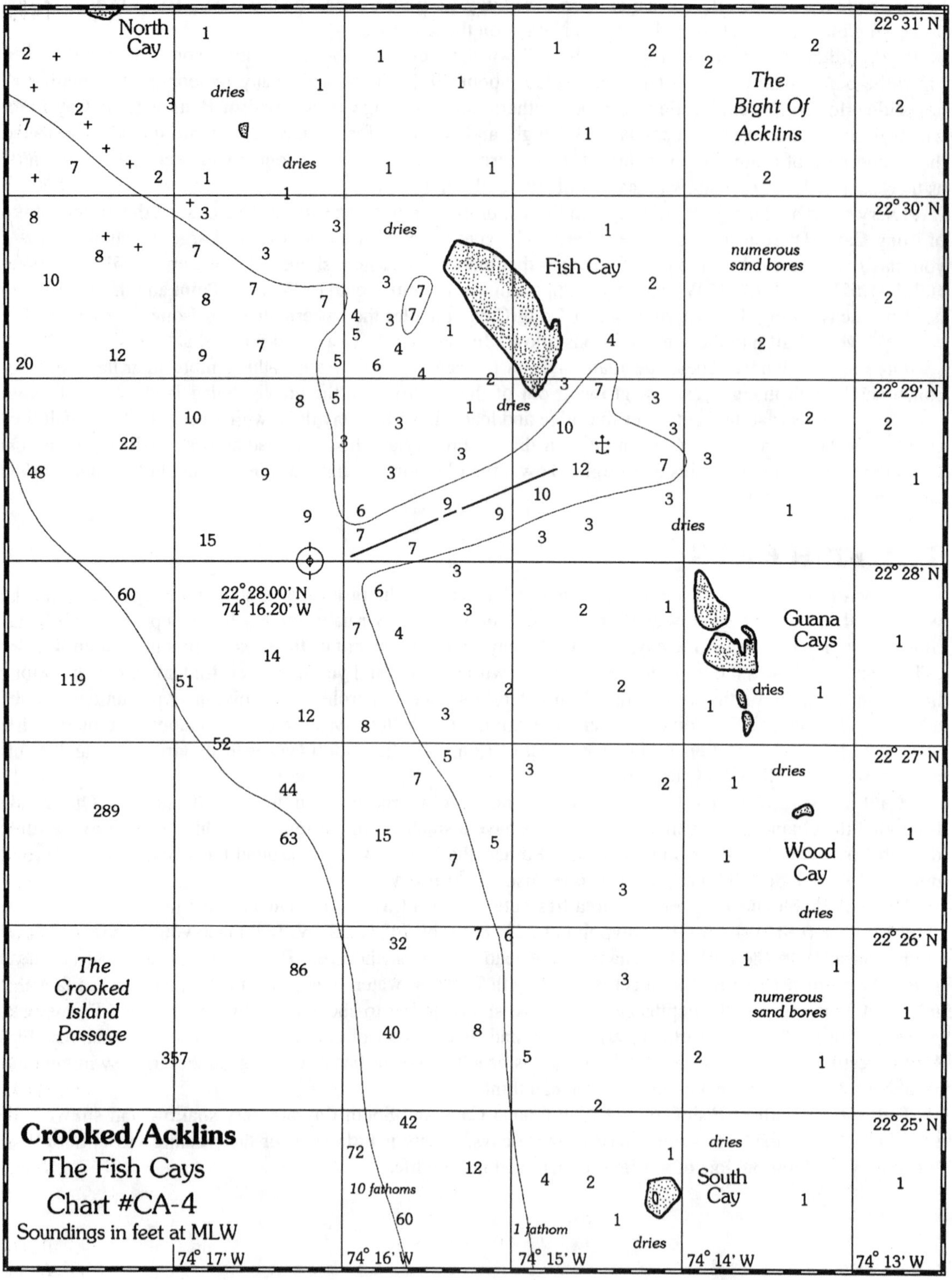

North Cay

dries

dries

dries

The Bight Of Acklins

Fish Cay

numerous sand bores

dries

dries

22° 28.00' N
74° 16.20' W

Guana Cays

dries

Wood Cay

dries

The Crooked Island Passage

numerous sand bores

Crooked/Acklins
The Fish Cays
Chart #CA-4
Soundings in feet at MLW

South Cay

dries

dries

10 fathoms

1 fathom

22° 31' N
22° 30' N
22° 29' N
22° 28' N
22° 27' N
22° 26' N
22° 25' N

74° 17' W
74° 16' W
74° 15' W
74° 14' W
74° 13' W

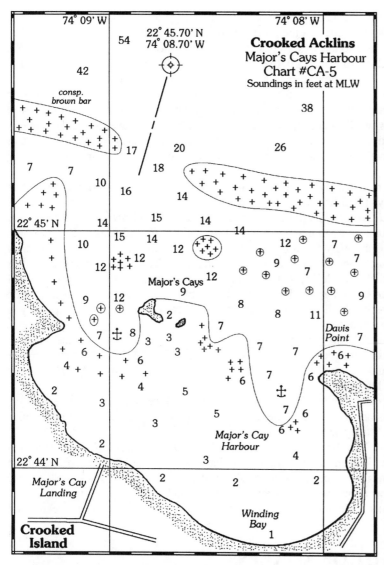

74° 09' W
22° 45.70' N
74° 08.70' W
54
42
consp. brown bar
Crooked Acklins
Major's Cays Harbour
Chart #CA-5
Soundings in feet at MLW
74° 08' W
38
17
20
26
7   7
18
10
16
14
22° 45' N   14
15
14
14
15   14
12
14
12   12
9
12
7   7
Major's Cays   12
9
12
9
12
8
8
11
Davis Point   7
10
12
7   8   3   3
3
7
6   6
4
5
2
3
5
3
Major's Cay Harbour
2
22° 44' N   3
4
Major's Cay Landing
2   2   2
Crooked Island
Winding Bay
1

THE NORTHERN SHORE OF CROOKED ISLAND

Travel close in along the northern shore of Crooked Island should only be attempted in good light and settled weather due to the absence of good protection and the abundance of shallow offshore reefs stretching eastward for over 25 miles with only an occasional break. There are only three anchorages along this route that I can in all honesty recommend and all should only be considered when seeking relief from the prevailing northeast to southeast winds. The north shore of Crooked Island and Acklins is no place to be caught in a fierce frontal passage if it can be avoided. The breaks in the reef are hard to find in poor to fair visibility and heavy seas. Use extreme caution if you plan to enter any of the harbours along the northern shore.

Vessels heading east along the northern shore of Crooked Island must first round Bird Rock and the reef just to its north. A GPS waypoint at 22° 51.85' N, 74° 22.10' W, will place you approximately ¼ mile north of the northwest tip of this reef. From this position, or preferably north of this position, you can begin to head east avoiding the reef that bears away east/southeast along the shore of Crooked Island.

Heading eastward along the northern shore some seven miles from Gun Bluff is Moss Town. Moss Town is accessible only by small boat from Attwood Creek, a shallow mangrove lined tidal creek. The town is a cluster of small houses decorated with yellow elder, the Bahamian National Flower. From the top of the hill in Moss Town you can gaze upon the brilliant blue-green waters of Turtle Sound, accessible from the southern part of Crooked Island at French Wells. Years ago fisherman could navigate the maze of twisting shallow mangrove creeks from Turtle Sound to gain access to Moss Town from various landing stations. The only station that is still in use is "#1" which connects with Cabbage Hill via a long road. Turtle Sound is a very attractive small boat anchorage with tall cliffs, mangrove lined waterways, and blooming cactus ashore. Cabbage Hill is the most populous of Crooked Island's settlements. There you will find the *Crooked Island Beach Inn* with 6 rooms available, also the *T & S Guest House*, two churches, the *One-Stop Shopping Center*, an auto repair shop, a barber shop, and a beauty salon. There are three bars including the *Bloom of the Valley Bar and Night Club* which is actually located in Johnny Hill.

Farther east is Colonel Hill, the capital of the Crooked Island District. At the top of the hill you will see the Commissioner's home and just below it the small Government complex consisting of a Post Office, Commissioner's Office, Police Station, Government Clinic, National Insurance Office, the central high school, and several teacher's residences. Here you will find *Sunny Lea*, a restaurant, guest house, bakery, and store all in one and run by Mrs. Eunice Deleveaux. The entrance to the unnamed harbour at Colonel

Hill is through a small reef passage northeast of McKay's Bluff. I cannot recommend this passage. The reef passage itself is not difficult bearing 205° on the conspicuous palm trees standing on McKay's Hill. The problem begins when you turn back to the west to pass McKay's Bluff to anchor in its lee. You must negotiate a series of reefs with small, narrow breaks between them. It is possible to pass over them with 6' at low water but you must certainly know how to read the water as you will be passing over reef while trying to dodge many shallower heads. Shallow draft vessels should have no problems. If you do plan to anchor west of McKay's Bluff, once you round the point you will find an uninhabited anchorage with shelter from east through south to west. On the southwest section of the bluff is a cave, only accessible by small boat, with a wide mouth and a series of natural skylights inside. Just outside the cave is a large lignum vitae tree covered with bromeliads. West of Colonel Hill is the airstrip with Bahamasair flights on Tuesdays and Saturdays.

Just past Colonel Hill along the northern shore you will come to Major's Cay with its impressive white church sitting high on a hill. Here you will find the *Peace and Plenty Bar* and the huge (as big as a garage by American standards) *South Land Grocery*, the largest store on the island. The bright orange *Peace and Plenty Bar* is actually someone's home and you must go around back for a drink and a chat. Entrance into Major's Cay Harbour as shown on Chart #CA-5 is relatively easy. The anchorage has 7'-12' over a sandy bottom and the town lies approximately one mile inland down a sandy path. The primary landmark in this area is the prominent wedge-shaped cliff at McKay's Bluff which lies approximately 12 miles southeast of Bird Rock. From this landmark head east for approximately 2 miles until the next break in the reef lines up with the two small cays bearing south. A GPS waypoint at 22° 45.70' N, 74° 08.70' W, will place you approximately ¼ mile north of the entrance. Use caution when entering this and any harbour entrance along the north side of Crooked Island. This particular cut is wide, deep, and easily seen. Steer roughly south/southwest and keep an eye out for the reefs on either side. The best anchorage is in about 7'-12' over a sandy bottom between the point and the small cays. Another option is to anchor east of Major's Cays in the lee of Davis Point in 7' at mean low water.

The small towns west of Major's Cay, Bullets Hill, Thompson Hill and True Blue were at one time the largest communities on Crooked Island. At one time there were more people in these three communities than the entire population (1200+) of today's Crooked Island.

There is an anchorage shown in *The Yachtsman's Guide to The Bahamas* just off True Blue and Brown's but I cannot recommend it. The anchorage, although it has good holding, offers no protection in the prevailing east to southeast winds and there is nothing ashore of interest. Brown's is deserted, only ruins on the shore today, and the waters off the beach are strewn with small, shallow patch reefs to avoid. Much better anchorages are at Major's Cay and Attwood Harbour which is discussed in the section on Acklins Island.

CROSSING THE BIGHT OF ACKLINS

Skippers wishing to cross the Bight of Acklins eastward towards the western shore of Acklins Island must do so from the eastern shore of Long Cay (unless you draw less than 4', then you can pass northwards along the western shore of Acklins from Castle Island). North of the conch shell islands mentioned in the previous section on Long Cay, as shown on Chart #CA-3, you will see a very conspicuous road that cuts over the ridge. The road leads down to a tiny dock with a very shallow small boat channel marked by a stake leading to it. The mailboat puts this road astern and steers 90° to head to Acklins Island. Skippers wishing to head across the bight of Acklins may use the following waypoints as shown on Chart #CA-3. From the GPS waypoint south of Windsor Point head to a waypoint at 22° 34.10' N, 74° 19.90' W. From this position head to a waypoint at 22° 34.65' N, 74° 16.90' W. From this position head generally east (approximately 92°-98°) with the road astern to a waypoint at 22° 34.00' N, 74° 09.90' W. From this position you can take up a course of approximately 155° to a waypoint at 22° 27.00' W, 74° 07.00' W, which places you in Pompey Bay, approximately ¼ mile west of Camel Point and southwest of Spring Point. From here eyeball your way in to anchor wherever your draft allows heading northeast to Spring Point or just off the settlement of Delectable Bay in Pompey Bay.

The western shore of Acklin's Island has places where the water is 8' deep and more but the further south you travel, the shallower the water gets. You were once able to travel southward along the western shore of Acklin's with a 6' draft all the way to Castle Island and points south. I believe those days may be over. I tried that passage with my 5' draft and bumped so many times I gave up and turned around. A local dive boat operator told me he has taken his 5½' draft into this area only to meet the same fate and he has been operating in these waters for years. This area definitely needs more exploration and I intend to have it fully sounded for a future edition of this guide. My sincerest apologies if I have failed you and caused you any inconvenience.

ACKLINS ISLAND

Acklins Island, the largest of the Crooked Island District, is one of the most beautiful islands in The Bahamas but is rarely visited by cruising yachtsmen due to a lack of sophisticated docking facilities. If you do not require the latest in marina accommodations then you will truly enjoy the beauty that Acklins Island has to offer. The cay was once covered in hardwoods such as lignum vitae, braziletto, and ebony. The entire eastern shore of Acklins Island is a beachcomber's paradise due to the prevailing winds and currents, however the only access to Acklins Island is by way of the Bight Of Acklins, from the west.

A word of warning about the waters in the Bight of Acklins. In the northern areas of the Bight of Acklins, strong northerly winds tends to push all the water out of the area to the extent that you may have a low tide for a day or two in the upper reaches of the Bight, especially in Turtle Sound. The tides along the northwestern shore of Acklins Island around Spring Point lag the tides at Nassau by about 3 hours while at Jamaica Cay they are 1 hour and 15 minutes behind Nassau.

Along the northern shore of Acklins Island you will find anchorages at Lovely Bay and at Attwood Harbour. Lovely Bay offers a good anchorage in prevailing winds as well as a good lee in winds from west to north.

Photo by Kelly Becker

Bird Rock Light, Crooked/Acklins.

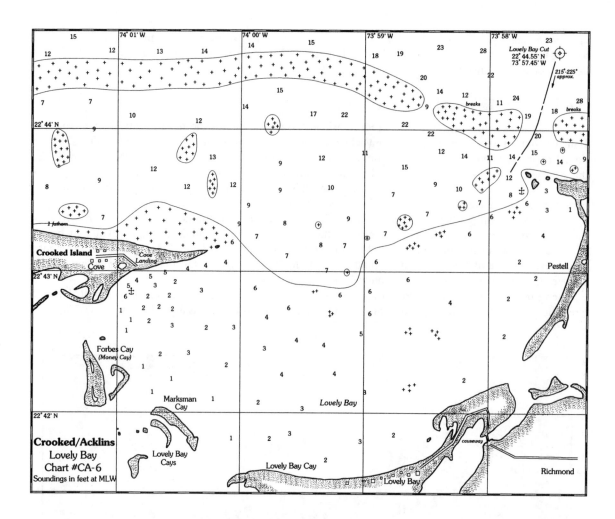

Lovely Bay is just that—lovely. There is a wide, deep break in the reef just north of the three rocks lying northeast of the Lovely Bay settlement. A GPS waypoint at 22° 44.50' N, 73° 57.50' W, will place you approximately ½ mile northeast of this break as shown on Chart #CA-6. Eyeball the opening and once you have located it, steer approximately 225° through the break in the reef and avoid the small patch reefs that lie on the inside of the fringing reef. If you seek shelter from northeast to east winds you can anchor just south of the three rocks just to port. If you proceed to Lovely Bay steer clear of the patch reefs that dot the area. If you have a draft of 5' or less and seek shelter from a front head west across the bay and work your way over the shallows south of Cove Point to anchor in the lee of Cove Landing in pockets of water from 5'-6' deep at MLW. Here you will have protection from west to north. Once the wind goes northeast you will probably want to head east to anchor under the three rocks. If you anchor here try not to block the ferry that shuttles between the landing and Lovely Bay. In settled weather you can anchor off the settlement of Lovely Bay as close in as your draft allows, the water shallows quite a way out from the shore. Just a few paces to the east of the dock lies the center of town where you will find a small store and a bar which also is the phone station.

Between Cove Landing and Lovely Bay is the entrance to the Bight Of Acklins called *The Going Through*. Here shallow draft vessels, less than 3' draft, will have a field day as they try to work their way through the maze of creeks and tidal passages. A hint—be sure to keep a mile away from the mangroves. Deeper inside, are some excellent hurricane holes for shallow draft vessels but searching for them will take most of your time. Watch the tide and have fun.

West of Lovely Bay, between Lovely Bay and Attwood Harbour, is the town of Chester's which lies approximately 8 miles east of Major's Cay. Shallow draft vessels can gain access to Chester's by heading east inside the reef from Lovely Bay. Chester's is probably most famous for its boatbuilding. Here the legendary Frank Moss, now retired and living in Nassau, built wooden boats with his bare hands for most of his 80 plus years. He has a 70 footer and a 100 footer to his credit, building them right on the beach. In

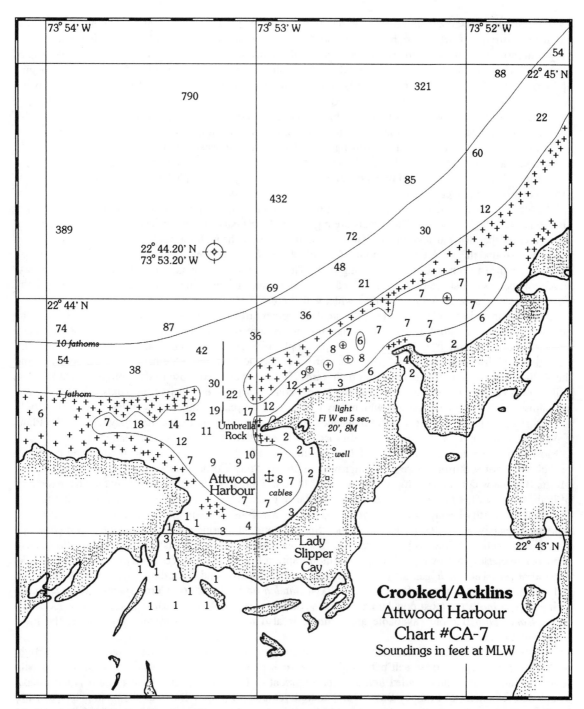

Crooked/Acklins
Attwood Harbour
Chart #CA-7
Soundings in feet at MLW

his latter years he built only dinghies. You can purchase food at *Moss' Store* and there is a phone available in town. If you need gasoline you may be able to convince someone to sell you some of their supply.

Four miles east of Chester's is Attwood Harbour, a lovely curving bay offering protection from winds from the east-northeast through south to almost west. Attwood Harbour is not exactly a part of Acklins Island, it actually is situated on Lady Slipper Cay. There is a light at the entrance but as most lights in the outer islands it should be considered unreliable at best. The best anchoring is in the northeast corner of the harbour. Although the outlying reefs and shallow entrance channel break most of the seas entering the harbour, Attwood Harbour is not the best spot to ride out a frontal passage. I have ridden out a weak front there and would not wish to be inside during a fierce, 30+ knot, norther. Van Sant calls Attwood Harbour a deathtrap in a norther, he is not overexaggerating.

A GPS waypoint at 22° 44.20' N, 73° 53.20' W, will place you approximately ½ mile north of the entrance to Attwood Harbour as shown on Chart #CA-7. The break through the reef is wide and deep and very straightforward and easy to see. Never attempt this entrance at night! From the waypoint head south. Your landmark will be Umbrella Rock and the light on the point on your port side. The deep water begins approximately 150 yards west of Umbrella Rock. Pilot your way in by eye and drop your hook in the eastern end of the harbour in 7'-10' in good holding sand.

Ashore you will see two small buildings that house cable equipment sitting just inland of the beautiful beach. About 50 yards south of the northern tip of the eastern beach is a path leading inland about 30-50 yards to a concrete lined well. This well has excellent water for washing and showers. In a pinch you could boil it and drink it. There is a small creek with a 1' bar at the entrance that winds back into the Bight of Acklins. There are some small pools inside where you will find 3'-4' at MLW. There are plenty of reefs around to arouse the interest of the divers and anglers in your crew.

Off the northeast tip of Acklins Island lies a reef strewn area known as Northeast Point and Hells Gate. Give this area a WIDE berth. These reefs are a graveyard for boats. Here you will find acres and acres of elkhorn coral that dries at low water. There is simply no way through the reefs and you must go around them, way around them! A GPS waypoint at 22° 48.00' N, 73° 47.00' W, will place you in deep water well north of Northeast Point and its surrounding reef. There are no settlements, no anchorages, and no access to any of the eastern shore of Acklins Island. The shore has a long fringing reef along its entire length. Give the eastern shore of Acklins Island a wide, wide berth.

On the mainland of Acklins Island is the small settlement of Pinefield, sitting south of Hell Gate on the northeastern tip of Acklins Island. Although no one is sure of how this area got its name it has been suggested that it came from the time when pineapple was grown on the islands. Most residents are fishermen who use their small boats in the mangrove creeks north of the settlement. In town you will find the Williamsons with a wingless plane in their yard. The plane crashed close to their property and Holston Williamson keeps it in good shape, applying a new coat of a paint every time he paints his house. The Williamsons have two guest houses which they rent to visitors year round. A few miles south of Pinefield is Hard Hill, the highest point on Acklins Island. Residents say that on a clear day they can see the Plana Cays to the east. Here in Hard Hill the main road running north to south on Acklins really begins.

Most of the communities on Acklins Island dot the western shore of Acklins Island adjoining the Bight of Acklins. Just south of where the mangroves begin sits Snug Corner, parts of which were once called Mason Bay but which are now mostly abandoned. Here in Snug Corner the residents say they have the best of both worlds. . . they have the same number of dance halls as they do churches. There is a blue hole in the Bight just north of Snug Corner. If you need gas see Mr. Bain in town.

Approximately ten miles further south lies Spring Point, the principal settlement on Acklins Island. This area is rich in fertile soil, and was the first area settled on Acklins Island. The plantations were primarily interested in growing tobacco and cotton. Spring Point has a fuel dock where the mailboat docks once a week. The *Shell* gas station is only open on Tuesdays and Saturdays, when the flights from Bahamasair land. If you need fuel contact Felix at *Batelco* on VHF ch. 16. Curtis Hanna's (*Red Devil* on VHF) *Airport Inn* is the most popular eating and socializing spot in Acklins. Here you will also find *Nai's Guest House* with 6 rooms available and a nurse is also to be found in town. Try *Rollex*, the local restaurant/bar.

Just past Spring Point is Delectable Bay. The town itself sits inland one mile separated from the Bight of Acklins by a large flooded salt pan. Follow the rock path to town. The residents are involved with sponging and growing aloe, called *halawis*, for shipment to Nassau. A little further south is the almost abandoned settlement of Pompey Bay. One hundred years ago Pompey Bay was the most active town in the district and the rock walls marking the old plantation boundaries are still in place. The tall church on the shore is the only semi-complete structure from the past. Just a little further south sits the large concrete dock marking Morant Bay, now all but deserted. Four feet can access the dock at high tide. Just around the point is Jamaica Cay. Next stop southbound is Binnacle Hill where a few houses can be seen overlooking the flats in the Bight of Acklins.

Off the southeastern tip of Acklins lies Jamaica Bay, a delightful lee anchorage providing adequate shelter in the prevailing northeast to southeast winds. For vessels with drafts of over 4½', the only entrance to this anchorage is from the south at Datum Bay. Head northward along the shore and round Salina Point and anchor where your draft allows. Jamaica Bay is good in prevailing east/southeast conditions.

74° 20' W   74° 19' W   74° 18' W   74° 17' W   74° 16' W   74° 15' W

The Bight of Acklins

60

22

7

117   44

7

22° 12' N

Acklins Island

Salina Point

378

2176

Datum Bay

9

39 ⌘ 7

22

7

59   21

72

awash at lw

22° 11' N

118

China Hill

32   15

32

awash at lw+

breaks 22

22° 10' N

66

60

22

South West Point

18

60

3348

98

1 fathom

7

36

7

37

7

awash at lw

David Morris Breaker

breaks

20

10 fathoms

60

348

15   50

72

22° 09' N

48

7

11

22° 08.50' N
74° 20.40' W
⊕

85

45   20

12

39

77

9

⌘

light
GP Fl W (2)
ev 2 sec
130', 22M

1262

Northwest Rock

Castle Island

consp. cliffs

Jim Bar

32

55

7

⌘

7
12

15

Mudian Harbour

9

7

44

58

The Mayaguana Passage

Castle Rock

12

31

18

9   18

32

44

48

44

60

66

59

60

64

673

32

32

60

60

22° 08' N

22° 07' N

Mira Por Vos Passage

231

22 07.00' N
74 19.00' W

343

1 kn

22° 06' N

2134

1583

4692

Crooked/Acklins
Castle Island
Chart #CA-8
Soundings in feet at MLW

22° 05' N

CASTLE ISLAND

Castle Island lies along the western edge of the Mira Por Vos Passage and just off the southern tip of Acklins Island. The northern end of the island is rather high and hilly, becoming low and sandy as it stretches southward. The cut between Castle Island and Acklins Island is guarded by a large reef system and this passage is suitable for shoal draft vessels or dinghies only.

The huge 135' white Castle Island Lighthouse (GP. FL W-2 ev 20 sec, 130', 22m), is one of the most important lights in the Caribbean, due to the tremendous amount of boat traffic plying the waters of the Crooked Island Passage, the Windward Passage, and the Old Bahama Channel along the Cuban coast. The light was manually operated until Bahamian Independence in 1973, today it is all battery and solar powered. If you wish to visit the cay you will notice the recent ruins of the lightkeeper's homes, cooking rooms, and the boathouse with its railway leading to the water. You can climb to the top of the lighthouse for some spectacular views and sunsets.

On the beach is the wreck of an old Belizian freighter. The ship, and sometimes the beach itself, is strewn with shoes. Closer examination of the hold will reveal clothes and shoes. One cruiser I know entered the hold to find a pair of boot soles, the right and left in the correct placement for a body lying in the dark water. She called to her companion and they soon discovered that the boots were simply floating upside down.

Anchorages can be found on the banks west of Castle Island or east if the need arises. A GPS waypoint at 22° 08.50' N, 74° 20.40' W will place you approximately ½ mile northwest of the anchorage on the western shore of Castle Island as shown on Chart #CA-8. There is a small reef encircled anchorage called Mudian Harbour (a corruption of *Bermudian Harbour*) on the southern side of Castle Island that is good in winds form the northwest to the north/northeast. The entrance is through a break in the reef approximately ½ mile east of the lighthouse. Two white beacons on the northwest side of the harbour form a range (003°) for the entrance channel which can carry 9' at low water. A GPS waypoint at 22° 07.00' N, 74° 19.00' W, will place you approximately ¼ mile south of the entrance to Mudian Harbour.

Vessels can also anchor north of Castle Island at Datum Bay in easterly conditions. It can get quite rolly in southeasterlies.

MIRA POR VOS

The Spanish named this tiny group of islets and reefs well. Their name means "watch out for yourself" and should be taken to heart when visiting this group. This 40 square mile area, unlit and unmarked, is best skipped unless you require shelter or seek to test the excellent fishing that abounds in the area. The islands only inhabitants are flocks of nesting sea birds. The area was once much more dangerous until the Imperial Lighthouse Service constructed the lighthouse on Castle Island.

Mira Por Vos, Chart #CA-9, lies about 7 miles west of Castle Island at its closest point and is essentially a large shallow bank less than 60' deep and thick with scattered heads and reefs. Land masses consist of a number of small barren reefs and rocks scarcely visible above water, the largest being only ½ mile long. The fishing is superb on the Mira Por Vos bank but this is not a place to ride out any type of threatening weather.

South Cay is the largest island and a temporary anchorage can be found in its lee if absolutely necessary. There is a shallow rocky bar extending from South Cay to Northeast Rocks that must be avoided. You can anchor in the lee of Northeast Rocks which in strong prevailing winds is actually quite calm. Two miles to the northwest of Northeast Rocks lies North Rock, a brown booby rookery but not much of an anchorage.

A GPS waypoint at 22° 07.00' N, 74° 32.50' W, will place you approximately 1 mile west of the Mira Por Vos bank. From this position you may head east to Northeast Rock, southeast to South Cay, or northeast to North Rock.

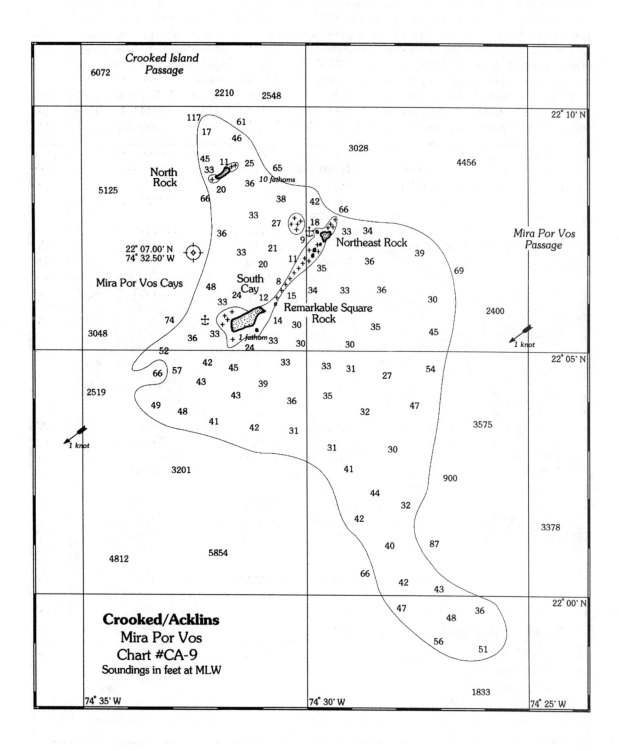

Crooked Island
Passage

6072

2210   2548

22° 10' N

117   61
17
46
3028
4456

45   11   25
North   33   65
Rock   20   36   10 fathoms

5125   66   38   42   66

33   27   18   33   34
36   9   Northeast Rock   39

22° 07.00' N   33   21   11   36   69
74° 32.50' W   20   35

Mira Por Vos Cays   48   South   8   34   33   36
24   Cay   12   15   Remarkable Square
33   Rock
74   14   30   35   45

3048   36   33   1 fathom   33   30
52   24   30   2400

1 knot

42   45   33   33   31   27   54   22° 05' N
66   57   43   39
2519   43   36   35   47
49   48   32
41   42   31   3575
31   30
3201   41
44   900
42   32
40   87   3378

4812   5854   66
42   43

47   22° 00' N
Crooked/Acklins   48   36
Mira Por Vos   56   51
Chart #CA-9
Soundings in feet at MLW

1833

74° 35' W   74° 30' W   74° 25' W

Mira Por Vos
Passage

1 knot

SAMANA

Samana (Chart #CA-10), is an uninhabited and very isolated little cay lying about 20 nautical miles north-northeast of Attwood Harbour on Acklins Island. There is a small body of evidence pointing to this nine mile long cay as being Columbus' first landing site in the New World, not San Salvador as is the popular belief. The cay was once populated by Lucayan Indians before the raiding Spanish decimated the population. Ashore you will find the ruins of an old settlement, a few fishermen's huts, and a well which is now brackish. In later years the island was called *Attwood Cay*, and eventually became *Samana*. The waters surrounding the cay are thick with coral reefs which have claimed many a vessel. You can still see the remains of an old freighter on the northeast side of Samana's eastern reef.

In the past Samana was actively farmed by Acklins Islanders. The farmers would stay for extended periods of time and large boats would sail to Samana to pick up the Cascarilla bark, conch, fish, crabs, and crops that the farmers harvested. This practice eventually ceased in the 1950's, and Samana was rarely

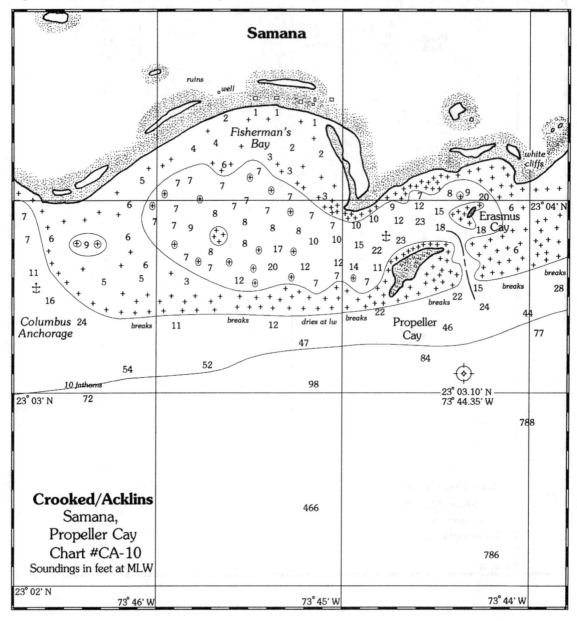

visited except by passing yachts for the next quarter of a century. The practice was revived in 1983, and carries on today. On the shores of Fisherman's Bay you will see the wooden shacks used by today's fishermen standing next to the stone ruins of past buildings. Today there is once again an active interest by fishermen in search of fish, lobster, conch, and land crabs, sometimes staying weeks at a time in the renovated shacks in Fisherman's Bay. When I last visited the island to finish my soundings in April of 1997, I met two fisherman from Lovely Bay that came over in a 16' boat with a 30 horsepower outboard. They were in search of black land crabs. The white crabs have more meat than the smaller black crabs but the meat is sweeter in the black crabs. The two gentleman had four huge bags of crabs that they told me would net them $110 a bag in Nassau. They asked me if I had any gas to spare and I told them I was down to my last 10 gallons but I could let them have 3 gallons. I did not ask for any recompense but they soon returned with a gallon size bag full of cleaned conch that took us three days to finish. In the outer islands courtesy shown is often rewarded many times over.

APPROACHES TO SAMANA

Samana is generally low and sandy along its western shore with a conspicuous white bluff along its southern shore. From Attwood Harbour it is 20.4 nautical miles on a course of 33° to the waypoint south of Propeller Cay. From Betsy Bay, Mayaguana, the Propeller Cay anchorage lies 50 miles away on a course of 326°. From Bird Rock, northwest of Crooked Island, Propeller Cay bears 80° at a distance of 36.6 nautical miles. From West Plana, Propeller Cay anchorage bears 357° at 28.2 miles but be careful to avoid the reefs off the northeastern tip of Acklins Island if headed to or from the Plana Cays.

A note on the passage between Acklins Island and Samana. The Antilles Current runs strong along the northeastern shores of The Bahamas, roughly at a speed of ½ knot but often higher. Through the 20 mile stretch between Acklins and Samana the Antilles Current is funneled somewhat with a resulting increase in speed to about ¾ knot at times. At times this current acts like the Gulf Stream in the sense that at its center, along its *axis*, the seas are generally higher than at its northern or southern edges. Another interesting note, an Acklins Islander told me that there is a spot in the center of this passage with only 90' of water over it. He told me the bank lies on a bearing of 210° from Propeller Cay, ". . . just as you make out the land, about 12 miles out from Acklins." I have searched for this area, a possible pinnacle, but have found no evidence of it. That does not mean that it doesn't exist. If you are in the area and notice anything strange in the sea conditions, this bank may have something to do with it. If you find it please contact me with its coordinates. An acknowledgment in and a free copy of the next edition of this guide will be your reward.

SAMANA

Samana, pronounced *Sa-MAN-a*, not *Sah-ma-NAH*, as the city in the Dominican Republic is called, offers good protection to vessels headed north or south if a frontal passage threatens. The best, and only anchorage as far as I am concerned, is in the lee of Propeller Cay off Samana's southern shore. You may find charts with Propeller Cay listed as Pimlico Cay or even Prickly Cay. This anchorage is open to the southwest and it can get pretty choppy inside with a stiff southwest wind blowing. Although a reef breaks the truly big seas on the outside, inside may develop a two foot chop in 25 knots of wind. Some skippers tout the Columbus Anchorage west of Fisherman's Bay but I find it entirely open from southeast through south to west-northwest. Little protection here, use it only as a settled weather anchorage and watch out for reefs upon your approach. The Columbus Anchorage lies just west of the end of the fringing reef that lies south of Fisherman's Bay. If you are not happy here the anchorage at Propeller Cay is not that difficult to enter if you have good visibility and it gives excellent protection.

For entrance into the Propeller Cay anchorage as shown on Chart #CA-10, a GPS waypoint at 23° 03.10' N, 73° 44.35' W will place you approximately ½ mile south of the entrance to the anchorage behind Propeller Cay. A good landmark as you approach is the very conspicuous white cliffs that lie just northeast of Propeller Cay. From this position head directly northward until you can pick up the channel which you should approach on a heading of approximately 350°-360°. The northern end of the slightly winding channel lies about 50-75 yards east of the northeastern tip of Propeller Cay. The moderate current flows east and west across the channel and through the anchorage as well. The ability to read the water is essential here but if you have made it this far you are probably pretty fair at picking out reefs and heads from sand. Never attempt this channel at night or with a heavy following sea, one small mistake and you will be up on a reef before you know it. This is a narrow channel, only about 40'-75' wide with a least depth of 9', but the bottom is easily seen as its green color (indicating sand) stands out from the surrounding brown reefs. A good idea is to approach the reefs and steer parallel to them about 100 yards off if weather permits to eyeball the channel before entry. Take your time and give the channel a good once over to familiarize yourself with it. If time and weather conditions permit you may wish to dinghy the channel first. Some skippers mark the channel with floats, often leaving them behind when they leave. Never, I repeat **never**, trust any range or buoys you see in this vicinity. Trust only what your eyes tell you! As you make out the channel, approach it on a heading of approximately 350°-360°. This heading is not that important, what is important is what you see and what your depth sounder indicates, trust your eyes. The channel makes two small doglegs before rounding the reef at the northeastern tip of Propeller Cay. Watch out for the shallow yellow coral amidst darker coral that lies to port just as you begin your entrance to the channel, this head is just awash at low water. Once you clear Propeller Cay round to port, not too soon mind you, you'll find excellent holding in soft sand in 10'-25' of water.

The shore of Propeller Cay is surrounded by beautiful reefs as are the beaches of Samana just north of Propeller Cay. Good snorkeling and fishing abound in this area, there are beautiful reefs everywhere. If you wish to land your dinghy the best spot is at the northeastern end of Fisherman's Bay just west of the entrance to the shallow creek area west of the palm trees. This area is very shallow and strewn with small rocks, conch shells, conch pens, and small patch reefs so use caution. A better spot, particularly if you wish to use the beach for swimming, is about ¼ mile east of the conspicuous white cliffs. Here the reefs break most of the seas and you can land your dinghy on a very nice, deep, sandy beach. The northern shore of Samana is excellent for beachcombing especially after a norther.

As I mentioned earlier, there is a moderate current that runs east-west through this anchorage. It is not as strong as say the current at French Wells but it can make your stay a little rolly. In east or west winds you will lie to the wind, and not roll very much, unless the wind pipes up. In any other winds you will be turned slightly to the current, not much, you'll barely notice, only enough to make the accompanying roll uncomfortable. To make the best use of the shelter offered, and to cut down on roll, you can lie to a bridle and adjust your position to the incoming surge, or you can play musical chairs and move around the anchorage. In winds from ENE through SSW the best anchorage with the least roll is close in the lee of Propeller Cay (watch out for the reefs along the shore). In winds from NE through N to W your best spot is on the northern side of the anchorage as close as you can get to shore (again, watch out for the inshore reefs). In strong SW to W winds, well, just pray they don't last long as there is no real lee and you will have to endure some chop depending on the wind strength.

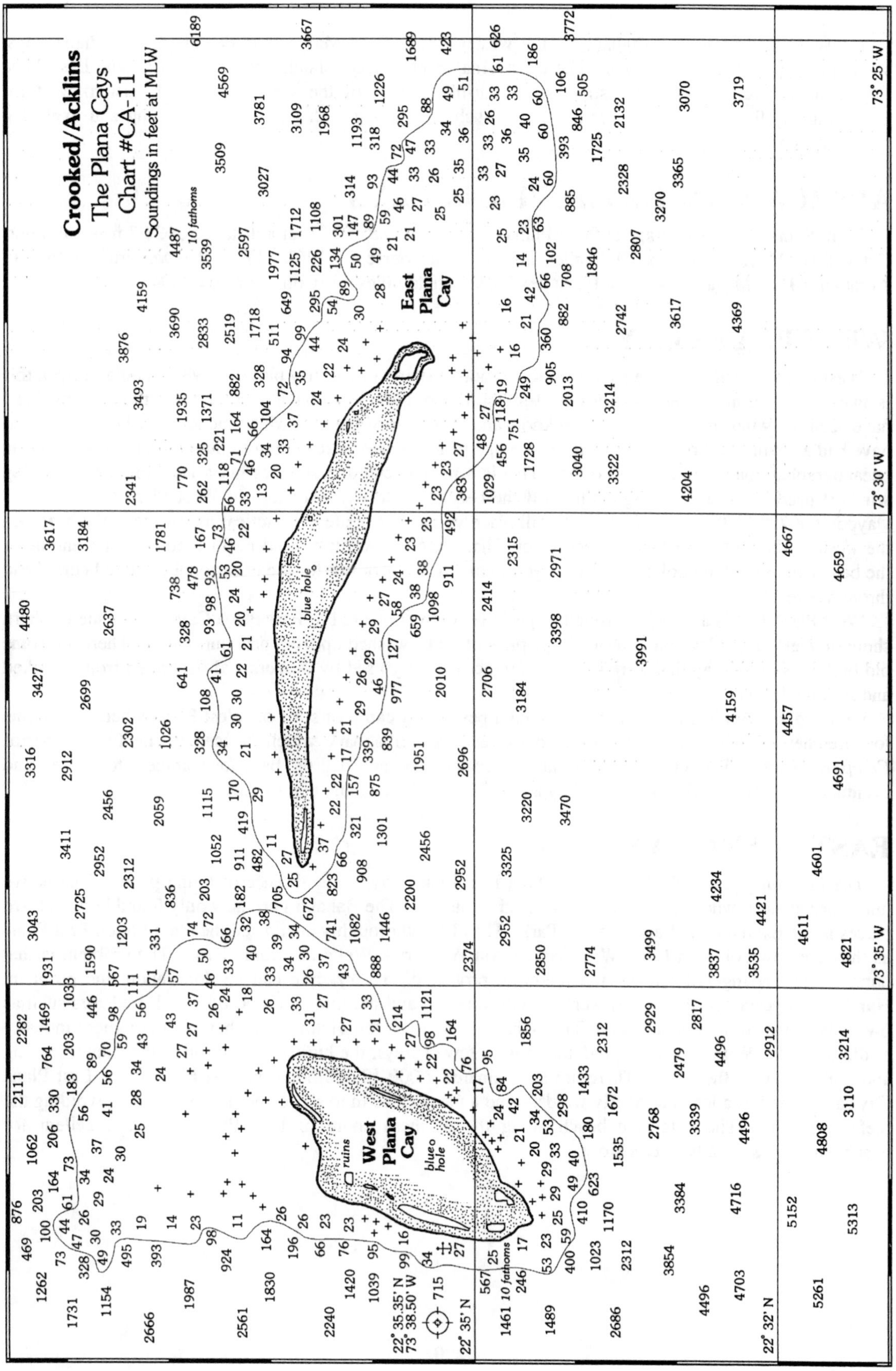

Crooked/Acklins
The Plana Cays
Chart #CA-11
Soundings in feet at MLW

East
Plana
Cay

West
Plana
Cay

ruins

blue hole

blue hole

10 fathoms

10 fathoms

73° 25' W

73° 30' W

73° 35' W

22° 35.35' N
73° 38.50' W

22° 35' N

22° 32' N

THE PLANA CAYS

Between Acklins and Mayaguana on the western side of the Mayaguana Passage lie the Plana Cays, sometimes called the French Cays. These two small reef fringed islands, West Plana Cay and East Plana Cay, actually the tops of two distinct seamount-like risings of the sea floor, stretch east to west for approximately 9 miles. They offer a lee side anchorage along with good fishing, diving and exploring possibilities ashore.

APPROACHES TO THE PLANA CAYS

From Samana, the anchorage at West Plana lies on a course of 177° at a distance of 28.2 nautical miles. Betsy Bay, Mayaguana, lies 29.7 miles distant on a course of 296°. From the western entrance to Abraham's Bay, Mayaguana, West Plana lies 36.3 nautical miles away on a course of 304°.

WEST PLANA CAY

West Plana Cay offers some lee protection in northeasterly or easterly blows. I wish I could tell you this is an excellent lee anchorage but it is not. I prefer to avoid it unless I have to stop. I don't know why, but I have seen the winds blow strong, 15-20 knots and more out of the east while anchored at West Plana and have had a small swell running into the anchorage from the west threatening to put me ashore. Perhaps an oceanographer could explain this to me. This is a rolly anchorage at times but a lee from the prevailing winds if needed. The anchorage is just off the beach on the western shore of West Plana Cay. A GPS waypoint at 22° 35.35' N, 73° 38.50' W, will place you approximately 1 nautical mile west of the beach on the western shore of West Plana as shown on Chart #CA-11. Simply head in for a point in the middle of the beach and drop the hook in sand with good holding. Watch out for the occasional scattered coral head through here.

West Plana Cay is a very lush island, especially when compared to East Plana Cay. Along the northern shore of West Plana Cay you will find large piles of rocks washed up from past hurricanes. There are some old buildings on the cay that were built and are occasionally used by farmers and fishermen from Crooked and Acklins Islands.

Crooked and Acklins Islanders have set up a permanent camp of sorts on West Plana where they come for stretches of two months at a time to harvest Cascarilla bark which is used in the Italian aperitif *Campari*. During this period the harvesters cut, soak, dry, and bag the bark for shipment to Nassau and eventually to Italy. While on the cay they also catch conch, fish, and black crabs.

EAST PLANA CAY

The first thing you will likely notice about East Plana Cay is the absence of living plants. The native hutia (pronounced who-tia), which once thrived throughout The Bahamas are now only found here and two places in the Exuma Cays Land and Sea Park. They have thoroughly decimated the plant life on East Plana as they are now doing on Little Wax Cay and on Warderick Wells in Exuma Park. The problem is that hutia are an endangered species and therefore protected so very little can be done about the problem. Hundreds of years ago these cays were heavily forested and the hutia had more natural predators such as owls. With the coming of settlers to The Bahamas, the trees fell victim to the burgeoning lumber industry as did the owls. With no natural predators, save a few ospreys, the hutia have the run of the island, feeding and multiplying as they will. There are an estimated 7,000-12,000 hutia on East Plana Cay. East Plana Cay can be used as a lee in northerly winds. Find a place close in to shore and drop your hook avoiding the reefs closer in. The extensive beach along the northern shore of East Plana Cay is excellent for beachcombing especially after a blow.

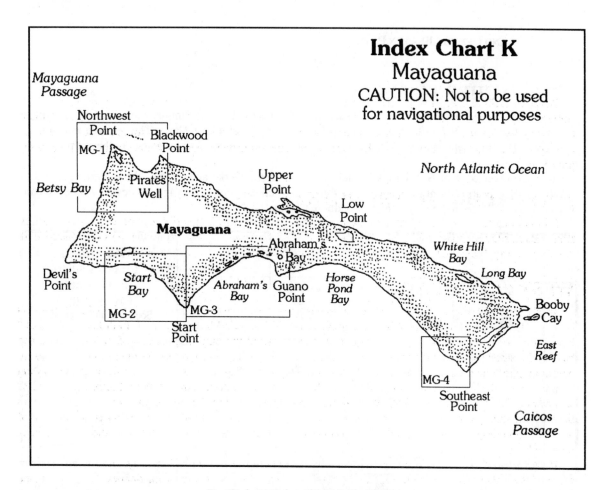

Index Chart K
Mayaguana
CAUTION: Not to be used
for navigational purposes

*Mayaguana
Passage*

Northwest
Point · · · Blackwood
Point
MG-1

North Atlantic Ocean

Betsy Bay

Pirates
Well

Upper
Point

Low
Point

Mayaguana

Abraham's
Bay

*White Hill
Bay*

Long Bay

Devil's
Point

*Start
Bay*

*Abraham's
Bay*   Guano
Point

*Horse
Pond
Bay*

MG-2   MG-3

Start
Point

Booby
Cay

*East
Reef*

MG-4

Southeast
Point

*Caicos
Passage*

MAYAGUANA

Mayaguana is almost as primitive as its ancient Lucayan name which was shown on some early charts as *Mariguana*. Some local residents tell me that the name is not Lucayan in origin, rather that the island is named after the many green iguanas found on Booby Cay lying off the eastern shore of Mayaguana. Of course the term *iguana* itself is Lucayan in origin. The island was uninhabited until around 1812 when a group of Turks Islanders settled here. Many of today's residents can trace their heritage to those early inhabitants.

The United States Government leased bases in Mayaguana for 99 years from the British government in exchange for 40 old destroyers during World War II. Although no base was ever really developed, an Air-Sea Rescue Station of the Caribbean Division of the U.S. Air Force was set up and maintained at Abraham's Bay on the south side of the island. This area was the site of a U.S. Missile Tracking Station, now long abandoned, which boosted the population of Mayaguana to over 3,000 for a few years. Abraham's Bay was sounded and a chart drawn up in 1941 (which is still in wide use today although the latitude and longitude lines are off considerably). A wireless station was also established at the same time on the west side of the island at Betsy Bay.

Mayaguana boasts one of the world's best shelling spots along it's weather shore and Abraham's Bay is a favorite stopover for those skippers bound to or from the Caribbean. Magnificent wall dives surround this tiny island (Did I say tiny? It's 24 miles long and 6 miles wide.) with the drop off just a few hundred feet offshore in some places while the offshore reefs are alive with food fish and lobsters (I have heard some local fishermen boast that the best fishing is along the northern and eastern reefs).

The island itself is thickly wooded and rather low-lying for the most part although its hills rise here and there throughout the land mass with the eastern end being generally more hilly and steep-to.

APPROACHES TO MAYAGUANA

Betsy Bay, Mayaguana bears 146° at a distance of 50.0 nautical miles from the Propeller Cay anchorage at Samana Cay, and 29.7 miles on a course of 116° from West Plana Cay. The western entrance to Abraham's Bay lies approximately 36.3 miles distant on a course of 124° from the southern tip of West Plana Cay.

From the outer edge of Sandbore Channel off Provo in the Turks and Caicos, the eastern entrance to Abraham's Bay bears 330° at a distance of 46.4 miles. Southeast Point, Mayaguana lies 37.7 miles distant on a course of 337° from the waypoint off Sandbore Channel.

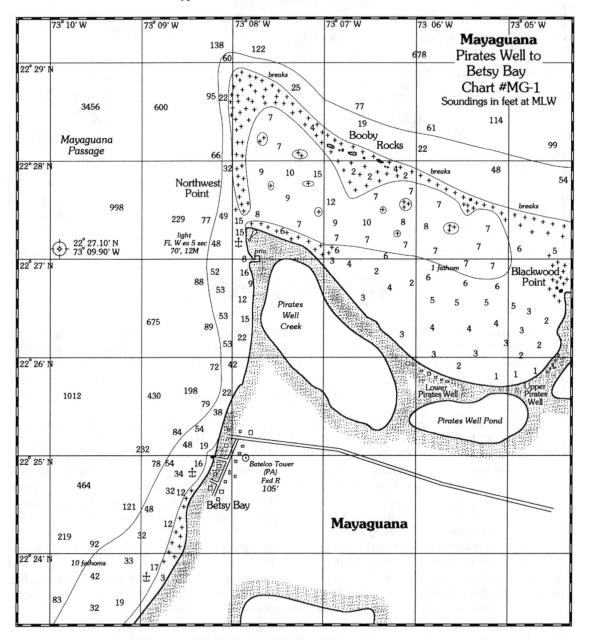

NORTHWEST POINT TO START BAY

For vessels heading southward across the Mayaguana Passage, Northwest Point and Betsy Bay make good stopovers at the end of a long day. Abraham's Bay lies almost twenty miles away around Devil's Point and in prevailing winds (with no chance of a westerly shift) many cruisers opt to anchor off

Northwest Point, Betsy Bay, or at Pirates Well for the night and then proceed to Abraham's Bay the next morning.

A GPS waypoint at 22° 27.10' N, 73° 09.90' W, will place you approximately 1½ miles west of Northwest Point as shown on Chart #MG-1. From here you can head through the cut to Pirates Well, anchor just below the light (Fl W ev 5 sec, 70', 12M), or head another two miles southeast and anchor off the settlement of Betsy Bay. My personal favorite in light easterly weather is to anchor off the small rocky beach just south of the light in 15' of water. Here, with the help of a bridle arrangement, you will get less roll than at Betsy Bay. The bottom is sand with scattered rocks and coral so pick a good sandy spot to drop your hook and hope that your rode doesn't wrap around a coral head or rock if the wind shifts. Years ago a whale skeleton washed ashore off the point and you may still find pieces of it strewn about.

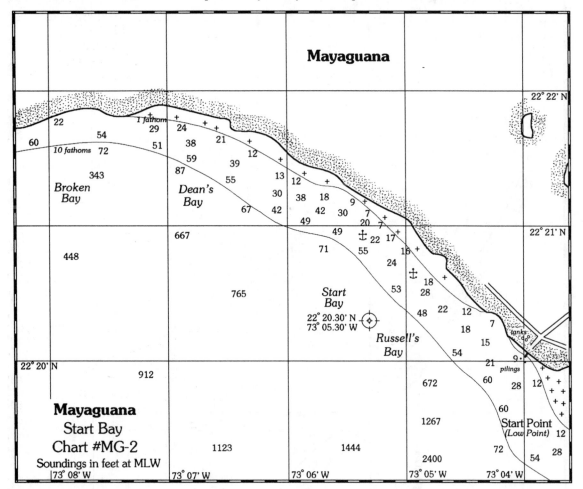

About ½ mile south of the light you will see what appears to be a marina with a range leading into its entrance channel. This is a private dock used only by the mailboat and there is usually no one around so don't even bother calling on the VHF. Although there is 8' of water at the entrance and 10' inside the sides are sharp rock and coral and not a place you would want to tie up to except perhaps in an emergency. I should add that this place is open to the west and would be a deathtrap in a strong westerly.

If you wish to anchor at Betsy Bay head southeast about two miles to anchor off the settlement in water from 15' to 40' deep. The very conspicuous Batelco tower and huge satellite dish, which is sometimes your first landfall when approaching from the northwest, mark the settlement. Here too the water is strewn with coral and rocks so take care in setting your anchor, the holding is good when you find a sandy spot. The anchorage at Betsy Bay is better in southeast winds than the anchorage south of Northwest Point Light though I like the anchorage by the light better in light easterly winds. There is a long beach just south of Betsy Bay that offers good protection in southeast winds but don't stray in too close as there is a rocky bar lying parallel to the beach about 50 yards or so out from the beach.

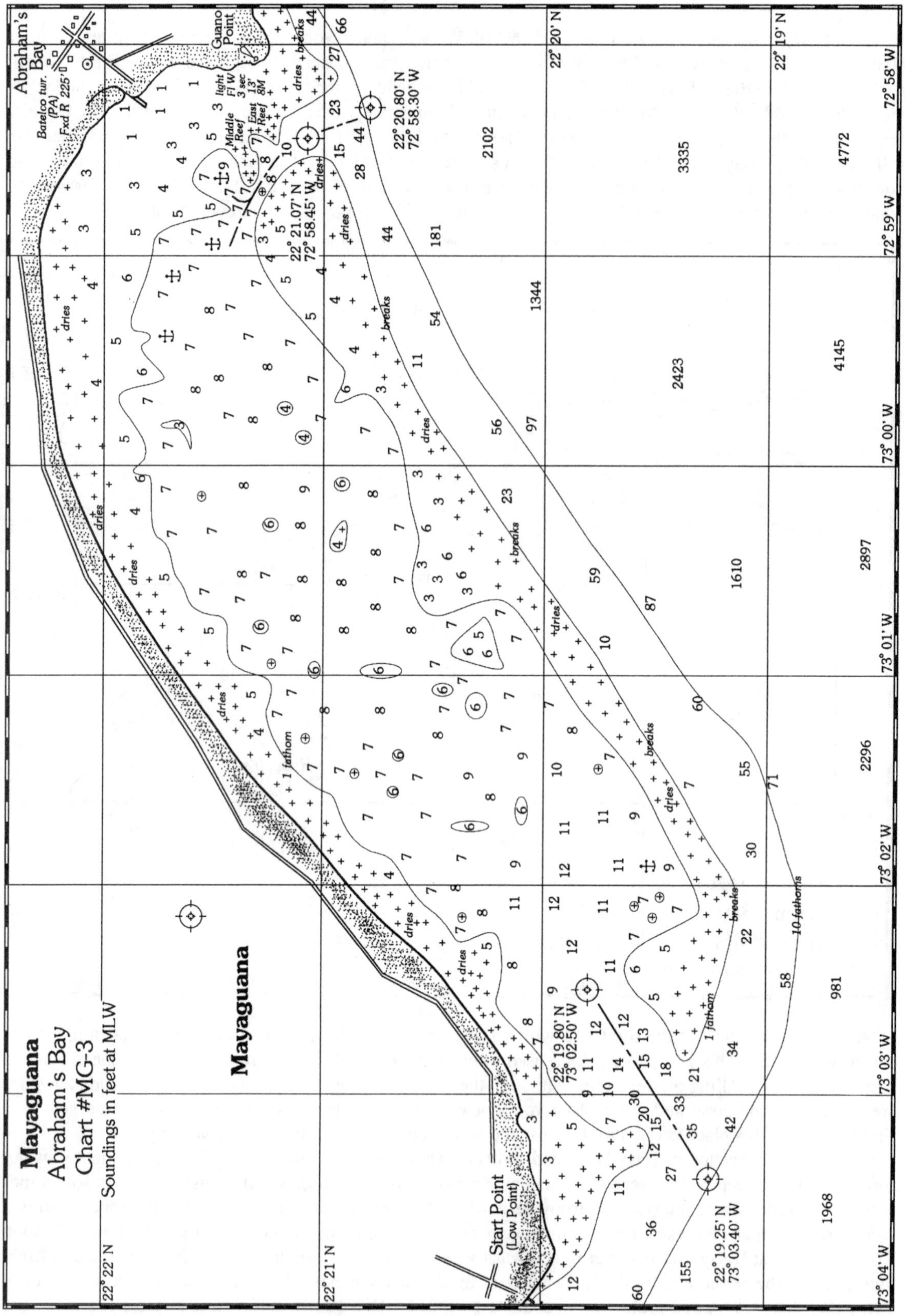

Mayaguana
Abraham's Bay
Chart #MG-3
Soundings in feet at MLW

Mayaguana

Abraham's Bay

Guano Point

Batelco tur. Bay (PA) Fxd R 225'0

Middle Reef

East Reef

light Fl W 3 sec 13' 8M

22° 21.07' N
72° 58.45' W

22° 20.80' N
72° 58.30' W

Start Point
(Low Point)

22° 19.80' N
73° 02.50' W

22° 19.25' N
73° 03.40' W

10 fathoms

1 fathom

dries

breaks

22° 22' N   22° 21' N   22° 20' N   22° 19' N

73° 04' W   73° 03' W   73° 02' W   73° 01' W   73° 00' W   72° 59' W   72° 58' W

1968   155   36   60   981   2296   2897   1610   2423   4145   3335   4772   2102   1344   181

Another option is to pass through the cut in the reef lying north of Northwest Point and anchor off Lower Pirates Well. The cut lies about 100 yards north of Northwest Point and has a minimum depth of 8' at MLW. Never try this cut in poor visibility or with a heavy onshore (westerly) swell as it breaks all the way across the cut and you will likely not see it. Once through the cut head eastward along the northern shore, not too close in) and anchor wherever your draft allows off Lower Pirates Well, the first community to starboard just east of the new, and very conspicuous hotel. The two communities of Upper Pirates Well and Lower Pirates Well are usually just called Pirates Well (I'll bet that by now you can guess how this community got its name). At one time you could take a 5' draft well into the bay to anchor off the shore of Upper Pirates Well which sits under the very pretty grove of coconut palms at the southeastern end of the bay. Today, unless you have a shoal draft multihull, you can't get very close at all. But Pirates Well, Upper and Lower, are lovely little communities with a small but very friendly population. In Lower Pirates Well you will see the new hotel that has just been constructed and you will also find *Gibson's Food Fair* and *Brown's Convenience Store*. If you need an outboard mechanic call *Bain Boys* on the VHF and ask to speak to Stafford Bain Jr. The Booby Rocks lying along the reef north of Pirates Well are aptly named as there is a colony of brown boobies that inhabit the rocks.

The entire northern shore of Mayaguana offers good beachcombing with a few very nice beaches. The coast has a few small, snug anchorages for boats but the cuts through the reefs are narrow, intricate, and very difficult to see, it's best to have a local guide if you intend to investigate this region. Once again, try Stafford Bain Jr. if you need a guide by calling *Bain Boys* on VHF.

When you have had your fill of this area and decide to move on to Start Bay or Abraham's Bay you can pass close in to the western shore of Mayaguana and round Devil's Point just a few hundred yards off. As you round Devil's Point you will immediately find yourself in the grip of a very strong current, sometimes as strong as two knots or more depending on wind speed and direction. This current runs very close in to Devil's Point but as you head more towards Start Bay or Broken Bay you will find yourself free of its effects. The only anchorage in this area is at Start Bay where you can anchor in good holding sand. Although it is possible to anchor anywhere between Broken Bay and Start Point, the area called Start Bay as shown on Chart #MG-2 has the best holding and least rock and coral clutter. Once again, find a nice sandy spot in which to drop your hook. A GPS waypoint at 22° 20.30' N, 73° 05.30' W, will place you approximately ¼ mile southwest of the best holding. Start Bay has the advantage of being easy to leave at night for a passage to Provo or northward. There is an almost continuous brown bar that often breaks lying about 50 yards offshore almost the entire length of the bay from Broken Bay to Russell's Bay so don't try to tuck in too close. This anchorage is good in north through east winds but it's time to move when the wind goes southeast. At the southeast end of the bay at Start Point is the small dock and pilings where the fuel ship ties up to unload her diesel and gasoline for Mayaguana.

ABRAHAM'S BAY TO SOUTHEAST POINT

As you head eastward around Start Point for Abraham's Bay the reef begins just past the fuel dock and continues, with only two breaks, to Guano Point just south of the settlement of Abraham's Bay. If approaching from the west the western entrance to Abraham's Bay is the widest, deepest, and easiest to enter. A GPS waypoint at 22° 19.25' N, 73° 03.40' W, will place you approximately ¼ mile southwest of the western entrance channel to Abraham's Bay as shown on Chart #MG-3. From this position head generally northeastward (you will be able, in good visibility, to make out the reef on both sides of you) until you are past the reef, about ¾ mile, and into Abraham's Bay proper. Never attempt this entrance in strong onshore conditions or at night, even using waypoints. Sometimes in strong southwest and west weather this entrance breaks all the way across and the break is impossible to see. Better to heave-to and wait for good visibility or settled conditions. If you do heave-to remember to keep a constant check on your position, plotting your position every 10-15 minutes at least as there are fluky currents in the area that push sometimes west, sometimes east, and sometimes north depending on wind strength and direction. In March of 1997, the 36' sloop *Hey Jude* was hove to eight miles south of Abraham's Bay in strong west/northwest winds. Taking positions every 30-40 minutes she drifted east and then north. She finally wound up on the southwestern tip of the reef, a total loss, don't let this happen to you. More on this wreck later. If leaving the western entrance to Abraham's Bay, a GPS waypoint at 22° 19.80' N, 73° 02.50' W, will place you approximately ¼ mile northeast of the entrance and is a good spot to begin your passage through the reef.

The eastern entrance to Abraham's Bay, just southwest of Guano Point, is narrower than the western entrance and there is a shallow rock lying almost in mid-channel. A GPS waypoint at 22° 20.80' N, 72° 58.30' W, will place you approximately ¼ mile south/southeast of the entrance channel. Never attempt this channel at night, in poor visibility, or with a heavy onshore swell running, you'll never see the channel. Government charts of this area, even those updated to 1996, show what appears to be two small cays on either side of the channel entrance. **CAUTION**: There are no such cays. The areas they show as cays are actually elkhorn coral that dries at low tide and has a height of approximately ½'-1' above MLW. With good visibility you will have no problem entering this channel. From the waypoint given above, head to an inner waypoint that lies halfway between the two stands of coral at the mouth of the eastern entrance at 22° 21.07' N, 72° 58.45' W. From this position head in the entrance following the green water between the very obvious reefs. You can parallel the western reef and follow it around in 7' at low water. This course is simply for alignment purposes, as you steer this course keep a good lookout. Pilotage by eye is essential here. Keep a sharp lookout for the small reef, little more than a handful of rocks, with only 4' over them that lies almost mid channel, it can be very difficult to see. Once past the small reef you can steer to starboard keeping the small sandbar shown to port to anchor in 7' at low water or pass west of the sandbar to anchor in 7' at low water a little further out. The light on Guano Point was working when I last passed that way in May of 1997. It flashes white every 3 seconds, is 13' tall, and is supposed to be visible for 8 nautical miles.

The people of Mayaguana have applied for a permit to place buoys to mark the entrance channels to Abraham's Bay. The Port Authority in Nassau is on the verge of allowing them to do so. If these buoys are ever installed yachtsman will have to thank the people of Mayaguana for this convenience as they have taken up this burden strictly for the benefit of cruisers, the Mayaguanians know where the channel is and don't need the buoys.

The best anchorage is all the way in to the eastern end of Abraham's Bay where you can anchor in 6'-9' of water in places. Keep a sharp eye out as you navigate eastward in Abraham's Bay. The bay has quite a few shallow spots and rocky heads here and there, all easily seen in good light. Never attempt this route with the morning sun right in your eyes. You'll be aground long before you see the shallows. At the eastern end of the harbour the bottom is strewn with rocks and small heads so be sure to pick a good sandy spot to drop your hook. The holding is good here when you are set in the sand though a constant roll is evident, more so in stronger winds. A bridle arrangement is helpful although during periods of strong winds, say 20+ knots, if you adjust your bridle to the wind-generated waves you will roll from the swell coming in from the reef. If you adjust for the swell coming in from the reef you will roll to the wind-generated waves. At times like these you'll just have to grit your teeth and bear it.

Visitors to town can dinghy in to the large concrete dock to tie up and visit ashore. The dinghy channel is narrow and extremely shallow at low water. About two hundred yards southwest of the dock is a white buoy. From the white buoy steer toward the end of the dock until you can pick up the white channel that leads between two shallow grassy areas to the dock. The channel is sandy white and kept clean from the amount of outboard traffic that passes through it. This channel has about 1' of water at low tide so keep an eye on your prop. When you get to the dock you will find some steps about halfway to the beach on the western side. This is where you will want to tie up. Pull out your dinghy anchor and wedge it into a crack on the dock as there are no cleats and nothing to tie to. A large concrete garbage receptacle is ashore at the end of the dock for your convenience.

The town of Abraham's Bay, once called Charlton Town, lies about ¼ mile up the sandy road from the dock. The first building on the left at the Batelco Tower is the pink Government Office building. Here you will find the Commissioner, Mildred Williamson, the Post Office, and Customs and Immigration (Abraham's Bay became a Port Of Entry in 1995). Abraham's Bay is the first and last Port Of Entry in The Bahamas depending upon your direction of travel. If you wish to clear in or out walk up to the Government Office during normal business hours and ask for Customs. Next door is the Batelco office where you can place a call seven days a week from 9:30 A.M.-5:30 P.M.

A hundred yards further up the road to the right is *Reggie's Villas and Satellite Lounge*. The building with the satellite dish is the lounge and next door is the restaurant and guest house. Reggie Charlton has a reputation for serving some downright strong drinks, he is an excellent bartender and a genial host. Reggie also sells cigarettes and can arrange for any parts you need to have flown in via the Bahamasair flights on Mondays and Fridays. If you need fuel you can also ask Reggie for assistance but be advised that you will have to jerry jug it back to the dock. Reggie has a wheelbarrow that you might be able to persuade him to

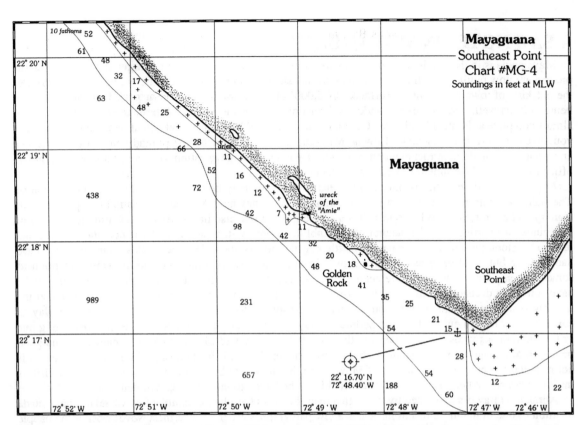

10 fathoms 52

Mayaguana
Southeast Point
Chart #MG-4
Soundings in feet at MLW

Mayaguana

wreck
of the
"Amie"

Golden
Rock

Southeast
Point

22° 16.70' N
72° 48.40' W

allow you to use for that purpose. The small blue and white building across the street is a nice little grocery store.

If you take a right at the crossroads in town you will find *Cha Cha's*, where owner Cha Cha serves lunch, dinner, and also takes in laundry. Hers is the peach colored concrete block building on the left (the second house on the left) with the concrete path to the door. Just past *Cha Cha's* on the other side of the road is the town cistern, a large V-shaped corrugated tin roof that collects rainwater into the cistern below. Here you can fill up your jugs but you must bring a bucket on a rope to haul up the water with. Again, you may be able to talk Reggie into letting you use his wheelbarrow to cart your jugs back to the dock. To the left of the crossroads, at the first street on the right, is the Police Station. The Mayaguana Police monitor VHF ch. 16 and have a range of 50 miles. If you need assistance call *Boys in Blue*. Just past the Police Station is *Cap and Doris Brown's Paradise Villas Guest House*. Cap and Doris used to serve food in their restaurant but they were closed when I last visited in April of 1997 and were unsure as to when they would reopen. Cap is somewhat of a diesel mechanic and you can purchase fuel from him also. Another knowledgeable diesel mechanic is Cleveland Brown who answers to *Papa Charlie* on the VHF. If you need propane look up Prince Pinder, anyone can tell you where to find him.

Many cruisers on their way to Provo usually leave Abraham's Bay and anchor in the lee of Southeast Point for a few hours to make a nighttime departure for Provo that much easier and shorter. A GPS waypoint at 22° 16.70' N, 72° 48.40' W, as shown on Chart #MG-4, will place you approximately 1 mile west/southwest of the anchorage area. Anchor off the beach in the shelter of the reef and you will be fairly comfortable in light to moderate northeast to east winds. Strong east winds make this an uneasy anchorage. Winds and/or seas out of the southeast may make this anchorage anywhere from uncomfortable to downright untenable. If you anchor here awaiting your departure for Provo you might wish to explore the wreck of the sailboat *Amie* which lies on a beach about 2 miles northwest of Southeast Point. I have seen pink flamingos wading in the shallows that dry about a mile northwest of the wreck.

To the east of the main island of Mayaguana lies Booby Cay. Booby Cay, besides being a home to brown boobies, is also home to a colony of small rock iguanas. These are the same iguanas that are found 50 miles to the southeast at Little Water Cay northeast of Provo. There is a small anchorage just inside the reef between Mayaguana and Booby Cay offering little save some shelter from westerly winds. The entrance through the reef is narrow and hard to find, if you intend to enter this anchorage I suggest you ask a local guide for assistance, perhaps Stafford Bain Jr. at Pirate's Well.

A SAD NOTE ON MAYAGUANA

Mayaguana is in the middle of a growth spurt. Mayaguanians are hoping for a larger slice of the tourism pie and are now putting an infrastructure in place that should bring that about. The 11,000' long airstrip on the outskirts of town is getting a resurfacing of 5,000' of its runway and a new airport terminal building is being built as well. New roads are under construction all over the island. A new and very large hotel is almost complete at Pirate's Well. The Commissioner, Mildred Williamson, would appreciate any feedback you have concerning Mayaguana and what Mayaguanians can do for tourists already enjoying their island and what they can do to attract any new visitors. If you have any suggestion stop in and see Mildred at her office in the pink Government Building by the Batelco tower.

Mayaguana and her citizens must realize that Mayaguana may be either the first or last impression of The Bahamas cruisers have upon passing through. As such they have a certain obligation to represent their country and countrymen. When one writes a cruising guide one also has a certain obligation to the user of that guide. Reporting must be accurate and truthful. Many writers will concentrate on the positive and tend to overlook the negative. I have very little negative to say about The Bahamas and her people, I have had nothing but good experiences throughout the years in these islands (with the possible exception of some incidents with poachers while acting as an Assistant Warden at Exuma Park). With this in mind I have come to a decision to inform cruisers of a series of events that have happened on Mayaguana over the last few years that give this island a bit of a bad reputation. What I am about to relate should in no way be considered an indictment of the good people of Mayaguana, rather it should be a warning concerning one or two individuals whose greed has given the respectable citizens of Mayaguana a bad name. To the good people of Mayaguana, and especially to the Commissioner, Mildred Williamson, I offer my apologies. It is not my intent to besmirch the people of Mayaguana, but it is my obligation to report the truth and visitors must be warned. When the situation is rectified I will be happy to inform people of that fact.

Abraham's Bay is surrounded by a reef that over the years has claimed quite a few vessels. I have made mention of one of the more recent instances a few paragraphs earlier. When these wrecks occur the people of Mayaguana are usually called upon to rescue the crew and whatever goods may be salvageable. In return these rescuers should be compensated for their time and fuel, though how can you put a price on a man risking his life in a small boat in severe conditions to come to your assistance? In the instance of *Hey Jude*, and another wreck that happened a few years earlier, the salvageable goods were stored ashore. In both cases electronics and other valuables were removed from the boxes of goods that were stored and locked in various places. Both times local residents suggested that the goods were being held for "ransom" to insure some type of compensation for the rescuers. In the instance that occurred previous to *Hey Jude* the items were returned when the skipper promised compensation if the goods were returned. In the case of *Hey Jude*, nothing was returned. These are the ways of wreckers, an occupation one would think is dead in today's Bahamas.

As I said before, this is the work of one or two individuals, and the general consensus amongst Mayaguanians is to let the Police handle the matter. Of course this is the proper course to take but there is little the Police can do unless they catch the perpetrators red-handed. Some of the citizens of Mayaguana, and Abraham's Bay in particular, know what is going on and do nothing (that I have noticed) to remedy the situation. I believe that it is the responsibility of the people of Mayaguana to create a climate of rejection for actions such as these. Only then will these activities cease. If that happens I will be happy to change the tone of this writing to reflect the changes in this community.

The events reported should not keep you from visiting Mayaguana. However, if you happen to come to grief upon the reef and you have to place your goods ashore, store them at the Police station. It's the safest place around.

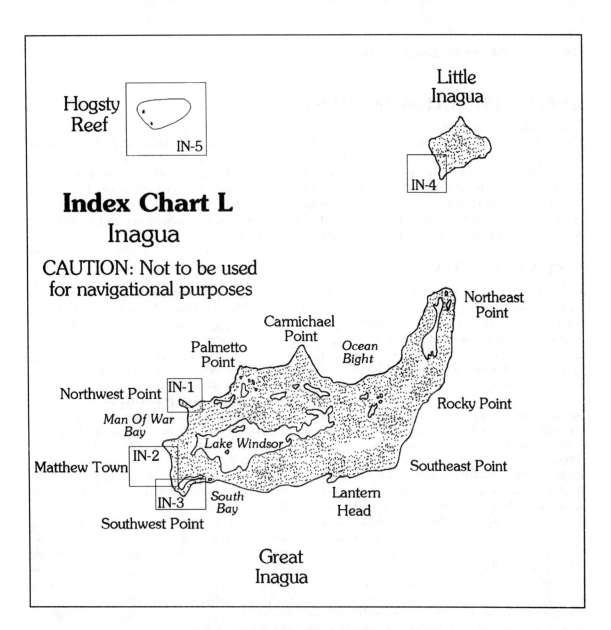

Index Chart L

Inagua

Hogsty Reef

IN-5

Little Inagua

IN-4

Northwest Point

IN-1

Palmetto Point

Carmichael Point

Ocean Bight

Northeast Point

Man Of War Bay

Rocky Point

Matthew Town

IN-2

Lake Windsor

IN-3

South Bay

Southwest Point

Lantern Head

Southeast Point

Great Inagua

GREAT INAGUA

Lying almost within sight of the mountains of Cuba and only sixty miles from Hispaniola, Great Inagua, the third largest and southernmost island in The Bahamas, is approximately 40 miles long and 20 miles wide. The island of Great Inagua is generally low-lying, flat, and wooded except for a few scrub covered hills along its eastern shore. Both Little Inagua and Great Inagua are fringed by reefs along their eastern shores that are a graveyard for all manner of vessels. Some say the island's name is a corruption of *heneagua,* which is derived from the early Spanish discoverer's word for a salty site, the way the Spanish viewed Inagua and which has changed little in 500 years. Other folks say the island's moniker is a corruption of the name of one of the island's many residents, the iguana. The island of Great Inagua is comparatively dry, most people use cisterns for catching rainwater, while incoming salt ships bring fresh water to the island.

APPROACHES TO GREAT INAGUA

From Castle Island at the south end of Acklins Island, Matthew Town bears 158° at a distance of 75.2 nautical miles. From the waypoint at Hogsty Reef, Matthew Town bears 176° at a distance of 44.2 nautical miles.

If approaching from Little Inagua, one must round Northwest Point well off then turn southward to Matthew Town. The waypoint off Northwest Point lies 38.8 nautical miles on a course of 248° from the anchorage at Little Inagua. If approaching the waypoint off Northwest Point from the anchorage at Little Inagua be sure to keep a sharp lookout as you approach within 10 miles of Northwest Point. There are several reefs lying northeast of Northwest Point that you must avoid.

GREAT INAGUA

Inagua is sort of the Wild West of The Bahamas and is definitely not set up for tourism. This isolated island is rarely visited by tourists. With the exception of three 100' high hills the terrain is flat and harsh and has more cacti than any other Bahamian island. Wild donkeys, cows, and hogs roam the land. The donkeys in particular seemed plagued by mosquitoes and it is not unusual to see one wade out into the water until only its head is above water. As the mosquitoes swarm over their exposed head they will dunk their head in the water and shake it until rid of the bothersome mosquitoes, for a little while at least.

Inagua's principal claim to fame is shared by some 60,000 pink flamingos and the Morton Salt Company. Inagua was once called the *El Dorado* of The Bahamas due to its productive salt industry, the second largest in the world. Little is known of the early history of Inagua. There is evidence of a prosperous salt industry as early as 1803 and some say salt was a commodity here as early as the 1600's. Wrecking seemed to be prosperous in Inagua as elsewhere in The Bahamas. Henri Christophe, the Black Emperor of Haiti, built a summer palace at Northeast Point in the early 1800's to take advantage of Inagua's close proximity to Haiti and is rumored to have been rowed back and forth the entire 110 miles from Haiti. There is a spot near the northeast point called Christoph (spelling correct) where there are still some ruins to be found. It is said Christophe hid a cache of gold in the area.

In 1849, a company upgraded salt production on Inagua by using mule powered rail cars. The salt was kept in a specially built storage building called the Salt House. Above the door to the Salt House, which still stands today, is a unique brick design whose bricks were imported from the sunken remains of the old Pirate haven of Port Royal, Jamaica. Just before the end of the first World War, the population on Inagua was 5,000. Matthew Town, along with Albert Town on Long Cay in the Crooked/Acklins District, was a main port of entry for ships plying the waters of the Windward Passage and Caribbean. Ships from both the Hamburg-American Line and the Netherlands Steamship Company regularly made stops at Inagua to take on salt, laborers, and supplies. The unionization of stevedores and migrant workers stopped a lot of the shipping activity around Inagua and the economy suffered somewhat until the arrival of the Erikson Brothers.

The modern history of Inagua can be traced to 1936 and the arrival of the Erikson brothers. The Erikson brothers moved into Inagua, much to the hostile discontent of the local inhabitants, with tractors, trucks, bulldozers, and modern machinery. They built up the salt works in the space of only 12 years to where they were, and still are, one of the most successful in the world. The salt industry here had flourished during the American Civil War years and until sometime thereafter. The price during this period rose from $.60 to $1.00 a bushel. This translates to somewhere between $18.00 and $30.00 a ton. During this time Matthew Town was a flourishing community of some 7,000 happy islanders. They lived in lavish luxury for such an out of the way place. They had horse drawn carriages, moonlight balls, French fashions, even a polo team. With falling prices, down to a low of $3.00 a ton, and a slumping market, the salt economy collapsed and Matthew Town became a ghost town. Many of the islanders shipped out to work on the Panama Canal, the Mexican railways, the *Hamburg-American Line*, the *Royal Netherlands Line*, or the mahogany industry in Central America. The three Erikson brothers had to import laborers from the Turks Islands to build a sufficient workforce to man all their machinery. The Eriksons were successful in revitalizing the salt industry to such a degree that it caught the interest of the giant Morton Salt Company which bought them out in 1955. For a first-hand account of the Erikson years and the lifestyle of the residents of Inagua during that period, read *Great Inagua* by Margery O. Erikson (*Capriole Press*, Garrison, N.Y., 1987), it is an excellent account of those years.

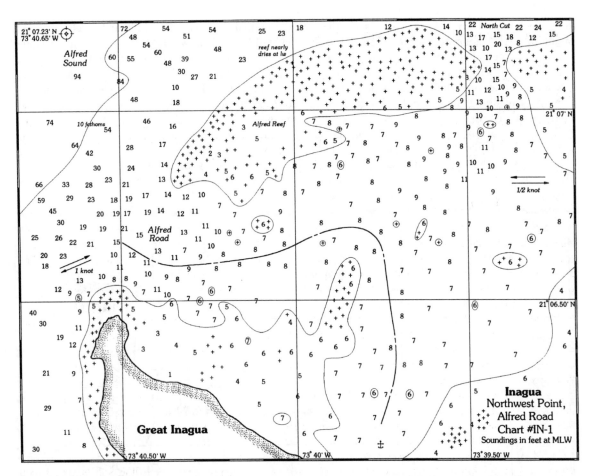

Inagua
Northwest Point,
Alfred Road
Chart #IN-1
Soundings in feet at MLW

Today, *Morton Bahamas, Ltd.* (MBL), employs over 300 people and operates some 80 odd salt ponds covering 12,000 acres. It is the second largest solar salt operation in the world producing over a million pounds of salt every year and its huge mountains of salt can be seen from many miles out at sea. Dikes hold back shallow but extensive reservoirs that hold water pumped from the sea for evaporation. Seawater is channeled from one reservoir to another by the pumps and aqueducts. The tropical sun evaporates the moisture and the seawater transforms first into a concentrated brine and finally layers of almost pure salt which are raked up and piled in huge white pyramids easily seen from offshore. Besides regular salt for consumer use, Inagua also produces a larger, coarser grain the size of peanuts for scientific and industrial applications. Today Matthew Town has a population of around 1200.

Inagua is home to a mercury driven, kerosene fueled, 25,000 candlepower lighthouse that was built in 1870, much to the dismay of the wreckers who were put out of business by the presence of the light. The light is the last manually operated light in The Bahamas. The light was of no help to a scientist named Gilbert Klingel whose *Spray* replica was wrecked on an Inaguan reef in a gale in the 1920's. On his way to a scientific expedition to the West Indies when shipwrecked, Klingel decided to use his salvaged equipment to study Inagua. Klingel stayed on for six months taking botanical specimens and wrote an excellent natural history book, *Inagua: The Ocean Isle*.

NORTHWEST POINT TO MAN OF WAR BAY

At the northwestern tip of Great Inagua lies Northwest Point as shown on Chart #IN-1. Vessels headed for Matthew Town or the Windward Passage via the western shore of Inagua can make for a GPS waypoint at 21° 07.23' N, 74° 40.65' W. This will place you approximately ¾ mile north/northwest of the point. Vessels headed to this waypoint from Little Inagua or Mayaguana should keep an eye out for the reefs north of Inagua and northeast of Alfred Sound and Northwest Point.

There is a fair anchorage inside Alfred Sound that is good in south to west winds which is great in the prelude to a frontal passage but not a good spot after the wind comes into the west/northwest. The entrance to the anchorage weaves through a break in the reef and around some smaller heads and patch reefs and should never be attempted at night. Use caution if anchored here, if the winds shifts into the north while you are anchored at night you will find yourself on a lee shore and you won't be able to find your way out until daylight. Inagua suffers from a lack of an all weather anchorage. Your only choices in a frontal passage are to leave, or hide inside Molasses Reef (more on Molasses Reef later). To enter the anchorage from the waypoint given above, head in through Alfred Road just north of Northwest Point. One can also enter through North Cut but that pass is very narrow though just as deep. Continue east and pass north of the long reef that works out from Great Inagua. Once past its northern tip, turn to starboard and work your way in as close to the shore of Inagua as your draft will allow.

Northeast of Northwest Point lies Sheep Cay. Some publications suggest anchoring in its lee, I cannot. The narrow entrance through the reef just east of Sheep Cay is hard to find even in good visibility and only allows vessels that draw 3'-4' inside at low water.

Just south of Northwest Point, along the northwestern shore of Great Inagua between Northwest Point and Devil's Point just north of Matthew Town is large, curving, Man Of War Bay. In winds from northeast to southeast this is a good lee anchorage though there are quite a few reefs just off the shoreline, especially on the northern shore. The northern shore is high and offers a fair lee in north to northeast winds. Keep an eye out as you approach the shore to drop the hook. Expect a surge throughout the bay.

The southern shore should not be considered as an anchorage as the water is relatively deep close in to the shoreline. You would be better off in southerly conditions to anchor inside Northwest Point.

MATTHEW TOWN

Matthew Town is the principal settlement on Great Inagua and the waters are fairly deep close in to shore. A GPS waypoint at 20° 57.10' N, 73° 41.50' W, as shown on Chart #IN-2, will place you approximately ¾ mile west of the town dock. The anchorage here is a good lee in light to moderate prevailing winds though there is often a surge. If a front approaches you must go elsewhere. The Erikson brothers made several attempts to build jetties but each met with disaster as gale after gale destroyed their finest efforts.

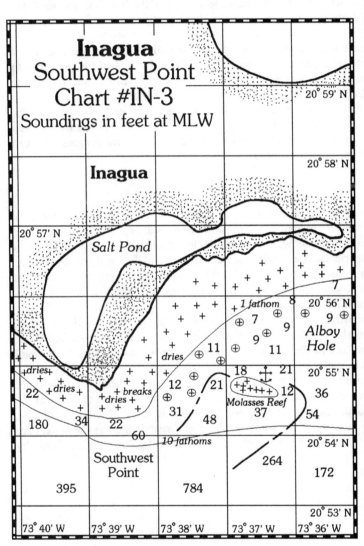

For those wanting to land a dinghy the best thing to do is head north of town into the small dredged harbour where you can tie up and walk or hitch a ride into town, only minutes away. Never attempt to use the small 200' by 200' harbour as a refuge from a frontal passage, it is a deathtrap as the wrecks inside will testify. If a front threatens either go elsewhere or seek whatever shelter you can find behind Molasses Reef. The entrance to the small harbour is on a course of 126° on the small pole at the southeast end of the harbour. Use caution upon entry as rock ledges line both sides of the narrow entrance channel that barely takes 5' at low water. The local *Shell* station will arrange for fuel at the southern wall of the small harbour if needed. Matthew Town is a Port Of Entry and clearance can be obtained at the pink Customs office in town near the dock.

In town you will find several restaurants and grocery stores. The *Topp's Restaurant and Bar*, owned by Cleveland Palacious, serves good Bahamian foods and is quite a night spot. Cleveland monitors VHF ch. 16 for those in need of local information. On the other side of town is Sheddie Fox's *Hide Out Cafe and Disco*, one of the more popular spots for nighttime entertainment. Matthew Town has an excellent phone system, almost every house has a phone. There is a *Royal Bank of Canada* branch in Matthew Town as well as a branch office of the *Bank of The Bahamas*. Sometimes films and slide shows are presented in the *Old Salt Theater*. The *Main House*, owned by *Morton Bahamas Limited*, is a four room hotel with restaurant in Matthew Town. Accommodations can also be found at the *Crystal Beach View Hotel* with 13 rooms and *Walker's Guest House* with 5 rooms. You'll also find *Ingraham's Variety Store*, the *MBL Store*, a *Shell Trading Ltd.* gas station and auto parts, and a clinic with a doctor and nurse.

In 1963 The Bahamas National Trust convinced the government of The Bahamas to set aside 287 square miles in the interior as a preserve for the long-necked, and equally long-legged pink flamingo. Thus was born Inagua National Park complete with a Warden and encompassing 12 mile long Lake Windsor and numerous mangrove salinas, the pink flamingo's breeding and feeding grounds. Resident Warden Henry Nixon has his hands full protecting the lives of some 60,000 pink flamingos. Henry's father Jimmy has been protecting "fillymingos" here since 1952, first as an Audubon Warden and recently as the Park Warden. Jimmy retired leaving Henry to battle poachers on a daily basis as "fillymingo steak" seems to be quite tasty. In Roman times flamingo tongue was a delicacy while here on Inagua Nixon can tell tales of "fillymingo" roundups when entire families chased the tasty pink flamingo. Besides worrying about poachers the Warden has to keep the wild boars from eating the flamingos. The pink flamingos do not breed in great quantities, usually laying just one egg per year. For this reason the Bahamas National Trust has begun a hatchling program with 10,000 flamingos being born in 1992 itself. The flamingos feed mostly on brine shrimp which helps maintain their pink color. The flamingo may be the only vertebrate that eats standing straight up with its head upside down. Henry can arrange jeep tours of the Park and you may stay at *Flamingo Camp* (the *Arthur Vernay Camp*) in the park in the rather Spartan surroundings offered at *Basil's Bunkhouse*.

Nearby *Union Creek* is a seven square mile hawksbill and green turtle preserve. Union Creek was started by the *Caribbean Conservation Society* and the late Sam Nixon. The purpose of the project is to develop a breeding and research ground for sea turtles. The *Caribbean Conservation Society* and the Bahamas Ministry of Agriculture and Fisheries release thousands of newly hatched turtles into Inaguan waters in hopes that they will grow to maturity and return to nest on Inagua. The park also protects the Bahamas parrot which only live on Inagua and Abaco. The Inagua Parrot nests in trees unlike their Abaco cousins which nest in the ground. Ask around in Matthew Town as there are several persons who can arrange private tours though it is best to contact Henry Nixon.

SOUTHWEST POINT

With the exception of the anchorage at Alfred Sound inside Northwest Point (Chart #IN-1), the only other place on Great Inagua to offer any sort of protection in southwest winds is approximately 2 miles east of Southwest Point in the lee of Molasses Reef as shown on Chart #IN-3. I cannot recommend this spot in strong southwesterlies as I have never experienced those winds at this location and the local opinion differs. Some folks say it is good place to anchor, most say no. I am inclined to believe the naysayers. I would not relish the thought of riding out a prefrontal wind shift to the west behind Molasses Reef. But since this is the only protection available I have sounded the area and offer the results.

From Matthew Town, parallel the coastline of Great Inagua southeastward toward Southwest Point staying at least ½ mile off the reef strewn shore. Many places along this reef dry and once past Southwest Point, the waters close in to the southern shore of Great Inagua are literally strewn with many, many small heads and patch reefs. Pilotage by eye is essential here.

Round Southwest Point giving it a berth of at least ½ mile and head east approximately 2½ miles until past very visible Molasses Reef where you can round up into its lee. You can also pass to the west of the reef but if you have strong westerly or southwesterly winds blowing, this would make Molasses Reef a lee shore. You will not be able to get very close in to the southern shore of Great Inagua as the waters are shallow and littered with dangerous heads and small patch reefs but you can still gain some lee simply by tucking in as close as your draft allows.

LITTLE INAGUA

Little Inagua lies a little over 5 miles north of Northeast Point on Great Inagua and is seldom visited by the cruising yacht. The island is relatively flat with a small ridge just inshore encircling most of the island. The inhospitable eastern shore is guarded by a very shallow and dangerous fringing reef extending from the northwestern tip of Little Inagua along the eastern shore to the southern tip.

APPROACHES TO LITTLE INAGUA

If approaching Little Inagua from southern end of West Caicos on the Turks and Caicos Banks, steer to a point just north of Little Inagua. From there you may pass to the west of Little Inagua to head to the anchorage described later or to head to Matthew Town on the western shore of Great Inagua. An added benefit for cruisers heading to Little Inagua from the east is the "pinnacles" lying northeast and east of Little Inagua. These "pinnacles" are actually the tops of undersea mountains that rise to within 90' of the surface. They are not a hazard to navigation and in fact are excellent fishing grounds, be sure to troll a line here. A lot of the sportfishermen from the Turks and Caicos come here for piscatorial action.

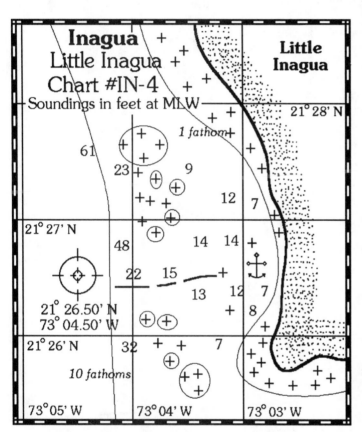

LITTLE INAGUA

The only anchorage is off the beach on the southwestern shore of Little Inagua as shown on Chart #IN-5. A GPS waypoint at 21° 26.50' N, 74° 04.50' W, will place you approximately 1½ miles west of the southwestern tip of Little Inagua. Find your way through the break in the reef and head in to the beach as far as your draft will allow and anchor in good holding sand. You'll have to dodge some heads and patch reefs here so only attempt this in good visibility, never at night. These same reefs and heads will probably supply your dinner if you take the time to look.

Some of the biggest lobsters I have ever seen outside of Exuma Park inhabit the coral heads in this area. This anchorage is only good in northeast to southeast winds and some swell may work its way in during periods of strong winds.

Inland are some very interesting formations. Here you will find 100' Royal Palms rising out of holes that are at times 30' deep. These same holes are often a reservoir for fresh water if you are in need. Boil the water before drinking.

The passage between Little Inagua and Great Inagua is about 5 miles wide and over a mile deep in places. There is a westward setting current here and this piece of water can get very rough in strong conditions so take care to avoid it if conditions dictate (say a strong west wind against the west setting current).

One final word (you're probably tired of that phrase by now, right?) about Little Inagua. A few years ago some cruisers that I know set up camp on the beach at the above mentioned anchorage. In a little while four "South American gentlemen" bearing automatic weapons entered their camp. They lined up the cruisers, took their camera, exposed the film, replaced it with new film and took photos of the not-so-happy campers. They then ordered them off the island sans camping equipment and camera but very much alive. My friends felt that they were very lucky. This happened in 1991. When I last visited this remote outpost in May of 1997 I found no evidence of any recent visitors save a few fishermen. There is an increased Defence Force presence in this region (the Southern Bahamas) and I hope that has helped convince the "South American gentlemen" to move on to greener pastures. This wonderful little island, about as far off the beaten path as you can get, is definitely worth exploring in settled weather and I sincerely believe that the event described will not happen again. But while the rest of The Bahamas is free of the violence that was associated with drug smuggling in the 1980's, Little Inagua is very removed from the mainstream of tourist traffic and any help is 50 miles away at Matthew Town. I can only urge you to use caution as the event described happened only a very few years ago.

HOGSTY REEF

Hogsty Reef was once shown on old charts as *Les Etoiles* and its present name was given to the area by early buccaneers. Hogsty Reef, along with Glover Reef and Lighthouse Reef off Belize and the Cay Sal Bank, is the closest thing that you will find to a true coral atoll in the North Atlantic. To understand how rare this is one must bear in mind that there are over 400 atolls scattered about the Pacific and Indian Oceans.

Hogsty Reef is basically a horseshoe shaped outer reef enclosing an inner lagoon with depths of 20'-30' over a sandy bottom with numerous scattered coral heads. The area is approximately 3 miles by 5 miles and good size seas can build up within the lagoon even though the outer reef breaks the ocean swells. The fringing reef rises almost straight up from mile deep water so rapidly that skippers rarely see the breakers from over a mile out and may not even come up on soundings until 100 yards away from the reef.

Visitors to Hogsty Reef today are primarily fishermen taking advantage of the abundance of marine life in the vicinity and cruisers seeking shelter. Do not attempt to use this anchorage in a strong blow from any direction unless absolutely necessary.

The outer reef offers excellent diving opportunities but only for the experienced diver due to tidal conditions, sea swells, and a strong current. The inner lagoon makes for excellent snorkeling and fishing over the scattered heads.

APPROACHES TO HOGSTY REEF

The most visible landmark during the day are the rusting remains of an old Liberty ship stranded on the northern reef by a hurricane in 1963. This may appear at first to be a ship underway on a heading of 142° so don't be misled. The hulk is approximately 4 miles east of the entrance to the lagoon which lies just south of Northwest Cay. Almost as visible is the 29' high red and white banded light tower standing on Northwest Cay. The light flashes white every 4 seconds and is visible for approximately 8 nautical miles.

Hogsty Reef lies approximately halfway between Castle Island in the Crooked/Acklins District and the Northeast Point of Great Inagua. From Castle Island a course of 139° for 38.8 miles will bring you to the waypoint off the western edge of Hogsty Reef. From Matthew Town, Great Inagua, the same waypoint bears 356° at a distance of 44.2 nautical miles.

HOGSTY REEF

The entrance to the reef enclosed basin is fairly simple, it lies between Northwest Cay and Southeast Cay, which actually lies at the southwestern tip of Hogsty Reef. A fair lee anchorage can be found along the western shore of Northwest Cay in 8'-30' of water as shown on Chart #IN-5. The two cays are little more than a couple of hundred yards long each and offer little protection. In settled weather you may anchor in the center of the lagoon in water from 6'-35' deep but take care to avoid the scattered coral heads. A GPS waypoint at 21° 40.50' N, 73° 51.50' W, will place you approximately one mile west of the entrance lying between Northwest Cay and Southeast Cay. Head generally east/northeast to enter the lagoon proper or simply steer for Northwest Cay to anchor in its lee. Remember, Hogsty Reef is no place to be when bad weather threatens, it is best avoided if conditions are forecast to deteriorate.

Inagua
Hogsty Reef
Chart #IN-5
Soundings in feet at MLv

Northwest Cay

Southeast Cay

light
Fl W ev 4 sec,
29', 8M

1 fathom

10 fathoms

dries

21° 42' N   21° 41' N   21° 40' N

21° 40.50' N
73° 51.50' W

73° 45' W   73° 46' W   73° 47' W   73° 48' W   73° 49' W   73° 50' W   73° 51' W

REFERENCES

AND SUGGESTED READING

A Cruising Guide to Abaco; Steve Dodge, White Sound Press, 1995

A Cruising Guide to the Caribbean and the Bahamas; Jerrems C. Hart and William T. Stone, Dodd, Mead and Company, New York, 1982

A Cruising Guide to the Exumas Cays Land and Sea Park; Stephen J. Pavlidis with Ray Darville, Night Flyer Enterprises, U.S.A., 1994

A History of the Bahamas; Michael Craton, Collins Press, London, 1969

A History of the Bahamas; Michael Craton, San Salvador Press, Ontario, Canada, 1986

American Practical Navigator; Nathaniel Bowditch, L.L.D., DMA Hydrographic Center, 1977

Bahamas Handbook and Businessmen's Manual; Etienne Dupuch, Jr., Etienne Dupuch Jr., Publications, Nassau, Bahamas, 1960

Bahamas Handbook and Businessmen's Manual; Etienne Dupuch, Jr., Etienne Dupuch Jr., Publications, Nassau, Bahamas, 1971

Bahamas Handbook and Businessmen's Manual; Sir Etienne Dupuch, Jr., Etienne Dupuch Jr., Publications Ltd., Nassau, Bahamas, 1991

Dictionary of Bahamian English; John A. Holm, Lexik House Pub., Cold Springs, N.Y., 1982

Great Inagua; Margery O. Erikson, Capriole Press, Garrison, N.Y., 1987

Island Expedition, The Central and Southern Bahamas; Nicolas and Dragan Popov, Graphic Media, Miami, FL, 1988

Mystical Cat Island; Eris Moncur, Northstar Press, Miami, FL, 1996

Out Island Doctor; Dr. Evans W. Cottman, Hodder and Stoughton, London, 1963

Reptiles and Amphibians of the Bahamas; Bahamas National Trust, 1993

Sailing Directions for the Caribbean Sea; Pub. #147, Defense Mapping Agency, #SDPUB147

Secrets of the Bahamas Family Islands 1989; Nicolas Popov, Dragan Popov, & Jane Sydenham; Southern Boating Magazine, May 1989

The American Coast Pilot; Blunt, 1812

The Aranha Report on the Berry Islands; Land and Surveys Dept., Nassau, New Providence, Bahamas, 1925

The Bahamas Handbook; Mary Moseley, The Nassau Guardian, Nassau, Bahamas, 1926

The Bahamas Rediscovered; Nicolas and Dragon Popov, Macmillan Press, Ltd., London, 1992

The Ephemeral Islands, A Natural History of the Bahamas; David G. Campbell, MacMillan Education, 1990

The Exuma Guide, A Cruising Guide to the Exuma Cays; Stephen J. Pavlidis, Seaworthy Publications, Inc., Port Washington, WI, 1995

The Gentleman's Guide to Passages South; Bruce Van Sant, Cruising Guide Publications, 1989 and 1996

The Ocean Almanac; Robert Hendrickson, Doubleday, New York, 1984

The Pirates Own Book; published by A. & C. B . Edwards, New York, and Thomas, Cowperthwait, & Co., Philadelphia, 1842

The Yachtsman's Guide to the Bahamas; Meredith Fields, Tropic Isle Pub., 1995 and 1996

APPENDICES

APPENDIX A: Navigational Aids

A-1: Lights

Navigational lights in The Bahamas should be considered unreliable at best. Their characteristics may differ from those published here and are subject to change without notice. It is not unusual for a light to be out of commission for long periods of time. Listing of lights reads from north to south.

LIGHT	CHARACTERISTICS	COLOR	HT.	RNG.
THE BIMINIS				
Great Isaac LH	FL ev 15 sec	W	37'	11 nm
North Rock	FL ev 3 sec	W	40'	8 nm
Gun Cay	FL ev 10 sec	W	80'	14 nm
Cat Cay Marina (Priv.)	FL ev 4 sec.	W	12'	5 nm
Ocean Cay Range	QK FL	W	35'	7 nm
South Riding Rock	FL ev 5 sec	W	35'	10 nm
THE GREAT BAHAMA BANK				
Russell Beacon	FL ev 4 sec	W	20'	8 nm
Mackie Beacon	FL ev 2 sec	W	20'	8 nm
Sylvia Beacon	FL ev 4 sec	W	20'	8 nm
Northwest Shoal Buoy	FL ev 2 sec	W	12'	5 nm
NW Channel Light	FL ev 3 sec	W	33'	8 nm
THE BERRYS				
Great Stirrup Cay LH	GP FL (2) ev 20 sec	W	82'	22 nm
Bullock's Harbour	FL ev 6 sec	W	20'	7 nm
Little Harbour Cay	FL ev 2 sec	W	75'	9 nm
Chub Point *	FL ev 10 sec	W & R	44'	7 nm
ANDROS	FL ev 6 sec	R		
Morgan's Bluff channel	FL	R & G		
Bethel Channel Range	FL ev 5 sec-two lights	W	60/65'	9 nm
AUTEC #1 sea buoy **	FL ev 4 sec	W		
AUTEC #1 channel	FL ev 4 sec	G #3		
AUTEC #1 channel	FL ev 4 sec	G #5		
AUTEC #1 channel	FL ev 4 sec	R #6		
AUTEC #1 channel	FL ev 4 sec	G #7	16'	
High Cay	FL ev 4 sec	W	70'	5 nm
AUTEC #2 sea buoy	FL ev 4 sec	R		
AUTEC #2 channel	FL ev 4 sec	G #3	16'	
AUTEC #2 channel	FL ev 4 sec	R #4	16'	
AUTEC #2 channel	FL ev 4 sec	R #6	16'	
AUTEC #2 channel	FL ev 4 sec	G #9	16'	
AUTEC #2 channel	FL ev 4 sec	R #10	16'	
AUTEC #2 channel	FL ev 4 sec	G #13	16'	
AUTEC #2 F. range	QK FL	W	22'	
AUTEC #2 R. range	FL ev 6 sec	W	42'	
AUTEC #3 sea buoy	Fl ev 4 sec	W		
AUTEC #3 channel	Fl ev 4 sec	G #3	19'	
AUTEC #3 channel	Fl ev 4 sec	R #4	19'	
AUTEC #3 channel	Fl ev 4 sec	W	33'	
AUTEC #3 channel	Fl ev 4 sec	R #6	16'	
AUTEC #3 channel	Fl ev 4 sec	G #9	16'	
Little Golding Cay	FL ev 5 sec	W	17'	7 nm
AUTEC #4 channel	Fl ev 4 sec	G #1	19'	
AUTEC #4 channel	Fl ev 4 sec	R #2	19'	

South Bight-Sirius Rock	FL ev 3 sec	W	29'	7 nm
Duncan Rock	FL ev 3.3 sec	W	37'	6 nm
Tinker Rock	FL ev 4 sec	W		8 nm
NEW PROVIDENCE				
Goulding Cay-W end	FL ev 2 sec	W	36'	8 nm
Fort Fincastle ***	FL ev 5 sec	W	216'	18 nm
Paradise Island ****	FL ev 5 sec	W or R	68'	W-10 nm R-5 nm
Nassau W entrance	FL ev 4 sec	G #1		
Nassau W entrance	FL ev 4 sec	R #2		
Nassau E breakwater	FL ev 5 sec	G		9 nm
Nassau W breakwater	FL ev 5 sec	R	30'	
Nassau W entrance	FL ev 4 sec	G #3		
Nassau W entrance	FL ev 4 sec	R #4		
Nassau W entrance	FL ev 4 sec	G #5		
Nassau W entrance	FL ev 4 sec	R #6		
Nassau W entrance	FL ev 4 sec	G #7		
Range Light-front	FXD	G	37'	7 nm
Range Light-rear	FXD	G	61'	7 nm
The Narrows-Athol Isl.	FL ev 5 sec	R	12'	2 nm
Chub Rock	FL ev 5 sec	W	25'	4 nm
Lyford Cay	FL ev 2 sec	W	25'	4 nm
Coral Harbour	FL ev 2 sec	W		
East Point	FL ev 6 sec	W		8 nm
NEW PROVIDENCE TO ELEUTHERA				
Porgee Rocks	FL ev 3 sec	W	23'	5 nm
The Narrows	FL ev 5 sec	W	12'	2 nm
Chub Rock	FL ev 5 sec	W	32'	4 nm
Fleeming Channel-west	FL ev 4 sec	R	37'	8 nm
Fleeming Channel-east	FL ev 4 sec	G	32'	10 nm
ELEUTHERA				
Egg Island	FL ev 3 sec	W	112'	12 nm
Royal Island	FL ev 5 sec	W	22'	5 nm
Man Island	Gp. FL (3) ev 15 sec	W	93'	12 nm
Hatchett Bay	FL (2-4 sec) ev 15 sec	W	57'	8 nm
Governor's Harbour	FL ev 4 sec	W	40'	8 nm
Poison Point	FL ev 15 sec	W	38'	8 nm
East End Point	FL ev 4½ sec	W	61'	6 nm
TMB2 Buoy	FL ev 4 sec	W	Red Buoy	
LITTLE SAN SALVADOR				
South shore	FL ev 2½ sec	W	69'	13 nm
CAT ISLAND				
Bennett's Harbour	FL ev 4 sec	W	53'	12 nm
Smith's Bay	FL ev 4 sec	W	38'	7 nm
Devil Point	FL ev 5 sec	W	143'	12 nm
EXUMAS				
Beacon Cay	FL ev. 3 sec.	W & R*	58'	8 nm
Elbow Cay	FL ev. 6 sec.	W	46'	11 nm
Dotham Cut	FL ev. 5 sec.	W	36'	8 nm
Galliot Cut	FL ev. 4 sec.	W	50'	7 nm
Conch Cay	FL ev. 5 sec.	W	40'	8 nm
Jewfish Cut	FL ev. 2½ sec.	W	38'	8 nm
Hawksbill Rock	FL ev. 3.3 sec.	W	40'	6 nm
CONCEPTION ISL.				
Southwest Point	FL ev 2 sec	W	84'	6 nm

RUM CAY

Cottonfield Point	Fl ev 8 sec	WYR	75'	10 nm
Port Nelson Dock	FXD	G	16'	5 nm

SAN SALVADOR

Dixon Hill Lighthouse	GP. FL (2) ev 10 sec	W	163'	19 nm

LONG ISLAND

Cape Santa Maria	FL ev 3.3 sec	W	99'	14 nm
Clarence Tn.-Booby R.	FL ev 2 sec	W	41'	8 nm
South End	FL ev 2½ sec	W	61'	12 nm

THE JUMENTOS

Nuevitas Rocks	FL ev 4 sec	W	38'	10 nm
Flamingo Cay	FL ev 6 sec	W	138'	8 nm
Ragged Island	FL ev 3 sec	W	118'	12 nm
Cay Santo Domingo	FL ev 5 sec	W	30'	7 nm
Cay Lobos Lighthouse	GP. FL (2) ev 10 sec	W	145'	22 nm

CROOKED ISLAND DISTRICT

Bird Rock Lighthouse	FL ev 15 sec	W	112'	23 nm
Attwood Harbour	FL ev 5 sec	W	20'	8 nm
Hell Gate	FL ev 6 sec	W	56'	10 nm
Windsor Point	FL ev 3 sec	W	35'	8 nm
Castle Island Lighthouse	GP. FL (2) ev 20 sec	W	130'	22 nm

HOGSTY REEF

Northwest Cay	FL ev 4 sec	W	29'	8 nm

MAYAGUANA

Guano Pt., Abrhm's Bay	FL ev 3 sec	W	13'	8 nm
Northwest Point	FL ev 5 sec	W	70'	12 nm

GREAT INAGUA

Matthew Town Canal	GP. FL (2) ev 10 sec	W	120'	17 nm

* Chub Point light has white and red sectors denoting safe entrance to the marina and anchorage at Chub. These sectors are unreliable and quite often red is not working.

** All AUTEC lights are subject to change without notice, especially offshore buoys which are often hard to see at night even when lit. AUTEC towers flash amber lights.

*** The Fort Fincastle light is a gray concrete water tower with a revolving white light atop, similar in appearance to a lighthouse.

**** The Paradise Island Light, a white stone tower, normally shows white but is obscured from 334° to 25°. When the bar at the western entrance to Nassau Harbour is dangerous the light shows red.

A-2: Batelco Towers

Towers over 50' in height have red lights at their tops, either fixed or flashing (Fxd or Fl). Taller towers may have fixed red lights at intermediate levels. Positions are approximate. Listing of Batelco towers is from north to south.

LOCATION	LIGHT	HT.	LOCATION	LIGHT	HT.
THE BIMINIS*			**ELEUTHERA**		
Alice Town	Fl-R	100'	Spanish Wells	Fxd-R	120'
Cat Cay	unlit	50'	Harbour Island	Fxd-R	40'
North Bimini	Fxd-R	50'	Lower Bogue	Fxd-R	200'
ANDROS			Hatchet Bay	Fl-R	265'
Cargill Creek	Fxd-R	100'	Governor's Harbour	Fl-R	180'
Fresh Creek	Fl-R	225'	Governor's Harbour	Fxd-R	59'
Kemp's Bay	Fl-R	150'	Savannah Sound	Fl-R	200'
Mangrove Cay	Fxd-R	100'	Tarpum Bay	Fl-R	200'
Mars Bay	Fxd-R	100'	Rock Sound	Fxd-R	100'
Mastic Point	Fxd-R	100'	Green Castle	Fl-R	240'
Nicholl's Town	Fl-R	255'	**CAT ISLAND**		
Red Bay	unlit	50'	Arthur's Town	Fl-R	200'
Staniard Creek	Fl-R	200'	New Bight	Fl-R	235'

THE BERRYS				Hawks Nest	unlit	50'
Bullock's Harbour	Fxd-R	235'		**SAN SALVADOR**		
Chub Cay	Fl-R	200'		Cockburn Town	Fxd-R	59'
NEW PROVIDENCE				Cockburn Town	Fxd-R	150'
Delaporte	Fxd-R	100'		**RUM CAY**		
Lyford Cay	Fxd-R	100'		Port Nelson	Fxd-R	100'
Coral Harbour-Batel.	Fl-R	160'		**CROOKED ISLAND**		
Coral Harbour-Def. F.	Fxd-R	100'		Cabbage Hill	Fxd-R	82'
Soldier Road	Fl-R	260'		Cabbage Hill	Fl-R	200'
Poinciana Drive	Fl-R	200'		**ACKLINS ISLAND**		
East Street	Fxd-R	80'		Spring Point	Fl-R	235'
Perpall Tract	Fxd-R	150'		Spring Point	Fxd-R	70'
Perpall Tract	Fxd-R	150'		**MAYAGUANA**		
Perpall Tract	Fxd-R	80'		Abraham's Bay	Fxd-R	225'
Perpall Tract	Fxd-R	80'		Betsy Bay	Fxd-R	105'
LONG ISLAND				**INAGUA**		
Stella Maris	Fxd-R	50'		Matthew Town	Fxd-R	70'
Simms	Fl-R	200'		Matthew Town	Fxd-R	59'
Roses	unlit	50'		Matthew Town	Fxd-R	50'
LONG ISLAND				**JUMENTOS**		
Deadman's Cay	Fl-R	200'		Duncan Town	Fl-R	118'
Clarence Town	Fxd-R	60'				

* In 1996, the very conspicuous tower on South Bimini, actually not a Batelco tower but a LF radio tower (Fl R ev 20 seconds, Morse code letter "B," -...), was removed and plans were uncertain as to when it was to be rebuilt and what its characteristics are to be. As of July, 1997, the tower was still down.

APPENDIX B: Marinas

Some of the marinas listed below may be untenable in certain winds and dockside depths listed may not reflect entrance channel depths at low water. Check with the Dockmaster prior to arrival. All the marinas can handle your garbage disposal problems however some may levy a charge per bag for those who are not guests at their docks. For cruisers seeking services "Nearby" may mean a walk or short taxi ride away.

MARINA	FUEL	SLIPS	DEPTH	GROCERIES	DINING
ANDROS					
Lighthouse Marina, Fresh Crk.	D & F	18	9'	Nearby	Y
THE BERRYS					
Chub Cay Marina	D & G	80	10'	Y	Y
Frazier Cay Marina	None	10	7'	N	Y
Great Harbour Cay Marina	D & G	86	9'	Nearby	Y
BIMINI					
Bimini Beach Club & Marina	None	50	8'	N	Y
Bimini Big Game Fishing Club	D & G	100	6'	Nearby	Nearby
Bimini Blue Water Resort	D & G	32	6'	Nearby	Nearby
Harcourt Brown's Marina	None	24	6'	Nearby	Nearby
Sun Crest Marina	None	32	8'	Nearby	Nearby
Weech's Bimini Dock	None	15	6'	Nearby	Nearby
CAT CAY					
Cat Cay Marina	D & G	75	8'	Nearby	Nearby
CAT ISLAND					
Hawk's Nest Resort & Marina	D & G	8	7½'	Some	Yes
ELEUTHERA					
Yacht Haven, Spanish Wells	D & G	40	10'	Nearby	Yes
Harbour Isl. Club, Harbour Isl.	D & G	32	10'	Nearby	Yes
Valentines, Harbour Island	D	42	10'	Nearby	Yes
Mar. Serv. of El., Hatchet Bay	D	10	12'	Nearby	Nearby
Cape Eleuthera, Powell Point	D & G	24	10'	No	No

Davis Harbour, Weymss Bight	D & G	8	7½'	No	No
LONG ISLAND					
Stella Maris	D & G	12	6'	Nearby	Nearby
NEW PROVIDENCE					
Lyford Cay					
Lyford Cay Marina	D & G	Avail.	9½'	Yes	Yes
Nassau					
Brown's Boat Basin	D & G	2	7'	Nearby	Nearby
East Bay Marina	D & G	25	10'	Nearby	Nearby
Hurricane Hole Marina	D & G	64	10½'	Nearby	Y
Maura's Marina (Bayshore)	D & G	0	15'	Nearby	Nearby
Nassau Harbour Club	D	65	15'	Nearby	Y
Nassau Yacht Haven	D & G	70	15'	Nearby	Y
Paradise Harbour Club	None	20	7'	Nearby	Y
Texaco Fuel Dock	D & G	36	10'	Nearby	Nearby
Port of New Providence					
Clareridge Marina	D & G	Avail.	6'	No	No
RUM CAY					
Sumner Point Marina	D & G	12	9'	Nearby	Yes
SAN SALVADOR					
Riding Rock Marina	D & G	10	9'	Nearby	Nearby

APPENDIX C: Service Facilities

As with any place, businesses come and go, sometimes seemingly overnight. Certain entries on this list may no longer exist by the time this is published.

FACILITY	LOCATION	TEL. #	VHF CALL ch.16
CAR RENTALS			
Andros Beach Hotel	Nicholl's Town, Andros		*Andros Beach*
Avis-West Bay St.	Nassau, New Providence	326-6380	
Avis-Airport	Nassau, New Providence	327-7121	
Avis-Paradise Island	Nassau, New Providence	363-2061	
Big Rock General Store	James Cistern, Eleuthera	335-6355	
Budget-Airport	Nassau, New Providence	327-7121	
Budget-Paradise Island	Nassau, New Providence	363-3095	
Chichcharnies Hotel	Fresh Creek, Andros	368-2025/6	
D & E Rent A Car	Love Hill, Andros	3368-2454	
Larry Dean's Car Rentals	Hatchett Bay, Eleuthera	332-2568	
Dollar-Airport	Nassau, New Providence	377-7301	
Dollar-British Colonial	Nassau, New Providence	325-3716	
Dollar-Cable Beach	Nassau, New Providence	327-6000	
Donna Lee Motel & Rest.	Nicoll's Town, Andros	329-2194	
Ethyl's Cottgs. & Car Rental	Tarpum Bay, Eleuthera		*Ethyl's Cottages*
Friendly Bob's	Powell Pt., Eleuthera		*Friendly Bob*
Griffin's Car Rentals	Governor's Harbour, Eleu.	332-2077/9	
Hawks Nest Resort & Marina	Hawks Nest Pt., Cat Island	357-7257	*Hawks Nest*
Hertz-Airport	Nassau, New Providence	377-6321	
Hertz-Paradise Island	Nassau, New Providence	377-6866	
Lighthouse Marina	Fresh Creek, Andros		*Lighthouse Marina*
Marine Serv. of Eleu.	Hatchet Bay, Eleuthera	335-0186	*Marine Services*
Moss Transportation & Tour	Nassau, New Providence	393-0771	
National	Nassau, New Providence	327-8300/1	
Nixon-Pinder Car Rentals	Governor's Harbour, Eleu.	332-2568	
New Bight Shell Service Sta.	New Bight, Cat Island	342-3014	*New Bight Service*
PK's Auto Rentals	Rock Sound, Eleuthera	334-4236	
Poinciana	Nassau, New Providence	393-1720	

Riding Rock Inn	Cockburn Town, San Salv.		*Riding Rock Inn*
Royal Palm Beach Lodge	Kemp's Bay, Andros	329-4608	*Royal Palm*
Stella Maris Marina	Stella Maris, Long Island	338-2055	*Stella Maris Marina*
Taylor's Garage	Burnt Ground, Long I.		*Taylor's Garage*
Thompson's Bay Inn	Salt Pond, Long Island		*Thompson's Bay Inn*
Wallace's U Drive	Nassau, New Providence	393-0650	
Williams Car Rentals	Glinton's, Long Island	338-5002	*William's Garage*

DIESEL REPAIR/PARTS

Atlantic Equipment & Power	Nassau, New Providence	323-5701	
Bahamas Diesel Sales & Ser.	Nassau, New Providence		
Cap Brown	Abraham's Bay, Maygna.		
Cleveland Brown	Abraham's Bay, Maygna.		*Papa Charlie*
Diesel Power	Nassau, New Providence	325-8319	*Diesel Power*
Great Harbour Cay Marina	Bullock's Hrbr., Berrys		*Great Harbour Cay Marina*
Frank Harding	Nassau, New Providence	393-2181	*Harding Marine*
Ingraham's Marine	Nassau, New Providence	323-5835	
Lightbourne Marine	Nassau, New Providence	393-5285	
Mal-Kemp Marine Co., Ltd.	Nassau, New Providence	322-7131	
Marine Diesel Ltd.	Nassau, New Providence	322-7135	*Marine Diesel*
Marine Garage	Nassau, New Providence	393-3177	
Marine Serv. of Eleu.	Hatchet Bay, Eleuthera	335-0186	*Marine Services*
Anthony Martin	Chub Cay, Berry Islands		*Chub Cay Marina*
Maura's Marine	Nassau, New Providence	393-7873	
Milander's Auto/Marine	Clarence Town, L.I.		*Milanders Auto*
On Site Marine	Spanish Wells, Eleuthera	333-4382	*On Site Marine*
Pinder's Tune Up	Spanish Wells, Eleuthera	333-4262	
Riding Rock Marina	Cockburn Town, San Salv.		*Riding Rock Marina-ch. 06*
Clifford Saunders	Alice Town, North Bimini		*ask at any marina*
Stella Maris Marina	Stella Maris, Long Island	338-2055	*Stella Maris Marina*
Sumner Point Marina	Port Nelson, Rum Cay		*Sumner Point Marina*
Sunpower Marine, Ltd.	Nassau, New Providence	322-2144	
Timothy Thompson	Landrail Pt., Crooked I.		*Cold Front*

ELECTRONICS-marine

Hi-Technology Comm. Sys.	Nassau, New Providence	322-6918	
JVC Electronics	Salt Pond, Long Island		

HAUL OUT

Brown's Boat Basin	Nassau, New Providence	393-3331	*Brown's Boat Basin*
Clareridge Marina	South Shore, New Prov.	364-2218/9	*Clareridge Marina*
George Town Marina & Rep.	George Town, Exuma		*George Town Marina*
Marine Serv. of Eleu.	Hatchet Bay, Eleuthera	335-0186	*Marine Services*
R & B Boat Yard	Spanish Wells, Eleuthera		
Stella Maris Marina	Stella Maris, Long Island	338-2055	*Stella Maris Marina*

HULL REPAIR/PAINTING

Brown's Boat Basin	Nassau, New Providence	393-3331	
Clareridge Marina	South Shore, New Prov.	364-2218/9	*Clareridge Marina*
Cooper's Marine Specialists	Nassau, New Providence	393-7475	
George Town Marina & Rep.	George Town, Exuma		*George Town Marina*
Marine Serv. of Eleu.	Hatchet Bay, Eleuthera	335-0186	*Marine Services*
R & B Boat Yard	Spanish Wells, Eleuthera	333-4462	
Spanish Wells Mar. & Hrdwr.	Spanish Wells, Eleuthera	333-4035	*Sp. Wells Hrdwr. & Mar.*
Stella Maris Marina	Stella Maris, Long Island	338-2055	*Stella Maris Marina*

MARINE SUPPLIES

Bimini General Store & Mar.	Alice Town, North Bimini		*Bimini General Store*
Brown's Boat Basin	Nassau, New Providence	393-3331	
Cooper's Marine Specialists	Nassau, New Providence	393-7475	
Ingraham's Marine	Nassau, New Providence	323-5835	

Lightbourne Marine	Nassau, New Providence	393-5285	*Lightbourne Marine*
Marine Serv. of Eleu.	Hatchet Bay, Eleuthera	335-0186	*Marine Services*
Maura's Marine	Nassau, New Providence	393-7873	*Maura's Marine*
Milander's Auto/Marine	Clarence Town, L.I.		*Milanders Auto*
Montagu Hts. Serv. Ctr.	Nassau, New Providence	393-1160	
Nautical Marine, Ltd.	Nassau, New Providence	393-3894	
Pinder's Marine	Deep Creek, Eleuthera	334-8330	*Pinder's Marine*
Ron's Marine and Auto Parts	Rock Sound, Eleuthera		*Ron's Marine*
Ronald's Marine	Spanish Wells, Eleuthera	333-4021	*Ronald's Marine*
Spanish Wells Hrdwr. & Mar.	Spanish Wells, Eleuthera	333-4035	*Sp. Wells Hrdwr. & Mar.*
Stella Maris Marina	Stella Maris, Long Island	338-2055	*Stella Maris Marina*
Sunpower Marine, Ltd.	Nassau, New Providence	325-2313	*Sunpower Marine*
Top To Bottom	George Town, Exuma		*Top To Bottom*
Under The Sea Marine Sply.	Mangrove Bush, Long I.		

OUTBOARD REPAIR

Stafford Bain Jr.	Pirates Well, Mayaguana		*Bain Boys*
Brown's Boat Basin	Nassau, New Providence	393-3331	
Derek Carter	Duncan Town, Ragged I.		*Monkey Man*
Great Harbour Cay Marina	Bullock's Hrbr., Berrys		*Great Harbour Cay Marina*
Harding's Supply Centre	Salt Pond, Long Island		
Lightbourne Marine-Merc.	Nassau, New Providence	393-5285	*Lightbourne Marine*
Marine Serv. of Eleu.	Hatchet Bay, Eleuthera	335-0186	*Marine Services*
Anthony Martin	Chub Cay, Berry Islands		*Chub Cay Marina*
Maura's Marine-Evinrude	Nassau, New Providence	393-7873	*Maura's Marine*
Nassau Bicycle Co.-Yamaha	Nassau, New Providence	322-8511/2	
Nautical Marine Ltd.-Mariner	Nassau, New Providence	393-3894	
Alpheas Nespitt	Duncan Town, Ragged I.		*Fish*
Pinder's Marine	Deep Creek, Eleuthera	334-8330	*Pinder's Marine*
Riding Rock Marina	Cockburn Town, San Salv.		*Riding Rock Marina-ch. 06*
Ronald's Marine-Ev. & John.	Spanish Wells, Eleuthera	333-4021	*Ronald's Marine*
Chris Saunders	Alice Town, North Bimini		*ask at any marina*
Clinton Scavella	Landrail Point, Crooked I.		*Snow White*
Sp. Wls M&H. Merc./Mar.	Spanish Wells, Eleuthera	333-4035	*Sp. Wells Hrdwr. & Mar.*
Stella Maris Marina	Stella Maris, Long Island	338-2055	*Stella Maris Marina*
Sumner Point Marina	Port Nelson, Rum Cay		*Sumner Point Marina*
Sunpower Mar.-OMC	Nassau, New Providence	325-2313	*Sunpower Marine*
Under The Sea Marine Sply.	Mangrove Bush, Long I.		

SAIL REPAIR

Phillip's Sails	Nassau, New Providence	393-4498	

APPENDIX D: GPS Waypoints

Caution: GPS Waypoints are not to be used for navigational purposes. GPS waypoints are intended to place you in the general area of the described position. All routes, cuts, and anchorages must be negotiated by eyeball navigation. The author and publisher take no responsibility for the misuse of the following GPS waypoints. There are places throughout The Bahamas, along *The Devil's Backbone* for instance, where some Skippers would feel comforted by GPS waypoints. Waypoints along any tight passage offer a false sense of security and any navigator who uses waypoints to negotiate a tricky passage instead of piloting by eye is, to be blunt, a fool and deserving of whatever fate befalls him or her. Waypoints are listed from north to south. Latitude is "**North**" and longitude is "**West**." Datum used is WGS84.

#	DESCRIPTION	Latitude	Longitude
	SOUTH FLORIDA		
1.	Hillsboro Inlet	26° 15.19'	80° 04.55'
2.	Ft. Lauderdale/Port Everglades	26° 05.57'	80° 05.40'
3.	Miami-Government Cut	25° 45.70'	80° 05.80'
4.	Cape Florida	25° 38.74'	80° 07.70'
5.	Angelfish Creek	25° 19.35'	80° 12.60'
	ABACO		
6.	Little Harbour Bar-½ nm SE of Cut	26° 19.30'	76° 59.32'
	THE BIMINIS		
7.	North Rock-½ nm W	25° 48.06'	79° 16.00'
8.	North Rock-2 nm E	25° 48.06'	79° 13.50'
9.	*Bimini Roads* Dive Site	25° 45.99'	79° 16.69'
10.	North Bimini-harbour entrance-½ nm W of and on range	25° 42.07'	79° 18.56'
11.	South Bimini-¼ nm W of entrance to Nixon's Harbour	25° 41.23'	79° 18.50'
12.	Gun Cay Channel-¼ nm NW	25° 34.48'	79° 18.15'
13.	South Cat Cay-½ nm W of entrance to Dollar Harbour	25° 31.00'	79° 16.00'
	ACROSS THE GREAT BAHAMA BANK		
14.	Mackie Shoal Light-200 yards N	25° 42.00'	78° 39.00'
15.	Russell Beacon-½ nm N of buoy	25° 29.00'	78° 25.54'
16.	NW Channel Light-250 yards N	25° 28.40'	78° 09.67'
	ANDROS		
17.	North Joulters-beginning of route to E of Joulter's Cays	25° 24.25'	78° 09.45'
18.	Joulters East-at E edge of bank clear of maze of sandbores	25° 22.30'	78° 07.35'
19.	Joulters Cay anchorage-¼ nm E of bar	25° 18.52'	78° 07.00'
20.	Morgan's Bluff-¼ nm W of entrance channel	25° 11.28'	78° 00.78'
21.	Bethel Channel-½ nm ENE of break in reef	25° 08.36'	77° 59.06'
22.	AUTEC Buoy-between Nassau and Andros	24° 57.36'	77° 43.94'
23.	Staniard Rock Passage-1 nm ENE of break in reef	24° 52.40'	77° 51.00'
24.	Fresh Creek-¼ nm ENE of entrance channel	24° 44.25'	77° 45.65'
25.	Salvador Point, AUTEC Base #2 channel-½ nm E of sea buoy	24° 29.95'	77° 41.40'
26.	Middle Bight, AUTEC Base #3 channel-¼ nm E of sea buoy	24° 20.10'	77° 39.45'
27.	South Bight-1 nm NE of entrance channel	24° 14.25'	77° 35.50'
	THE BERRY ISLANDS		
28.	Great Harbour Marina-entrance channel-1 nm NNW	25° 49.64'	77° 57.41'
29.	Great Stirrup/Slaughter Harbour entrance-½ nm N	25° 49.60'	77° 55.66'
30.	Great Stirrup/Panton Cove entrance-½ nm NE	25° 49.40'	77° 53.30'
31.	Great Harbour Route-RG2-200 yards E of	25° 46.11'	77° 56.59'
32.	Great Harbour Route-RG4-200 yards E of	25° 45.73'	77° 54.96'
33.	Great Harbour Route-RG6-200 yards E of	25° 45.32'	77° 53.62'
34.	Great Harbour Route-RG8-200 yards E of	25° 45.08'	77° 52.95'
35.	Great Harbour Route-RG10-200 yards E of	25° 44.86'	77° 52.50'
36.	Great Harbour Route-R daymark below range-200 yds. W of	25° 44.81'	77° 52.10'
37.	Great Harbour Cay-entrance to eastern anchorage	25° 46.03'	77° 49.41'

38.	Devil's Hoffman Anchorage-¼ nm E of	25° 36.56'	77° 43.49'
39.	Little Harbour/Frozen Alder Anchorage entrance-½ nm W	25° 33.93'	77° 42.50'
40.	Little Whale Cay-¼ nm E of entrance to anchorage	25° 26.77'	77° 45.13'
41.	Frazier-Hogg/Bird Cay	25° 23.45'	77° 51.05'
42.	Chub Cay-1 nm S of and on the 35° range	25° 23.90'	77° 55.08'
	NEW PROVIDENCE		
43.	Nassau Harbour-W entrance	25° 05.30'	77° 21.30'
44.	Lyford Cay-¼ nm N of light that marks entrance channel	25° 04.00'	77° 30.94'
45.	W tip of New Providence-1¼ nm NW of Golding Cay	25° 02.15'	77° 35.35'
46.	*Nassau Blue Hole*	25° 01.70'	77° 08.50'
47.	Port of New Providence entrance channel	25° 00.14'	77° 15.68'
	NEW PROVIDENCE TO ELEUTHERA		
48.	Little Pimlico Island-½ nm SW of	25° 18.10'	76° 53.60'
49.	Fleeming Channel-¼ nm N of channel entrance	25° 16.00'	76° 55.30'
50.	Fleeming Channel-¼ nm S of channel entrance	25° 15.50'	76° 54.50'
51.	Douglas Channel-1 nm NW of	25° 10.00'	77° 05.50'
52.	Douglas Channel-1 nm SE of	25° 07.80'	77° 03.00'
53.	Chub Rock-¼ nm N of	25° 06.85'	77° 14.60'
54.	Porgee Rocks-¼ nm S of	25° 03.45'	77° 14.50'
	ELEUTHERA		
55.	Pilot pickup point N of Ridley Head Channel	25° 34.50'	76° 44.30'
56.	Bridge Point-N waypoint	25° 34.32'	76° 43.03'
57.	Ridley Head Channel-N waypoint	25° 34.00'	76° 44.30'
58.	Bridge Point-S waypoint, just off Bridge Point	25° 33.90'	76° 43.18'
59.	Ridley Head Channel-S waypoint, just off Ridley Head	25° 33.54'	76° 44.33'
60.	Hawk's Point-just N of point on Devil's Backbone route	25° 33.53'	76° 40.85'
61.	Current Point-just N of point on Devil's Backbone route	25° 33.05'	76° 39.88'
62.	Spanish Wells Harbour-just E of pilings at eastern entrance	25° 32.60'	76° 44.35'
63.	Turning point on Devil's Backbone route to Harbour Island	25° 32.26'	76° 39.17'
64.	Spanish Wells Harbour-just S of pilings at western entrance	25° 32.10'	76° 45.40'
65.	Meek's Patch-¼ nm NW of northern tip of	25° 31.60'	76° 47.30'
66.	Royal Island-¼ mile S of entrance	25° 30.60'	76° 51.73'
67.	Egg Island Cut-1½ nm WNW of Cut	25° 29.60'	76° 54.75'
68.	Harbour Island-½ nm ENE of Whale Point	25° 28.70'	76° 37.30'
69.	Harbour Island-S entrance, outer waypoint of N route	25° 28.50'	76° 37.81'
70.	Harbour Island-S entrance, outer waypoint of S route	25° 28.43'	76° 37.78'
71.	Harbour Island-S entrance, inner waypoint of N route	25° 28.32'	76° 38.50'
72.	Harbour Island-S entrance, inner waypoint of S route	25° 28.11'	76° 37.94'
73.	Wreck of the *Arimora*-¼ nm SW	25° 27.87'	76° 53.75'
74.	Current Rock-½ nm NW of	25° 24.50'	76° 51.42'
75.	Current Cut-½ nm NW of western entrance	25° 24.40'	76° 48.00'
76.	Current Cut-1 nm SSE of eastern entrance	25° 22.94'	76° 46.61'
77.	Current Island-½ nm SW of southwestern tip	25° 18.45'	76° 51.29'
78.	Little Pimlico Island-½ nm SW of	25° 18.10'	76° 53.60'
79.	Gregory Town-¼ nm SW of	25° 23.15'	76° 33.75'
80.	Hatchett Bay-¼ nm S of entrance	25° 20.50'	76° 29.70'
81.	Pelican Cay-½ nm SW of	25° 16.30'	76° 20.50'
82.	Holmes Bay-½ nm SW of	25° 14.40'	76° 18.90'
83.	Governor's Harbour-1 nm W of	25° 11.75'	76° 16.25'
84.	Palmetto Point-1 nm SW of	25° 07.70'	76° 11.40'
85.	Davis Channel-E end	24° 52.25'	76° 16.30'
86.	Davis Channel-W end	24° 51.30'	76° 20.63'
87.	Rock Sound-½ nm W of entrance	24° 50.30'	76° 11.70'
88.	Powell Point-¼ nm W of entrance to marina	24° 50.23'	76° 21.09'
89.	Davis Harbour-¾ nm W of entrance buoy	24° 43.80'	76° 15.75'
90.	East End Point-1 nm SW of	24° 35.90'	76° 09.25'

THE EXUMAS

91.	Beacon Cay-¼ nm NW of	24° 53.18'	76° 49.50'
92.	Ship Channel-2 nm SE of Beacon Cay in Exuma Sound	24° 51.73'	76° 47.81'
93.	Highborne Cay Cut-¼ nm ESE	24° 42.20'	76° 48.60'
94.	TMB2 Buoy in North Exuma Sound	24° 38.20'	76° 31.30'
95.	Norman's Cay Cut-¼ nm E	24° 35.76'	76° 47.48'
96.	Warderick Wells Cut-½ nm N	24° 24.86'	76° 38.24'
97.	Conch Cut-½ nm NE	24° 17.55'	76° 31.43'
98.	Sampson Cay Cut-¼ nm NE	24° 12.78'	76° 27.55'
99.	Big Rock Cut-½ nm NE	24° 11.66'	76° 26.38'
100.	Dotham Cut-¼ nm E	24° 07.14'	76° 23.85'
101.	Farmer's Cay Cut-½ nm E	23° 57.95'	76° 18.32'
102.	Galliot Cut-¼ nm E	23° 55.62'	76° 16.50'
103.	Cave Cay Cut-¼ nm E	23° 54.00'	76° 15.20'
104.	Rudder Cut-¼ nm NNE	23° 52.52'	76° 13.48'
105.	TMB Buoy in South Exuma Sound	23° 50.40'	75° 43.20'
106.	Adderly Cut-¼ nm ENE	23° 47.45'	76° 06.33'
107.	Children's Bay Cut-¼ nm N of	23° 44.60'	76° 03.03'
108.	Rat Cay Cut-¼ nm N	23° 44.31'	76° 02.82'
109.	Square Rock Cay Cut-¼ nm ENE	23° 43.56'	76° 00.90'
110.	Glass Cay Cut-¼ nm N	23° 42.50'	75° 59.44'
111.	Soldier Cay Cut-¼ nm NE	23° 41.10'	75° 57.40'
112.	Conch Cay Cut-½ nm NNW	23° 34.30'	75° 48.50'
113.	Eastern Channel, Elizabeth Harbour-¼ nm NE	23° 29.81'	75° 39.95'
114.	Jewfish Cut-1 nm N	23° 27.85'	75° 57.56'
115.	Jewfish Cut-1 nm S	23° 25.37'	75° 56.25'
116.	Hawksbill Rock-200 yards W	23° 25.31'	76° 06.31'
117.	Hog Cay Cut-¼ nm N	23° 24.75'	75° 30.82'
118.	Sandy Cay- ½ nm N of NE tip of sandbank	23° 24.93'	75° 21.62'
119.	Hog Cay Cut-¼ nm S	23° 23.50'	75° 30.92'

LITTLE SAN SALVADOR

120.	West Bay-1 nm W of anchorage	24° 34.48'	75° 58.60'
121.	Little San Salvador-1 nm S of light	24° 32.70'	75° 56.30'

CAT ISLAND

122.	Arthur's Town-½ nm SW of	24° 36.80'	75° 41.20'
123.	Bennett's Harbour-½ nm W of entrance	24° 33.75'	75° 39.00'
124.	Alligator Point-½ nm SW of southwestern tip	24° 31.00'	75° 41.50'
125.	Smith's Bay--¾ nm W of	24° 19.75'	75° 29.55'
126.	Fernandez Bay-¾ nm W of	24° 19.10'	75° 29.55'
127.	Bonefish Point-¾ nm SW of western tip of shoal	24° 16.50'	75° 28.90'
128.	New Bight-¾ nm SW of Batelco Tower	24° 16.75'	75° 25.75'
129.	Old Bight-¾ nm NW of anchorage	24° 13.40'	75° 25.20'
130.	Hawks Nest Point-1 nm W of point	24° 08.55'	75° 32.45'

CONCEPTION ISLAND

131.	North of reef off northwestern tip of Conception Island	23° 55.18'	75° 05.40'
132.	West Bay-¾ nm W of anchorage	23° 51.00'	75° 08.00'
133.	Southeast point-clears reef SE of Conception	23° 47.25'	75° 04.66'

RUM CAY

134.	Flamingo Bay-¼ nm N of wreck at entrance to Bay	23° 42.45'	74° 56.80'
135.	Sandy Point-clears Sandy Point for eastward jog to Port Nelson	23° 38.50'	74° 57.30'
136.	Port Nelson-¼ nm SW of western end of Sumner Point Reef	23° 37.75'	74° 51.20'
137.	Rum Cay-1½ nm SE of southeastern tip clear of reef	23° 37.00'	74° 47.00'

SAN SALVADOR

138.	Graham's Harbour-1 nm W of entrance channel at Green Cay	24° 08.15'	74° 31.60'
139.	Cockburn Town-1 nm W of anchorage off town	24° 02.75'	74° 32.75'
140.	French Bay-¾ nm SW of Sandy Point	23° 56.10'	74° 34.80'

LONG ISLAND

141.	Cape Santa Maria-clears reefs off NW tip of the Cape	23° 42.00'	75° 21.50'
142.	Cape Santa Maria anchorage-¾ nm W of beach below light	23° 39.70'	75° 21.60'
143.	Calabash Bay-½ nm W of 90° entrance between the reefs	23° 38.70'	75° 21.40'
144.	Joe Sound-½ nm SW of entrance channel at Galliot Cut	23° 36.85'	75° 21.55'
145.	Dove Cay Passage	23° 33.53'	75° 20.83'
146.	Dove Cay Passage	23° 34.61'	75° 21.15'
147.	Dove Cay-W of entrance to Stella Maris Marina channel	23° 33.03'	75° 19.90'
148.	Simms-¾ nm SW of settlement	23° 28.10'	75° 14.90'
149.	Comer Channel #1	23° 20.82'	75° 19.95'
150.	Salt Pond, Long Island-¼ nm SW of Indian Hole Point	23° 20.70'	75° 10.30'
151.	Comer Channel #2	23° 19.53'	75° 24.00'
152.	Comer Channel #3-western end of Comer Channel	23° 20.30'	75° 32.00'
153.	Dollar Harbour-¾ nm S of	23° 10.00'	75° 15.55'
154.	Clarence Town-½ nm NW of Booby Rock at entrance	23° 07.35'	74° 57.65'
155.	Little Harbour-½ nm E of entrance	22° 58.65'	74° 50.30'
156.	Southern tip of Long Island-½ nm S of	22° 50.35'	74° 51.70'

THE JUMENTOS

157.	Nuevitas Rocks-banks side-½ nm N of	23° 10.00'	75°22.10'
158.	Nuevitas Rocks-offshore side-½ nm SE of	23° 09.30'	75° 21.60'
159.	Pear Cay Pass-½ nm NNW of	23° 08.65'	75° 31.20'
160.	Pear Cay Pass-½ nm SE of	23° 07.80'	75° 30.65'
161.	Water Cay Cut-¼ nm SE of	23° 02.20'	75° 40.35'
162.	Water Cay-banks side-¾ nm NW of	23° 02.00'	75° 44.00'
163.	Flamingo Cut-¼ nm W of	22° 54.30'	75° 51.00'
164.	Flamingo Cay-1 nm NW of	22° 54.30'	75° 53.10'
165.	Man Of War Shoal-outer break-N of	22° 48.75'	75° 54.46'
166.	Man Of War Shoal-inner break-N of	22° 48.75'	75° 54.00'
167.	Man Of War Shoal-outer break-S of	22° 48.05'	75° 54.46'
168.	Man Of War Shoal-inner break-S of	22° 48.05'	75° 54.00'
169.	Jamaica Cay-½ nm W of	22° 44.55'	75° 55.10'
170.	Nurse Channel-½ nm W of Channel Cay	22° 31.30'	75° 50.40'
171.	Nurse Cay-½ nm W of	22° 28.60'	75° 52.70'
172.	Raccoon Cut-¾ nm NNE of	22° 21.45'	75° 47.00'
173.	Hog Cay-¼ nm W of southernmost beach	22° 14.60'	75° 45.50'
174.	Little Ragged Island-¾ nm SW of	22° 08.65'	75° 40.00'

CROOKED ISLAND DISTRICT

175.	Bird Rock-¼ nm N of northwestern tip of reef	22° 51.85'	74° 22.10'
176.	Portland Harbour-½ nm W of entrance SW of Bird Rock	22° 50.40'	74° 21.90'
177.	Landrail Point-½ nm W of anchorage off beach	22° 49.10'	74° 21.40'
178.	North of Acklins Island-clear of Northeast Reef	22° 48.00'	73° 47.00'
179.	Majors Cays-½ nm north of entrance through reef	22° 45.70'	74° 08.70'
180.	Lovely Bay-½ nm NNE of entrance through reef	22° 44.55'	73° 57.45'
181.	Attwood Harbour-½ nm N of entrance through reef	22° 44.20'	73° 53.20'
182.	French Wells-1¼ nm NW of entrance	22° 41.40'	74° 18.90'
183.	Albert Town-½ nm WNW of	22° 36.35'	74° 21.50'
184.	Long Cay-turning point to head east across Bight of Acklins	22° 34.65'	74° 16.90'
185.	Long Cay-i¼ nm south of stake leading to small dock	22° 34.10'	74° 19.90'
186.	Turning waypoint to Pompey Bay in Bight of Acklins	22° 34.00'	74° 09.90'
187.	Long Cay-southern tip-¾ nm S of Windsor Point	22° 31.65'	74° 22.80'
188.	Anchorage between Fish Cay and Guana Cay-entrance	22° 28.00'	74° 16.20'
189.	Pompey Bay-¼ nm W of Camel Point	22° 27.00'	74° 07.00'
190.	Castle Island-½ nm NW of anchorage on W shore	22° 08.50'	74° 20.40'
191.	Castle Island-¼ nm S of Mudian Harbour entrance	22° 07.00'	74° 19.00'
192.	Mira Por Vos-1 nm W of Mira Por Vos Bank	22° 07.00'	74° 32.50'

SAMANA

193.	Propeller Cay anchorage-½ nm S of entrance channel	23° 03.10'	73° 44.35'

PLANA CAYS

194.	West Plana Cay-½ W of anchorage	22° 35.35'	73° 38.50'

MAYAGUANA

195.	Northwest Point-1½ nm W of light	22° 27.10'	73° 09.90'
196.	Abraham's Bay-inner waypoint at eastern entrance	22° 21.07'	72° 58.45'
197.	Start Bay-½ nm SW of best holding	22° 20.30'	73° 05.30'
198.	Abraham's Bay-¼ nm SSE of eastern entrance	22° 20.80'	72° 58.30'
199.	Abraham's Bay-¼ nm NE of western entrance	22° 19.80'	73° 02.50'
200.	Abraham's Bay-¼ nm SW of western entrance	22° 19.25'	73° 03.40'
201.	Southeast Point-1 nm WSW of anchorage	22° 16.70'	72° 48.40'

INAGUA

202.	Hogsty Reef-1 nm W of entrance to lagoon	21° 40.50'	73° 51.50'
203.	Little Inagua-1½ nm W of anchorage	21° 26.50'	73° 04.50'
204.	Northwest Point-¾ nm NNW of point	21° 07.23'	74° 40.65'
205.	Matthew Town-¾ nm W of	20° 57.10'	73° 41.50'

TURKS AND CAICOS ISLANDS

206.	Sandbore Channel-¼ nm W of entrance (WGS72)	21° 44.53'	72° 27.25'

APPENDIX E: Magnetic Variation For Each Island Group

Magnetic variation differs slightly from island group to island group. In some cases there are three different rates of variation for on island such as Cat Island or Mayaguana where the variation differs by 16' between the northern shore of Mayaguana and the southern shore at Abraham's Bay. These figures are approximate and may change.

Area	1999	2000	2001	2002	2003	Yrly. Change
North Andros	6° 38' W	6° 46' W	6° 54' W	7° 02' W	7° 10' W	8' W
Berrys	6° 33' W	6° 41' W	6° 49' W	6° 57' W	7° 05' W	8' W
Biminis	5° 28' W	5° 36' W	5° 44' W	5° 52' W	6° 00' W	8' W
Cat Island	7° 40' W	7° 48' W	7° 56' W	8° 04' W	8° 12' W	8' W
Conception Island	8° 18' W	8° 26' W	8° 34' W	8° 42' W	8° 50' W	8' W
Crooked/Acklins	8° 09' W	8° 17' W	8° 25' W	8° 33' W	8° 41' W	8' W
Eleuthera	7° 52' W	8° 00' W	8° 08' W	8° 16' W	8° 24' W	8' W
Exumas	7° 30' W	7° 38' W	7° 46' W	7° 54' W	8° 02' W	8' W
Inagua	8° 50' W	8° 59' W	9° 08' W	9° 17' W	9° 26' W	9' W
Jumentos	7° 20' W	7° 29' W	7° 38' W	7° 47' W	7° 56' W	9' W
Long Island	8° 06' W	8° 14' W	8° 22' W	8° 30' W	8° 38' W	8' W
Mayaguana	9° 16' W	9° 24' W	9° 32' W	9° 40' W	9° 48' W	8' W
Nassau	6° 45' W	6° 53' W	7° 01' W	7° 09' W	7° 17' W	8' W
Plana Cays	8° 41' W	8° 49' W	8° 57' W	9° 05' W	9° 13' W	8' W
Rum Cay	8° 18' W	8° 26' W	8° 34' W	8° 42' W	8° 50' W	8' W
San Salvador	8° 18' W	8° 26' W	8° 34' W	8° 42' W	8° 50' W	8' W
Samana	8° 09' W	8° 17' W	8° 25' W	8° 33' W	8° 41' W	8' W

APPENDIX F: Tidal Differences

All tides mentioned in this guide are based on Nassau tides. Times of tides in other locations throughout The Bahamas vary from a few minutes, to a few hours before or after Nassau tides. Times and heights are affected by local conditions, the season, and the phase of the moon. The tidal differences in this table are to be used as a general guideline only. Actual times may vary from times shown in this table. Time is "B" for before Nassau, and "L" for later than Nassau.

LOCATION	LAT. N	LON. W	TIME HW	TIME LW
Abraham's Bay, Mayaguana	22° 22'	73° 00'	10 min. L	13 min. L
Allan's-Pensacola, Abacos	26° 59'	77° 40'	35 min. L	45 min. L
The Bight, Cat Island	24° 19'	75° 26'	35 min. B	35 min. B
Cat Cay, Biminis	25° 33'	79° 17'	23 min. L	23 min. L
Clarence Town, Long Island	23° 06'	74° 59'	49 min. L	54 min. L
Datum Bay, Acklins Island	22° 10'	74° 18'	15 min. B	15 min. B
Elbow Cay, Cay Sal Bank	23° 57'	80° 28'	1h 26 min. L	1h 31 min. L
Eleuthera, eastern shore	24° 56'	76° 09'	19 min. L	26 min. L
Eleuthera, western shore	25° 15'	76° 19'	2h 17 min. L	2h 36 min. L
Freeport, Grand Bahama	26° 31'	78° 46'	same	same
Fresh Creek, Andros	24° 44'	77° 48'	13 min. L	5 min. L
George Town, Exuma	23° 32'	75° 49'	20 min. B	20 min. B
Great Stirrup Cay, Berry I.	24° 49'	77° 55'	25 min. L	25 min. L
Green Turtle Cay, Abacos	26° 46'	77° 18'	5 min. L	5 min. L
Guinchos Cay	22° 45'	78° 07'	14 min. L	19 min. L
Little Inagua	21° 27'	73° 01'	10 min. L	10 min. L
Mastic Point, Andros	25° 03'	77° 58'	5 min. L	5 min. L
Matthew Town, Great Inagua	20° 57'	73° 41'	15 min. L	15 min. L
Memory Rock, Abacos	26° 57'	79° 07'	24 min. L	29 min. L
North Bimini	25° 44'	79° 18'	13 min. L	25 min. L
North Cat Cay	25° 33'	79° 17'	30 min. L	35 min. L
Nurse Channel, Jumentos	22° 31'	75° 51'	15 min. L	10 min. L
Pelican Harbour, Abacos	26° 23'	76° 58'	26 min. L	31 min. L
Royal Island, Eleuthera	25° 31'	76° 51'	5 min. L	5 min. L
San Salvador	24° 03'	74° 33'	35 min. B	35 min. B
Ship Channel, Exuma	24° 52'	76° 48'	15 min. B	15 min. B
South Riding Rock, Biminis	25° 14'	79° 10'	40 min. L	40 min. L
Start Point, Mayaguana	22° 20'	73° 03'	25 min. L	25 min. L
Walker's Cay, Abaco	27° 16'	78° 24'	1h 25 min. L	1h 25 min. L

APPENDIX G: Logarithmic Speed Scale

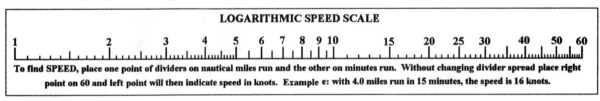

APPENDIX H: Depth Conversion Scale

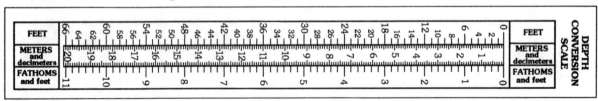

APPENDIX I: Metric Conversion Table

Visitors to The Bahamas will find the metric system in use and many grocery items and fuel measured in liters and kilograms. As a rule of thumb, a meter is just a little longer than a yard and a liter is very close to a quart. If in doubt use the following table.

1 centimeter (cm) = 0.4 inch	1 inch = 2.54 cm
1 meter (m) = 3.28 feet	1 foot = 0.31 m
1 m=0.55 fathoms	1 fathom=1.83 m
1 kilometer (km) = 0.62 nm	1 yard = 0.93 m
1 km=0.54 nautical nm	1 nautical mile=1.852 km
1 liter (l) = 0.26 gallons	1 gallon = 3.75 l
1 gram (g) = 0.035 ounce	1 ounce = 28.4 g
1 metric ton (t) = 1.1 tons U.S.	1 pound = 454 g

APPENDIX J: Weather Broadcast Frequencies

Frequencies sometimes change with little notice, and may differ by the time of publication.
All frequencies are upper sideband except where noted.

VOICE BROADCASTS
NMN
Coast Guard Portsmouth, Virginia

AREA	TIME UTC	FREQ. KHz
Offshore Forecast-W. Cental N. Atl., Car., SW N. Atl., Gulf of Mexico	0330	4426, 6501, 8764
Offshore Forecast-same as above plus the offshore waters east of New England	0930 1600, 2200	4426, 6501, 8764 6501, 8764, 13089
High Seas Forecast-N. Atl, Car., Gulf	0500 1130, 2330 1730	4426, 6501, 8764 6501, 8764, 13089 8764, 13089, 17314

CW BROADCASTS

STATION	AREA	TIME UTC	FREQUENCY, KHz
WNU-Slidell, La.	SW. N. Atl. & Car. Gulf of Mexico	0350, 0950 1550, 2150	4310, 8570, 12826.5, 17117.6, 22575.5
WCC-Chatham, Mass.	**High Seas**-Atl., Car., Gulf of Mexico	1250, 1650	4331, 6376, 8586, 8630, 13033, 16972

AMTOR/SITOR (FEC)

STATION	AREA	TIME UTC	FREQUENCY, KHz
NMF-Boston, Mass.	**High seas**-Atl., Car., Gulf	0140, 1630	6314, 8416.5 12579, 16806.5
WCC-Chatham, Mass.	**High seas**-Atl., Car., Gulf **Offshore**-New Eng., W Centl. N. Atl., SW N Atl., Car., & Gulf of Mexico	0440, 1240, 1640	4216.5, 6324, 8424 8426.5, 12589.5 12598, 16817, 16825 22386.5 (ATOR-LSB and 1.4 KHz higher)
WNU-Slidell, La.	**Offshore**-SW N Atl., Car., Gulf of Mexico	0350, 0950 1550, 2150	4210.5, 6327, 8425.5 12588.5, 16834.5

WEATHERFAX

STATION	TIME UTC	FREQUENCY KHz
NAM-U.S. Navy, Cutler, Maine	0000-1200 only	3357
	1200-0000 only	10865
	24 hours	8080, 15959, 20015
NMF-U.S.C.G., Boston, Mass.	24 hours	6340.5, 9110, 12750
NMG-U.S.C.G., New Orleans, La.	24 hours	4317.9, 8503.9, 12789.9
NMN-U.S.C.G., Chesapeake, Va.	The U.S.C.G. is scheduled to commence WeFax transmissions from NMN in the Fall of 1997.	

NAVTEX

STATION	TIME UTC	FREQUENCY	FORECAST
NMA-Miami, Florida	0000, 0400, 0800 1200, 1600, 2000	518 KHz	SW N. ATL. & Car., Coastal Florida
NMF-Boston, Mass.	0045, 0445, 0845 1245, 1645, 2045	518 KHz	Offshore New England
NMG-New Orleans, La.	0300, 0700, 1100 1500, 1900, 2300	518 KHz	Offshore Gulf, Coastal Gulf
NMN-Chesapeake, Va.	0130, 0530, 0930 1330, 1730, 2130	518 KHz	W. Cntl. N. Atl.
NMR-San Juan, P.R.	0200, 0600, 1000 1400, 1800, 2200	518 KHz	SW N. ATL. & Car., W. Cntl. N. Atl.
ZBM-Bermuda	0100, 0500, 0900 1300, 1700, 2100	518 KHz	SW N. ATL. & Car., W. Cntl. N. Atl.

TIME

STATION	FREQUENCY
WWV-Ft. Collins, Colorado	2.5, 5, 10, 15, 20, 25 MHz
WWVH-Kekaha-Kawai, Hawaii	2.5, 5, 10, 15, 20 MHz.

The National Bureau of Standards broadcasts voice time signals continuously 24 hours a day, and storm alerts at 8 minutes after the hour.

INDEX

About The Author
Stephen J. Pavlidis

Stephen J. Pavlidis has been cruising and living in The Bahamas aboard his 40' sloop IV Play since the winter of 1989. In January of 1990 he began cruising and living in the Exumas where he met Ray Darville, the new Warden of the Exuma Cays Land and Sea Park in Feb. of 1993. Ray soon drew him into a working relationship with the Park as a volunteer Deputy Warden. In this role he quickly gained an intimate knowledge of the waters of the Exumas. Subsequently, Steve and Ray produced A Cruising Guide to the Exuma Cays Land and Sea Park. The favorable response to that publication in turn led to The Exuma Guide which covers the entire Exuma island chain. The excellent response to that work has in turn led to the complete coverage of the Central and Southern Bahamas with this guide. Steve, N4UJP, is a member of the Waterway Radio and Cruising Club.

Jack Blackman

Jack Blackman designed and painted the cover for this guide. Jack has had a varied and successful career as an artist and designer. His fine art studies were obtained from *The School of Fine Arts* at *Columbia University* and *The Art Students League* in New York City. Jack's talents have involved many disciplines, such as designing sets for The Broadway Stage, Network television, and Art Direction for several major motion pictures. Several years ago Jack sailed his cutter *Sea Rogue* to The Bahamas, where he fell in love with the brilliant colors of the islands and their waters. Since then, his watercolors have been inspired by the graceful lines of racing sloops, time worn facades of Out Island buildings, and the warm, honest Bahamian people at work and play. Having had a number of successful shows, many of Jack's paintings reside in private and corporate collections internationally, as well as The Bahamas. His original works and reproductions are well represented in local galleries. Jack has a studio in the Berry Islands where he paints daily, completing commissions and new works for his next show.

Don Reynolds

Don Reynolds is a painter and sculptor who divides his time by working in the woods in his Tree House Studio in Sanford, Florida and sailing with his wife Lynn on *Ppalu*, a 36' cutter crafted by his own hand. Don's eye catching murals in the heart of Orlando have become true landmarks. His glorious woodcarvings show a great love of the natural world. Don has developed a reputation for variety in his work, from a 64' bas-relief cast concrete cooling tower, to bronze, aluminum, and copper pieces, to internationally recognized centerpiece sculptures used in Europe by the United States Culinary Team. Now Don had found a unique way of blending his art and his desire to sail. As he took *Ppalu* on her first island voyage, he captured the beauty of each stop along the way with the most basic artistic medium, and his personal favorite, the pencil sketches which grace several pages in this guide. Don likes taking that "second look," which drawing demands. Don's sketches are a record of cruising the islands in the style dreamed of through 15 years of boatbuilding. Resisting the urge to see The Bahamas in any other way proved provident. The adventure was such a success, another is soon to follow.

NOTES